Systematic Instruction of Persons with Severe Handicaps

Third Edition

Systematic Instruction of Persons with Severe Handicaps

Martha E. Snell, editor
University of Virginia

Charles E. Merrill Publishing Company
A Bell & Howell Information Company
Columbus   Toronto   London   Melbourne

The cover art was created by Terry Verdine, a young adult with severe physical and mental handicaps. Using a melting crayon technique, Terry selected both the colors and the pattern. He attends West Central Training Center, a facility in Columbus, Ohio that provides vocational training and a sheltered work environment. Terry enjoys swimming, music, and art.

Published by Merrill Publishing Company
A Bell & Howell Information Company
Columbus, Ohio 43216

This book was set in Univers

Administrative Editor: Vicki Knight
Production Coordinator: Linda Hillis Bayma
Cover Designer: Cathy Watterson

Photo Credits: All photos copyrighted by individuals or companies listed. Philippa H. Campbell and the Children's Hospital Audiovisual Department, pp. 176, 177, 178, 180, 181, 184,185,208; Dan Grogan, pp. 157, 277, 278, 279, 285, 290; Martha E. Snell, pp. 335, 364, 380, 386, 397, 422, 429, 430.

Chapter 3 was supported in part by Cooperative Agreement #G0083C0040 from the U.S. Department of Education, Office of Special Education and Rehabilitative Services, Special Education Programs. This material does not necessarily reflect the position or policy of the U.S. Department of Education, and no official endorsement should be inferred.

Library of Congress Catalog Card Number: 86-62348
International Standard Book Number: 0-675-20468-2
Printed in the United States of America

For all the people with handicaps who have not received an appropriate education and for their current teachers, and their teachers-to-be. And for my mentors, Ed Keller and Don Burke.

Preface

The first two editions of this book were published 4 and 9 years ago. These were times when appropriate services for people with severe handicaps were commonly nonexistent; later, these services existed but were often inadequate. During this passage of 9 years, specialized personnel have taken the place of many who did not know how to work effectively with these students; a growing number of teachers have accepted the importance of teaching useful skills, not simply targeting developmental milestones; programs more frequently reflect the once ideal characteristics of being community-based, integrated, functional, and age appropriate; and many professionals and parents have come to see that active planning for each student's adult years and the transition into that period is an advised, although often difficult, practice. These changes in our services, practices, and attitudes are significant. Most important, these changes mirror what we currently know about working effectively with students who have severe handicaps.

This third edition retains the same goal of the first two: to describe and explain proven teaching methods with people who have severe handicaps. Although coverage is broad, some readers will find that it relies on much prerequisite information: these readers will find some assistance in two general review chapters on assessment (Chapter 4) and intervention (Chapter 5). Comprehensive reference lists at each chapter's end will aid the reader in seeking out supplementary material.

The book is organized so that the important basics are addressed first: parents, assessment, and general intervention principles. Then, the focus shifts to four areas of related services: emergency and routine medical procedures; positioning, handling, and programming for people with movement difficulty; recreation and leisure instruction; and communication. The last section of the book reviews the literature in domestic skills, community skills, functional academics, vocational skills, and postschool options.

Many people have assisted in the task of developing this edition: the content is too voluminous for one or even several individuals to present meaningfully. The first group of people whose contributions deserve merit are those who reviewed the strengths and shortcomings of the second edition and made recommendations for the writing of this one. These people are David Gast, University of Kentucky; Linda McCormick, University of Hawaii; Rosanne Silberman, Hunter College; and Barbara Sirvis, University of Illinois.

Next are those who provided reviews of one or several chapters and, thus, guided the final revision of each of the 17 chapters in this edition: Irene Carney, University of Virginia; Robert Gaylord-Ross, San Francisco State University; Jennifer Holvoet, Institute of Logopedics, Wichita, Kansas; Ian Pumpian, San Diego State University; and Jennifer York, University of Wisconsin at Madison.

Four people reviewed the entire book in its final draft stage and offered suggestions both for individual chapters and for improving the flow and consistency of the entire book: Hank Bersani, Jr., Syracuse University; Felix Billingsley, University of Washington; Michael D. Orlansky, The Ohio State University; and Rosanne Silberman, Hunter College.

Next, the contributions of Vicki Knight, administrative editor, and Linda Bayma, production editor, deserve notice. I would also like to thank freelancers Mary Kuhner and Shirley Nyhan.

Finally, thanks is owed to the children, adolescents, and adults who appear in this edition's photographs, their parents who granted their permission, and their teachers who are responsible for the programs that warranted either photographic illustration or description in the text.

Contents

Martha E. Snell
University of Virginia

1

What Does an "Appropriate" Education Mean?

The number of students with severe handicaps is small (.05% of the population) in contrast to those having milder disabilities. The severely handicapped often have a second or third disability such as cerebral palsy, a sensory impairment, or serious maladaptive behavior. When this group is characterized by their service needs, the following definition holds true:

[*These individuals*] *"who require ongoing support in several major life areas in order to participate in the mainstream of community life, and who are expected to require such support throughout life."* (Bellamy, 1985, p. 6)

Since 1978, public schools have been required by law to educate all school-aged students, even those with severe handicaps. Many schools have demonstrated problems meeting this mandate citing reasons such as an absence of trained teachers, poor prognoses for learning by these students, and inadequate funds to cover the many extra services needed. The U.S. Department of Education has responded by bolstering funds for personnel preparation and for the development of school interventions programs that demonstrate models of excellence. Also, in response to inappropriate school programs, parent and professional organizations have gone to the courts for judgment and settlement. Both responses have served as checks and balances on the way we educate those with severe handicaps.

Basic issues contested have centered upon what constitutes "appropriate" education for students with severe handicaps. What should the teacher teach? How is instruction implemented to profit the student's independent, responsible functioning in society? How much instructional time is needed both annually and cumulatively? In what settings should learning take place? In what ways should the student's family be involved? Whose responsibility is the student's success after the school services end? These are only some of the questions. The answers, however, are harder to generate; they are complex, but there *are* answers.

WHAT SHOULD BE TAUGHT?

It is not unusual for teachers of students with severe handicaps to have little or no training relevant to their task. The following classroom description is based on an actual situation. It is a situation that unfortunately repeats itself in many school programs.

Bev was hired at the last minute, just several days before school started because the Genova Public Schools had been unable to hire any other teacher for nine students with severe handicaps. Bev had worked some in a residential facility, but her training was geared toward teaching students with mild handicaps. She readily admitted ignorance about lifting and positioning students with orthopedic involvement. The school system was desperate and felt that extra staff (two classroom aides) and plenty of support people would compensate for Bev's lack of training (an extra occupational therapist, etc.) After several weeks, the parents and administrators were distressed: the program fell far short of their dreams, and even the teacher admitted problems although she also felt alone and defensive.

Picture a typical day in Bev's classroom. The students are young (ages 6 to 10) and varied in their handicaps, as is often the case in such classes. Several students are in wheelchairs, more than half are not toilet trained, only one has reliable vocal communication skills, three are frequently noncompliant as if they are bored with the tasks, and several have extensive medical problems requiring close supervision. Bev has a daily circle time when the aides stand by and watch. Then instruction is given on a one-to-one basis while the other students are grouped for supervision by the aides. Speech and physical therapy is given in therapy rooms located outside the classroom, although the teacher and her staff do not know the proper techniques and have little opportunity to observe therapists. Last year's programs and recommendations by other teachers remain in files because Bev is too busy planning day-by-day. The teachers who wrote these recommendations are angry that their work has been forgotten, as are many parents.

Classroom teaching materials are largely Fisher-Price toys along with the traditional puzzles, blocks, felt shapes, and pegboards found in nursery schools. There is little time to think about what to order, and Bev does the best she can. "When you teach children aged 6 through 10 who have very few skills," she had been taught by her university professors, "you should aim for their thinking age, their mental age, their developmental age—not 6 years or 10 years, but more like 6 months to perhaps 3 or 4 years at best. Get on their level," they advised.

Bev's aides also don't know what they should do to teach these students. They have many problems with managing the behavior of a few students and often resort to threats and physical and verbal abuse. They feel frustrated and even guilty at times; *though one aide maintains that it's the only way those students can learn. No one has shown her otherwise.* [*]

The main instructional goals are developmental, but at the infant and preschool levels these include: receptive identification of shapes, colors, common animals and objects; using scissors, scribbling with a crayon, answering to one's name, tracking objects, following simple directions. By contrast, most daily routines are entirely prompted rather than taught. Thus, students are pulled and hand-guided down the halls to and from the bus, the gym, and the cafeteria; they are not allowed to try the tasks with less than total assistance. Students are not taught to get their tray in the cafeteria or to lower and raise their pants before toileting but are "put through" the motions because performance of these self-help routines generally is not targeted for instruction. Again the teacher is following her training: she is being consistent with the tenets of most developmental assessment devices, which suggest that items to teach first are those that are failed on the list of skills normally performed by infants and toddlers.

The problems are many and all too typical. The teacher does not know how to program for learning, nor does she know what to teach. She is frustrated, as are the students, their parents, and other staff. She will not last in the classroom beyond this year unless she can make significant changes. Bev feels no one appreciates her hard work, and she is probably right!

Some teachers who share problems in common with Bev are far less noticeable. These teachers have good relationships with their co-workers, the parents, and administrators, in addition to effective teaching techniques. Although these teachers *can* teach their students, they teach the wrong things: skills that have little or no relevance to the student's daily life, skills that will be forgotten through disuse, or skills that, if learned, will emphasize the student's handicaps because they are meant only for children much younger. *Both* types of teachers did not get their money's worth at college; like Bev, they are targeting the wrong behaviors because they do not know how to select relevant teaching objectives.[†]

---

[*]Effective methods for teaching appropriate behavior are described in Chapter 12.

[†]The research on teaching leisure, domestic, community, and vocational skills to students like Bev's is set forth in Chapters 13–16.

Teachers must take the time necessary to determine what should be taught. To do so requires close and frequent contact with the student's care providers in order that the families' regular routines and expectations for their child become known. This information is perhaps the single most important set of information for drawing up instructional objectives. Further, teachers will need to examine the nearby services that may be available to each student (the living possibilities for later years and their entry requirements, vocational options, leisure opportunities). Such a survey often reveals inadequate service options and thus may stimulate changes before the student becomes older. Also, the upcoming school setting will be visited by the teacher as a possible source of objectives for each student. This assessment process is referred to as an "ecological inventory" of the student's current and future environments.*

HOW IS INSTRUCTION IMPLEMENTED?

As Bev's story illustrates, the teacher's first problem is to determine *what* to teach. Knowing *how* to teach the targeted skills is altogether another matter, which is equally complex. "Best-practices" techniques for teaching students with severe handicaps have been defined in many current publications and in several important courtroom settlements of disputes between parents of children with severe handicaps and school systems (e.g., *Fialkowski v. Shapp*, 1975). Such appropriate methods for these difficult-to-teach students include those that reduce errors, and that facilitate generalization of skills learned under one set of conditions to other conditions.† Further, teachers need to collect accurate student performance data so that progress can be monitored, and so that programs that don't work can be improved.‡

Related services provided by speech therapists, adaptive physical educators, occupational and physical therapists and school nurses need to be integrated into the student's daily routine for several reasons. First, teachers need to learn from parents, medical staff, and therapists who also must communicate with, feed, move, and position students, as well as maintain their health, during the school day. Second, when teaching methods used by staff are consistent and the focus of instruction is common across instructors, students are more likely to generalize their learning across situations. Related services staff need to focus upon skills useful to a particular student rather than upon "useful" skills selected once ecological inventory data are combined with health, communication, or movement assessment data.*

The daily schedule must allow for planned interactions between students having handicaps and those without so that social behavior can be taught under realistic conditions to replace maladaptive behavior. These interactions should be regular enough to allow learning to occur and should involve same-age peers rather than only staff or age-different students.

Because our students experience difficulty generalizing skills, the teacher must use a variety of procedures to facilitate transfer of learning. Both learning and later skill use appear to be best promoted when instruction occurs in the actual place where the skill is needed, involves the real materials, and is taught at the time of day the skill normally will be used. Instead of isolated skills being taught, teachers should target the relevant cluster of related skills so students can learn to function as independently as is possible.† These latter requirements mean that students cannot be isolated in their classrooms. As students grow out of their elementary years, they will spend less and less time in the school, and more time in the community, domestic and leisure sites, and vocational training settings. In community-based instructional settings, students have the benefit of learning to recognize the natural stimuli that ultimately must control their skill performance when teachers are no longer present to assist, to correct, and to praise. Instruction must include proven techniques, systematic implementation with ongoing monitoring of students' performance, the help of ancillary staff, and

---

*Chapters 3 and 4 further define and illustrate the ecological inventory phase of assessment.

†Chapter 5 addresses these and other intervention strategies.

‡Chapter 4 describes methods for teachers to collect, display and use student performance data.

---

*In Chapter 6, routine and emergency medical procedures are delineated; movement and positioning considerations and their impact on programming are the topics of skills rather than their impact on skills chosen from standard lists of "therapeutic" tasks. Chapters 7 and 8, and Chapters 10 and 11 address communication assessment and intervention.

†These practices are described further in Chapter 5.

the goal of meaningful participation in activities relevant to the student's current and future life.*

WHERE SHOULD STUDENTS BE TAUGHT?

Where students should be taught is a question that has been partially addressed, but it still seems to confuse many educators as well as parents, administrators, lawyers, and even judges. As in the following real situation, many people believe that the best education for students with severe handicaps is the private, expensive, residential school that offers "intensive training" to its residents.

Ronny is 7 years old. Like very few other people in this world, he was born with the inability to metabolize an essential amino acid, phenylalanine, common to many foods. His condition, more often known as PKU, is very rare, and when it does occur now, it is detected at birth with tests required in all states. When Ronny was born, two mistakes were made: the first PKU blood or urine test, to be given shortly after birth, was forgotten; while the second, backup test, given several weeks later, was given but misread. If the first test had been given, it would have shown that Ronny had PKU; the second test, if not misread, would have verified this diagnosis. Once positive readings are obtained on PKU tests, a phenylalanine-free diet is prescribed that enables the child to grow and develop normally without the progressive brain damage that results from a failure to metabolize the essential amino acid.

At age 4, it was clear that Ronny was not like other 4 year olds. Medical tests revealed the errors made early in his life. The state was named responsible in a suit, which was upheld in court. But what settlement would be appropriate for Ronny and his family? The error could not be undone. Ronny could not be healed, no matter how much money was awarded. His level of mental retardation measured in the severe range. The lawyers, in planning the parents' case, sought advice on what should constitute the settlement. Because of the clear-cut evidence of error on the state's part, it was likely that almost any program component or services asked for would be awarded. What, then, to ask for? Acting on their assumptions, the lawyers appointed a psychologist to identify the best program possible—perhaps some modern, residential program with a high staff-to-student ratio, lots of the most advanced equipment available, and trained staff. Ideally, a program that would run 24 hours a day,

---

*Chapters 9 and 14 through 16 detail how to build functional skills that generalize and maintain.

12 months a year, and in all this intensity, would make the most of Ronny's potential. Or would it? Such a program would cost a lot of money; in fact, $100,000 per year would not be unusual.

The psychologist talked to Ronny's family and sought the advice of psychologists, doctors, and special educators. "Where are these programs? Money is absolutely no issue, we want the best program no matter where it is located. Travel to and from Ronny's home for visitation can be covered, since we are pretty sure there aren't any of these programs in his state."

When interviewing one special educator, the psychologist, who knew the family, was asked if the family was close to their son. She replied that they were very close, and that a separation would not be easy, but that the family wanted what was best for their son even if it meant living away from him. Next, the discussion turned to the features of a good program: the importance of targeting useful skills, and applying teaching methods to deal with the problems of slow learning, easy forgetting, and poor transfer of skills. Several special educators suggested that realistic goals for Ronny would include attainment of some level of independence in the daily routines, mastery of some skills in domestic living, and community use and leisure time that would be compatible with his preferences and his family's. The psychologist was urged to program vocational training early in Ronny's schooling, not wait until high school. The psychologist agreed with the need to teach a meaningful system for communicating with others; several special educators stressed the importance of learning to interact with other people his own age who did not have handicaps, in addition to his family and neighbors. Due to Ronny's generalization problems, they indicated that social skill learning would be unlikely in a setting where all Ronny's peers had handicaps. (Unfortunately, because many private, and public, schools are still segregated, not only within the school but also from the nearby community, students do not have realistic interaction opportunities.)

When the psychologist was asked about Ronny's home town, its available school programs and its post-school services (respite care for families, community residential options, vocational training programs), the information was not too favorable: "They aren't equipped to deal with Ronny," was the answer. When one special educator asked: "What would it take to build the best program in Ronny's own community?" the discussion became exciting and the pessimism was replaced with optimism.

After several weeks, and numerous contacts with others in bordering states who reinforced these ideas, the psychologist developed a plan to bring the best program to Ronny rather than to search for one. The program proposed to the court involved three phases: current until age 12, age 13 until 21, and age 21 and beyond. Initial plans included setting up a classroom in which Ronny would be one of the members. The classroom would be in the elementary school during phase 1, but during later phases it would be shifted first to the middle school and then to the high school, although much of the instruction would occur in the community as Ronny grew older. The teachers would be provided with the necessary consultants to guarantee a quality program; assistance would be given to the administrators and related services personnel. The community services would be strengthened so that the family would have respite services available. During later phases there would be money to build and staff a small group home and the necessary vocational training program.

This may sound like a dream situation because most communities do not provide families with adequate support, and educational programs are often still evolving. Ronny's situation should not be a dream but, rather, the reality that our public laws have promised for citizens with handicaps.

The court awarded the program and the needed settlement that was requested by Ronny's family and his lawyers. The costs may not be significantly less than the price of a private, residential program one thousand miles from Ronny's home. Further, Ronny will stay with his family and will obtain the extensive ongoing support necessary to participate in his community, in the company of his family and friends, and to enjoy a life.

HOW SHOULD THE STUDENT'S FAMILY BE INVOLVED?

How the family can be involved is a question that has no "right" answer. Many families will be active in their involvement with the school and the development of their child's program, though school staff may not always look favorably upon their involvement. In the first case study, Bev's classroom, involved parents working with a school system were responsible for starting services for their children. The same parents also rightfully complained when the program did not live up to their expectations.

Some families will be viewed by professionals as not being concerned or involved enough with their son's or daughter's program. The next case you will read is about such a family. Usually there are good reasons for the amount of involvement any family has with their child's school program. These reasons include past experiences with schools (good and bad), the number of other demands on a family besides school, fears about the future, advice given by professionals on their child's potential, and the child's current chronological age.

Families and schools can differ in opinion. If these differences are open and strong, they may stimulate constructive change or they may contribute further to the communication barriers. When the differences between families and schools go unstated, interactions may be guarded and defensive or simply very infrequent.

Various school personnel and families will not always agree on how many services are needed or what kinds of services are appropriate. For example, in Ronny's situation, some professionals would have praised the choice of a private school that specialized in serving only students with severe disabilities. Other professionals would have criticized the family for choosing a segregated school that allowed no interaction with the community or nonhandicapped peers. Another area of difference concerns expectations. Families may have different expectations for their sons or daughters than do teachers and other professional staff. When teachers and parents recognize that they will not always agree on how to describe or realize a student's potential whatever that may be, then disagreement is less likely to be mistaken for *not caring*. What is certain about how schools and families work together is that they must *do so*. To the extent that all parties work to express and understand their differences, the student's educational program is likely to be richer in its individual reflection of the best thinking of all concerned.*

DILEMMAS IN SERVICE PROVISION

Students with extensive handicaps sometimes fall between the cracks in our system of service provision. David is an example of this phenomenon.

David is 13. When he was 11, he had no handicaps; but after a near-fatal car accident, David suffered head trauma and lost most of his abilities. The accident had other tragic effects: David's family split apart; and because there were inadequate facilities to deal with head trauma in David's own

---

*Chapter 2 discusses this topic of interaction between families and professionals.

state, he was moved to the nearest hospital in the next state where he remained for 2 years. Not only was the distance too great to allow much visiting, but David's extensive handicaps and loss of previous skills made him very different to his family and friends. The family still loved David, but they felt his placement in a small hospital was the best that could be done. Each parent considered taking David home, but neither was able to arrange home care for him; the community offered no support services. Because he was not officially a resident of the state where he was living, he was not enrolled in an educational program; if re-classified as a resident of that state, he might lose his insurance eligibility, and the hospital would be unable to keep him. David was in a no-man's land, a mire of red tape and regulations.

Meanwhile, the hospital staff became concerned about David's lack of progress in the various therapies he was provided. Some of the therapists withdrew him from their service, feeling that other patients would benefit more. Other staff saw clear, untapped potential and requested assistance and new approaches for "reaching" David. But David's day was and still is an unbusy one, despite the flurry of papers concerning his predicament. He spends his best times with a few staff who recognize the personality that is still there. He is also guided through traditional therapy tasks that seem to make no impact. David lives among other patients who are much older than he, but who also have suffered some form of neural trauma from accidents or strokes. David spends a lot of time sitting in his wheelchair; he rarely leaves the third floor of the hospital.

David's situation is all too common, though most people in his place are adults. David's lack of appropriate services is not due to an absence of caring people in his life, but to a set of service-provision laws that still require knowledgeable, active advocates to make them work as they should. Not just anyone can fill this role; successful advocates must (a) know well and believe in what they are asking for, (b) know the legal rights that justify their advocacy, (c) identify and address effectively the public avenues of power, and (d) persist doggedly in their pursuit of appropriate services despite the odds against them.* Many of us—teachers and other professionals—serving those with severe handicaps do not view all of these advocacy tasks as being our responsibility, certainly not as our forte. All too often we have relied upon the parents of these people to advocate for changes, citing our conflicts of interest or inadequate time. When and if changes do arrive, we complain. Apathy and inaction undermine the potential to effect change. David is waiting.

REFERENCES

Bellamy, T. (1985). Severe disability in adulthood. *Newsletter of The Association for Persons with Severe Handicaps, 11,* pp. 1 and 6.
Fialkowski v. Shapp, 405 F. Supp. 946 (E. D. Pa. 1975).

---

*Chapters 2 and 17 address in-school and post-school service provision laws.

Last week I talked with a parent of a young child with severe emotional problems. "I need to know my rights. I heard you talking about the public law, and I'm worried that I don't know enough about what rights my son has to special services." She sounded calm, but as we talked she sounded tired and anxious about her son. "He's only 4 and has had special services for a year, and I feel like the school is already telling me I want too much. They say he needs a more intensive program, but then when I move him to one, they only pay for half of it. Now they want him back in their program, to save money I think, but he's just starting to make progress. I belong to a parent group, and there are others who want to learn more about this law."

In another town, two teachers who feel defeated in their efforts with a teenage student share some of their emotions with each other. "You just cannot reason with those parents, they still feel guilty about the accident and what it did to John, and they take it out on everyone who touches John. No one can do anything right for him. They either drive him to school or the dad follows the bus, and they would still be sitting in the classroom observing every move we make if the administration hadn't gotten them out. It's really an impossible situation. I just can't teach the things they want John to learn; it will never make him what he was, and it will only make him more dependent."

These are not typical situations, but they exist periodically in most special programs. Parents and professionals who have too many barriers between them to move beyond their disagreements. Parents who feel outpowered by smooth-talking administrators. Teachers and administrators who feel a student's needs are the "top priority" and that over-involved or under-involved parents (or parents who have goals for their children that differ from the school's) probably do not care as much as they do. Negative beliefs like these add to the barrier. The public law says that parents must be involved, but it does not emphasize that the amount and type of involvement must vary depending upon the family and their other demands at any point in life. Families are as individual in their characteristics as are their children, to whom we readily give credit for being individuals.

Most working relationships between parents of children with disabilities and professionals are smoother than those just described. In fact, surveys of parents generally show that they report satisfaction with their child's program. And teachers say

Introduction to Chapter 2

they can communicate fairly well with their students' parents. But when the students have severe handicaps and begin to advance in years, teachers feel pressure to plan ahead for the student's future; parents may feel some anxiety but be less able to face the years ahead. They may not know the choices that exist, and, like most of us who never plan much beyond several months or a year in advance, they may prefer to deal with the complexities of living on a day-to-day basis.

In the next chapter Buzz and Ann give us a new perspective on parents through the family-systems approach. This view does not focus simply on the student with disabilities; it focuses on the family as a dynamic, complex, functioning system and on the student as a member of that family. This perspective requires more from professionals but appears to be more accurate than the conventional, narrow focus on the person with handicaps, who is enrolled in our class. This approach implies that professionals will need to individualize their approach to families in terms of school involvement and planning. It also implies that greater harmony will develop between teachers and parents that will promote better atmosphere to address our students' education.

G. J. "Buzz" Bronicki
University of Kansas

A. P. Turnbull
University of Kansas

Family-Professional Interactions

2

In the following paragraphs Rud Turnbull (1985), a professional and the father of a son with moderate mental retardation, describes an early experience with professionals. His description is characteristic of those reported by other parents of children with severe handicapping conditions (Akerley, 1985; Ziskin, 1985).

One of the first things I noticed about Jay was that he had a large, egg-shaped lump on the top of his head where most babies have a concave impression; in photographs at home it is so noticeable that it is remarkable that nobody seemed to pay it much heed. Another early warning sign was his plain dullness—not that he wasn't a beautiful child with an abundance of blond curls; it is just that he didn't turn over, move about, push himself up on his elbows, or do the other things that my friends' children of his age had done. His pediatrician, now the head of the Department of Pediatrics at a large eastern state school of medicine, seemed to pooh-pooh my concerns. After measuring the circumference of Jay's head, he simply said Jay was within the high range of normalcy, bordering on a bit slow. When my ex-wife tearfully cross-examined him, giving ample display of our anxieties, his responses became even vaguer.

Had it not been for Jay's hernia in the first year of his life, we might have waited far longer to have our suspicions confirmed. Upon detecting the rupture, the pediatrician admitted Jay to Hopkins for what should have been a fairly simple operation, but it turned out to be rather more than that. The Hopkins surgeon gave Jay a thorough examination the day before the scheduled operation and immediately called off the surgery, explaining to me on the telephone that Jay's retina was unusually flat and he wanted a neurologist to look at him. Later that week, after the pediatrician, surgeon, and neurologist had examined Jay, I learned that they wanted to do more tests before deciding on his surgery.

My antennae were up—I was seeing danger signals in every phrase the doctors uttered. My questions—"Can't you be more specific? Have you had cases like this before? Why is the neurologist involved? Is something wrong with his eyes?"—went unanswered. I was told, "We can't say yet; we're still checking things (not him) out."

On one of my frequent visits to the hospital to see Jay, I saw a nurse I used to date and asked her to come see Jay with me. His curls had been shaved off his head (they are in an envelope in our safe deposit box, remnants of our age of innocence), and he was in a crib next to a child whose chart read, "Nothing by mouth or intravenously," and whose head was far larger than Jay's. While we were visiting Jay, I picked up his chart and asked her to read the neurologist's report. After scanning it quickly, she said, "It's better for you not to know, Rud." And she left, suddenly saddened and taking with her my hopes for knowledge. The nurse in charge of the ward promptly appeared on the scene, admonishing me not to read the chart. "Jay's doing fine, Mr. Turnbull." Of course he was: no worse and no better than at home. But I wasn't doing fine at all.

A day or two later, still ignorant but scheduled for the neurologist to undertake some minor surgical procedure, we waited and waited and waited for him to come to see us before the surgery. When at last he appeared, I turned all my anger and ignorance on him. "Before you so much as lay a hand, much less a scalpel on Jay, I want to know, I demand to know, what the hell's going on! And where have you been all this time!"

"Saving a life down the hall—and you've got the right to be angry, Mr. Turnbull. Let's talk."

Had it not been for Dr. Neal Aronson, the neurologist who leveled with me, the entire staff of Johns Hopkins Hospital might have kept me in eternal ignorance. Simply, deliberately, humbly, and patiently he explained all: Jay's flat retina, the little egg on his head, his slowness, and his "high range of normalcy" were signs of either macrocephaly or hydrocephaly. Jay, I heard him say, was retarded and very seriously so, although the exact degree was hard to pinpoint at his early age and would remain so for several years. He ran a serious risk with surgery for the hernia. To better evaluate the risk, the doctors needed to do an "exploratory"— that is, take a look at his brain through a very small incision, maybe blow air around his brain, or put fluid in and take pictures, nothing unusual or unusually risky. He let me know so gently that all I felt was absolution, the soft vanishing of my present and past anxiety—not the pain of the future (Turnbull, 1985, pp. 109-110)

Pointing fingers at those who made mistakes in the past will not protect us from doing the same things in the future. But being aware of those mistakes will help us all avoid repeating history. Establishing a new and meaningful partnership between parents and professionals depends upon all of us knowing what has been done wrong. The professionals have not made all the mistakes. Parents have made mistakes, too. But, in all fairness, we should realize that many mistakes made by parents were aided and abetted by misguided professional advice. Perhaps keeping parents in ignorance is one of the gravest disservices and most devastating mistakes. Other mistakes illustrate fears and feelings, disrespecting parents' time, and failing to communicate honestly and emphatically.

Just as professionals sometimes slight parents, parents' attitudes and behaviors also contribute to negative interactions. There is no easy way to tell a mother and father that their child has a substantial handicap. Some parents can handle the hard truth; others need to be eased into it. Professionals may choose their words with great sensitivity, yet still offend the parents. Parents may not realize the difficult position of the professional. They may vent their anger at the professional by becoming publicly critical of those with whom they and their children have worked.

Community advocacy groups sometimes exclude professionals on the grounds that it is impossible for them to understand parents' feelings and needs. Parents may form cliques with the primary goal of ostracizing and criticizing professionals.

There are situations in which parents fight long and hard for services for their child. After the services are found and the child is receiving an appropriate education, the parents continue their intense advocacy until minor issues with professionals become major confrontations. As one mother stated, "For years I have scrapped and fought for services. Now I come on like gangbusters over issues that are really not that important. I don't like what has happened to me. I've ended up to be an aggressive, angry person." This posture leads to unproductive interactions between parents and professionals.

Only in the last decade has significant national attention been focused on the importance of a parent-professional partnership based on mutual respect and equal decision-making authority. The factors contributing to recognizing the importance of the parent-professional partnership include

1. Experimental evidence that parents can positively influence the development of their children through teaching them at home (Atkeson & Forehand, 1979; Atkeson, Sturgis, & Forehand, 1977; Bronfenbrenner, 1974; Clark & Baker, 1983; Gordon, 1971; Karnes, Teska, Hodgins, & Badger, 1970; Schaefer, 1972).
2. The positive influence of early intervention in ameliorating the developmental deficits asso-

ciated with actual and "at-risk" handicaps (Bronfenbrenner, 1974; Buchman, 1983; Consortium for Longitudinal Studies, 1979; Gray & Klaus, 1970; Horowitz & Paden, 1973; Tjossem, 1976).

3. The success of parents in bringing litigation to establish the educational rights of their children (*Armstrong v. Kline*, 1979; *Fialkowski v. Shapp*, 1975; *Hines v. Pittsburgh County Board of Education*, 1980; *Mills v. Board of Education*, 1972; *Pennsylvania Association for Retarded Children v. Commonwealth of Pennsylvania*, 1972; Turnbull, 1986).

4. The resulting federal legislation, P.L. 94–142 (Education for All Handicapped Children Act), which sets forth clear standards for parent involvement in the educational process.

The major principles of P.L. 94–142 have profoundly shaped the nature of parent-professional interaction on issues related to identification, evaluation, programming, and placement for students with disabilities. All special educators need to have a thorough knowledge of P.L. 94–142 principles and requirements. The next section will provide an overview with emphasis on parent rights and responsibilities.

P.L. 94-142: PARENT RIGHTS AND RESPONSIBILITIES

The Education for All Handicapped Children Act, which became law in 1975, was implemented in 1977. It is commonly called P.L. 94–142 (the 142nd bill passed into law by the 94th Congress of the United States). It guarantees certain rights to parents and guardians of students enrolled in special education classes and the professionals who work with these students.

In addition to federal law, all states have laws to guarantee a free, appropriate education for their students. The rights guaranteed under state law may exceed those prescribed in the federal statute. Education professionals should be aware of any differences between federal law and the law of their state.

Six principles of P.L. 94–142 provide a foundation for many of the interactions among educators and parents. These principles include Zero reject, nondiscriminatory evaluation, individualized education programs, least restrictive environment, due process, and parent participation. Turnbull (1986)

provides a more detailed discussion and analysis of these principles for readers interested in more in-depth information.

Zero Reject

The zero reject principle requires that all children with handicaps be provided a free, appropriate public education. As the term implies, *no child*, regardless of the type or severity of the handicap, may be rejected by the public education system.

The zero reject principle prevents a child from not only being totally excluded, but also functionally excluded. *Total exclusion*, as the term implies, is when a child is denied the right to attend school of any type because of a disability. Total exclusion of some children with disabilities was widely practiced in the past. For example, some children with moderate or severe mental retardation were not allowed to attend school, but children identified as experiencing mild mental retardation were allowed. *Functional exclusion* occurs when a child receives services not appropriate to his or her needs. To prevent functional exclusion, the individualized education program (IEP) specifies the goals and objectives appropriate for each student.

In addition to standard educational services, students have rights to related services that address individual needs. Related services include transportation, speech and audiology, occupational and physical therapy, psychological services, counseling, physical education, recreation, school health services, social work services, and medical services for diagnostic purposes. Many states mandate other specific related services such as music therapy and dance. Students with severe handicaps may require a constellation of related services to meet their needs.

The zero reject principle mandates that educational services will be provided for children with severe handicaps who were previously excluded from school. In the past, parents had to beg for programs; sometimes they found no public programs and were forced to find other resources. Private schools, which have been tremendous financial burdens for parents, have led to feelings of alienation from the public schools. Many educators have been similarly frustrated: they want to provide for students with disabilities but have been stopped by constraints in school budgets. Zero reject requirements are creating new relationships between educators and parents, based on the premise that appropriate educational services will be provided at public expense. Interactions can begin by defining the types of curricula and services that constitute an appropriate education rather than by deciding whether or not the school will provide services for the student.

Nondiscriminatory Evaluation

Nondiscriminatory evaluation ensures that evaluation procedures are broadly based, fairly administered, and, initially, given only with the parents' informed consent. (Obtaining parents' informed consent throughout the evaluation process is discussed under "due process.") Broadly based testing must be sensitive to cultural factors (e.g. administered in the child's native language; validated for the specific purpose for which the tests are to be used; the use of two tests [minimum] and information from nontest sources, including data on physical condition, socio-cultural background, and adaptive behavior in home and school). Although not specifically required by the law, parents may be members of the evaluation team charged with collecting and interpreting educational data. If parents are not formal team members, the professionals on the evaluation team can solicit information from them.

Parents have other rights related to evaluation, such as challenging the appropriateness of particular data and obtaining formal evaluations of their children from private sources. Because these rights are procedural safeguards, they are discussed under "due process."

Thus P.L. 94–142 involves parents in the education process from the starting point of identification of service needs. As parents participate at different levels of involvement in the evaluations, they begin to interact with professionals and to lay foundations for future cooperation.

Individualized Education Programs

The individualized education program (IEP) is a primary mechanism set forth by P.L. 94–142 to ensure that students with disabilities receive a meaningful education appropriate to their needs and abilities.

It is beyond the scope of this chapter to describe, in-depth, the numerous requirements pertaining to the IEP process. Some of the major implications for

parent involvement will be highlighted. Turnbull, Strickland, and Brantley (1982) provide a more comprehensive analysis for developing, implementing, and evaluating IEPs.

Congressional intent for strong parental involvement in the IEP process is evident in the following statement by former Senator Harrison Williams:

The individualized planning conference is also intended as a method of providing additional parent counseling and training so that the parent may bolster the educational process at home. This involvement is important to assure the educational services are meeting the child's needs, and so both parents and child may be part of the process from which they're so often removed. . . .

One of the greatest benefits that can come to the handicapped child is to have the parents brought into the conferences, because the education of the child continues after the school doors close and the child is at home. This is one of the reasons the idea of the mandatory conference was developed, to make sure the parent is part of the education of the child. (126 Congressional Record S1950, daily ed., June 18, 1975)

The idea of the mandatory conference implies an expectation that parents will assume an active decision-making role in the conference. Educational professionals must provide either an oral or written notice to parents informing them of the purpose, time, location, and names of persons who will be in attendance at the IEP conference. The meeting must be scheduled at a time and place convenient for the parents.

The IEP conference is the crucial process for achieving an appropriate education program for students with handicaps. The implications of parent involvement in developing the IEP are tremendous. This requirement has the potential of bringing parents to the forefront in specifying what is an appropriate curriculum for their children and significantly influencing the degree of mutual decision making. The *actual* participation of parents in IEP conferences is discussed later in the chapter. Current research is reviewed to suggest that the parent-professional partnership in the IEP process is now more the exception than the rule.

Least Restrictive Environment

In P.L. 94–142, placement is considered the *least* restrictive when it meets two criteria: (a) it is nearest the education provided for students without handicaps, and (b) it provides a curriculum that is appropriate to the needs of the student.

There is no simple formula for determining the least restrictive educational placement. This principle addresses students' rights to associate with other students who do not have disabilities as well as the right to receive an appropriate education. If a student is placed in a regular classroom in which her specific needs are not being met, the placement is not the least restrictive. Likewise, placement in a special school attended only by students with disabilities is not the least restrictive placement.

The concept of least restriction also applies to extracurricular activities such as school clubs and special-interest groups. Skills to prepare students for meaningful involvement in extracurricular activities can be included on the IEP.

Many parents of students with disabilities have concerns about least restrictive placements (Turnbull & Winton, 1984). One study investigated the perspectives of parents of students with mild and moderate disabilities who were mainstreamed in kindergarten classes. The parents reported that the two major drawbacks of mainstreaming are their perception that their children do not receive the special help or individualized instruction they need, and that teachers are not qualified or trained to deal with the needs of their children. They identified major benefits as preparation for the real world and opportunities to learn from children who do not experience handicaps (Winton, Turnbull, Blacher, & Salkind, 1983). It is important to address these perspectives with parents directly and encourage them to participate in making placement decisions. Professionals can also be responsive by assisting all parents—those with and without children having disabilities—to gain more information on the goals of integrated placements. Many different strategies for providing information to parents on issues associated with integration are provided by Bautz, Barber, Brotherson, and Turnbull (1984).

Due Process

The due process principle addresses consent, proper notification, due process hearings, and surrogate (legally appointed) parents. It provides a system of checks and balances to protect the rights of the students, parents, and educators. It guarantees the right to protest the actions a government (a school district is a government unit) plans to take.

Due process makes school districts, as well as parents, accountable for their actions. It provides for fair procedures to produce acceptable, correct, and fair results.

In a larger sense, the due process principle is found in all aspects of both federal and state laws pertaining to special education. The laws specify the process to be followed in providing for the educational needs and rights of the students.

Consent
Parents have the right to give or refuse consent for their child's *initial* evaluation for special education services and *initial* placement in a special education program. Although consent is given in writing, parents have the right to withdraw it.

Notice
Parents must be notified in writing by the school before any changes are made in their child's placement or identification. The notice must contain a statement of the parents' legal rights, an explanation of the actions proposed by school personnel, the rationale for the actions, and any additional factors school personnel used in making their decision.

Independent Evaluations
Parents and guardians may request independent evaluations if they disagree with those performed by the school district. The school district has the responsibility to provide information concerning where such evaluations can be obtained at no expense or low expense.

Hearing
The due process hearing, guaranteed under both federal and state law, provides parents and educators with a means to resolve differences. Both parties may be represented by counsel, present evidence, examine, and cross-examine witnesses, and be assured of an impartial hearing officer to make a decision concerning the appropriateness of the student's education. The hearing should not be viewed as always being an "us against them" situation. It can provide a structured setting in which educators and parents can arrive at fair decisions that will result in an appropriate education for students with disabilities.

Obviously, due process stipulations create opportunities for parents to have access to educational information and to influence or change educational decisions. The opportunity for due process hearings provides checks and balances for both the parents and educators. Many parent-professional relationships are characterized by dissatisfaction with the behavior of one party by the other. Due process hearings provide an opportunity to examine these issues objectively and systematically. Thus, due process is a method of resolving conflict. A model for professional and parent participation in the due process hearing is described by Turnbull and Strickland (1981).

Surrogate Parents

If the parents of a child are unknown or unavailable, the question arises, "Who speaks for that child's rights?" In the case of a child who is a ward of the state, the same question arises. Understanding the importance of parents in the special education process, federal and state lawmakers have made provisions to ensure that all children with disabilities have someone to look after their interests. Surrogate parents (sometimes called educational advocates) are made available to all children and youth without parents or legal guardians.

The state education department appoints surrogate parents for students needing them. The person appointed must have the skills needed to represent a child properly, and there can be no conflict of interest. That is, the person cannot have conflicting loyalties as might be the case if an employee of the state education department or a local school district were appointed to be an advocate.

In some states, surrogate parents are paid. The laws make it clear that a person paid by a public agency, such as a state department of education, only to represent the interest of a student, does not become an agency employee. As a result, there is no conflict of interest issue to consider.

Surrogate parents have a right to (a) exercise all the duties, responsibilities, and rights that are given to parents or guardians concerning the education of the child they are appointed to represent and (b) receive assistance from school personnel to meet their responsibilities as advocates.

Parent Participation

The five principles already discussed have implications for parent participation in the special education process. Parent responsibility, as it pertains to such things as notice and consent, are all forms of parent participation.

Parents are also entitled to inspect and review all educational records kept on their children (unless prevented by state laws pertaining to matters such as guardianship, separation, and divorce) within 45 days after their request for access. They may request an interpretation of the records and may request that amendments be made. If the education agency refuses to amend the records, the parents may initiate a due process hearing.

Access to records equalizes decision-making power. The equalization of power stops the inclusion of negative, subjective information in the students' records. Such subjective information can influence the students' future teachers and prospective employers.

Parental access to records and the right to request amendments places them on equal footing with professionals who no longer control a domain that is off-limits to parents. Professionals are accountable for the manner in which they collect and maintain student data.

Before personally identifiable information is released to anyone other than authorized agency officials, school personnel must obtain parental consent. Because such records may contain private family and student information, this consent safeguard allows parents to control their children's records.

Agencies are required to inform parents when a need no longer exists for the collection and maintenance of confidential information. Parents can request that all unneeded information be destroyed. Certain types of information can be destroyed, but some information must be maintained for social security and other governmental benefits in the future. A permanent record of name, address, phone number, grade, attendance record, classes attended, grade level completed, and year completed may legally be maintained. Again, interested parties should consult state laws covering the maintenance of records.

Finally, parent involvement in the education process extends beyond the classroom. P.L. 94–142 charges state and local education agencies with conducting public hearings to solicit parental input concerning annual state and local program plans. Public comments must become components of such plans. Further, state education agencies must establish advisory panels with parent representation to establish guidelines for special education efforts and to review regulations.

P.L. 94–142 clearly provides opportunities for parents—biological, guardian, and surrogate—to be full partners with teachers, therapists, and other professionals in the special education process.

School personnel are responsible for educating children and youth while ensuring that their rights are safeguarded.

For each parent right there is also a responsibility. Parents should attempt to keep educators informed of developments that affect their children's education. Parents fulfill their responsibilities by participating in the IEP conference, giving consent, and by communicating openly with educators. Cooperation and respect for the rights and responsibilities of parents by educators is half of the picture; parent cooperation and respect for educators is the other half.

Partnerships between parents and professionals cannot be actualized through a legal mandate alone. Although the first decade of P.L. 94–142 has been reached, there is still a discrepancy between the intention of P.L. 94–142 and prevalent practices that continue to sidestep parent involvement in planning. Some of these discrepancies are discussed in the next section with recommendations for improvement.

PARENTS AS EDUCATIONAL DECISION MAKERS

The many requirements for parent involvement in P.L. 94–142 are integrated into a systematic process involving the identification, evaluation, and placement of students with disabilities. This process is summarized in Figure 2.1. Many parents participate in all functions, from the point of referral to reviewing and revising the IEP. Other parents prefer a less active role. Professionals may view parents of students with disabilities as homogeneous rather than heterogeneous. They sometimes assume that all parents have similar interests and capabilities. Recent research on parent involvement (from the parents' perspective) reveals diverse opinions and preferences in assuming an active decision-making role (Winton & Turnbull, 1981).

Turnbull and Turnbull (1982) examined the assumptions underlying parent participation in the educational process. They found that professional assumptions regarding active participation by parents are not based on sound research data. The assumptions are based more on ways that advocates, policy makers and legislators *think* parents should participate. The assumption that *many* parents want to be involved has led, in some cases, to the assumption that *all* parents want this involvement. Parent participation in the decision-making

process may be detrimental to some and extremely helpful to others (Turnbull & Turnbull, 1982; Turnbull, Turnbull, & Wheat, 1982).

Professionals must ensure that parents have opportunities for decision making; however, each parent must decide the degree to which he or she will assume the role of an educational decision maker. Special attention will be given here to two types of decision making, parent involvement in evaluation and in IEP development.

Parent Involvement in Evaluation

Involving parents in the evaluation of their child helps educators understand the parents' view of the child's developmental level and educational needs. Active parent involvement also enhances the probability that the parents will understand the information they receive. Parents should have the opportunity to share information with educators and to receive information and interpretations from them. They should also be assured of the strict confidentiality of this information.

Marion (1980) has stated that compared to other issues, evaluation has caused the most friction between schools and culturally diverse populations. Parents of children from culturally diverse backgrounds are concerned about the disproportionate number of ethnically different children assigned to special education classes. By sharing and receiving information, parents can help educators guard against discrimination.

Valuable information can be obtained from parents immediately after referral and before the initial educational evaluation of the student (McLoughlin, Edge, & Strenecky, 1978). Parents can provide information on the child's developmental history, previous diagnostic reports, and any special concerns to be considered in planning the evaluation. Guidelines for constructing a behavioral inventory to use with parents to pinpoint the child's strengths and weaknesses are provided by Heward, Dardig, and Rossett (1979). It is important to remember, however, that sometimes parents are asked to provide information repeatedly (developmental history) that should be in the cumulative record. These requests show disrespect for parents' time and also waste professionals' time. Records of important information should be maintained to avoid redundant questioning. Parents should also be afforded the right to privacy of family information unrelated to their child's disability.

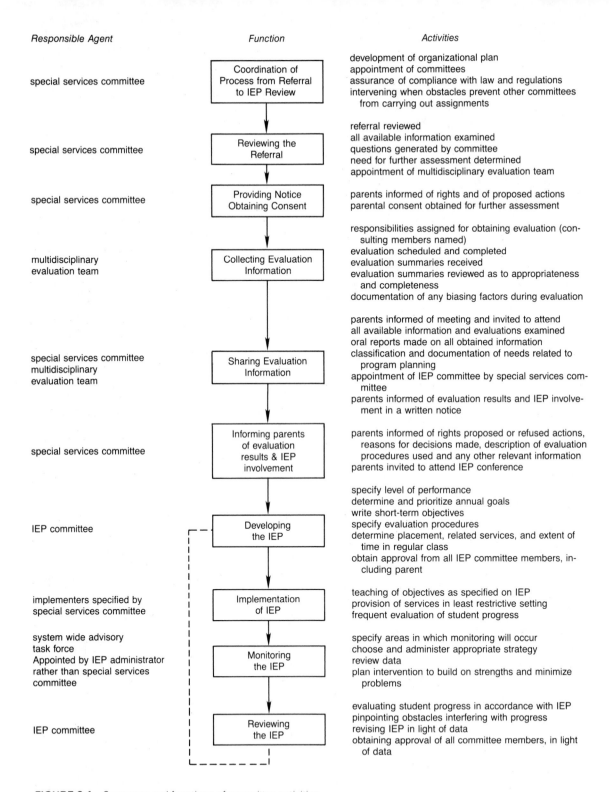

Responsible Agent	Function	Activities
special services committee	Coordination of Process from Referral to IEP Review	development of organizational plan appointment of committees assurance of compliance with law and regulations intervening when obstacles prevent other committees from carrying out assignments
special services committee	Reviewing the Referral	referral reviewed all available information examined questions generated by committee need for further assessment determined appointment of multidisciplinary evaluation team
special services committee	Providing Notice Obtaining Consent	parents informed of rights and of proposed actions parental consent obtained for further assessment
multidisciplinary evaluation team	Collecting Evaluation Information	responsibilities assigned for obtaining evaluation (consulting members named) evaluation scheduled and completed evaluation summaries received evaluation summaries reviewed as to appropriateness and completeness documentation of any biasing factors during evaluation
special services committee multidisciplinary evaluation team	Sharing Evaluation Information	parents informed of meeting and invited to attend all available information and evaluations examined oral reports made on all obtained information classification and documentation of needs related to program planning appointment of IEP committee by special services committee parents informed of evaluation results and IEP involvement in a written notice
special services committee	Informing parents of evaluation results & IEP involvement	parents informed of rights proposed or refused actions, reasons for decisions made, description of evaluation procedures used and any other relevant information parents invited to attend IEP conference
IEP committee	Developing the IEP	specify level of performance determine and prioritize annual goals write short-term objectives specify evaluation procedures determine placement, related services, and extent of time in regular class obtain approval from all IEP committee members, including parent
implementers specified by special services committee	Implementation of IEP	teaching of objectives as specified on IEP provision of services in least restrictive setting frequent evaluation of student progress
system wide advisory task force Appointed by IEP administrator rather than special services committee	Monitoring the IEP	specify areas in which monitoring will occur choose and administer appropriate strategy review data plan intervention to build on strengths and minimize problems
IEP committee	Reviewing the IEP	evaluating student progress in accordance with IEP pinpointing obstacles interfering with progress revising IEP in light of data obtaining approval of all committee members, in light of data

FIGURE 2.1 Sequence and functions of committee activities

Source: From *Developing and Implementing Individualized Education Programs* (p. 22) by A. P. Turnbull, B. Strickland, and J. C. Brantley, 1982, Columbus, OH: Charles E. Merrill. Copyright 1982 by Charles E. Merrill Publishing Company. Reprinted by permission.

Parents also can share useful information on the child's adaptive behavior, self-help skills, peer interaction in the neighborhood, medication schedule, and language development. This information can be collected through informal discussions, structured interviews, and written questionnaires. Vincent and her colleagues have developed the *Parent Inventory of Child Development in Non-school Environments* that enables evaluators to identify skills important to parents and that are relevant for the student's home and community environment (Vincent, Davis, Brown, Broome, Miller, & Gruenewald, 1983).

Parents can also provide information about their child's preferences and choices, especially when a student with severe disabilities is unable to communicate in the IEP conference. Parents can complete an inventory, such as the one in Table 2.1, to share important information on their child's preferences. Special educators recognize the importance of identifying student preferences and choice-making skills (Guess, Benson, & Siegel-Causey,

1985; Shevin & Klein, 1984; Turnbull & Turnbull, 1985).

In order to plan an IEP tailored to their child's strengths and weaknesses, parents need information from educators on the child's performance during the evaluation. Most children with severe handicaps are diagnosed before they enter the educational system. Thus, parents typically learn that their child has some serious problems during the preschool years. The educational evaluation usually confirms the presence of a handicap and provides additional information on the child's pre-academic and academic performance.

Professionals should listen to the parents' concerns and gear the interpretation of the data to those concerns, answering questions, using examples to illustrate developmental concepts (visual tracking), minimizing or eliminating the use of jargon, and sharing information rather than withholding aspects that are unpleasant or difficult to discuss.

It is helpful to parents to have an immediate follow-up meeting to the interpretative conference

TABLE 2.1   Student preference and choice questionnaire

1. How does _____ indicate his/her likes/dislikes?

	Likes	*Dislikes*
a. Laughs	_____	_____
b. Cries	_____	_____
c. Facial Expression	_____	_____
d. Screams	_____	_____
e. Tantrums	_____	_____
f. Looks at people	_____	_____
g. Looks at objects	_____	_____
h. Moves body	_____	_____
i. Points/Reaches	_____	_____
j. Imitates actions	_____	_____
k. Vocalizes	_____	_____
l. Gestures	_____	_____
m. Other _____	_____	_____
n. _____	_____	_____
o. _____	_____	_____

TABLE 2.1 (continued)

2. What kinds of choices does _____ usually have the opportunity to make? Please provide examples:

_____

_____

_____

_____

3. What types of choices are most comfortable for _____ to make?

_____

_____

Why do you think these are most comfortable?

_____

_____

4. Do you want an objective included in _____'s individualized education program (IEP) that will help him/her learn the skill of making choices. (Circle one)

YES   NO

5. Has _____ ever indicated what kind of job he/she would like to have? If so, what is it?

_____

_____

Have you or the school personnel identified the critical skills _____ will need to perform this job?

YES   NO

If yes, which skills would you like included in _____'s next IEP?

_____

_____

_____

If no, discuss with the school personnel how these skills could be identified and by whom.

6. Has _____ ever indicated where he/she would like to live after high school or later in adulthood?

YES   NO

If yes, where? _____

_____

Have you or the school personnel identified the critical skills _____ will need in the place he/she chooses to live?

YES   NO

TABLE 2.1 (continued)

If yes, which skills would you like included in _____'s next IEP?

_____

_____

_____

If no, discuss with the school personnel how these skills could be identified and by whom.

7. In general, at what time of day does _____ prefer to be active and productive?

_____

8. At what time of day does _____ prefer to rest and relax?

_____

9. Most of the time, _____ prefers to be:
   (circle the appropriate response)

   a. alone   with 1 other   with small   with large   unable to
                     person   group   group   assess

   b. independent   supervised   dependent   unable to
                                                         assess

   c. with age   with persons   with persons   unable to
      peers   older   younger   assess

   d. Involved in:

      activities of activities of   activities of   unable to
      fast pace   moderate pace   slow pace   assess

   e. Engaged in:

      highly   moderately   non-repetitive   unable to
      repetitive   repetitive   activities   assess
      activities   activities

   f. in highly   moderately   non-competitive   unable to
      competitive   competitive   situations   assess
      situations   situations

   g. in highly   moderately   loosely   unable to
      structured   structured   structured   assess
      situations   situations   situations

The information in this questionnaire can help parents and educators develop an individualized education program (IEP) based upon the choices and preferences of your child. This questionnaire can help identify the appropriate evaluations, goals, objectives, and related services that need to be included in the IEP document. It can also help identify the time of day and in what environment your son or daughter prefers to learn. It can be a valuable tool for planning an individualized education program.

Source: Adapted from *How to Plan for My Child's Adult Future: A Three-part Process to Future Planning* by A. P. Turnbull, M. J. Brotherson, G. J. Bronicki, H. A. Benson, J. Houghton, C. Roeder-Gordon, and J. A. Summers, 1985, Future Planning Project, University Affiliated Facility, Bureau of Child Research, Lawrence, KS.

(a week later) where they can ask for clarification or interpretations soon after they have reflected on what was said. Regardless of how many times parents have been told about the developmental deficits of their children, interpretative sessions are usually stressful. The information parents receive may be clouded by the stress they feel.

When students are reevaluated (P.L. 94–142 requires reevaluation every 3 years), some parents may prefer to receive a written summary of the evaluation results before the interpretative conference. This advance information allows parents to identify parts of the report that are unclear and make notes on information to share and questions to ask. Their confidence is boosted by knowing they will not be caught by surprise when they meet face to face with educators.

Parent Involvement in IEP Development

Parents must be invited to attend conferences, but a review of the research on parent participation in the IEP meeting suggests that parental participation is usually passive rather than active. The National Committee for Citizens in Education (1979) surveyed approximately 2,300 parents from 438 school districts. Slightly over half the parents said that the IEP was completed before the meeting. Observations of IEP conferences for elementary school students with mild disabilities revealed that a typical conference involved a resource teacher describing an already developed IEP to the parent (Goldstein, Strickland, Turnbull, & Curry, 1980). The mean length of these conferences was 36 minutes. Gilliam and Coleman (1981) surveyed participants at IEP meetings to determine the roles of persons with the strongest influence and contributions. Parents were ranked high in importance before the meeting, but low in actual contribution after the meeting.

Lynch and Stein (1982) surveyed 400 parents concerning the nature of their IEP participation. (A small subset of these parents had children with severe handicaps.) Parents reported that they had actively participated in IEP development. The active participation they cited included expressing opinions and making suggestions (14.6%), helping and trusting the professionals (11.2%), listening to and agreeing with the teacher's recommendations (7.5%), and understanding everything going on (6.3%). These examples do not necessarily indicate *active* involvement.

The manner in which professionals conduct IEP conferences can greatly influence the nature of parent participation. One model for conducting IEP conferences is to conceptualize the conference as having six components:

1. *Preconference preparation.* Plan the conference agenda and logistics in advance to ensure meaningful parent participation.
2. *Initial conference proceedings.* Establish rapport at the beginning of the meeting to ensure that the purpose of the meeting is understood and the agenda is organized.
3. *Interpretation of evaluation results.* Identify the student's strengths and weaknesses as a foundation for planning an appropriate IEP.
4. *Development of the curriculum portion of the IEP.* Specify the student's current level of performance, annual goals, short-term objectives, and evaluation procedures to be used in measuring progress.
5. *Placement decision and related services.* Determine the least restrictive, appropriate setting and the necessary related services to ensure that the student will benefit from special education.
6. *Conclusion of the meeting.* Summarize the decisions made, the methods to be used in maintaining communication between parents and professionals, and the nature of follow-up responsibility.

Table 2.2 includes suggestions for each of the six components of the conference. These suggestions help provide opportunities for parents to participate according to their preferences and increase the effectiveness and efficiency of team decision making.

A resource for more information on individualizing IEP conferences to accommodate parental interests is Turnbull, Turnbull, Summers, Brotherson, and Benson (1986), which includes an inventory parents can complete in advance of the conference to specify their preferences for time and location of the meeting, family members and professionals to attend, and information that would be helpful to exchange in advance. Furthermore, they include a comprehensive review of research on parental participation in IEP conferences.

In summary, there are extensive legal requirements pertaining to parent-professional partnerships. Many school systems are using different strategies to meet both the letter and the spirit of the law in enhancing opportunities for parents to

TABLE 2.2 Suggestions for involving parents in the IEP conference

Preconference Preparation

1. Appoint a conference chair to coordinate all aspects of the conference. The conference chair should assume responsibility for coordinating preconference preparation, chairing the conference, and coordinating follow-up.
2. Solicit information from parents on their preferences related to their participation: persons who should attend, convenient time, convenient location, needed assistance (child-care, transportation), and the type of information that they would like to receive in advance. (See Table 10.2 for a sample questionnaire.)
3. Specify the persons appropriate to attend the IEP conference in light of parent and professional preferences. Be sure to consider carefully the possibility of including the student.
4. Arrange a convenient time and location for the meeting.
5. If needed, work with parents in assisting them with logistics such as childcare and transportation.
6. Inform parents (in writing or verbally) of the purpose, time of conference, location, and names of participants.
7. In light of parents' preferences, share information in advance of the conference that they believe will help them prepare for participation—e.g., evaluation reports, evaluation checklists to complete, list of subject areas which school personnel think should be covered by the IEP, summary of child's strengths and weaknesses in each subject area, ideas from school personnel on possible goals and objectives, information on legal rights, and information on placement options and related services.
8. If several placements are being considered for the student, encourage parents to visit each program prior to the conference.
9. Discuss the conference purpose and procedures with students and assist them in specifying their own preferences for educational programming. Encourage students to discuss their preferences with their parents.
10. Encourage parents to share any information with school personnel in advance of the conference that the parents believe will be helpful during the preparation period.
11. Gather all information from school personnel that will help prepare for the IEP conference.
12. Prepare an agenda to cover each of the remaining five components of the conference.

Initial Conference Proceedings

1. Greet and welcome parents upon arrival and welcome any persons whom the parents bring with them.
2. Introduce all conference participants and share sufficient information to identify roles and areas of responsibility. If parents are being introduced to several professionals for the first time, consider the use of name tags or make a list of the names and positions of conference participants for the parents.
3. State the purpose of the conference and review the agenda. Ask the parents and their guests if there are any issues they would like to add to the agenda.
4. Ask participants the amount of time they have available for the conference. State the intention to use time wisely but to avoid rushing through important decisions. Share the option of re-scheduling another meeting if necessary.
5. Ask parents and their guests if they would like to have a clarification of legal rights. If so, fully provide the information they request.

Review of Formal Evaluation and Current Levels of Performance

1. If a formal evaluation of the student has been conducted and a separate evaluation conference to review results has not been held, ask the appropriate diagnostic personnel to identify the tests administered, the specific results of each, and the options for consideration based on the evaluation results.
2. After evaluation information has been shared, summarize the major findings and encourage parents to point out areas of agreement and disagreement and their corresponding reasons.
3. Ask parents if they would like to have a written copy of evaluation results. If so, provide it to them.
4. If a formal evaluation has not been conducted (one must be conducted every three years), review the child's developmental progress and present levels of performance in each subject area.
5. Identify current implications of all test results for instructional programming and future implications for the next lifecycle stage of the child.
6. Clarify any diagnostic jargon that is used.
7. Solicit parental input on the student's current performance levels. Identify areas of agreement and disagreement.
8. Strive to resolve disagreement through discussion or examples of student performance. If your disagreement cannot be resolved within the conference, develop a plan for collecting further evaluation information by school personnel or an independent evaluator. Solicit parental suggestions on the procedures to follow in collecting further information.
9. Proceed with the development of the IEP only when you and the parents agree on the student's type of exceptionality and current levels of performance.

TABLE 2.2   (continued)

Development of Goals and Objectives

1. Based on the current levels of performance, identify all subject areas requiring specially designed instruction. For each subject area, collaboratively specify appropriate goals and objectives.
2. Encourage parents and their guests to share goals and objectives they believe are important for current and future functioning in the home, school, or community environment.
3. Prioritize goals and objectives in light of relevance for the student. Discuss future educational and vocational options for the student to insure that the goals and objectives provide sufficient preparation for future needs.
4. If the student receives instruction from two or more teachers, clarify the manner in which the responsibility for teaching the objectives will be shared.
5. Ask parents if they are willing to assume responsibility for teaching or reviewing some of the objectives with their son or daughter at home. If so, discuss their preferences for which goals and objectives they will work on.
6. Insure that evaluation procedures and schedules are identified for goals and objectives.
7. Explain to parents that including goals and objectives in the IEP does not represent a guarantee that the student will achieve them; rather, it represents a good faith effort that school personnel will teach these goals and objectives.

Determination of Placement and Related Services

1. Based on the student's current levels of performance and the goals and objectives deemed appropriate, review the full continuum of viable placement options by identifying benefits and drawbacks of each. Solicit parent input on benefits and drawbacks from an academic and social perspective of the different placement options for their child.
2. If parents have not already visited possible placements, encourage them to do so. Agree on a "tentative placement" until the parents can visit and confirm its appropriateness.
3. Select the placement option consistent with the goals and objectives to be taught. The placement should be as close to peers who do not have exceptionalities as possible. Specify the extent of the student's participation in the regular education program.
4. Identify the related services the student needs. Discuss the benefits and drawbacks of each service and options for scheduling (i.e., frequency, the portion of class that will be missed).
5. Specify the dates for initiating each related service and the anticipated duration of each.
6. If the parents have not had an opportunity to meet the teacher of the selected placement or the related service providers, share the names and qualifications of these professionals.

Concluding the Conference

1. Summarize to review major decisions and follow-up responsibility. Take notes to record this summary.
2. Assign follow-up responsibility for any task (e.g., arranging for physical therapy) requiring attention.
3. Review with parents the responsibility (teaching objectives, increasing socialization opportunities during after-school hours, visiting adult programs) they have expressed interest in assuming.
4. Set a tentative date for reviewing the IEP document on at least an annual basis and preferably more frequently.
5. Identify strategies for ongoing communication with parents, in light of the preferences of all involved parties.
6. Express appreciation for the shared decision making that occurred and reiterate to parents how much their participation is valued.

Source: From *Families and Professionals: Creating an Exceptional Partnership* (pp. 238–240) by A. P. Turnbull, H. R. Turnbull, J. A. Summers, M. J. Brotherson, and H. A. Benson, 1986, Columbus, OH: Charles E. Merrill. Copyright 1986 by Merrill Publishing Company. Reprinted by permission.

participate in educational decisions. Research over the last 5 years suggests that parents participate passively in educational decision making. This finding has led researchers and practitioners to examine the needs of families and to propose a model that recognizes the complex needs of families as well as their role in their child's educational development. The next section will review the progress that has been made in working within this family-systems perspective.

A FAMILY-SYSTEMS PERSPECTIVE

Family-systems theory searches for the causes of behavior, not in the individual alone, but in the interactions among the members of a system or group. This theory operates on the premise that all parts of the family are interrelated; furthermore, each family has unique properties, understood only through careful observation of the relationships and interactions among all members. There is a growing interest in the family systems model (Berardo, 1980; Holman & Burr, 1980; Olson, Russell, & Sprenkle, 1980; Olson, Sprenkle, & Russell, 1979; Turnbull, Brotherson, & Summers, 1985; Turnbull, Summers, & Brotherson, 1984; Turnbull, Turnbull, Summers, Brotherson, & Benson, 1986). This model requires a multidisciplinary effort involving sociologists, social workers, psychologists, counselors, and special educators.

The application of family-systems theory to special education requires fundamental changes in answering the question: Who is the consumer of the services delivered by special education professionals? In the past, the student has been viewed as the sole consumer. The family-systems approach identifies the whole family as the consumer of services. Figure 2.2 depicts the family-systems framework (Turnbull, Summers, & Brotherson, 1984). The components of the framework and their interrelationships within the system are as follows:

1. *Family resources* consist of the descriptive characteristics of the family, including the characteristics of exceptionality, characteristics of the family, and personal characteristics of each member. These characteristics are the *input* into the interactional system—the resources, the perception of the world—that shape the way in which the family interacts.

2. *Family interaction* is the hub of the system, the *process* of interaction among individual family members and subsystems. Subsystem interactions are influenced by and, in turn, influence the responses made to meeting individual and collective family needs.

3. *Family function* is the *output* of the interactional system. Using its resources (input), the family interacts (processes) to produce responses that fulfill family economic, social, vocational, and affectional needs.

4. *Family life cycle* introduces the element of *change* into the family system. As the family moves through time, developmental and nondevelopmental changes alter the family's resources and/or the family's needs; these, in turn, produce change in the way the family interacts.

The dominant features of the family-systems model are the family's complexity and uniqueness. Each family is composed of so many attributes that it can interact in an almost endless variety of ways. Furthermore, a family is not a static entity. It is constantly changing as well as resisting change. This section will briefly discuss each of the four components outlined in Figure 2.2 and highlight issues relevant for special educators.

Family Resources

If you will think of the range of families in your community, you will see that family resources are infinitely diverse. This diversity greatly influences the impact of a child with severe disability on the family and their response to meeting the needs of that child. Three considerations in understanding the diversity of a family's resources are the characteristics of the disability itself, the characteristics of the family as a whole, and the personal characteristics of each member of the family.

Characteristics of the exceptionality will vary. A nonambulatory child can place restrictions on the mobility and spontaneity of activities for all members. A child with medical complications can move the focus of parent-child interaction from the home to the hospital room. A child with a later onset of disability (disability caused from an accident during school years) can cause major readjustments from "normality" to "special needs." A child with an intense need for structure and routine can clash with the flexible temperament of other family members. A child able to complete domestic chores can be helpful to the family in meeting its responsibilities. A child with a special gift for expressing affection can greatly enhance the love and warmth within the family. Special educators have long recognized the need for individualization in the classroom. The overlooked fact is that there is also individualization in the way each child affects the family, depending upon the child's characteristics and the family's response to them. A more severe disability does not always produce greater stress. As one parent of a young adolescent commented:

Don has been labelled profoundly retarded. He is not able to do anything to take care of himself, cannot walk, and has no language. Sure, he creates strains and stresses. But I remind myself that I never have to chase him around the house, he never talks back or sasses, he doesn't have to enter the rat race of teen-age years like my other sons, and he does not try to hurt himself.

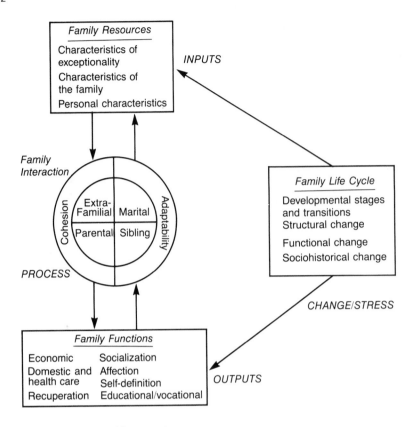

FIGURE 2.2   Family systems conceptual framework

Source: From *Working with Families with Disabled Members: A Family Systems Approach* (p. 60) by A. P. Turnbull, J. A. Summers, and M. J. Brotherson, 1984, Lawrence, KS, Kansas University Affiliated Facility, University of Kansas.

Second, *family characteristics* vary in areas such as size (Trevino, 1979), form (dual vs. single parents, original vs. reconstituted family) (Vishner & Vishner, 1982), cultural background (McGoldrick, Pearce, & Giordano, 1982), socioeconomic status (Dunlap & Hollingsworth, 1977), and geographic location (McGill & Pearce, 1982). Ethnicity, an aspect of the family's cultural background, provides an example of variations in family characteristics.

Ethnicity involves more than race, religion, or country of national origin. It is a sense of "we-ness" handed down through generations (Turnbull, Summers & Brotherson, 1984). McGoldrick and her colleagues (1982) noted:

Ethnicity patterns our thinking, feeling, and behavior in both obvious and subtle ways. It plays a major role in determining what we eat, how we work, how we relax, how we celebrate holidays and rituals, and how we feel about life, death and illness. (p. 4)

The United States as a "melting pot" is a myth. Recent research has shown that traditional values and attitudes continue to influence third- and fourth-generation families (McGoldrick et al., 1982). It would be more accurate to describe American society as an "exotic stew" composed of various ingredients (ethnic groups) that maintain certain characteristics despite the blending that occurs in the "simmering" of the mixture.

A family may not even identify its own behavior patterns as being influenced by cultural roots. Marriage ceremonies, religious beliefs and practices, rites of passage (bar or bas mitzvah), celebrations of holidays, observations of holy days, rituals surrounding deaths and burials, a person's perception of his relationship to the world, political beliefs, attitudes toward independence and work, and achievement orientation may be peculiarly influenced by ethnicity. For example, vocational training for a teen-ager with severe mental retardation will be viewed differently by persons from different ethnic traditions because of different work values. Many professionals may mistakenly interpret parents' lower priority on vocational training as a failure to recognize the potential abilities of their son or daughter with mental retardation, when, in fact, the lower priority is consistent with their ethnic values and is not at all related to their views of mental retardation.

Professionals must be aware of influences rooted in ethnic backgrounds. They must be able to integrate this phenomenon into the delivery of service, but remain ever vigilant against stereotyping. There is no such thing as a "typical" Black, Italian, German, or Jew. There may, however, be shared traits and understandings that can make a difference in the success of parent-professional interactions (Brotherson, 1984; McGoldrick et al., 1982). Just as with ethnicity, other diverse characteristics of families can influence their relationship with their child and with special education professionals.

Individuals comprise families, and individuals have their own *personal characteristics:* physical and mental health, intellectual capacity, and coping styles. For example, Olson and his associates (Olson, McCubbin, Barnes, Larsen, Muxen, & Wilson, 1983) categorized five types of coping strategies:

1. Passive appraisal (ignoring a problem or setting it aside, either temporarily or permanently).
2. Reframing (changing the way one thinks about a problem in order to solve it and/or to make it seem less stressful).
3. Spiritual support (deriving comfort and guidance from spiritual beliefs).
4. Social support (receiving practical and emotional assistance from friends and family).
5. Professional support (receiving assistance from professionals and human service agencies).

Families use various combinations of these strategies with different degrees of success in response to stress created by the presence of a disability.

Consider the similar needs of two families. They both have young children with severe mental retardation and major health complications. Both children require 24-hour per day care, and both families are committed to keeping their children at home. One family enlists the assistance of a respite-care program along with members of their church who assist with care of the child and household duties. The second family adamantly opposes asking anyone for help. They turn to extended family members and friends who volunteer. In the first family, the father does not involve himself in providing personal care to his child and says "he just can't handle it." His cultural background influences his decision about what he as a male should and should not handle. This is a major source of family conflict because the mother believes that he places unrealistic expectations on her. In the second family, the father and mother share childcare duties. Their major source of support is their cooperative partnership. The major source of stress for them is that the mother wants to pour out her feelings and get on with making long-term plans. The father, on the other hand, stoically insists that talking about it only makes matters worse. It is obvious that these families differ in their coping styles and that individuals within the same family differ from each other.

In summary, families vary widely in the resources available to them. Professionals can best help families by helping them recognize their unique resources for providing support to their child and by forming partnerships with them that are respectful of their individual characteristics and values.

Family Interaction

Parent-professional relationships are typically mother-professional relationships. Frequently, the assumption is made that "mother" and "family" are synonymous (Benson & Turnbull, 1986). This is a faulty assumption. Some families' members are related by blood or marriage whereas others are related by preference (a close family friend who is regarded as a family member). The family is a unit of interaction. Each family member is affected by the child's disability and the child is affected by each family member.

Professionals should always recognize that any interaction with the child or any other member has ripple effects throughout the whole family. A home visit can create family stress because of a perception of having the privacy of one's own turf violated or because of the need to alter the family's schedule of activities or responsibilities. Scheduling a parent conference to discuss the child's progress can create an argument between two working parents about which one will take time off from employment. Working with the child to improve social skills can enhance a sibling relationship that was threatened by embarrassment over inappropriate public behavior. Expecting parents to follow through on home programs can strengthen their relationship with their child, but may also create major tensions. These tensions between parent and child can then spill over into the marriage, sibling interactions, and interactions with extended family, neighbors, bosses, and co-workers. Interaction with any member of the system has implications for all members.

The family-systems framework highlights four major subsystems within traditional nuclear families:

1. Marital subsystem—Husband and wife interactions.
2. Parental subsystem—Parent and child interactions.
3. Sibling subsystem—Child and child interactions.
4. Extrafamilial subsystem—Whole family or individual member interactions with extended family, friends, neighbors, and professionals.

Variations in subsystems exist in many families, such as single parents, step parents, the one-child family, "live-in" members, and the extrafamilial network.

The impact of a child with a severe disability can vary across different subsystems of the family by strengthening or impinging upon marriages (Kazak & Marvin, 1984; Murphy, 1982), creating greater sensitivity in siblings or contributing to adjustment problems (Grossman, 1972; Vadasy, Fewell, Meyer, & Schell, 1984), creating parental satisfaction or disappointment (Turnbull & Turnbull, 1985), and drawing the extended family closer together or farther apart (Vadasy, Fewell, & Meyer, 1986). Professionals should recognize that supporting families are important in developing relationships that are as positive and gratifying as possible. IEP goals can foster successful family integration. For example, students can be taught leisure skills consistent with the recreational interests of parents and siblings, or priority can be given to self-help, communication, or social skills that could lead to increasing contact with members of the extrafamilial network. Professionals can provide information to extended family or friends and help them gain confidence in handling seizures, feeding techniques, positioning, and responding to perseverative language.

Families have responsibilities for meeting the needs of *all* members, not just the child or youth with a disability. Professionals may perceive a parent's absence from a conference or failure to follow through on home teaching as not giving the child adequate attention. An alternative explanation is that the parents are attending to the needs of the marriage, other family members or their own personal needs. Successful families balance the needs of *all* members, rather than placing a *single* member in a focal position and meeting that person's needs at the expense of other members. Family therapists have identified two dimensions in establishing balance in family relationships—cohesion and adaptability.

Cohesion is the bridge between close emotional bonding and individual independence. Carnes (1981) uses an example of "the touching of hands" to describe cohesion:

The dilemma is how to be close yet separate. When the fingers are intertwined, it at first feels secure and warm. Yet when one partner (or family member) tries to move, it is difficult at best. The squeezing pressure may even be painful. . . . The paradox of every relationship is how to touch and yet not hold on. (pp. 70–71)

Professionals can be sensitive to supporting families to learn to "touch and yet not hold on" by encouraging them to have a balanced rather than focal view of their child in the family, to obtain respite care when it is needed, to assist their child in building a social support network, and to acquaint them with the range of community resources upon which they can draw.

Adaptability is the ability of the family to change and create new responses when necessary to respond to emerging situations (Olson et al., 1980). Many families establish routine patterns of interaction. For example, the mother in a family may assume responsibility for bathing, dressing, feeding, and toileting a child with severe physical disabilities. This pattern may become so engrained that the mother is unable to leave town for a vacation or a visit with extended family or even to have a break from these duties. If the mother is ill or an emergency arises, a crisis is likely to occur. One way to support families to achieve successful family interactions is to encourage them to develop an array of alternatives and options to enhance their adaptability.

Families vary greatly in how they choose to interact. The families' resources influence their interaction patterns, and interaction patterns influence how families respond to individual or collective needs.

Family Functions

As with other complex social organizations, families exist to serve the individual and collective needs of their members (Turnbull, Summers, & Brotherson, 1984). Serving these needs is the function of the family system; functions are the product or output of the various family interactions. Family functions can be characterized in many ways; one of those ways is the identification of seven functions (Turnbull, Turnbull, Summers, Brotherson, & Benson, 1986).

These functions, and some tasks performed by family members to meet them, are:

1. Economic—Generating income and handling family finances, paying bills, earning allowances, handling insurance matters.
2. Domestic/Health Care—Purchasing food, preparing meals, health care and maintenance, home maintenance, transportation activities, general safety measures.
3. Recreation—Vacations, developing and participating in hobbies or clubs, setting aside everyday demands.
4. Socialization—Developing individual and collective friendships, social skills, and engaging in social activities.
5. Self-definition—Establishing self-identity and self-image, awareness of personal strengths and weaknesses, feelings of belonging and acceptance.
6. Affection—Developing intimate personal relationships, expressing one's sexuality, giving and receiving nurturance and love, expressing emotions.
7. Educational/Vocational—Participating in school-related activities, continuing education for family adults, homework, career development, development of work ethic.

It is apparent that the functions are not independent of each other. One function may facilitate another function, as might be the case when the socialization function of developing an individual friendship eventually leads to an intimate personal relationship which meets an individual need for affection. On the other hand, one function may impede progress in another functional area. Con-

sider the case where economic insolvency affects a family's nutrition or other health-related needs, which in turn can affect an individual member's feeling of personal security which is related to self-definition.

Professionals must examine all family functions. Educational/vocational needs represent but one function. There may be a tendency for educational professionals to concentrate on the educational/ vocational functions of parents to the exclusion of all others. Education professionals can best support students with disabilities and their families by recognizing the complex, interrelated needs of families.

A youth with a disability can influence a family in negative, neutral and positive ways (Skrtic, Summers, Brotherson, & Turnbull, 1984; Turnbull, Turnbull, Summers, Brotherson, & Benson, 1986; Wikler, Wasow, & Hatfield, 1981; Wikler, Wasow, & Hatfield, 1983). We will discuss the economic and affection functions as examples of the differential impacts of a disability in the family.

Economic Needs

All families have a need for income and a way to spend the money earned to meet the family's food, clothing, shelter and miscellaneous needs. The presence of a member with a disability can create economic problems. There are costs associated with rearing a child with a disability that are not associated with children without disabilities. Adaptive feeding utensils, special clothing, lift-equipped vans, bathroom adaptions such as support and safety bars, ongoing medications required for seizures and other physiological maladies, various body braces, voice synthesizers, hearing aids, adaptive seating equipment, ongoing evaluations by specialists, specially adapted furniture to facilitate lifting, hospital beds, respirators, suctioning equipment, adaptive exercise equipment, remote control devices for televisions, radios and lights, positioning equipment such as side lyers and prone standers, adaptive toys, and adaptive mobility devices such as walkers and crutches are but some of the devices and services a person with a disability may require.

Many of the devices require ongoing servicing and periodic replacement. Even families fortunate to have the best health insurance coverage find that many of the adaptive devices and medical services are not fully covered. The costs associated with medically fragile people can be even greater.

Brotherson (1985) offered the following quote on financial matters by one of the fathers in her study:

I don't know where the money is going to come from. We've had to have help over the years. I quit counting when Ron's hospital bill topped $600,000. (p. 205)

Costs associated with providing for the needs of one family member can limit the funds available for other family members. Parents and other family members may forgo attending to their own needs to be able to afford services for their children. Parents may know that a child could benefit from the purchase of some special piece of equipment and not be able to afford it. Such a situation can have a detrimental impact on the parents' self-image as providers.

The presence of a family member with a disability may prevent parents from obtaining employment because of the level of care and supervision required. This is especially true of parents of preschool children with disabilities, because of the shortage of preschool programs and day care options available for children with handicaps. Often, when such programs are available, their hours of operation are such that full-time employment is precluded.

Many families report that their child with a disability requires less money. Some less active children require less frequent clothing and footwear replacements. The child may not request some of the more expensive items associated with growing up such as complex stereo systems, personal telephones, cars, undergraduate and graduate education and extensive travel.

The brother of a young man with severe disabilities made the following comment:

We could all learn from Michael: he cares about his appearance but does not need to buy the latest styles that New York dictates are "in" and just as quickly "out." He works as a carpenter's helper and is proud of his savings account. He stretches a dollar bill three ways and then cuts it down the middle before he spends it. He'll go out with his girlfriend and spend an entire Saturday having a great time, he foots the entire bill—a whole five dollars. He does his share of real work around the house. His tastes are simple yet his life is so very complete—I envy him.

Many parents turn to educators for needs beyond the traditional scope of education. Professionals who keep abreast of the range of community services available can save families much aggravation in accessing needed services. Turnbull and her colleagues (1986) offer the following suggestions for providing information to families:

1. Collect information on financial planning and maintain it as part of a family resource library. Periodic updating is a must.
2. Collect information on general community services and programs. Included in such a list would be vocational services, advocacy groups, residential service providers, parent support groups, respite care services, and attorneys, to mention but a few. The names of people to contact and their telephone numbers is part of such lists.
3. Organize presentations to parent groups by representatives of community agencies. Parents who have successfully negotiated the maze of some service agencies could share their knowledge with others at such presentations.
4. Schedule IEP conferences and other meetings with families so these do not adversely affect work schedules.
5. Understand that each family's economic function is possibly one of the most important needs the unit addresses. As with other aspects of life, financial situations are not static; they change and require adaptations in family life styles.

Affection Needs

Receiving and giving affection is a basic human need. The family provides an environment in which needs for affection can be met (Turnbull, Turnbull, Summers, Brotherson, & Benson, 1986). Affection is more than touching and kissing; it is also the feeling of giving and receiving unconditional love and achieving emotional mastery (Caplan, 1976). Emotional mastery involves learning to express feelings of anger, guilt, anxiety, psychic pain, and fear in an acceptable framework. It further involves expressions of more positive emotions such as love, contentment, and happiness.

Meeting one's own needs as well as assisting others to meet their needs is important in establishing a positive self-image. A positive self-image, in turn, affects a person's general physical health. Again, it is clear that the seven family functions are interdependent.

There are conflicting data in the literature concerning the impact of a family member with a disability on the affection needs of other members (Skrtic, Summers, Brotherson, & Turnbull, 1984).

Recent research indicates that the special bond which usually develops between a newborn and his or her parents may be delayed, distorted, or even absent in the case of a child with a severe disability (Blacher, 1984; Kaiser & Hayden, 1984). Family members may have difficulty working through their feelings of anger about the situation. Parents may experience recurring feelings of guilt (Sewell-Wright, Granger, & Sammeroff, 1984). "Was it something I did or did not do that led to the disabling condition?" Brothers and sisters may experience feelings of embarrassment that can cause resentment and anger being directed against the "source" of the situation (Skrtic, Summers, Brotherson, & Turnbull, 1984).

The child with a disability can have a positive impact on a family's affection needs. The perception that a family is different from other families because of the presence of a member with disabilities can draw a family together, a kind of "we are all in this together" approach to life (Turnbull, Summers, & Brotherson, 1984). Such a feeling can lead to close bonding among the members of the immediate family and can draw extended family members closer.

The special need of a member can lead to cooperation among other members; responsibilities may be shared for some or all tasks. Accomplishments or gains made by the member with a disability can lead to a feeling of satisfaction and pride by the rest of the family. After all, the entire family worked together to achieve the gain: it was team work. Brothers and sisters can develop close bonds, resulting from their roles as models and helpers of the siblings with handicaps.

The member with a handicap can be the catalyst that enables a family to see that all people, and life itself, have inherent value. Turnbull (1984) reviewed over 200 letters submitted to the Department of Health and Human Services in response to proposed "Baby Doe" regulations in the summer of 1983. The letters were from parents, relatives, and persons with disabilities. Many stressed the inherent sanctity of life, which is evident in the description of one parent:

I am a 35-year-old parent of a 16-month-old child diagnosed as having Down syndrome and a severe congenital heart defect. And yet, as imperfect as he may appear to many "professionals" and "intellectuals" of our day, I wouldn't trade him for any other child in this world. I cannot begin to sufficiently articulate the profound joy this child has brought into our lives. He has added a dimension of completeness and fulfillment that I have never experienced previously. He may never grow up to be president of anything, but that surely doesn't mean that he does not contribute in a positive way. His life is so very precious to us.

Many families have difficulty facing the sexual needs of a member with a disability. Families may fear that a member with a disability may become sexually active without understanding the consequences. Others may fear sexual abuse at the hands of others in the community. Also, there is mixed sentiment in the general community regarding sexual expression by persons with disabilities, from those who would deny any expression to those who lobby for liberated attitudes.

The emotional upheaval occasioned by the emergence of sexuality leads many people to deny that it is present. One mother of an adolescent son stated: "He has no needs along this line. I don't see any sexual desires expressed" (Brotherson, 1985, p. 211). Another mother of an adolescent girl stated: "People that are retarded don't need sex, now stop talking about it." Some persons with disabilities may never express sexual interest. For others, sex is an important issue, and sexual expression is a major need.

Professionals must be aware of the range of issues that can be associated with the family's efforts to meet the affection needs of its members. The following are but a few suggestions that professionals may find useful in helping families with their affection needs:

1. Understand that all family members have needs for affection and those needs change.
2. Attending to home-based programs addressing a child's educational goals may adversely affect the quantity and quality of "together" time the family can have. Some families may choose not to sacrifice affection needs for other functions.
3. Understand that people have differing views regarding affection and sexuality. Our personal views may work well for us and only us. Respect for different opinions must be standard operating procedure.
4. Provide material and information through resource libraries, discussion groups, ongoing seminars and individually to family members regarding issues of affection and sexuality.
5. Some students may benefit from IEP goals regarding affection issues. An example might

be a program designed to teach an adolescent to express sexuality in private.

6. Identify resources available in the community that may help families with affection-related problems. These resources may include counseling, planned parenthood and support groups.
7. Recognize and reinforce the positive impacts of children with disabilities on the abilities of individual family members to meet their affection needs.

The family is a busy organization trying to address many distinct but related functions. Education represents but one of these functions. If parents are not involved in a child's education, it does not mean the parents are not actively involved with the child in other functions.

Family Life Cycle

Families differ in resources, and those differences influence interaction patterns affecting the ability of the family to meet their functional needs. Each family is a unique unit. Similar families may exist but no two are exactly alike. Each unique family unit changes as it progresses through stages and transitions.

The family life cycle can be described as a series of developmental stages which are periods of time in which family functions are relatively stable (Duvall, 1957). Many tasks facing families of adolescents are different from those facing families of preschoolers. Researchers and theorists disagree concerning the number of life cycle stages that exist. Some have identified as many as 24 while others have identified as few as 6 (Turnbull, Turnbull, Summers, Brotherson, & Benson, 1986). The number is not nearly as important as the tasks families are responsible for accomplishing at each stage. Six stages are identified here: birth and early childhood, elementary school years, adolescence, young adulthood, post-parental years, and aging. Table 2.3 identifies possible issues encountered at the first 4 life cycle stages, which are the stages in which families and educators have the most contact.

Transitions are changes from one developmental stage to another. The changes brought on by a transition can alter the characteristics of families (children leaving home affects family size), their interaction patterns (dealing with the liberated child as an adult), and their needs (the smaller family may now have added economic potentials).

Transition of the child into public school marks the beginning of a long association between parents and professionals. This association may be rewarding for all family members, or may prove to be a road strewn with dissent and unfulfilled promises. As the child grows older, the full extent of the disability starts becoming apparent. One father commented that when his son was about 10 years old it finally became clear to him that, "What I saw is what I got."

Adolescence presents its own set of challenges. The person with the disability experiences physical and psychological changes which may present new concerns for the rest of the family. It is also at this point that many families first begin struggling with the looming unknown called the future. "What will happen after there is no more school eligibility?" "Where will she live?" "Where will she work?"

The successful launching into adulthood for people with disabilities requires careful planning in diverse areas; however, attention to transition has not typically occurred until the student approaches the end of eligibility in the secondary special education program. A parent who had received information on future planning asked that a representative of a local vocational training program attend the IEP conference in hopes of better coordinating her son's high school education with later employment options. The representative responded as follows when asked what goals might be included in the IEP to facilitate transition for the student.

As Paul is now only 15 years old, we will not even be looking at him for seven more years. He will apply for admission about a half year before he wants to work at the workshop. We will then see if he meets our criteria and if he does he will be accepted.

The big questions are: What if he does not meet the criteria? What if his IEP could have been written in such a manner that it could have taught him the criteria skills? The above questions represent the heart of a future planning process.

A program at the University of Kansas assists adolescents with disabilities and their families in making successful transitions from secondary education into adulthood. The program focuses on four future planning strategies.

1. Identifying criteria important for the family and the member with a disability in choosing places to live, work, and interact in the community— the criteria that constitute quality of life.

TABLE 2.3   Possible issues encountered at life cycle states

Life Cycle Stage	Parents	Siblings
Early Childhood, ages 0–5	Obtaining an accurate diagnosis Informing sibling(s) and relatives Locating services Seeking meaning in the exceptionality Clarifying a personal ideology to guide decision making Addressing issues of stigma Identifying positive contributions of exceptionality	Less parental time and energy for sibling needs Feelings of jealousy over less attention Fears associated with misunderstandings of exceptionality
School Age, ages 6–12	Establishing routines to carry out family functions Adjusting emotionally to educational implications Clarifying issues of mainstreaming v. special class placement Participating in IEP conferences Locating community resources Arranging for extracurricular activities	Dividing responsibility for any physical care needs Oldest female sibling may be at risk Limited family resources for recreation and leisure Informing friends and teachers Possible concern over surpassing younger sibling "Mainstreaming" into same school Need for basic information on exceptionality
Adolescence, ages 13–21	Adjusting emotionally to possible chronicity of exceptionality Identifying issues of emerging sexuality Addressing possible peer isolation and rejection Planning for career/vocational development Arranging for leisure time activities Dealing with physical and emotional change of puberty Planning for postsecondary education	Overidentification with sibling Greater understanding of differences in people Influence of exceptionality on career choice Dealing with possible stigma and embarrassment Participation in sibling training programs Opportunity for sibling support groups
Adulthood, ages 21–	Planning for possible need for guardianship Addressing the need for appropriate adult residence Adjusting emotionally to any adult implications of dependency Addressing the need for socialization opportunities outside the family for individual with exceptionality Initiating career choice or vocational program	Possible responsibility for financial support Addressing concerns regarding genetic implications Introducing new in-laws to exceptionality Need for information on career/living options Clarify role of sibling advocacy Possible guardianship

Source: From *Families and Professionals: Creating an Exceptional Partnership* (pp. 106–107) by A. P. Turnbull, H. R. Turnbull, J. A. Summers, M. J. Brotherson, and H. A. Benson, 1986, Columbus, OH: Charles E. Merrill. Copyright 1986 by Merrill Publishing Company. Reprinted by permission.

2. Identifying programs that offer services to meet the quality-of-life criteria and determining what skills the person will need to be eligible for entry into a program and successful within the program.

3. Incorporating goals and objectives into the IEP to teach the student the skills needed for successful transition to and placement in adult services.

4. Making lifelong plans addressing important legal/ethical/financial considerations such as guardianship, estate planning, accessing financial benefits, and consent.

Professionals can offer valuable help to families during all the stages involved in the process. First, professionals can help parents identify the criteria that constitute a quality of life for the family, understanding that each family has unique ideas regarding what they consider important. Some families may consider it necessary for a residential program to be located within easy driving distance while such a consideration might be unimportant for other families.

Educators also help families identify the preferences of students regarding vocational, educational, and community options. The teacher may notice that a particular student performs tasks with greater accuracy and speed when working alone but not in groups. Such information could be important in considering the kind of work place or living environment that would best match that student's preference for solitude. Professionals and families combine the information obtained in school and nonschool settings to acknowledge the student's preferences as well as those of other family members in determining what is necessary for a quality adult life.

As a second step, professionals offer considerable assistance during the second stage of the process; they serve as referral sources to help families locate options. Professionals should visit local and regional adult service programs to become familiar with entrance criteria and with the skills students will need to be successful in the various community options; they can offer to accompany families on visits to various programs. During this second step, families and professionals should identify the admissions criteria and determine which skills the individual with a disability possesses, and lacks, in order to gain entrance into a specific community option. Needed skills can then be prioritized for the IEP.

The third step involves using the established IEP process to prepare the student for a smooth and successful transition into adulthood. Professionals assist parents and students in identifying needed goals and determining the most appropriate teaching strategies to achieve them. Incorporating adult needs into the IEP transforms the IEP process from an annual view of the student's needs to a more lifelong view.

The fourth step focuses on legal/ethical/financial information. Many families do not know the best way to secure the disabled family member's future plans in finances, access to services, autonomy to make decisions, and ability to enter into contracts. Few lawyers, trust officers at banks, and financial advisors know about disability-related regulations, benefits, and programs. Families need accurate information to make lifelong plans that are tailored to their unique resources, interactional patterns, and approaches to meeting needs.

Viewing the approaching adulthood of an individual with a disability as a cooperative planning process helps design the student's education to meet present as well as future needs. Changes over the life cycle produce stress in all families (McCullough, 1980) and possibly greater stress for those families that have a member with a disability (Brotherson, 1985; Wikler, 1981). Others (Brotherson, Backus, Summers, & Turnbull, 1986), however, suggest that stress can be minimized when families are more aware of what the future holds.

SUMMARY

Historically, parent-professional interactions have not been as positive and productive as they might have been. The passage of P.L. 94–142 has established ground rules for both educational professionals and parents for their interactions with one another. Associated with each of the six major principles of the law—zero reject, nondiscriminatory evaluation, individualized education programs, least restrictive alternative, due process, and parent participation—are requirements for shared decision making and responsibility in ensuring that students receive an appropriate education.

Legislation alone will not ensure collaboration among parents and professionals. All parties must work within the guidelines to develop partnerships to meet the individual needs and preferences of families. The roles of parents and other family members in the evaluation and IEP process will vary from one family to the next. Likewise, the level of involvement sought by different family members can be expected to fluctuate.

Professionals are encouraged to view students within the broader context of family life. A family-systems perspective recognizes the true complexity of the family and offers a framework that professionals can use to understand the resources, interactions, functions, and changing needs and actions of families.

The challenge is exciting. Appropriately preparing individuals with severe disabilities with the academic, social, emotional, and vocational skills to function in society is a complex process. It requires innovative efforts by family members and professionals working toward shared goals. The possibilities are boundless, and the benefits for persons with disabilities are unlimited if we can apply our energies and our imaginations together in a partnership of progress.

REFERENCES

Akerley, M. S. (1985). False gods and angry prophets. In H. R. Turnbull & A. P. Turnbull (Eds.), *Parents speak out: Then and now* (pp. 23–32). Columbus, OH: Charles E. Merrill.

Armstrong v. Kline, 476 F. Supp. 583 (E.D. Pa. 1979).

Atkeson, B. M., & Forehand, R. (1979). Home-based reinforcement programs to modify classroom behavior: A review and methodological evaluation. *Psychological Bulletin, 86*, 1298–1308.

Atkeson, B. M., Sturgis, E., & Forehand, R. (1977). Training a parent to teach communication skills: A case study. *Behavior Modification, 1*, 259–276.

Bautz, B. J., Barber, P., Brotherson, M. J., & Turnbull, A. P. (1984). Preparation of parents for mainstreaming. *A Journal for Remedial Education and Counseling, 1*, 157.

Benson, H. A., & Turnbull, A. P. (1986). Approaching families from an individualized perspective. In R. H. Horner, L. H. Meyer & H. D. Fredericks (Eds.), *Education of learners with severe handicaps: Exemplary service strategies* (pp. 127–157). Baltimore: Paul H. Brookes.

Berardo, F. M. (1980). Decade preview: Some trends and directions for family research and theory in the 1980s. *Journal of Marriage and the Family, 42*(4), 723–728.

Blacher, J. (1984). A dynamic perspective on the impact of a severely handicapped child on the family. In J. Blacher (Ed.), *Severely handicapped children and their families* (pp. 3–50). Orlando, FL: Academic Press.

Bronfenbrenner, U. (1974). *A report on longitudinal evaluations of preschool programs: Is early intervention effective?* (Vol. 2). Washington, DC: United States Department of Health, Education and Welfare.

Brotherson, M. J. (1984, May). *Working with families in a transcultural setting.* Paper presented at the 108th Annual Conference of the American Association on Mental Deficiency, Minneapolis, MN.

Brotherson, M. J. (1985). *Planning for adult futures: Parents' self-report of future planning and its relationship to family functioning and stress with sons and daughters who are disabled.* Unpublished doctoral dissertation, The University of Kansas, Lawrence.

Brotherson, M. J., Backus, L. H., Summers, J. A., & Turnbull, A. P. (1986). Transition to adulthood. In J. A. Summers (Ed.) *The right to grow up* (pp. 17–44). Baltimore: Paul H. Brookes.

Buchman, B. M. (1983). *Review of research methods and benefits of behavioral parent training with handicapped children: A call for research.* Unpublished manuscript, the University of Kansas, Department of Human Development and Family Life, Lawrence.

Caplan, G. (1976). The family as a support system. In G. Caplan & M. Killilea (Eds.), *Support systems and mutual help: Multidisciplinary explorations* (pp. 19–36). New York: Grune & Stratton.

Carnes, P. J. (1981). *Family development I: Understanding us.* Minneapolis: Interpersonal Communications Programs, Inc.

Clark, D. B., & Baker, B. L. (1983). Behavioral training for parents of retarded children: Prediction of outcome. *American Journal of Mental Deficiency, 87*, 14–19.

Consortium for Longitudinal Studies. (1979). *Summary report: Lasting effects after preschool.* Washington, DC: United States Department of Health and Human Services.

Dunlap, W. R., & Hollingsworth, J. S. (1977). How does a handicapped child affect the family? Implications for practitioners. *The Family Coordinator*, 286–293.

Duvall, E. (1957). *Family development.* Philadelphia: Lippincott.

Fialkowski v. Shapp, 405 F. Supp. 946 (E.D. Pa. 1975).

Gilliam, J. E., & Coleman, M. C. (1981). Who influences IEP committee decisions? *Exceptional Children, 47*(8), 642–644.

Goldstein, S., Strickland, B., Turnbull, A. P., & Curry, L. (1980). An observational analysis of the IEP conference. *Exceptional Children, 46*(4), 278–286.

Gordon, I. J. (1971). A home learning center approach to early stimulation (Grant No. MH 16037-02). Gainesville, FL: Institute for Development of Human Resources.

Gray, S. W., & Klaus, R. A. (1970). The early training project: A seventh year report. *Child Development, 41*, 909–924.

Grossman, F. K. (1972). *Brothers and sisters of retarded children: An exploratory study.* Syracuse, NY: Syracuse University Press.

Guess, D., Benson, H. A., & Siegel-Causey, E. (1985). Concepts and issues related to choice making and autonomy among persons with severe handicaps. *The Journal of the Association for the Severely Handicapped, 10*, 79–86.

Heward, W. L., Dardig, J. C., & Rossett, A. (1979). *Working with parents of handicapped children.* Columbus, OH: Charles E. Merrill.

Hines v. Pittsburgh County Board of Education. 497 F. Supp. 403 (E.D. N.C. 1980).

Holman, T. B., & Burr, W. R. (1980). Beyond the beyond: The growth of family theories in the 1970s. *Journal of Marriage and the Family, 42*(4), 729–741.

Horowitz, F. D., & Paden, L. Y. (1973). The effectiveness of environmental intervention programs. In B. M. Caldwell & H. N. Ricciuti (Eds.), *Review of child development research* (Vol. 3, pp. 331–402). Chicago: University of Chicago Press.

Kaiser, C. E., & Hayden, A. H. (1984). Clinical research and policy issues in parenting severely handicapped infants. In J. Blacher (Ed.), *Severely handicapped children and their families* (pp. 275–317). Orlando, FL: Academic Press.

Karnes, M. B., Teska, J. A., Hodgins, A. S., & Badger, E. D. (1970). Educational intervention at home by mothers of disadvantaged infants. *Child Development, 41*, 925–935.

Kazak, A. E., & Marvin, R. S. (1984). Differences, difficulties and adaptation: Stress and social networks in families with a handicapped child. *Family Relations, 33*, 67–77.

Lynch, E. W., & Stein, R. (1982). Perspectives on parent participation in special education. *Exceptional Education Quarterly, 3*(2), 56–63.

Marion, R. L. (1980). Communication with parents of culturally diverse exceptional children. *Exceptional Children, 46*(8), 616–625.

McCullough, R. P. (1980). Launching children and moving on. In E. A. Carter & M. McGoldrick (Eds.), *The family life cycle: A framework for family therapy* (pp. 171–196). New York: Gardner Press.

McGill, D., & Pearce, J. K. (1982). British families. In M. McGoldrick, J. K. Pearce & J. Giordano (Eds.), *Ethnicity in family therapy* (pp. 457–479). New York: The Guilford Press.

McGoldrick, M., Pearce, J. K., & Giordano, J. (Eds.). (1982). *Ethnicity and family therapy.* New York: The Guilford Press.

McLoughlin, J. A., Edge, D., & Strenecky, B. (1978). Perspective on parental involvement in the diagnosis and treatment of learning disabled children. *Journal of Learning Disabilities, 11*(5), 32–37.

Mills v. Board of Education of the District of Columbia. 348 F. Supp. 866 (D.D.C. 1972).

Murphy, A. T. (1982). The family with a handicapped child: A review of the literature. *Developmental and Behavioral Pediatrics, 3*(2), 73–82.

National Committee for Citizens in Education (1979). Unpublished manuscript serving as basis for Congressional testimony.

Olson, D. H., McCubbin, H. I., Barnes, H., Larsen, A., Muxen, M., & Wilson, M. (1983). *One thousand families: A national survey.* Beverly Hills, CA: Sage.

Olson, D. H., Russell, C. S., & Sprenkle, D. H. (1980). Marital and family therapy: A decade review. *Journal of Marriage and the Family, 42*(4), 973–993.

Olson, D. H., Sprenkle, D. H., & Russell, C. S. (1979). Circumplex model of marital and family systems I: Cohesion and adaptability dimension, family types and clinical applications. *Family Process, 18,* 3–28.

Pennsylvania Association for Retarded Children v. Commonwealth of Pennsylvania, 343 F. Supp. 279 (E.D. Pa. 1972).

Schaefer, E. S. (1972). Parents as educators: Evidence from cross-sectional longitudinal and intervention research. *Young Children, 27,* 227–239.

Sewell-Wright, J., Granger, R. D., & Sammeroff, A. J. (1984). Parental acceptance and developmental handicaps. In J. Blacher (Ed.), *Severely handicapped children and their families* (pp. 51–90). Orlando, FL: Academic Press.

Shevin, M., & Klein, N. K. (1984). The importance of choice-making skills for students with severe disabilities. *The Journal of the Association for the Severely Handicapped, 9*(3), 159–166.

Skrtic, J. M., Summers, J. A., Brotherson, M. J., & Turnbull, A. P. (1984). Severely handicapped children and their brothers and sisters. In J. Blacher (Ed.), *Young severely handicapped children and their families: Research in review* (pp. 215–246). New York: Academic Press.

Tjossem, T. D. (Ed.). (1976). *Intervention strategies for high-risk infants and young children.* Baltimore: University Park Press.

Trevino, F. (1979). Siblings of handicapped children: Identifying those at risk. *Social Casework: The Journal of Contemporary Social Work, 60*(8), 488–492.

Turnbull, A. P., Brotherson, M. J., & Summers, J. A. (1985). The impact of deinstitutionalization on families: A family systems approach. In R. H. Bruininks & K. C. Lakin (Eds.), *Living and learning in the least restrictive environment* (pp. 115–140). Baltimore: Paul H. Brookes.

Turnbull, A. P., & Strickland, B. (1981). Parents and the educational system. In J. L. Paul (Ed.), *Understanding and working with parents of children with special needs* (pp. 231–263). New York: Holt, Rinehart & Winston.

Turnbull, A. P., Strickland, B., & Brantley, J. C. (1982). *Developing and implementing individualized education programs* (2nd ed.). Columbus, OH: Charles E. Merrill.

Turnbull, A. P., Summers, J. A., & Brotherson, M. J. (1984). *Working with families with disabled members: A family systems approach.* Lawrence: The University of Kansas, University Affiliated Facility.

Turnbull, A. P., & Turnbull, H. R. (1985, April). *Families with children having disabilities: Issues for the eighties.* Testimony before the Select Committee on Children, Youth, and Families, Anaheim, CA.

Turnbull, A. P., Turnbull, H. R., Summers, J. A., Brotherson, M. J., & Benson, H. A. (1986). *Families, professionals, and exceptionality: A special partnership.* Columbus, OH: Charles E. Merrill.

Turnbull, A. P., & Winton, P. J. (1984). Parent involvement policy and practice: Current research and implications for families of young severely handicapped children. In J. Blacher (Ed.), *Severely handicapped children and their families: Research in review* (pp. 377–397). New York: Academic Press.

Turnbull, H. R. (1985). Jay's story. In H. R. Turnbull & A. P. Turnbull (Eds.), *Parents speak out: Then and now* (pp. 109–118). Columbus, OH: Charles E. Merrill.

Turnbull, H. R. (1986). *Free appropriate public education: Law and implementation.* Denver, CO: Love.

Turnbull, H. R., & Turnbull, A. P. (1982). Parent involvement in the education of handicapped children: A critique. *Mental Retardation, 20*(3), 115–122.

Turnbull, H. R., Turnbull, A. P., & Wheat, M. J. (1982). Assumptions about parental participation: A legislative history. *Exceptional Education Quarterly, 3*(2), 1–8.

Vadasy, P. F., Fewell, R. R., & Meyer, D. J. (1986). Grandparents of children with special needs: Insights into their experiences and concerns. *Journal of the Division for Early Childhood, 10,* 65–72.

Vadasy, P. F., Fewell, R. R., Meyer, D. J., & Schell, G. (1984). Siblings of handicapped children: A developmental perspective on family interactions. *Family Relations, 33,* 155–167.

Vincent, L., Davis, J., Brown, P., Broome, K., Miller, J., & Gruenewald, L. (1983). *Parent inventory of child development in nonschool environments.* Madison, WI: Madison Metropolitan School District Early Childhood Program, Active Decision Making by Parents Grant.

Vishner, J. S., & Vishner, E. B. (1982). Step-families and step-parenting. In F. Walsh (Ed.), *Normal family processes* (pp. 331–353). New York: The Guilford Press.

Wikler, L. (1981). Chronic stresses of families of mentally retarded children. *Family Relations, 30*(2), 281–288.

Wikler, L., Wasow, M., & Hatfield, E. (1981). Chronic sorrow revisited: Parent vs. professional depiction of the adjustment of parents of mentally retarded children. *American Journal of Orthopsychiatry, 51,* 63–70.

Wikler, L., Wasow, M., & Hatfield, E. (1983). Seeking strengths in families of developmentally disabled children. *Social Work,* 313–315.

Winton, P., & Turnbull, A. P. (1981). Parent involvement as viewed by parents of preschool, handicapped children. *Topics in Early Childhood Special Education, 1*(3), 11–19.

Winton, P. J., Turnbull, A. P., Blacher, J. B., & Salkind, N. (1983). Mainstreaming in the kindergarten classroom: Perspectives of parents of handicapped and nonhandicapped children. *Journal of the Division of Early Children, 6,* 14–20.

Ziskin, L. (1985). The story of Jennie. In H. R. Turnbull & A. P. Turnbull (Eds.), *Parents speak out: Then and now* (pp. 65–74). Columbus, OH: Charles E. Merrill.

Introduction to Chapters 3, 4, and 5

In the next three chapters, both the rationale for and the mechanics of program development and evaluation are set forth. Thus, the main topics addressed are educational assessment and intervention. During the life of a student with severe handicaps, *assessment* of various aspects of performance is frequent; in the opinion of many educators, assessment is *too frequent* and *not too meaningful*. In contrast, educational interventions are more often accused of being too *infrequent*, although intervention is often judged as not being meaningful as well. These chapters provide rules and guidelines to avoid these common errors.

Just as many different people assess the student, so do many fill the role of teacher. All of these individuals are members of a changing team of people influencing the educational program of each student with severe handicaps as he grows older. Each team member—teachers, parents, occupational, physical, and speech therapists, psychologists, doctors, and other medical personnel—has a rightful role in the complex task of providing an appropriate educational program.

Educational intervention may be viewed as having five phases: (a) assessment, (b) curriculum development, (c) analysis of behavior, (d) program development, and (e) program evaluation. The individuals serving on the intervention team have varying responsibilities across these five phases, with the teacher's role being dominant at all points. Teachers usually are charged with "synthesizing" the input of others, a job that requires many talents among which include: (a) familiarity with and respect for others' roles on the team, (b) diplomacy, (c) a clear view of the student's current life and future options, (d) understanding and value for student's and family's hopes and preferences, and (e) an emphasis on advancing the student's level of independence.

In Chapter 3, Fredda Brown gives an overview of assessment, its changing form and function when applied by members of the team, and its connection to program development. In addition to current assessment practices, Chapter 3 addresses the trends we can expect to see in educational assessment during the next decade, trends which are aimed at improving the value which assessment results have for teachers and their students.

In Chapter 4, Nancy Grigg and Marti Snell describe the current technology involved in all five phases of the educational process. Particular attention is focused upon the teacher's development and evaluation of an educational program and, therefore, upon informal observation and measurement of student behavior. These targeted behaviors have been carefully chosen to satisfy two overriding criteria: behavior that currently is or will be functional in the student's life and behavior that is suited to the student's chronological age.

Then, in Chapter 5, Tom Zirpoli and Marti Snell describe the wide range of educational intervention strategies which have proven effective with our students. They suggest what the teacher can do to change a student's behavior once the targeted skill is identified, and they also discuss teaching techniques that will lead to meaningful behavior change—skills that will be used by the student in a variety of settings and not be forgotten through disuse or a failure to generalize.

For many readers, these three chapters will review concepts learned earlier, but for all readers, the content of these chapters delineates the complex procedures and considerations which will characterize instructional programs of students in *all* domains.

Fredda Brown
Institute for Professional Practice
New Haven, Connecticut

3

Meaningful Assessment of People with Severe and Profound Handicaps

Testing has long been a controversial component of the educational process. Because assessment procedures influence so many aspects of a student's educational experience, both the instruments and their uses have been extensively criticized (Ysseldyke & Algozzine, 1982). Traditionally, classification and placement decisions in special education relied on assessments of intellectual functioning, academic achievement, and perceptual-motor skills (Gresham, 1983). The use of these tests with special education students, especially students with severe and profound handicaps, failed to provide meaningful information to special educators. In 1975, P.L. 94–142, the Education of All Handicapped Children Act, was passed. The importance of appropriate assessment is emphasized in this law by its extensive guidelines. Sec. 121a.532 requires that assessment address several major points (Gaylord-Ross & Holvoet, 1985):

1. Tests and other evaluation materials must be validated for the specific purpose for which they are used and must be administered by trained personnel.
2. Tests and other evaluation materials must include assessment of specific areas of educational need; a single intelligence quotient is not sufficient.
3. Tests and other evaluation materials must be selected and administered to ensure that what is measured is aptitude rather than simply impaired sensory, motor, or speaking skills.
4. Interpretations of evaluation data must draw upon a variety of sources including aptitude and achievement tests, teacher recommendations, social or cultural background, physical condition, and adaptive behavior.
5. Evaluators must have procedures to assure that information from all such sources will be documented and considered.
6. The placement decision resulting from the evaluation must be made by a group of people knowledgeable about the specific child and the evaluation data.
7. The parents may request an independent educational evaluation at public expense if they have reason to believe that the test results are not valid. (Public Law 94–142, *Federal Register*)

These criteria underscore the need for a variety of assessment sources conducted by a multidisciplinary team. Students with severe and profound handicaps are likely to have difficulties in areas such as mobility, self-help, language, social interaction, health, or any combination of these. Finding a single instrument that can measure such a student's capabilities, despite these difficulties, is impossible; even when several instruments are used that have been adapted to bypass his handicaps, interpretation of the multifactored assessment is troublesome.

The issue of testing and assessment is integrally related to the way one defines a disability. Ysseldyke and Algozzine (1982) point out that definitions provide the basis from which identification practices evolve but caution that we should remember that labels or "categories are simply terms used to confirm that individuals in our society differ from each other" (p. 43). It follows then that definitions of disability and evaluation strategies constantly change to reflect changing societal values and attitudes (White, 1985; Ysseldyke & Algozzine, 1982). This is illustrated by the change in the definition of mental retardation. The current acceptable definition is "significantly subaverage, general intellectual functioning existing concurrently with deficits in adaptive behavior, and manifested during the developmental period" (Grossman, 1977, p. 5). This definition is a revision of earlier ones by Heber (1959, 1961) that did not include the criteria of adaptive behavior. The addition of the concept of adaptive behavior reflected a tremendous change in the approach to persons with retardation, away from the sole measurement of "intelligence," and toward the gathering of more meaningful and relevant information. This change has naturally expanded the types of instruments used to measure the behavior of individuals with handicaps and has added a new dimension to assessment—the measurement of an individual's adaptation to environmental demands.

The type of assessment that a professional perceives as appropriate and meaningful, will be strongly influenced by two variables. First, the purpose of the inquiry or the ways in which the assessment data are to be used will determine which instruments are appropriate. Second, the instructor's educational philosophy will determine the types of educational goals seen as appropriate for the students and, consequently, will influence the selection of instruments. This chapter will discuss ways that the purpose of the assessment and educational philosophy determine what meaningful assessment is. Several current theories of educa-

tional assessment will be discussed within this framework, and considerations for the meaningful assessment of severely and profoundly handicapped students will be addressed.

PURPOSE OF ASSESSMENT

Different types of assessments offer the user different types of information. A teacher must look for an instrument that will match the purpose of the assessment inquiry. Just as a teacher should select an educational intervention to match the particular targeted skills, so must an assessment match the purpose. Assessments are used to gain information for the purposes of screening, placement, curriculum development and student evaluation (cf. Salvia & Ysseldyke, 1984). The professionals involved in each of these areas, the types of instruments or strategies used, and the timing of the measurement will vary according to the purpose of the assessment. Table 3.1 describes these variations.

Assessment for Screening

Screening is the first step in the assessment process. The purpose of this step is to identify students who may have a handicapping condition. Medical personnel and psychologists use screening instruments with young children having severe handicaps; such instruments, however, have little value as the child grows older and contribute little to curriculum development. It is a very broad and quickly administered measure, and its intention is not to obtain information precise enough to make instructional decisions, or to determine why a problem exists, but rather to determine whether a student is significantly different from his peers and requires further testing. Screening may begin as early as the prenatal period with the use of amniocentesis to determine the presence of certain genetic disorders. Immediately following birth, screening occurs as physicians check for obvious handicapping conditions or genetic and metabolic disorders (White, 1985). The Apgar Scoring System (Apgar, 1953; Apgar & Beck, 1973) and the Brazelton Neonatal Behavioral Assessment Scale (BNBAS) (Brazelton, 1973) are screening instruments designed to detect potential problems in newborns. The Apgar Scoring System assesses the neonate's heart rate, respiration, reflexes, muscle tone, and general appearance. In addition to these types of neurological measures, the BNBAS also looks at 27

TABLE 3.1 Varying purposes and characteristics of assessment in the education of students with severe handicaps

Assessment Purpose	Types of Assessment	Assessor(s)	Time of Assessment
Screen	Newborn and infant measures Motor and sensory functioning measures Specific domains	Medical staff Occupational, physical, and speech therapists Psychologists	Early in child's life or after head injury
Diagnose and place	IQ tests Adaptive behavior tests Motor and sensory functioning tests	Psychologist or educational specialist Occupational, physical, or speech therapists	Early in the child's life or after head injury
Curriculum and program development	Ecological inventory Adaptive behavior tests Task analytic assessment	Teacher or psychologist	Throughout school years at regular intervals
Student evaluation	Direct observation of IEP behaviors/skills under criterion conditions Training and probe data	Teacher	Daily, weekly, or bi-weekly

behavioral measures. These include general measures, such as alertness, activity level, self-quieting activity, smiles; other measures which examine sleep patterns; and specific behaviors that look at the newborn's response to environmental stimuli such as a light, sounds, and a pinprick on the bottom of the foot. These two screening instruments alert hospital staff to newborns who may be in distress or have neurological damage; however, they should not be used to predict long-term outcomes (Fewell & Cone, 1983).

Screening instruments for infants and older children may cover a variety of domains such as the Denver Developmental Screening Test (DDST) (Frankenburg, Dodds & Fandal, 1975) which includes personal-social, fine motor, adaptive, language, and gross motor skills. This screening test is intended for use with children from birth to 6 years of age. The Developmental Profile II (Alpern, Boll, & Schearer, 1980) was developed for children up to the age of 9 and includes physical, self-help, social, academic, and communication screening. Other screening instruments may specifically focus on only one domain of interest, such as the Parson's Visual Acuity Test (Spellman, DeBriere, & Cress, 1979). Many students with severe or multiple handicaps do not go through a formal screening evaluation, as they are obviously handicapped, and the assessment process then begins with diagnostic testing (Gaylord-Ross & Holvoet, 1985).

Assessment for Diagnosis and Placement

The next step in the assessment process is to further test the child to identify the disorder and possible cause of the delay to make eligibility, classification and/or placement decisions (Salvia & Ysseldyke, 1984). Once a problem is suspected, either through screening or observation, diagnostic testing may be initiated to probe sensory deficits, mental ability, or a student's adaptive functioning. Neurological tests, intelligence tests, and tests of adaptive behavior are used to assess students in each of these areas. These tests are usually administered by psychologists, therapists and presented at an IEP meeting. Each of these types of tests yields very different information, and just how much a teacher uses the results in the classroom depends on his or her philosophical orientation to program development.

Assessment for Curriculum Development

A major purpose of the assessment process is the development of an appropriate educational program. Assessment conducted to determine which skills should be taught is considered educational assessment (Gaylord-Ross & Holvoet, 1985; Switzky, 1979). It is this step of the process that makes assessment so important because a teacher may use selected instruments to determine what to teach. Some assessments, such as criterion-referenced tests and certain adaptive behavior scales, are more suited than others for this purpose, whereas others, such as intelligence tests, are inappropriate for this purpose. The use of ecological inventories (see Chapter 4) is an informal assessment strategy that provides crucial information for the development of an age-appropriate and functional curriculum for students with severe handicaps. This phase of the assessment process is usually the responsibility of the teacher who will directly assess and observe the student, as well as elicit additional pertinent information from parents, psychologists, and therapists. A teacher must carefully inspect an instrument to determine if it was developed with this type of decision-making capability.

Student Evaluation

Finally, evaluation of student progress is another component of the assessment process. Teachers must be responsible for providing continuous and meaningful evaluations of their individual educational programs. Documentation of successful student outcomes has extended beyond the use of single-subject methodology and must now include more qualitative measures as well. The idea of "social validity" (Kazdin, 1977; Wolf, 1978), has added this qualitative dimension to evaluation of educational interventions by asking us to look at the importance and social acceptability of the behavior change.

APPROACHES TO ASSESSMENT

There are two basic ways of conceptualizing the nature of a student's needs. Students may be viewed as having a composite of discrete units of behavior or individual skills, which are determined by behaviors manifested by normally developing individuals. When combined, these individual skills should result in a "competent" student. Another way to conceptualize the development of skills is to view the many skills a student needs as being interdependent and determined by environmental demands. Gaylord-Ross and Holvoet (1985) identified two approaches to assessment that parallel these philosophies. The developmental approach compares the handicapped student with normally developing children, and the environmental approach compares the student's current adaptive skills in home and school environments with those likely to be needed in the future.

The Developmental Approach

The developmental approach looks at the normal sequence of development to determine what it is that the handicapped person should be achieving. Justification for this approach rests on at least three assumptions: (a) normal development constitutes the most logical ordering of behaviors, (b) many behaviors within normal development are prerequisite behaviors, and (c) behaviors acquired by a nonhandicapped child are appropriate measures for a handicapped child of the same developmental level (Guess & Noonan, 1982). Tests sequenced according to normal development are termed norm-referenced tests. Norm-referenced tests are used to determine the extent of deviation from the norm (Fewell & Cone, 1983). This type of measure usually compares the performance of the student to nonhandicapped students of the same age. It allows the evaluator to determine whether the child is developing the same skills as the majority of children in the normative sample.

IQ Tests

The IQ test is the most popular norm-referenced test, and along with adaptive behavior scales, typically make up the diagnostic component of assessment. There are many problems in applying this type of test to students with handicaps, and certainly, the more severe the handicap is, the less appropriate is the application of the IQ test. Students with severe or profound handicaps many times do not even score on these tests; consequently, infant intelligence tests are used (Gaylord-Ross & Holvoet, 1985). The inappropriateness of the intelligence test is further exacerbated by the lack of age-appropriateness. Some frequently used intelligence tests are the Bayley Scales of Infant Development (Bayley, 1969), Cattell Infant Intelligence Scale (Cattell, 1940), Stanford-Binet Intelligence Scale (Terman & Merrill, 1973), The Wechsler Intelligence Scale for Children–Revised (Wechsler, 1974), and the Wechsler Preschool and Primary Scales of Intelligence (WPPSI) (Wechsler, 1967). There has been much controversy over the use of intelligence tests in special education. A major disadvantage of these measures is the misuse of the information that they provide: they are too often used to make decisions about students and services based on very limited data, and they are too often inappropriately used to measure student progress (Fewell & Cone, 1983). Litigation, such as *Mills v. Board of Education* (1972) and *Hobson v. Hansen* (1969), ruled that exclusion or grouping of students on the basis of standardized tests is unconstitutional.

Developmental Scales

There are several advantages to using developmental scales in the assessment process. These scales provide items that are presented in observable terms so that presence or absence of a skill can usually be reliably determined. Student progress on these measures can then be noted by periodic administration of the instrument. The scales give information on developmental functioning in various skill areas, and because skills are listed chronologically, they may provide direction for the next skills to be taught. When used for educational assessment, the items that a student can and cannot do are determined. The first items that a student cannot do are then targeted for intervention. And finally, the familiarity of many disciplines with normal developmental theory may increase communication between disciplines. Tables detailing extensive information on available developmental scales can be found in Fewell and Cone (1983), and Switzky (1979).

There are, however, many problems with applying the developmental approach to students with severe and profound handicaps. First, this approach assumes that those sequences of behavior typical of nonhandicapped students are relevant for the student with severe or profound handicaps. A person who is handicapped may develop in a very different sequence, and the relationship among skills may be different. Providing students with prostheses or arranging for environmental adaptations may render typical developmental sequences inappropriate. White (1985) points out that although head control is a prerequisite for normal walking, it is not a prerequisite for a motorized wheelchair. Therefore, although the student failed the head control item, the evaluator should not stop probing higher level gross motor skills. This particular student, given individualized adaptations, may score on many other higher level functional skills.

Second, because this approach assumes that certain behaviors must be present before other behaviors can be acquired, results may influence some teachers to instruct students on skills that are neither age appropriate or functional for adapting to their daily environments (Guess & Noonan, 1982). For example, a 15-year-old student who is severely handicapped may fail the item "Points to parts of doll" on the Bayley Scales of Infant Development (Bayley, 1969), that is usually passed by non-handicapped babies by the time they are 26 months. Instruction on this skill would require materials that are not appropriate for a 15-year-old person and a skill that would have little relevance for him.

A third potential danger is that skills within and across curricular or environmental domains may be seen in isolation and, thus, remain unrelated to each other. For example, the skill of grasping is certainly important and necessary for most physical interactions with the environment. However, unless grasping is related to other skills, or looked at within functional contexts, it has little meaning. Grasping a brush, or spoon, or toy certainly will provide more relevant assessment information than grasping a 2-inch wooden dowel. "Scans objects" begins to have meaning if it precedes a skill such as "functional object use."

Fourth, the purpose or reason for assessing a skill may not be apparent and therefore be left open to inappropriate assessment, administration, and interpretation. For example, White (1985) points out that it is not clear what an item such as "imitates three-block bridge" is supposed to assess. If it is to assess the fine-motor ability of a student, then a child without limbs and unable to manipulate a prosthetic device would fail the item. However, if the intent of the item was to assess "imitation" then some strategy should be developed to allow the child to demonstrate this cognitive ability given his physical capabilities.

Similarly, some teachers may assume that because an item is on an assessment it must be meaningful for instructional purposes. It has been argued by many professionals that a normal developmental sequence does not provide information that can be directly used in the educational context (Hogg, 1975; Switzky, 1979). For example, the Portage Guide to Early Education (Bluma, Shearer, Frohman, & Hilliard, 1976) includes the skill "builds tower of three blocks." Before considering instruction on such an item the teacher must again question the purpose of assessing this particular skill. Is it to determine the motor ability of the student, or whether the student can play with blocks? If a specific rationale for the assessment of that particular item (motor ability) was determined, then the teacher must decide if this basic function is a relevant instructional objective for the student. If the teacher concludes that the function of the item may be relevant, the teacher must then translate the item into a form that is most meaningful for the student's age and specific environment. Figure 3.1 presents a form that may assist a teacher in translating potential items from a developmental assessment. This form encourages a teacher to question the reason for a particular item, and will further assist her in translating a useful item into a relevant activity for the student. Although this procedure will help implement an item, there is still the danger of contriving situations that would not otherwise be considered for instruction.

Some developmental instruments have been devised to relate more directly to the program development component of the assessment process. These instruments are accompanied by a curriculum guide. The *Portage Guide to Early Education* includes a color and number coded card file containing a behavioral description and intervention suggestions for each item on the checklist. Other instruments that have a programming component are

- *Cambridge Assessment Development Rating and Evaluation (CADRE)* (Welch, O'Brian, & Ayers, 1974)
- *Learning Accomplishment Profile (LAP)* (Sanford, 1974)
- *Learning Accomplishment Profile for Infants (Early LAP)* (Griffin & Sanford, 1981)
- *RADEA Program* (Dallas County Mental Health/ Mental Retardation Center, 1972)

Although these instruments were developed with instructional implications in mind, a teacher must still carefully evaluate the relevance of the particular items for a student as illustrated in Figure 3.1. As will be shown in Chapter 4, the student's age, interests, motor or sensory disabilities, and home and community environments must all be considered in the decision-making process.

The Adaptive Behavior Approach

The second approach looks at environmental demands to determine what skills to assess. This approach reflects an individual's adaptive behavior or "the effectiveness or degree with which indi-

viduals meet the standards of personal independence and social responsibility expected for age and cultural group" (Grossman, 1983, p. 1). The concept of adaptive behavior has encouraged educators to look at behaviors that are more relevant to a student's functioning in society. Measures of adaptive behavior are usually checklists which focus on skills required to adapt to one's daily environment. The AAMD Adaptive Behavior Scale (Nihira, Foster, Shellhaas, & Leland, 1974) includes the domains of independent functioning, physical development, economic activity, language, number and time, domestic and vocational activity, self-direction, responsibility, and socialization.

Adaptive behavior measures have been criticized on several counts. First, adaptive behavior is difficult to measure because the concept is still vague and inadequately defined, making interpretation subjective (Fewell & Cone, 1983). Second, although these measures focus on skills required in daily living, they often do not assess an individual's ability to adapt to changing circumstances in their environments. An item, such as "able to catch a bus to work," may assess a skill necessary for functioning in the work world; however, it does not address the individual's ability to solve the problem that would arise if the correct bus failed to come on time (Evans & Brown, in press). Third, the high correlation between adaptive behavior and IQ leads many to conclude that functionally they are measuring the same variables (Adams, 1973; Baumeister & Muma, 1975). Finally, the information obtained from tests of adaptive behavior do not indicate much more about the severity of the problem or its cause than do more simplified screening instruments (Gaylord-Ross & Holvoet, 1985).

Although norm-referenced tests can be used to measure adaptive behavior, criterion-referenced tests are more commonly used. Unlike the norm-referenced test, which compares a student's performance to other students, the criterion-referenced test compares a student's performance to a predetermined level of mastery (criterion), regardless of the performance of other students. The specific adaptive or functional criterion behavior identified in a test provides the measure for the assessment. The tremendous advantage of this approach is that the environment may be used to determine the skills needed for a student. Many of these tests may be appropriate sources for determining, at least in part, what to teach individual students. Table 3.2 describes the content areas covered by some frequently used scales that either measure only adap-

Item Evaluation

Assessment Instrument: _____

Item for Revision: _____

_____

Rationale: _____

_____

_____

Substitute Functional Activity	Domain	Materials	Time/Settings

FIGURE 3.1 Sample of completed form for translating selected items from an instrument into functional activities

tive behavior or include extensive sections on adaptive behavior.

TRENDS IN EDUCATIONAL ASSESSMENT

Instruments that are useful for educational assessment are based on the task analysis model. The ecological inventory strategy (Brown, Branston, Hamre-Nietupski, Pumpian, Certo, & Gruenewald, 1979) has been used to determine the adaptive behavior skills on which the student should be assessed in order to define the content for further task analysis. Special educators have also begun to focus more on the purpose that a behavior is supposed to serve, and less on exactly the way that behavior is accomplished. Brown, Evans, and Weed (1984) have described these foundations and

TABLE 3.2 Adaptive behavior measures used for children with severe handicaps

Instrument, Author, and Publisher	Assessment Methods			Ages Covered			Content Areas									
	Interview	Observation	Direct Testing	0–3 Yrs	3–6 Yrs	6+ Yrs	Sensory	Gross Motor	Fine Motor	Language	Cognition/ Academic	Social/ Emotional	Self-Help	Independent Living	Vocational	Recreation/ Leisure
Adaptive Behavior Scales (Lambert, Windmiller, Cole, & Figueroa, 1975) American Association on Mental Deficiency 5201 Connecticut Avenue, N.W. Washington, D.C. 20015	X	X		X	X	X	X	X	X	X		X	X	X	X	X
Balthazar Scales of Adaptive Behavior (Balthazar, 1976) Consulting Psychologists Press 577 College Avenue Palo Alto, CA 94306			X	X	X	X	X	X	X	X		X	X	X		X
Camelot Behavioral Checklist (Foster, 1974) Camelot Behavioral Systems P.O. Box 607 Parsons, KS 67357	X	X		X	X	X	X	X	X	X	X	X	X	X	X	X
Callier Azusa Scale (Stillman, 1978) Callier Center for Communication Disorders University of Texas/Dallas 1966 Inwood Road Dallas, TX 75235		X	X	X	X		X	X	X	X		X	X			
Pennsylvania Training Model: Individual Assessment Guide (Somerton-Fair & Turner, 1975) Pennsylvania Dept. of Education Bureau of Special Education Harrisburg, PA 17111	X	X		X	X		X	X	X	X	X		X			

trends in educational assessment in terms of their contribution to the assessment process and how they can most efficiently be used for valid assessment purposes.

Task Analysis

White (1971) defined the task analysis model as "a detailed description of each behavior needed to accomplish a behavioral objective given the student's current ability level" (p. 175). As it relates to assessment, the student is asked to perform a selected task or activity, and the components on which the student is not proficient are recorded. The teacher then knows which components of the chain need to be taught. Although task analysis offers one of the most useful approaches to assess-

TABLE 3.2 (continued)

Instrument, Author, and Publisher	Assessment Methods			Ages Covered			Content Areas									
	Interview	Observation	Direct Testing	0–3 Yrs	3–6 Yrs	6+ Yrs	Sensory	Gross Motor	Fine Motor	Language	Cognition/ Academic	Social/ Emotional	Self-Help	Independent Living	Vocational	Recreation/ Leisure
Pyramid Scales (Cone, 1984) PRO ED 5341 Industrial Oaks Blvd. Austin, Texas 78735	X	X	X		X	X	X	X	X	X	X	X	X	X	X	X
Scales of Independent Behavior (Bruininks, Woodcock, Weatherman, & Hill, 1984) DLM Teaching Resources One DLM Park Allen, Texas 75002	X			X	X	X	X	X	X			X	X	X	X	X
TARC Assessment Inventory for Severely Handicapped Children (Sailor & Mix, 1976) H&H Enterprises P.O. Box 3342 Lawrence, KS 66044		X		X	X		X	X	X	X		X	X	X		
Uniform Performance Assessment System (White, Edgar, & Haring, 1982) Merrill Publishing 1300 Alum Creek Drive Box 508 Columbus, OH 43216		X	X	X	X	X	X	X	X		X	X	X			
Vineland Adaptive Behavior Scales (Sparrow, Balla, & Chicchetti, 1984) American Guidance Service Inc. Circle Pines, MN 55014	X			X	X	X	X	X	X			X	X	X		X

Source: From "Identification and Placement of Severely Handicapped Children" by R. R. Fewell and J. D. Cone in *Systematic Instruction of the Moderately and Severely Handicapped* (p. 60) by M. E. Snell (Ed.), 1983, Columbus, OH: Charles E. Merrill. Copyright 1983 by Merrill Publishing Company. Reprinted by permission.

ment, Brown et al. (1984) delineated three areas of concern about the traditional use of task analysis in the assessment process.

Inconsistency

One problem with the task analytic model is that the beginning and end points of behavioral chains are arbitrary or inconsistent, that is, there are no guidelines to establish where a task analysis begins and where it ends. One teacher may break down the task of washing dishes in the following way: "turn on water, put soap on sponge, wet dish, wash dish, rinse dish, put dish in drainer." Another teacher, however, may begin the chain with getting the materials needed to wash the dishes and end the chain with "put away the sponge and soap." Still another teacher may have started the chain with "go to the kitchen." Further, the components within the chain are also identified in a very arbitrary fashion by the instructor. In the above example of dishwashing, the instructor may have included additional steps such as "wet sponge," "squeeze sponge," "wash bottom of dish," etc.

Limited Scope

The limited scope of skills included in a task analysis presents another issue. Traditionally tasks are broken down within the context of observable motor skills. There may be, however, many fewer observable skills that may be crucial to the competent performance of the chain. Using the dishwashing example, the student should also know when it is time to wash the dishes, how to problem solve if something out of the ordinary happens, and should be able to perform the task in an appropriate amount of time as well as make sure that the dishes are clean.

Equal Weighting

Finally, a very crucial limitation to the use of the traditional task analysis is the equal weighting given to the components of the chain. That is, when a task is analyzed, each component of the chain is treated the same. It may be, however, that certain components of the chain have different characteristics and must therefore be assessed in different ways. A task analysis of "brushes teeth" may include components such as "obtains necessary materials for brushing teeth" and "squeezes toothpaste onto toothbrush." These two components are likely to have very different characteristics. Although the materials may change, the first component mentioned above is similar to what is required in many other tasks: preparation of materials is necessary in most activities we do. The second component above is not required in many activities that we do. The difference in the generality of these two components will likely affect the assessment procedures. If the instructor wanted to know whether the student could "obtain materials," then assessment would need to sample this item within the context of many activities. If, however, the instructor was only interested in the toothbrushing activity, then sampling would be limited to the toothbrushing context.

Ecological Inventory

The ecological inventory strategy, or the top-down approach, focuses on the natural environment both as the source of curriculum content and as a location for training these identified needs (Brown et al., 1979). This strategy examines current environments in which the student is expected to function. These may include domestic, general community, recreation/leisure, vocational, and educational environments (Brown, Branston-McClean, Baumgart, Vincent, Falvey, & Shroeder, 1979). These environments are then divided into subenvironments, and activities and skills that are needed to participate in each subenvironment are identified (see Chapter 4 for a detailed description on how to implement this strategy). Students then can be assessed in terms of the discrepancy between their present skills and those identified as needed to function in various current and subsequent environments. Although this process is very time-consuming for an individual teacher to carry out, it is likely that completed and tested inventories will become increasingly available (Freagon, Wheeler, McDannel, Brankin, & Costello, 1983; Neel, Billingsley, McCarty, Symonds, Lambert, Lewis-Smith, & Hanashiro, 1983).

This approach has several advantages in the assessment process. The "top-down" strategy focuses on those skills needed to be an independent adult. This is in contrast to the more traditional developmental approach, or "bottom-up" approach, that starts with the skills of a normal infant and then progresses to the skills needed by an adult (Brown et al., 1979). With this "bottom-up" approach, it is unlikely that the student would progress to the skills necessary for independent living.

Another advantage of using the ecological inventory approach to assess students is that it is flexible in terms of its content (Brown et al., 1979). The content is not predetermined but rather depends on each student's individual situation. This is an important consideration in assessing a student's competence considering the variability in environments and their subsequent demands. That is, some students are expected to function in urban settings and others in rural settings, still others in settings with city buses or subways. And certainly, the recreational options in various communities differ greatly. If one's goal is to assess a student's ability to adapt within his own environment, the content of the assessment should reflect the unique requirements of his community.

To provide a more formal use of this approach as an assessment strategy, however, a structured framework is needed. Without structure, two instructors could inventory the same environments for the same student but identify very different skills. A systematic approach to the observation of behavior using this strategy would enhance the reliability of this process. Brown et al. (1984) have identified several areas that teachers should address in order to utilize this strategy more effectively as an assessment tool. First, the ecological inventory may result in sequences of skills needed to perform various functional activities. An assessment procedure should provide a formal process to relate the skills identified across the various sequences. An ecological inventory of the work domain may identify the activity of "purchasing a snack" during breaktime. Another inventory of the leisure domain may indicate "purchasing groceries." A teacher should be able to systematically identify activities or sequences of skills that may be the same (purchasing a snack at the mall and purchasing a snack during a work break) or that may be similar (purchasing a snack at the mall and purchasing groceries). Identifying skills that are the same or similar has direct implications for assessment: performance of one activity may or may not represent performance of the other activities.

The same isolated look at sequences of skills may occur on a more basic skills level. If basic skills such as grasping, object identification and functional object use are not somehow related across situations or contexts, then we are in the unfortunate situation where we

must attempt to teach a likely unobtainable number of discrete skills to achieve even the beginning of effective adaptive behavior.

. . . If, for example, a large number of task-analyzed instructional programs were to be lined up side-by-side, we might be able to identify a number of "critical skills" common across the various programs." (Guess & Noonan, 1982)

Second, the teacher needs to be sure that the ecological inventory will identify not only the observable activities and skills that are associated with competent performance in natural environments, but also related skills that may not be quite so apparent. Other types of skills that may not be readily apparent are subtle social skills such as smiling at a waitress and giving eye contact to the cashier at a restaurant. These behaviors, although not critical to the performance of the routine, may nonetheless be crucial to socially appropriate performance of an activity. Similarly, some language competencies may not be observable because they do not occur at that specific place or time of the activity. That is, "going to a movie" may be identified as an activity within the community domain and divided into its component parts. "Communicating about the movie" later in the day or "inviting a friend to go to the movies" would not likely be identified in an inventory.

Third, the teacher should attempt to identify not only those activities necessary to the independent functioning of a person that occur on a consistent or daily basis, but those that occur on a more intermittent or episodic basis. For example, "going to the dentist for a checkup" should be identified as a desirable outcome for some students when doing the inventory.

Form versus Function

The concept of *function* or *critical effect* has been increasingly used in special education assessment (Meyer, Reichle, McQuarter, Evans, Neel, & Kishi, 1983; White, 1971; White, 1980; White & Haring, 1976; White & Liberty, 1976). White distinguishes between *form* and *function;* whereas *form* refers to a specific motor act, *function* focuses attention on the purpose the behavior is supposed to serve. White notes that the form approach overlooks the possibility that there may be many ways to accomplish the same basic outcome. The function "prepares a simple meal" may be accomplished in any number of ways (making a sandwich or heating up canned soup). It is the meal preparation (function) that is the focus in this example, and not the more specific motor activities (form) (Evans, Brown, & Weed, 1984). This concept of "function" is crucial to the assessment of student competence because it is the accomplishment of the function that is important. The function of "gets to work on time" does not specify whether this is done by using public transportation, a taxi, or getting a lift from a neighbor. The advantage of defining accomplishments according to function is that success is determined by the outcome of the behavior. Individuals who happen not to have a particular "form," either because they lack instruction or have a physical disability, are not penalized if they can accomplish the critical effect in another way. This concept also allows success to be determined according to the unique demands of any particular setting.

Unfortunately, some instruments include items that rigidly call for specific forms of a skill. The Vineland Adaptive Behavior Scales (Sparrow et al., 1984) include the possibility of scoring 'N' (no opportunity) to address the concern with some items that may be too concerned with form. The item, "Names one or more favorite television programs when asked, and tells on what days and channels the programs are shown," may be rated "N" so that if a family did not own a television or did not approve of television, the student would not be penalized.

THE COMPONENT MODEL OF FUNCTIONAL LIFE ROUTINES: AN ASSESSMENT STRATEGY

The Component Model of Functional Life Routines (Brown, Evans, Weed, & Owen, in press) (see Figure 3.2) was developed to provide a synthesis of the practices and trends discussed above so that they might better address current assessment needs for students with severe and profound handicaps. The component model breaks down a person's daily activities into a series of routines which are composed of different components or skills. Routines are defined as skill sequences that begin with a natural cue and end with the achievement of the critical effect or function of the behavior (Neel, Lewis-Smith, Hanashiro, McCarty, & Billingsley, 1983). The focus on routines provides a conceptual model that reflects the broad competencies needed to function in the natural environment. Unlike the traditional ecological approach, the Component Model systematically divides routines into a structured subset of skills to provide parameters for further reliable identification of components to be assessed.

Routine Function

In order to address the importance of assessing the "function," rather than "form," the component model identifies routines that are either substitutable or fixed. A *substitutable* routine may be accomplished in many different ways. As long as the routine is accomplished in a way that is appropriate to the criterion environment and acceptable to others, it matters little what the form is. A substitutable routine, "spends free time with a friend," can be accomplished by playing pinball with a friend, playing a simple board game with a friend, listening to music with a friend or going jogging with a friend. Each of these routines accomplishes the same basic function. The form of the routine will be determined by the type of community the student lives in, student preference, age, the cognitive and motor skills, and the resources provided by the family. An assessment strategy should allow for the substitution of some routines so that students are not penalized by irrelevant criteria. Other routines, however, are *fixed* and do not lend themselves to different forms of accomplishing the critical effect of the routine. Many personal management routines such as toileting, brushing teeth, or dressing require very definite behaviors to be performed in order to accomplish the critical effect. Any alternative activity would lose the intent of the activity.

All routines, however, are composed of skills or components that may be substitutable. An individual skill can be accomplished in many ways. Although "dressing" is not substitutable at the routine level, the specific way that the dressing occurs can vary: one student may use velcro straps instead of shoelaces, hold on to a chair for support when putting on pants, or use pants with an elasticized waistband in order to dress independently. Similarly, when asking for assistance from a workshop supervisor, a student may communicate using a communication board, speech, or sign. The assessment should be looking at the critical effects of the behavior and be flexible enough to allow students with various levels of cognitive and motor skills to accomplish critical effects with adaptations, prostheses, or any other environmental arrangements.

Domains

In the Component Model of Functional Life Routines, routines may be classified into the domains of personal management, leisure, vocational/school (depending on the age of the student), and mobility. The two-directional arrows connecting the domains indicate possible interaction among the domains. A routine is given meaning by the context in which it is performed or the intent of the routine: "doing the dishes" may be thought of as a personal management activity. If the intent, however, is to perform the same routine as a dishwasher in a restaurant, some of the skills needed to perform the routine would change, whereas the basic skills needed may remain the same across both domains. Characteristics of the task that may change include how frequently the routine is done

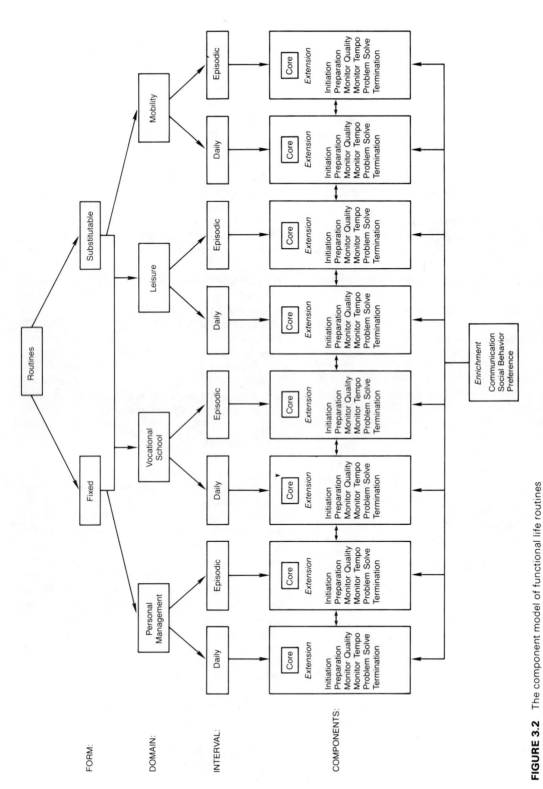

FIGURE 3.2 The component model of functional life routines

Source: From '"Making Functional Skills Functional: A Component Model" by F. Brown, I. M. Evans, K. Weed, and V. Owen, in press. *Journal of the Association of Persons with Severe Handicaps.* Reprinted by permission of the author.

(dishes may need to be washed three times a day at home for a total of ½ hour, but as a vocational skill may need to be repeated continually for 3 hours), where the routine is performed (home versus large restaurant kitchen), the precision with which it needs to be done (housemates may have a lower standard of what is considered clean than a supervisor), the materials used (different types of detergents, sponges or perhaps type of dishwasher), and the sequence or order in which the skills need to be performed (at home limited counter space may require one to clean off each dish and then place in dishwasher, and a vocational site may require one to wash several dishes before placing them all at once in the dishwasher). Simply assessing "washing dishes" would not give adequate information to the evaluator; assessment must consider the unique requirements of each domain. This will be addressed further in the section, "Component Skills."

Routine Interval

There are two types of routines under each domain. *Daily* routines occur on a daily basis and are integral or critical to the individual's functioning given the demands of his or her typical environments. Examples of daily routines are eating, brushing teeth, using the bathroom, going to school or work, and occupying one's time after school. *Episodic* routines occur on a more intermittent basis. Some episodic routines do not have to be accomplished every day but are still crucial to independent functioning; others may never need to be accomplished but may have a qualitative impact on a person's life. For example, shopping for food and menstrual care do not have to be accomplished daily but are crucial to independent functioning. Going to the movies never really has to be accomplished but certainly adds an enriching dimension to one's usual routine. Assessors must make sure to include evaluation of episodic routines that may not be obvious in a behavioral sampling of typical environments.

Component Skills

Three different types of skills make up a routine. These skills provide the crucial structure for a comprehensive assessment of functional routines. The structure also adds reliability to the ecological approach by enabling two professionals inventorying the same subenvironments to observe the environment in the same way.

Core Skills

Core skills are those smaller components of a routine that are absolutely necessary for the intent or purpose of the routine to be accomplished. These skills are directly related to the critical effect or purpose of the routine and are bound to the context of the routine. For example, if a student were to brush his hair (routine), the core skills would include: picking up the brush, applying the brush to his head, pulling the brush through all sections, and placing the brush down. Core skills are typical of the traditional task analysis or breakdown of skills in many assessments. To exemplify this, the AAMD Adaptive Behavior Scales-Public School Version (Lambert, Windmiller, Cole, & Figueroa, 1975) breaks down "washing hands and face" into the following components: washes hands with soap, washes face with soap, washes hands and face with water, and dries hands and face. Does successful performance of these four parts imply that the student has mastered this skill? These core skills do not sample the range of behaviors necessary for functional use of the routine in natural environments. To use this skill in the natural environment, a student would also be expected to know, for example, when his hands needed washing and to check to make sure they are clean.

Extension Skills

As described above, a traditional task analysis may result in a list of skills that do not represent the broad range of skills needed to function in criterion environments. Extension skills extend the core skills in order to delineate a more comprehensive routine, and thus provide a more meaningful evaluation of student competence. Six specific extension skills are included in this model: *initiating* the routine, *preparing* or planning for the routine, *monitoring* the *quality* of performance, *monitoring the tempo* (rate and duration) of performance, *problem solving* if something out of the ordinary should occur within the realm of the routine, and *terminating* or doing the things necessary to end a routine. Thus, in addition to the core skills listed on the ABS item "washing hands and face," the student could also be expected to: "know when it's time to wash" (initiate), "obtain the soap and towel" (plan), "wash for an appropriate amount of time" (monitor rate/duration), "be sure hands and face are clean" (monitor quality), "negotiate any problems encountered while washing" such as not finding the soap or towel, or dropping the soap on the floor (problem solve), hang up the towel, and clean up any mess if necessary (terminate).

Extension skills are required in all routines (note the two-way arrows connecting the component tier of Figure 3.2). Even though there may be some generality of extension skills across routines there are not sufficient data at this point to determine if performance of an extension skill in one routine implies that the person has the skill in other routines. Motivation will likely be one influence on the variable performance of one extension skill across different routines. For example, a 10-year-old student would be more likely to initiate playing with a friend than brushing his teeth. More investigation is needed, but to date we must assume that these extension skills should be assessed in each of the criterion environments and routines (Weed, Brown, & Evans, 1985).

Enrichment Skills

Enrichment skills are not critical to the independent performance of a routine. They do, however, enrich or add to the quality of the routine, and as such may be considered to be equally as important, if not more important than the previous skills mentioned. If as educators we are concerned with the quality of our students' lives, then our assessment procedures should reflect this concern. This category of skills includes expressive communication, social behaviors, and preference or choice. If one were doing the laundry, talking or signing about the activity may not be crucial to accomplishing the task, but it may make the task a bit more pleasant, and certainly offers functional practices of language instruction. Certain social interactions such as smiling at the supermarket cashier when checking out is not critical to the performance of the routine, but it would enhance the quality of the routine. Choosing between two or more feasible alternatives (a hairstyle) is also not crucial to the performance of a routine, but adds to the quality of a student's experience as well as providing him with some control of the environment. The same enrichment skills may be found across the three domains, and therefore like extension skills, may require assessment procedures that sample many contexts.

Each of the components in the component model represents meaningful units of behavior. As such, all items that a student is assessed on are relevant to the demands of the natural environment. This becomes particularly important for students with severe physical handicaps. For example, a student may not be able to perform the "core" skills of eating (grasps spoon, lifts spoon to mouth, takes food off spoon, chews, swallows). It is likely that this student would also not be able to perform the motor skills required in many other self-help skills; this student is likely to "bottom out" of most assessments. Interpretation of this type of assessment information would likely conclude that the student should begin to learn the specific motor movements of the skill as determined by a detailed task analysis. According to the component model, however, this student may be able to engage in other very meaningful aspects of "eating" such as: indicating to someone that he would like to eat (initiate), moving his electric wheelchair to the table (transition) and choosing what he would like to eat (choice). With this type of approach, the student is not only being assessed on relevant items, and scoring on meaningful dimensions of behavior, but interpretation of his performance on these types of items will influence a teacher to include these as relevant goals in the student's educational program. Figures 3.3 and 3.4 are examples of ways the routines of "grooms hair" (a *fixed* routine) and "engages with play activity with family" (a *substitutable* routine) are analyzed for assessment.

FACTORS RELATED TO MEANINGFUL ASSESSMENT

In order to understand assessment, familiarity with certain terms and issues is necessary. The following sections will introduce specific assessment concepts that can be used when evaluating the potential utility of assessment instruments being considered for use in the classroom.

Test Reliability

Reliability refers to the extent to which an instrument is consistent in measuring whatever it is measuring. If an assessment is repeated within a short interval of time a student should receive the same score or rating. Reliability is usually measured by some form of reliability coefficient ranging from 0 to 1 or by the standard error of measurement derived from it. Salvia and Ysseldyke (1984) state that tests should have reliability coefficients in excess of .60 if the scores are for administrative purposes or are reported for group scores; however, when tests are to be used to make decisions

Domain: Personal Management

Interval/Form: Daily/Fixed

Routine: Grooming Hair

Which of the following aspects of hair grooming does your child do independently?

	Yes	No	NA	With Adapt.	Comments
1. Grooms or indicates need to groom at such times as when hair is messy, before going out, after gym (initiate)					
2. Finds and selects needed items such as comb, brush, or pick (prepare)					
3. Combs, brushes, or picks hair (core)					
4. Checks hair for neatness (monitor quality)					
5. Grooms hair within acceptable time (monitor tempo)					
6. If a problem arises, such as a tangle or can't find brush, will take action to remove problem (problem solve)					
7. Puts comb or brush away, cleans up loose hairs if necessary (terminate)					
8. Expresses or communicates about any aspect of hair grooming, such as need for haircut or style (communication)					
9. Makes choices concerning hair grooming, such as choosing between comb or brush, type of barrett, hairstyle (choice)					
10. Grooms hair according to social standards, in acceptable settings, responds appropriately to comments of others (social behavior)					

FIGURE 3.3 Items comprising the routine "Grooming hair," as determined by the component model of functional life
Source: Adapted from Figure 2 in "Making Functional Skills Functional: A Component Model" by F. Brown, I. M. Evans, K. Weed, and V. Owen, in press, *Journal of the Association of Persons with Severe Handicaps.* Reprinted by permission of the author.

regarding individual students a reliability coefficient should be over .90.

This term does not address the *content* of what is being assessed, only its consistency. A teacher could reliably measure a student's ability to "place pegs in a pegboard within one minute," as part of an assessment of vocational readiness. The measure may be very consistent, or reliable, across time, and two evaluators may very well agree on the student's performance on the assessment (inter-rater reliability). Although reliability may be estab-lished, this skill has no relationship to the janitorial tasks on which the student will be trained. Thus, whereas this may be considered a reliable measure, the concept does *not* address the purpose, or the content (validity) of what is being measured.

Test Validity

Test validity refers to the extent to which a test measures what it is supposed to measure; in other words, it looks at the *content.* This is a very impor-

Domain: Leisure

Interval/Form: Episodic/Substitutable

Routine: Engages in play activity with family at home: _____

Based on the leisure activity you indicated above, which aspects of this activity does your child do independently?

	Yes	No	NA	With Adapt.	Comments
1. Approaches family member(s) or lets you know in some way when he/she wants to do this activity (initiate)					
2. Arranges play area, obtains needed materials, turns equipment on, or arranges with family member for these types of things to be done (prepare)					
3. Student performs the basic steps of the activity (core)					
4. Attempts to improve skills or increase enjoyment for self and family (monitor quality)					
5. Spends appropriate amount of time engaged in activity (monitor tempo)					
6. If a problem arises, such as if he/she can't find the game, a piece is missing or broken, will take action to remove problem (problem solve)					
7. Puts away materials, arranges for family member to put away, or helps straighten up (terminate)					
8. Expresses or communicates about any aspect of the activity, such as things that happened during game, enjoyment (communication)					
9. Makes choices concerning activity, such as which board game to play, which color playing piece, who to play with (choice)					
10. Responds appropriately with family members during game, follows general rules, shares, etc. (social behavior)					

FIGURE 3.4 Items comprising the routine "Engages in play activity with family at home," by the component model of functional life routines

Source: Adapted from Figure 3 in "Making Functional Skills Functional: A Component Model" by F. Brown, I. M. Evans, K. Weed, and V. Owen, in press, *Journal of the Association of Persons with Severe Handicaps.* Reprinted by permission of the author.

tant variable to consider because important decisions may be made on the basis of tests that measure irrelevant information. If a test is not valid we cannot meaningfully interpret the results. For example, if the receptive language skills of a quadraplegic student were being assessed, but the test required that the student respond by pointing, it would not be valid for this particular student. Instead, this test would be measuring a motor skill and not the receptive language of the student, thus lacking *content* validity. However, if the student's vision was good and eye glance was a reliable response, then receptive language test results assessed in this manner could be regarded as valid. Content validity would also be lacking if a test did not adequately sample a broad enough range of skills to determine whether competency was sufficient. If the self-help domain of a particular test included only toileting, dressing, and hairbrushing, we must conclude that three skills are insufficient for making a judgment of a student's general self-help skills and thus are invalid.

Criterion-related validity refers to the extent to which scores on the test are in agreement with (*concurrent* validity) or predict (*predictive* validity) some given criterion measure. For example, if we were questioning the criterion-related validity of a hypothetical "Smith's Test of Adaptive Behavior," we would determine if the person's test score on this test related to his scores on perhaps the AAMD Adaptive Behavior Scales (Nihira, Foster, Shellhaas, & Leland, 1974), a test that is presumed to be a valid measure of adaptive behavior, or if the score could accurately predict the person's chances for success in living in the community.

Data Gathering

There are three basic methods of gathering assessment information. Each of the methods provides different information and has its own advantages and disadvantages.

Direct Testing

This method of data collection requires the teacher to systematically provide the student with the opportunity to respond to the stimuli. The teacher may provide the student with certain materials or instructions to determine if he can perform the behavior that is being assessed. Direct testing may occur in either isolated settings or in more representative settings. A teacher may take a student into the bathroom, provide a toothbrush, tooth-

paste, cup, and towel, and then ask him to brush his teeth. The teacher will then observe what components of the task he performs. In this situation the student is not being assessed, however, for whether he brushes his teeth at the appropriate times; rather the testing is done in an appropriate setting and with the same materials that the student is expected to use in his natural environment. *Direct testing, whenever possible, should occur in the criterion environment and using the criterion materials.* If a teacher were to assess the student in this example by bringing him into the classroom and providing him with an electric toothbrush, the information gathered might not be representative of his performance in the bathroom and with the type of toothbrush used at home. The selection of materials to use in the assessment process, as well as in instruction, must be made with several considerations in mind: availability of materials at home, physical status and preferences of the student, and school resources.

This approach provides the student with the opportunity to demonstrate the behavior. Many times students lack a skill not because they are unable to do the behavior, but because they have not had the opportunity to engage in it. This may be a difficult approach to use, however, because some behaviors do not naturally occur, or do not occur frequently, in the classroom but still may be important to assess. A teacher may want to assess a student on handling money. Although the criterion environment is the community, she may want to first gather information by direct testing in the classroom to get a general idea of the student's skill. She must, however, keep in mind that the student's performance in the classroom may be different than it would be in the criterion environment. If it is revealed that the student demonstrates the desired skills in the classroom, a second assessment of the skill should take place in the community. Similarly, showering may not be a typical part of the school day, but if the teacher was interested in directly assessing this skill she would need to arrange the situation.

The disadvantage of this approach is that very often the cues and materials are only similar, and not the same, as the natural environments. In the showering example, the teacher can arrange to use some of the same materials that the parents use at home; however, there may not be much she can do if the school has a stall shower, and the parents have a tub shower.

Observation in the Natural Environment

In this type of information gathering, the teacher observes the student in the setting in which the behavior(s) naturally occur. The major advantage of this situation is that she has the opportunity to observe a wider range of behaviors. In other words, she can see if the student demonstrates associated skills such as mobility to the location of the activity, initiation of the skill, ways he addresses problems that may arise in the natural environment, as well as noting any inappropriate social behavior. A classroom environment may not offer the same natural opportunities to demonstrate the competencies that are really needed for skill use in the criterion environment. When assessment occurs in the natural environment, the teacher does not have to be concerned about attempting to simulate materials and cues that approximate the natural environment. In order for this type of data gathering to be the most useful, the observations should sample all of the appropriate settings (classroom, home, playground, bathroom), the appropriate times of the day (before or after lunch, morning, afternoon), and the criterion situations (group, one-to-one, free play). Each of these variables are likely to influence the student's performance of any skill or activity, and so in order to obtain data that accurately represents the student, several observations may be necessary.

One major disadvantage of this approach is that the behavior teachers are interested in observing may not naturally occur at the time of the observation. A teacher may decide to take the student into the community to assess him on "responds appropriately to strangers." The ideal way of assessing this would obviously be to take him to a mall and observe his behavior if a stranger was to approach him; however, there is a good chance that no stranger will approach on that particular day, at that particular time. Furthermore, assessing the student on some items may, in fact, be dangerous or unethical. Exploring a student's skill in "crossing the street" has obvious problems! Similarly, allowing the student to be in the vulnerable situation where a stranger may approach may also not be a good idea. Finally, another disadvantage of this approach is the great amount of time and resources that may be involved.

Interview

Some assessments require that information be obtained by interviewing others who know the student very well. The Adaptive Behavior Scales (Nihira et al., 1974), the Camelot Behavioral Checklist (Foster, 1974), and the Vineland Adaptive Behavioral Scale (Sparrow et al., 1984) are a few examples of instruments that obtain assessment information by interview. This may include one or both parents, staff from a residential facility if the student does not live at home, or the student if possible. The major advantage of this approach is that the information provided by the informants is likely to reflect the student's performance in natural settings with naturally occurring cues and consequences.

Interviewing parents is also the most direct method of finding out about the types of activities the family does, student likes and dislikes, and parents' preferences for particular activities. Used in conjunction with the other types of information gathering, a teacher will get a very broad picture of the student's home environment. This method is also a very constructive way of involving parents in the program and letting them know that their input is necessary for development of a good educational program.

If a parent, for whatever reason, is not available for the interview, an informal written format may help the teacher to elicit necessary information. If she was developing some type of informal environmental inventories, she could send the parents a questionnaire that could be filled out easily. The questionnaire would allow the teacher to find out about the home environment, likes, dislikes, and preferences. When done prior to an IEP meeting, the questionnaire may help prepare the parents to think about educational outcomes that are functional and relevant to present and potential environments. Figure 3.5 provides a sample of an informal questionnaire of this type. (Chapters 4, 14, and 15 provide additional examples of this process to select IEP objectives.)

Scoring

The types of scoring systems required in any assessment vary widely. Some tests may require a simple dichotomous response ("yes" the student has the skill or "no" the student does not have skill), while other instruments require a more complex or multiple level response on dimensions such as independence or frequency (can do skill given no assist, minimal assist, maximum assist; can do the skill never, some of the time, frequently, or always).

Parent Input Questionnaire

Parent's Name: _____

Child's Name: _____

Date: _____

Please answer the following questions so that we may get a better idea of your child's present needs at home and your feelings about his or her needs in the future.

At Home

1. What would you like your child to be doing at home now that he or she is not doing at the present time (for example, play by self, help clear off table, keep room neater)?
2. Where do you expect your child to live in the future?
3. What types of things may be expected from your child in this setting that your child is not expected to do now (for example, set the table, do the laundry, shower)?

Leisure Activities

4. What places have leisure opportunities for your child at the present time (for example, school, playroom at home, community center)?
5. What types of leisure activities would you like your child to participate in at these places (for example, watch T.V., computer games, boardgames, playground games)?
6. Are there other places that may have leisure opportunities for your child sometime in the future (for example, breaktime at work, shopping at the mall, community center)?
7. What are the types of leisure activities that will likely be available to your child in these settings (for example, playing cards, video games, bingo)?

At Work

8. What type of work setting (or post-school setting) do you expect your child to participate in after completing this present educational program?
9. What types of technical skills do you think will be required there (for example, assembly skills, janitorial skills, bussing tables)?
10. What types of work-related skills do you think will be required there that your child will probably need to work on (for example, getting along with others, getting along with supervisor, waiting in line for lunch, finding something to do during breaktime)?

In the Community

11. What types of community settings would you like your child to participate in now (for example, restaurant, shopping mall, grocery store)?
12. What are the specific activities that you would like your child to do at these settings (for example, ordering food in a restaurant, purchasing items in a store, walk and not run)?
13. Are there any other community settings or activities that may be available in the future that are not available now? If so, please list.

FIGURE 3.5 Sample of an informal parent questionnaire to elicit information about the student's present environments and potential future environments

There are advantages and disadvantages to each approach, and each approach may adequately serve different purposes. The dichotomous scoring method is appropriate to represent broader student outcomes or skill mastery. In terms of assessing what skills a student has to use in the community, he either has or has not mastered the skill suffi- ciently for independent use in the natural environ- ment. If he can cross a street "some of the time," certainly the teacher would conclude that this does not represent a sufficient level of mastery!

Similarly, if teachers are interested in what the student can do independently in the community, then scoring must be related to *meaningful* units of behavior (Brown et al., 1984). She will then know that an increase in the total score indicates an increase in functional competence of the person being assessed. This is compared to scoring items of an instrument that may be less significant components of a task analysis. When this is the case, a student may increase his total score, but the increase may represent fairly insignificant increases across several skills and not any increase that would help him function independently in the community. In the Pennsylvania Training Model (Somerton-Fair & Turner, 1975), there are 75 equally-weighted dressing items. Each dressing skill is task-analyzed into 4 to 7 increasingly complex items. "Putting on a shirt," for instance, includes the following six items:

1. Child pulls shirt down from midstomach
2. Child pulls shirt down from under armpits
3. Child puts one arm in armhole and pulls shirt into position
4. Child puts both arms in armholes and pulls shirt into position
5. Child pulls shirt down from eye level, puts both arms in armholes and pulls shirt into position
6. Child puts shirt on independently

The skill of "putting on a shoe" includes the following four items:

1. Child puts shoe on by pushing heel into proper position
2. Child puts shoe on when heel is completely out of shoe
3. Child puts shoe on when just tips of toes are in shoe
4. Child puts shoe on independently

In September, a student may do the first three items of "putting on a shirt" and the first two items of "putting on a shoe," for a total of five items passed. The student could not, however, do either skill independently. In June, the student's total score on these two skills may increase to 7. An increase of 2 offers little information about what the student has mastered. It is possible that the student passed an additional item on each dressing skill, still not doing either one independently. Or the student could have passed the two remaining items of "putting on a shoe," and can now independently put on his shoes. In terms of independent functioning, the latter increase of 2 items is more significant than the former.

Indeed, a student may have only some part of a skill or may be able to partially engage in an activity.

The Principle of Partial Participation (discussed in detail in Chapter 4) argues that although some persons with severe or profound handicaps may not be able to function independently in all environments, they should be taught to perform or to participate at least partially, or to whatever extent possible, in identified least restrictive environments (Baumgart, Brown, Pumpian, Nisbet, Ford, Sweet, Messina, & Schroeder, 1982). If a student's participation in an activity is going to be partial, attention to meaningful components of an activity as an index of progress becomes especially important. A teacher must be sure to work toward participation on components of the activity that the student, or others, perceives as meaningful (see section on the *Component Model of Functional Life Routines*). For example, a student who has severely limited range of arm motion may partially participate in grocery shopping by touching a can of food placed three inches from his hand. This same student could also participate by extending his arm to touch a picture of a particular food item to indicate a preference or choice. Having control over the environment and causing desired effects is a more meaningful form of participation in the activity (Brown et al., 1984).

The multiple-level scoring method is most appropriate when used to monitor student progress in any given instructional program; in terms of instruction, movement from performing a skill with maximum assistance to performing the same skill with minimal assistance may represent significant progress for a student in the acquisition phase of learning that skill. Thus, a scoring system sensitive to small student changes in independence or consistency of performance would be most appropriate for instructional purposes. Similarly, progress on small components of a task analysis, as in the example of "putting on a shirt," provides information that a teacher needs to determine adequacy of his instructional interventions.

In conclusion, there are many factors related to meaningful assessment of students with severe and profound handicaps. Teachers should be aware of issues related to test reliability and test validity in order to help determine what instruments are suitable for their particular needs. Understanding the various data gathering and scoring methods and issues will help prevent the teacher from making inappropriate conclusions about student progress and will assist in adapting instruments for student needs.

The Assessment Rating Scale (Figure 3.6) summarizes some of the main issues discussed in this

---

Assessment Rating Scale

Instrument Name: _____

Author(s): _____

Domains Covered:

_____ domestic   _____ community   _____ other:

_____ vocational   _____ leisure

Administered by:

_____ teacher   _____ psychologist   _____ other:

_____ aide   _____ OT/PT

_____ parent(s)   _____ speech therapist

Administration Time: _____

Data Collection Strategy:

_____ interview   _____ direct testing

_____ natural observation   _____ other:

	Yes	Somewhat	No, but can be adapted	No
Reliability:				
1. Administration method clear?				
2. Scoring method clear?				
Relevance:				
3. Items meaningful?				
4. Skill breakdown meaningful for instruction?				
5. Skill breakdown meaningful as outcome indicators?				
6. Data collection reflects natural environment?				
7. Items cover adequate range of behaviors?				
Individualization by:				
8. Chronological age?				
9. Physical abilities?				
10. Student preference?				
11. Parent input?				
12. Current environmental requirements/resources?				

Conclusions:

FIGURE 3.6 Assessment rating scale for systematic examination of an instrument on dimensions that are relevant for meaningful assessment

chapter that contribute to meaningful assessment of students with severe and profound handicaps. The intent of this scale is not to get a numeric score for rejecting or adopting an instrument. Rather, it provides a systematic approach to evaluate any given instrument on dimensions that are relevant for meaningful assessment. A teacher may find that a certain assessment is excellent in its coverage of administration and scoring methods, spans a functional and comprehensive range of skills, requires data collection in natural environments, is appropriate for the student's age; *but* it does not adequately address ways a student with severe physical handicaps can be assessed and what environmental adaptations might be helpful in assessing him. The teacher may choose, on the basis of this information either to reject the instrument or to adapt specific items by accepting responses that use environmental adaptations and alternate modes of communication. Similarly, she may find that an instrument is adequate across all of the items on the Assessment Rating Scale, but does not include parent input into the assessment process. The teacher is, thus, given a reminder to include parent input.

SUMMARY

This chapter reviews the importance of meaningful assessment of students with severe and profound handicaps. It describes the various purposes for and approaches to assessing these students. The contribution of various approaches to the assessment process are discussed in addition to their most efficient and valid use. General factors related to meaningful evaluation are also presented with strategies for selecting appropriate instruments. Although there is a lot of work yet to be done in this area, if a teacher is aware of the issues and ways information from testing is best used, interpreted, and too often abused, assessment can be the cornerstone of the educational process.

REFERENCES

Adams, J. (1973). Adaptive behavior and measured intelligence in the classification of mental retardation. *American Journal of Mental Deficiency, 78*(1), 77–81.

Alpern, G. D., Boll, T. J., & Shearer, M. S. (1980). *Developmental profile II* (Rev. Ed.). Aspen, CO: Psychological Development Publications.

Apgar, V. (1953). A proposal for a new method of evaluation of the newborn infant. *Current Researches in Anesthesia and Analgesia, 32*, 260–267.

Apgar, V., & Beck, J. (1973). *Is my baby all right?* New York: Trident Press.

Balthazar, E. E. (1976). *Balthazar scales of adaptive behavior for the profoundly and severely mentally retarded, I and II.* Palo Alto, CA: Consulting Psychologists Press.

Baumeister, A. A., & Muma, J. R. (1975). On defining mental retardation. *The Journal of Special Education, 9*(3), 293–306.

Baumgart, D., Brown, L., Pumpian, I., Nisbet, J., Ford, A., Sweet, M., Messina, R., & Schroeder, J. (1982). Prin-

cipal of partial participation and individualized adaptations in educational programs for severely handicapped students. *Journal of the Association for the Severely Handicapped. 7*(2), 17–27.

Bayley, N. (1969). Bayley scales of infant development. New York: Psychological Corporation.

Bluma, S., Shearer, M., Frohman, A., & Hilliard, J. (1976) *Portage Guide to Early Education.* Portage, WI: Cooperative Educational Service Agency.

Brazelton, T. B. (1973). *Neonatal behavioral assessment scale.* Philadelphia: J. B. Lippincott.

Bricker, W. A., & Campbell, P. H. (1980). Interdisciplinary assessment and programming for multihandicapped students. In W. Sailor, B. Wilcox, and L. Brown (eds.). *Methods of instruction for severely handicapped learners.* Baltimore: Paul H. Brookes.

Brown, F., Evans, I. M., & Weed, K. (1984). *A component model of functional life routines* (Technical Report No. 6). Binghamton: State University of New York, Department of Psychology and Division of Professional Education, Project SPAN.

Brown, F., Evans, I. M., Weed, K., & Owen, V. (in press). Making functional skills functional: A component model. *Journal of the Association of Persons with Severe Handicaps.*

Brown, L., Branston-McLean, M., Baumgart, D., Vincent, L., Falvey, M., & Schroeder, J. (1979). Using the characteristics of current and subsequent least restrictive environments in the development of curricular content for the severely handicapped students. *AAESPH REVIEW, 4*, 407–424.

Brown, L., Branston, M. B., Hamre-Nietupski, S., Pumpian, I., Certo, N., & Gruenewald, L. (1979). A strategy for developing chronological-age-appropriate and functional curricular content for severely handicapped adolescents and young adults. *Journal of Special Education, 13*, 81–90.

Bruininks, R. H., Woodcock, R. W., Weatherman, R. F., & Hill, B. K. (1984). *Scales of independent behavior; Woodcock-Johnson psychoeducational battery, part four.* Allen, TX: DLM Teaching Resources.

Cattell, P. (1940). *Infant intelligence scale.* New York: Psychological Corporation.

Cone, J. D. (1984). *The pyramid scales.* Austin, TX: Pro Ed.

Dallas County Mental Health/Mental Retardation Center. (1972). *The RADEA program.* Dallas: Metton Peninsula Company.

Evans, I. M., & Brown, F. (in press). Outcome assessment of student competence: Issues and implications for special service providers. *Special Services in the Schools.*

Evans, I. M., Brown, F., & Weed, K. (1984). *Participant research on parental concerns: A report on the parent verification (Report No. 4).* Binghamton: State University of New York, Department of Psychology and Division of Professional Education, Project SPAN.

Fewell, R., & Cone, J. (1983). Identification and placement of severely handicapped children. In M. E. Snell (Ed.), *Systematic instruction of the moderately and severely handicapped,* 46–73. Columbus, OH: Charles E. Merrill.

Foster, R. W. (1974). *Camelot behavioral checklist.* Lawrence, KS: Camelot Behavior Systems.

Frankenberg, W. K., Dodds, J. B., & Fandal, A. W. (1975). *Denver developmental screening test*. Denver: Ladoca Project and Publishing Foundation.

Freagon, S., Wheeler, J., McDannel, K., Brankin, G., & Costello, D. (1983). *Individual student community life skill profile system for severely handicapped students*. (Available from DeKalb County Special Education Association, 145 Maple, Cortland, IL 60112.)

Gaylord-Ross, R. J., & Holvoet, J. (1985). *Strategies for educating students with severe handicaps*. Boston: Little, Brown.

Gresham, F. M. (1983). Social skills assessment as a component of mainstreaming placement decisions. *Exceptional Children, 49*, 331–336.

Griffin, P. M., & Sanford, A. R. (1981). *Learning accomplishment profile for infants*. Chapel Hill, NC: Chapel Hill Training Outreach Project.

Grossman, H. J. (Ed.) (1977). *Manual on terminology and classification in mental retardation*. American Association on Mental Deficiency, Special Publication, Series No. 2.

Grossman, H. J. (Ed.) (1983). *Classification in mental retardation*. Washington, DC: American Association on Mental Deficiency.

Guess, D., & Noonan, M. J. (1982). Curricula and instructional procedures for severely handicapped students. *Focus on Exceptional Children, 4*, 1–12.

Heber, R. (1959). *A manual on terminology and classification in mental retardation*. Willimantic, CT: The American Association on Mental Deficiency, *64*(2).

Heber, R. (1961). Modifications in the manual on terminology and classification in mental retardation. *American Journal of Mental Deficiency, 65*(4), 499–500.

Hobson v. Hansen, 269 F. Supp. 401 (D.D.C. 1967).

Hogg, J. (1975). Normative development and educational programme planning for severely educationally subnormal children. In C. C. Kiernan & F. P. Woodford (Eds.) *Behavioral modification with the severely retarded*. Amsterdam: Associated Scientific Publishers, 1975.

Kazdin, A. E. (1977). Assessing the clinical or applied importance of behavior change through social validation. *Behavior Modification, 1*, 427–452.

Lambert, N., Windmiller, M., Cole, L., & Figueroa, R. (1975). *AAMD adaptive behavior scale, public school version* (1974 Rev.). Washington, DC: American Association on Mental Deficiency.

Meyer, L., Reichle, J., McQuarter, R. J., Evans, I. M., Neel, R. S., & Kishi, G. S. (1983). *Assessment of social competence (ASC): A scale of social competence functions*. (No. 300-82-0363) Minneapolis: Minnesota Consortium Institute for the Education of Severely Handicapped Learners.

Mills v. Board of Education of the District of Columbia. 348F. Supp. 866 (D.D.C. 1972).

Neel, R. S., Billingsley, F. F., McCarty, F., Symonds, D., Lambert, C., Lewis-Smith, N., & Hanashiro, R. (1983). *Teaching autistic children: A functional curriculum approach*. (Available from R. S. Neel, 103 Miller Hall, University of Washington, Seattle WA 98195.)

Neel, R. S., Lewis-Smith, N., Hanashiro, R., McCarty, F., & Billingsley, F. F. (1983). *Validation of a functional curriculum: The IMPACT project*. Unpublished manuscript, University of Washington, Seattle.

Nihira, K., Foster, R., Shellhaas, M., & Leland, H. (1974). Adaptive behavior scales: Manual (Rev. ed.), Washington, DC: American Association on Mental Deficiency.

Sailor, W., & Mix, B. J. (1976). *The TARC assessment system*. Lawrence, KS: H & H Enterprises.

Salvia, J., & Ysseldyke, J. E. (1984). *Assessment in special and remedial education* (3rd edition). Boston: Houghton Mifflin.

Sanford, A. R. (Ed.). (1974). *Learning accomplishment profile*. Chapel Hill, NC: Chapel Hill Training Outreach Project.

Somerton-Fair, M. E., & Turner, K. D. (1975). *Pennsylvania training model: Individual assessment guide*. Harrisburg, PA: Pennsylvania Department of Education.

Sparrow, S. S., Balla, D. A., & Cicchetti, D. V. (1984). *Vineland adaptive behavior scales*. Circle Pines, MN: American Guidance Service Incorporated.

Spellman, C. R., DeBriere, T. J., & Cress, P. J. (1979). Final report, from the project Research and Development of Subjective Visual Acuity Assessment Procedures for Severely Handicapped Persons (BEH Grant #G00-76-02592). Parsons, KS: Parsons Research Center.

Stillman, R. (1978). *Callier-Azusa Scale-Revised*. Dallas: Callier Center for Communication Disorders.

Switzky, H. N. (1979). Assessment of the severely and profoundly handicapped. In D. A. Sabatino & T. L. Miller (Eds.). *Describing learner characteristics for special education instruction*. New York: Grune & Stratton, 415–477.

Terman, L. M., & Merrill, M. A. (1973). *Stanford-Binet intelligence scale*. Boston: Houghton Mifflin.

Wechsler, D. (1974). *Wechsler Intelligence Scale for Children-Revised*. New York: Psychological Corporation.

Wechsler, D. (1967). *Wechsler preschool and primary scale of intelligence (WPPSI)*. New York: Psychological Corporation.

Weed, K., Brown, F., & Evans, I. M. (1985). *Observations of component skills in functional life routines of handicapped and nonhandicapped students*. (Technical Report No. 12). Binghamton: State University of New York, Department of Psychology and Division of Professional Education, Project SPAN.

Welch, R. J., O'Brian, J. J., & Ayers, F. (1974). *Cambridge assessment development rating and evaluation (CADRE)*. Cambridge, MN: CADRE Center, Cambridge-Isanti Public Schools.

White, O. R. (1971). *A glossary of behavioral terminology*. Eugene, OR: Research Press.

White, O. R. (1980). Adaptive performance objectives: Form versus function. In W. Sailor, B. Wilcox, & L. Brown (Ed.), *Methods of instruction for severely handicapped students*, 47–70. Baltimore. London: Paul H. Brookes.

White, O. R. (1985). The evaluation of severely mentally retarded individuals. B. Bricker and J. Filler (Eds.). *Severe mental retardation: From theory to practice*, 161–184. Reston, VA: Council for Exceptional Children.

White, O. R., Edgar, E., & Haring, N. G. (1982). *Uniform performance assessment system (UPAS)*. Columbus, OH: Charles E. Merrill.

White, O. R., & Haring, N. G. (1976). *Exceptional teaching.* Columbus, OH: Charles E. Merrill.

White, O. R., & Liberty, K. A. (1976). Behavioral assessment and precise educational measurement. In N. G. Haring and R. L. Schiefelbush (Eds.), *Teaching special children.* New York: McGraw-Hill.

Wolf, M. M. (1978). Social validity: The case for subjective measurement, or how applied behavior analysis is finding its heart. *Journal of Applied Behavior Analysis, 11,* 203–214.

Ysseldyke, J. E., & Algozzine, B. (1982). *Critical issues in special and remedial education.* Boston: Houghton Mifflin.

4

Instructional Assessment and Curriculum Development

Martha E. Snell
University of Virginia

Nancy C. Grigg
University of Virginia

The process of developing relevant curricula for students having severe handicaps consists of five interrelated phases. As the teacher systematically moves through each phase of the process, he or she will solicit different types of information and require varying degrees of involvement from the student's parents or guardians, professionals representing other disciplines, as well as other significant persons in the student's environment. Therefore, it is clear that the successful completion of the various steps involved in the development of functional curricula cannot be accomplished in a single meeting, but rather should be thought of as a dynamic, flexible process that results in a product which is open to revision and improvement.

As can be seen in Figure 4.1, during the first phase of the curriculum development process, necessary information concerning the student is gathered through a number of assessment techniques and involves the teacher and all persons able to provide relevant information. In the second phase, the major task is to synthesize the information gathered and determine the most pressing areas of instructional need, so that long- and short-term goals can be identified. The priority activities and skills represented by these goals are more finely analyzed in phase three, in order to facilitate program development, which is completed in the fourth phase. Following this, procedures which allow continuous monitoring of the instructional programs are planned and implemented within the final phase of the process. It should also be noted that these program evaluation procedures can, if necessary, lead the teacher to one of the two major feedback loops. The first loop leads back to phase 1 for the gathering of more assessment information, while the second goes back to phase 3 for reevaluation of the behavior targets and the possible revision of the instructional plans. The use of these feedback loops allow staff to be responsive to the student's level of performance, shifting parent priorities, changes in the student's environment, etc., and ensures that the curriculum remains relevant to the student's needs.

Indeed, since the curriculum and the resulting IEP will be the central driving force guiding a student's educational experiences, it is critical that it truly reflect the student's individual strengths and instructional needs. The long- and short-term goals which are identified will dictate the type of educational opportunities that the student will be exposed to, often for long periods of time. Ensuring that these goals are appropriate for a given student is particularly important when considering education for individuals with handicaps, because as the severity of the handicap increases, the more likely it is that learning will be slowed. Further, approximately 48% of individuals exhibiting moderate to profound levels of retardation have one or more additional handicap, either physical or emotional (Hill & Bruininks, 1981). When an individual with a mental handicap also has impaired vision or hearing that cannot be corrected, accurate perception of the surroundings is less likely. An inability to control or voluntarily move one's limbs adds greatly to difficulty in acquiring skills. Frequent aberrant behavior also has a negative impact on learning. Therefore, it is important that instructional time be spent only on those skills which will be of maximum benefit to the student.

Further, while some may debate the learning potential of persons with severe handicaps, there is considerable evidence that these individuals can learn functional skills if they receive appropriate instruction (Snell & Browder, 1986; Stainback & Stainback, 1983). At the same time, it must be acknowledged that there has been less attention paid to the problems encountered when teaching the small number of individuals having profound mental handicaps and/or severe motoric impairments. Yet, as noted by Donald Baer, this lack of documentation does not prove that the students cannot be educated.

All this implies that there is no way to be sure that a given behavior is unteachable in a given child. The set of procedures to be tried is too large and not yet totally invented; the set and sequence of possible reasonable prerequisite skills that, if taught first, would then render easy the teaching of the original target, is too large with even a moderately imaginative behavior analyst. A child cannot be declared unteachable in fact until teaching has been tried and has failed; teaching is too large a set of procedures (even in its known world) to have been tried and to have failed in its entirety, within the lifetimes of the child and the child's teachers. The point can also be stated in more mundane terms: The cost of truthfully affirming a child to be unteachable is no less than the cost of continuing to attempt teaching the child. (Baer, 1981, pp. 96–97)

In view of Baer's arguments, then, the development of a functional curriculum must be guided by the overriding assumption that *all* people with severe handicaps can learn although learning is likely to be slow in contrast to those with less severe impairments. Further, in order to help these students to attain the highest level of self-sufficiency, instructional time must not be wasted.

PHASE ONE: ASSESSMENT

Norm-referenced and Developmental Assessment Devices

Traditional assessment approaches with individuals having severe handicaps include norm-referenced or informal developmental tests. When using this approach, the teacher tries to identify those tasks, normally performed by infants and young children, that the student with severe handicaps has not yet mastered. Failed items are then rewritten as instructional goals based upon the assumption that students with handicaps should acquire the same orderly progression of skills seen in children without such impairments. Unfortunately, this approach to selecting objectives rarely yields behaviors that are actually needed by a particular person, or that serve to reduce their dependency on others. In fact, if the student with a handicap is much beyond infancy, a developmentally-based curriculum is likely to have little impact upon the ultimate attainment of self-sufficiency (Holvoet, Guess, Mulligan, & Brown, 1980).

Consider the two students we will be examining in detail in this chapter, each of whom had very different instructional needs. The first, Christine, is a 4-year-old girl who has cerebral palsy, and is therefore nonambulatory and experiences great difficulty when attempting to move her limbs voluntarily. Although Christine is nonverbal, her teachers believe that she has an extensive receptive vocabulary, and testing estimates that she has moderate to severe levels of mental retardation. The second, Robert, is a 19-year-old male living in an institutional setting, who has been tested and found to be profoundly mentally retarded. He does not have any motoric impairments, but frequently exhibits severe self-injurious behaviors.

When these students were assessed with a typical normative instrument, it was found that both

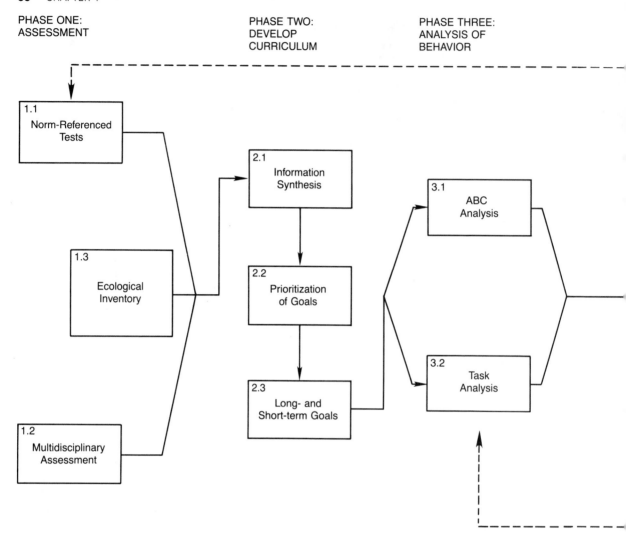

PHASE ONE:
ASSESSMENT

PHASE TWO:
DEVELOP
CURRICULUM

PHASE THREE:
ANALYSIS OF
BEHAVIOR

1.1
Norm-Referenced
Tests

1.3
Ecological
Inventory

1.2
Multidisciplinary
Assessment

2.1
Information
Synthesis

2.2
Prioritization
of Goals

2.3
Long- and
Short-term Goals

3.1
ABC
Analysis

3.2
Task
Analysis

FIGURE 4.1   Curriculum development process

failed the time requiring them to complete a simple inset puzzle. Since this is a behavior typically demonstrated by normally developing children, should both students be taught to place a circle, square and triangle in a puzzle board? Is this a necessary prerequisite skill for later independent functioning? Is this skill age-appropriate and/or functional? Is this skill related to other skills or useful in other contexts? Is this skill important enough to deserve valuable instructional time?

It would appear that sole reliance on developmental instruments for the selection of instructional objectives will be unlikely to result in the development of curricula relevant to the needs of either student. Although these two students may perform similarly on some developmental scales, it is clear their instructional programs should be very different. Even if Christine could learn to complete such a puzzle, would it not be a better investment of instructional time to teach her, for example, a functional method of communication? And would puzzle completion be a useful skill for Robert, who has been mandated by court order to move to a group home soon but cannot dress or feed himself?

However, as discussed in Chapter 3, some norm-referenced instruments, such as the AAMD

PHASE FOUR:
PROGRAM·
DEVELOPMENT

PHASE FIVE:
PROGRAM
EVALUATION

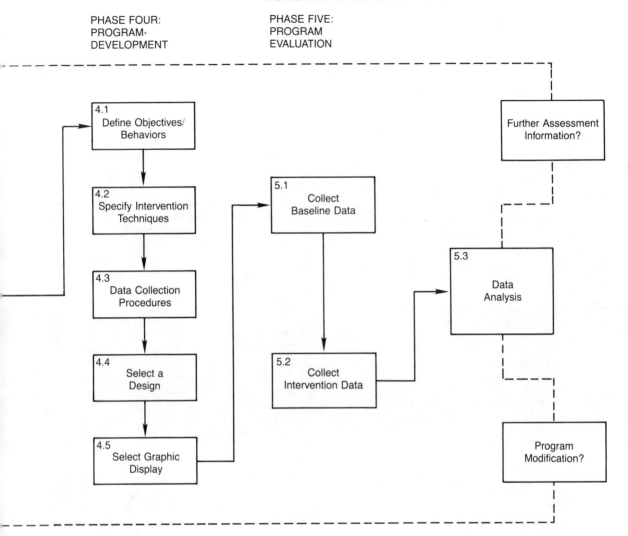

Adaptive Behavior Scales (Lambert, Windmiller, Cole, & Figueroa, 1975) or the Scales of Independent Behavior (Bruininks, Woodcock, Weatherman, & Hill, 1984) may be useful for teachers of students with severe handicaps for two purposes. First, these tools may provide a global picture of an unfamiliar student's abilities, thereby giving direction for more precise information assessment procedures. Second, because these published tests have wide familiarity among special educators and psychologists, the results, if considered accurate, provide common ground for reporting performance levels. However, since they are not intended to detect small changes in behavior and do not address all areas where instruction is likely, they cannot be used to evaluate student performances.

Thus, with the limited exception of some norm-referenced instruments, most assessment information gathered for the purpose of curriculum development will be collected through precise individualized behavior observation. Prior to the presentation of these teacher-mediated techniques, however, information gathered through assessment by professionals from other disciplines will be discussed.

Multidisciplinary Assessment

P.L. 94–142 requires that each special education student be provided with the related services, such as speech pathology and audiology, physical and occupational therapy, medical and counselling services, and recreational services, which are necessary to meet the individual needs of the student. As a result, there is often a large number of professionals who are charged with gathering assessment information as well as providing services to the student. Although it has been found that teams make more accurate decisions than do individuals (Thurlow & Ysseldyke, 1979), multidisciplinary teams have also been criticized as failing to deliver coordinated services to the student. In the next phase of the curriculum development process, we will discuss methods which can be used to integrate the information gathered by members of the team more effectively, thereby ensuring that necessary services are provided in the most efficient and effective manner.

Ecological Inventory

Dissatisfaction with the information gathered through norm-referenced and other standardized assessment instruments has led to the widespread need for techniques which better assist the schools to fulfill the mandate of P.L. 94–142 to teach the "skills a student needs, to optimize his or her independent, responsible functioning in society" (Hawkins & Hawkins, 1981, p. 13). For those with severe handicaps, instruction should focus upon partial or total independence in skills that have a high probability of being required at home, in school, at work, or in the community, and that will increase self-sufficiency within those environments (Brown, Branston, Hamre-Nietupski, Pumpian, Certo, & Gruenewald, 1979).

Because of differences in a myriad of factors affecting each student's life (cultural and community expectations, family preferences and priorities, administrative policies), skills that are useful or functional for one student cannot be assumed to be so for another. Therefore, instructional goals must be determined individually: what appears to be "functional" may not be so for each student.

The skill assessment and selection process, to be described, involves surveying the student's current and future environments to identify needed domestic, leisure-recreational, community, and voca-

tional skills (Brown et al., 1979; Vincent, Salisbury, Walter, Brown, Gruenewald, & Powers, 1980). This practice differs from the developmental approach in which instructional objectives are chosen from the "bottom up," starting with skills normally performed by infants and proceeding to those considered more advanced (motor, social, and cognitive). Brown and his colleagues (1979) refer to their functional survey for objectives as a "top-down" approach to skill building. That is, they *begin* with the requirements of independent adult functioning in four skill categories or domains: domestic, leisure/recreation, community, and vocational.

The domestic domain includes skills performed in and around the home: self-care, clothing care, housekeeping, cooking, and yard work. To the extent that an adult might be paid for performing domestic tasks, this domain has some overlap with vocational skills (janitorial or hotel maid jobs). In the leisure-recreational domains are spectator or participant skills; those required in the community domain include street crossing, using public transportation, purchasing in stores, eating in restaurants, and using other public facilities (such as theaters and parks). Finally, vocational-domain skills include those involved in attaining sheltered and competitive employment. Motor skills, communication, social behavior, and, for some, modified academic skills are likely to play a part in all four domains.

In order to accurately assess the skills necessary for successful functioning within these four domains, the teacher must acquire information from a variety of sources. Perhaps the most important source of information are the parents, guardians, or residential staff, since students will spend a great proportion of their time within their living environment. Indeed, the careful and thorough gathering of information from these informants can often reveal many potential instructional targets that could enhance the student's independent functioning within nonschool environments. As pointed out by Hawkins and Hawkins (1981):

A teacher in a school environment is unlikely to see that a particular child wanders into the kitchen occasionally and plays with knobs on the kitchen range, does not get in or out of an automobile or a bathtub without a great deal of help, does not imitate his parents' or siblings' speech, eats out of the pet's dish, gets food out of the cupboard or refrigerator without permission, requires repeated requests to get out of bed in the morning, does not stay alongside the family when walking, or squeals offensively sometimes when entering a restaurant. (p. 15)

Involving these informants during the earliest phase of the curriculum development process can make the teacher aware of many additional skill targets that might otherwise be overlooked. Further, when parents, guardians or staff are meaningfully involved in the development of the student's curriculum, they will be more likely to understand the goals and objectives identified and will be able to express their agreements and disagreements before a final draft is produced (Hawkins & Hawkins, 1981). Interaction with care-takers also should not be limited to any one phase in the curriculum development process: for example, in phase four, it is logical for the teacher to involve these informants when planning teaching programs, identifying reinforcers, or assessing "typical" or generalized performance.

Information also must be gathered from other individuals familiar with the environments in which the student will be involved. In Robert's case, the teacher could facilitate his successful transition to a vocational or group home placement by identifying the skills considered most crucial by those who will work with him in the future. Christine's teacher may survey other school staff to determine the types of demands and expected behavior in environments such as the school playground and cafeteria.

The process of developing a functional curriculum for a given student has been precisely defined by Brown and his colleagues (1979); we will summarize its first five phases by briefly illustrating its use with the two students previously discussed. We will first give a more complete description of the students, and then delineate how the functional curriculum is developed for each.

Robert *is a nonverbal 19-year-old male with profound mental retardation. Because of his age, he is in his final few years of public schooling. He has lived in an institution since he was 10 years old, but a nearby U.S. District court has ruled that he be transferred to a group home in the near future, along with his fellow residents. Currently, he attends a public school program in a community high school and is placed in a self-contained classroom for eight students with severe handicaps. Robert has minimal self-help skills: he is able to eat finger foods and drink independently; but when he uses utensils, the result is usually very messy. As a result, staff members often feed him meals. He is habit*

trained in toileting, but requires assistance to perform personal hygiene (washing his face and hands, brushing his teeth, shaving) as well as dressing and undressing.

Robert has not received any relevant vocational training, even though he would be eligible for placement in a workshop when he moves. Although he is ambulatory, he rarely goes out into community environments such as stores or restaurants, and has never used public transportation. He does not use his leisure time appropriately: when he is not receiving one-to-one attention, he usually engages in stereotypic behavior. In addition, he will exhibit severe self-injurious behavior when he is required to engage in activities he does not like.

Christine *is a 4-year-old student with cerebral palsy, which manifests itself in a severe restriction of voluntary movement in all extremities. She is capable of performing some movements on request (gross pointing responses and moving her head to one side or up and down); however, these voluntary responses are often difficult to discriminate because of extraneous involuntary movements which are almost constantly in evidence.*

Christine typically communicates with others through idiosyncratic facial expressions and body movements, as well as some vocalizations. She has been trained to drop her head to her chest to indicate "yes" and move her head to one side to indicate "no"; however, this behavior is only recognized by those familiar with her. Her lack of expressive ability concerns her teachers because they believe she understands most of what is said to her. She is very socially responsive and seems to enjoy interacting with others.

Christine is unable to perform any self-help skills and is not toilet trained. She does not have any independent leisure skills although she enjoys playing games when given assistance. She is often taken to a variety of community environments by her parents, with whom she lives in their city apartment. Her parents are very involved with her education but are concerned about their ability to care for her in the future when she is larger and more difficult to lift and position. They think that a group home in the community would be an acceptable alternative but will not consider an institutional placement.

Phases of the Ecological Inventory

There are five phases of the ecological inventory process which Robert and Christine's teachers will need to implement. These include:

1. Identify curriculum domains;
2. Identify and survey current and future natural environments;

3. Divide the relevant environments into subenvironments;
4. Inventory these subenvironments for the relevant activities performed there;
5. Examine the activities to isolate the skills required for their performance (Brown et al., 1979).

Identify Curriculum Domains For most students, including Robert, all four domains will be relevant. It is possible, however, that planning for very young students like Christine will focus primarily on domestic, leisure, and community skills, delaying vocational domain until after preschool. These curriculum domains rather than the traditional academic or developmental categories are used because they (a) represent the major life areas, (b) lead to the selection of practical skills, and (c) emphasize the functional goals of self-sufficiency. This practice does not mean that skills such as "language" or "fine motor" are forgotten.

Identify and Survey Current and Future Natural Environments The next step requires the teacher to identify and examine the environments in which the student presently lives, works, and plays. Further, to prepare the student to function in the settings she eventually will be placed in, future environments also must be added to the inspection list. Although it is difficult to predict future environments, (as long periods of training time may be needed to ensure a successful transition to alternate schools, residences, and work settings), it is necessary to identify these placements as early as possible. Figure 4.2 lists a *sample* of the current and future community environments that have been identified for Robert and Christine.

Divide the Relevant Environments into Subenvironments Further subdivision of environments is necessary to isolate activities most likely to be required. As with all other steps in this process, the subdivision must be completed with the individual needs of the student in mind. Figure 4.2 lists the manner in which some of these environments were divided for both Christine and Robert.

Inventory These Subenvironments for the Relevant Activities Performed There What are the essential clusters of behaviors a student is or will be required to perform in these settings? The teacher should identify only those activities necessary for basic acceptable performance, rather than isolating every possible activity (See Figure 4.2). Where possible,

attempts should be made to identify those activities that are considered to be *mandatory* for successful functioning in the various environments. Extensive considerations should also be given to how many times an activity (or a variation of it) is needed in other subenvironments, the student's current skills, his or her interests, the priorities of the parents, and the specific physical characteristics of the setting which dictate behaviors. Thus, as we discussed in Chapter 3, it is clear that the ecological assessment process is a complex strategy which requires the teacher to simultaneously consider a variety of issues which influence the instructional needs of each student.

Examine the Activities to Isolate the Skills Required for Their Performance As can be seen in Figure 4.2, this step requires activities to be broken down into teachable units. If selected for instruction, these units or separate skills will be further task analyzed into more precise sequences of behaviors. Although each skill is separated for measurement and teaching, the teacher must not lose sight of the end goal—clusters of related skills that must be performed together in the natural environment. Robert's success in using a fast-food restaurant will rely on his ability to exit from the vehicle, enter the restaurant, indicate desired food items to a companion, find seating, and wait until his companion orders and pays for food, eat, dispose of his trash, and leave. At some point, either during acquisition or after, this sequence of skills must be performed in combination.

Although the procedures used to conduct an ecological inventory described by Brown and his colleagues (1979) allow the practitioner to identify the skills that will be most functional for an individual student, it is clearly a complex and time-consuming process; however, some authors have suggested some extensions or variations of this procedure which have the potential for reducing the workload required. Wilcox and Bellamy (1982) described a process for cataloguing a community's opportunities for vocational, leisure, and domestic activities. This process initially involves a great deal of work, but it could be completed by a group of teachers working in the same area and used as a basis for developing curricula for individual students. Such information would preclude the need for repeatedly surveying common environments although specific activities would necessarily be individualized for each student. An assessment format has also been developed that can be used to identify functional skills for adolescents and adults with severe handicaps (Peterson, Trecker, Egan, Fredericks, & Bunse, 1983). Alternately, the Individualized Curriculum Sequencing Model not only specified methods for facilitating responses of students with severe handicaps, but also described how clusters of collateral behaviors frequently needed by students can be targeted as IEP objectives (Holvoet, Guess, Mulligan, and Brown, 1980; Sailor & Guess, 1983). Freagon and her colleagues (1983) described a routine domestic skills checklist and the process for developing it for a given geographic area.

By the end of the first phase of the curriculum development process, the teacher and other professionals who will be working with the student will have amassed a large body of information. Thus, the next phase of the process requires that the teacher, in consultation with the parents and other informants, identify the most pressing instructional needs.

PHASE TWO: DEVELOPING A FUNCTIONAL CURRICULUM

Information Synthesis

The special education teacher must be considered as the primary coordinator of all of the various data that are gathered during phase one. Although the task of integrating the wealth of information can be somewhat cumbersome, the different types of assessment data collected by the various professionals should be considered as complementary rather than competitive. Given the diverse needs of students with severe handicaps, no one professional or method of assessment will be adequate to fully document the needs of the student; however, when the entire body of assessment information is considered as a whole, we can obtain a comprehensive view of the capabilities and deficits demonstrated by the individual student.

Further, effective integration of information goes beyond the common practice in which various professionals simply tell each other what they intend to do with the student. Rather, teachers must ensure that the various services are provided in a coordinated, coherent fashion. Since educational services place the highest priority upon training the student to function in a variety of least-restrictive environ-

ments, we recommend that the teacher use the information obtained in the ecological inventory as a framework to assist in the identification of priority targets for intervention, as well as to coordinate the delivery of related services. Information gathered about various less restrictive settings can be used by the teacher and speech therapist to focus on the student's most critically needed communicative skills, as well as allowing instruction to occur in natural settings rather than in an isolated therapy room. Similarly, physical therapists could integrate their services by conducting training in conjunction with programs targeting other necessary skills such as teaching mobility skills when the student walks to a grocery store for training in a community environment (Sailor, Halvorson, Anderson, Goetz, Gee, Doering, & Hunt, 1986). Further, close and continuing consultation among the various professionals involved in the curriculum development process allows the integration of common goals and objectives across all services. If the vocational specialist has targeted specific grooming and social skills as necessary for the student's successful transition to a competitive work site, the objectives and training methods used should be shared with the student's teacher, caretakers, and therapists so that the same targets can be worked on across the day.

Prioritization of Goals

When information from a "top-down" approach to curriculum development is combined with that gathered by other professionals, there will be a large number of functional activities and skills identified; however, instruction could not possibly begin simultaneously on all skills and be very effective. Some choices must be made about which skills to teach before others. The main guide for prioritizing skills is to select for immediate instruction those skills the student requires most often to function more independently in least restrictive settings. Informants in this process include those persons already questioned: parents and guardians; workshops or other vocational training staff; group home or foster care parents, or other residential living staff; teaching staff in the upcoming educational settings; multidisciplinary staff (occupational, physical and speech therapists); and individuals familiar with community programs for which the student may be eligible. Time is saved if the teacher asks each informant to prioritize activities and skills during the initial assessment process. Observations

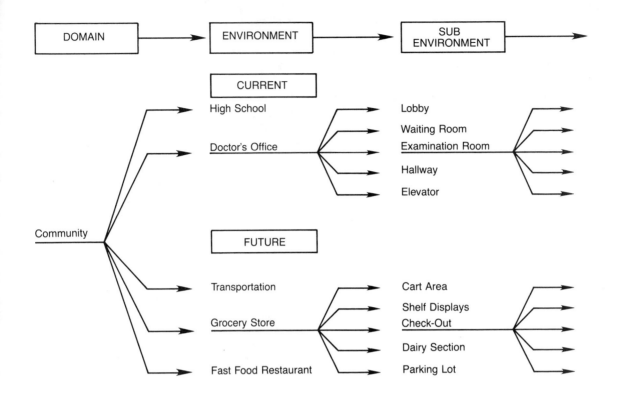

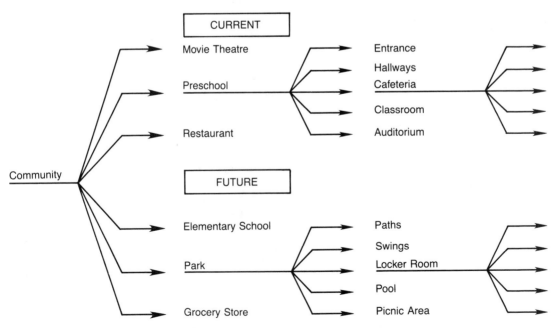

FIGURE 4.2 A partial listing of the ecological inventory procedures used with Robert and Christine

ACTIVITY	$\longrightarrow$	SKILL

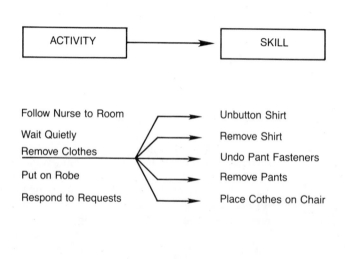

Follow Nurse to Room	Unbutton Shirt
Wait Quietly	Remove Shirt
Remove Clothes	Undo Pant Fasteners
Put on Robe	Remove Pants
Respond to Requests	Place Cothes on Chair

ROBERT

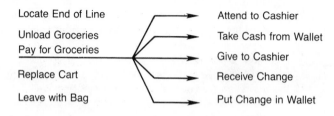

Locate End of Line	Attend to Cashier
Unload Groceries	Take Cash from Wallet
Pay for Groceries	Give to Cashier
Replace Cart	Receive Change
Leave with Bag	Put Change in Wallet

- -

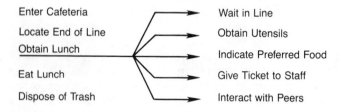

Enter Cafeteria	Wait in Line
Locate End of Line	Obtain Utensils
Obtain Lunch	Indicate Preferred Food
Eat Lunch	Give Ticket to Staff
Dispose of Trash	Interact with Peers

CHRISTINE

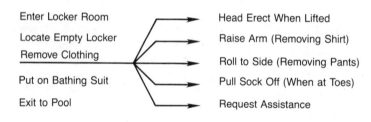

Enter Locker Room	Head Erect When Lifted
Locate Empty Locker	Raise Arm (Removing Shirt)
Remove Clothing	Roll to Side (Removing Pants)
Put on Bathing Suit	Pull Sock Off (When at Toes)
Exit to Pool	Request Assistance

of the typical performance demonstrated by others within the targeted environments should also be used to validate existing entry requirements and the subjective opinions of the informants, and may reveal additional important skills.

There are several important issues which should be considered when selecting those skills that should be taught:

1. Has the skill been designated by any of the informants as critical for entry into a future program or crucial for the student's health or safety?
2. Does the skill occur more than once in the inventory (e.g., named by more than one informant, used in more than one subenvironment?)
3. Is the skill required in future environments?
4. Is the skill appropriate for the student's chronological age?
5. Does the teacher have the time, materials and the appropriate setting available to teach and maintain the skill?

The teacher could conduct a review of all skills identified as potential instructional targets, recording "yes" or "no" responses for each of the questions listed above. Additional questions may also be addressed, depending upon the individual teaching situation. The skills identified as critical to entry into future environments or crucial to the student's health or safety (question 1) are usually considered to be of the highest priority for immediate instruction. Remaining instructional targets are selected from those skills receiving the largest number of affirmative answers.

Chronologically Age-appropriate Skills

As noted, the prioritization process must consider the degree to which the skills are appropriate for the student's chronological age. Brown and his colleagues explain the importance of this selection factor.

If one goal of education is to minimize the stigmatizing discrepancies between the handicapped and their nonhandicapped peers, it is our obligation to teach the former the major functions characteristic of their chronological age using materials and tasks which do not highlight the deficiencies in their repertoires. (Brown et al., 1979, p. 86)

The importance of this issue is underscored by a study which examined the attitudes of persons without handicaps as expressed toward a young woman having Down syndrome who was performing different activities. Two groups were shown different slide presentations: for example, when discussing fine motor skills, the first presentation showed the woman putting coins into a parking meter; the second showed her putting small pegs in a board. It was found that the group viewing slides of functional and age-appropriate activities made significantly higher estimates of the woman's IQ, earning capacity, and level of retardation. They also made less restrictive predictions about her residential and classroom placement and employment than did the group observing the same woman engaging in nonfunctional, age-appropriate activities (Bates, Morrow, Pancsofar, & Sedlak, 1984). Therefore, it would appear that the selection of appropriate skills can have a significant impact on the manner in which students with severe handicaps are perceived by others in the community.

Further, as students with severe handicaps are likely to require longer periods of time to acquire skills, it is best to select those activities that will be age appropriate in future environments as well. The teacher may choose to teach Christine to operate an adapted Fisher Price musical toy, since this item has been observed to be used by other nonhandicapped preschool children; however, an examination of future environments would reveal that this type of toy is not used outside preschool programs, thus requiring Christine to be taught new leisure skills when she gets older. A more efficient use of instructional time would teach her to use adaptive devices to operate a regular tape recorder, radio or record player, which would be appropriate at any age.

Partial Participation

Not all materials, activities, or instructional objectives suited to nonhandicapped persons will be appropriate for individuals of the same age who have severe handicaps. Rather, the teacher must also consider the motoric and/or cognitive requirements of the skills identified in the ecological inventory. Some of these requirements may appear to present insurmountable obstacles for an individual student. For students like Christine, a teacher may hesitate to select skills which require motor skills not demonstrated by the student, such as toothbrushing or face washing. Or, in Robert's case, calculating the cost of a fast-food order and giving the cashier the correct amount of money may appear too difficult for him to master in any reasonable period of time, if ever.

Rather than deleting these skills from consideration, and thereby restricting the student's ability to function in some environments, the teacher can employ the "principle of partial participation" (Brown et al., 1979). This principle affirms that persons with severe handicaps can acquire many of the skills that will allow them to participate, at least to some degree, in age-appropriate and functional environments and activities (Brown et al., 1979). Although the student's ability to participate in these activities can be facilitated through direct and systematic instruction, in some cases the motoric and/or cognitive requirements of certain parts of the task may prevent complete mastery. However, the inability of the student to perform some component skills independently should not be used as a justification for excluding the student from participating in the entire activity or environment.

Baumgart and her colleagues (1982) have delineated several types of adaptations which may allow or enhance a student's partial participation in less restrictive environments. For example, handwashing has been identified as a priority skill for Christine, but it is clear that the teacher could not teach her this skill using the same task analysis that was developed for Robert (Table 4.1). The various adaptations which could be employed to allow Christine to participate in the task of handwashing, at least partially, are listed in Table 4.2. Although this task analysis is similar in some ways to the one delineated for Robert, provisions have been made to compensate for motoric impairments, which

TABLE 4.1   Task analysis for hand washing

1. Go to bathroom sink.
2. Grasp the cold water faucet.
3. Turn on the water.
4. Wet your hands.
5. Pick up the soap (with the dominant hand).
6. Rub the soap on the other hand.
7. Put the soap down.
8. Rub palms together.
9. Rub back of hand (with palm of opposite hand).
10. Rub back of other hand (with palm of opposite hand).
11. Put hands under water.
12. Rinse palm of hands (until all visible suds removed).
13. Rinse back of hands (until all visible suds removed).
14. Grasp the cold water faucet.
15. Turn off the water.
16. Pick up towel.
17. Dry your palms.
18. Dry the back of your hands.
19. Hang towel over rack.

would otherwise prevent Christine from completing the task.

One type of adaptation illustrated in Christine's task analysis is the use of prosthetic devices, which are used to either improve her ability to perform the task or allow the performance of a behavior that would otherwise be impossible. The use of basins of water makes it possible for her to wash her hands at home and school where the sinks are not wheelchair accessible. The use of an adapted soap dispenser (with an enlarged plunger surface on the pump making it easier to push) allows her to complete a step independently that she otherwise would not be able to perform.

Prosthetic devices have also been used to simplify the cognitive or "thinking" requirements of a task without changing the ultimate result. A priority skill for Robert is the purchasing of grocery store items. Assessment has revealed that he does not have the reading skills necessary to construct or read a shopping list or the money skills needed to handle many of the steps involved in paying for selected items. Considering Robert's age and his imminent departure from school, as well as the slow rate of learning demonstrated in previous training programs, the use of prosthetic devices would appear to be a viable alternative.

Table 4.3 presents an adapted task analysis developed to teach Robert to partially participate in the grocery store environment. A prosthetic shopping device similar to that described by Gaule, Nietupski, and Certo (1985), allows him to construct a shopping list of needed items not exceeding a designated budget. This is accomplished by pasting labels from the canned items used in his meal preparation program onto cards, the size of which is determined by the approximate price of the item. After each meal preparation training session in which he uses a canned item, he is required to select the card that matches the used can, and then place the card in the tabs cut in the prosthetic shopping list. The list is sized so that it will hold only those cards representing less than a five dollar total. Thus, he will not have to determine the amount of money needed to pay for his selections, but can simply hand the cashier the five dollar bill given to him prior to each shopping trip. Similar procedures could also be used to train him to purchase produce or dairy items.

Picture communication cards which allow nonverbal students to purchase snacks at a fast-food counter are another prosthetic device which has

TABLE 4.2 Task analysis for handwashing: Partial participation

PLACE SOAP DISPENSER ON WHEELCHAIR TRAY WITHIN REACH OF STUDENT'S RIGHT HAND. PLACE ONE SPONGE BENEATH SPOUT OF SOAP DISPENSER.
1. Press the plunger (on the soap dispenser with right hand, until small amount of soap falls on sponge).
PLACE SOAP DISPENSER WITHIN REACH OF STUDENT'S LEFT HAND.
PLACE SECOND SPONGE BENEATH SPOUT.
2. Press the plunger (on the soap dispenser with left hand, until small amount of soap falls on sponge).
3. Rub palm of right hand on sponge (approximately three times).
4. Rub right palm on the back of left hand (approximately three times).
5. Rub left palm on left sponge (approximately three times).
REMOVE SPONGES AND SOAP DISPENSER FROM WHEELCHAIR TRAY.
PLACE BASIN OF WATER IN FRONT OF RIGHT HAND.
6. Place right hand in water.
7. Move hand up and down in water (to rinse off suds).
SPLASH WATER ON REMAINING AREAS OF THE HAND TO RINSE SUDS OFF.
8. Remove right hand from water.
PLACE BASIN OF WATER IN FRONT OF LEFT HAND.
9. Place left hand in water.
10. Move hand up and down in water (to rinse off suds).
SPLASH WATER ON REMAINING AREAS OF THE HAND TO RINSE SUDS OFF.
11. Remove left hand from water.
REMOVE BASIN FROM TRAY, AND SPREAD TOWEL ON TRAY.
12. Wipe right palm on towel (approximately three times).
13. Wipe left palm on towel (approximately three times).
DRY BACK OF STUDENT'S HANDS.

Steps in CAPITAL LETTERS are completed by the teacher.

Source: Credit from this task analysis must be given to Anne Graham and Patrice Lewis, Community Based Instruction Program, Woodbrook Elementary School, Albemarle County Schools, Charlottesville, VA.

been used (Christoph, Nietupski, & Pumpian, 1980). Similarly, the difficulty of functional tests could be modified by simplifying the rules of leisure games or teaching students to cook using commercial mixes or precooked frozen foods, rather than preparing food from scratch.

The second type of adaptation employed in Christine's task analysis (Table 4.2) falls under the category including verbal, gestural, physical, or supervisory assistance provided by another person (Baumgart et al., 1982). This adaptation should be distinguished from the type of assistance provided during the training process, or "prompting," which is gradually faded out (prompting will be discussed in Chapter 5). The type of assistance associated with partial participation is intended to be permanent. Since Christine will be motorically incapable of drying her hands, the plan calls for assistance to be given whenever she reaches this step in handwashing. This procedure maintains her ability to partially participate in a difficult part of the activity, and avoids the automatic completion of the entire activity by a careprovider—a situation often encountered by students with severe motoric dys-

function. Similarly, it can be seen in Table 4.3 that adult assistance allows Robert to find the correct aisle location since it was predicted that he would be unable to master this part of the grocery shopping sequence in a reasonable time period.

Some task adaptations enable students to participate in a variety of less restrictive environments, but there may be some disadvantages associated with their use. As pointed out by Baine (1982), the visibility of some adaptive devices can be stigmatizing, drawing attention to the student's functional inadequacies. Further, unless all task simplifications are field tested, they may actually be found to disrupt performance. Will the staff in the fast food restaurant correctly identify the food represented on picture cards presented by nonverbal students? Is an electronic switch reliable? How much and what type of pressure is need to trigger the switch, and can the student accomplish it? Do Christine's hands get clean using modified procedures? Are the procedures considered useful by her parents? Validation must be thorough and completed before instruction begins to avoid wasting the student's time. Finally, wherever possible, temporary rather

TABLE 4.3 Task analysis for purchasing items in grocery store

1. Unfasten seat belt.
2. Open car door and get out of car.
3. Lock and close car door.
4. Walk to sidewalk (maintain close proximity to trainer; observe appropriate safety precautions).
5. Walk to entrance door and enter store.
6. Walk to shopping cart storage area.
7. Pull out one cart and push to open area (out of way of other shoppers).
8. Push down seat and put shopping list open on seat.
9. Point to picture of first item.
10. Push cart and follow adult (to correct area of store).
11. Stop cart and push to side of aisle (when given verbal cue "Here is the right shelf"; cart is placed so it does not obstruct aisle).
12. Pick up can from shelf and place in cart (item that matches picture card).
13. Take picture out of the list and put away in pocket (picture card that matches previously selected item; pocket located on back cover of shopping list)
14. Point to picture of next item.
15. (Repeat steps 10 to 14 until all items are selected).
16. Push cart and follow adult to cashier line.
17. Wait quietly in line (with hands at side).
18. Push cart forward (when needed; repeat as required).
19. Place items from cart onto counter (when close enough in line to do so).
20. Wait quietly (while cashier totals and bags items; with hands at side).
21. Take money from pocket and hand it to cashier (when total announced).
22. Take change from cashier and put in pocket.
23. Push grocery cart out of cashier line (forward to open area of store, avoiding other shoppers).
24. Pick up bag of groceries.
25. Walk to exit door and leave store.
26. Walk to car (maintain close proximity to trainer; observe appropriate safety precautions).
27. Put bag in trunk (adult unlocks trunk and closes).
28. Walk to passenger door and wait (until adult unlocks door).
29. Open car door and get in the car.
30. Close door.
31. Fasten seat belt.

than permanent adaptations should be used, and their use should be systematically faded as soon as possible (Baine, 1982).

Long- and Short-term Goals

Once the student's most pressing instructional needs have been identified, these priorities are restated as long- and short-term goals. Long-term goals describe specific skills or activities (eating in a school cafeteria or making purchases in a grocery store), but as they typically consist of complex clusters of related behaviors, it is unlikely that instruction can begin simultaneously on all aspects. Therefore, the long-term goals are broken down into segments representing realistic instructional targets for an individual student. The number of these short-term goals will be determined by the complexity and/or difficulty of the long-term goals, but represent behaviors or skills that can be mastered by an individual student at some time during the following school year.

Further, the expected date for the achievement of each long- and short-term goal should be specified in order to provide a standard against which student progress can be evaluated. Such predictions about expected learning rates will be difficult to make when the teacher does not have access to information concerning the student's previous performance in instructional programs. Recommendations concerning procedures which can be used in such situations will be discussed later in this chapter.

In summary, the goal of Phase Two is to gather all of the information obtained during the assessment process in order to identify those skills and activities which are the most critically needed by a particular student. These priorities are then translated into long- and short-term IEP goals.

PHASE THREE: ANALYSIS OF BEHAVIOR

Before attempting to develop instructional objectives directed towards the accomplishment of the long- and short-term goals, we must gather more detailed information about the specific behaviors than has been obtained in previous phases of the curriculum development process. Thus, when short-term goals represent behaviors which are to be taught (rather than inappropriate behavior being reduced) task analytic procedures will be used to expand the existing short-term goal into the behavioral objective to be used during instruction. Further, although most short-term goals will focus on the mastery of new skills or the generalization of existing skills, some will be concerned with the reduction of excessively maladaptive or harmful behavior. An ABC analysis is essential when teachers, parents, and others are trying to sort out the relationship between a student's inappropriate behavior and the environment.

ABC Analysis

"ABC analysis" or a functional analysis of behavior is a systematic procedure which is used to observe and record events that occur before and after the behavior of interest, as well as other general setting characteristics typically associated with the occurrence of the behavior (White, 1971). Thus, the teacher attempts to identify the aspects of the physical and social environment which appear to precipitate the behavior, as well as events which reinforce or maintain it. That is, the observed behavior is hypothesized to be a function of specific variables in the external environment (Evans & Meyer, 1985).

The teacher's observation focuses upon external events that appear to influence the behavior. Robert's teacher may say he engages in stereotypic behaviors when he is "frustrated" or "bored," but such conclusions cannot be used in the development of an intervention program; however, if the ABC analysis reveals that his stereotypic behavior is consistently preceded by teacher requests, and that he is usually excused from instruction after persisting in this behavior for a period of time, the behavior's function seems to be escape from work. Treatment strategies that we could use to reduce or eliminate this behavior become more apparent from such an analysis. In this case, the teacher would *not* select a timeout procedure to consequate this behavior as this would only serve to further reinforce the inappropriate behavior.

Table 4.4 illustrates a simple form which was used by the teacher examining Robert's self-injurious headbanging behavior. Although more observations would actually be conducted before the teacher would attempt to develop a treatment program, the following section describes those factors which should be considered during each observation session.

Antecedents Within this category, the teacher should consider all aspects of the physical setting (heat, light, time of day, location, materials provided or taken away, number of people present) as well as social stimuli (commands, requests from adults or peers) that are present prior to the emission of the target behavior. Although antecedent conditions have been demonstrated to have a significant impact on behavior, and may be easy to manipulate, they often are ignored in the development of intervention programs (Bates & Hanson, 1983). In Table 4.4 higher noise levels appear to be associated with increased rates of self-injurious behavior. Further, headbanging is usually preceded by some type of verbal cue or reinforcement from the teacher.

Behavior Recording a precise description of the behavior observed will not only contribute to accuracy in defining the behavior but also may reveal the relevant dimensions of the behavior (whether the frequency, magnitude, or duration of the behavior is important). Other behaviors noted during the observation sessions should also be recorded (other positive or negative behaviors are typically seen under these conditions). It can be seen in Table 4.4 that Robert occasionally demonstrates appropriate use of leisure materials during the observation period. Some additional undesirable behaviors (handbiting and tearing of clothing) occurring at a lower frequency than headbanging, are also observed to occur under these conditions. Further, it may be possible to identify chains of behaviors which predictably precede the behavior of interest. An analysis of the behaviors reported in Table 4.4 reveals that Robert usually engages in frequent vocalizations and handflapping immediately before episodes of headbanging. Such information will be critical during intervention planning so that the teacher may be alerted to potential positive behaviors (appropriate use of leisure materials) that could be increased to take the place of the self-injurious behavior, while being warned of potential negative behaviors (tearing clothing, handbiting) that may spring up to replace headbanging in the absence of positive alternatives. Further, as a predictable chain of behaviors appears evident, we may find that intervening earlier in this chain (when vocalizations or handflapping are observed) may prevent the occurrence of the more serious targeted behavior.

Consequences These include all reinforcing, punishing, and/or neutral events which follow the target behavior. Decisions concerning the nature of the events should be made only following an analysis of their effect on the behavior: praise is assumed to be reinforcing, but observations recorded in Table 4.4 reveal that praise appears to punish or suppress appropriate leisure activity. Further, consequences may perform a dual role: they not only follow a behavior, but may serve as the stimuli for the next (Bates & Hanson, 1983). Negative attention ("Stop that!") may suppress the

TABLE 4.4 ABC analysis of Robert's self-injurious behavior

Student Name: Robert	*Observer Name:* Carol	
Target Behavior: Headbanging		
Setting: Classroom: leisure recreation area		
Time Begins: 11:45 a.m.	*Time Ends:* 11:50 a.m.	

Antecedent	Behavior	Consequence
Training ends. Teacher (T) tells R. to go to leisure area.	R. walks to leisure area	Aide: (A) "Pick a game, R."
Area crowded, 8 peers, variety of age appropriate leisure games available	R. turns on tape machine, sits on carpet near wall	Music
A. kneels in front of R. and hands him hand-held video game	R. pushes buttons on game, looking at video display	A. stands up, saying "Good, Robert! That's the way to play the game!"
	R. throws game on floor, and starts to wave hand in front of face, (rate: 1 to 2/second) and vocalizing quietly ("Bah, bah, bah.")	A. watches briefly, then walks to another group of students 3–4 feet away
T. calls from 5 feet away: "R. play with the game."	R. increases speed of hand flapping, (4/second) vocalizations increase in volume (can be heard 10 feet away)	T. walks to within 2 feet saying: "Stop that!"
	R. leans backward until head touches wall, then rapidly bangs head back and fourth, (3/second)	T. rushes to R.'s side placing hand on R.'s back to stop movement
	R. sits motionless vocalizing intermittently	T.: "Nice sitting, R." Stays sitting beside R.
	R. places fist in mouth, biting down (does not break skin). Places other hand inside front opening of shirt, pulling on lapel with sufficient force to pull button through hole, causing small tear in fabric	T.: "No, R., put your hands down!", and places her hand on top of R.'s hand (one pulling shirt)
	R. takes fist out of mouth, puts hand in lap. Sits motionless	T. stands up, "Time to go to lunch." Walks over to group of other students
Peers begin to leave area, noise level increases, A. supervises, back to R.	R. puts fist in mouth, bangs head against floor. (3/second, causes redness on forehead)	T. rushes to R.'s side, "No!", stops movement with hand on chest.
	R. sits, erect, hand still in mouth. Pulls at front of shirt, but not with sufficient force to tear.	T: "Let's go to lunch", stands up, holding R.'s arm.
	Stands up, hand in mouth (not biting down)	T. moves toward door
	Walks behind T. to door, hand still in mouth	

preceding behavior (handflapping) but also serves as a stimuli for the next behavior, headbanging.

The ABC analysis will facilitate the development of intervention strategies by allowing the careful examination of the social and physical environment which surround the behavior of interest. Although this procedure is amenable for use within applied settings, other methods for examining the functions of specific behaviors have been described by Donnellan, Mirenda, Mesaros, and Fassbender (1984), Evans and Meyer (1985), as well as Iwata, Dorsey, Slifer, Bauman, and Richman (1982). These procedures are addressed in more detail in Chapters 5 and 12. Regardless of the procedures used to collect the relevant information, a full understanding of events surrounding the behavior of concern will greatly assist in the development of effective intervention programs in the following phase.

Task Analysis

There are a variety of methods used to break tasks into their component steps (Baine, 1982; Becker, Engelmann, & Thomas, 1975; Resnick, Wang, & Kaplan, 1973). Use of these procedures will allow the teacher to facilitate learning by developing an individualized task analysis that takes into consideration the skills and disabilities exhibited by a specific student. Although some authors recommend more extensive procedures than others, most include the following three steps:

1. Identify a functional skill that is considered to be an important instructional target for a particular student.
2. Define the target skill, including a description of the setting and materials most suited to the natural performance of the skill.
3. Perform the task as it is completed in the selected setting using the chosen materials and/or observe others who are skilled at the task performed (handicapped or nonhandicapped). Develop and validate the task analysis.

As seen in Figure 4.1 the information that has been gathered to this point in the curriculum development process will enable the teacher to fulfill the requirements of the first step, the identification of functional skills. The teacher will thus move to the second step and carefully define the behavior, the type of materials used, the environmental conditions for performing the task, as well as the standards or quality of performance expected. As previously noted, one skill identified for Robert in the community domain was purchasing food in a grocery store. A task analysis of this skill will be affected by the materials and method to be used by the student. Will Robert use a shopping cart or a basket? What format will be used for his shopping list? How will he pay for his purchases? What will the environmental conditions be (large chain store versus small convenience store)? The quality or standards also must be determined. Must he complete his purchases within a certain period of time? Must he simply select needed items, identify certain brands, and/or find the best buy?

When a specific task is selected for instruction, efforts must be directed towards the ultimate use of the required skills in the natural environment. Some researchers have argued that training in artificial or simulated settings rather than in the natural environment may: (a) be more efficient (omitting the need for travel time, waiting in lines), (b) permit repeated practice of skills that occur infrequently in the natural environment, and (c) reduce the likelihood of potentially embarrassing or dangerous situations (Page, Iwata, & Neef, 1976). However, when using simulated training environments, the instructor must not assume that students who can perform correctly in the classroom will generalize the skills to the natural environment (Stokes & Baer, 1977). Rather, generalization must be directly and regularly tested, and if satisfactory skill transfer is not observed, supplemental instruction must be provided in the natural environment (Brown et al., 1979). Time spent teaching skills in artifical settings is wasted if the student does not demonstrate competency in the appropriate setting and in the presence of persons other than the original trainers (Billingsley, 1984).

Unfortunately, although studies examining simulated setting training conducted with students having mild and moderate handicaps have typically reported satisfactory generalization (Neef, Iwata, & Page, 1978; Page et al., 1976; van den Pol, Iwata, Ivancic, Page, Neef, & Whitley, 1981), comparisons of the relative efficacy of simulated and *in vivo* training with students having severe handicaps have been mixed. Browder, Snell, and Ambrogio (1984) found that students learned to use vending machines and the specific associated coin values whether taught on a simulated machine in the classroom setting or on a real machine in a community site. However, all students were trained and tested in the community setting at some time during the course of the study. In contrast, Marchetti, McCartney, Drain, Hooper, and Dix (1983) found that training pedestrian skills in the community was significantly more effective than using a simulated 4 ft by 4 ft model of a street.

In general, a review of the literature confirms the anticipated result: difficulty in generalizing trained skills across environments appears to increase with the severity of the handicap (Snell & Browder, 1986). Further, it also appears that the degree to which the simulated setting replicates the relevant stimuli present in the natural setting is often predictive of the positive transfer of skills. If the teacher wished to teach Robert some of the more difficult grocery shopping skills within a simulated setting, all relevant stimuli should be duplicated. Thus, when teaching him to select a specific can from a grocery store shelf, he must view a display similar to that which would be encountered in the grocery store, as making a selection from a large array of items is more difficult than choosing one can from a small group on a classroom desk. Further, even if the teacher is able to construct a simulation which is relatively authentic, it still will be impossible to duplicate many of the stimuli that can have a deleterious effect on performance (noise levels, crowds of shoppers).

Thus, whenever possible, it is recommended that training should be conducted in the natural setting. If simulated settings are used to train portions of difficult or potentially hazardous skills, frequent assessments of skill generalization to the natural environment should be conducted, so that appropriate modifications can be made if skill transfer is unsatisfactory. Further, when the teacher and student are in the community setting for such purposes, it will be possible to provide some training there as well. Use of a single opportunity probe (to be explained later in this chapter) will allow the teacher to implement training on the remaining steps of the task analysis following the student's first error. Thus, both assessment and training can occur in a relatively limited amount of time.

Once these decisions concerning training conditions are made, the teacher will analyze the task as it is performed with the same materials, in the same manner and under the same conditions that the student will be expected to perform. This can be accomplished either by the teacher's performing the task, or by observing those judged proficient in the performance of the targeted behavior. Alternatively, Cuvo (1978) has suggested that expert models be videotaped so that two or more observers can watch the tape and break the task into steps. Any disagreements between the resulting task analyses can be resolved by: (a) discussing the differences, resolving them verbally, and repeating the modified task analysis until agreement is obtained; (b) resolving differences through repeated observations of the behavior with revision of the task analysis; or (c) consulting a third person more skilled in the selected behavior.

It must be remembered that the overriding objective is to identify the simplest sequence of behaviors that will allow the completion of the task; however, the typical manner of completing a task may not be the most simple or straightforward (Baine, 1982). Experimenting with a variety of methods of performing the task, as well as observing a variety of performers can often reveal a number of potential alternatives. Finally, the teacher must ensure that the task analysis is individualized for the student so that it will: "(a) employ the skills she already possesses, (b) require acquisition of the least number of new skills, and (c) avoid the need to revise existing skills or habits" (Baine, 1982, p. 10).

Once the first draft of the task analysis has been completed, you may wish to further check the accuracy of the task analysis by consulting with "experts" in the targeted behavior. Cronin and Cuvo (1979) asked a home economist to evaluate preliminary task analyses of mending skills and then to perform each task using the steps to verify (or improve upon) their inclusion and order. Similarly, to ensure that task analyses which target self-care skills for Christine are realistic and/or appropriate, they should be checked by an occupational or physical therapist. A task analysis developed as part of Robert's vocational training should be validated by the actual personnel who will supervise and evaluate his performance on the job.

During the process of breaking down the task into its component parts, there is often considerable confusion about the degree of specificity, or the appropriate "size" of the steps that should be delineated. Referring to vocational tasks, Bellamy, Horner, and Inman (1979) recommend that tasks be broken into functional response units or steps that result in "distinct observable change in the item being assembled" (p. 68). Although the degree of specificity used in the task analysis will necessarily be related to the learner's characteristics, it has been found that students taught with a fine-grained task analysis (one response per step) made significantly fewer errors during training than students taught with a task analysis requiring two or four responses per step (Crist, Walls, & Haught, 1984). Although more research is needed concerning the optimum degree of specificity required, it appears that the number of steps included in the task analysis will have a considerable impact on student performance.

Further, if the teacher uses the principle of partial participation to make permanent, rather than temporary adaptations in the task analysis, these should be made before finalizing the task analysis, as any change in the task analysis will change the assessment as well. Results obtained from assessing a skill with one task analysis are not comparable with those obtained when a different task analysis of the same task is used. The differences will be in the number, order, or type of steps that constitute the task analysis, and thus influence the student's performance.

To enhance the teacher's use of the task analysis during instruction, all steps of the task analyses presented in this chapter (see Tables 4.1, 4.2, and 4.3), are phrased in the second person so that, when spoken, they could serve as a verbal prompt; however, when an excessive amount of detail must be used to describe a step adequately its wording will be too complex to serve as a verbal prompt. In these cases, the descriptive words which are not spoken by the teacher are set apart by parentheses.

In summary, the task analyses which have been developed for Christine and Robert have the following characteristics:

1. Steps are stated in terms of observable behavior.
2. Each step results in a visible change in the product or process.
3. Steps are ordered from first performed to last performed.
4. Steps are phrased in the second person, with detail not to be used as a verbal prompt set apart by parentheses.

Both task analysis and ABC analysis yield information that lets the teacher formulate treatment strategies and specify conditions and performance criteria more accurately, therefore facilitating the next step of the curriculum development process, when instructional objectives and intervention programs are developed.

PHASE FOUR: PROGRAM DEVELOPMENT

Define Instructional Objectives

Behavioral objectives are clear and precise statements describing the skill or behaviors that the student will be expected to acquire as a result of intervention. Similarly, when we determine that intervention is required to reduce or extinguish a maladaptive behavior, an equally precise descrip-

tion must be formulated. The statements must therefore describe: (a) the *behavior* that will be changed as a result of intervention, (b) the *conditions* under which the behavior will be performed/observed, and (c) the *standards* or *criterion* that will be used to judge the success of the intervention. These statements should be as concise as possible but also must include sufficient detail so that independent observers would agree upon each occurrence or nonoccurrence of the behavior under the same conditions. The following section discusses these three features in more detail.

Behavior The behavior to be changed as a result of intervention must be described in observable and measurable terms. When teaching Robert to purchase canned grocery items, the teacher wants him to select the can from the shelf that matches the picture contained in his shopping list. When describing this skill, verbs such as "will identify . . ." or "will discriminate . . ." must be avoided, because these do not describe observable behaviors. Rather, we must determine how Robert will demonstrate this knowledge: he will be required to "pick up" the correct item, and place it in the grocery cart (Baine, 1982).

The "size" of the behavior to be monitored will depend on the student's skills and the goals of intervention, as well as the precision of the observation instrument used. In the initial stages of training, "handwashing" is too "large." It can be measured more effectively if we evaluate the specific behaviors involved (turns on the cold water, wets hands, picks up soap); however, when Robert has mastered a series of self-help skills, we simply may count each skill completed before he goes to work (handwashing, toothbrushing, shaving, and appropriate dressing). If performance on the components of each skill is satisfactory, more precise breakdowns of the specific tasks would be unnecessarily cumbersome.

Conditions It is necessary to delineate clearly the conditions under which observations of the student's behavior will take place. This will include factors such as the physical setting, people present, the instructional materials and cues to be provided, and any other relevant variables that are expected to influence the student's performance. Further, teachers must specify the most rigorous conditions under which they expect the student to perform. Even if some training will be conducted in a simulated setting, the objective should include a description of the features of the natural environment(s) in which the behaviors are needed (Baine, 1982). This last consideration is critical, because it has been demonstrated that many objectives written for persons with severe handicaps target functional skills but fail to describe the settings where the skill is to be performed. Although this does not mean that teachers failed to assess performance in natural settings, the lack of a description of such conditions will reduce the usefulness of these objectives for both designing instructional programs as well as evaluating the effectiveness of training (Billingsley, 1984).

Standards or Criteria   The standards delineated in the behavior statement describe the type or quality of performance that the student will be expected to achieve as a result of intervention. Depending upon the target behavior, the teacher will delineate the performance standards of response latency (the student must respond appropriately within 5 seconds of the waitress' query, "What do you want?"), frequency (the student will complete two assembly tasks per minute) or the number and/or type of errors that cannot be tolerated. Standards must not be set arbitrarily, but rather must be carefully tailored to the type of behavior taught. It is important not to prolong training by insisting upon unnecessarily rigorous performance standards; however, teachers must ensure that the student demonstrates an acceptable level of performance (Baine, 1982; Sobsey & Ludlow, 1984).

Factors of safety, public appearance, or social standards may need to be considered when writing the criterion for an intervention program. Safety concerns would dictate that errors cannot be tolerated in a street crossing program. Some social standards may dictate a particular criterion, as forgetting to put socks on occasionally is acceptable, but going outside without pants is not (Sobsey & Ludlow, 1984). Conversely, for other skills, the criterion can be less stringent and still guarantee that the student demonstrates a functional level of performance: social manners need not be "perfect," and some errors made when engaging in a leisure activity are probably acceptable. Therefore, the teacher must describe errors that are considered acceptable (if any), and their acceptable frequency, as well as errors that cannot be allowed under any circumstances (Baine, 1982; Sobsey & Ludlow, 1984).

Social Validation

The degree of proficiency required for most tasks is more difficult to establish than it is for an activity such as street crossing. Thus, social validation procedures can be used in order to determine whether or not the learned behavior is functional or meaningful (Kazdin, 1980). Indeed, at this phase in the curriculum development process, the teacher has already addressed one aspect of social validation—social validation of instructional goals. When goals are selected which will facilitate a student's independent functioning, one can say that these goals are socially valid; however, social validation is a broad concept and addresses the results of intervention as well. Will the student be able to perform the target skill at a level or standard that is needed in the natural environment?

The first method of social validation, *social comparison*, ensures that the criteria set for the student's posttreatment performance will represent a standard of behavior comparable to that demonstrated by nonhandicapped peers. Such a comparison will prevent the teacher from either imposing unnecessarily rigorous performance criteria, or stopping training before the student reaches a socially acceptable level of performance. Van den Pol and his colleagues (1981) observed diners without handicaps in fast food restaurants to determine the normative rate of errors. They found that on the average, the diners completed 70% of the steps in the task analysis correctly. This information allowed the researchers to establish realistic criteria to evaluate posttraining behavior. Similarly, before setting standards to teach women having retardation to color coordinate their clothing, Nutter and Reid (1978) observed the color combinations worn by over 600 women in nearby public settings.

A second means of socially validating performance, *subjective evaluation*, requires that the opinions of those people who by their expertise or familiarity with the student(s) are able to judge performance or to set standards. For example, Voeltz, Wuerch, and Bockhaut (1982) validated the outcome of training by asking parents, institutional and community program staff, and nonhandicapped peers to view pairs of videotapes taken two months apart which portrayed adolescents with severe handicaps during their free time. The students who received leisure skill training during the intervening 2 months were viewed as being more interested in their activity, "looking more OK" and as having a more worthwhile activity than were students who had not received training. Similarly, Wilson, Reid, Philips, and Burgio (1984) demonstrated that videotapes of the students' dining skills following training were rated as superior to their pretraining performance. Such procedures provide some assurance that the student's behavior change is meaningful and will, thus, facilitate functioning within the intended environments.

Specify Intervention Techniques

It almost goes without saying that a curriculum of functional objectives, no matter how good, is useful only if intervention follows. The curriculum development process described here is based upon the assumption that behavioral principles are the instructional method of choice with students having severe handicaps. Behavioral principles, or more specifically principles of operant conditioning, "describe the relationship between behavior and environmental events (antecedents and consequences) that influence behavior" (Kazdin, 1980, p. 27). What occurs before a behavior (instructional cues, materials, prompts to respond) or after a behavior (reinforcement, extinction, or punishment) will ultimately affect whether that behavior is acquired, is forgotten, or occurs more or less frequently. When behavioral principles are applied to humans in natural settings, such as the home and school, to modify socially significant problems, then the term "applied behavior analysis" is appropriate. This approach rests firmly upon direct and frequent measurement of behavior, individual rather than group analysis of behavior, replicable teaching procedures and single subject rather than group experimental control. The manner in which this approach is operationalized will be discussed in greater detail in the next sections of this chapter as well as in the following one.

Data Collection Procedures

In order to evaluate the impact of intervention programs developed in this phase of the curriculum development process, specific strategies for collecting frequent, repeated, objective measures of student performance must be formulated. Such monitoring is crucial, since there is no way to predict accurately whether or not a teaching strategy will work with an individual student or for a specific skill. Further, it has been demonstrated that when staff fail to use systematic data collection procedures, they are unable to judge student progress

accurately (Holvoet et al., 1983). Since the average teacher has eight or more students with severe handicaps to supervise, it is impossible to keep track of each student's progress on every program, without using systematic data collection procedures (Tawney & Gast, 1984). In order to know whether the student makes progress towards achieving the instructional goals, the teacher must collect and analyze performance data for each student. Programs that do not result in satisfactory rates of learning can be modified, so that valuable instructional time is not wasted on ineffective procedures.

Although the type of data collection procedure selected will be largely determined by the characteristics of the target behavior, the teacher must also select the most simple method possible (Tawney & Gast, 1984). Unnecessarily complex data collection procedures are likely to interfere with classroom activities, and are difficult to implement, thus raising questions about the accuracy of the obtained data.

The teacher must also determine how often data will be collected. Although many recommend that data be obtained every day, such a standard may be unnecessarily rigorous in some situations. Rather, the teacher must consider the type of behavior, the rate of learning, as well as balance the convenience of less frequent data collection with the risks of unnecessarily prolonging a program which is not yielding satisfactory learning. This issue will be discussed in greater detail later in this chapter.

There are a large number of data collection procedures suitable to teaching settings. These procedures can be classified as either direct observation of behaviors, of which five types will be described, or measurement of permanent products. Prior to implementing any of these behavior measurement procedures, the observer must proceed meticulously through a sequence of steps.

1. Clearly define the target behavior in observable terms.
2. Specify the conditions for observation that will yield accurate measurement (when, where and for how long the behavior will be observed).
3. Identify the characteristics of the target behavior (its duration, frequency), and select the appropriate measurement procedure.
4. Construct a data recording form or specify the way data will be recorded.

Clearly Define the Behavior

Once the teacher has reached this stage of the curriculum development process, each behavior targeted for intervention (to be increased, maintained or decreased) will be clearly and precisely defined. In addition, to select the appropriate measurement technique, she must determine the relevant characteristics of the behavior (the frequency, rate, duration, or magnitude) that need monitoring. Finally, the definition must be tested for its inter-rater reliability—whether two or more observers will agree on the occurrence or nonoccurrence of the behavior.

Intervention with a single behavior may lead to changes in other related behaviors. Therefore, rather than focusing on specific behaviors in isolation, we must consider the complex interrelationships surrounding the behavior and expect that any significant change may have additional positive and/or negative side effects. Such efforts cannot be assumed, but rather need to be monitored carefully. VanBiervliet, Spangler, and Marshall (1981) demonstrated that eating family style rather than institutional style led to increased communication among peers; however, such positive "side effects" were not observed in a group of adults having profound mental retardation who were trained to dine in this format (Wilson et al., 1984). Similarly, if a treatment were implemented to eliminate Robert's self-injurious behavior, the influence of the program on the other associated negative behaviors could not be predicted. The ABC analysis can help teachers become more aware of the relationships between behaviors, but collecting objective data on multiple behavior targets will allow the accurate analysis of such effects. Further, teachers must be sensitive to the occurrence of unanticipated effects, and willing to modify procedures as necessary.

Specify the Conditions for Observation

In order to evaluate the effect of an intervention, each assessment must be carried out in the same way, and under the same conditions. Since changes in the environmental conditions can have a significant impact on performance, measurements made under different conditions cannot be compared meaningfully. Further, evaluating the student's performance under the most difficult conditions that she will normally encounter is the only way to determine whether the skill has been mastered or whether a target maladaptive behavior is under control. These conditions will include a variety of factors, such as physical setting, people present, materials, or comments, and assistance provided.

When specifying conditions for assessment, the teacher should also be aware of the various natural prompts which may be available to the student. In a study targeting aerobic exercise skills, student performance was assessed while the trainer modeled each exercise and gave a verbal cue, since such assistance was naturally present during aerobic lessons (Stainback, Stainback, Wehman & Spagiers, 1983). Similarly, Aeschleman and Schladenhauffen (1984) reported that the unplanned presence of naturally provided prompts from store clerks ("Come over here if you are finished shopping." p. 256) and models provided by other shoppers resulted in some improvement across the baseline probes in the relatively simple behaviors involved in shopping skills. If naturally occurring prompts with the potential to enhance the student's performance will be available in the environment, their presence should be specified in the conditions statement and incorporated into the assessment process. Otherwise, our assessment data may not be an accurate reflection of the student's actual level of competency in the natural environment.

Finally, the teacher should be aware of more transitory factors which can affect behavior, including less obvious physiological conditions, such as the presence of a fever or changes in medications (Breuning & Davidson, 1981; Singh & Aman, 1981). Although it is often not possible to control such extraneous factors, wherever possible, a record should be maintained to obtain an accurate interpretation of the data collected.

Selection of the Measurement Procedure

Once the targeted behavior and the conditions for observation are defined, the teacher can decide how frequently data are to be collected and which data collection procedure will be used. The six observation procedures summarized in Table 4.5 are addressed below.

Measurement of Lasting Products Frequently with academic, domestic and vocational skills, student performance results in a product (correctly placed table setting, coins matched to a price card, number of plastic dinnerware and napkin combinations properly packaged, etc). The tangible evidence may be measured more conveniently after the student has completed the task—an advantage over behavior observation techniques. Also, teachers may examine products for error patterns and thus select

TABLE 4.5 Classroom evaluation measurement procedures

Procedures for the Measurement of Behavior	Advantages	Disadvantages	Examples of Behaviors Measured
Direct measurement of lasting products—A frequency record from appropriate or inappropriate behavior	1. Measurement is taken after behavior has occurred 2. Specification of a tangible behavior is easier	1. Behavior must have a tangible result 2. Inaccurate measurement may occur for individual counts when others are producing similar products during period before measurement	*Appropriate*—Number newsletters folded and stapled, places set at the dinner table *Inappropriate*—Number of buttons ripped from clothing, wet diapers
Observational recording 1. *Frequency or event*—A running tally of a given target behavior	1. Useful with a wide variety of discrete classroom behaviors 2. Often part of the regular classroom routine 3. Often only paper and pencil are needed 4. May be converted to rate	1. Necessitates continuous attention during observation period 2. Yields less accurate results with very high rate behaviors and/or behaviors taking varying amounts of time 3. Inappropriate for long-duration behaviors	*Appropriate*—Accurate ball throws, hand raising, spontaneous requests for needed materials, all types of *correct* responses *Inappropriate*—talkouts, hits, obscene gestures, all types of *incorrect* responses
2. *Task analytic*—A frequency record of correct and incorrect responses made for each step in a sequence of behaviors comprising a task	1. Useful for most skills in domestic, vocational, leisure/recreational, and community domains 2. May be used to guide instruction 3. Enables the measurement of each behavior that comprises a skill 4. Meaningfully reported as percentage *or* number of steps	1. Requires a good task analysis of skill 2. Not suitable for measuring inappropriate behaviors	*Appropriate*—Bedmaking, playing a record, hair combing, mopping floors, assembly tasks *Inappropriate*—Not suitable

remedial teaching procedures; however, the specific product or bit of tangible evidence still must be defined clearly. When teaching ironing, a piece-rate measurement (number of articles correctly ironed per unit of time) could be the measurement procedure. Daily piece-rate data would be essential to evaluate the instructional program for someone who has learned to iron but is so meticulously slow that the skill is not functional.

Measurement of Observed Behavior Unfortunately, most behaviors do not result in tangible products and, therefore, are more difficult to measure. Transitory behaviors must be measured as they occur. Examples of such behaviors measured with the following techniques include appropriate behaviors which are targeted for instruction (staying on-task, street crossing, requesting needed materials), or inappropriate or aberrant behaviors that are to be reduced and replaced (hitting, stereotypic movements, masturbation in public). The method of measurement selected will vary depending upon (a) the duration of the behavior, (b) its visibility, (c) the number of other behaviors being recorded simultaneously, (d) the level of measurement precision required, and (e) the time and attention available for measurement (Hall, Hawkins, & Axelrod, 1975).

TABLE 4.5 (continued)

Procedures for the Measurement of Behavior	Advantages	Disadvantages	Examples of Behaviors Measured
3. *Duration*—The total amount of time a targeted behavior was engaged in	1. Yields precise record of a behavior's length of occurrence 2. May be used to record total duration of each incident of behavior	1. Necessitates continuous attention during observation period 2. For best accuracy requires a stop watch 3. Inappropriate for high-rate behaviors of short duration	*Appropriate*—Attending, completion of tasks (eating, dressing, cleaning), work production, physical fitness activities *Inappropriate*—Temper tantrums, stereotypic behavior
4. *Interval*—The occurrence or nonoccurrence of a target behavior during a defined amount of time	1. Requires less effort than continuous event or duration procedures 2. Yields sufficiently precise duration and frequency data 3. Does not require definition of a precise unit of behavior 4. Applicable to a wide variety of behaviors	1. Difficult to use with less visible behaviors 2. Low-frequency behavior 3. Size of interval must be appropriate to behavior frequency. Accuracy is facilitated by timers or a tape-recorded counting of intervals	Any of those listed for frequency or duration
a. *Whole interval*—Continuous occurrence throughout an interval	Useful when it is important to know that the behavior is not interrupted.	Underestimates magnitude of target behavior	More useful with appropriate behaviors such as toy sharing or attending
b. *Partial interval*—Occurrence at any time in an interval	Useful for behaviors that may occur in fleeting moments.	Overestimates magnitude of target behavior	
5. *Momentary time sampling*—Occurrence or nonoccurrence of a target behavior during a randomly timed check	Useful for behaviors that tend to persist for a while	Must be frequent, random, and relatively short intervals	

Frequency or event recording refers to counting the number of times the behavior (appropriate or inappropriate) occurs within a specified period of time. Behaviors measured this way must be relatively uniform in length, readily divided into discrete units with a beginning and end, and easily visible. Stereotypic hand waving, pinching, hitting, errors in requesting task, or incorrect coin combinations matched to a price may be inappropriate and too frequent. Some behaviors may be appropriate but too infrequent and in need of acceleration: hand raising prior to speaking, toy sharing, quantities correctly counted, or responses to "come here" commands. Since *frequency* provides a direct measure of the amount of behavior occurring, it is sensitive to changes produced by intervention.

When a behavior occurs at a very high rate, it is often difficult to count and record each incidence accurately; however, accuracy can be enhanced by substituting hand-held counters or wrist-worn golf counters (Lindsley, 1968) for the typical paper and pencil tally. Alternately, the teacher may wish to use a duration or interval recording method (to be discussed later). When counting the frequency of several behaviors simultaneously, multiple-channel manual counters are useful.

When behaviors which occur for long periods of time (out of seat for entire class periods) or for varying periods of time (stereotypic behavior), are measured with a frequency count, the result is deceiving. The number of times the behavior is recorded, (as frequency or as rate of behaviors per minute), does not accurately reflect the amount of behavior which occurs. For these types of behaviors, duration or interval records would be more descriptive.

If the opportunity for the behavior occurs only a fixed number of times per observation session, but the duration of each is similar, then the data may be reported as the *percentage* of behaviors observed out of the total possible (the number of correct manual signs demonstrated divided by the number of object identification trials provided, multiplied by 100) or as *rate* (when given 50 assembly tasks, the number of correctly completed items per minute). When the number of behaviors emitted is variable, the observer cannot predict the frequency ceiling or the maximum behaviors possible per unit of time. These data are reported either by a simple frequency (the total number of behaviors observed each day or in a 20-minute teaching session) or by rate (number of behaviors per minute or hour) but *not* by percentage.

Frequency measures must be taken for equal units of time which are long enough to obtain a representative behavior sample. If the observation time cannot be uniform, then frequency counts must be interpreted with caution: the number of opportunities to perform in a 1-minute period cannot be equated with those in a 30-minute period. When sessions of unequal duration must be used, frequency data must be converted into rate per standard unit of time: if a child vocalizes 30 times during a 20-minute observation, and 60 times during a 30-minute observation, the vocalization rate per minute is calculated by simple division (number of behaviors observed divided by the number of minutes observed). The resulting rates are 1.5 and 2 vocalizations per minute; however, with students having severe handicaps, attention span and fatigue may make this "equation" practice unwise when there are wide discrepancies between observation periods (White & Haring, 1976). Therefore, observation periods should be equal whenever possible.

Task analytic assessment is a variation of a frequency measure in that a sequence of behaviors is measured at one time. It is probably the most valuable method for the informal assessment of a student's performance on specific tasks, such as those listed in Figure 4.2. Unlike a frequency method, it is *not* useful for assessing inappropriate behavior.

Before using task analytic assessment procedures, the teacher will have developed a task analysis using the methods described earlier. To conduct the assessment, the steps of the task analysis are entered on a data sheet (as shown in Table 4.6) so they can be used to guide the observation. The student will be observed under the conditions specified in the instructional objective, and the teacher then judges the quality of performance on each step in the task analysis. A symbol for correct (+) or incorrect (−) performance is entered on the data sheet beside each step.

At least two different task analytic procedures can be used within the classroom setting: single opportunity or multiple opportunity. The *single opportunity method* is carried out as follows:

1. Conditions (including materials) are arranged as described on the data sheet.
2. The instructional cue (if any) is given when the student is attending.
3. The student's response to each step in the task analysis are recorded as correct or incorrect (performed incorrectly or not performed at all). The following rules can be used to handle errors, periods of no response, and inappropriate behavior.
   a. Testing is stopped after the first error, and all remaining steps are scored as errors.
   b. After a specified period of no response (3 seconds), testing is stopped and all remaining steps are scored as errors.
   c. After a specified period of inappropriate behavior (10 seconds of stereotypic behavior) or after a single inappropriate response (throwing soap or towel), testing is stopped and all remaining steps are scored as errors.
4. In most cases, steps performed are scored as being correct if they correspond to the task description, regardless of the order in which they are carried out, as long as the end result is satisfactory; however, in some cases, such as assembly tasks, performing each step in order may be crucial to the successful completion of the activity. Therefore, the first step out of sequence will be scored as an error. In addition, when rate of performance is important, (as specified in the criteria or standards) the maximum length of time might be specified for testing.

The single opportunity method can be illustrated using the handwashing task and the data recording sheet shown in Table 4.6.

First, the teacher reviewed the instructional objective and checked whether the setting and available materials (soap, towel) conformed to the conditions stated. Further, as the objective stated that

TABLE 4.6 Single and multiple opportunity probes

	Single Opportunity				Multiple Opportunity			
1. Go to bathroom sink	−	+	+	+	−	+	+	+
2. Grasp the cold water faucet	−	+	−	+	+	+	+	+
3. Turn on the water	−	+	−	+	+	+	+	+
4. Wet your hands	−	−	−	+	−	−	+	+
5. Pick up the soap (with the dominant hand)	−	−	−	−	−	−	+	+
6. Rub the soap on the other hand	−	−	−	−	+	+	+	+
7. Put the soap down	−	−	−	−	+	−	−	−
8. Rub palms together	−	−	−	−	+	+	+	+
9. Rub back of hand (with palm of opposite hand)	−	−	−	−	−	−	−	+
10. Rub back of other hand (with palm of opposite hand)	−	−	−	−	+	−	+	+
11. Put hands under water	−	−	−	−	+	+	+	+
12. Rinse palm of hands (until all suds removed)	−	−	−	−	+	+	+	+
13. Rinse back of hands (until all suds removed)	−	−	−	−	+	+	+	+
14. Grasp the cold water faucet	−	−	−	−	+	+	+	+
15. Turn off the water	−	−	−	−	+	+	+	+
16. Pick up towel	−	−	−	−	+	+	+	+
17. Dry your palms	−	−	−	−	+	+	+	+
18. Dry the back of your hands	−	−	−	−	+	+	+	+
19. Hang towel over rack	−	−	−	−	−	−	−	+
Percentage performed independently	0	16	5	21	73	68	84	95

Robert was to perform the task in response to naturally occurring cues (following a meal, before going to the cafeteria, or immediately following toileting), his behavior was assessed at these times.

Thus, as the first step in the task analysis required the student to respond appropriately to natural cues in the environment, the teacher did not give an instructional request to begin assessment. In this case, the bell signaling the lunch break rang, indicating that students were to get ready to go to the cafeteria, and the teacher observed whether or not Robert responded appropriately by going to the bathroom to wash his hands. In addition, since a slightly longer latency between the natural cue and the initiation of the response would be acceptable within a natural environment, the task analysis specified that he should be allowed 10 seconds to initiate this response. However, for the rest of the task, 3 seconds was specified as the maximum amount of time that could elapse between each step in the task analysis.

On the first assessment day, Robert heard the bell and immediately left the classroom. However, in the hallway, he passed the bathroom where he was to wash his hands and headed straight for the cafeteria. Since this was an error, the teacher scored the first step as an error, as well as all remaining steps in the task analysis. As assessment was stopped at this point, the teacher was free to train the skill using the procedures outline in the instructional program.

At the same time on the second assessment day, Robert heard the bell and, although he hesitated for a few seconds, he walked to the bathroom and stood before the sink within the 10-second limit. He grasped the cold water tap and immediately turned on the water. The teacher scored a plus for the first three steps in the task analysis; however, *rather than wetting his hands (step 4), Robert picked up the towel. Since this was an error, the teacher stopped him, thanked him for his effort, and scored the remaining steps as errors.*

On the third day, Robert again behaved correctly within 10 seconds of the naturally occurring stimulus; however, rather than grasping the faucet, he started flapping his hands in front of his face. After 10 seconds of this inappropriate behavior, testing was discontinued and all steps counted as errors. On the fourth day, Robert performed the first four steps correctly, but hesitated longer than 3 seconds before picking up the soap (step 5). The four days of test performance resulted in the percentage scores shown in Table 4.6.

The single opportunity method generally is completed quickly and provides a conservative estimate of the student's skills. Less instructional time is wasted because training can begin immediately following the first error. Further, learning is less likely to occur during testing; therefore it should provide a more accurate estimate of the effect of instruction. One disadvantage of this method is that performance on steps in a task analysis occurring after the first error cannot be observed, as testing is terminated at this point; thus, probes (testing done once intervention has started) will not initially reflect learning on later steps because testing always ends before the student reaches the learned steps. If the teacher is using a backward chaining progression (last step following second-to-last step and so on), then the single opportunity probe will not reflect any progress until training advances to the first step in the chain. In these cases, the multiple opportunity probe would produce more information.

The *multiple opportunity method*, although started in the same way as the single opportunity methods, differs in a number of ways.

1. Materials are readied as described on the data sheet.
2. The instructional cue (if any) is given when the student is attending.
3. The student's responses to each step in the task analysis are recorded as correct or incorrect.
4. Whenever an error occurs or after a specified period of no response or inappropriate behavior, the step is then completed by the assessor, using as little effort as is needed. The student is positioned for the next step.

To understand the multiple-opportunity probe method, we will describe this process as it is used to assess the same handwashing task.

First, the teacher reviewed the instructional objective and checked whether the setting and available materials (soap, towel) conformed to the conditions stated. Further, as the objective stated that Robert was to perform the task in response to naturally occurring cues (following a meal, before going to the cafeteria, or immediately following toileting), his behavior was assessed at these times.

On the first assessment day, Robert heard the bell, and immediately left the classroom; however, in the hallway, he passed the bathroom where he was to wash his hands, heading straight for the cafeteria. Since this was an error, the teacher scored the first step as an error. Rather than terminating assessment at this point, she brought the student to the bathroom sink, without making any comment about the error, and positioned him for the next step in the task analysis. Standing in front of the sink, Robert hesitated, but not for more than the 3-second limit. He grasped the cold water tap, and immediately turned on the water. The teacher scored a plus for the steps 2 and 3 in the task analysis. However, instead of wetting his hands (step 4), Robert tried to pick up the towel. The teacher stopped the error by gently interrupting his action and used her cupped hands to splash water over his hands, thereby completing this step without requiring his participation (step 4 scored as an error). Since Robert was then ready to attempt the next step, the teacher took her hands away and waited 3 seconds for him to initiate the next step in the task analysis. He did not make any response within the 3-second period, so the teacher scored step 5 as minus, and placed the soap in his dominant hand. Robert immediately rubbed the soap on his other hand, put the soap down and rubbed his palms together, scoring pluses for steps 6, 7, and 8. Robert then dropped his hands to his side, and did not initiate the next step within the next 3 seconds so the teacher rubbed soap on the back of one of his hands to complete the next step, scoring minus for step 9. Robert immediately rubbed soap on the back of his other hand, thus scoring a plus for step 10. He then hesitated briefly, placed his hands under the water, rinsing the back of his hands (step 11 and 13 scored correct) and then his palms (step 12 scored correct: although the steps were completed in an order different from that specified on the task analysis, they are scored "correct" since the end result was not adversely affected). Robert grasped the cold water tap and turned it off, picked up the towel and dried off the palms and backs of his hands (step 14 to 18 scored as correct). The teacher waited 3 seconds, but Robert did not move to hang up the towel. She took the towel, hung it up for him, scored step 19 as an error, then thanked him for his work. The assessment was completed. The multiple opportunity method was used for an additional 3 days of testing, and the results are represented in the percentage scores shown in Table 4.6.

In both examples, no feedback is provided to the student on performance of the targeted skill in order to differentiate between conditions of testing, which represent the most difficult conditions specified in the objective, and the conditions of teaching, when prompts and reinforcement are available. In the multiple opportunity method, the student is not physically assisted through incorrectly performed steps, but rather, the step is performed by the examiner *for* the student, to avoid teaching during testing.

An examination of Table 4.6 gives a much more accurate picture of Robert's performance level because the multiple opportunity method let him attempt each step in the task analysis. When relying on information from the single opportunity probe alone, Robert appears to be much less proficient at the task of hand washing, while the multiple opportunity probe reveals that he has mastered a number of steps in the task analysis, however, the multiple opportunity probe requires much more instructional time than does the single opportunity probe. Therefore, the teacher may wish to use this method only part of the time to have an idea of progress on steps later in the chain. When doing so, the results of the multiple opportunity assessment would be presented separately on the graph to distinguish them from the data obtained using the single opportunity method.

Although the collection of accurate probe data is necessary to evaluate performance, it is obtained at the sacrifice of valuable instructional time. Unfortunately, there are no clear guidelines concerning how frequently probes should be conducted or for the selection of the appropriate probe procedure. This issue will be discussed later in this chapter.

Duration recording focuses on the length of time a particular behavior is performed and has been used to measure length of time required to complete a buttoning task (Kramer & Whitehurst, 1981), or the time that students were engaged in social interaction (Gaylord-Ross, Haring, Breen, & Pitts-Conway, 1984). Similarly, a comparison of the duration of time spent operating various battery-controlled devices allowed the identification of specific reinforcer preferences of persons having multiple handicaps (Wacker, Berg, Wiggins, Muldoon, & Cavanaugh, 1985).

Duration is recorded by accumulating the number of seconds or minutes of behavior observed. Since Robert was observed to engage in stereotypic behavior during handwashing instruction, the teacher was interested in monitoring the behavior, in order to see whether it decreased as his handwashing skills improved, or if the duration remained unchanged. In the latter case, the teacher may decide to intervene directly with this behavior, as it will adversely affect his ability to perform this task. To monitor this behavior, the teacher could start an unobtrusively held stopwatch whenever the behavior occurred during the training session. As soon as the behavior was discontinued, the stopwatch would again be stopped, started again when the behavior occurred, and so on. At the end of the session, the total time accumulated on the stopwatch would equal the total duration of stereotypic behavior during a single observation. Although duration recording may sound simple, accuracy rests upon precise delineation of what constitutes the behavior's onset and termination.

Duration may be reported in terms of the total number of minutes or the percentage of time a behavior is engaged in during each observation. Percentage reporting is especially useful if the observation sessions vary in length, since the resulting percentages are roughly comparable. The percentage of time a behavior occurs during a given observation is calculated by a simple percentage formula: $A/B \times 100 = X$. If A equals the total amount of time a behavior occurs and B equals the total length of observation, then X is the percentage of time the behavior occurred during observation; however, as with frequency data, caution must be exercised when comparing data obtained during observation sessions of varying lengths.

Duration records also may be kept when a teacher is interested in the amount of time a student takes to complete a specific task for which no minimum or maximum time has been set. Meal eating may range from 5 minutes to more than an hour, yet there still may be no time limitations set. A slow-eating student's baseline duration over five lunches, measured in minutes, could consist of 75 minutes, 50 minutes, 67 minutes, 43 minutes, and 70 minutes. Behaviors for which no time criteria are set are reported in time units (seconds, minutes), since percentages are meaningless without a maximum or minimum criterion.

Duration recording, like event recording, requires the observer's complete attention during each observation. Duration records are most appropriate for behaviors which either have a high or even rate or which simply may be variable in length from onset to end, making frequency less meaningful. Stereotypic behavior, or time spent eating, for example, may vary in length from a few seconds to long periods. Although stopwatches facilitate more accurate duration measurements, wall clocks or wristwatches with second hands may be used, as long as the observer can write down the duration of each occurrence of the behavior. These separate occurrences are later totaled to yield the total duration for each unit of observation. Since interval measures are more adaptable to a variety of behaviors and are also time based, they are often used in place of duration measures.

Interval recording may be conducted using either a partial or a whole interval method. In both procedures, the observer divides the observation unit (2 minutes, 10 minutes) into equal intervals (5 seconds, 10 seconds, etc.). With *whole interval* recording, an interval is checked only when the target behavior occurs continuously throughout the entire interval. With *partial interval* recording, the interval is checked although the behavior occurs only in part of the interval. In addition, regardless of the number of times a target behavior occurs during any single interval, only one tally is recorded for that interval.

As with frequency and duration recording, the teacher's total attention must be directed toward the student during the entire observation period. In addition, the observer must have some method of keeping track of the intervals in order to know when to move from one interval to the next on the data sheet. A watch or clock with a second hand can be used to time the intervals, but checking the time will interrupt the observer's concentration on the student. If available, a portable tape recorder with a tape of prerecorded interval counts and ear plugs will eliminate this problem; a timer with a light or sound signaling at regular intervals may also be used. For longer intervals (3 to 5 minutes), inexpensive egg timers, kitchen timers (with cotton taped around the bell to muffle the sound), and Memo Timers (Foxx & Martin, 1971) have been used effectively.

Interval recording may be applied to many behaviors (discrete, continuous, or sporadic) as long as the behavior can be classified as "observed" or "not observed" during any interval. Selection of the appropriate interval method will be guided by the characteristics of the behavior as well as the goals of intervention. When a behavior is brief (verbalizations), a partial interval method must be used to detect the behavior; however, it will overestimate the occurrence of behaviors of long duration. When monitoring a behavior such as "attending," this method should not be used because the behavior will be scored as present even if it occurs very briefly during the interval. In such cases, when it is important to know that the behavior occurs continuously, a whole interval method should be used, although it will underestimate the amount of behavior, just as brief interruptions in the target behavior will result in a failure to score the behavior for the interval.

When behavior characteristics do not clearly dictate the type of interval system to be used, the teacher should generally choose the most conservative measure so that treatment effects are not inflated. When instruction is implemented in order to increase an appropriate behavior such as correct use of recreational equipment, the whole interval method will provide the most conservative measure: the behavior will be scored only when it occurs for the entire interval. Conversely, if the whole interval method was used to monitor the effects of a behavior reduction program, the obtained data could be misleading: the behavior could occur frequently, but not be recorded because it did not last for the entire interval. Use of a partial interval will ensure that the behavior was totally absent from all intervals not scored.

The length of the interval will depend both on the behavior being observed (its average length and frequency) and the observer's ability to record and attend. The more frequent the behavior, the smaller the interval for observation should be, so the data will yield a more accurate representation of the behavior. For example, if 15-minute intervals are used to measure a student's appropriate use of signs, a tally in one interval would not begin to reflect the behavior's density (whether the student used signs 35 times, or once). For behaviors that occur infrequently, longer intervals can be used within applied settings, although they are probably inadequate for experimental purposes. When Repp, Roberts, Slack, Repp, and Berkler (1976) compared the accuracy of observations taken by interval procedures with frequency measures of the same behavior for the same time period, low and medium rates of responding were accurately measured with 10-second intervals, but high-rate response patterns (either continuously high rate or with bursts of high rates) were grossly underestimated by interval measurements. They recommended either using intervals of less than 10 seconds or frequency procedures to measure high rate behaviors.

Momentary time sampling is another interval procedure useful in teaching settings. Although the same procedures are used for dividing the observation periods into small units, this method does not require the teacher to watch the student for the entire interval; rather, the teacher merely glances over at the student at the end of the interval, and records whether or not the behavior is occurring at that time.

Time samples need not be taken at regular intervals. One procedure that has been suggested requires the teacher first to decide how many samples of the student's behavior will be observed in a given session (6 times during a one-hour session). During the observation session, the teacher will set a timer randomly and then record the student's behavior immediately after hearing the signal. This sequence is repeated during the session until the predetermined number of observations are obtained (Hall, Hawkins, & Axelrod, 1975). As with the previously described interval systems, the teacher should use a signaling device which is as unobtrusive as possible, as the obtained data could be misleading if the student's behavior is influenced by signal.

An alternate type of time sampling, reported by Quilitch and Risley (1973), allows a teacher to assess the behavior of an entire group. Placheck (Planned Activity Check) is conducted as follows:

1. Define the planned activity or behaviors (on-task during math period, engaged in aggressive behavior) the teacher wants to measure in a group;
2. At given intervals (5 minutes, 10 minutes) count and record how many students are engaged in the activity.
3. Immediately count and record the total number of students present in the area of activity.

The number of students engaged in the target behavior is divided by the total number present and multiplied by 100, which yields the percentage of the group engaging in the behavior during the sampled interval. When used with longer sessions, it is best to sample once in the middle or at equally spaced points (beginning, middle and end of session).

Momentary time sampling requires less intensive involvement on the part of the observer but does not provide as accurate a reflection of low frequency behavior as could be obtained with the interval or frequency procedure. When using time sampling to measure low frequency or short duration behavior, the results may indicate that the behavior never occurred if the samples are too infrequent. With both low frequency and short duration behavior, the intervals must guarantee enough observation samples to obtain an adequate measure of the behavior.

Continuous- and time-sampling interval recording are often used in applied settings. Besides being appropriate to observe a wide variety of behaviors, they may also be used to observe one or multiple behaviors across a group of people. This is done very effectively by sequentially rotating observations across the group until all have been observed and repeating the sequence until the observation period is over (Thomson, Holmberg, & Baer, 1974). An additional advantage of interval methods is the convenient conversion of the data into percentages for graphing. Interval percentages are calculated simply by dividing the total number of intervals where behavior was observed and multiplying by 100. When data are reported as "the percentage of intervals" an individual engaged in a particular behavior, they are easier to understand.

Construct a Data Recording Form
Data recording forms must be constructed to conform to the constraints set by

1. The measurement procedures selected: permanent products, interval, frequency, etc.;
2. The number of individuals observed: Sufficient space should be allowed so data for each individual are clearly separated and identifiable;
3. The number of behaviors observed: Intervals or observation periods (as with frequency and duration) need to be subdivided and coded so tallies or number of instances observed are identified with the behavior they represent;
4. The frequency of the behavior: When frequency measures are used, enough space must be allowed for recording more frequent behaviors.

A rough draft of the data collection form should be field tested, modified, and converted to a ditto master for easy reproduction, since its repeated use will be necessary before, during, and following the intervention. Data forms may be constructed so that several days' observation can be recorded on one form.

Every data form, regardless of the measurement procedure used, should include space for basic information: (a) name of individual(s) observed; (b) observer's name; date, time and place of observation; (c) length of each observation period; (d) behavior(s) observed (with brief definitions); (e) data totals and/or percentages; (f) and perhaps comments.

Select a Design

Once the program is written for a target behavior and the measurement procedure selected, the design to be used must be determined. Although there is similarity between the designs used by researchers and those recommended for use by teachers or clinicians, there are some critical differences.

In research, one goal is to demonstrate a functional relationship between specific behaviors and intervention strategies. This is important, for it is only through researchers' careful and meticulous efforts that practitioners will have a basic knowledge necessary to select the most efficient and effective teaching strategies for their students. For researchers to provide this information with any certainty, they must control the environment, systematically and consistently apply the procedure(s), ensure the reliability of measurement, and determine the functional relationship of the treatment and behavior in question. This stringent attention to details is generally not the role of the practitioner.

Teachers must teach students new skills and help them remain proficient on skills already mastered. Their responsibility is to select proven techniques, to schedule interventions in accord with their students' performance, and to monitor performance to ensure that satisfactory progress is being made. Procedures delineated in this chapter are not as rigorous as those required in research, but will allow the teacher to be accountable for student learning through the careful collection of objective performance data. Therefore, we will describe only those designs suitable for classroom use.

AB or Baseline-Intervention Design

In an AB design, repeated measures of the target behavior(s) are obtained under baseline (A) and intervention (B) conditions. This design is referred to as a quasi-experimental design because it is not possible to conclusively demonstrate a cause-effect relationship between the intervention and the observed changes in behavior. Since there is no withdrawal of the intervention and/or replication of treatment effects, it is impossible to rule out rival hypotheses based on factors not controlled by the teacher that may have caused the changes in behavior. Given the lack of experimental control, this design rarely is used by researchers, but it *is* considered to be adequate for monitoring student performance within teaching settings. Indeed, when teachers are familiar with the student's typical learning patterns and are aware of various events which may affect performance, it is usually possible to judge treatment effects with a considerable degree of certainty. Since student performance is monitored before teaching (baseline) and during different phases of teaching (acquisition, maintenance, and generalization), this design provides an objective description of the student's behavior before and after training, giving us an adequate record of student progress towards the accomplishment of instructional goals.

An example of an AB design is presented in Figure 4.3, to illustrate the presentation of data collected during Robert's grocery shopping program. As can be seen, the AB design can be extended to include an additional C phase (or more phases) if data analysis indicates that program modifications are required. In this case, analysis of the performance data indicated that Robert was not demonstrating a satisfactory rate of learning. The teacher hypothesized that the lack of success was due to his failure to respond to the model cues provided, so these were replaced by physical guidance prompts. When such changes are made, a solid vertical line is used to separate the phases, and they are concisely labeled so the reader can immediately identify when the change occurred, as well as the type of program modification made.

In some cases, the teacher may wish to obtain more convincing demonstrations of treatment effects and/or compare the use of a specific method across different behaviors, settings or students. One of the following designs could be selected, as they allow more rigorous experimental control than the AB design, yet are easily implemented within teaching settings.

Multiple Baseline Across Subjects, Behaviors, or Settings

The multiple baseline design, described by Baer, Wolf, and Risley (1968), measures the effect of a

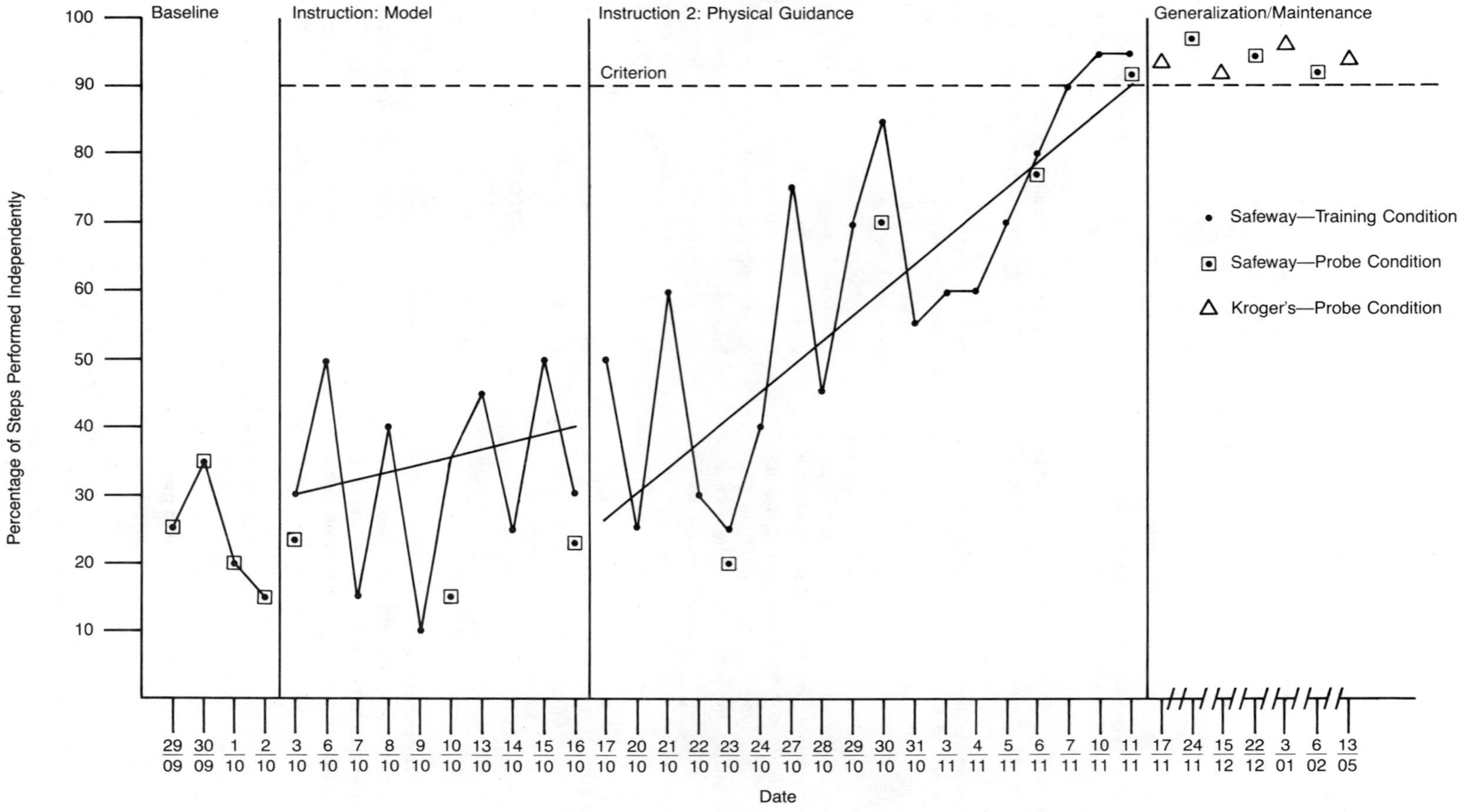

FIGURE 4.3 AB design for instruction of grocery shopping skills

single treatment on: (a) several behaviors of the same individual; (b) one behavior of a single individual across a variety of settings (classroom, school cafeteria, and the home); or (c) two or more students in the same situation exhibiting the same class of behavior. The initial step in the use of this design requires the simultaneous collection of baseline data across all targeted behaviors, subjects or settings. When all baselines appear to be stable, intervention is started with the first behavior target. The effectiveness of the treatment is demonstrated when the graphic display indicates that the data from the treated behavior has moved in the desired direction, while the baseline measures for the remaining behaviors remain unchanged. Once the effect of the treatment has been clearly demonstrated, the same intervention procedure is applied to the second behavior until the desired change is again obtained and so on, until all behaviors have been treated.

If, in each instance, the target behavior alters *only when the treatment is applied*, it can be said with a considerable degree of certainty that intervention is the reason for the observed changes in behavior. Thus, when using a multiple baseline across behaviors, the teacher must be able to predict that the targeted behaviors are independent: that is, intervening with one behavior will not also result in changes in the other behaviors. Similarly, it may be found that intervention in one setting or with one subject may affect the remaining baselines. When this occurs, it is unclear whether the effect of the treatment has generalized to the untreated behaviors or whether the treatment was ineffective, and the observed changes were due to other factors (Tawney & Gast, 1984).

Multiple Probe Design

The multiple probe design (Horner & Baer, 1978) is similar to the multiple baseline design, in that baselines are taken simultaneously on three behaviors (or on one behavior across students or settings) before intervention begins with the first behavior or person. However, in contrast to the multiple baseline design, where continuous measures of behaviors not receiving treatment are obtained, the multiple probe design requires less frequent measures of these untreated behaviors (see Figure 4.4). This design is not only more practical in teaching settings, but it also reduces the probability that the behavior will change as a result of the baseline assessment process. When a multiple baseline design across subjects was used by Horner and

Kelitz (1975) in an examination of toothbrushing training, the fourth subject, who had undergone weeks of baseline assessment, developed a number of inappropriate behaviors such as playing in the water and with the toothpaste. Conversely, since reinforcement is not provided during the baseline phase, desirable skills may be extinguished by excessive baseline measures (Horner & Baer, 1978). Finally, this design can be used when there is a low probability that the student will learn a behavior without training. If a student is not expected to learn new manual signs in the absence of direct instruction, it is not necessary to repeatedly probe performance or untrained signs. Similarly, a multiple probe design is appropriate when the instructional program targets a sequence of skills in which later behaviors are dependent upon mastery of previous skills (sequences such as supported sitting with head steady, sits self-supported by arms, sits with no support).

Briefly, the procedures used to implement a multiple probe include: (1) collecting a minimum of three baseline measures for all behaviors to be treated; (2) intervening with the first behavior, and continuing treatment until the criterion level has been achieved; (3) probing all behaviors, obtaining at least three measures or until performance is stable; (4) intervening with the second behavior, continuing to criterion level; (5) probing all behaviors again (including behaviors at criterion) and intervening with the next behavior, continuing until all behaviors have been treated.

Changing Criterion Design

This design, originally described by Wolf, Risley, and Mees (1964) and discussed in some detail by Hartmann and Hall (1976) consists of three general phases: baseline, changing criterion, and followup. After a traditional baseline or assessment period, an intervention program (usually a contingency) is implemented in a series of phases. In the beginning, minimal behavior change is required. Gradually, however, stepwise changes in the criterion brings the rate of behavior closer and closer to the targeted level.

This design is typically used when compliance and/or fluency problems, rather than skill deficits, are responsible for the student failing to meet the designated criterion. If a student is able to perform a specific task, but the rate or quality is adversely affected by the demonstration of an inappropriate behavior (excessive requests for assistance), this design could be used to reduce systematically or

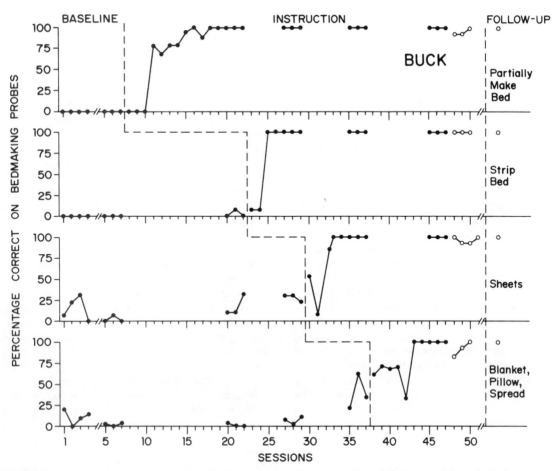

FIGURE 4.4 A multiple probe design across behaviors teaching bedmaking skills to an adolescent having severe handicaps

Source: From "Analysis of Time Delay Procedures for Teaching Daily Living Skills to Retarded Adolescents," by M. E. Snell, 1982, *Analysis and Intervention in Developmental Disabilities, 2,* p. 150. Reprinted by permission.

eliminate the problem behavior. Similarly, this design was used to establish a more acceptable work production rate for the assembly of a drapery pulley through stepwise increases in the criterion established for obtaining self-administered reinforcement (Bates, Renzaglia, & Clees 1980).

The length of each phase, as well as the magnitude of each criterion change must be determined after an analysis of student performance. In general, Hartmann and Hall (1976) recommend that each phase must be long enough to allow the behavior to restabilize at the new rate, as stability (the behavior matches the designated criterion each time it is changed) is the most convincing demonstration of the effect of the intervention. Further, although the magnitude or size of the changes in the criterion

should be large enough to guarantee that differences in the behavior can be detected, it must also represent a realistic criterion for the student. Finally, highly variable data should be carefully interpreted because it is possible that factors other than the treatment contingency are affecting the behavior. Treatment effects are clear only when a close correspondence between the rate of behavior and each new criterion level is repeatedly demonstrated.

Multielement or Alternating Treatment Design

When using a multielement design, the teacher is able to compare the effects of two different treatments on a single behavior (either intervention and baseline or two different interventions). This design has been used to compare the effects of two different types of reinforcement on the performance of a vocational assembly task (Koop, Martin, Yu, & Suthons, 1980). Similarly, it was demonstrated that music delivered contingently for an erect head position resulted in the maintenance of this position for longer periods of time than was seen under baseline conditions (Murphy, Doughty, & Nunes, 1979). Although such comparisons could be made using other designs, the multielement design is more efficient, as different treatments are implemented at the same time rather than one after another.

Following the collection of baseline data, the multielement design requires that the two different conditions be quickly alternated. The teacher can either alternate conditions within a single day or across days, but care should be taken to counterbalance the presentation schedule so that neither treatment is consistently associated with a particular time of day, location or staff member. Further, each treatment or condition should be presented an equal number of times. The data contained under each condition are separately presented on the same graph, so that the teacher can determine if each treatment results in a distinctively different performance. As soon as it is clear that one treatment is more effective in producing the desired effect, the other can be discontinued.

This design has been successfully used to evaluate various treatments for appropriate and inappropriate behaviors in students having severe handicaps; however, it is difficult to interpret the data when effects of the treatments are not immediate, or if the two conditions do not result in distinctly different patterns of behavior. Further, procedural reliability is critical: each treatment must be implemented accurately according to the schedule (Tawney & Gast, 1984). As this strict adherence to a schedule can be difficult to maintain when coping with the other demands of a classroom, accuracy can be enhanced by establishing some type of system that will remind staff of the schedule to be used in implementing the various treatments. Further, intermittent checks should be made to monitor the consistency and accuracy with which staff apply the different procedures.

Designs to Assess Response Maintenance

It can be seen that use of previously outlined research designs place primary emphasis on determining a functional relationship between treatment and the observed behavior change; however, when teaching students to perform successfully in natural environments, we must not only evaluate skill acquisition but also monitor the maintenance of behavior over time. A brief discussion of three strategies which can be used to assess maintenance follows (Rusch & Kazdin, 1981).

The *sequential withdrawal* design requires that the teacher systematically withdraw one component of a multicomponent intervention plan (tangible reinforcers), then a second (prompts), and a third, until all components have been withdrawn. Treatment components can be either abruptly discontinued or systematically faded over time. This strategy has been used in combination with reversal designs (O'Brien, Bugle, & Azrin, 1972) or a multiple baseline design (Sowers, Rusch, Connis, & Cummings, 1980). Regardless of the design used, this strategy allows the teacher to monitor the student's behavior after each withdrawal and to determine which, if any, part of the intervention program is essential to the long-term maintenance of the desired behaviors. If indicated, modifications to maintenance procedures can be made as required.

The *partial withdrawal* strategy is used in combination with a multiple baseline design, and requires that one component of a treatment, or the complete treatment, be withdrawn from one baseline (representing measures taken for one behavior, student, or setting). Thus, the teacher is able to observe the effects of withdrawing the treatment by comparing these baselines to those for which treatment was continued. Again, if the desired behavior levels are not satisfactorily maintained, the teacher can implement procedures which will facilitate response maintenance.

Finally, the *partial-sequential withdrawal* initially replicates the procedures used in the previous strategy: the entire treatment or one component of the treatment is removed from one baseline, and the effects of the partial withdrawal are assessed; however, if the withdrawal results in a deterioration in performance levels, rather than modifying the original treatment, sequential withdrawals are used for the remaining baselines. Rusch and Kazdin (1981) provide an example using this strategy, withdrawing the entire treatment (prompts and praise) from the first subject in a multiple baseline design (partial withdrawal); however, this withdrawal was followed by a deterioration of performance levels, indicating that a similar withdrawal of all components of the treatment from the second subject would result in similar losses. Thus, only one component (prompts) was withdrawn from the second subject (sequential withdrawal). Once the resulting data indicated that the remaining aspect of the treatment (praise) maintained the behavior, praise was withdrawn. The same sequential withdrawal strategy would be used for the first subject after the reestablishment of criterion performance.

Select Graphic Display

Behavioral data are usually charted on graphs, as changes in a behavior's duration, frequency, and rate are more visible in this format. Basic behavior graphs are simple, equal interval graphs on which days of the week or sessions are plotted along the horizontal line (abscissa). The scores or behavior measurement tools are stated in percentage, duration, rate per minute or frequency and are plotted in equal intervals along the vertical line (ordinate).

Both the horizontal and the vertical axes are labeled before the data are plotted. In Figure 4.3, the abscissa is labeled "Date," and the exact dates are recorded, so the teacher and others are able to identify when probes were conducted on the grocery shopping skills. As a task-analytic, assessment procedure was used for this task, the ordinate is labeled "Percentage of Steps Performed Independently" and represents the percentage of steps in the task analysis performed without assistance. The vertical axes should always be marked in units that allow the measurement of the entire range of possible behavior. Thus, the graph in Figure 4.3 ranges from 0 to 100 percent. When there is no definite upper and lower limit, the range should extend from the baseline level to the target level, with some extra space added at both ends to allow for variability in data.

Data points within each phase of a program are connected by straight lines, but should not be connected across phase changes (baseline, intervention 1, intervention 2). Each phase is separated by a vertical line, and should be labeled to indicate what type of intervention was used ("Instruction: Modeling"). If one wishes to measure more than one behavior or the same behavior performed in different settings or by different individuals, the behaviors can be plotted on the same graph as long as they are measured in the same units;

however, to prevent confusion, usually no more than three different data paths are included on one graph. Further, different shaped data points, or solid and broken lines, are used to distinguish between the different behaviors, settings, or individuals. When these graphing conventions are used, the graph will be interpreted more accurately by professionals and parents.

Another type of graph teachers may use is the ratio chart or standardized semilogarithmic grid, which displays a student's daily rate data stated in movements or behaviors per minute. Although ratio charts may seem somewhat more confusing than interval charts, they may be mastered quickly and appear to permit more accurate instructional decisions to be made (Haring, Liberty & White, 1980). Ratio charts offer greater precision and flexibility in recording the rate changes of a wide range of behaviors from very slow (0.01 per minute) to very fast (1,000 per minute).

PHASE FIVE: PROGRAM EVALUATION

The final phase of the IEP process—evaluation of learning—is perhaps the most crucial. The teacher is now ready to collect frequent measures of student performance on functional tasks, but these data are not useful unless they are analyzed and used to make decisions concerning the effectiveness of the various intervention programs. The following is a brief description of ways that data should be collected within baseline and intervention phases. Included also are recommendations concerning procedures to be used when analyzing data and making instructional decisions.

Collecting Baseline and Intervention Data

Data that are collected during the baseline phase to establish the student's current level of performance, provide a standard against which the effects of training can be judged. That is, it is assumed that without treatment, the level of performance would remain unchanged. A comparison of the repeated measures obtained before and during the intervention would determine whether the program had yielded the desired change in the student's behavior. To facilitate accurate comparisons, baseline assessment should take place under conditions as similar as possible to those the student will be expected to perform after training.

The trainer's performance during assessment in the baseline and intervention phases will be determined by a number of factors. In some situations, such as the task analytic procedure described earlier, the observer is able to interact with the student in a specified way and collect data simultaneously. At other times, the observer's presence may influence the student's behavior, and distort the accuracy of the obtained data (interaction with peers, rate of maladaptive behaviors), so the observer should be as unobtrusive as possible. In some cases, it may be necessary to conduct pre-baseline observations until the novelty of the observer's presence has diminished, and the behavior returns to more typical rates (Kazdin, 1980). Data obtained during this phase are usually not included in subsequent data analysis procedures.

In other situations, observer presence may be troublesome only in the generalization/maintenance phase of instruction. Since the presence of a trainer might have unintentionally cued performance, Coon, Vogelsberg, and Williams (1981) used observers who were unknown to the student to monitor posttraining bus-riding performance. Similarly, Aeschleman and Schladenfauffen (1984) instructed their trainers to accompany clients at a distance in the store when assessing their shopping skills.

Teachers must balance the advantages of less frequent data collection (increased instructional time, convenience for staff) with the need for accurate information on which to base instructional decisions. The frequency with which data are collected during skill acquisition programs and behavior reduction programs is influenced by different factors, and thus will be discussed separately.

Skill Acquisition

When conducting skill acquisition programs, the teacher typically collects two different types of data: training data, which records student performance when prompts and reinforcement are available; and probe data, which measures student performance under targeted posttraining conditions (no assistance or praise). In the former case, recording the student's performance on each step usually requires brief interruptions of training. Conversely, failure to record data or at least use a data sheet with the task analysis could lead to inconsistency in training (skipped steps, incorrect verbal cues).

If training data are graphed, they should always be presented separately from data obtained under probe conditions, since this allows the teacher to distinguish easily between the student's behaviors under different conditions. However, even if training data are not graphed, they must be referred to when the teacher makes decisions concerning the effectiveness of instruction. Analysis of both measures of performance is important because a sole reliance on data obtained under probe conditions can mask significant learning. If the student has learned to perform a particular step on the task analysis with increasingly less assistance (moving from physical assistance to a verbal prompt), this learning would not be reflected under probe conditions where credit is given only for steps completed without help. The resulting graph of probe data, therefore, would not reflect this progress and could lead a teacher to modify an instructional program which, in reality, was producing learning.

Further, although the collection of probe data is necessary to evaluate performance, it is obtained at the sacrifice of valuable instructional time; therefore, in the absence of clear guidelines to use when making decisions concerning frequency of data collection, following factors should be considered.

Typical Learning Rate If training and probe data are not collected daily, they should be gathered more frequently at the beginning of the program (so the teacher can assess whether the instructional methods are promoting learning) and towards the end of programming, so that training is not unnecessarily prolonged. Data collected between these two phases of learning must be obtained with sufficient frequency to ensure that the student's optimal rate of learning is being maintained; therefore, data collection will be more frequent with students who learn quickly or show greater inconsistency in their performance.

Task Characteristics If the task is long and/or instruction occurs infrequently (one trial per day or less), noninstructional probes of performance should be conducted approximately once a week or every five sessions. This practice will guarantee that sufficient training is provided: in general, a ratio of no fewer than *four training trials to each probe trial* should be maintained. The use of the single opportunity probes when assessing such tasks would also permit at least some instruction to occur on test days (Snell & Browder, 1986), since this method allows instruction to begin immediately following the first error in the probe.

Stage of Learning   Naturally, data will be obtained more frequently during acquisition than during the generalization/maintenance phase of learning. Further, maintenance probes should be obtained more often soon after the cessation of intensive training so that programming could be immediately reinstated if the student's performance deteriorates. Once the student has demonstrated satisfactory maintenance over a period of time, the frequency of probes can be greatly reduced. In fact, students may simply be observed, rather than formally probed, when they routinely carry out the task.

Behavior Reduction

In general, the time spent observing targeted inappropriate behaviors will be dependent on the following considerations:

When and Where the Behavior or Its Absence Is Most Troublesome   In some cases, this decision is easily made (sloppy eating occurs only at mealtime), whereas in other situations, such decisions can only be made following an evaluation of the ABC analysis.

Behavior Characteristics Observation System   For low frequency behaviors, longer and/or more observation periods will be needed to obtain a representative sample of the behavior than is required for behaviors occurring more frequently. Further, some behaviors are more easily observed and recorded than others (loud verbalizations or thrown objects versus off-task behavior), and different types of observation systems will place varying levels of demands on the observer (whole-interval versus momentary time sampling). These factors must be taken into account so that observation periods are scheduled only when it is possible to obtain accurate measures of behavior.

Accuracy of Performance Measures

Before making instructional decisions on the basis of performance data, the teacher must be confident that the data are truly reflective of the student's behavior and that the intervention was actually implemented as planned. These concerns are referred to as *interobserver reliability* or *agreement* and *procedural reliability*, respectively. The issue of

reliability is complex (see Kazdin, 1980 for a more complete discussion), and published research studies typically devote a considerable amount of time and resources towards establishing the reliability of their observational codes and procedures. Although standards within teaching settings will, for practical purposes, be less rigorous, the degree of confidence in the information used to make instructional decisions can be increased if occasional checks are made.

The primary measure used to assess the accuracy of performance measures taken in classrooms determines *interobserver agreement*, or the degree to which two independent observers agree on the occurrence or nonoccurrence of the targeted behavior. Whenever possible, the teacher should try to recruit the second observer from outside the classroom, because it has been demonstrated that staff who work together often develop similar idiosyncratic methods of scoring behavior. Therefore, while they may achieve high levels of agreement, the actual level of accuracy declines (Kazdin, 1980). In general, accuracy should be checked at least once per phase; however, if an observation code of measurement procedure is complex, accuracy is more difficult to maintain and therefore should be checked more frequently.

The simplest method for determining the accuracy of frequency, duration, or interval recording is to compare the totals (number of behaviors/intervals scored, total minutes) obtained by the two observers, using the following formula:

$$\frac{\text{Smaller total}}{\text{Larger total}} = \text{Percentage of agreement}$$

Agreement scores obtained this way must be viewed cautiously, since this only reflects total agreement: if both observers scored 10 behaviors, they would achieve 100% agreement. However, this does not mean that they were both counting the same 10 behaviors; in reality, they may not have agreed on any specific instance of the target behavior.

A more precise measure of agreement has been used most frequently with interval data although it also can be used to determine agreement on task analytic assessments. It requires that each interval or task step recorded by the two observers be compared separately in order to determine whether or not the observers agreed or disagreed on the occurrence or lack of occurrence of the behavior. The following formula is used:

$$\frac{\text{Agreements}}{\text{Agreements} + \text{Disagreements}} = \text{Percentage of agreement}$$

The standards used to judge acceptable agreement scores will partially depend on the type of measurement system used, as well as the characteristics of the target behavior. Data obtained from the permanent product should be 100% accurate; when agreement for counting permanent products is less than 100%, the products simply may be recounted and the data made accurate. If data are gathered from observations, 80% agreement is usually the minimum acceptable level (Kazdin, 1980). Lower percentage-of-agreement scores indicate a need to increase the number of reliability checks. If problems persist, the behavior definitions, the task analysis, and/or observation system should be modified until more accurate results are obtained. Such modifications are important: when the teacher is analyzing the results of training, inaccurate data are likely to result in the making of inaccurate instructional decisions.

The second area of concern, *procedural reliability* or the degree to which program procedures are implemented accurately, must also be assessed (Billingsley, White, & Munson, 1980). Before trying to judge the effectiveness of a specific instructional method, teachers must be sure that the procedures were implemented accurately and consistently. Did the trainer use the correct prompts in the right order? Was the selected reinforcer delivered/given at the right time? Unless we establish that the instructional procedure was implemented properly, it is again possible that the teacher may make inaccurate instructional decisions. A teacher may decide that a certain instructional system does not "work" with a student, when it was not implemented properly, and/or was used inconsistently over time.

Data Analysis

Visual analysis of graphed, performance data necessarily involves some degree of subjective interpretation, but some general guidelines exist which can be used to judge the adequacy or inadequacy of instructional procedures. A brief explanation of these issues follows (see Barlow and Hersen (1984), Parsonson and Baer (1978) and Tawney and Gast (1984) for more detailed information).

In general, at least *three data points* are required before changing phases, since this is the minimum required to determine the level of stability and trend in the data. Obtaining a clear picture of the student's performance may require a longer period of time when the data are extremely variable (if the student's performance is inconsistent from one measurement period to the next). Given that the observations are accurate, variability in performance data may indicate that there are inconsistent environmental factors (persons present, events preceding or following the session, noise level) that are affecting the student's performance. In such cases, fluctuations in the student's performance can often be reduced by identifying and controlling these influences so that each observation occurs under more similar conditions (Parsonson & Baer, 1978). For example, if it is observed that Robert typically demonstrates a higher level of proficiency in his vocational tasks when he is placed in closer proximity to peers with less severe handicaps, we may wish to specify in his program that he should always sit by these co-workers. Similarly, if Christine's ability to partially participate in handwashing is negatively affected by high noise levels, we may modify the training setting (close the door, change the position of other students) in order to minimize the deleterious effect of such stimuli.

When considering the baseline phase, the primary objective is to obtain a stable and accurate measure of the student's performance against which to judge the effects of the treatment. In the ideal case, the charted data will appear as a relatively straight line; however, a countertherapeutic trend—a trend in which the data are ascending or descending in a direction opposite to that expected after intervention—is also acceptable. Since baseline data are critical to subsequent attempts to evaluate intervention effects, this requirement of a stable or an acceptable baseline trend should be fulfilled whenever it is practical; however, long baseline periods will be unwise and/or unethical when the observed behavior is dangerous to the student, other people and/or the environment.

More data points are obtained during an intervention phase than are gathered during baseline (at least 7 to 10) so that the treatment is given a "fair chance" before we make judgments concerning its effectiveness. If satisfactory learning is occurring, the program is continued until the student meets the criterion. On the other hand, if the behavior shows little or no change in the desired direction, or the rate of change is unacceptably low, changes should be made in the program.

When judging the effects of intervention, the teacher usually will take two properties of the data into consideration. The first is the change in *level* between the two phases. If a student had an average score of 10% correct during baseline, but immediately improved to an average score of 70% correct after introduction of the instructional program, and if this increase was maintained over time, the effect of our intervention would be clearly demonstrated. However, such an ideal pattern, which shows a large and abrupt change in the level of data, is rarely found in behavioral research or school programs, since most treatments take a longer time to affect behavior (Parsonson & Baer, 1978).

The second major consideration involves the *trend* of the data, including the direction (ascending, descending or neutral) as well as the slope or steepness of the data path (Tawney & Gast, 1984). As noted, when a trend occurs in the baseline data that is in the same direction as that expected after intervention, the teacher will have difficulty interpreting the data. That is, unless the intervention has a large effect, it is difficult to judge whether the change in the data is the result of the intervention or merely a continuation of the trend seen during baseline (Parsonson & Baer, 1978). When this phenomenon occurs, the teacher can either wait until the data become more stable before beginning instruction, or implement treatment using a multi-element design, which will allow the evaluation of the effect each condition has on the existing trend (Kratochwill, 1978).

Visual analysis of trends in the baseline or intervention phases can be facilitated by fitting a trend line to existing data. Methods such as the freehand method (Parsonson & Baer, 1978) or the more accurate split middle procedure (White & Haring, 1976) can be readily used in teaching settings. These lines summarize data, therefore clarifying the general direction of change in the data as well as the relative rate of change (reflected in the slope of change). The split middle procedure was used to help visually analyze the effects of grocery shopping program (see Figure 4.3). It can be seen that as Robert's performance was somewhat variable, the effects of the intervention are more evident when the trend lines in the different phases are compared.

Use of the split middle technique has been illustrated in Figure 4.5. The first figure represents the first intervention phase of Robert's grocery shopping program. As can be seen in the second figure, Step 1 requires the phase to be divided in half, and then for these halves to be divided in half again. Thus, the entire phase is divided into quarters, with an equal number of data points within each section. Note that because there were an odd number of data points, the vertical lines were drawn through an existing data point; had there been an even number, the line would have been drawn between two data points. Next, a horizontal line is drawn through the median rate of performance for the first and second half of the phase. This can be accomplished by simply counting down from the top to the bottom of the graph and noting the middle value within each half; thus, an equal number of data points will fall on either side of the horizontal line.

Step 2 is illustrated in the third figure: a line is drawn which connects the points in each half where the horizontal and vertical lines intersect. This line is then adjusted so that it "splits" the data: half of the data falls on or above the line, and half falls on or below the line. Thus, the line may be shifted either up or down, but the slope or angle of the line is *not* changed. As seen in Figure 4.5, the original line (dotted line) did not split the data in equal halves, so a parallel adjusted line (solid line) is drawn (White & Haring, 1976).

An examination of performance data characteristics is important but not sufficient to demonstrate that the "trend" or "level" of the data has changed significantly as a result of intervention. Rather, the teacher must be sure that the student's performance is changing at a rate which will allow successful performance in the natural environment at, or before, the target date specified in the IEP goal. Thus, the predictions concerning the student's expected learning rates made during the second phase of the curriculum development process (when establishing long- and short-term goals) will play an important role in the evaluation of instructional programs.

As noted earlier, the accuracy of these target dates will be enhanced when the teacher has access to information concerning the student's typical performance during instruction. Since Robert's teacher had graphed data from previous programs, examining his past performance on skills of a similar type and/or difficulty would enable the teacher to be more accurate when establishing a target date for the acquisition of grocery shopping

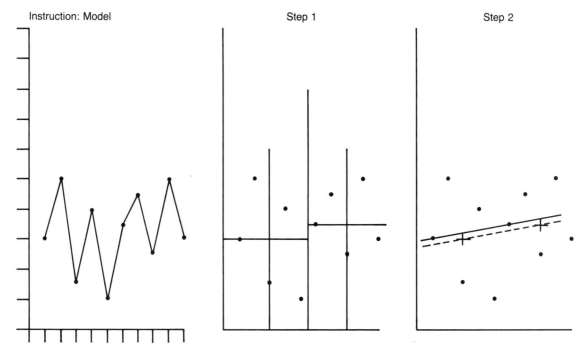

FIGURE 4.5   Drawing a split-middle trend line

skills. Further, when trend lines have been fitted to previous performance data, the teacher will have an objective standard against which to judge the actual rate of learning seen as a result of a new program. Thus, the teacher could see that the rate of learning shown in the first intervention phase of the grocery shopping program (as reflected in the slope or steepness of the trend line) was less rapid than had been previously demonstrated by Robert. Since these instructional procedures did not appear to result in the expected rate of learning, the teacher predicted that continuation of the existing program would not allow him to obtain criterion by the target date scheduled in the IEP. This prediction could be further substantiated if the teacher drew an extension of the existing line which maintained the same slope. This projected line would have graphically illustrated that continued learning at the same rate would not allow Robert to meet the target date; thus, program modifications were needed (see Figure 4.3).

When the teacher had obtained 6 to 10 data points following the introduction of the second intervention, a second split middle trend line was drawn. The slope of this line indicates the rate of learning occurring as a result of the second program. Again, the teacher could have extended

this line (maintaining the same slope) to the point at which it intersects with the criterion level of performance. Assuming that Robert will maintain a similar rate of learning, the teacher can estimate when he will reach criterion and make it possible to predict whether or not Robert will master the IEP objective by the target date. In this case, as the slope of the line appeared to be satisfactory, the teacher continued the second intervention, occasionally redrawing the trend line to ensure that the necessary slope is maintained.

In some cases, however, the teacher will not have access to data describing the student's typical performance under systematic instruction. If Christine had not previously been exposed to structured intervention programs, predictions concerning her achievement of various IEP goals would be more difficult to make. In such a situation, the teacher must rely more heavily upon the initial assessment information, including the reports of previous care providers, when establishing target dates. Further, once programs are implemented and performance data obtained, frequent reevaluation of the IEP target dates will be warranted.

In addition, as the teacher will not have previous performance data, it is not possible to make comparisons with the slope of past trend lines; however, it is possible to construct "progress lines" which can be used in place of trend lines (Haring et al., 1980). Although this method is typically used with logarithmic charts, when cautiously interpreted, it can also be a valuable aid for a teacher employing equal interval graphs. In particular, the teacher should remember that the line of progress as represented on an equal interval chart may be a less accurate reflection of the actual slope of progress which will be required to meet the criterion at a specific data, particularly in the early stages of learning. That is, the equal interval chart represents equal *absolute* changes: the distance between 5 to 10% correct is the same as the distance between 80 and 85% correct. In contrast, on a logarithmic chart, equal *relative* changes in performance are represented by equal distances: change from 5 to 10% correct in performance is a doubling of performance and is therefore represented by a greater distance than a change between 80 and 85% correct (Bailey, 1984). Thus, it is possible that data charted on a logarithmic chart more accurately reflect the effort required for learning, as improving performance from 5 to 10% correct may be more difficult for the student than moving from 80 to 85% correct.

To chart a "progress line," the teacher uses a calendar-synchronized chart and marks the first point where the targeted standard of performance intersects with the date specified in the IEP for achieving that standard. A second point is marked at the intersect between the current level of performance and the date. The "progress line" connects these two points, and describes the minimum rate of progress which must be made by the student if the goal is to be reached by the target date; however, it must be stressed that given the lack of previous data, the teacher cannot be confident that the progress line represents a realistic target for the student. Only with continuing experience with the learning rates typically demonstrated by a student will the teacher be able to estimate the adequacy of the predictions, and adjustments in the target date and resulting progress line must be made as is appropriate.

Thus, when using this procedure, we have an objective standard to use when charting performance from each session. That is, the progress line is used as a reminder of the rate of change which must be seen if criterion performance is to be achieved by the target date. If the data meet or exceed the progress line, the student will probably achieve the goal on schedule. If not, changes in the intervention program may be indicated.

Methods which assist the teacher to make instructional decisions on the basis of performance data have also been examined by Haring and his colleagues (1980) who have validated a series of decision rules for use with students with moderate to severe handicaps. These rules not only help the teacher to identify the types of data patterns which indicate whether or not it is appropriate to make instructional changes, but they also provide guidance concerning the type of change which should be made.

It should be stressed, however, that making instructional decisions is, at best, an inexact process. Although the preceding discussion indicates some methods which can enhance the probability that appropriate decisions will be made, the teacher must be aware that many factors will influence the manner in which the above guidelines are used. In particular, the teacher must be aware that the appropriate use of progress lines or other decision rules will be affected by the *type* of data that is collected, including the conditions under which it is gathered. This problem is particularly acute in the evaluation of instructional programs when the student's performance can be judged under training or probe conditions.

As previously noted, the teacher who chooses to collect single-opportunity probe data must be aware that the graphic presentation of such data can be misleading: the student may have learned a number of steps but does not have the opportunity to demonstrate new learning if it occurs on steps following the first error (when the probe is discontinued). Thus, if the rate of learning is estimated only through the visual analysis of graphed probe data, the teacher may not be adequately aware of the actual rate of progress. In such cases, it may be advantageous to graph training data instead of, or in addition to, probe data. This reasoning was used in determining the graphic presentation to be used for the instructional program represented in Figure 4.5. In this case, a complex task analysis dictated the use of the single opportunity probe. Such probes were conducted intermittently to assess the student's performance under conditions when no assistance or reinforcement was available. However, to reflect actual learning more accurately, the teacher also graphed training data (percentage of steps performed independently) during the intervention phases, in order to evaluate the student's rate of progress. Further, it was this latter data which was used to establish trend lines, and therefore judge the rate of learning; thus, it can be seen that the choice of data to be examined can have a significant impact on the instructional decisions which will be made.

Strategies for Change

When an analysis of performance data indicates that the rate of learning is unsatisfactory, what must be done to obtain more satisfactory progress? There are no simple answers; however, it can be seen that, in Figure 4.1, the teacher may select one of two feedback loops when making such modifications. In the first, it may be determined that additional assessment information is needed. If the teacher suspects a previously unidentified sensory deficit may be inhibiting performance, he may wish to consult a professional not originally involved in the curriculum development process. Similarly, he may determine that more information is needed from an existing team member, for example, to more precisely define the demands of a natural environment or to update information about a physical impairment. After this information is gathered, program modifications are made by moving systematically through the remaining phases of the curriculum development process again.

More often, the teacher will choose to reevaluate information obtained in phase 3 in light of recent student performance. In particular, information from an ABC or task analysis may be interpreted differently once the teacher has gained more experience with the student's typical learning style and/or skill deficits. All three components will be reexamined: (a) behavior (Is the behavior target realistic?), (b) conditions (Is performance inhibited by the characteristics of the social or physical environment, or the materials used?) (c) standards (Are standards set too high or too low for this particular student?). If the answer to any of these questions is affirmative, the teacher may wish to modify some components of the original objective in a manner that will better promote student learning.

If these components do not appear to be the likely culprits, the teacher moves to the next phase to reevaluate the instructional program. Factors such as the instructional methods (both antecedents and consequences provided to the student), frequency of instruction, length of sessions, and group size should be considered. Once modifications are made, instruction is again implemented, and the resulting data charted and analyzed. It should be noted that these data should be separated from previous data by a vertical phase line, so that data obtained after the program modification can be distinguished from the rest of the performance data (see Figure 4.3). Further, the written instructional program must be updated to ensure that it accurately reflects the instructional procedures to be used.

CONCLUDING COMMENTS

The development of a functional curriculum starts with the thorough assessment of the student's needs by all team members, with primary emphasis on the use of the ecological inventory procedures. This information is then integrated so that the student's strengths and most pressing areas of instructional need are identified, and individualized long- and short-term goals are established. Following the identification of these instructional targets, task analytic and ABC analysis provides specific information which will be used to write instructional objectives and intervention programs. Once the programs are established, precise measurement procedures are implemented and data graphed, so that the teacher can effectively monitor the impact of intervention and make modifications as required. This consistent monitoring allows the teacher to ensure that the program is indeed meeting the student's needs, and that precious instructional time is not being wasted.

The next chapter focuses upon intervention strategies to build skills as well as to increase and reduce existing behaviors. Further, the concepts and related teaching strategies of learning stages (acquisition, maintanence, and generalization learning) are addressed.

REFERENCES

Aeschleman, S. R., & Schladenhauffen, J. (1984). Acquisition, generalization and maintenance of grocery shopping skills by severely mentally retarded adolescents. *Applied Research in Mental Retardation, 5,* 245–258.

Baer, D. M. (1981). A hung jury and a Scottish verdict: "Not proven". *Analysis and Intervention in Developmental Disabilities, 1,* 91–97.

Baer, D. M., Wolf, M. M., & Risley, T. R. (1968). Some current dimensions of applied behavior analysis. *Journal of Applied Behavior Analysis, 1*(1), 91–97.

Bailey, D. B. (1984). Effects of lines of progress and semilogarithmic charts on ratings of charted data. *Journal of Applied Behavior Analysis, 17*, 359–365.

Baine, D. (1982). *Instructional design for special education.* Englewood Cliffs, NJ: Educational Technology Publications.

Barlow, D. H., & Hersen, M. (1984). *Single case experimental designs: Strategies for studying behavior change.* New York: Pergamon Press.

Bates, P. E., & Hanson, H. B. (1983). Behavioral assessment. In J. L. Matson, & S. E. Bruening (Eds.), *Assessing the mentally retarded* (pp. 27–64). New York: Grune and Stratton.

Bates, P., Morrow, S. A., Pancsofar, E., & Sedlak, R. (1984). The effect of functional vs nonfunctional activities on attitudes/expectations of non-handicapped college students: What they see is what we get. *Journal of the Association for the Severely Handicapped, 9*, 73–78.

Bates, P., Renzaglia, A., & Clees, T. (1980). Improving the work performance of severely/profoundly retarded young adults: The use of a changing criterion procedural design. *Education and Training of the Mentally Retarded, 15*, 95–104.

Baumgart, D., Brown, L., Pumpian, I., Nisbet, J., Ford, A., Sweet, M., Messina, R., & Schroeder, J. (1982). Principle of partial participation and individualized adaptations in educational programs for severely handicapped students. *Journal of the Association for the Severely Handicapped, 7*, 17–27.

Becker, W. C., Englemann, S., & Thomas, D. R. (1975). *Teaching 2: Cognitive learning and instruction.* Chicago: Science Research Associates.

Bellamy, G. T., Horner, R. H., & Inman, D. P. (1979). *Vocational habilitation of severely retarded adults.* Baltimore: University Park Press.

Billingsley, F. F. (1984). Where are the generalized outcomes? (An examination of instructional objectives). *Journal of the Association for Persons with Severe Handicaps, 9*, 186–192.

Billingsley, F. F., White, O. R., Munson, R. (1980). Procedural reliability: A rationale and an example. *Behavioral Assessment, 2*, 229–241.

Bruening, S. E., & Davidson, N. A. (1981). Effects of psychotropic drugs on intelligence test performance of institutionalized mentally retarded adults. *American Journal of Mental Deficiency, 85*, 575–579.

Browder, D., Snell, M., & Ambrogio, B. (1984). *Using time delay to transfer stimulus control within the behavioral chain of vending machine use with a comparison of training sites.* Unpublished manuscript. Lehigh University, Department of Special Education.

Brown, L., Branston, M. B., Hamre-Nietupski, S., Pumpian, I., Certo, N., & Gruenewald, L. A. (1979). A strategy for developing chronological age appropriate and functional curricular content for severely handicapped adolescents and young adults. *Journal of Special Education, 13*, 81–90.

Bruininks, R. H., Woodcock, R. W., Weatherman, R. S., & Hill, B. K. (1984). *Scales of independent behavior.* Allen, TX: D.L.M. Teaching Resources.

Christoph, D., Nietupski, J., & Pumpian, I. (1980). Teaching severely handicapped adolescent and young adults to use communication cards to make purchases at a fast food counter. In L. Brown, M. Falvey, D. Baumgart, I. Pumpian, J. Schroeder, & L. Gruenewald (Eds.), *Strategies for chronologically appropriate functional skills to adolescent and young adult severely handicapped students* (pp. 333–386). Madison: University of Wisconsin and Madison Metropolitan School District.

Coon, M. E., Vogelsberg, T., & Williams, W. (1981). Effects of classroom public transportation instruction on generalization of the natural environment. *Journal of the Association for the Severely Handicapped, 6*, (2), 46–53.

Crist, K., Walls, R. T., & Haught, P. A. (1984). Degree of specificity in task analysis. *American Journal of Mental Deficiency, 89*, 67–74.

Cronin, K. A., & Cuvo, A. J. (1979). Teaching mending skills to retarded adolescents. *Journal of Applied Behavior Analysis, 12*, 401–406.

Cuvo, A. J. (1978). Validating task analyses of community living skills. *Vocational Evaluation and Work Adjustment Bulletin, 11*(4), 13–21.

Donnellan, A. M., Mirenda, P. L., Mesaros, R. A., & Fassbender, L. L. (1984). Analyzing the communicative functions of aberrant behavior. *Journal of the Association for Persons with Severe Handicaps, 9*, 201–212.

Evans, I. M., & Meyer, L. H. (1985). *An educative approach to behavior problems. A practical decision model for interventions with severely handicapped learners.* Baltimore: Paul H. Brookes.

Foxx, R. M., & Martin, P. L. (1971). A useful portable timer. *Journal of Applied Behavior Analysis, 4*, 60.

Freagon, S., Wheeler, J., Hill, L., Brankin, G., Costello, D., & Peters, W. M. (1983). A domestic training environment for students who are severely handicapped. *Journal of the Association for the Severely Handicapped, 8*(4), 49–61.

Gaylord-Ross, R. J., Haring, T. J., Breen, C., & Pitts-Conway, V. (1984). The training and generalization of social interaction skills with autistic youth. *Journal of Applied Behavior Analysis, 17*, 229–248.

Gaule, K., Nietupski, J., Creto, N. (1985). Teaching supermarket shopping skills using an adaptive shopping list. *Education and Training of the Mentally Retarded, 20*, 53–59.

Hall, R. V., Hawkins, R. P., & Axelrod, S. (1975). Measuring and recording student behavior: A behavior analysis approach. In R. A. Weinberg & R. H. Wood (Eds.), *Observation of pupils and teachers in mainstream and special education settings: Alternate strategies* (pp. 193–217). Minneapolis: University of Minnesota, Leadership Training Institute.

Haring, N. G., Liberty, K. A., & White, O. R. (1980). Rules for data-based decisions in instructional programs. In W. Sailor, B. Wilcox, & L. Brown, (Eds.), *Methods of instruction for the severely handicapped* (pp. 159–192). Baltimore: Paul H. Brookes.

Hartmann, D. P., & Hall, R. V. (1976). The changing criterion design. *Journal of Applied Behavior Analysis, 9*, 527–532.

Hawkins, R. P., & Hawkins, K. K. (1981). Parental observations on the education of severely retarded children: Can it be done in the classroom? *Analysis and intervention in Developmental Disabilities, 1*, 13–22.

Hill, B. K., & Bruininks, R. H. (1981). *Physical and behavioral characteristics and maladaptive behavior of mentally retarded people in residential facilities*. Minneapolis: University of Minnesota, Department of Psychoeducational Studies.

Holvoet, J., Guess, D., Mulligan, M., & Brown, F. (1980). The individualized Curriculum Sequencing model (II): A teaching strategy for severely handicapped students. *Journal of the Association for the Severely Handicapped, 5,* 337–351.

Holvoet, J., O'Neill, C., Chazdon, L., Carr, D., & Warner, J. (1983). Hey, do we really have to take data? *Journal of the Association for the Severely Handicapped, 8*(3). 56–70.

Horner, R. D., & Baer, D. M. (1978). Multiple-probe technique: A variation of the multiple baseline. *Journal of Applied Behavior Analysis, 11,* 189–196.

Horner, R. D., & Kelitz, I. (1975). Training mentally retarded adults to brush their teeth. *Journal of Applied Behavior Analysis, 8,* 3301–3319.

Iwata, B. A., Dorsey, M. F., Slifer, K. J., Bauman, K. E., & Richman, G. S. (1982). Toward a functional analysis of self-injury. *Analysis and Intervention in Developmental Disabilities, 2,* 3–20.

Kazdin, A. E. (1980). *Behavior modification in applied settings* (2nd ed.). Homewood, IL: Dorsey Press.

Koop, S., Martin, G., Yu, D., & Suthons, E. (1980). Comparisons of two reinforcement strategies in vocational skill training of mentally retarded persons. *American Journal of Mental Deficiency, 84,* 616–626.

Kramer, L., & Whitehurst, C. (1981). Effects of button features on self-dressing in young retarded children. *Education and Training of the Mentally Retarded, 16,* 277–283.

Kratochwill, T. R. (1978). Foundations of time-series research. In T. R. Kratochwill (Ed.), *Single subject research: Strategies for evaluating change* (pp. 1–100). New York: Academic Press.

Lambert, N., Windmiller, M., Cole, L., & Figueroa, R. (1975). *AAMD Adaptive Behavior Scale: Public school version* (1974 rev.). Washington, DC: American Association on Mental Deficiency.

Lindsley, O. R. (1968). A reliable wrist counter for recording behavioral rates. *Journal of Applied Behavior Analysis, 1,* 77.

Marchetti, A. G., McCartney, J. R., Drain, S., Hooper, M., & Dix, J. (1983). Pedestrian skills training for mentally retarded adults: Comparison of training in two settings. *Mental Retardation, 21,* 107–110.

Murphy, R., Doughty, N., & Nunes, D. (1979). Multielement designs: An alternative to reversal and multiple baseline evaluation strategies. *Mental Retardation, 17,* 23–27.

Neef, N. A., Iwata, B. A., & Page, T. J. (1978). Public transportation training: In vivo versus classroom instruction. *Journal of Applied Behavior Analysis, 11,* 331–344.

Nutter, D., & Reid, D. H. (1978). Teaching retarded women a clothing selection skill using community norms. *Journal of Applied Behavior Analysis, 5,* 475–487.

O'Brien, F., Bugle, C., & Azrin, N. H. (1972). Training and maintaining a retarded child's proper eating. *Journal of Applied Behavior Analysis, 5,* 67–72.

Page, T. J., Iwata, B. A., & Neef, N. A. (1976). Teaching pedestrian skills to retarded persons: Generalizing from the classroom. *Journal of Applied Behavior Analysis, 9,* 433–444.

Parsonson, B. S., & Baer, D. M. (1978). The analysis and presentation of graphic data. In T. R. Kratochwill (Ed.), *Single subject research: Strategies for evaluating change* (pp. 101–166). New York: Academic Press.

Peterson, J., Trecker, N., Egan, I., Fredericks, H. D., & Bunse, C. (1983). *Teaching research assessment procedures for the secondary student with severe handicaps*. Monmouth: Oregon State System of Higher Education.

Quilitch, R. H., & Risley, T. R. (1973). The effects of play materials on social play. *Journal of Applied Behavior Analysis, 6,* 573–578.

Repp, A. C., Roberts, D. M., Slack, D. J., Repp, C. F., & Berkler, M. S. (1976). A comparison of frequency, interval, and time-sampling methods of data collection. *Journal of Applied Behavior Analysis, 9,* 501–508.

Resnick, L. B., Wang, M. C., & Kaplan, J. (1973). Task analysis in curriculum design: A hierarchically sequenced introductory mathematics curriculum. *Journal of Applied Behavior Analysis, 6,* 697–710.

Rusch, F. R., & Kazdin, A. E. (1981). Toward a methodology of withdrawal designs for the assessment of response maintenance. *Journal of Applied Behavior Analysis, 14,* 131–140.

Sailor, W., & Guess, D. (1983). *Severely handicapped students and instructional design*. Boston: Houghton-Mifflin.

Sailor, W., Halvorson, A. Anderson, J., Goetz, L., Gee, K., Doering, K., & Hunt, P. (1986). Community intensive instruction strategies (pp. 251–288). In R. Horner, L. Voeltz, & B. Fredericks (Eds.), *Education of learners with severe handicaps: Exemplary service strategies*. Baltimore: Paul H. Brookes.

Singh, N. N., & Aman, M. G. (1981). Effects of thioridazine dosage on the behavior of severely mentally retarded persons. *American Journal of Mental Deficiency, 85,* 580–587.

Snell, M. E. (1982). Analysis of time delay procedures for teaching daily living skills to retarded adolescents. *Analysis and Intervention in Developmental Disabilities, 2,* 139–155.

Snell, M. E., & Browder, D. M. (1986). Community-referenced instruction: Research and issues. *Journal of the Association for Persons with Severe Handicaps, 11,* 1–11.

Sobsey, D., & Ludlow, B. (1984). Guidelines for setting instructional objectives. *Education and Treatment of Children, 7,* 157–165.

Sowers, J., Rusch, F. R., Connis, R. T., & Cummings, L. T. (1980). Teaching mentally retarded adults to time manage in a vocational setting. *Journal of Applied Behavior Analysis, 13,* 119–128.

Stainback, S., Stainback, W., Wehman, P., & Spagiers, L. (1983). Acquisition and generalization of physical exercises in three profoundly retarded adults. *Journal of the Association for the Severely Handicapped, 8*(2), 47–55.

Stainback, W., & Stainback, S. (1983). A review of research on the educability of profoundly retarded persons. *Education and Training of the Mentally Retarded, 18,* 90–100.

Stokes, T. F., & Baer, D. M. (1977). An implicit technology of generalization. *Journal of Applied Behavior Analysis, 10,* 349–367.

Tawney, J. W., & Gast, D. L. (1984). *Single subject design in special education.* Columbus, OH: Charles E. Merrill.

Thomson, C., Holmberg, M., & Baer, D. M. (1974). A brief report on a comparison of time-sampling procedures. *Journal of Applied Behavior Analysis, 7,* 623–626.

Thurlow, M. L., & Ysseldyke, J. E. (1979). Current assessment and decision making practices in model programs for learning disabled students. *Learning Disability Quarterly, 2,* 15–24.

VanBiervliet, A., Spangler, P. F., & Marshall, A. M. (1981). An ecobehavioral examination of a simple strategy for increasing mealtime language in residential facilities *Journal of Applied Behavior Analysis, 14,* 295–305.

van den Pol, R. A., Iwata, B. A., Ivancic, M. T., Page, T. J., Neef, N. A., & Whitley, F. P. (1981). Teaching the handicapped to eat in public places: Acquisition, generalization and maintenance of restaurant skills. *Journal of Applied Behavior Analysis, 41,* 61–69.

Vincent, L. J., Salisbury, C., Walter, G., Brown, P., Gruenewald, L. J., & Powers, M. (1980). Program development and curriculum development in early childhood/special education: Criteria of the next environment. In W. Sailor, B. Wilcox, & L. Brown (Eds.), *Methods of instruction for severely handicapped students* (pp. 303–328). Baltimore, Paul H. Brookes.

Voeltz, L. M., Wuerch, B. B., & Bockhaut, C. H. (1982). Social validation of leisure activities training with severely handicapped youth. *Journal of the Association for the Severely Handicapped, 7*(4). 3–13.

Wacker, D. P., Berg, W. K., Wiggins, B., Muldoon, M., & Cavanaugh, J. (1985). Evaluation of reinforcer preferences for profoundly handicapped students. *Journal of Applied Behavior Analysis, 18,* 173–178.

White, O. R. (1971). *A glossary of behavioral terminology.* Champaign, IL: Research Press.

White, O. R., & Haring, N. G. (1976). *Exceptional teaching.* Columbus, OH: Charles E. Merrill.

Wilcox, B., & Bellamy, G. T. (1982). *Design of high school programs for severely handicapped students.* Baltimore: Paul H. Brookes.

Wilson, P. G., Reid, D. H., Philips, J. F., & Burgio, L. D. (1984). Normalization of institutional mealtimes for profoundly retarded persons: Effects and noneffects of teaching family style dining. *Journal of Applied Behavior Analysis, 17,* 189–202.

Wolf, M. M., Risley, R., & Mees, H. (1964). Application of operant conditioning procedures to the behavior problems of an autistic child. *Behavior Research and Therapy, 1,* 305–312.

5

Intervention Strategies

Martha E. Snell
University of Virginia

Thomas J. Zirpoli
University of Virginia

In Chapter 4 it was shown that skills taught must be functional and age appropriate. This chapter will discuss other characteristics of instruction that can serve as guidelines for applying intervention strategies both to build skills and to reduce inappropriate behavior.

CHARACTERISTICS OF APPROPRIATE INSTRUCTION

Systematic Instruction

When teaching is systematic, it is a defined, replicable process which reflects currently accepted "best" practices, uses performance data (both probe and instructional) to make modifications, and includes acquisition, proficiency, maintenance, and generalization learning. Though systematic instruction is complex, it appears to be the most certain route to learning for students with severe handicaps. For these students the ultimate goals of learning must be skills that will function despite the passage of time, variations in materials, setting, or the presence of people.

Unfortunately, systematic training is frequently associated with rote training procedures conducted in sterile settings. It is falsely believed that teaching cannot be conducted in a systematic manner while using natural cues within natural environments, and that community instruction cannot or should not be systematic. However, as Ford and Mirenda (1984) emphasize, even in natural settings, students with severe handicaps "must learn to respond to relevant cues and corrections in the midst of the spontaneous happenings and general variability of events that naturally occur in community environments" (p. 85). Thus, systematic instruction may not be confined to any one setting. Rather, it refers to 'state of the art' techniques which are necessary for effective and efficient learning across environments.

Figure 5.1 shows an abbreviated analysis of systematic instruction that includes program development through evaluation. This chapter reviews some intervention strategies found successful with students having severe handicaps

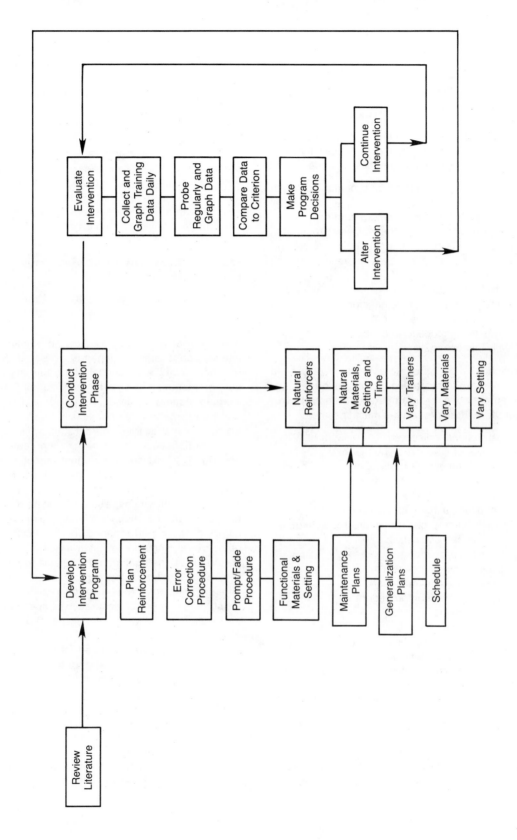

FIGURE 5.1 Implementing and monitoring the IEP

which are thus used to implement and monitor the IEP.

Planning and Writing Programs

Although many teachers feel that paperwork takes too much time, some written documents cannot be ignored. At the very minimum these include

1. Emergency and medical information for each student (Chapter 6);
2. A complete IEP (Chapters 2, 3, and 4);
3. Descriptions of probe and teaching procedures for each objective being taught (Chapters 4 and 5) with notes on changes made in teaching procedures and why;
4. Dated graphs of baseline and probe performance data and training data for each objective being taught (Chapter 4) with changes in instructional procedures denoted in each graph;
5. Daily instructional schedule.

Teaching procedures (lesson plans) also need certain ingredients to be complete guides for implementing a program. As demonstrated in Figure 5.2, these procedures must specify the

1. Instructional objective;
2. Student or students being taught;
3. Training time and setting;
4. Instructor;
5. Date initiated;
6. Instructional materials needed;
7. Baseline and probe procedure and schedule;
8. Student characteristics;
9. Teaching procedures:
   a. Discriminative stimulus,
   b. Prompt/fade methods,
   c. Error correction procedure,
   d. Reinforcers,
   e. Reinforcement schedule;
10. Skill maintenance plan;
11. Skill generalization plan;
12. Data collection sheets (if a task analysis is used to teach the skill these data sheets will detail the task analysis; see Figure 5.3).

If programs are described in this detail, they are more likely to be implemented consistently, regardless of who teaches. For example, since the washing hands program in Figure 5.2 outlines the specific order in which steps will be trained, consistency in the sequence of skill training is ensured. Although this particular program was developed to teach

handwashing to Robert, introduced in Chapter 4, the basic format used in this program may be employed to teach other skills. Moreover, programs that lead to learning can be replicated, whereas those that yield little or no learning can be modified more precisely.

In addition, note in Figure 5.3 that some programming details (cues, delay levels) are also outlined in the handwashing data sheet to remind the teacher of pertinent training information. However, this information does not substitute for a much more detailed training program.

Stages of Learning to Achieve Success in the Community

Research (Ayllon & Azrin, 1964; Csapo, 1981; Smith & Lovitt, 1976; White & Haring, 1976; White & Liberty, 1976) indicates that there is more than one stage of learning, and that the influence of intervention strategies depends on stage. Since one tactic might be influential in one learning stage but not another, it is important to determine which learning stage an individual is in for a particular skill before intervening on that skill.

There are at least four different stages of learning: acquisition, fluency, maintenance, and generalization. During acquisition, the student cannot perform the skill accurately. Initially, the percentages correct are zero, indicating the need to acquire competency in the target skill. Once the student can perform the task correctly, the fluency stage begins. At this point speed of performance (proficiency) is the objective. In addition to accuracy and speed of performance, the student must be able to perform new skills, after formal training is completed, under different conditions. Maintenance training teaches the student to maintain accuracy and speed of performance in the absence of instructional prompts and reinforcement. In generalization training, the objective is accurate and fluent skill performance across materials, settings, and/or trainers.

In many cases, accuracy is the only target in instructional programming; however, through the following example of Robert, the 19-year-old institutionalized student described in Chapter 4, you can see why this goal is not sufficient. While in an institutional setting, Robert learned how to wash the dishes and set them in a dish rack for someone else to dry. He needed to know how to wash the dish because this was one of many skills he would be required to perform in the group home, his future placement. Before initiating training, Robert's teacher conducted a task analysis of the target skill and assessed his ability to wash the dinner dishes. She then initiated an instructional program, carefully measured daily performance, and kept daily records. She determined that three consecutive days of washing dinner dishes without an error would indicate mastery. Finally, after three months of instruction, Robert reached this objective.

Two months later, Robert was scheduled to stay at the group home during a 48-hour evaluation. During this period, he was asked to perform many skills (bedmaking, laundry, washing and drying dishes) while the group home director documented his performance. After the 48-hour evaluation, Robert returned to the institution with a report indicating that his skills were not sufficient for him to live at the group home.

What was the cause of this apparent failure? Simply that the teacher had not completed her instruction. Two very important phases of training were omitted. First, after Robert learned how to wash the dishes, he was no longer required to perform the skill. Thus, the teacher did not ensure that Robert's dishwashing performance was maintained after training. Indeed, when asked to wash the dishes at the group home, Robert had forgotten many of the steps. In addition, Robert did not maintain skill performance under conditions which were different from the training environment. That is, he did not learn how to wash dishes following different cues from different staff, with different materials, in a different kitchen sink. Robert's teacher should have checked with the group home to inquire about their materials and procedures in order to include them in the training program. If Robert's teacher did not know whether Robert might be discharged to a family home or a group home, then generalization could be ensured by training across different teachers and materials. In addition, as the skill was being learned, varying cues (to more general and natural) would also be an important consideration. Perhaps the teacher could ask the group home for the use of their facilities for the purpose of conducting probes and training in a different environment. Even if she does not do this, that particular group home *will be* Robert's future placement. Use of the actual residence would greatly enhance Robert's skill performance there. This is important since a recent court order has mandated that Robert *will reside* in that particular group home within a year. After all,

the goal of generalization training is to ensure skill performance across all relevant environments.

Billingsley (1984) suggests that IEP objectives specify performance of generalization skills. Thus, instructional considerations for generalization of new skills would be integrated into program plans from the *onset* of program development.

Clearly, there are two important reasons for attending to all four stages of learning. First, students with severe handicaps will not succeed in community environments unless they can perform their new skills fluently and as conditions fluctuate naturally over time. Second, tactics selected for instruction must facilitate all stages of learning. Thus, the teacher must consider carefully the materials, prompts, and instructional settings selected. In addition, the effective teacher must look beyond the student's current instructional needs and program for future opportunities.

Natural versus Simulated Training Conditions

Students who have severe handicaps do not easily retain known skills or transfer them to new situations, and the more severe the student's handicaps, the more critical are the problems of maintenance and generalization (Liberty, Haring, & Martin, 1981). If students are taught functional skills, their natural daily use helps to maintain them. If students are taught to perform skills using real materials (wall clocks, groceries in a store) rather than simulated or teacher-made materials (paper plate "clocks," empty food cartons, pictured groceries), they are more likely to be able to perform the skill outside the classroom.

When the training setting itself is natural, skill generalization is even further facilitated. When teaching a student to cross streets, the skill will more likely be usable if instruction takes place on a side street and then is moved to a busier street, as students gain independence. Whereas, simulated training in the classroom presents no dangers to the student, skill generalization is likely to be more difficult since the classroom differs drastically from a real street. Thus, actual use of pedestrian skills *learned* under simulated conditions may ultimately be more dangerous.

If a teacher adopts the principle of teaching in the natural setting whenever possible, then less time will be spent in the classroom. This is especially true as students grow older, and vocational and community skills become priorities (Brown, Shiraga,

---

Program: Handwashing   Date Initiated: _____

Student(s): Robert   Instructor: _____

Training Time(s): Before meals

Setting(s): Classroom restroom, home restroom, and other restrooms in school and community

Instructional Objective: Given a restroom sink, bar of soap, and some paper towels, the student will wash and dry his hands with 100% accuracy, according to the task analysis, during probe conditions for 3 consecutive sessions.

Rationale: Hand washing is important for maintaining hygiene and will help achieve independence in self-care skills across domains. In addition, it is a required skill for admission into community group homes.

Student Characteristics that: (1) Assist—Ambulatory, good gross motor control, normal vision, and good eye-hand coordination. (2) Hinder—Profound mental retardation and poor expressive and receptive language skills.

Baseline/Probe Procedures: Conduct baseline until natural performance of skill is stable. Use a single opportunity procedure. Give instructional cue "Wash your hands" and wait 5 seconds for the initiation of the response. If the student responds correctly, record (+) and continue observing performance of steps in the task analysis. If the student responds incorrectly or no response occurs within the 5-second latency period, record (–) for that step and all following steps. Do not provide reinforcement or assistance during baseline/probe sessions. During training, probe the entire task once weekly at the beginning of the training session. Graph all baseline and probe data.

Behavior Change Procedures: Simultaneously train all steps in the task analysis using a time delay procedure with a physical prompt.
1. Give the instructional cue "Wash your hands."
2. If student initiates an incorrect response, interrupt response immediately in order to prevent error, provide student with verbal prompt for appropriate step ("Turn on the water"), and physical prompt to complete step correctly.
3. Use time delay levels of 0, 2, 4, 6, and 8 seconds. Provide 10 trials per delay level except provide unlimited trials at 8 seconds once this delay level is reached.
4. During the 10 trials at 0 time delay, use physical prompt immediately to guide student through correct response immediately while giving the verbal prompt on each per step in task analysis.
5. During 2-, 4-, 6-, and 8-second time delay, if student performs step correctly during delay period, provide verbal reinforcement for completion of specific step ("Good job turning on the water!").
6. If the student does not respond correctly during the delay period (no response or an incorrect response), provide verbal and physical prompt at the end of the delay to assist student to complete step. Then provide student with appropriate verbal reinforcement.

FIGURE 5.2 A program designed to teach handwashing

York, Kessler, Strohm, Rogan, Sweet, Zanella, VanDeventer, & Loomis, 1982). Realistic training settings available to most schools include cafeterias (eating, social, language and janitorial skills), a variety of bathrooms (self-care and janitorial skills), sidewalks (pedestrian skills and social behaviors), school buses (loading and unloading), and hallways (social interaction and mobility). Thus, it is not essential to leave the school to teach generalization of all skills.

Planning for Interaction with Nonhandicapped Peers

P.L. 94-142 requires education in the least restrictive setting possible, regardless of the degree of handicap. Some researchers have set about to show the positive outcome of interactions between students with severe handicaps and nonhandicapped students. Brinker (1985) found significantly higher rates of social interaction (verbal and non-

7. If student makes three consecutive errors at any delay level, go back to 0 delay. Conduct five trials at each delay level until the original delay level is reached. The original number of trials (10) for each subsequent delay level is then reinstated.

Data Collection Method for: (1) Baseline/probes—Record (+) for an independent correct response or (–) for an incorrect response or no response within the 5-second latency. (2) Intervention—Record (+) for an independent correct response ($\sqrt{}$) for a prompted correct, (–) for an error during the time delay period, (=) for an error made after the prompt, or (0) for no response.

Reinforcement—Type and Schedule: Provide the student with social praise on a continuous schedule, specific to each step in the task analysis. Once a specific step is being correctly performed at an independent level for 5 consecutive trials, discontinue social praise for that step. Continue fading social praise per step in the above manner until praise is given only for task completion.

Generalization Procedures: Teacher and aide will rotate responsibility of training this skill. Parents will also be given a copy of the program and data sheets and taught how to complete this program and collect data. They will be asked to help maintain skill performance in the home. In addition, training will be conducted once per week in different restrooms within the school and once per two weeks in different restrooms outside of school (excluding home) by teacher or aide. Training materials (soap or soap dispenser, faucets, paper towel dispenser) at different training settings should vary, but include materials used within future placements (group home, work site).

Maintenance Procedures: Once the student has reached criterion, provide student with natural reinforcement for washing hands before meals (allowed to secure meal) and natural consequences for not washing hands ("Did you forget to wash before you eat" or "You can't eat until you wash your hands"). Also, task performance will be probed once per month. If the student does not perform task independently, probe again after 24 hours but within one week. If performance is still unacceptable, reintroduce training at step where error occurs at 8-second delay level until program criterion is reached.

Task Analysis for Handwashing:
1. Turn on the water.
2. Wet your hands.
3. Pick up the soap.
4. Rub soap on your other hand.
5. Put the soap down.
6. Rub your hands together.
7. Rinse your hands.
8. Turn off the water.
9. Pick up a paper towel.
10. Dry your palms.
11. Dry the back of your hands.
12. Throw away the paper towel.

verbal) between students having severe handicaps and nonhandicapped peers when the students came from an integrated educational setting than when students came from segregated settings. Voeltz (1980, 1982a) showed that favorable attitude changes in nonhandicapped students attending public schools can result from carefully planned integration of students with severe handicaps. Others currently are investigating the reciprocal effects of integration. For those with handicaps,

these benefits should include more age-appropriate social skills, better skill generalization due to freer movement in the school and community, and ultimately more acceptance in the local community, which would lead to more certain acceptance of residential facilities and would improve job opportunity.

But mere mixing of the students with handicaps with their nonhandicapped peers in school buildings probably will not yield attitude changes as

Student(s): Robert

Teacher: Hawkins

Program Title: Handwashing

Instructional Cue: "Wash your hands"

Target Behavior: Given materials, the student will wash his hands with 100% accuracy, according to the task analysis, during probe conditions for three consecutive sessions.

_X_ Training Data   ___ Baseline/Probe Data

Date:	7/30	7/31	8/1																					
Delay Level:	4	4	4																					
Turn on the water.	O	–	–																					
Wet your hands.	+	+	+																					
Pick up the soap.	o	o	–																					
Rub soap on your other hand.	O	–	+																					
Put the soap down.	+	–	+																					
Rub your hands together.	+	+	+																					
Rinse your hands.	–	–	–																					
Turn off the water.	+	+	+																					
Pick up a paper towel.	O	–	+																					
Dry your palms.	–	–	+																					
Dry the back of your hands.	+	–	+																					
Throw away the paper towel.	–	+	–																					

Materials: Soap, paper towels, sink

Setting: School + community restrooms

Recording Key: (+) for independent correct response, (√) for physically prompted correct, (–) for error during time delay period, (=) for error made after prompt; (0) for no response.

Response Latency: 5 seconds during baseline and probe sessions.

Delay Levels: 0, 2, 4, 6, and 8 seconds

FIGURE 5.3 Task analysis data sheet for washing hands training program

positive as those obtained from structured interactions (Voeltz, 1980; 1982a). Instead, formal and informal efforts must be made to promote integration (Bellamy, Rhodes, Wilcox, Albin, Mank, Boles, Horner, Collins, & Turner, 1984; Brown et al. 1984; Stainback, Stainback, Strathe, & Dedrick, 1983;

Voeltz, 1982a). Hamre-Nietupski and Nietupski (1981) reported on a variety of integration methods used in the Milwaukee Public School to mingle 80 students with severe handicaps into an elementary school, two middle schools, and a high school. These include the following strategies:

1. A faculty member was employed to plan and conduct integration activities.
2. Before integration began, faculty, administrators, and students were given sensitization sessions and information on integration and the severely handicapped.
3. Preintegration planning with faculty and administrators facilitated scheduling, cafeteria and gym use, hall movement, use of home economics area, and other school facilities.
4. Students with severe handicaps were taught the age-appropriate behavior expected of them in the regular school.
5. Parents were included in the planning.
6. Faculty were given sensitization media to use with nonhandicapped students.
7. An "open-door" visitation policy was initiated for special education classrooms.
8. Special education teachers mixed regularly with regular education teachers.
9. Students with severe handicaps were involved in school jobs and participated in school activities.
10. Nonhandicapped students served as partners or tutors of students with handicaps, assisted in conducting sensitization sessions for their peers, and wrote articles for the school paper on integration.

Group versus One-to-One Instruction

One-to-one instruction has not proven to be as beneficial for students with severe handicaps as many had thought. Recent investigations show that groups of 2 to 6 students with moderate to severe handicaps acquire a variety of skills at rates comparable to or even better than one-to-one instruction (Favell, Favell, & McGimsey, 1978; Kohl, Wilcox, & Karlan, 1978; Oliver & Scott, 1981; Oliver, 1983; Storm & Willis, 1978; Westling, Ferrell, & Swenson, 1982). Since group instruction maximizes instructional time, these findings are encouraging.

Furthermore, as emphasized both in the above studies and those by Brown, Holvoet, Guess, and Mulligan (1980), group instruction promotes opportunities not available in one-to-one instruction. These include "(a) increased control of motivational variables; (b) opportunities to facilitate observational learning, peer interaction, and peer communication; and (c) generalization of skills" (p. 353).

In motivation, timeout from reinforcement for a nonresponsive student in a group allows the teacher to work with a responsive student rather than creating a nonproductive time. Learning by observation is more likely to occur when students are intentionally arranged and reinforced in groups. Students, rather than teachers, may present cues and consequences to other students in the group, as the group independence work of Matson and his colleagues in showering (Matson, DiLorenzo, & Esveldt-Dawson, 1981) and family style eating (Matson, Ollendick, & Adkins, 1980) has so successfully demonstrated. Students are actively involved in the learning process even during the "turns" of other students.

Finally, groups create more natural reinforcement conditions. These "natural" conditions include: learning to take turns, to attend to others, to wait for teacher and peer attention, to obtain a turn contingent on responsiveness, to tolerate intermittent attention, and to receive reinforcers and cues from peers rather than only adults. All these conditions approximate the real world and prepare students to perform new skills and behaviors under those conditions.

Even with all the previously mentioned advantages of group instruction, Reid and Favell (1984) cautioned special educators that more research is needed that compares group and one-to-one instruction with students having severe disabilities. Indeed, the decision to use one-to-one or group instruction may depend on the skill to be taught. Although group instruction has been demonstrated to be effective in teaching simple receptive language skills such as pointing to objects (Oliver, 1983), group instruction has not been as effective as one-to-one instruction in teaching self-help with this population (Alberto, Jobes, Sizemore, & Doran, 1980). In addition, Reid and Favell (1984) found that group instruction in vocational and community living skills for students with severe disabilities has not yet been addressed in the literature.

Massed, Distributed, or Spaced Trial Learning

Most teachers use a 15- to 30-minute daily teaching slot to teach each program. During that time, the student has many trials on the same skill. If the skill can be performed in a single discrete trial (requesting or labeling objects, identifying prices, using signs), the repetitions are often *massed,* one right after the other. Group instruction, in which students take rotating turns, may break up these trials (creating a *spaced* trial situation); but because students take turns, no teaching time is lost. When the skills taught are chained (multiple-step sequences), as are most functional skills such as ironing and folding clothes, then performance of the skill is actually a *distributed* performance of a series of responses rather than massed practice on a single response. Other possibilities for distributed trials include teaching one student a cluster of related discrete behaviors (select a game, sign to request, play game) or teaching in a group but involving students in cue and reinforcer presentation during the turns of other students, thus eliminating the "wait" time.

A review of trial scheduling by Mulligan, Guess, Holvoet, and Brown (1980) emphasizes the *distributed* trial schedule as a more efficient use of time than either massed or spaced trials. Evidence available thus far suggests the following practices:

1. Use distributed trials rather than spaced to minimize "down time";
2. Use massed trials initially to obtain speedier acquisition or to correct errors, and change to distributed trials to maintain and generalize skills.

Massed trials should be used mainly when learning time is critical whereas most instruction should distribute trials across tasks, to yield fewer actual trials required for learning each separate skill; however, not all tasks lend themselves to distributed-trial training. In some instances it may be natural to repeat a single task, such as buttoning a row of buttons on a shirt and eating one bite after another. In these cases, massed trial training may be appropriate (Bambara & Warren, 1985).

Serial or Concurrent Training

Skills can be taught in *serial training order* (one at a time) to a set criterion, adding a second, then mixing the two; adding a third, then mixing the three; and so on. However, a number of researchers have made a good case for *concurrent task sequencing,* in which two or more skills are taught at the same time (Holvoet, Guess, Mulligan, & Brown, 1980; Panyan & Hall, 1978; Waldo, Guess, & Flanagan, 1982). Using this approach, signs would be taught in groups of two to four, with multiple trials on each sign, rotating across the group in a mixed fashion. After the student learns the first group of signs to a set criteria, a second group is introduced along with review trials on the first group. Two advantages of *concurrent task sequencing* over serial training is that instruction periods are more interesting to both student and teacher and may more readily be integrated into the daily routine (Dunlap & Koegel, 1980).

INTERVENTION STRATEGIES AIMED AT INCREASING BEHAVIOR

When a behavior increases because specific consequences (reinforcers) consistently follow instances of that behavior in a planned manner—but are not available in the absence of that behavior—a reinforcement contingency is in operation. This interdependent or contingent arrangement between behaviors and consequences lets us change behaviors purposefully. This is commonly called *contingency management.* Positive reinforcement occurs when the presentation of rewarding consequences (called *positive reinforcers*), made contingent upon a behavior, leads to an increase in the performance of that behavior. To reinforce, thus, means to strengthen behavior by increasing its frequency, duration, or intensity.

Types of Reinforcement

Although reinforcers have unlimited range and vary from tangible items and activities to abstract thoughts of self-approval, all reinforcers are either *primary* (unlearned or unconditioned) or *secondary* (learned or conditioned). The first category includes the "universal" or automatic reinforcers to which everyone responds (although not continuously) without instruction. Primary reinforcers for someone who is feeling hungry, thirsty, or cold include food, drink, and warmth respectively.

Secondary Reinforcers
Secondary reinforcers have developed reinforcing value through conditioning. Secondary reinforcers begin as neutral pairings with already existing (primary or other secondary) reinforcers. Eventually these events take on reinforcing value of themselves when, for example, students learn to enjoy playing with toys, riding a bike, listening to music, receiving pay for work, receiving praise, and accomplishing a goal.

Generalized Reinforcers

Generalized reinforcers are highly effective secondary reinforcers that acquire their reinforcing power by association with many other primary and secondary reinforcers. Money, affection, attention, and approval by others all fit this caregory because each requires learning and is associated with many additional reinforcers (money purchases food, entrance to various activities, clothes, toys).

Generalized reinforcers commonly used in educational settings include attention, approval, money, and tokens. A token system or economy is analogous to a currency-payment system, except that the value of a token is limited to the immediate setting and is controlled by the person who implements the system. Tokens come in many forms (pennies, slips of specially marked paper, or simply checkmarks on an "official" checksheet). As with other reinforcers, tokens are given, contingent upon behaviors and, in turn, are exchangeable for the "purchase" of back-up primary and secondary reinforcers. Tokens have advantages over many other reinforcers because they may be distributed conveniently to students and, because of their exchange power, are durable in reinforcing quality. Unlike wages, tokens generally have no value outside the intervention program, and the exchange value within the program may be easily and quickly adjusted. Tokens have been used in combination with praise as reinforcers to modify a wide variety of behaviors in the moderately and severely handicapped (Kazdin & Bootzin, 1972): math skills (Baker, Stanish, & Fraser, 1972; Dalton, Rubino, & Hislop, 1973), language skills (Baer & Guess, 1973; Baker et al., 1972), bedmaking (Snell, 1982), and social skills (Bates, 1980).

Most token economies have a specific and additive exchange value, much like our own currency system. Although counting may be taught with a token system, many of our students may be unprepared to learn counting and the concept of purchasing. In these cases, the usual token economy may be modified. First, and most common, is the use of counters. The student places earned pennies on a card with circles or squares or on a wooden block with coin-sized holes. When all the spaces are filled with coins, the student can purchase a reinforcer. In other cases a token economy based on varying, rather than specific, values may be used (Kent, 1974). With varying value systems, tokens are given, contingent upon specific behavior(s); however, they can be ex- changed for back-up reinforcers either singly or, more often, in varying amounts whenever the teacher feels a more tangible reinforcer is necessary to maintain the generalized reinforcing value of the tokens. The individual is "token trained" before implementing such a system. This type of token system has been used effectively with learners who were nonverbal and had profound retardation (Snell, 1979). In addition, Kent-Udolf and Sherman (1983) state that if a student is participating in a "comprehensive token economy" during the day, tokens used to reinforce task performance during a specific training program should be different from those used in the token economy (p. 17).

The following steps comprise token training and can establish an association between tokens and their back-up reinforcers.

1. Identify a behavior or class of behaviors easily performed by the individual (imitation of movements, following simple commands with gestures like, "Come Here").
2. Prepare a choice of known back-up reinforcers (arranged on a tray or cupcake pan), a token container (a coin holder or a one-pound coffee can), and a set of at least 30 tokens at a training table.
3. Ask the individual to perform the behavior, and
   a. Reinforce immediately following the behavior with a single token placed in the individual's hand and with enthusiastic praise; or
   b. Prompt if the behavior is not forthcoming, and then reinforce with a token and praise immediately following the behavior.
4. Immediately hold out a hand to collect the token (with prompting, if necessary) and present the reinforcer tray. Prompt the student to select one reinforcer.
5. Repeat this cycle (request for behavior, praise and token reinforcement, and immediate exchange) until the individual, without any prompts, begins to associate tokens and token exchange. If the student reaches for the token after a response, in order to speed up the exchange process, increase the exchange schedule gradually from one token to four or five tokens before the exchange.
6. While remaining at four or five tokens, introduce the token container to facilitate the collection and exchange process. Next, drop tokens into the can and show the student how to lift and empty the contents at exchange time.

7. Increase the exchange ratio gradually over the remainder of the token-training session, which should not last beyond 15 to 20 minutes.
8. At this point, tokens can be used as reinforcement during actual teaching sessions. Initially, a brief review (a few immediate or low-ratio exchanges) may be necessary to remind the student of the tokens' exchange value.

Tokens may be used to help teach a new skill if praise or other more natural reinforcers are not effective. However, because token systems described here are not found in the real world, students must be weaned from them as the skill reaches mastery. This process, called *fading*, is discussed in a later section of this chapter.

Selection of Positive Reinforcers

Particular items or events themselves do not serve as positive reinforcers for everyone. Reinforcers are defined by their effect upon an individual's behavior. If the object or event, when made contingent upon a behavior, does not cause an increase in that behavior, it is not a positive reinforcer. Because of past experiences or personal preference, what is reinforcing to one individual may not be to others. Not all students like M&M's, and neither do all people with handicaps find social praise to be reinforcing. In addition, secondary reinforcers, such as money and praise, are effective only if the learner knows that they are associated with primary or unlearned reinforcers, such as food is to a hungry person.

Potential reinforcers should not be determined by guessing. This information may be gained with the following general techniques:

1. Ask the student directly about his likes and dislikes. Direct questioning, although often effective with verbal individuals, is ineffective with those who have severe handicaps because it relies on communication.
2. Ask others who are familiar with the student's likes and dislikes for a list of potential reforcers, and be sure to verify their responses with one of the other three methods. Although both questioning methods may seem to be efficient, they can yield limited information: what is reinforcing in one setting may be impractical, ineffective, or unavailable for use in another.
3. Observe the student over a period of days in the natural setting, and list observed reinforcing events. If carried out systematically for long enough, direct observation of his preferences (for foods, toys, songs, people, activities, clothes) probably yields the most accurate list of reinforcers. A teacher may use the measurement procedures described in Chapter 4 to record these preferences (time spent in various activities, frequency of selecting various toys). In addition, Wuerch and Voeltz (1982) suggest using picture choices to determine preferred leisure activities.
4. Structure the environment to observe a reinforcement period. As with natural observations, structured observations do not depend upon language skills, an advantage with many students having severe handicaps. Structured observations let a teacher observe a student's reaction to potential reinforcers that are normally unavailable. In a structured observation, a student is first allowed to sample briefly a small group of similar items (foods, toys) or events suitable to his chronological age (listening to a tape recorder, looking at magazines, being pushed in a wagon). Then he is given the entire group of potential reinforcers, and the frequency or duration of choices is recorded. After a group of possible reinforcers is sampled and the free-choice observation is recorded, other groups may be observed similarly. Wacker, Berg, Wiggins, Muldoon, and Cavanaugh (1985) trained six students (13 to 18 years of age) with profound handicaps to use simple motoric responses (raise arm or head) to activate microswitches in order to indicate a preference between two reinforcers (toys). They found that four of the six students demonstrated preferences between two toys as measured by the frequency and duration of "interaction" with each device.

Besides arranging reinforcers from most to least preferred, they also can be arranged along a continuum from those perceived by our culture as less natural or immature (unlearned, primary) to those perceived as more natural or mature (conditioned, secondary, and generalized). At more mature levels of reinforcement, the student has learned to expect less immediate and less frequent reinforcement. The following *reinforcer hierarchy* is arranged from primary to secondary and generalized reinforcers:

1. Food;
2. Toys and leisure activities;

3. Tokens or payment with back-up reinforcers from categories 1 and 2;
4. Parental, peer, and teacher approval;
5. Self-praise for accomplishment of a goal.

Within the level of reinforcement preferred, the teacher should select actual reinforcers that are appropriate to the individual's chronological age. For example, if observation indicates that an adolescent boy likes food and preschool toys best, the teacher probably would want to

1. Reinforce with food less often and eventually not at all when other reinforcers are established.
2. Select suitable "toys" or leisure activities that are liked and easily used (tape-recorded music, magazines); avoid the use of preschool toy reinforcers if you can substitute others that are not age bound or food.
3. Reinforce with praise before every instance of tangible reinforcement, while gradually reducing tangible reinforcement.
4. Teach the use of new, potentially reinforcing, age-appropriate activities (the Simon electronic game by Milton Bradley, velcro dart boards, pinball, and video games) which would expand the group of activity reinforcers and replace food.
5. Reduce the frequency of activity reinforcers through intermittent reinforcement or by teaching the use of tokens.

Teachers and parents must reduce excessive use of reinforcers, eliminate inappropriate reinforcers, and encourage students to function at more natural levels of reinforcement suitable to their chronological age.

In addition to being age appropriate, selected reinforcers should be as natural as possible. *Natural reinforcers* approximate the type of response the learner is most likely to receive from others or the environment, contingent upon his/her behaviors. When learning to ask for objects during expressive communication training, the most natural reinforcer is the object asked for since this will be the most natural response to the learner's behavior. Teaching the student to ask for "juice" and reinforcing a correct response with a cookie is inappropriate. Of course, the appropriate response would be to give him some juice after each correct request for juice, and research shows that this stimulus-specific reinforcement *is* more effective than reinforcement by "random" reinforcers or those unrelated to

the skill (Litt & Schreibman, 1981; Williams, Koegel, & Egel, 1981).

Teaching within natural settings and times promotes the use of natural reinforcers. It is easier to reinforce requests for food and drink when teaching these language skills during meals rather than the traditional isolated setting when the student may not be hungry.

Selection of reinforcers is a critical part of program development. Failure to use one or more of the above considerations in the selection process could seriously decrease teaching effectiveness and may cost the student a lot of learning time later on.

Reinforcement Schedules

Schedules of reinforcement indicate how many and which responses are reinforced. Thus, they affect the response pattern. Reinforcement schedule is the A (arrangement) element in Lindsley's (1964) operant framework: $E^a \rightarrow B \rightarrow A \rightarrow E^c$. Reinforcement may be given according to the number of responses performed (ratio schedules) or the passage of time in relation to the performance (interval schedules). Both types of schedules may be based either upon absolute numbers of responses or amounts of time (fixed schedules). The presentation of one reinforcer for every occurrence of the target behavior is a fixed ratio schedule of one (FR:1). This is commonly called *continuous reinforcement*. All other schedules may be generally called *intermittent reinforcement*. An FR:5 would be a fixed pattern of reinforcement for every fifth response; in a VR:5 schedule, reinforcement would be variable rather than regularly applied to an average of every fifth response. This VR:5 pattern might consist of three, seven, two or eight occurrences of a target behavior followed by reinforcement. In interval schedules, the first target response occurring after a regular time period of so many seconds or minutes (fixed interval or FI) or an average period (variable interval or VI) is reinforced.

In many classrooms, reinforcement schedules are time based (at the end of a class period), and teacher-dispensed social reinforcers may be as meager as one per minute. In a classroom of 30, this converts to a schedule of one reinforcement every half-hour, a rather sparse schedule. Classroom reinforcement schedules are more often variable than fixed. Teachers may provide reinforcement when they judge enough work has been done or sufficient time has passed. Because *sufficient* and *enough* tend to vary from one day to the next, a variable schedule results. If the students are unaware of the reinforcement schedule, they probably will not learn as predictably as if schedules are planned. For example, students can learn to count money faster if they use fixed-ratio schedules that are adjusted as they improve (initially one reinforcement per correct counting, later one reinforcement every other counting, then one reinforcement every correct third, fifth, and so on).

Differential reinforcement of high rates of behavior (DRH) is a useful schedule that also requires the teacher to identify a target rate of performance that may be achieved gradually. *Differential reinforcement of low rates of behavior* (DRL) complements DRH. DRL is used to reduce frequent misbehaviors. Due to the powerful influence of reinforcement schedules upon behavior, some related considerations on scheduling reinforcement should be applied when arranging the learning conditions for instruction.

1. Reinforcers should be available only when they are contingent upon the performance of appropriate behavior or a realistic approximation of that behavior.
2. During the acquisition stage of learning, every instance of behavior should be encouraged by the continuous provision of small amounts of contingent reinforcement (small bits of food plus praise, a few seconds of music plus praise) rather than larger amounts less often. Continuous reinforcement yields a high rate of performance.
3. After a higher rate of behavior has been established (late in acquisition or in the fluency or maintenance stage), reinforcers should be provided on an intermittent schedule. That is, the reinforcement schedule should be thinned slowly so that more behavior is required for each reinforcement. This will "strengthen" the behavior; the individual will learn to tolerate periods of nonreinforcement rather than to abruptly "give up" and stop responding when reinforcement is not forthcoming.
4. Variable schedules generally produce more even patterns of behavior than fixed schedules because the individual cannot predict the occasions for reinforcement.

5. Reinforcers should be arranged in order from the most preferred/most powerful to the least preferred/least powerful. This allows the teacher to match reinforcers with the effort required by the student to perform a particular behavior and to reserve the most powerful reinforcers for more "difficult" teaching programs (behaviors on which the student, after a lot of instruction, has shown minimal progress).

OTHER CONSIDERATIONS

Immediacy of Reinforcement

An additional consideration of effective positive reinforcement, which affects the degree of behavior change, is "timing." The relationship is direct: the more immediately the reinforcers are presented after the behavior, the greater is their effect. Immediacy promotes the association of the reinforcer with performance of the target behavior (an understanding of the contingency used by the teacher). Immediacy is especially important for children and adults with limited language skills. They are less able to learn contingencies from verbal contracts such as, "After you perform a certain behavior, you may have a particular reinforcer". Immediacy also decreases the chance of accidentally reinforcing behaviors not targeted for positive reinforcement.

Immediacy is more essential during acquisition than during the later stages of learning, when the behavior is performed more reliably. Further, after a behavior is in the fluency or maintenance stage, the student should be taught to tolerate delays as well as less reinforcement.

Satiation

Satiation results from the overuse of a reinforcer. It is quite possible to tire of an event so that it is no longer reinforcing, especially if it is given too frequently or in large amounts. If too much of an edible reinforcer is offered too frequently, the reinforcing effect may be lost. After extensive involvement with certain toys or activities, the novelty lessens and the desired behavior is no longer effectively reinforced. This same outcome occurs when reinforcers are given freely or noncontingently (unlimited access to certain events devalues their contingent effect on the target behavior).

Because of satiation, a teacher must preserve the "special" quality of objects or activities selected as reinforcers. The use of intermittent reinforcement helps avoid satiation because it uses fewer reinforcers for more behavior. In addition, whenever feasible, a variety of natural reinforcers should be used instead of a single reinforcer. When a student learns to request "juice," different types of juice should be used as natural reinforcers. Whenever, as in this case, different kinds of natural reinforcers are available, the student should, when feasible, select the reinforcer.

Negative Reinforcement

Negative reinforcement is frequently confused with punishment; however, the intent of negative reinforcement, like positive reinforcement, is to *increase* targeted behavior. The intent of punishment, to be discussed later in this chapter, is to *decrease* targeted behavior.

Positive reinforcement involves "providing" a stimulus, contingent upon a desired behavior, with the intent of increasing the desired behavior. Negative reinforcement involves the "removal" of an "aversive" stimulus, contingent upon a desired behavior. If a student's behavior is inappropriate during a training session, the teacher makes him stand in a corner to decrease the inappropriate behavior. If she succeeds, then this method may be referred to as "punishment." But this strategy does not work if the student continues to act inappropriately while standing in the corner. If the teacher makes the removal of this aversive stimuli (standing in the corner) contingent upon appropriate behavior, she is using "negative reinforcement" to increase appropriate behavior while the student stands in the corner. If the student returns to his seat and demonstrates 5 minutes of appropriate behavior, then he receives praise from the teacher to increase appropriate behavior during training sessions. This is an example of "positive reinforcement."

Obviously, positive reinforcement is the preferred method for increasing appropriate behavior and, as an indirect result, decreasing inappropriate behavior. Furthermore, negative reinforcement as a planned classroom intervention is not common although many times teachers negatively reinforce behaviors without being aware of it. The teacher who yells at students until they are quiet removes the aversive stimuli (teacher yelling) contingent upon appropriate student behavior. If appropriate student

behavior increases as a result, then the students behavior has been negatively reinforced. But yelling is seldom conducted in a systematic manner and is not likely to be successful in decreasing inappropriate behavior. A plan to reinforce appropriate behavior systematically and either ignore or punish inappropriate behavior should prove more effective.

ANTECEDENT TECHNIQUES

In Chapter 4 we discussed the ABC arrangement of antecedent conditions, behavior, and consequences. Intervention strategies used to build skills usually involve careful programming not only of consequences for various responses, but also of stimuli that precede performance of the target behavior.

Discriminative Stimulus

Learning is a process of understanding how to respond to specific and changing signals or cues. Students who have learned to ask for things they want at meals find that sitting (a) in the presence of food, (b) at the dining room table, and (c) when they are hungry, all serve as discriminative stimuli for the behavior of saying "Want milk" (or some other food). This behavior in the presence of these stimuli has been reinforced long enough to have been learned. Discriminative stimuli (more commonly referred to as S^Ds) may include the natural cues of the setting, materials, time of day, weather, or the person's physical state (empty stomach, full bladder). They may also include a teacher's request and various prompts provided to get students responding.

In other words, some stimuli are "known" S^Ds for some individuals, but other S^Ds have not yet been discriminated. When first teaching students to clean a bathroom mirror, the instructional cue or S^D of "clean the mirror" may not be meaningful, and may not result in a response. The stimulus "clean the mirror" has not become associated with the behavior of mirror cleaning, so it is a to-be-learned S^D. However, if the teacher provides some meaningful S^Ds, such as a model of the first step plus directions (teacher says "Get the glass cleaner" and then reaches into the cupboard and removes the spray bottle), students can perform the first step in the task. If similar meaningful S^Ds are provided over time for all the remaining steps in the task, subsequently, students may respond independently to the S^D provided by the request ("clean the mirror") and the situation.

Eventually students must be able to respond in the presence of natural cues rather than teacher-applied stimuli (see Falvey, Brown, Lyon, Baumgart, & Schroeder, 1980; Ford & Mirenda, 1984 for more comment). They should respond by cleaning mirrors that are dirty rather than only when requested by the teacher. Similarly, students should initiate requests for materials rather than responding only after the teacher asks "What do you want?". To have natural S^Ds control a behavior, a teacher must incorporate them into the instructional plan. Teaching in natural settings and at natural times lets the teacher use environmental cues. Initially, however, for most tasks, the instructional cues constitute one or more of the following to-be-learned S^Ds:

1. Should be stated in terms easily understood by the student;
2. Should be phrased as commands, not questions ("Tie your shoes");
3. Should be provided only when the student is attending;
4. Should be given only once at the beginning of the task rather than repeated over and over (prompts, which will be described next, are used when the student is unable to follow the instructional cue);
5. Should reflect the conditions stated in the instructional objective ("Given the request 'Clean the mirror,' a dirty mirror and a cabinet with cleaning materials inside...");
6. May include the presentation of materials (cleaning materials handed to the student) or may require the student to locate them;
7. Should include the natural cues provided by realistic settings (real bathrooms with mirrors) and materials (dirty mirrors and actual glass cleaner).

Stimulus and Response Prompting

Behavior must occur before it can be shaped. To ensure that a new behavior will occur, various types of assistance can be given prior to the response to increase the likelihood that the learner will perform the desired behavior or a better approximation. This assistance (directions, models, cues, or physical prompts) primes the desired behavior, hence Skinner's term *response priming*.

The term *prompting* often is used interchangeably with priming. Prompts may be associated primarily with the task stimuli, materials or the response. The former, *stimulus prompts*, would include color coding various parts of bicycle brake pieces to make the assembly task easier (Gold, 1972). The workers simply color matched the parts to be joined. The use of a picture to prompt reading is another example. *Response prompts* include verbal instructions, gestures or pointing movements, models, and physical assists.

Prompts help students make responses they do not know, which can be reinforced and eventually learned; however, prompts are generally introduced only to "get the behavior going" and must be removed so that the student learns to respond independently. Wolery and Gast (1984) state that the goal of response and stimulus prompts is to "gradually shift stimulus control to naturally occurring stimuli without errors or with a minimum of errors" (p. 66). Thus stimulus and response prompts are only temporary means to obtain behavior during acquisition. Eventually, this guidance must be eliminated so that stimulus control transfers from the priming stimuli to the appropriate natural discriminative stimuli (S^Ds), those stimuli in the presence of which the target behavior is reinforced.

Stimulus and response prompts can be illustrated using Robert's washing hands program. If Robert is always reminded to dry his hands after washing, he will not learn to perform the skill independently. Instead, he will learn to wait for the training prompt ("Dry your hands") before performing the task. Teachers must fade prompt supports gradually so students can practice independent performance and gain mastery. Knowing when and how to help or withhold help constitutes effective teaching.

Falvey et al. (1980) suggest that most teaching prompts are artificial. Artificial prompts are more likely to foster excessive dependence on a trainer. Directing the learner's attention toward the cues in the natural setting ultimately promotes self-prompting and self-correction. When instruction takes place in unnatural settings, instructional procedures are not likely to focus on natural cues to correct or prompt the student. If Robert's hand washing program is never conducted in a bathroom, and he doesn't have opportunities to wash his hands in a real sink, he may not learn to respond to natural prompts presented by water faucets indicating that he needs to turn the water on or off, however, less "natural" procedures (verbal instructions) can be successfully applied to teach a new skill in a natural setting.

Natural procedures appear to be used less often, however, because they are less systematic: the trainer has less control over their presentation. Another problem with using natural procedures is the wide variety of cues present across every step in a task-analyzed skill. A prompt hierarchy, such as system of least intrusive prompts (which will be discussed next), is easily used across steps in a task: first wait for independent performance, then give verbal instructions; next, if needed, give a model plus verbal prompts; finally, if still necessary, give physical assistance along with instructions. When natural cues are used, the teacher must vary the prompts (or correction procedure) by focusing the learner's attention on cues related to each step in a task, making instruction much more complex. Clearly more research is needed to develop and test natural prompt and correction procedures in order to resolve the above difficulties since independent performance in natural settings is the only defensible goal of teaching.

Teachers still may promote the presence of natural cues during teaching by

1. Carefully validating each task analysis, including all necessary steps and selecting appropriate methods for completing that task (Chapter 4);
2. Matching verbal prompts with the actual terminology used in the setting where the skill ultimately will be performed (Liberty et al., 1981);
3. Emphasizing the type of prompt (models, verbal directions, pictorial instruction) most prevalent in the natural setting (watching others use dryers at a laundromat);
4. Using natural prompts and correct procedures whenever possible, especially during the fluency, maintenance, and generalization phases when performance is more complete;
5. Teaching students in the later phases of learning to ask for assistance when no prompts are forthcoming.

Types of Instructional Prompts

Verbal directions offered before and during the performance of a behavior often serve as guides for responding. When a teacher asks a student to select seven forks and knives from a tray of silverware by saying, "Count out forks and knives,"

many different behaviors are being requested. The S^Ds, which come to control the individual's behavior, also demand action, number selection, and object discrimination. Initially, the teacher may need to give additional directions that prompt the correct behavior. If the student begins to count out spoons, the teacher might repeat the word "forks." If the student miscounts, the teacher might say the numerical sequence for the student; if he hesitates, the teacher could prompt him to "count faster." Above all, the student must understand the directions. Sometimes the teacher must speak slowly, use simple word combinations and vocabulary, and even use accompanying gestures, signs, or cues.

Instructions provided for moderately and severely handicapped individuals may take a variety of modes and formats: verbal, verbal with gestures, verbal with models or demonstrations, a single picture or a sequentially arranged set of pictures, verbal with partial or complete physical assistance. Pictures promote independence from the teacher and create opportunities to practice the more cognitively demanding skills of picture comprehension. Of course, the student must make the picture-object associations before illustrated instructions will be appropriate.

Cuvo and Davis (1980) list the following three methods of verbal instruction used successfully with moderately to severely handicapped students:

1. Stating or re-stating the response (reminding a student to, "Set the table")'
2. Asking questions (asking a student who has hesitated 5 seconds "What is next?");
3. Procedural description (for the first step in table wiping, "Go get the sponge").

Procedural descriptions, cited above, effectively prompt students who understand simple verbal instructions. Once a student has partially or completely mastered a task, questioning prompts may act as less intrusive, but still very helpful, prompts. Initially, verbal instructions that simply state the response are used as the to-be-learned S^D for the entire task ("Cross the street when it's safe"); however, once the skill has been mastered, students should be taught to respond to natural S^Ds (the need to get to the other side of a street). At these times, if a student hesitates, stating the response serves as a prompt.

The teacher's instructions must match certain aspects of the student's language abilities. These include the number of instructions given simultaneously, their length, complexity, and whether there are accompanying gestures and demonstrations.

Modeling consists of demonstrating part or all of the desired behavior to the student who imitates or repeats the action immediately. The modeled response may be performed by the teacher or peers, or through models or illustrations (copying a printed name card, using a coin equivalency card to make change, following a series of pictures to make ice tea or soup).

Since the student must see the demonstration in order to imitate, visual-attending skills are important and imitative skills are essential. The effectiveness of modeling as a prompt with students having severe handicaps is increased when

1. The student's attention is gained prior to presenting the model. If he attends part of the time, verbal or physical prompts may be used along with shaping to improve attending behavior.
2. The student readily imitates the model (movements or sounds) and this imitative behavior is under stimulus control.
   a. If the student imitates part of the time, physical prompts may be used after the model is presented in conjunction with shaping to encourage better imitations.
   b. If the student does not imitate or imitates only infrequently, imitation skills may be taught before using modeling as a method to prompt behavior.
3. If direction of the response is important, the orientation of the viewed model should be the same as it will be when the student performs the skill (Parton, 1976).
4. The length or complexity of the modeled response or the chain of responses should be short and simple. When errors occur in a student's imitations, the task analysis of the skill may need revision.

Cuing a behavior, at times similar to modeling, is different from manual guidance in that cuing directs the learner's attention to the teaching materials without physical contact. In a multiple-choice task, a student is taught to associate a coin set with a particular price card made from vending machine photos, in the presence of the instructional cue (S^D), "Which coins go with this price?" The correct choice may be cued in the following ways:

1. Movement cues—Pointing to, touching, or tapping beside the correct choice;
2. Position cues—Placing the correct choice closest to the student;
3. Redundancy cues—Pairing one or more dimensions of color, shape, size, or position (as in position cues) with the correct choice (color: a white piece of paper is always placed under the correct choice while other choices all have red paper or perhaps no paper; size: the correct choice is always physically larger than the other choices as with some coins).

In an effort to learn more about cuing, Gold (1972) compared the effectiveness of color-redundancy cuing with form cuing for individuals having severe handicaps who were learning to assemble bicycle brakes in a sheltered workshop. Color cues were placed on one side of every part so that when assembled correctly the colored part faced the worker. The presence of color cues led to significantly faster acquisition and longer retention of the task than did cues provided only by the form or shape of the individual brake parts.

A fourth type of cuing, "match-to-sample," is similar to modeling. When prompting by means of match-to-sample, the teacher simply gives the instruction (S^D) ("Which coins go with this price," displays vending machine photo of 45 cents) and cues the correct response by showing the student a sample of the correct choice (two quarters). The student merely must select the matching coins from a group of mixed coins. Although movement cues rely on attending and imitation skills to prompt a response, redundancy and match-to-sample cues depend on the ability to discriminate between dimensions such as color, size, and shape. In addition, the ability to use match-to-sample cues requires the learner to compare stimuli. If a student has difficulty discriminating between different samples of a single dimension (different shapes of the same color and size), additional redundant cues should help (Fisher & Zeaman, 1973; Zeaman & House, 1963). That is, a person will learn to select a standard screw driver with a large, silver handle more quickly when shown with a phillip's screw driver having a small, black handle. The difference between the choices is made more obvious by redundant stimuli. Likewise, difficulties in matching may be overcome by offering fewer choices and, more importantly, by making all the nonmatching choices differ widely from the stimulus object.

Prompt Systems and Hierarchies

Prompts may be used singularly, in combination, or as part of a hierarchy. If they are arranged in order of complexity and rely on prerequisite skills, manual guidance is the easiest because it relies on cooperation and minimal attention; however, the learner performs very little of the response alone. Manual guidance would be followed in decreasing intrusiveness and increasing difficulty by cuing (movement cues, position cues, and match-to-sample cues), modeling, verbal direction (oral, then written), and naturally occurring prompts and cues.

Prompt hierarchies consist of a sequence of two or more "levels" of prompts arranged and used in a "least-to-more" intrusive order or "most-to-least" intrusive order. Lent and McLean (1976) have used a prompt hierarchy in which a teacher advances to increasing levels of instructional assistance depending on the student's ability to respond in a task. Since their first use of this least-to-most system, many other researchers have applied this three-level hierarchy of (a) verbal instructions, (b) verbal instruction plus a model, and (c) verbal instruction plus physical assistance. As shown in Figure 5.4, the system of least intrusive prompts is applied one level at a time until the student is able to complete the response successfully. A short latency period (usually from 3 to 5 seconds) is allowed for the response after the instructional cue is presented, as well as after each successive prompt. If no response occurs during this time, the more intrusive prompt is provided. If an error is made, it is interrupted immediately, and the next level of prompt is given. A correct response from the student is usually followed by verbal reinforcement regardless of the prompt level.

Tucker and Berry (1980) used this least-prompt system to teach six severely handicapped students to put on their hearing aids. The "least-prompts" method also has been used to teach students having moderate to profound handicaps the following skills: janitorial (Cuvo, Leaf, & Borakove, 1978), cooking (Johnson & Cuvo, 1981), sewing and mending (Cronin & Cuvo, 1979), reach-grasp (Correa, Poulson, & Salzberg, 1984), and basic photography (Giangreco, 1983).

The least prompt system of verbal, model, and physical prompts lends itself well to a variety of tasks (and will be referred to in later chapters of this book); however, it must be matched carefully to the student's skills. Students who do not imitate will

generally be unable to use the first two prompt levels. For these students, variations using two or three simpler prompts may be employed. Those students who do not respond well to verbal cues but *do* imitate or follow gestural prompts (such as pointing) might be given prompts in the following order:

1. Model plus verbal (or gestural plus verbal depending upon the behavior being prompted),
2. Partial physical plus verbal (less than half of the behavior prompted),
3. Full physical plus verbal (the entire behavior prompted).

It would be possible to omit a partial physical and use only two prompt levels. Students unskilled in using model prompts might be given two or three levels of physical plus verbal prompts ranging from partial to complete assists. The same general procedures used with the verbal-gestural-physical prompt hierarchy and shown in Figure 5.4 would be applied with these simpler systems. That is, teachers should always allow an independent response first, interrupt errors with the next level of prompt, and wait the latency period before and between prompts.

Cuvo et al. (1978) used two interesting variations of this prompting system when teaching janitorial tasks. On an extra difficult few steps, a most-to-least order of prompts was used; thus, physical plus verbal prompts were used first. At some point, the trainer switched to the model-plus-verbal prompt; later a verbal prompt was used, followed by no prompts at all. (It also would be possible to task analyze these difficult steps, creating more steps, and continue the least-to-most intrusive system.)

A second novel variation of this prompt system by Cuvo et al. (1978) included two even more minimal prompts during maintenance training, after the student had met acquisition criteria. Before using the verbal-model-physical sequence, a teacher would try a confirmation prompt followed by a nonspecific-question prompt. Confirmation consisted of saying "yes" to a student who had begun a step in the task. If this did not work or there was no opportunity to use a confirmation prompt, then the student would be asked, "What's next?" Remaining prompts in the hierarchy would be used only if necessary. The complete sequence would include the following prompts:

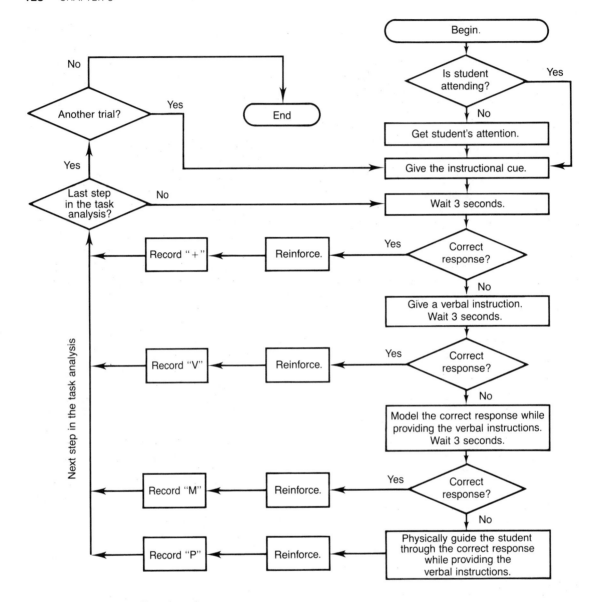

FIGURE 5.4 System of least intrusive prompts

Source: Credit for this illustration must be given to Joan Miller, University of Virginia, 1981.

1. Confirmation,
2. Nonspecific question ("What's next?"),
3. Verbal,
4. Verbal plus model,
5. Verbal plus physical assistance.

Not all research on prompt strategies is in agreement. Some researchers feel that a least-to-most prompt system, described above, promotes dependence upon prompts. For example, Glendenning, Adams, and Sternberg (1983) compared different prompt sequences while teaching a 48-step, string-tying task analysis to students with moderate and severe handicaps. They found that a verbal + full physical assistance prompt was significantly more effective than verbal + lessening amounts of physical assistance, verbal prompts only, or physical prompts only in promoting self-initiated responses.

Thus, they advocate the most-to-least intrusive prompt sequence and warn that the least-to-most intrusive prompt system may be reinforcing students for "being passive because by not responding, they get a greater and greater amount of help until finally the task is accomplished" (p. 325). However, these findings may be a result of the specific task, which was very long.

A system of least prompts appears to work with learners because of reinforcer density (the sooner they respond correctly the sooner they obtain reinforcement). But, it also is true that this effect, for some students, may be overshadowed if physical assistance from the teacher seems more "reinforcing" than the reinforcement intentionally given by the teacher.

Graduated guidance is a second response-prompt system. Unlike the system of least intrusive prompts, graduated guidance uses most intrusive prompts first followed by less-to-least intrusive prompts. A few variations of graduated guidance have been described to teach eating (Azrin & Armstrong, 1973; O'Brien & Azrin, 1972; Richman, Sonderby, & Kahn, 1980; Stimbert, Minor, & McCoy, 1977); dressing (Azrin, Schaeffer, & Wesolowski, 1976; Foxx, 1981); aspects of toileting (Azrin & Foxx, 1971); and physical fitness exercises (Moon, Renzaglia, Ruth, & Talarico, 1981).

The most frequently applied version of graduated guidance uses "constant contact" physical assistance, which is applied by the teacher to the student first at the hand, then the wrist, the forearm, the elbow, and finally the shoulder. This order gradually reduces the physical prompt. Initially, the student is guided through the steps of the task—the teacher's hand over the student's hand—with *only as much physical assistance as is necessary* for the student to complete the task. Over successive trials, the teacher reduces the physical assistance by shifting her hand to the student's wrist. The teacher will return her hand to the student's hand when more control is necessary or if errors or long hesitations occur.

Graduated guidance moves the student forward through all the steps in the task, like most applications of a least intrusive prompt system; however, both prompt systems can be applied singly to one step in a task, as in backward chaining. The two systems differ in the fading procedure. In least prompts, because the student is given an opportunity to respond on every step with increasing assistance, he is generally given only as much

prompting as needed. Over successive trials, the student uses less and less assistance as learning occurs. In graduated guidance, the teacher must gauge the reduction in physical assistance mainly on the moment-to-moment, subtle pressure cues between her guiding hands and the student's. Although it might be possible to systematize fading by designating a certain number of trials at each level of prompt (20 trials at hand, 20 at wrist, 20 at forearm), this schedule is difficult to estimate, and there is no research to substantiate this use of graduated guidance.

A second type of graduated guidance (Foxx, 1981) uses the following progression of physical prompts:

1. *Full graduated guidance*—Teacher holds her hand over the student's hand using as much physical guidance as is needed to guide him through the steps in the task.
2. *Partial graduated guidance*—Teacher maintains only thumb and forefinger contact with the student's hand, requiring, for example, that he grasp a spoon alone.
3. *Shadowing*—Teacher keeps a hand within one inch of the student's hand but does not actually touch it.

Moon et al. (1981) used three levels of graduated guidance to teach severely handicapped young adults sit-ups, push-ups, sit, bob and reach, chin-ups, and squat-thrust exercises. The levels all included (a) a verbal plus a full hand prompt (molding of the hand around the body part involved in the movement), (b) fingertip guidance using little force, and (c) a verbal prompt alone.

In most forms of graduated guidance, verbal reinforcement is given continuously for steps completed. In many applications, an edible or an activity reinforcer is provided at the end of the chain. Whenever the student resists or tries to pull away from the physical guidance, the trainer holds his resistive hand in place until he relaxes. No movement is prompted by the trainer until the student stops "fighting" the physical assistance.

Physical guidance may be a mild irritant to the student (Foxx, 1981) who, in order to avoid being guided, may attempt independently to imitate movement on various steps in the chain. It is critical for the teacher to be sensitive to any pressure cues indicating the student is performing more independently; these cues should result in immediate reduction of physical assistance.

Fading of Prompts

Fading is the *gradual* changing of prompts and reinforcers controlling a student's performance to less intrusive and more natural prompts and reinforcers, without reducing student performance. Fading may also include reducing the *number* of prompts provided (demonstration and instructions faded to just instructions).

Although it is important to transfer behavior control from training prompts to natural cues quickly, removal of prompts too quickly is certain to hamper successful transition. Fading is most successful when it is planned and completed systematically.

Moving Through a Prompt Hierarchy

In a system of least prompts and more structured forms of graduated guidance, prompts are faded naturally. On every teaching trial, the student has an opportunity to perform without assistance and then with increasing amounts of help. The sooner he responds correctly, the sooner he receives reinforcement, which contributes to fading. At times, especially in difficult steps and after lapses in training sessions, students will require more assistance. This apparent backtracking should be only temporary, until he returns to earlier performance levels. Sometimes, however, learning can be assisted by reanalyzing a difficult step and breaking it down further. It may even be necessary to select an alternative method and eliminate the difficult step altogether.

At times the teacher may want to provide more intrusive reinforcement for responses made independently than for prompted responses. This strategy, which can apply to any prompt procedure, is called *differential reinforcement*. It may be used most effectively when students seem to rely on verbal prompts or less intrusive prompts. Differential reinforcement motivates students who have already made progress to perform without prompts. However, those who appear to rely on physical prompts more than a week or two may need more reinforcement, a simplification of difficult steps, or more training each day rather than differential reinforcement. In addition, the student may be engaging in behavior that is incompatible with learning (Etzel & LeBlanc, 1979). For example, poor visual attention and excessive self-stimulation may need to be modified as part of the skill instruction procedure.

Reducing Saliency of Stimulus Prompts

Stimulus prompts such as color or pictures are more commonly faded by gradually reducing their visibility. If words are taught by pairing a picture cue with each word, the teacher can use three to six successively less obvious variations of the picture (as shown in Figure 5.5) while providing perhaps five trials with each of the levels of picture fading. It is critical that the student attend to the S^D (in this case, the word) rather than simply the picture. Otherwise the S^D will be meaningless when the picture is finally faded. Because they require a variety of materials (six different versions of each picture prompt), procedures like these fading stimulus prompts are less common in classrooms than response prompts.

Time Delay

Progressive time delay procedures are another means of gradually fading prompts (Touchette, 1971). In time delay, the prompt is delayed by gradually increasing increments of time, allowing the learner to anticipate the correct response without assistance. Although less frequently used than other prompt-fading procedures, time delay has been applied to teach learners with severe handicaps to follow instructions (Striefel, Bryan, & Aikins, 1974; Striefel, Wetherby, & Karlan, 1976); to read manual signs (Smeets & Striefel, 1976a) and to sign (Browder, Morris, & Snell, 1981; Kleinert & Gast, 1982; Smeets & Striefel, 1976b; Stremel-Campbell, Cantrell, & Halle, 1977); to use a vending machine (Browder, Snell, & Ambrogio, 1984); to partially participate in toothbrushing (Houghton, Snell, & Lewis, 1985); to request lunch (Halle, Marshall, & Spradlin, 1979) and other activities (Halle, Baer, & Spradlin, 1981); and to make beds (Snell, 1982).

In sign training the teacher must first decide whether physical or model prompts are best since a single prompt is used more easily with time delay; however, a hierarchy of prompts may be used, as illustrated in Browder, Morris, and Snell, 1981. If the student is a good imitator, a model is best, with physical assistance used only to correct errors; but if he cannot accurately reproduce a modeled sign, a physical prompt is appropriate.

After selecting functional signs and reinforcers, the teacher identifies the amounts or levels of time delay in seconds. As described in more detail in Snell and Gast (1981), there are many possibilities;

FIGURE 5.5   Fading levels for a picture cue

Source: *Teaching Sight Words to the Moderately and Severely Mentally Retarded* by D. M. Browder, 1981, Unpublished doctoral dissertation, University of Virginia. Used with permission.

however, a no-delay or 0-seconds level is always used initially with the prompt given immediately after the S^D. Next, gradually increased increments of time are introduced, delaying the prompt and giving the student more time to respond independently. Delay levels may consist of 0, 2, 4, 6, and 8 seconds; 0, 1, 2, 3, . . . 8 seconds; 0, 4 seconds; or other combinations. It is important to end with a delay period long enough for the student to respond (some motorically impaired learners take longer than 8 seconds).

Once delay levels are chosen, the teacher may specify the number of trials to be presented out at each level. A wide variety of tasks have been taught using time delay and the number of trials per delay level have varied. Other teachers may wish to be less structured and advance to the next level after several successive prompted corrects and backtrack to the previous level whenever an error is made during the delay period.

As illustrated in Figure 5.6, time delay requires rather different teacher responses from other

instructional procedures; however, it is an effective procedure to teach students with a minimum of errors. Research with a variety of skills indicates that students having moderate to severe handicaps correctly anticipated the delayed prompt (responded correctly before the prompt) in 2 to 8 seconds. At the longest delay level, unlimited trials are often allowed, although students may learn the behavior before getting to this level.

STRATEGIES INVOLVING CONSEQUENCES

Shaping

Shaping and chaining are two major reinforcement strategies used to build new behaviors and to improve or expand present behaviors. Both involve providing reinforcement for improvements in behavior or for specific amounts of behavior. The teacher must focus carefully on the learner's responses and make instant judgments about a response in comparison to earlier occurrences and the targeted criterion level.

Shaping consists of reinforcing successive approximations or improved "attempts" at the target response. When a speech therapist teaches a student to say a new word, she reinforces any close approximation to the correct articulation of the word as a stepping stone to the appropriate sound. When a physical therapist teaches weight bearing, she may begin by reinforcing 3 seconds of the correct response, then 6, then 10, and so on. Although the target response may be 5 minutes of weight bearing, since the student has never used his legs to support his weight, using the 5-minute criterion at the start may cause both pain and physical harm. In addition, since student failure, in this case, is almost guaranteed at first, the student would have little opportunity to receive reinforcement and may become frustrated with failure. Knowing which response classes represent earlier approximations of a target behavior is part of the skill of shaping.

A closer examination of shaping reveals that extinction compliments reinforcement. As each closer approximation of the desired response is reinforced, the earlier, less precise approximations are no longer reinforced. Once the student has mastered weight bearing for 3 seconds and is working toward the 6-second objective, the physical

Time Delay

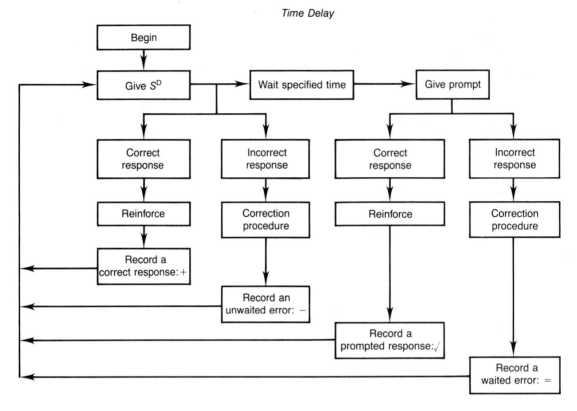

FIGURE 5.6 Flow chart illustrating time delay procedure

Source: Credit for this illustration must be given to Sherri Owen, University of Virginia, 1981.

therapist no longer reinforces him after 3 seconds. He must now perform at a closer approximation of the desired response (6 seconds of weight bearing) in order to be rewarded.

Response Chaining

At times called *forward* and *backward shaping,* *response chaining* differs from shaping. Whereas shaping is used to develop new behaviors, chaining is used (usually with shaping) to "link together" a series of functionally related responses. Most skills actually consist of a chain of smaller component responses: self-care behaviors (toileting, eating), daily living skills (vacuuming a room, grocery shopping), and vocational tasks (parts assembly, "punching in" at work). In order to learn a chain or sequence of responses, the student must attend to the stimuli in each successive step as the S^D for the next step in the chain.

To teach these chains, the response is first divided into an ordered list of separate "teachable" behaviors, usually through task analysis. Since chaining may proceed forward or backward across the sequence of behaviors, the teacher must select the order in which the components will be taught. The number of responses a chain is divided into will vary with different levels of beginning skills. It must meet the following general criteria:

1. Each step must be observable and easily measured.
2. The chain must be divided finely enough so that the addition of each successive step does not result in excess errors.
3. There must not be too many steps, or instruction becomes inefficient. If chaining proceeds forward, one of at least three of the following methods may be used:
   a. All steps may be taught simultaneously in their natural order of performance,

b. Steps may be taught one at a time in a forward progression, or

c. A long chain may be divided into several shorter chains, and each shorter chain taught in a forward, all-steps-at-a-time, manner.

When teaching a student to perform one step at a time, the first unmastered step in the chain is identified through baseline observations. Instruction begins at that point, with his performing earlier steps independently. If the baseline performance is inconsistent and only some nonsequential steps are mastered, instruction should start with the first step. It may be necessary to prompt him or to shape this first behavior until no errors occur. Successive approximations are reinforced until he can adequately perform the first teaching step without help. Then he can be taught to perform the next step by shaping or prompting, while correctly completing the preceding, already mastered step. The student is reinforced only after completion of the teaching step. He may or may not be assisted through all the remaining steps in the chain but is not expected to perform independently until each step in the sequence is mastered. If, for example, shoe tying is to be taught through forward chaining, the first skill in the sequence to be mastered is the half-knot (or just crossing the two shoelaces). Later, the bow loop and remaining steps in the chain are taught.

In backward chaining, teaching generally begins with the last step and progresses toward the beginning of the chain. Sometimes baseline performance indicates that the student has mastered one or more steps at the end of the chain. Teaching, therefore, would begin on the step immediately before the mastered step. With some behaviors that need to be performed in entirety as part of the daily routine (eating, toileting, dressing), he actually may be guided through the preceding steps in the chain until the teaching step is reached. At other times, he may be started at the teaching step. Then, by shaping or prompting, this unmastered step is taught. Reinforcement is given only after the last step in the chain is completed. When teaching steps that precede the last one, the teacher may prompt the student to perform the target step but expect him to perform all remaining steps in the chain without assistance before he receives reinforcement. Eventually, as the remaining steps are learned and added in a backward order, the entire chain is performed, and the learner is reinforced.

It is possible to use forward and backward chaining together when teaching certain skills or particular students, including students whose baseline performance shows scattered success across the chain (the ability to perform more than a single step or a single group of steps). Both chaining procedures may also be combined when a skill's primary behavior occurs in the middle of a longer chain rather than at its end. In the basic self-care skills of eating with a spoon and elimination on the toilet, both the eating and toileting responses are preceded and followed by preparatory or related behaviors. The first step in teaching spoon use probably would be for the student to eat the food from the spoon after it is guided to his lips since this step involves natural reinforcement. Teaching could proceed both backward and then forward from this step.

Teaching the total task (all steps simultaneously) can be a more natural and faster method of instruction than training one step at a time (Azrin et al., 1976; Cuvo et al., 1978; Johnson & Cuvo, 1981). In comparisons of total task and backward chaining procedures, Martin, Koop, and Turner (1981) and Spooner (1984) found the total task method more effective in training assembly skills to students with severe handicaps. In addition, Walls, Dowler, Haught, and Lawlocki (1984) found this procedure "as effective in reducing errors as forward chaining when it is coupled with a progressive delay of prompts" (p. 284). However, some researchers (Bellamy, Horner, & Inman, 1979) suggest that difficult steps (vocational assembly tasks) should be taught in isolation until an accuracy rate of 80% is achieved and then the responses chained together. As stated by Spooner and Spooner (1984) after a review of chaining techniques, "In the final analysis, it may be that different learners do better with different procedures, and that when different tasks are used (e.g., dressing vs. vocational) different results are obtainable" (p. 123).

Error Correction Procedures

In order to maintain a reinforcing environment for learning over time, it is important to minimize the potential for student errors. When teaching new skills, teachers should prevent or reduce the potential for error "from the outset of the learning process" (LeBlanc & Ruggles, 1982, p. 130). When errors do occur, however, the teacher can interrupt and correct them in several ways.

One way to correct error is to repeat the S^D immediately, giving the student another opportunity to perform but increasing the amount of assistance provided, as in the system of least intrusive prompts. This could include verbal instructions, a model, a gestural cue, or physical assistance. For example:

While teaching a student to eat with a spoon, the teacher says, "Pick up the spoon." After he does not respond, she repeats the verbal cue and points to spoon. He touches the spoon but does not grasp it. This time, she says, "Pick up the spoon like this," while physically guiding the student to grasp the spoon correctly. She releases his hand and he continues the response. She responds, "Right, you picked up the spoon."

A second error correction procedure is to interrupt the error and follow it immediately with the least assistance needed to obtain a correct response and not repeating the S^D. For example:

A student is learning to set the table while a teacher prompts him through the steps using a system of least prompts. On the first step (go to the kitchen) a verbal prompt is required. He errs on the second step (open the dish cupboard) by opening the wrong cupboard. She sees this error develop and stops his hand as he tries to open the wrong cupboard. Next she immediately gives the verbal prompt, "Open the dish cupboard," and waits 5 seconds. He does not respond and looks confused. She then repeats the verbal cue while modeling which cupboard to open. He responds correctly and is praised.

A third approach to correcting errors is to interrupt the error and follow it immediately with a verbal prompt and repeated practice, with physical assistance, on the incorrect step. Using the vocational assembly task illustrated next, Close, Irvin, Prehm, and Taylor (1978) demonstrated a repeated practice procedure to be more effective than a single verbal-physical prompt or a verbal-gestural correction.

A student is learning a nut and bolt assembly task which requires (a) picking up an axle nut from one compartment in the left hand, (b) rotating the nut with the right hand until the raised side faces up, (c) picking up an axle post from the other compartment with the right hand, (d) inserting it into the flat side of the nut, and (e) placing the completed assembly between the compartments. When he forgets to rotate the nut, the teacher says, "Flat side up," and physically prompts the correct response, saying, "Good." Then the nut is replaced in the bit, flat side up, and the teacher helps him pick it up.

The teacher then prompts, "Flat side in," and physically assists the correct positioning of the nut in his hand. After five repetitions of this correction procedure in steps (a) and (b), the nut and bolt are assembled with physical assistance given only as needed. (pp. 272–273)

Once the student has learned all, or most, of the skill and moved to the fluency or maintenance stage, slightly different error correction procedures may be used. Because he is more proficient at the skill, errors are infrequent and may be caused by distraction or carelessness rather than not knowing what to do. In these cases, one of the following procedures may be chosen:

1. The student who makes an error or hesitates may be given a brief time (10 to 15 seconds) to self-correct. Some errors, if uninterrupted, will provide *natural correction cues*. If the student learning to set the table was allowed to open the wrong cupboard, the absence of dishes in the opened cupboard would provide a natural cue that he made an error. He may then correct his own error and complete the correct response without prompts from the teacher. If a correction is not forthcoming, then one of the other procedures can be tried.
2. The error might be followed by a mild reprimand ("No," or "That's not right") plus a request to try the step again. If a second error results, some assistance would be given.
3. A minimal prompt ("What's next?") or verbal rehearsal of the last step correctly performed ("You just finished getting the plates, now what's next?") may be applied as soon as the error is stopped. If the student stops before a step is complete, the teacher may confirm and urge him to continue ("That's right, keep going.").
4. The teacher may provide a mildly aversive statement ("No, that's not how you empty the trash"), possibly mention that the reinforcement will be withheld ("You can't be paid this time"), and physically assist the student through the step. This procedure should always be followed by an opportunity to repeat the task with reinforcement. If the same error is repeated for two to four consecutive trials, the teacher may want to reinstitute the prompt procedure.

There are other possible methods of correcting errors; however, to be effective, error correction procedures must

1. Be matched to the learner's present level of functioning,
2. Be applied immediately and consistently,
3. Provide enough help to correct the error quickly if in acquisition or to help the learner discriminate that correct responses are followed by reinforcement while errors are not (if in fluency or maintenance),
4. Be suited in their amount of assistance and aversiveness (if any) to the student's stage of learning for that task, and
5. Be followed by additional opportunities to respond on the same task or step.

INTERVENTION STRATEGIES AIMED AT DECREASING INAPPROPRIATE BEHAVIOR

Is There Really a Problem?

As coherently illustrated by Evans and Meyer (1985) and Gaylord-Ross (1980) in their models for the treatment of aberrant behavior, careful assessment of the so-called "behavior problem" must precede any intervention. Teachers must not bias their perceptions of students' behavior based on labels or word of mouth. This danger was demonstrated by Evans and Meyer (1985) when they asked teachers to view a videotape of a child participating in a training session. The teachers were given one of two different background reports on the child and asked to design an IEP for the child. Although all the teachers viewed the same video of the child, the experimenters found that "teachers were much more likely to focus on excess behavior if the child was described as having several excess behaviors" than if the same child was described in more positive terms (p. 26).

Gaylord-Ross (1980) suggests that the teacher and parent first answer the following four questions and decide whether the problem behavior is severe or obtrusive enough to require intervention.

1. Is the behavior causing physical harm to the student or others?
2. Is the behavior disrupting overall classroom instruction to a significant degree?
3. Does the behavior appear to be triggering collateral, emotional reactions (excessive crying or screaming, extreme withdrawal)?
4. Is the behavior so contextually inappropriate that it is leading to social exclusion and a limitation in the number of places and experiences in which the student can engage? (p. 140)

If any of these questions is answered yes, baseline data must be collected to further substantiate the problem.* If the data do verify that a problem exists, Gaylord-Ross (1980) suggests that before planning an intervention, illnesses or other medical explanations for the behaviors should be considered. Chronic ear infections, fevers, and changes in medications can result in visible behavioral changes. If medical factors can be identified as causing the problem, a corresponding medical intervention is the logical solution.

If medical causes are ruled out as the problem's source, then a behavioral analysis is continued until causative or maintaining factors are identified and corresponding intervention procedures selected. The best way to decrease a behavior problem is to increase one or more replacement skills. While this strategy may not be the easiest, it is a far better choice than attempting to eliminate the inappropriate behavior, for at least four reasons. First, students having severe handicaps often have too few appropriate behaviors, and just eliminating inappropriate behaviors without building new skills does not remediate the problem over the long term. Further, as Iwata, Dorsey, Slifer, Bauman, and Richman (1982) and Donnellan, Mirenda, Mesaros, and Fassbender (1984) have shown, inappropriate behavior often serves a function for persons with severe handicaps. Iwata and his colleagues found that self-injurious behavior (SIB) was inadvertantly maintained by school personnel and others. Whenever it occurred one or a combination of things happened to the student: (a) demands were briefly terminated, (b) teacher attention was provided (even if in the form of a reprimand), or (c) sensory stimulation was provided by the SIB when the student had nothing else to do. Donnellan, Mirenda, Mesaros, and Fassbender (1984) also described incidents showing that inappropriate behaviors (yelling in shopping malls and aggression during a task) served a communication function (to say "I'm overwhelmed" and "This task is too difficult") for two students.

Other reasons for attacking behavior problems by building appropriate skills include the human rights of the individual in view of the intrusive and ethically questionable use of most punishment.

---

*See chapter 4

Finally, there is serious question about the generality of behavior supression obtained through punitive means (Axelrod & Apsche, 1983). (See Chapter 11 for more information.) the student's IEP would therefore reflect those new skills prioritized to replace that student's severe deficits instead of many behavior reduction objectives (Evans & Meyer, 1985).

The Least Restrictive Alternative

Withholding reinforcement (extinction), reinforcing other behaviors, removing reinforcers and presenting aversives (punishment) are four different classes of consequences for inappropriate behavior to reduce or eliminate it. For many severely handicapped students, the antecedent application of classroom rules may also prevent undesirable behavior from occurring. Environmental modifications (changes in temperature, noise, amount of space available, number of activities or toys available) may make a strong, positive impact upon aberrant behavior. Finally, improvements in a student's curriculum may be needed to reduce inappropriate behaviors. Tasks that are too simple, involve too much free time, or provide inadequate variety or reinforcement appear to yield more inappropriate behavior. Dunlap and Koegel (1980) found that a "varied task" resulted in better student responding than a "constant task." Moreover, the students were judged to be "more enthusiastic, interested, happier, and better behaved during the varied task sessions" (p. 619).

These intervention procedures vary considerably in complexity, ease of implementation, and suitability to various students, behaviors, and environments. They cannot be selected haphazardly or based on personal preference. Procedures selected to reduce inappropriate behavior must meet the following four criteria:

1. Proven effective with the moderately and severely handicapped,
2. Matched to the likely causative or maintaining factors,
3. Simplest to use but still effective,
4. Least restrictive (least intrusive or punitive) and most socially accepted procedure.

If intervention procedures have been carefully chosen, planned, and applied, but the program still fails to reduce the inappropriate behavior, modifications must be made. The four criteria are still applied. The student's existing program first should be examined closely for logical improvements. If this alternative is unsuccessful, then more intrusive procedures may be used, but *only after* the input and approval of the student's parents, program administrators and review of teachers.

The "Fair Pair"

Although strengthening or shaping desirable behaviors is clearly the goal of education, teachers are also concerned with the reduction of behaviors that upset classroom routine. The "fair pair" rule (White & Haring, 1976) states that when it is necessary to decrease an undesirable behavior, teachers should select one or more desirable behaviors to increase at the same time. In addition, these selected behaviors should provide a more functional substitute for the inappropriate behavior (learning functional ways of expressing needs to replace tantrums) (Donnellan et al., 1984; Iwata et al., 1982). This procedure results in a repertoire of appropriate behaviors, providing the student with alternative responses rather than merely eliminating behavior. More opportunities to reinforce students positively are also created.

The desirable half of the "fair pair" of behaviors may be the behavior opposite of that to be eliminated (out-of-seat and in-seat, incorrect labels and correct labels). However, if this rule of thumb produces the absence of behavior (no crying and excessive crying), a better strategy might be to select a behavior found to be important to the individual through an ecological inventory that can be accelerated but cannot occur at the same time as the undesirable behavior. Depending upon the child's abilities, the positive half of "excessive crying" could be "requests items by name"; "hand-waving and staring" could be replaced with "eye contact with teacher and objects presented by the teacher." Teachers or parents using these procedures are differentially reinforcing behaviors or teaching new skills that are incompatible with the problem behavior while ignoring (or placing on extinction) the problem behavior. This procedure is called *differential reinforcement of incompatible behavior* or DRI. It is especially useful when the average amount of reinforcement the student obtains is fairly low and the behavior problem is either reinforcing in itself (stereotypic behavior) or results in attention from others (Gaylord-Ross, 1980).

A second procedure similar to DRI is DRO or *differential reinforcement of other behavior*. In this procedure the student is reinforced for performing other appropriate behavior that may not necessarily be incompatible with the problem behavior but provides another way to get attention. When a 5 year old sucks his thumb, it may not only damage future tooth formation but also have a negative effect on social acceptance. Giving the child praise or tokens to exchange for favorite activities when he is not sucking his thumb is a DRO strategy while teaching him to play table games involving the use of his hands is a DRI strategy.

Curriculum Modifications

An important set of variables that may cause or maintain behavior problems are related to instructional curriculum. Possible modifications in curriculum should be investigated if inappropriate behavior increases when certain instructional tasks are scheduled (Gaylord-Ross, 1980). Iwata et al. (1982) state that efforts to decrease or terminate demands may be a function of inappropriate behavior exhibited during tasks; however, teachers should not eliminate important learning tasks because inappropriate behavior increases when they are scheduled. Indeed, this action will surely reinforce the inappropriate behavior. Thus, it is necessary for teachers to analyze each behavior problem in order to identify their antecedents and consequences *before* deciding on a treatment method. There are at least four types of curriculum problems.

Task Is Too Difficult

A student making many errors is obtaining little or no reinforcement. If the task is a high priority (toilet training), and there are no medical or physical reasons to explain the high error rate (the student is older than two years and does not have damage to the nerves controlling the bladder and bowel sphincters), then the task should be retained and the teaching procedure changed. The task analysis may need more steps, prompts may be added or modified, and possibly more time could be spent daily on the task (a 30 minute toileting schedule instead of a two-hour schedule). Crist, Walls, and Haught (1984) found that students with mental retardation, especially severe cases, made less errors during training (assembly tasks) when the task analysis included 28 small steps compared to 7 or 14 larger steps. They concluded that "By breaking a task into fine steps, the subject was forced to attend to each physical movement or response . . ." (p. 72). Thus, in some cases, the task

itself may be too difficult and should be preceded by easier skills.

Task Is Too Simple

In some cases, skills students have already mastered are still actively "taught" by teachers rather than maintained through natural use. Boredom or unmotivated performance often results in behavior problems during instruction.

Task Is Not Reinforcing to the Student

A student may have a long history of failure on a given task and come to dislike it although it is still unmastered. Reinforcers may need to be changed completely or perhaps a new reinforcer hierarchy needs to be developed. A choice of reinforcers could be offered to avoid satiation. In addition, it may be more functional for the student to learn the task in a community setting where there may be more motivation to participate in training. Learning to order a hamburger and french fries at McDonald's may increase the student's enthusiasm and responsiveness. If he continues to respond below unacceptable levels, it may be best to ask first whether the skill's mastery will contribute to his independence more than other skills. If it cannot be dropped altogether, it may be best to postpone work on it since the task is associated with failure.

There Is Little or No Instruction

The obvious solution to excessive "down time" is to develop and implement a functional curriculum. No matter how handicapped a student may be, boredom is likely to cause inappropriate behavior.

Classroom Environment

Gaylord-Ross (1980) provides good arguments for examining the effect of ecological variables on a student's misbehavior. Factors such as amount of space per student (Rago, Parker, & Clelend, 1978), heat, light, noise, and interesting activities (Dunlap & Koegel, 1980), or objects available (Iwata et al., 1982) may influence behavior. When the living environment of five women with profound retardation in an austere institutional setting (many residents and few engaging objects) was enriched with activities, manipulable objects, and differential reinforcement for engaging with these items, the women exhibited more adaptive behavior and far less maladaptive behavior (Horner, 1980).

Rules

The use of rules may also help set the atmosphere of a teaching setting and provide an effective means of behavior management. The first and most essential guide for developing rules is that rules must describe behavior in ways understandable to the students. In many situations, pictures and simple wording yield comprehensible rules; at other times, role playing will result in more complete understanding. Invariably, however, it is the consistent enforcement of the rules that leads to this comprehension. In groups of students whose comprehension skills are only in the beginning stages, the use of simply stated rules is still justifiable for two reasons. First, even in early stages of language development, the student learns to associate an adult's facial expressions, tone of voice, and some words like "No!" or "Good!" with punishing or reinforcing consequences. Second, the rules may increase the teacher's consistency in applying various consequences to behavior.

In addition to putting rules in comprehensible terms, (a) rules should be stated positively whenever possible, so that appropriate behavior is described; (b) the number of rules should be limited so they can be enforced; and (c) the teacher should review new classroom rules daily until infractions decrease. Rules must be periodically revised if they are to remain relevant to the school situation, curriculum, and individuals within the class. Whenever possible, class members should help formulate and revise rules.

If a rule is stated positively ("We eat with a spoon"), the teacher should attempt to reinforce those who follow the rule, restating the rule as they are praised ("Good eating with a spoon!"). If positively stated rules are broken, the teacher may choose either to punish the behavior ("No, use the spoon!" with removal of food for 30 seconds) or to ignore it. If a rule is stated negatively ("No swearing in class"), infractions cannot be ignored but must be punished in some way, or the rule becomes meaningless. However, with both types of rules, whenever an individual is punished for an infraction, the teacher should ask him to restate the rule before punishment. Prompts should be provided if he cannot state the rule. This verbal rehearsal of rules before punishment will help him understand the contingency. The eventual self-rehearsal of rules is critical in self-control. Finally, if punishment is used, the teacher must determine the consequences in advance and when they will be applied in relation to rule infractions (whether a single warning will be given before punishment is applied or whether the child will be punished after the first infraction). The discussion of punishment provided in the next section should aid in answering these questions.

Classroom Schedule

Another important variable contributing to the classroom environment is the classroom schedule. The purpose of the schedule is threefold. First, it provides the teacher with an additional planning tool during curriculum development. Given the teacher's classroom resources (materials and equipment), space, support services (number of aides, professional therapist), and number of students, only a limited number of skills may be taught in the classroom at any given time. These considerations help the teacher prioritize the list of skills for which students need training. Second, the classroom schedule is a critical organizational tool because of the variety of training needed by students with severe handicaps in a single classroom and the number of resource personnel necessary to assist the teacher. In addition, an organized pattern or flow of classroom activities will positively affect the attitudes and behaviors of both teachers and students. Third, and finally, the classroom schedule provides additional documentation of the frequency and duration of classroom training, meals, toileting schedules, recreational activities, field trips, therapy sessions, and "down time." A quick review of the classroom schedule can provide teachers, parents, and other observers with important information regarding the services provided to students. The elementary classroom schedule provided in Figure 5.7 clearly outlines the types of services received by students (6 to 10 years of age) having severe handicaps. It also provides the teacher with an overview of student training and an opportunity to evaluate programming.

1. Q: Are skills taught during natural times of the day?
   A: Yes, handwashing is taught before meals and putting on coat is taught before going outside.
2. Q: Are skills taught across teachers and aides?
   A: Yes, training is rotated whenever possible.
3. Q: Are resource services integrated into classroom activities?

Teacher: Hawkins (T)
Aide: Garris (A)
Others: Smith, physical therapist (PT)   Houch, recreation therapist (RT)   Sanford, speech therapist (ST)   Peer Volunteer (PV)

Date Begun: 8/1/85
Day of Week: Monday

Student Name	9:00	9:30	10:00	10:30	11:00	12:00	1:00	1:30	2:00	2:30	3:00
John	T-3a	T-18 / T-2	T-6	RT-8	RT-15/16 / RT 1/M	→	RT-10 / RT-8 / RT-2	A-6	T-16	T-17b	A-8b
Mike	A-3a / A-2	A-17b	T-6	RT-8	RT-15/16 / RT-11	→	RT-10 / RT-8 / RT-2	A-6	T-16	T-17b	A-3b
Jill	T-3a	T-18 / T-2	A-5	RT-3	A-11 / A-9a	T-13	T-9b / T-10	T-5	T-16	T-17b	A-3b
Jeremy	A-3a / A-2	A-17a	ST-7	RT-8	T-11 / A-9a	T-13	T-10 / T-2	PV-3b / PV-19			→
Tommy	T-3a	T-18 / T-1	T-6	RT-8	A-18 / A-1 / A-11	A-12M	T-10 / T-18 / T-1	A-6	PT-4	A-17a	A-1 / A-3b
Jason	A-3a / A-1	PT-4 / A-17a	A-5	RT-8	T-1 / T-11	A-12M	A-10 / A-1	ST-5	A-5	A-17a	T-1
Chris	T-3a / T-1	A-17a	A-5	RT-8	T-1 / T-11	A-12 / A-14	T-10	PT-4	A-5	A-17a	A-1 / A-2b
Melissa	A-3a / A-1	PT-4	T-1 / A-5	RT-8	T-1 / T-11	PT-12 / PT-14	A-10 / A-1	ST-5	A-5 / A-1	A-17a	T-1 / T-3b

Program Key:

1. Urination Habit Training
2. Toilet Training Maintenance
3a. Taking Off Coat 3b. Putting On Coat
4. Physical Therapy - Classroom
5. Communication Training - Board
6. Communication Training - Sign
7. Speech Training - Classroom
8. Recreation/Leisure - Gym
9a. Setting Table 9b. Clearing Table
10. Toothbrushing   10M Maintenance
11. Washing Hands   11M Maintenance
12. Eating with a Spoon   12M Maintenance
13. Eating with a Fork   13M Maintenance
14. Drinking from a Cup
15. Purchasing - Fast Food - McDonald's
16. Coin Selection - Small Purchase - Class and McDonald's
17a. Dressing - T-Shirt Off 17b. T-Shirt On - Bathroom
18. Dressing - Pants On and Off - Bathroom
19. Out of School Appointment
20.

FIGURE 5.7 An example classroom schedule format

A: Yes, the speech therapist (ST) provides training in the student's classroom, not in an isolated therapy room.
4. Q: Are skills taught across settings?
   A: Yes, coin selection and small purchases are taught in the classroom and at McDonald's.

These questions and others such as, "How much 'down-time' is there in the classroom?" are more easily answered when all activities are organized on a classroom schedule.

A classroom schedule should contain certain key information in order to be beneficial to the overall classroom regime. As illustrated in Figure 5.7, this includes students' names, time periods, specific activities, persons conducting individual training sessions, and setting for each activity. An outside observer should be able to look at a classroom schedule and know what should be going on with each student and where it will occur at any given time during the school day.

When behavior problems continue even after careful review and modification of the curriculum and classroom environment, targeting specific behaviors may be the next alternative. The teacher has many behavior change procedures to choose from, and these procedures—from least to most intrusive—will be reviewed below.

Extinction

Extinction is the intentional withholding of positive reinforcement by the teacher because of the student's response. Reinforcement is not withdrawn, which would constitute punishment; rather it simply is not presented. To ignore a behavior that was formerly rewarded decreases its frequency. Because it is fairly easy to use and is less intrusive than most other behavior reduction procedures, extinction is the first treatment of choice when the behavior problem appears to be maintained by others' positive reinforcement of it.

With extinction, the decrease of a behavior's frequency rate relates directly to its earlier schedule(s) of reinforcement. If a behavior was always reinforced, the change to extinction would be abrupt and highly noticeable to the individual, so the behavior would extinguish rapidly. However, an individual who performs well on an intermittent schedule (perhaps reinforcement of every 10th response) has learned to perform a number of times without reinforcement. During extinction, that person will continue with these bursts of performance before an eventual decline in frequency. Histories of gradually developed, variable, lean schedules (with many responses occuring before each reinforcement) lead to the strongest responses and are most resistant to extinction.

Although extinction is useful to reduce a large range of undesirable behaviors, there are some situations and some classes of behavior for which extinction is not recommended. First, extinction is not effective unless the reinforcers that are maintaining the undesirable behavior are known and can be controlled by the teacher. Controlling peer reinforcement is difficult, which makes extinction ineffective for reducing mildly annoying behaviors such as swearing, burping, and showing off. When the mere performance of the behavior produces the reinforcement, such as self-stimulation (rocking, arm movements, hand waving), the teacher cannot withhold the reinforcers.

Second, because extinction is slow, it is not recommended for use with destructive behaviors or self-injurious behaviors. Although extinction may eventually decrease the frequency of these behaviors, the student may physically harm himself or others before the behavior is eliminated. Clearly the use of extinction would be unethical here.

Because most serious undesirable behaviors tend to have a long, varied, reinforcement history, the rate of extinction may be very slow. Since *consistency* in the use of extinction *is essential* for its effectiveness, teachers must determine their ability to tolerate the behavior. If it is particularly disruptive and annoying to others in the classroom, even if not destructive, then using extinction is demanding for the teacher and the entire class. The requirement for consistency is strongly threatened in these situations.

In general, extinction is used easily and effectively as a consequence with misbehaviors that occur less frequently, when their performance will not endanger the individual or others, and they are not self-reinforcing. In addition, the effects of extinction are greatly magnified when one or more desirable behaviors are reinforced. Reinforcing a student for all efforts made toward completing a task but ignoring him when he screams and pushes away his task materials will be more effective than simply ignoring the inappropriate behavior.

When extinction is first applied, the target behavior may increase in frequency and intensity before it decreases. This effect, called extinction burst, appears to be due to the individual's prior learning that the behavior was followed by reinforcement. Temper tantrums and whining are shaped when we give in to the increased demands of a student placed on extinction. Reinforcing behavior during extinction bursts makes extinction take longer or renders it ineffective for that behavior. If extinction for 5 to 10 days does not eliminate or reduce the behavior to an acceptable level, another intervention procedure should be selected.

Punishment

Punishment is defined by its effect on behavior: it decreases the behavior which it follows. There are two different punishing operations: the presentation of an aversive event (reprimand) and the removal of positive reinforcers (loss of privileges, removal of tokens, isolation from an enjoyable situation) immediately following a behavior. The first type of punishment includes aversive conditioning, overcorrection, and reprimands; the second includes response cost and timeout. Both types of punishing consequences decrease the frequency of a behavior. If the behavior is not decreased, punishment has not occurred; the "aversives" presented actually were not aversive to that person, or the events or objects removed were not reinforcing in the first place. In fact, the inappropriate behavior may have served its self-maintaining function (removal from a demanding situation, attention, or self-stimulation). As with reinforcers, punishers range along a hierarchy and must be identified individually.

Along with a reduction in the punished behavior, other less desirable effects may also occur. Newsom, Favell, and Rincover (1983) refer to these effects as "secondary effects of a punisher" and may include a suppression of unpunished behaviors (desirable or undesirable); emotional reactions such as counteraggressive behavior, avoidance, escape, or anxiety in the punishment situation to the punisher; a future recurrence of the punished behavior; and failure to suppress the behavior completely. Because of these potential side effects and because some forms of punishment are unacceptable, it is essential that teachers know and follow guidelines when seeking to decelerate behavior. Whenever punishment is used, the teacher should monitor any side effects and be prepared to revise or drop the program if they become extreme.

MacMillan, Forness, and Trumbull (1973) identified six variables which alter the effects of punishment, discussed below.

Timing

The punishment should be delivered immediately after the misbehavior. The longer the delay between the undesirable act and its punishment, the less effective the punishment is in inhibiting the behavior. If a student has completed the behavior and punishment is delayed for some reason, it may be best to wait for the next instance of the behavior rather than risk punishing the wrong behavior or a desirable behavior.

Consistency

Punishment must be consistently applied for every instance of the behavior and by all persons involved with the student. Consistency includes carrying out threats. The punishment for a behavior will be learned most quickly if the same consequence is applied every time the misbehavior occurs, at a point early in its performance or immediately after its termination.

Intensity

The initial administration of the punishment should be at full intensity, rather than escalating the intensity with each successive occurrence of the behavior. First, the teacher must determine the intensity that constitutes punishment for an individual and always apply that level of punishment. If brief removal of dessert is not sufficiently aversive to control food stealing, then perhaps the entire meal must be removed temporarily. When using verbal aversives, intensity involves firmness, not loudness. In fact, soft, firm reprimands directed toward the appropriate person are more effective in the classroom than loud reprimands, that avoid any spillover effect (the suppression of behavior in others located near the punished individual). In implementing the intensity rule, the teacher must be careful not to overpunish.

Adaptation or satiation lessens the effects of a punisher upon a behavior and is related to both consistency and intensity. Escalating the intensity of a punisher often allows the student to adapt to each degree of punishment. The use of the same punishers to the exclusion of others can lead to satiation. Varying aversive consequences of the same intensity tends to increase awareness of the punishment.

Alternatives to the Behavior

Whenever punishment is used to reduce a behavior's frequency, alternatives to the punished behavior should be provided*. This can be done by reinforcing behavior that competes with the punished behavior. When the competing behaviors are not in the student's repertoire, various prompts and shaping procedures should be used so that alternative behaviors can be learned and thus compete with undesirable or inappropriate behaviors.

Prior Relationship

The more positive the prior relationship of the one who punishes is with the individual being punished, the more immediate will be the effects. When teachers who are "liked" by the students apply punishment, they also automatically withdraw the reinforcing consequences of their attention and affection. This increases the effectiveness of the punishment.

Cognitive Variables

Finally, cognitive variables are of utmost importance in influencing the effects of punishment upon persons having severe handicaps. Since the goal of punishment is to decrease a behavior by teaching the recipient to associate aversive consequences with it, the student obviously must understand which behavior is being punished. Either the teacher should use simple terms to identify the behavior being punished, or the student should be asked to state the rule which was broken. Furthermore, if punishment must be delayed, these simple verbal explanations become essential.

Selection of a Behavior Change Procedure

Teachers frequently target behavior problems as priority training in order to "prepare" the student for skill acquisition. It is strongly recommended here and by others (Evans & Meyer, 1985) that behavior change procedures, for students exhibiting inappropriate behavior, should target the development of new skills as the first priority. Further, when a punishment is necessary, the training program should be implemented only *after* some type of review process (human rights committee, program review team, behavior management committee) (Barton, Brulle, & Repp, 1983; Brakman, 1985;

Cook, Altman, & Haavik, 1978). The primary purpose of these "program review committees" is to protect the rights of students to be treated with dignity and to ensure that less intrusive alternatives have been applied competently and have been documented as being unsuccessful. Approval to use any type of punishment should be granted for only a limited time period. At the end of this time, reapproval must be based on data which documents a significant trend toward success.

Aversive conditioning using strong primary aversives, such as electric shock, to eliminate behavior is defensible only when the behavior is clearly life-threatening to self or others and when less aversive methods are not feasible due to the high frequency and intensity of the behavior. In most districts and public school settings, use of these procedures is not permitted. In settings where these procedures are allowed, some type of formal review process and consultation with experienced professionals must be required before program implementation. It should be noted, however, that even electric shock will not prove successful in decelerating behaviors within an environment which does not reinforce other behaviors and teach new skills (Carr & Lovaas, 1983).

Firm Verbal Statements

A common punishment consists of reprimands or firm verbal statements made as soon as the misbehavior occurs. Although very little research has been conducted on reprimands, Van Houten and Doleys (1983) state that "it is clear that eye contact, touch, intensity of reprimand, physical proximity, and other variables influence the efficacy of reprimands . . ." (p. 68). Verbal statements and threats are often overused, ineffective, and may even be reinforcing. However, when backed up by other methods (overcorrection, response cost, or timeout) and combined with positive reinforcement of appropriate behaviors, firm verbal statements may serve as effective immediate punishment.

Generally reprimands are short, negative imperatives ("No!" "Stop!") or brief restatements of the broken rule ("No hitting!" "Stop eating with your hands!"). In addition, the teacher may firmly, but carefully, grasp the child's hands to get his attention and stop or restrain the behavior. Azrin and Wesolowski (1980) decelerated behavior stereotypy in several students having profound handicaps using a reprimand, response interruption, and reinforcement of appropriate behavior. In a program to teach proper mealtime behavior, O'Brien

---

*See "Fair Pair."

and Azrin (1972) decreased incorrect responses such as touching food with hands, taking oversized bites, and drooling by the use of an "interruption-extinction" procedure. The trainer gave a verbal reprimand ("No!"), returned the food to the plate, wiped the student's hand and mouth, and removed the student's food for 30 seconds.

Response Cost

This procedure removes reinforcers the learner already has, through a fine or penalty system for inappropriate behavior. Fines may include the removal of money, tokens, points, stars, extra food (desserts, snack beverages), free time, or privileges. The removal of colored slips of paper on which the individual's name had been written constituted an effective punisher for emotionally disturbed boys (Hall, Axelrod, Foundopulos, Shellman, Campbell, & Cranston, 1971). Iwata and Bailey (1974) used a response-cost system to increase appropriate, and decrease inappropriate, classroom behaviors of students.

For response cost to be used as a decelerating strategy, the punished individual must already have a valued commodity that can be removed, and the economy must be planned carefully so that the student does not go into debt, in which case, motivation to perform can be severely dampened. In addition, basic necessities such as meals, clothing, or other ordinary belongings must not be removed or response cost becomes unethical. Response cost is easily used as part of a primary positive intervention program in which the students earn reinforcers, such as in a token economy. As with other forms of punishment, the effectiveness of response cost increases when careful attention is given to the seven variables described earlier.

Timeout from Positive Reinforcement

Timeout achieves its punishing effects by removing the student from opportunities to receive positive reinforcers, generally teacher and peer attention. Applied to misbehavior, the student is immediately removed for a specified period of time. As a method to reduce inappropriate behaviors in students having severe handicaps, timeout has been applied successfully to self-destructive behavior (Lucero, Frierman, Spoering, & Fehrenbacker, 1976), agression (Calhoune & Matherne, 1975), and disruption during mealtime (Barton, Guess, Garcia, & Baer, 1970).

In the simplest form of timeout, the teacher merely turns away from the misbehaving student

and refuses to interact or present instructional stimuli for a specific period of time. Foxx and Shapiro (1978) paired the cessation of teacher attention with the temporary removal of a ribbon previously given to each student and associated with appropriate behavior. In addition, students received reinforcement for appropriate behavior. This procedure was more effective than just reinforcement of appropriate behaviors in decelerating inappropriate classroom behaviors. As a more complex punishment, the student is removed from a reinforcing situation and taken or sent to a neutral place for some period. Return to the reinforcing situation, of course, depends on the absence of misbehavior. A neutral place can be as simple as a chair facing the wall or a screened corner of a room; however, for students unlikely to remain in a chair, a small, empty room with adequate lighting and ventilation may be necessary. As with any punisher, consistency and immediacy of application are critical for success of deceleration of inappropriate behaviors. In addition, the user should use the following guidelines when planning a timeout program:

1. Use a neutral timeout area that is not reinforcing to the student. Generally this means that no books, windows, toys, or peers are available but that the space is well lighted and ventilated.
2. When the individual is sent or accompanied to the timeout area, the teacher should not communicate with him except to restate the broken rule or the reason for timeout ("No hitting!"). Long explanations provide attention to him and potential reinforcement for the inappropriate behavior (Harris, 1985).
3. To facilitate immediacy of punishment, the timeout area should be close to but visually isolated from the teaching areas.
4. The length of timeout may vary. With students having moderate and severe retardation, White, Nielsen and Johnson (1972) found that short timeouts (1 minute) were as effective as longer timeouts (15 to 30 minutes). However, if a teacher first used 1-minute timeouts and then switched to longer ones, the reapplication of 1-minute timeouts lessened their punishing effect. Therefore, it is best to select shorter timeouts (1 to 5 minutes) and, with a kitchen timer, apply them consistently so that more time is left for instruction and the chance to obtain a positive reinforcement.

5. After the timeout has ended, the individual returns to the reinforcing situation only if he is not disruptive. If tantrums or other inappropriate behavior are still occurring at the end of the timeout period, the teacher should wait until the first quiet moment available to remove the individual from timeout.

6. For timeout to be successful, there must be an ongoing program of positive reinforcement from which the individuals are removed. Although this last point is obvious, it cannot be overstated. Timeout relies upon the student's perception of the contrast between the neutral conditions of timeout and the reinforcing conditions that precede and follow it.

7. For some students, timeout may function as a reinforcer when the classroom environment is too demanding and timeout is preferred (Harris, 1985). The use of timeout, therefore, must be monitored and reviewed on a daily basis.

Overcorrection

In this punishment procedure, the individual must either correct the consequences of a misbehavior by restoring the disrupted situation to a "better-than-normal" state (restitutional overcorrection) or practice an exaggerated form of the behavior after each performance of the misbehavior (positive practice). Restitutional overcorrection has been used to eliminate food stealing (Azrin & Wesolowski, 1974), pica (Singh & Winton, 1985), in toilet training (Azrin & Foxx, 1971), and to reduce self-stimulatory behaviors such as rocking, handweaving, and handstaring (Azrin, Kaplan, & Foxx, 1973). Positive practice has been used to eliminate stripping (Durana & Cuvo, 1980), noncompliance (Doleys, Wells, Hobbs, Roberts, & Cartelli, 1976), talking out and out-of-seat (Azrin & Powers, 1975), and self-stimulatory behaviors (Denny, 1980).

There is also evidence, however, that overcorrection can have negative side effects and may not produce consistent effects on the target behavior. In a review of 23 studies reporting side effects of overcorrection, Foxx and Bechtel (1983) found that "12 reported positive side effects, 4 reported negative side effects, and 7 reported both" (p. 189). Negative side effects of overcorrection included increases in nontargeted inappropriate behaviors, physical resistance to the procedure, aggression, and escape behaviors. In addition, Rollings et al. (1977) found no spontaneous generalization of behavior changes from training to

living environments and poor maintenance of effects after training.

Corporal Punishment

The use of corporal punishment is never an appropriate punishment alternative; however, even with the availability of proven methods of behavior management, many school administrators and teachers still practice corporal punishment. Viano (1974) found that 66% of educators condoned "spanking" as a form of discipline. Rose (1983) found that 51% of 232 principals from 18 states reported using physical punishment with students in special education classes. In many schools, the use of corporal punishment is illegal or may only be administered by the principal. In any case, corporal punishment is usually ineffective in changing students' behavior since it is typically administered without regard to the guidelines defining effective punishment (planned, systematic, consistent). Corporal punishment provides students with inappropriate modeling, especially when teachers are trying to decrease aggressive behaviors in the classroom. Moreover, the use of corporal punishment is an attack on the student, not his behavior. Given the already low self-esteem of many students with handicaps, this should be avoided at all cost and educators are encouraged to use proven, effective methods of changing behavior while preserving the student's dignity.

Conclusions

There are a number of variations of punishment, all designed to decrease the frequency of undesirable behavior. These strategies will only be implemented if positive tactics such as instruction or reinforcement of incompatible behaviors *alone* are not successful. Even in these cases, a positive program to increase appropriate behaviors must be initiated *with* the punishment program. Accurate data records (taken prior to and during each day of intervention) must be kept to make program decisions and to prevent abuse of the student. Clearly written program procedures must be posted and understood by all staff who come in contact with the student. Punishment procedures should be chosen and implemented in a least-to-most intrusive order. Not only is parental participation in program planning especially important, it is also critical that parents be consulted and give their permission when an instruction program uses any form of punishment. Furthermore, the use of more intrusive punishment often requires formal examination by a professional review board. Teachers should be aware of procedures in their school district and insure due process for students whenever more intrusive punishment is considered.

SUMMARY

This chapter reviews basic intervention strategies to increase and decrease behavior, and also provides the teacher with research-based guidelines for their application. Methods available to teach behaviors which do not readily occur are explained, as are the means by which training prompts may be ultimately faded to promote independence in skill performance. Positive reinforcement is described and its parameters outlined—types of reinforcement, selection, reinforcement schedules, and procedures. The importance of reinforcing alternative behaviors and teaching new skills, rather than emphasizing the deceleration of problem behaviors is discussed. Modifying the curriculum, classroom environment and schedule, and extinction are discussed as nonpunitive strategies to decrease inappropriate behavior in the classroom. In addition, specific methods of punishment (reprimands, response cost, timeout, and overcorrection) are described. Cautions in the application of all decelerations strategies and the importance of having a committee to review and evaluate these programs are emphasized.

REFERENCES

Alberto, P., Jobes, N., Sizemore, A., & Doran, D. (1980). A comparison of individual and group instruction across response tasks. *Journal of the Association for Severely Handicapped, 5,* 285–302.

Axelrod, S., & Apsche, J. (1983). *The effects of punishment on human behavior.* New York: Academic Press.

Ayllon, T., & Azrin, N. H. (1964). Reinforcement and instructions with mental patients. *Journal of Experimental Analysis of Behavior, 7,* 327–331.

Azrin, N. H., & Armstrong, P. M. (1973) The "mini-meal"—A method for teaching eating skills to the profoundly retarded. *Mental Retardation, 11,*(1), 9–13.

Azrin, N. H., & Besalel, V. A. (1980). *How to use overcorrection.* Lawrence, KS: H & H Enterprises.

Azrin, N. H., & Foxx, R. M. (1971). A rapid method of toilet training the institutionalized retarded. *Journal of Applied Behavior Analysis, 4,* 89–99.

Azrin, N. H., Kaplan, S. J., & Foxx, R. M. (1973). Autism reversal: Eliminating stereotyped self-stimulation of retarded individuals. *American Journal of Mental Deficiency, 78,* 241–248.

Azrin, N. H., & Powers, M. A. (1975). Eliminating classroom disturbances of emotionally disturbed children by positive practice procedures. *Behavior Therapy, 6,* 525–534.

Azrin, N. H., Schaeffer, R. M., & Wesolowski, D. M. (1976). A rapid method of teaching profoundly retarded persons to dress by a reinforcement-guidance method. *Mental Retardation, 14*(6), 29–33.

Azrin, N. H., & Wesolowski, D. M. (1974). Theft reversal: An overcorrection procedure for eliminating stealing by retarded persons. *Journal of Applied Behavior Analysis, 1,* 241–248.

Azrin, N. H., & Wesolowski, D. M. (1980). A reinforcement plus interruption method of eliminating behavior stereotype of profoundly retarded persons. *Behavior Research and Therapy, 18,* 113–119.

Baer, D. M., & Guess, D. (1973). Teaching productive noun suffixes to severely retarded children. *American Journal of Mental Deficiency, 77,* 498–505.

Baker, J. G., Stanish, B., & Fraser, B. (1972). Comparative effects of a token economy in nursery school. *Mental Retardation, 10*(4), 15–19.

Bambara, L. M., & Warren, S. F. (1985). *A close look at the development of the individualized curriculum sequencing model.* Unpublished Manuscript.

Barton, E. S., Guess, D., Garcia, E., & Baer, D. M. (1970). Improvement of retardates' mealtime behaviors by timeout procedures using multiple baseline techniques. *Journal of Applied Behavior Analysis, 3,* 77–84.

Barton, L. E., Brulle, A. R., & Repp, A. C. (1983). Aversive techniques and the doctrine of least restrictive alternative. *Exceptional Education Quarterly, 3*(4), 1–8.

Bates, P. (1980). The effectiveness of interpersonal social skills training on the social skills acquisition of moderately and mildly retarded adults. *Journal of Applied Behavior Analysis, 13,* 237–248.

Bellamy, G. T., Horner, R. H., & Inman, D. P. (1979). *Vocational habilitation of severely retarded adults.* Baltimore: University Park Press.

Bellamy, G. T., Rhodes, L. E., Wilcox, B., Albin, J. M., Mank, D. M., Boles, S. M., Horner, R. H., Collins, M., & Turner, J. (1984). Quality and equality in employment services for adults with severe disabilities. *Journal of the Association for Persons with Severe Handicaps, 9*(4), 270–277.

Billingsley, F. F. (1984). Where are the generalization outcomes? *Journal of the Association for Persons with Severe Handicaps, 9*(3), 186–192.

Brakman, C. (1985). A human rights committee in a public school for severely and profoundly retarded students. *Education and Training of the Mentally Retarded, 20,* 139–147.

Brinker, R. P. (1985). Interactions between severely mentally retarded students and other students in integrated and segregated public school settings. *American Journal of Mental Deficiency, 89*(6), 587–594.

Browder, D. M., Morris, W. W., & Snell, M. E. (1981). The use of time delay to teach manual signs to a severely retarded student. *Education and Training of the Mentally Retarded, 16,* 252–258.

Browder, D. M., Snell, M. E., & Ambrogio, B. M. (1984). *Using time delay to transfer stimulus control within the behavioral chain of vending machine use and a com-*

parison of training sites. Manuscript submitted for publication.

Brown, F., Holvoet, J., Guess, D., & Mulligan, M. (1980). The Individualized Curriculum Sequencing Model (III): Small group instruction. *Journal of the Association for the Severely Handicapped, 5,* 352–367.

Brown, J., Shiraga, B., York, J., Kessler, K., Strohm, B., Rogan, P., Sweet, M., Zanella, K., VanDeventer, P., & Loomis, R. (1984). Integrated work opportunities for adults with severe handicaps: The extended training option. *Journal of the Association for Persons with Severe Handicaps, 9*(4), 262–269.

Carr, E. G., & Lovaas, O. I. (1983). Contingent electric shock as a treatment for severe behavior problems. In S. Axelrod & J. Apsche (Eds.), *The effects of punishment on human behavior.* New York: Academic Press.

Calhoune, K. S., & Matherne, P. (1975). The effects of varying schedules of time out on aggressive behavior of a retarded girl. *Journal of Behavior Therapy and Experimental Psychiatry, 6,* 139–143.

Close, D. W., Irvin, L. K., Prehm, H. J., & Taylor, V. E. (1978). Systematic correction procedures in vocational-skill training of severely retarded individuals. *American Journal of Mental Deficiency, 83,* 270–275.

Cook, J. W., Altman, K., & Haavik, S. (1978). Consent for aversive treatment: A model form. *Mental Retardation, 16,* 47–51.

Correa, V. I., Poulson, C. L., & Salzberg, C. L. (1984). Training and generalization of reach-grasp behavior in blind, retarded young children. *Journal of Applied Behavior Analysis, 17,* 57–69.

Crist, K., Walls, R. T., & Haught, P. A. (1984). Degrees of specificity in task analysis. *American Journal of Mental Deficiency, 89,* 67–74.

Cronin, K. A., & Cuvo, A. J. (1979). Teaching mending skills to retarded adolescents. *Journal of Applied Behavior Analysis, 12,* 401–406.

Csapo, M. (1981). Comparison of two prompting procedures to increase response fluency among severely handicapped learners. *Journal of the Association for the Severely Handicapped, 6*(1), 39–47.

Cuvo, A. J., & Davis, P. K. (1980). Teaching community living skills to mentally retarded persons: An examination of discriminative stimuli. *Gedrag, 8*(1), 14–33.

Cuvo, A. J., Leaf, R. B., & Borakove, L. S. (1978). Teaching janitorial skills to the mentally retarded: Acquisition, generalization, and maintenance. *Journal of Applied Behavior Analysis, 11,* 345–355.

Dalton, A. J., Rubino, C. A., & Hislop, M. W. (1973). Some effects of token rewards on school achievement of children with Down's syndrome. *Journal of Applied Behavior Analysis, 6,* 251–259.

Denny, M. R. (1966). A theoretical analysis and its application to training the mentally retarded. In N. R. Ellis (Ed.), *International Review of Research in Mental Retardation* (Vol. 2). New York: Academic Press.

Denny, M. R. (1980). Reducing self-stimulatory behavior of mentally retarded persons by alternative positive practice. *American Journal of Mental Deficiency, 84,* 610–615.

Doleys, D. M., Wells, K. C., Hobbs, S. A., Roberts, M. W., & Cartelli, L. M. (1976). The effects of social punishment of noncompliance: A comparison with timeout and positive practice. *Journal of Applied Behavior Analysis, 9,* 471–482.

Donnellan, A. M., Mirenda, P. L., Mesaros, R. A., & Fassbender, L. L. (1984). Analyzing the communicative functions of aberrant behavior. *Journal of the Association for Persons with Severe Handicaps, 9*(3), 201–212.

Dunlap, G., & Koegel, R. K. (1980). Motivating autistic children through stimulus variation. *Journal of Applied Behavior Analysis, 13,* 619–627.

Durana, I. L., & Cuvo, A. J. (1980). A comparison of procedures for decreasing public disrobing of an institutionalized profoundly mentally retarded women. *Mental Retardation, 18,* 185–188.

Etzel, B. C., & LeBlanc, J. M. (1979). The simplest treatment alternative: The law of parsimony applied to choosing appropriate instructional control and error-less-learning procedures for the difficult-to-teach child. *Journal of Autism and Development Disorders, 9,* 361–382.

Evans, I. M. & Meyer, L. H. (1985). *An educative approach to behavior problems: A practical decision model for interventions with severely handicapped learners.* Baltimore: Paul H. Brookes.

Falvey, M., Brown, L., Lyon, S., Baumgart, D., & Schroeder, J. (1980). Strategies for using cues and correction procedures. In W. Sailor, B. Wilcox, & L. Brown (Eds.), *Methods of instruction for severely handicapped students* (pp. 109–134). Baltimore: Paul H. Brookes.

Favell, J. E., Favell, J. E., & McGimsey, J. F. (1978). Relative effectiveness and efficiency of group vs. individualized training of severely retarded groups. *American Journal of Mental Deficiency, 83,* 104–109.

Fisher, M. A., & Zeaman, D. (1973). An attention-retention theory of retardate discrimination learning. In N. R. Ellis (Ed.), *The international review of research in mental retardation* (Vol. 6). New York: Academic Press.

Ford, A. & Mirenda, P. (1984). Community instruction: A natural cues and correction decision model. *Journal of the Association for Persons with Severe Handicaps, 9*(2), 79–87.

Foxx, R. M. (1981). *Effective behavioral programming: Graduated guidance and backward chaining.* Champaign, IL: Research Press.

Foxx, R. M., & Shapiro, S. T. (1978). The timeout ribbon: A nonexclusionary timeout procedure. *Journal of Applied Behavior Analysis, 11,* 125–136.

Gaylord-Ross, R. (1980). A decision model for the treatment of aberrant behavior in applied settings. In W. Sailor, B. Wilcox, & L. Brown (Eds.), *Methods of instruction for severely handicapped students* (pp. 135–158). Baltimore: Paul H. Brookes.

Giangreco, M. F. (1983). Teaching basic photography skills to a severely handicapped young adult using simulated materials. *Journal of the Association for the Severely Handicapped, 8*(1), 43–49.

Glendenning, N. J., Adams, G. L., & Sternberg, L. (1983). Comparison of prompt sequences. *American Journal of Mental Deficiency, 88,* 321–325.

Goetz, L., Schuler, A., & Sailor, W. (1979). Teaching functional speech to the severely handicapped: Current issues. *Journal of Autism and Development Disorders, 9,* 325–343.

Gold, M. W. (1972). Stimulus factors in skill training of the retarded on a complex assembly task: Acquisition, transfer, and retention. *American Journal of Mental Deficiency, 76,* 517–526.

Hall, R. V., Axelrod, S., Foundopulos, M., Shellman, J., Campbell, R. A., & Cranston, S. S. (1971). The effective use of punishment to modify behavior in the classroom. *Educational Technology, 11*(4), 24–26.

Hall, R. V., & Hall, M. C. (1980a). *How to use planned ignoring (extinction).* Lawrence, KS: H & H Enterprises.

Hall, R. V., & Hall, M. C. (1980b). *How to use systematic attention and approval (social reinforcement).* Lawrence, KS: H & H Enterprises.

Hall, R. V., & Hall, M. C. (1980c). *How to use time out.* Lawrence, KS: H & H Enterprises.

Halle, J. W., Baer, D. M., & Spradlin, J. E. (1981). Teacher's generalized use of delay on a stimulus control procedure to increase language use in handicapped children. *Journal of Applied Behavior Analysis, 14,* 389–409.

Halle, J., Marshall, A., & Spradlin, J. E. (1979). Time delay: A technique to increase language usage and facilitate generalization in retarded children. *Journal of Applied Behavior Analysis, 12,* 431–439.

Hamre-Nietupski, S., & Nietupski, J. (1981). Integral involvement of severely handicapped students within regular public schools. *Journal of the Association for the Severely Handicapped, 6*(2), 30–39.

Harris, K. R. (1985). Definitional, parametric, and procedural considerations in timeout interventions and research. *Exceptional Children, 51*(4), 279–288.

Holvoet, J., Guess, D., Mulligan, M., & Brown, F. (1980). The individualized curriculum sequencing model (II): A teaching strategy for severely handicapped students. *Journal of the Association for the Severely Handicapped, 5,* 337–351.

Horner, R. D. (1980). The effects of an environmental "enrichment" program on the behavior of institutionalized, profoundly retarded children. *Journal of Applied Behavior Analysis, 13,* 473–491.

Houghton, A., Snell, M. E., & Lewis, A. P. (1985). *Teaching students with severe handicaps to partially participate in toothbrushing.* Unpublished manuscript.

Iwata, B. A., & Bailey, J. S. (1974). Reward versus cost token systems: An analysis of the effects on students and teachers. *Journal of Applied Behavior Analysis, 7,* 567–576.

Iwata, B. A., Dorsey, M. F., Slifer, K. J., Bauman, K. E., & Richman, G. S. (1982). Toward a functional analysis of self-injury. *Analysis and Intervention in Developmental Disabilities, 2,* 3–20.

Janssen, C., & Guess, D. (1978). Use of function as a consequence in training receptive labeling to severely and profoundly retarded individuals. *AAESPH Review, 3,* 246–258.

Johnson, B. F., & Cuvo, A. J. (1981). Teaching mentally retarded adults to cook. *Behavior Modification, 5,* 187–202.

Kazdin, A. E. (1980). *Behavior modification in applied settings.* Homewood, IL: Dorsey Press.

Kazdin, A. E., & Bootzin, R. R. (1972). The token economy: An evaluative review. *Journal of Applied Behavior Analysis, 5,* 343–372.

Kent, L. R. (1974). *Language acquisition program for the severely retarded.* Champaign, IL: Research Press.

Kent-Udolf, L., & Sherman, E. R. (1983). *Shop talk: A prevocational language program for retarded students.* Champaign, IL: Research Press.

Kleinert, H. L., & Gast, D. L. (1982). Teaching a multi-handicapped adult manual signs using a constant time delay procedure. *Journal of the Association for the Severely Handicapped, 6*(4), 25–32.

Kohl, F. L., Wilcox, B. L., & Karlan, G. R. (1978). Effects of training conditions on the generalization of manual signs with moderately handicapped students. *Education and Training of the Mentally Retarded, 13,* 327–331.

LeBlanc, J. M., & Ruggles, R. R. (1982). Instructional strategies for individual and group teaching. *Analysis and Intervention in Developmental Disabilities, 2,* 129–137.

Leitenberg, H. (Ed.). (1976). *Handbook of behavior modification and behavior therapy.* Englewood Cliffs, NJ: Prentice-Hall.

Lent, J. R., & McLean, B. M. (1976). The trainable retarded: The technology of teaching. In N. G. Haring & R. L. Schiefelbusch (Eds.), *Teaching special children* (pp. 197–231). New York, McGraw-Hill.

Liberty, K. A., Haring, N. G., & Martin, M. M. (1981). Teaching new skills to the severely handicapped. *Journal of the Association for the Severely Handicapped, 6*(1), 5–13.

Lindsley, O. R. (1964). Direct measurement and prosthesis of retarded behavior. *Journal of Education, 147,* 62–81.

Litt, M. D., & Schreibman, L. (1981). Stimulus-specific reinforcement in the acquisition of receptive labels by autistic children. *Analysis and Intervention in Developmental Disabilities, 1,* 171–186.

Lucero, W. J., Frieman, J., Spoering, K., & Fehrenbacker, J. (1976). Comparison of three procedures in reducing self-injurious behavior. *American Journal of Mental Deficiency, 80,* 548–554.

MacMillan, D. L., Forness, S. R., & Trumbull, B. M. (1973). The role of punishment in the classroom. *Exceptional Children, 40,* 85–89.

Martin, G., Koop, S., & Turner, G. (1981). Backward chaining versus total task presentation to teach assembly tasks to severely retarded persons. *Behavior Research of Severe Developmental Disabilities, 2*(2), 117–136.

Matson, J. L., DiLorenzo, T. M., & Esvendt-Dawson, H. (1981). A comprehensive dining program for mentally retarded adults. *Behavior Research and Therapy, 19,* 399–405.

Matson, J. L., Ollendick, T. H., & Adkins, J. (1980). A comprehensive dining program for mentally retarded adults. *Behavior Research and Therapy, 18,* 107–112.

McHale, S. M., & Simeonsson, R. J. (1980). Effects of interaction on nonhandicapped children's attitudes toward autistic children. *American Journal of Mental Deficiency, 85,* 18–24.

Moon, S., Renzaglia, A., Ruth, B., & Talarico, D. (1981). *Increasing the physical fitness of the severely mentally retarded: A comparison of graduated guidance and a hierarchy of prompts.* Unpublished manuscript, University of Virginia.

Mulligan, M. Guess, D., Holvoet, J., & Brown, F. (1980). The individualized curriculum sequencing model (I): Implications from research on massed, disturbed, or spaced trial training. *Journal of the Association for the Severely Handicapped, 5,* 325–336.

Newsom, C., Favell, J. E., & Rincover, A. (1983). The side effects of punishment. In S. Axelrod & J. Apsche (Eds.), *The effects of punishment on human behavior* (pp. 285–316). New York: Academic Press.

O'Brien, F., & Azrin, N. H. (1972). Developing proper meal time behavior of the institutionalized retarded. *Journal of Applied Behavior Analysis, 5,* 389–399.

Oliver, P. R. (1983). Effects of teaching different tasks in group versus individual training formats with severely handicapped individuals. *Journal of the Association for the Severely Handicapped, 8*(2), 79–91.

Oliver, P. R., & Scott, T. L. (1981). Group versus individual training in establishing generalization of language skills with severely handicapped individuals. *Mental Retardation, 19,* 285–289.

Panyan, M. C., & Hall, R. V. (1978). Effects of serial versus concurrent task sequencing on acquisition, maintenance, and generalization. *Journal of Applied Behavior Analysis, 11,* 67–74.

Parton, D. A. (1976). Learning to imitate in infancy. *Child Development, 47,* 14–31.

Pendergrass, V. E. (1972). Timeout from positive reinforcement following persistent, high-rate behavior in retardates. *Journal of Applied Behavior Analysis, 5,* 85–91.

Premack, D. (1959). Toward empirical behavioral laws: 1. Positive reinforcement. *Psychological Review, 66,* 291–333.

Rago, W. V., Parker, R. M., & Cleland, C. C. (1978). Effect of increased space on the social behavior of institutionalized profoundly retarded male adults. *American Journal of Mental Deficiency, 82,* 554–558.

Reid, D. H., & Favell, J. E. (1984). Group instruction with persons who have severe disabilities: A critical review. *Journal of the Association for Persons with Severe Handicaps, 9*(3), 167–177.

Richman, J. S., Sonderby, T., & Kahn, J. V. (1980). Prerequisite vs. *in vivo* acquisition of self-feeding skill. Behavior Research and Therapy, 18, 327–332.

Rollings, J. P., Baumeister, A. A., & Baumeister, A. A. (1977). The use of overcorrection procedures to eliminate the stereotyped behaviors of retarded individuals. *Behavior Modification, 1*(1), 29–46.

Rose, T. L. (1983). A survey of corporal punishment of mildly handicapped students. *Exceptional Education Quarterly, 3*(4), 9–19.

Saunders, R., & Sailor, W. (1979). A comparison of three strategies of reinforcement on two-choice learning problems with severely retarded children. *AAESPH Review, 4,* 323–333.

Singh, N. N., & Winton, A. W. (1985). Controlling pica by components of an overcorrection procedure. *American Journal of Mental Deficiency, 90*(1), 40–45.

Smeets, P. M., & Striefel, S. (1976a). Acquisition and cross modal generalization of receptive and expressive signing skills in a retarded deaf girl. *Journal of Mental Deficiency Research, 20,* 251–260.

Smeets, P. M., & Striefel, S. (1976b). Acquisition of sign reading by transfer of stimulus control in a retarded deaf girl. *Journal of Mental Deficiency Research, 20,* 197–205.

Smith, D. D., & Lovitt, T. C. (1976). The differential effects of reinforcement contingencies on arithmetic performance. *Journal of Learning Disabilities, 1,* 32–40.

Snell, M. E. (1979). Retarded residents as language trainers of profoundly retarded students. *Education and Training of the Mentally Retarded, 14,* 77–84.

Snell, M. E. (1982). Analysis of time delay procedures in teaching daily living skills to retarded adults. *Analysis and Intervention in Developmental Disabilities, 2,* 139–156.

Snell, M. E., & Gast, D. L. 1981). Applying delay procedure to the instruction of the severely handicapped. *Journal of the Association of the Severely Handicapped, 5*(4), 3–14.

Spooner, F. (1984). Comparisons of backward chaining and total task presentation in training severely handicapped persons. *Education and Training of the Mentally Retarded, 10,* 15–22.

Spooner, F., & Spooner, D. (1984). A review of chaining techniques: Implications for future research and practice. *Education and Training of the Mentally Retarded, 10,* 114–124.

Stainback, S. B., Stainback, W. C., Strathe, M., & Dedrick, C. (1983). Preparing regular classroom teachers for the integration of severely handicapped students: An experimental study. *Education and Training of the Mentally Retarded, 18,* 204–209.

Stainback, W. C., Payne, J. S., Stainback, S. B., & Payne, R. A. (1973). *Establishing a token economy in the classroom.* Columbus, OH: Charles E. Merrill.

Stimbert, V. E., Minor, J. W., & McCoy, J. F. (1977). Intensive feeding training with retarded children. *Behavior Modification, 1,* 517–530.

Storm, R. H., & Willis, J. H. (1978). Small-group training as an alternative to individual programs for profoundly retarded persons. *American Journal of Mental Deficiency, 83,* 283–288.

Stremel-Campbell, K., Cantrell, D., & Halle, J. 1977). Manual signing as a language system and as a speech initiator for the nonverbal severely handicapped student. In E. Sontag, J. Smith, & N. Certo (Eds.), *Educational programming for the severely and profoundly handicapped* (pp. 335–347). Reston, VA: Council for Exceptional Children.

Striefel, S., Bryan, K. S., & Aikins, D. (1974). A transfer of stimulus control from motor to verbal stimuli, *Journal of Applied Behavior Analysis, 7,* 123–136.

Striefel, S., Wetherby, B., & Karlan, G. (1976). Establishing generalized verb-noun instruction-following skills in retarded children. *Journal of Experimental Child Psychology, 22,* 247–260.

Sulzer-Azaroff, B., & Mayer, G. R. *Applying behavior-analysis procedures with children and youth.* New York: Holt, Rinehart & Winston.

Touchette, P. E. (1971). Transfer of stimulus control: Measuring the moment of transfer. *Journal of the Experimental Analysis of Behavior, 15,* 347–354.

Tucker, D. J., & Berry, G. W. (1980). Teaching severely multihandicapped students to put on their own hearing aids. *Journal of Applied Behavior Analysis, 13,* 65–75.

Van Houten, R., & Doleys, D. M. (1983). Are social reprimands effective? In S. Axelrod & J. Apsche, *The effects of punishment on human behavior* (pp. 45–70). New York: Academic Press.

Viàno, E. C. (1974). *Attitudes towards child abuse among American professionals.* Paper presented at the biennial meeting of the International Society for Research on Aggression, Toronto, Canada.

Voeltz, L. M. (1980). Children's attitudes toward handicapped peers. *American Journal of Mental Deficiency, 84,* 455–464.

Voeltz, L. M. (1982). Effects of structured interactions with severely handicapped peers on children's attitudes. *American Journal of Mental Deficiency, 86,* 180–190.

Voeltz, L. M. (1982b). Program and curriculum innovations to prepare children for integration. In N. Certo, N. Haring, & R. York, (Eds.), *Public school integration of the severely handicapped: Rational issues and progressive alternatives* (pp. 155–184). Baltimore: Paul H. Brookes.

Wacker, D. P., Berg, W. K., Wiggins, B., Muldoon, M., & Cavanaugh, J. (1985). Evaluation of reinforcer preferences for profoundly handicapped students. *Journal of Applied Behavior Analysis, 18,* 173–178.

Waldo, L., Guess, D., & Flanagan, B. (1982). Effects of concurrent and serial training on receptive labeling by severely retarded individuals. *Journal of the Association for the Severely Handicapped, 6*(4), 56–65.

Walls, R. T., Dowler, D. L., Haught, P. A., & Zawlocki, R. J. (1984). Progressive delay and unlimited delay of prompts in forward chaining and whole task training strategies. *Education and Training of the Mentally Retarded, 19*(4), 276–284.

Weeks, M., & Gaylord-Ross, R. (1981). Task difficulty and aberrant behavior in severely handicapped students. *Journal of Applied Behavior Analysis, 14,* 449–463.

Westling, D. L., Ferrell, K., & Swenson, K. (1982). Intraclassroom comparison of two arrangements for teaching profoundly mentally retarded children. *American Journal of Mental Deficiency, 86,* 601–608.

White, G. D., Nielsen, G., & Johnson, S. M. (1972). Timeout duration and the suppression of deviant behavior in children. *Journal of Applied Behavior Analysis, 5,* 111–120.

White, O. R. (1971). *A glossary of behavioral terminology.* Champaign, IL: Research Press.

White, O. R., & Haring, N. G. (1976). *Exceptional teaching.* Columbus, OH: Charles E. Merrill.

White, O. R., & Liberty, K. A. (1976). Behavioral assessment and precise educational measurement. In N. G. Haring & R. L. Schiefelbusch (Eds.), *Teaching special children* (pp. 31–71). New York: McGraw-Hill.

Williams, J. A., Koegel, R. L., & Egel, A. L. (1981). Response-reinforcement relationships and improved learning in autistic children. *Journal of Applied Behavior Analysis, 14,* 53–60.

Wolery, M., & Gast, D. L. (1984). Effective and efficient procedures for the transfer of stimulus control. *Topics in Early Childhood Special Education, 4*(3), 52–77.

Wuerch, B. B., & Voeltz, L. M. (1982). *Longitudinal leisure skills for severely handicapped learners.* Baltimore: Paul H. Brookes.

Zeaman, D., & House, B. J. (1963). The role of attention in retardate discrimination learning. In N. F. Ellis (Ed.), *Handbook of mental deficiency* (pp. 159–223). New York: McGraw-Hill.

As a teacher of students with severe handicaps, you are and will be faced with many medical terms, routine medical procedures, and more emergencies than most educators. Some of your students have seizures that you will need to recognize, handle, record, and report. Others will be on medication that you will need to dispense daily. Some students will have bowel and bladder disorders that require special attention. Controlled movement will be very limited in several of your students, and their abnormal muscle tone will need to be dealt with as will their positioning and their equipment. In some cases, these muscular control problems will be so extensive that chewing and swallowing will be slow and ineffective, making choking and food aspiration a daily risk. In addition to these situations more commonly limited to students with severe handicaps, your students will face the usual childhood illnesses and traumas: strep throat, ear infections, vaccinations and reactions, allergies, nose bleeds, burns, and broken bones.

Although you are a teacher and not a doctor, your responsibilities are not limited to teaching. You must teach through, in, and around the physical handicaps but cannot ignore them. At other times, you must stop teaching and deal quickly and competently with medical emergencies that arise. These will happen more often with your students and you need to be ready.

In this next chapter Toni McCubbin explains some of the essential information you will need in order to carry out the routine and emergency medical procedures presented by your students. In her nursing practice Toni has worked extensively with young children who have disabilities. The chapter is an abbreviated resource filled primarily with the basics. Your training should extend beyond this resource to include hands-on, supervised practice in feeding, positioning, and lifting students with cerebral palsy, a Red Cross course in cardiopulmonary resuscitation (CPR), and experience in handling seizures, fevers, and other emergencies.

Introduction to Chapter 6

6

Routine and Emergency Medical Procedures

Toni McCubbin
Pediatric Nurse Practitioner
Columbus, Ohio

Because of recent legislation and a developing philosophy promoting the educational rights of the developmentally disabled, handicapped individuals are moving out of their homes and institutions into their communities. Schools are facing medical concerns beyond their routine scope of expertise. Teachers are handling seizures and intermittent clean catheterization as well as chicken pox and skinned knees. Many schools do not have a full-time nurse, so the immediate responsibility for emergencies is shifted to the teacher.

As handicapped students attend school regularly, the teacher becomes a critical observer of behaviors that may be the first indications of serious medical problems. It is important that the family, school, and medical professionals work together as a team. The teacher needs some knowledge of the child's disability to plan an appropriate educational program, as well as to recognize potential problems and deal with medical emergencies. It is not our purpose to make teachers diagnosticians, but rather to help them understand and manage medical concerns in the classroom.

SCHOOL PROTOCOL

The legal implications of medical management in the classroom vary according to state laws and individual policies within each school system. Of primary concern are policies regarding bowel and bladder management in the school and administration of prescription medications. The teacher should clarify specific guidelines on these issues with the school administration. Issues like intermittent clean catheterization should be included in the child's IEP, and it should be determined at the IEP meeting who will carry out this procedure and how and where it will be done.

Planning a school protocol for emergencies is critical. Phone numbers of the rescue squad, emergency room, and poison control center should be posted. Every child should have an emergency card in a central office, listing the child's full name, parents' names, address, home phone number, parents' work phone numbers, the name and phone number of another person who may be contacted in an emergency and the name and phone number of the child's doctor. In addition, any disability or chronic disease should be noted along with particular related concerns. All known allergies should be recorded. Medications should be listed with the prescribed dosage, the time it is given, the prescribing physician's name, and pertinent side effects. Any medications taken at school should have this information on the bottle and should be kept in a locked cabinet. It may also be useful to keep the child's immunization record on this card.

All responsible citizens should be trained in cardiopulmonary resuscitation (CPR) and in the care of a choking victim. This training, available through the American Red Cross, is especially important for people who work with the handicapped population. These individuals are frequently at higher risk for cardiac or respiratory compromise. Many students with Down syndrome have an associated cardiac defect; cerebral palsied children often have oral dysfunction, which may result in aspiration and choking. We strongly recommend that teachers become certified by the American Red Cross in CPR and in first aid. These emergency techniques are briefly described later in this chapter. Another reference to childhood medical problems, which is easily understood and available, is the *Handbook of Pediatrics* (Silver, Kempe, & Bruyn, 1983).

SPECIFIC CONDITIONS

Cerebral Palsy

Cerebral palsy describes a nonprogressive insult to the brain that results in motor dysfunction. It is *not* a disease. Vining, Accardo, Rubenstein, Farrell, and Roizen (1976) state that 50% to 70% of children with cerebral palsy are mentally retarded, though there is a wide range of intellectual impairment. Any child who suffers a brain insult, such as anoxia prenatally, during the birth process, or postnatally, is at risk for cerebral palsy.

There are three types of cerebral palsy classified according to muscle tone and motor characteristics: spastic, extrapyramidal, and mixed. The spastic group is further classified by the area of the body involved:

1. *Hemiplegia*—the arm and leg on the same side are involved;
2. *Paraplegia*—only the legs are involved;
3. *Quadriplegia*—all four extremities are involved;

4. *Diplegia*—the lower extremities are more involved than the upper extremities; and
5. *Double hemiplegia*—the upper extremities are more involved than the lower extremities and often one side is more involved than the other (Bleck & Nagel, 1982).

Spastic cerebral palsy implies hypertonicity in the affected muscles. These children are prone to joint contractures. Extrapyramidal cerebral palsy usually involves all four extremities and may involve variable muscle tone. Rigidity, choreoathetosis (writhing movements), ataxia, or tremor may be noted. Mixed cerebral palsy involves components of both spastic and extrapyramidal abnormalities (Vining et al., 1976). Children with cerebral palsy may have a variety of other, related disabilities such as oral dysfunction resulting in feeding and language problems, hearing loss, poor visual acuity and strabismus, seizures, mental retardation, and behavior problems.

Drug therapy is sometimes used to minimize hypertonicity and involuntary movements. Valium and Dantrolene have been used to reduce the tone of hypertonic muscles. Fonazine has been used to minimize severe rigidity but can have a sedative effect (Vining et al, 1976).

Orthopedic surgery is frequently used to improve ambulation and self-care and may be necessary to prevent deformity. Bracing, casting, and intensive physical therapy are often combined with the efforts of the orthopedic surgeon.

Myelomeningocele

The child with a neural tube defect has an anomaly of the spinal column. There are several types of neural tube defects.

1. *Myelomeningocele*—an anomaly of the vertebral column allowing the spinal cord and its covering (the meninges) to protrude through the bony defect into a sac on the back;
2. *Meningocele*—a bony defect in the vertebral column with protrusion of the meninges, but not the spinal cord itself, into a sac on the back;
3. *Spina bifida occulta*—a bony defect in the vertebra.

Myelomeningocele is more common than meningocele. There is marked sensory impairment over and below the level of the myelomeningocele, resulting in motor impairment, immobility, poor circulation, and osteoporosis (brittle bone) (Holt, 1980).

Hydrocephalus

Hydrocephalus, sometimes referred to as "water on the brain," is a condition seen in 85% to 90% of children with myelomeningocele and less frequently with other disorders. Hydrocephalus is due to an obstruction such as a cyst in the brain, an overproduction of cerebrospinal fluid (CSF), or poor reabsorption of cerebrospinal fluid. The excess fluid causes dilation of the ventricles (the cavities in the middle of the brain), resulting in increased intracranial pressure and compression of the brain's cortex. This increased pressure, if left untreated, can cause illness and even death. Surgical intervention is necessary to insert a plastic tube, called a *shunt*, into the brain to drain the excess fluid.

The teacher must be alert to the signs of increased intracranial pressure in the child with hydrocephalus and a shunt. These signs indicate increasing intracranial pressure that is usually progressive and requires prompt attention:

1. Headache;
2. Irritability, restlessness;
3. Drowsiness, lethargy;
4. Behavior/personality changes;
5. Tense or bulging fontanelle in an infant;
6. Swelling, redness at shunt site;
7. Fever, if infection is present;
8. Decreased appetite;
9. Prominent forehead veins;
10. Ataxia (clumsiness);
11. Diplopia (double vision);
12. Change in muscle tone;
13. "Sunset eyes";
14. Twitching, seizures.

The signs may be subtle and noticeable only to those who know the child well, such as a teacher and parents. The teacher, as part of the team involved with the child, can share with the physician and parent vital information like changes in behavior and academic achievement that may indicate a shunt malfunction.

The child with a shunt does not require any special handling or management in the classroom. Head gear that may compress the shunt tubing should be avoided. Use of one-way valves in the shunt eliminates the concern about backflow of fluid into the brain, so activity and exercise need not be restricted.

Bladder and Bowel Management

Most children with a neural tube defect have permanent bowel and bladder incontinence. Lack of appropriate innervation and sensation leads to urinary tract infections and fecal impaction. There are several options for managing the incontinent bowel and bladder to prevent long-term complications. Goals for management should include preservation of a healthy urinary tract and bowel, skin integrity, social acceptance, and maximum independence.

The incontinent bladder may be spastic or flaccid, depending on innervation. Either situation may result in incomplete emptying of the bladder, resulting in urinary stasis. Stagnant urine acts as a medium for bacterial growth, resulting in frequent urinary tract infections. Poor sphincter control may allow urine to leak, which irritates the skin in the perineal area.

Several alternatives to bladder management are outlined in Table 6.1. Initially, a child with bladder incontinence should receive a complete urological evaluation and recommendation for management. Intermittent clean catheterization has become popular recently with physicians and individuals with spinal cord defects. A child functioning on a 5-year level may be able to perform a self-catheterization, allowing more independence and an improved self-image. This is a clean rather than sterile procedure, making it relatively convenient. Most importantly, the bladder is completely emptied, discouraging urinary stasis and infection. Table 6.2 and Figure 6.1 shows one procedure for intermittent clean self-catheterization.

Clean intermittent catheterization (CIC) has been a difficult issue for educators. There has been national debate as to whether CIC is a "related service," which must be provided to a child who is handicapped in accordance with the Federal Education for All Handicapped Children Act of 1975, or if CIC is unrelated to educational requirements.

The case of *Irving Independent School District v. Tatro* (1984) brought this issue to the Federal courts. On July 5, 1984, the U.S. Supreme Court ruled that Amber Tatro, a 9-year-old with spina bifida, must be provided with CIC during the school

TABLE 6.1 Bladder management alternatives

Options	Implications	Problems
Diapers or pads	Requires constant use of absorbent pads or diapers to catch leaking urine	Skin irritation Odor Poor social acceptability
Toilet	Requires scheduled potty times combined with straining or "grunting" to increase intra-abdominal pressure onto the bladder	Poor success rate Requires additional protection (diapers, pads)
Credé	Use firm pressure above the pubic bone to press in and down on the bladder to express urine. May be used together with techniques to increase intra-abdominal pressure (sitting up, straining)	Should not be done on individual with an abnormal urinary tract (reflux of urine from bladder to ureters)
External devices for males (penile sheath)	Requires constant use of device and collecting bag	Skin irritation Leaking Odor Poor social acceptability
Intermittent clean catheterization	A painless, nonsterile procedure requiring insertion of clean catheter through the urethra into the bladder to drain urine	Requires equipment (catheter container, wash cloth, soap water, toilet, or container for urine) and privacy Should be done every 2–4 hours depending on the individual May use credé to assist in complete bladder emptying May need pads between catheterizations to absorb dampness if bladder leaks urine
Ileal conduit	Ureters are detached from the bladder and joined to a segment of bowel. One end of the bowel is attached to the abdominal wall to form a stoma. Urine drains from the kidneys to the bowel segment and through the stoma into a collecting bag attached to the skin	Surgical procedure Surgical revision of stoma may be needed throughout life Skin irritation Odor Poor social acceptance Potential kidney damage Interference with bracing and appliances

day. The court held that CIC is a "related service" and necessary for Amber, and other children like her, to receive a free and appropriate public education in the least restrictive environment.

Bowel management should be initiated at the time toilet training would normally begin. Prevention of constipation is a major goal. Chronic constipation may lead to fecal impactions with leaking stool, distended bowel, hemorrhoids, foul breath, abdominal pain, and vomiting. Continued use of diapers with frequent stooling results in skin irritation, odor, and poor self-concept.

Constipation can frequently be managed with dietary adjustments and increased activity. Constipating foods (rice, bananas, applesauce, milk products) should be avoided, and whole grains, fiber foods (leafy vegetables, fruits) and fluids should be encouraged. Dependence on laxatives is not desirable. Table 6.3 lists some alternatives for bowel management. A bowel program such as the sample in Table 6.4 is the most generally desirable alternative because it promotes a total bowel evacuation routine, allowing the individual to discard diapers, avoids accidents and odors, and enables independence in bowel management. This protocol takes advantage of the gastrocolic reflex, the increased bowel activity after the individual has eaten or drunk a large amount. It is imperative that a convenient daily routine be established. Patience, perseverance, and motivation are critical to the success of a bowel routine. Many people are able eventually to discontinue the suppositories and maintain the routine. Stool softeners may become unnecessary with adequate fluids intake.

TABLE 6.2 Sample of clean intermittent self-catheterization program

1. Collect all the things you need: catheter, soap and washcloth or towelettes, lubricant, container for urine, absorbent pads, paper towel, clean container for storing catheter, and mirror. If you catherize yourself in your wheelchair or on the toilet, you probably won't need a urine container or absorbent pads. A mirror is only necessary when first learning to catheterize.
2. Wash your hands with soap and water. Rinse well.
3. Get yourself into a comfortable position, lying on an absorbent pad if you're on the bed. Arrange equipment so you can reach it easily.
4. *Girls:* Clean between your legs with a washcloth and soap and water. Rinse. Remember to clean from front to back, wiping at least 3 times.
   Boys: Retract the foreskin (if not circumcised) and wash the penis with soap and water. Rinse with clean water.
5. Apply lubricating jelly to small end of catheter (girls may prefer not to use lubricant).
6. *Girls:* Open labia with one hand and insert catheter gently with the other—do not force it.
   Boys: Grasp the penis on the sides (not top and bot-
tom) with one hand and hold it up straight; use the other hand to insert the catheter gently into the urinary opening. When the catheter comes to an area where it meets resistance, use gentle but firm pressure until the internal muscle relaxes.
7. Direct your urinary stream into the toilet; if you're on the bed, use the container.
8. When the urine stops flowing, strain as though you were having a bowel movement and then press firmly on your bladder to make sure there is no more urine. Remove the catheter gently, stopping if urine flows again.
9. *Boys:* If uncircumcised, pull foreskin back to normal position.
10. Wash your hands and the catheter with soap and water; rinsing catheter carefully. Shake catheter to remove water inside it; then dry very well.
11. At home you may hang catheter up to dry. Otherwise place it in a clean container such as plastic sandwich bag, envelope, or small covered jar.
12. Collect your equipment and put it away. Throw away soiled absorbent pad and empty urine container. Rinse out container and wash cloth.

Source: Adapted with permission from Barbara Deaver, OTR, Children's Rehabilitation Center, University of Virginia, Charlottesville.

Genetic and Metabolic Disorders Associated with Developmental Disability

There are multiple chromosomal disorders that result in significant handicaps and retardation. Down syndrome is the most widely known and most commonly diagnosed cause of retardation (Peterson & Cleveland, 1975). This disorder is also characterized by microcephaly, flat nasal bridge, small ears, large protruding tongue, short thick neck, and short hands with transverse palmar ("simian") creases. Approximately one-third have congenital heart disease, most often a defect in the septum between the right and left chambers. Generalized hypotonia and umbilical hernia are common. Sexual development is delayed. Leukemia is 20 times more common in individuals with Down syndrome than the normal population (Kempe, Silver, O'Brian, 1978). Individuals with this disorder tend to be more susceptible to infection.

Recently, the Special Olympics has drawn much attention to the relationship between Down syndrome and atlantoaxial instability, which is due to an abnormality of the two upper cervical vertebrae (Diamond, Lynne, & Sigman, 1984). This condition occurs in 17% of all individuals with Down syndrome who may suffer serious spinal cord injury if the neck is forcibly flexed causing dislocation of the vertebrae. Symptoms include changes in gross motor skills and in muscle tone, loss of bowel and/or bladder control, weakness, neck pain, or limited neck movement. It is strongly recommended that all individuals with Down syndrome be evaluated for atlantoaxial instability including X-rays of the neck, flexed and fully extended. Individuals with this anomaly, or those not yet evaluated, should be restricted from participation in gymnastics, diving, the butterfly stroke in swimming, the high jump, the pentathlon, soccer, and any exercise or activity placing pressure on the head and neck muscles (Cooke, 1984). Level of function and life expectancy vary with the number and severity of associated anomalies.

Metabolic disorders are variable in their clinical presentation and implication for the classroom. Some, such as phenylketonuria, are controllable. Others, such as Lesch-Nyhan syndrome and the mucopolysaccharidoses (Hurler's syndrome), imply progressive loss of function, mental deterioration, and severe behavior problems. Seizures and dysmorphic features are not uncommon.

Complete descriptions of these disorders are beyond the sope of this text. *Recognizable Patterns of Human Malformation: Genetic, Embryologic and Clinical Aspects* (Smith, 1976) may be a useful

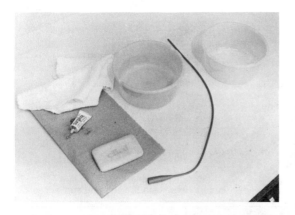

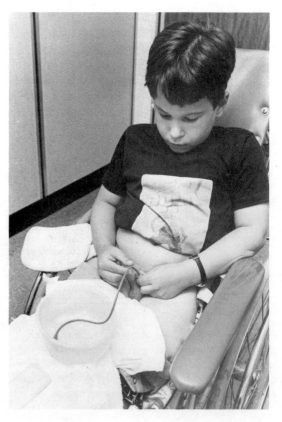

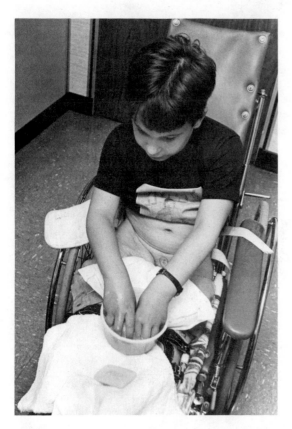

FIGURE 6.1 This boy with myelomeningocele is catheterizing himself to empty his bladder, eliminating the need for diapers. He carries the equipment in a clean container and clean, rather than sterile, technique is used. Jimmy is quite proud of this step toward independence.

Source: Photos by Dan Grogan, Children's Rehabilitation Center, University of Virginia Medical Center.

TABLE 6.3   Bowel management alternatives

Options	Implications	Problems
Diaper	Requires the individual to wear diaper constantly to catch stool	Skin irritation Constipation/fecal impaction Poor social acceptance Odor
Toilet	Requires scheduled potty times combined with straining or "grunting" to increase intra-abdominal pressure	Low success rate Requires continued use of diapers Frequent accidents Constipation/fecal impaction Poor social acceptance
Bowel Program	Combined use of scheduled potty times, straining, and suppository with daily stool softener to insure complete emptying of bowel	May require occasional enemas or digital evacuation Takes time to regulate the bowel
Colostomy	Lower bowel is brought out to abdominal wall to form a stoma. Stool is collected in bag attached to the skin.	Surgical procedure Skin irritation at stoma site Odor Poor social acceptance Interference with bracing and appliances

resource. It is especially important with these children that the team of school, parents, and medical professionals work together closely to share concerns and recommendations, and frequently reassess the children's capabilities and needs.

ROUTINE PEDIATRIC CONCERNS

Several routine health-related concerns for the child with handicaps are important to the teacher. Vision and hearing screening should be done for every preschool child, more frequently for children at risk for vision or hearing impairments as part of their disability. Communicable diseases are a concern in any group setting and particularly with children having handicaps. The responsibility for disease control frequently falls into the hands of the teacher, who must be aware of the symptoms and contagious periods for the more common communicable diseases. We have purposefully listed seizures with routine concerns to emphasize the nonemergency nature of a convulsion in a child with a known seizure disorder.

Vision Screening

Every child with developmental delays or perceptual problems deserves screening for visual impairments. Delayed diagnosis of significant visual impairments may lead to social and intellectual delays and permanent visual disorders. Any child with cerebral palsy, myelomeningocele, or many of the chromosomal disorders such as Down syndrome or metabolic disorders such as Hurler's syndrome is at risk for visual impairment.

Acuity and muscle imbalance problems are frequently found in handicapped people. The following disorders are commonly found:

1. *Strabismus*—commonly called "squint"; an imbalance of the eye muscles;
2. *Esotropia*—a type of strabismus in which the eye turns inward;
3. *Exotropia*—a type of strabismus in which the eye turns outward;
4. *Amblyopia*—a functional decrease in acuity in one eye due to untreated strabismus, where the child becomes dependent on one eye for vision and suppresses vision in the amblyopic eye;
5. *Nystagmus*—abnormal rapid eye movements in either the horizontal or vertical plane;
6. *Hyperopia*—poor acuity for close vision; and
7. *Myopia*—poor acuity for distance (Vaughan & McKay, 1975).

Strabismus may be due to:

1. Organic causes—tumors (brain tumors or retinoblastoma), congenital cataracts, PKU, hyperthyroidism;
2. Poor vision or blindness in the deviant eye.

Strabismus is not "outgrown" and, untreated, may result in significant loss of vision. Treatment is geared towards prevention of amblyasia and maintenance of binocular vision. Patching the deviant

TABLE 6.4 Sample bowel program

1. Well balanced diet
     3 quarts of liquid per day (water, fruit juices)
     Raw fruits (with peels), stewed or dried apricots,
     figs, prunes, dates, raisins
     Vegetables
     Whole grain cereals and bread
     (Avoid constipating foods—rice, bananas, milk, and
     milk products)
2. Plenty of exercise.
3. Fleets enema until clear first night
4. Colace—50 mg (age 2–8 years) before bed *each*
     night.
     100 mg (age 8 years +).
5. Ducolax suppository—½–1 suppository ages 2–8
     years.
     1+ suppository ages 8 years +
     given at the *same time* every *other* night after eating
     a big meal or drinking large amounts of fluids
     Retain suppository 20–40 minutes (it may be neces-
     sary to pinch the buttocks together), then sit on the
     toilet, massage abdomen, rock back and forth and
     strain to aid in expelling the stool.
6. If no bowel movement (BM) after 30–40 minutes, use
     digital stimulation (insert lubricated finger into rec-
     tum and rotate) to evacuate the bowel manually.
7. If no BM for 3 days, give milk of magnesia.
8. To establish a bowel habit:
     Routine should be done every night with suppository
     every other night regardless of any stooling during
     the day or lack of results after routine. It may take
     several weeks for a routine habit to be established.

eye, alternate partching, corrective lenses, and/or
surgery may be used. Early detection and treatment
significantly improve the outcome. Two simple tests
may be used to screen for strabismus:

1. *Corneal light reflex*—Shine a penlight into the
   face from approximately two feet away. Sym-
   metric light reflection in the pupils indicates
   normal alignment although this test alone is not
   definitive.
2. *Cover test*—Attract the child's attention to a toy
   or object held approximately two feet in front of
   his face. Cover the right eye with your hand or a
   card and observe the left eye for movement to
   fixate on the object. Uncover the eye, wait a
   minute, and repeat with the left eye. Any movement of the uncovered eye indicates that eye
   was not previously fixated on the object and
   implies eye muscle imbalance.

Assymmetric light reflex, abnormal cover test, or
other symtoms of eye disorders (squinting, headtilt,
blinking, photophobia, cloudy or white pupil, unusual eye movements, or inappropriate distances

between eyes and object) warrants referral to an
ophthalmologist. When in doubt, refer!

Visual acuity is often difficult to assess in the
child with handicaps. There are several tools that
may be used for different developmental ages. The
well-known Snellen chart requires a knowledge of
the alphabet. The "illiterate E" chart requires some
manual dexterity or verbal expression to describe
the direction of the E; however, the Lighthouse
Vision Test[*] uses simple pictures and matching
flash cards for the very young or nonverbal child.

The Parson's Visual Acuity Test was developed
for the difficult to test handicapped child or adult.
Pictures are used as test targets. Response does
not require a verbal or directional response but
rather "point to" or "match a picture" responses
using the universal symbols for hand, cake, and
bird. Near and far testing is administered at 13
inches making this useful for individuals who are
distractible and impulsive.[†]

In addition to acuity, peripheral fields and color
vision should also be evaluated where possible.
*Look At Me: A Resource Manual for the Develop-
ment of Residual Vision in Multiply Impaired Children* (Smith & Cote, 1982) is an excellent resource
for the teacher with discussion of disorders of the
eye, vision assessment, and vision stimulation.
Finally, the *Functional Vision Inventory for the Multiple and Severely Handicapped* (Langley, 1980) is
another useful vision assessment test.

The teacher should be aware that many medications used with the handicapped population have
significant ocular side effects. The following list
briefly cites some common drugs and their more
frequent side effects related to vision. The reader is
referred to Fraunfelder (1976) for a more complete
discussion.

1. *Phenobarbital* (convulsions)—ptosis (drooping
   eyelids), dilated or constricted pupils, decreased
   pupil reactivity to light, jerky or random eye
   movements, diplopia (double vision), nystagmus, change in color vision, decreased acuity,
   visual hallucinations, photosensitivity.

---

[*]Available through the New York Association for the Blind,
111 E. 59th St., New York, NY 10022.

[†]The Parsons Visual Acuity Test was developed by the
Bureau of Child Research, University of Kansas, under a
grant from the Bureau of Education for the Handicapped,
Department of Health, Education, and Welfare, and is
being manufactured and marketed by Bernell Corporation, 750 Lincolnway East, P.O. Box 4637, South Bend,
Indiana 46634.

2. *Mellaril* (psychoses, depression, schizophrenia)—decreased visual acuity, night blindness, change in color vision, abnormal dilation or constriction of the pupil, oculogyric crisis (involuntary deviation and fixation of the eyes, usually upward that may last minutes to hours), decreased tearing, diplopia, Horner's syndrome (pupil constriction, ptosis, loss of sweating on one side of the face), photophobia.

3. *Valium* (anxiety, agitation, muscle spasms, neuroses)—decreased acuity, abnormal eye movements, oculogyric crisis, abnormal depth perception, diplopia, nystagmus, visual hallucinations.

4. *Dilantin* (convulsions)—nystagmus, diplopia, decreased acuity, visual sensations and hallucinations, eye muscle weakness (Fraunfelder, 1976).

Hearing Screening

In addition to vision screening, any child with developmental delay deserves a hearing screening. Far too many hearing impaired children have been misdiagnosed as mentally retarded or hyperactive.

Causes for hearing impairments may be congenital, as with maternal rubella, or acquired, as with chronic ear infections. There are four types of hearing losses:

1. *Conductive*—Usually a temporary loss resulting from some obstruction, such as ear wax or middle ear pathology that interferes with the transmission or sounds to the inner ear. Most cases of conductive hearing loss can be corrected medically or surgically.

2. *Sensorineural*—A permanent loss involving damage to the eighth cranial nerve due to disease processes (maternal rubella, anoxia at birth, excessive jaundice) or ototoxic drugs. This type of loss may be progressive, is irreversible, and may benefit from a hearing aid.

3. *Mixed*—A combination of sensorineural and conductive losses.

4. *Central auditory dysfunction*—An impairment in the central nervous system (the brain), resulting in poor auditory comprehension despite normal audiogram and a healthy ear (Northern & Downs, 1978).

The teacher should be alert to signs of hearing impairment, including poor articulation, poor response to verbal instructions, frequent requests to repeat what has just been said, inattention and distractibility, and hyperactivity.

Hearing screening ascertains the intensity level at which sound is perceived as well as the capacity for speech discrimination. The pediatrician or audiologist may use several different tools. A tuning fork is useful for gross assessment.

A vibrating tuning fork placed at midline on the skull or forehead tests bone conduction of sound. If the sound is heard of equal intensity in both ears, normal hearing is assumed. If there is a conductive loss, more intense sound is heard in the ear with the loss. If there is a sensorineural loss, greater sound is heard in the normal ear. Another test with the tuning fork compares bone and air conduction sound. The stem of the vibrating tuning fork is placed against the mastoid bone just behind the ear. When the individual indicates that sound is no longer heard, the tuning fork is removed from the bone, and the prongs are held close to the ear. Air conduction of sound should be approximately twice as long as bone conduction. If bone conduction is longer than air conduction, a conductive hearing loss is presumed. There are several formal tests that may be performed by an audiologist.

1. *Behavioral Observation Audiometry (BOA)*—Behavioral responses to controlled sounds (speech, warble tone, pure tone) are observed. Difficulties with this test include low interobserver reliability and habituation to sound.

2. Stimulus Control procedures
   a. *Visual Reinforcement Audiometry (VRA)*—The individual is seated between two visual reinforcers (flashing lights, blinking toys). The individual is initially conditioned with visual and sound cues to look to the reinforcer on the right side when a sound is heard in the right ear and again for the left side with a left ear sound. The auditory cues are dropped, and visual response to various frequencies and decibels is recorded.
   b. *Play Audiometry*—The individual is conditioned to a play response (placing a block in a bucket) with sound.
   c. *Tangible Reinforcement Operant Conditioning Audiometry (TROCA)*—This test is especially good for individuals who are difficult to test since it requires no verbal instructions. A simple motor response, such as pushing a lever on sound cue, results in immediate reinforcement with a tangible or edible

reinforcer; responses without the cue get no reinforcer. (Goetz, Utley, Gee, Baldwin & Sailor, 1982).

Other objective tests require no response from the individual and little or no cooperation. *Impedence audiometry* (tympanometry) tests the integrity of the middle ear (the functional capability of the middle ear to transmit sound), but it does not evaluate hearing acuity. It is a brief (30 seconds/ear), painless, noninvasive test that only requires the individual to sit still for the testing period. *Brainstem-evoked Response Audiometry* measures the brain's response to auditory stimuli by evaluating changes in brain wave activity; however, the individual must be absolutely motionless for the 30- to 45-minute test; therefore, most children and uncooperative individuals are tested under general anesthesia. This is an expensive test, but it is worthwhile for those at risk for hearing loss who cannot cooperate with more standard procedures. Whatever test is used, the audiologist should work with therapists and teachers to position the handicapped individual so that any responsive capabilities can be used. An individual with cerebral palsy who is positioned to normalize her muscle tone, will be better able to respond purposefully with less abnormal reflexive movements that may cofuse the results (Goetz, Utley, Gee, Baldwin, & Sailor, 1982).

For further information on testing procedures, hearing loss and programming for the deaf or deaf/blind student, the reader is referred to *Auditory Assessment and Program Manual for Severely Handicapped Deaf-Blind Students* (Goetz et al., 1982).*

Children should be routinely screened during the preschool period, and children at risk (Table 6.5) should be followed closely by an audiologist.

Seizures

Epilepsy is abnormal, unpredictable, yet temporary paroxysmal discharge of neurons resulting in alterations of consciousness (Sharpe, 1975). It is perhaps one of the most feared and least understood disorders of handicapped individuals. In fact, the social stigma may be more disabling than the seizures. Teachers should educate themselves and their students about epilepsy, thereby alleviating

the mystery around the student with a seizure disorder.*

There are many known causes of seizures, including head trauma, infection, poisoning, metabolic disorders, and fever; but there are many seizure disorders that have no known etiology. The types of seizures are even more varied than their causes. Seizures are classified primarily according to their clinical picture as well as the age of the child and characteristic electroencephalographic (EEG) patterns.

The EEG is an often misunderstood diagnostic tool. Small electrical discharges within the brain are amplified through electrodes placed over the head and recorded graphically. Abnormalities may be localized, but the EEG is not conclusive and may record a transient event. There is certainly no relation between the EEG tracing and measurement of intelligence. The EEG may be normal in individuals who have a documented history of seizures (Peterson & Cleveland, 1975) as well as abnormal in individuals with no history of seizures.

A well-recorded history of seizure activity is the most important aspect of diagnosis. The teacher who sees the child every day can make critical observations of atypical behaviors such as staring spells, nodding, picking at one's clothes, or lip smacking, that can lead to early diagnosis and treatment.

Any child with a known seizure disorder should have information on file as to the type of seizure, severity, average length of seizure activity, and length of recovery period. Prodromal, or anticipatory, signs of the seizure should be noted, as well as individual precautions and instructions for emergency care. Medications, dosages, side effects, and the prescribing physician should be listed (Bryan, Warden, Berg, & Hauck, 1978).

Children with disorders of the central nervous system are at risk for seizure disorders. The seizures may become evident at any age or may remain subclinical or barely noticeable to the untrained eye. The characteristics or type of seizure may change as the child grows older. Table 6.6 briefly summarizes some of the more common seizure

---

*Available from the Association for Persons with Severe Handicaps, 7010 Roosevelt Way NE, Seattle, WA 98115.

*It is not the purpose of this chapter to describe fully the history, etiology, symptoms, or treatment of seizures. Those readers desiring further information should refer to publications by the Epilepsy Foundation of America, 1828 L Street, N.W., Washington, DC 20036.

TABLE 6.5 Children with high risk of hearing impairment

Positive Family History for deafness
Congenital Anomalies—Craniofacial
Ear, Nose, or Throat including cleft palate.

Prenatal	Postnatal
Maternal toxemia	Birth trauma
Maternal alcoholism	Hypoxia
Congenital infections	Jaundice
Rubella	Prematurity
Toxoplasmosis	Low birth weight (1500 gram)
Cytomegalic virus	Ototoxic drugs
Syphilis	Gentamycin
Herpes	Streptomycin
Rh incompatibility	Infection
Chromosomal abnormalities	Meningitis
Trisomy 21—Down syndrome	Measles (Rubeola)
Trisomy 13–15	Mumps
	Acoustic nerve tumor
	Chronic ear infections
	Head trauma
	Trauma to the acoustic nerve

types described in the International Classification of Epileptic Seizures.

Partial seizures, also called *focal* seizures and *temporal lobe* seizures, begin in a particular area of the brain and exhibit symptoms related to that area. Included in this category are seizure types previously known as *Jacksonian* seizures, with the familiar "marching" of motor activity up the body, and *psychomotor* seizures, with more complex behavioral symptoms including chewing, lip smacking, picking at clothes, and other purposeless activity. It is important to differentiate between partial seizures with complex symptoms and emotional disturbances.

Generalized seizures involve more diffuse electrical activity in the brain, resulting in symptoms that involve both sides of the body. One of the best known types of generalized seizures is the simple *absence* seizure, including the *petit mal* seizure. This type most frequently occurs in school-aged children. It is characteristically very brief, lasting only a few seconds, and frequently goes unnoticed. Changes in behavior and academic performance may be the only indications. The child is often described as day-dreaming or inattentive. Some children may exhibit some mild motor involvement such as eye blinking or a loss of muscle tone.

Tonic-clonic seizures, previously called *grand mal* seizures, are what most people identify when someone mentions epilepsy. Witnessing a tonic-clonic seizure may be frightening. There is sudden loss of consciousness as the individual falls to the ground, the entire body becomes extended and rigid, and the extremities jerk rhythmically. The individual may cry out at the beginning of the tonic phase. There may be loss of bowel or bladder control. Often respirations cease, and the individual may be cyanotic or bluish. Following the seizure activity (the postictal or recovery phase), the individual may remain unconscious or sleep for a long period of time.

Febrile seizures are not considered a type of chronic epilepsy. There are generally tonic-clonic in nature and occur in children 6 months to 5 years old following an abrupt onset of high fever. Febrile seizures are frequently associated with viral infections, upper respiratory infections, and immunizations, often with a family history of febrile seizures. Children who are normal before the incident rarely have any sequelae, though they are at a slightly higher risk for future febrile seizures and epilepsy. Prompt treatment of fever is preferable to anti-convulsant therapy in this distinctly different population.

Status epilepticus is prolongued seizure activity without regaining consciousness. It is important to know the average length and severity of an individual's seizures to determine if he is in status

TABLE 6.6   Common characteristics and treatment of seizures

Seizure Type	Characteristics	Drugs

Partial seizures
  Partial with elementary symptomatology
	Focal
	Includes Jacksonian; motor, sensory, and/or
	  autonomic symptoms
		Phenobarbital
		Depakene
		Dilantin
		Tegretol
		Mysoline

Partial with complex symptomatology	Includes psychomotor; confusion, behavioral symptoms (automatisms)	Phenobarbital Zarontin Depakene Dilantin Tegretol Mysoline

Generalized seizures
  Absence
	Bilateral, symmetrical
	Includes petit mal; sudden onset; brief unre-
	  sponsiveness
		Clonopin
		Depakene
		Zarontin

Myoclonic	Sudden, uncontrolled, severe jerking; brief
	  loss of consciousness; associated with
	  severe mental retardation
		Depakene
		Clonopin
		Valium
		ACTH
		Ketogenic diet

Infantile spasms	Sudden flexion and extension of extremities;
	  associated with severe and progressive men-
	  tal retardation
		Clonopin
		ACTH
		Ketogenic diet

Tonic-clonic	Massive contraction then rhythmic jerking of muscles followed by CNS depression	Phenobarbital Depakene Dilantin Tegretol Mysoline
Akinetic	Complete relaxation of muscle tone	Depakene Clonopin Valium Ketogenic diet

epilepticus as there is no fixed definition for the condition. This is the one situation with seizures which is a medical emergency and requires immediate transportation to a hospital for treatment with intravenous anticonvulsants.

First aid for seizures consists primarily of protecting the individual from injuring herself and protecting her privacy. Some people may benefit from helmets to prevent head injuries from falling. If a student begins to have a seizure with major motor components, allow or help her to lie down, move away any nearby furniture, loosen restrictive clothing, and tilt her head to one side if possible to allow saliva to drain out. Never try to hold the child, stop the seizure, or force any object in her mouth. Try to provide privacy during and after the seizure. Accurate observation and recording of the seizure are of utmost importance (Table 6.7). This information may help the medical team classify and therefore appropriately treat the seizure.

The primary goal of anticonvulsant therapy is to achieve maximum control with the fewest possible drugs and side effects (Hawken & Ozuna, 1979). Drug therapy is based on the seizure type, emphasizing the importance of accurate observation and recording of seizures. The teacher should be alert to symptoms, behavior changes, and possible side effects of anticonvulsant medication. Table 6.8 lists some common anticonvulsants by trade name with generic name in parentheses, the seizure type most

TABLE 6.7 Describing and recording seizure activity

Why It's Important to Be Accurate

Anticonvulsants are prescribed according to seizure type; therefore, it is necessary to know the type and frequency of seizure(s) to determine appropriate treatment and control.

Few people are trained in observing seizure behavior, and it is essential for all those who come in contact with the child (teachers and allied health professionals) to be aware of the importance of their observations and to know specifically what to look for and record.

I. Activities Prior to Seizure
  A. Environmental or situation.
    1. Fatiguing (too much exercise; not enough sleep night before)
    2. Stressful (argument with parent, sibling)
II. Seizure Activity
  A. Warning (part of the seizure; begin recording time)
    1. Fear
    2. Headache
    3. Specific smell
    4. Specific noise
    5. Visual impression, experience
    6. Unusual feeling (butterflies in the stomach)
  B. Record in proper sequence
    1. Where did activity begin: face, extremities (can begin as blank stare and be missed)?
    2. Did the individual fall, thrash, go limp, jerk?
    3. Did the individual lose consciousness?
    4. Did the individual make strange sounds or cry out?
  C. What parts of the body were involved?
    1. Arms: right, left, both
    2. Legs: right, left, both
    3. Head: drop, turned to left or right, ache
    4. Eyes: turn to right, left, up, down, blinking; were pupils dilated? did they react to light?

    5. Autonomic system: gastric disturbances, flushing of the face
  D. Did any of these activities take place during the seizure?
    1. Talk
    2. Walk
    3. Pick at clothes
    4. Demonstrate any purposeless movement
  E. Miscellaneous activities
    1. Teeth clamped, bite tongue
    2. Incontinent of urine or feces
    3. Characteristic of respirations
    4. Skin changes during seizure
    5. Vomiting
    Record time activity ends
III. Postictal Phase (after seizure)
  A. Degree of alertness—oriented to person, place and things
  B. Degree of confusion—how long
  C. Was sleep necessary—for how long
  D. Any weakness in the extremities
    1. Where?
    2. Degree?
    3. Length of time until full strength returned?
  E. Did the child remember anything unusual occurring prior to seizure?
IV. Did This Seizure Vary from Past Seizures?
  1. Record date and time of day each seizure occurs.
  2. All who come in contact with an individual having seizures should be taught how to describe and to keep seizure records accurately. It is necessary for the clinician, the family, and the school to have this information on seizure activity and frequency.
  3. If you are not sure an individual is having seizures, observe that person for 5 minutes out of every hour for a day or two. (This is very helpful when identifying absence seizures.)

Source: From "Screening for Seizures" by Nancy Santilli and Stephen Tonelson, 1981, *Pediatric Nursing*, 7(2), p. 14. Reprinted with permission.

frequently treated by the drug, and the more common side effects. Some of the side effects are transient, some are related to dosage or blood levels of the drug, and some are idiosyncratic. Blood levels of the drug are monitored regularly to prevent toxicity and evaluate compliance. Some drugs, such as Valproic Acid, require blood tests of liver and other organ function to monitor adverse effects. As a general rule, it seems the greater the number of drugs used in combination, the longer the individual has been on drug therapy, and the poorer the general state of health, the greater the risk of significant side effects.

Communicable Diseases

Infectious diseases are an integral part of growing up. Rarely does a child survive her first 10 years without contracting chicken pox.

Modern medicine has provided us with immunizations against many illnesses, significantly reducing childhood morbidity and mortality. Currently, state laws require children receive the DPT (Diphtheria-Pertussis [Whopping Cough]-Tetanus), OPV (Oral Polio Vaccine), MMR (Measles-Mumps-Rubella [German Measles]) immunizations prior to preschool entry. It is recommended infants receive the DPT and OPV at 2, 4, and 6 months with boosters at 18 months, and 5 years. The MMR is routinely given at 15 months. Children should begin Tuberculin screening prior to their first birthday and every two years thereafter, unless they are at high risk for exposure.

Particular religious groups as well as individuals may refuse immunization. It should be noted that these disease entities, in particular pertussis and polio, have not been eradicated in our society and continue to pose an especially serious threat to the neurologically impaired or debilitated individual.

B CAPSA I, a vaccine against *haemophilus influenza* type *b* which is a primary causative agent in meningitis, and other overwhelming septic diseases has been developed (Peltola, Kayhty, Virtanen, & Makela, 1984). The U.S. Center for Disease Control is currently recommending this one-time immunization for all children between 2 and 6 years of age.

The communicable disease chart (Table 6.9) may be used as a reference for some of the more common infectious diseases found in schools. Herpetic disease has become a significant problem in recent years (American Academy of Pediatrics, 1982). *Herpes simplex* (HSV) is a contagious viral disease. HSV is typically referred to as oral (HSV Type 1) and genital (HSV Type 2) although both types may be found in either oral or genital cultures. The virus may cause a variety of illnesses including:

1. *Gingivostomatitis*—Common in young children; presents with painful, often bleeding ulcers in the mouth and pharynx, and fever; self-limited disease resolves in 7 to 14 days.
2. *"Cold sores"*—Recurrent lesions on the lips or nose; triggered by fever, sunburn; resolve within a week to 10 days.
3. *Keratoconjunctivitis*—Presents as a weeping, red eye with little purulent discharge; requires prompt identification and treatment to avoid visual impairment from corneal scarring.
4. *Genital Herpes (Vulvovaginitis)*—Inflamed, painful ulcers on the genital mucose; self-limited disease resolves in 7 to 14 days with recurrence triggered by menses, stress; recurrences are generally less painful.

HSV 2 is transmitted by sexual contact. HSV 1 is transmitted primarily by saliva and respiratory droplets. Incubation period is generally 2 to 12 days.

Treatment is geared towards accelerating healing and decreasing painful symptoms. Drugs such as Acyclovir (Zovirax) do not affect the frequency of recurrence. There is no immunization prevention other than common sense precautions such as hand washing and avoidance of contact with open lesions. Secondary bacterial infection of the ulcerated lesion is a potential problem.

Cast Care

The physically handicapped child may undergo frequent orthopedic surgery requiring casting. Prolonged periods of postoperative or therapeutic casting make casts a common concern in the classroom. The primary concerns here are continued adequate circulation and maintenance of a clean dry cast. Swelling or pressure may impair circulation at any time during casting and result in severe problems. Skin breakdown due to rubbing and pressure is a significant concern with sensorily impaired children. The cast checklist below provides guidelines for daily assessment.

1. Can the child wiggle the toes/fingers?
2. Are the toes/fingers pink and warm to touch?
3. Does the child notice any tingling or numbness?
4. If you pinch the nail beds, do they quickly become pink again?
5. Is there any odor or drainage?
6. Is there any redness or blistering around the edges of the cast?

Any change in status requires immediate evaluation by a physician.

The child in a cast, especially body casts and hip spica casts that limit mobility, should change position frequently to avoid pressure areas. Pressure sores are most common at bony prominences, ankles, heels, hip bones, spine, and ribs. The skin area around the edges of the cast are subject to irritation from rubbing and pressure. Moleskin, a special soft nonabrasive fabric, may be used to protect the edges of the cast. Alcohol may be rubbed on the skin which is irritated to toughen it, preventing blistering and skin breakdown. Never use lotions on the skin around the cast!

The child may itch under the cast. Coat hangers, toys, and other items should never be pushed under the cast. It is best to divert the child's attention from this discomfort.

TABLE 6.8 Common anticonvulsants used with seizure disorders

Drug	Seizure Type	Side Effects
Clonopin (clonazepam)	Absence Infantile spasms Myoclonic Akinetic	Ataxia Hypotonia Muscle weakness Aggression Hyperactivity Irritability Attention deficits Drowsiness Slurred speech Confusion Psychosis Increased salivation
Depakene (valproic acid/sodium valproate)	Absence Partial elementary Partial complex Tonic-clonic Myoclonic Akinetic	Drowsiness Irritability Aggressive behavior Hyperactivity Resting tremor Anorexia Nausea, vomiting, alopecia—transient Alteration in bleeding time Hepatotoxicity Abdominal pain
Dilantin (phenytoin)	Tonic-clonic Partial elementary Partial complex	Ataxia Nystagmus Diplopia Vertigo Dysarthria Gum hypertrophy Coarse facial features Hirsutism Metabolic problems Skin rash
Mysoline (primidone)	Tonic-clonic Partial elementary Partial complex	Drowsiness Ataxia Nausea, vomiting—transient Hyperactivity Psychosis Anemia

Efforts should be made to keep the cast clean and dry, which is a particular problem for the incontinent child in a hip spica or body cast. Plastic wrap may be tucking around the perineum and used to funnel urine into a bedpan when the child is on a special frame. If diapers are used, they should be changed frequently.

Frequent change of position, usually every 30 minutes during the day, is recommended to prevent pressure areas and ulceration (decubitus ulcers) under the cast. Any skin breakdown should be reported to the physician. The *Manual of Ortho-* *pedics* (Hilt & Cogburn, 1980) is recommended for a more in-depth discussion of orthopedic concerns.

ACUTE PEDIATRIC CONCERNS

This section deals briefly with various emergency situations the teacher may encounter in the classroom, focusing on identification and management.

Cardiopulmonary Arrest

Cardiopulmonary arrest is the cessation of spontaneous respiration and heart activity, resulting in a

TABLE 6.8 (continued)

Drug	Seizure Type	Side Effects
Phenobarbital (luminal)	Tonic-clonic Partial complex Partial elementary Febrile Status epilepticus (I.V.)	Drowsiness—transient Agitation Irritability Behavior problem Ataxia Nystagmus Dysarthria (slurred speech) Paradoxical excitement
Tegretol (carbamazepine)	Tonic-clonic Partial elementary Partial complex	Nausea, vomiting Drowsy Dizziness Ataxia Diplopia Hypotension Skin rash Blood dyscrasias
Valium (diazepam)	Myoclonic Akinetic Status epilepticus (I.V.)	Drowsy Ataxia Dullness Vertigo Hypotension Irritability
Zarontin (ethosuximide)	Absence Partial complex	Nausea, vomiting Drowsiness Headache Dizziness Behavior changes Photophobia Parkinson-like symptoms Blood dyscrasias
ACTH & Corticosteroids	Myoclonic Infantile spasms	Hypertension Muscle weakness Osteoporosis Cushingoid symptoms Glaucoma Cataracts
Ketogenic diet	Myoclonic Infantile spasms	

lack of oxygen to vital tissues, including the brain. This is a life-threatening emergency requiring prompt intervention by trained individuals. Cardiopulmonary resusitation (CPR) is a technique that requires discussion and hands-on training beyond the scope of this chapter. Specialized instruction in CPR for the adult and child is available through the American Red Cross and the American Heart Association and should be incorporated into school in-service programs. Yearly recertification is recommended to keep these skills current.

For the teacher who is not trained in CPR, the American Red Cross ABC (Airway Breathing Circulation) assessment of the collapsed victim should serve as a guideline for intervention. The first step is to be sure there is an open airway (clear the mouth of any debris); listen or feel for air exchange to assess spontaneous breathing; and check the

TABLE 6.9 Communicable disease chart

1. CHICKEN POX
   Age: 2–8 years.
   Symptoms: Malaise, mild fever followed in approximately 2–3 days by sudden onset of small raised pimples beginning on the head and mucus membranes and spreading to the extremities. Pimples become filled with clear fluid. Later formation of scabs. Successive crops of pox appear. Itching.
   Incubation: 11–21 days.
   Contagious: From 24 hours before onset fever until rash vesicles are dry—approximately 5–7 days from appearance of rash.
   Transmission: Highly communicable. Direct or indirect contact. Droplets spread by airborne transmission; direct contact with lesions.
   Prevention: No vaccine available. Immune after one attack.
   Complications: Rare, occasionally encephalitis, pneumonia, or secondary to bacterial skin infection, conjunctivitis.

2. INFECTIOUS HEPATITIS
   Age: School age
   Symptoms: Abrupt onset of fever, headache, abdominal pain, mild upper respiratory infection, dark urine, sluggishness, fatigue, anorexia, nausea, vomiting. Jaundice is a later symptom.
   Incubation Period: 14–40 days.
   Contagious: As long as 2 months.
   Transmission: Oral fecal contact.
   Prevention: Injection of gamma globulin gives temporary immunity if exposed.
   Complications: Hepatic failure, fluid retention, blood disorders, hemorrhage. Usually mild in childhood.

3. STREP THROAT
   Age: any age
   Symptoms: Sudden onset of severe sore throat, high fever, headache, nausea, sometimes vomiting. Sometimes followed by a fine red rash on body (scarlatina or scarlet fever).
   Incubation Period: 2–5 days.
   Contagious: Throughout the acute stage; 7–10 days.
   Transmission: Direct or indirect contact with nasal phalangeal secretions.
   Prevention: None.
   Complications: Glomerulonephritis approximately 1–2 weeks after disease. Rheumatic fever 2–3 weeks after disease. Peritonsillar abscess, pneumonia, otitis media.

4. SYPHILIS
   Age: Any age.
   Symptoms: Primary syphilis—painless chancre on mucus membranes. Secondary syphilis—rash, sores in mouth, fever, sore throat, headache.
   Incubation Period: 10–60 days.
   Contagious: Until cure.
   Transmission: Sexual contact, transplacental and congenital.
   Prevention: Sexual discretion; premarital serology.
   Complications: Multiple and severe including the cardiovascular system, central nervous system, and skeletal system as well as congenital syphilis.

5. IMPETIGO (Streptococcus, Staphylococcus)
   Age: Toddler through preschool.
   Symptoms: Blisters with pus that later become crusted. Usually on face or extremities.
   Incubation Period: 1–5 days.
   Contagious: While lesion is active.
   Transmission: By direct or indirect contact.
   Prevention: Cleanliness.
   Complications: Acute glomerulonephritis, rheumatic fever..

6. RINGWORM
   Age: Toddler through school age.
   Symptoms: Round or oval lesion with red scaly ring and central clearing. Border spreads very slowly.
   Transmission: By contact with infected animals or humans.

7. SCABIES (Itch Mite)
   Age: Any age.
   Symptoms: Small, raised, red bumps in linear lesions, especially at fingers, wrist, skin folds. Severe itching especially at night or after bath.
   Incubation Period: Symptoms appear approximately 1 month after infestation.
   Transmission: By direct contact with infected persons or indirect contact with bedlinens, clothing, etc.

8. LICE
   Age: Any age.
   Symptoms: Itching scalp. Tiny, white eggs (nits) fasten to the hair shaft. Red pimples seen on scalp. Itching.
   Incubation Period: 1 week to 1 month.
   Transmission: By direct contact with infected person or indirect contact with infected person's articles.

carotid pulse in the neck as well as for severe bleeding. The teacher untrained in CPR should immediately call for help in any situation of cardiopulmonary arrest.

Choking

If a child appears to be choking on a foreign object, the teacher should first assess for air transfer and the degree of effective breathing. If the child appears cyanotic, very pale, or cannot talk, she may need help expelling the foreign body. Check the child's mouth to see if the object can be removed with your fingers. If not, place the child over your knees or have her bend over at the waist, and give a sharp blow between the shoulder blades. This may need to be repeated several times. If the child continues to choke, the Heimlich maneuver, or thrust, should be used. Standing behind the child or sitting her in a chair, place your fists between the umbilicus and sternum or breastbone, and thrust sharply inward and and upward. This may be alternated with the backslapping technique. The American Red Cross publication *First Aid for Foreign Body Obstruction of the Airway* (1978) has a more detailed discussion.

Bleeding and Hemorrhage

Nose bleeds are perhaps the most common bleeding injury and can be frightening. The child should sit quietly and apply direct pressure to the bleeding nostril. Ice packs to the nose may alleviate pain or swelling if the bleed is due to trauma and may hasten clotting. Severe nose bleeds may require the nostril be packed with gauze in an emergency room.

Bleeding from a *laceration* is usually most effectively managed by direct pressure over the wound with a clean bandage. If possible, the extremity should be elevated. Only severe, life-threatening bleeding should be treated with a tourniquet. In an emergency, a scarf, necktie, or strip of cloth may be used as a tourniquet and applied above the bleeding site. Once applied, never release the tourniquet. It is very important to mark somewhere on the person the time the tourniquet was applied.

Musculoskeletal Problems

Children with gait disturbances, seizures, and hypotonia are subject to frequent falls and therefore at risk for bony and soft tissue injuries.

Fractures involve some type of break to a bone. A child may have pain, swelling, and deformity at the fracture site. *Crepitus*, a grating noise, may be noted if the bone ends rub together when moved. The child should lie down and the extremity be supported and kept immobile. A splint should be applied to insure immobility during transfer to a hospital. Popsicle sticks for fingers, pillows for arms, or padded broomsticks for legs are possible splints. If the bone is exposed, bleeding should be controlled and the wound covered.

Sprains are injuries to the soft tissue (ligaments, and tendons) around a joint. Symptoms (rapid swelling, pain, discoloration) are similar to those of a fracture and require X-ray to differentiate. Elevation of the extremity, cold, and immobilization are necessary before diagnosis.

A *strain* due to overstretching of a muscle results in a sharp pain or spasm. The muscle becomes stiff and sore but requires no emergency treatment.

Dislocations of bones in a joint result in severe pain and sudden swelling. Deformity is usually obvious. There is loss of joint function and shortening of the extremity may be observed. The individual may show signs of shock (pallor, cold and clammy skin) and should be encouraged to lie down with the feet slightly elevated, if possible. The joint should be immobilized and a cold pack used to minimize swelling. No attempts should be made to realign the joint before transporting to a hospital.

Closed head injuries due to falls and trauma may present an emergency situation. Care should be taken to be certain there is no cervical spine injury. Be certain the individual is breathing effectively and the airway is open. Table 6.10 describes assessment and management of head injuries.

Burns

Burns may be caused by heat, scalding water, chemicals, or electricity. They are described as partial thickness or full thickness burns, referring to the extent of tissue damage. *Partial thickness* burns are pink or red, sensitive to pain, and may blister. Of greater concern are *full thickness* burns, which may be white, red, brown, or black. They become edematous or swollen, feel leathery to touch, and are not painful. Children with electrical burns should be transported immediately to the emergency room because the burn is always more severe than it appears. Chemical and thermal burns should be immediately flushed with cold water. Oils, ointments, or lotions should never be applied to a burn. A dry, clean dressing may minimize the sensitivity.

Foreign Objects in the Eyes, Ears, and Nose

Beans and small toy pieces frequently become lodged in ears and nostrils of little children. Tweezers may be used to grasp and remove a very superficial object, but referral to an ENT (Ear, Nose, and Throat) specialist may be necessary. Foreign particles in the eye are painful and cause profuse tearing. The child may effectively wash the particle out on his or her own, or a damp, clean swab may be used to carefully remove the particle. Flushing the eye with warm water may rinse away the

TABLE 6.10   Advice on head injuries

1. The head injury is considered trivial or mild if the child falls, hits head, cries a few moments, and resumes normal activity.
  A. No loss of consciousness, no vomiting, or change of color is present.
  B. May complain of a mild headache.
  If the abrasion is minor, clean with antiseptic. if necessary, go to the ER for sutures. Apply cold compresses to slight swelling and observe closely for 24 hours.
2. The head injury is moderate if:
  A. There is brief loss of consciousness and return to normal alert state.
  B. There is a decreased level of consciousness for some time and the child needs rousing.
  C. There are one or two episodes of vomiting shortly after the injury.
  The decision of whether the child should be seen in the hospital depends on how far away the child is and whether the parent/guardian is competent to observe
	accurately for a 48-hour period for:
	  Persistent vomiting
	  Unequal pupil size
	  Excess drowsiness or lethargy
	  Weakness of an arm or leg
	  Continuous crying
	  Change of color from normal to pale
	3. The severe head injury that requires immediate hospitalization is one in which the child has:
	  A. Loss of consciousness and remains unconscious.
	  B. Persistent vomiting.
	  C. Convulsions.
	  D. Irregular respirations.
	  E. Pale color.
	  F. Bleeding from the external ear canal (basal skull fracture).
	  G. Worsening of any of the symptoms of moderate head injury.

Source: From *Assessment and Intervention in Emergency Nursing* (p. 324) by Nedell Lanros, 1978, Bowie, Md.: Robert J. Brady. Copyright 1978 by Robert J. Brady Company. Reprinted with permission.

particle. If there is any concern that the particle is embedded in the eye, cover the eye and transport immediately to the emergency room.

Anaphylactic Shock

Anaphylactic shock is a severe allergic reaction (to drugs and insect bites) resulting in respiratory distress, low blood pressure, swelling, and collapse. This is an emergency situation that may require CPR. The child should immediately be transported to an emergency room. Children with known severe allergic reactions to insect bites should have an emergency kit with injectable epinephrine with them at all times.

Poisoning

Because of mouthing behaviors, impulsiveness, and indiscretion, developmentally delayed children are at high risk for poison ingestion. Many substances are potentially poisonous—drugs, plants, cleaning solutions, and other household items. The school should post the phone number of the local poison control center at a central location. Syrup of Ipecac, which can be purchased at a drug store, should be on hand to give at the recommendation of a physician to induce vomiting. Do not routinely induce vomiting after a suspected poison, as some chemicals may be severely caustic.

Vomiting, Diarrhea, and Fever

Teachers of the handicapped are especially concerned with episodes of vomiting, diarrhea, and fever because these problems may be far more threatening to handicapped children than they are to normal, healthy children. A fever may be due to an ear infection or a viral illness, or it might be due to an infected shunt, a serious urinary tract infection, or a decubitus ulcer under a cast. The teacher should always be alert to the following signs of dehydration:

1. Decreased quantity and frequency of urination,
2. Dry mucous membranes (decreased salivation, decreased tearing),
3. Lethargy,
4. Skin cool and dry with poor turgor,
5. Sunken fontannel ("soft spot") in babies.

Prolonged vomiting, diarrhea, or fever should be evaluated by a physician.

Child Abuse and Neglect

The handicapped child is at a significantly higher risk for abuse and neglect than the normal population. Bonding and parental expectations are frequently inappropriate. Marital and financial stresses are prevalent, and sexual abuse is more common with retarded children. The teacher should be alert to physical signs of abuse such as unexplainable bruises, lacerations, or burns; bruises on the head, back, and shoulders in various stages of healing; and repeated fractures. The child may demonstrate behavior changes or give verbal cues about the home environment. The teacher should document specific occurrences and observations. Each state has guidelines for reporting suspected abuse or neglect. The teacher should be well aware of the state and school policy and not hesitate to follow up accordingly on any suspicions of abuse or neglect.

SUMMARY

Medical problems in the classroom are of particular concern to the special educator. The teacher should be aware of the diagnosis and its implications before the child's entrance into the classroom. Thereafter, the teacher's ongoing relationship and daily contacts with the child make him or her an integral part of the team providing optimal comprehensive care for the disabled child.

Regular communication between all members of the team—teacher, parents, and medical professionals—cannot be emphasized strongly enough. The nature of the disability and the impact of the child's environment on development require frequent reassessment of medical, educational, and psychosocial goals.

This chapter briefly touched upon some of the more common routine and acute problems encountered by the teacher. The discussion should serve as a guideline for identification, management, and referral of specific concerns. We encourage you to seek out further in-depth medical and educational information on specific concerns.

REFERENCES

American Academy of Pediatrics (1982). *Report of the committee on infectious diseases.* American Academy of Pediatrics.

American Red Cross (1978). *First aid for foreign body obstruction of the airway.* American Red Cross.

Bleck, E. E., & Nagel, D. A. (1982). *Physically handicapped children: A medical atlas for teachers.* New York: Grune & Stratton.

Bryan E., Warden, M., Berg, B., & Hauck, G. (1978). Medical considerations for multiple-handicapped chil-

dren in the public schools. *Journal of School Health, 48*(2), 84–90.

Cooke, R. E., (1984). Atlantoaxial instability in individuals with Down syndrome. *Adapted Physical Activity Quarterly, 1*(3), 194–196.

Diamond, L. S., Lynne, D., and Sigman, B. (1984). Orthopedic disorders in patients with Down syndrome. *Orthopedic Clinics of North America, 1,* 57–71.

Fraunfelder, F. T. (1976). *Drug induced ocular side effects and drug interactions.* Philadelphia: Lee and Febriger.

Goetz, L., Utley, B., Gee, K., Baldwin, M., and Sailor, W. (1982). *Auditory assessment and program manual for severely handicapped deaf-blind students.* Parsons, KS: Words and Pictures.

Hawken, M., & Ozuna, J. (1979). Practical aspects of anticonvulsant therapy. *American Journal of Nursing, 79* 1062–1068.

Hilt, N. E., & Cogburn, S. B. (1980). *Manual of orthopedics.* St. Louis: C. V. Mosby.

Holt, K. (1980). Neurological and neuromuscular disorders. In S. Gabel & M. Erickson (Eds.), *Child development and developmental disabilities.* Boston: Little, Brown.

Irving (Texas) Independent School District v. Tatro, 104 S. Ct. 3371, 82 L. Ed. 2d 664 (1984).

Kempe, C. H., Silver, H., and O'Brian, D. (Eds.) (1978). *Current pediatric diagnosis and treatment* (5th ed.). Los Altos, CA: Lange Medical Publications.

Langley, M. B. (1980). *Functional vision inventory for the multiple and severely handicapped.* Chicago: Stoelting.

Northern, J., & Downs, M. (1978). *Hearing in children.* Baltimore: Williams and Wilkins.

Peltola, H., Kayhty, H., Virtanen, M., and Makela, P. H. (1984). Prevention of Hemophilus influenzae type b bacterimic infections with the capsular polysaccharide vaccine. *New England Journal of Medicine, 310,* 1566–1569.

Sharpe, K. (1975). Epilepsy and diseases of the nervous system. In R. Peterson & J. Cleveland (Eds.), *Medical problems in the classroom.* Springfield, Ill.: Charles C. Thomas.

Silver, H., Kempe, C. H. and Bruyn, H. (Eds.) (1983). *Handbook of pediatrics* (14th ed.). Los Altos, CA: Lange Medical Publications.

Smith, A. J. and Cote, K. S. (1982). *Look at me: A resource manual for the development of residual vision in multiply impaired children.* Philadelphia: Pennsylvania College of Optometry Press.

Smith, D. W. (1976). *Recognizable patterns of human malformation: Genetic, embryologic, and clinical aspects* (2nd ed.). Philadelphia: W. B. Saunders.

Vaughan, V., & McKay, R. J. (Eds.) (1975). *Nelson textbook of pediatrics* (10th ed.). Philadelphia: W. B. Saunders.

Vining, E., Accardo, P., Rubenstein, J., Farrell, S., & Roizen, N. (1976). Cerebral palsy: A pediatric developmentalist's overview. *American Journal of the Disabled Child, 130,* 643–649.

The students were in their travel chairs all day except when their diapers were being changed. Although they looked well-positioned when they arrived at 8:30 A.M., they were slumped and crooked within the hour. When the teacher and aides lifted Cindy, John, and Rhonda out of their chairs for a change, their muscle tone dominated. Cindy's arms flopped while her head rolled back into extension, and John and Rhonda's muscles became so stiff that they almost pushed themselves out of the teacher's arms. During instruction, the performance of the three students seemed to deteriorate along with their smiles. At 1:00 P.M. on alternate days, the therapist took them to the therapy room for 30 minutes of position and exercises. They returned to their teacher in the proper position but still in the same seating, soon drooping back into misalignment.

When educators do not know how to physically manage and handle students with movement dysfunction, there are both short and long-term consequences for the student, not to mention the physical risks to the teacher. Short-term problems for students include physical discomfort, an inability to focus on the task or to respond motorically although mentally capable, and thus, frustration. Long-term problems will include changes in muscle length, leading to later malformations of the bones and joints.

In the next two chapters, Pip Campbell, an occupational therapist, describes a framework both for understanding and programming for the motor difficulties typically associated with neurological disorders such as cerebral palsy. It is true that these skills of physical management and handling cannot be learned from reading alone. Neither will therapists and teachers learn to integrate their instructional efforts if they have not questioned the traditional approach for providing therapy. When teachers and therapists serve each other in facilitative roles, skills and techniques can be exchanged; and content acquired through reading may be supplemented with practice opportunities supervised by each other. Thus, teachers and aides can develop and expand upon their management and handling methods, and therapists can use the student's functional IEP content as a meaningful medium for therapy.

Introduction to Chapters 7 and 8

7

Physical Management and Handling Procedures with Students with Movement Dysfunction

Philippa H. Campbell
Director, Family Child Learning Center
Children's Hospital Medical Center of Akron
and Kent State University

Students with a variety of different movement disorders require conscientious management of physical needs while in home, school, and community environments. Proper lifting, carrying, positioning, feeding, toileting, dressing, and other similar procedures, however, are not specifically instructional. Management programs include passive activities where the posture and movement of the student are *managed* in ways that are therapeutic for the muscles, bones, joints, and overall muscle tone. Instructional or active therapy programs, in contrast, work to develop specific movement responses that can be used functionally by the student in a variety of environments. To lift a student from an adaptive chair in a way that maintains muscle tone at as normal levels as possible is good management of that student's physical status. To specifically train a student to perform an assisted standing transfer from the chair, however, is an instructional program that is designed to teach the student a new skill. Programming for students with movement disorders should include both instructional and management programs.

GOALS OF PROPER PHYSICAL MANAGEMENT

Some students with movement disorders demonstrate atypical muscle tone. Assessment procedures that can be used to identify discrepancies in muscle tone are described in Chapter 8. Secondary disorders in the muscular and structural systems of the body can occur where muscle tone deviates significantly from normal limits. Changes in muscle length, where muscles become too short or too long (over-lengthened), may result when a student is unable to move normally due to discrepancies in muscle tone. These changes in muscle length may produce subsequent changes in the bones and joints of the body. The first goal of proper management is to physically handle the student in ways that will normalize muscle tone and prevent the development of secondary muscular and structural disorders.

The second goal of proper management is to maintain normal body alignment. Structural alignment is related to muscle tone. Muscle tone must first be made as normal as possible in order to attain and maintain structural alignment. Structural alignment can be achieved when a student is properly positioned and moved in ways that maintain both normalized tone and body alignment. In contrast, improper positioning and handling of a student may develop body misalignment and physical abnormalities. These secondary physical changes in the bones and joints may impede functional movement as well as result in deformity that may only be correctable through surgical procedures.

Ideally, the methods that are used to physically handle each student should specifically relate to the goals and objectives of the active intervention program that the student is receiving. In other words, physical management should *carry over* the methods that are used in active intervention to other environments in which the student is positioned and moved. For example, an active intervention program designed to develop mobility in a student's pelvis and hips could be carried over into other environments by providing him with situations in which to achieve pelvic mobility while being lifted, carried, transferred, positioned, bathed, dressed, or even being fed. The third goal of proper physical management, then, is to move and position the student in ways that incorporate an objective of the active intervention program into as many other situations as possible.

A goal of physical management procedures used with every student is to allow him to perform as many components of the task as independently as possible. This allows the student to practice selected movements while being managed but also reduces the physical stress on the adult who is working with him. Many students may always remain dependent on others to physically move or significantly assist them due to the degree of impairment that may be present in posture and movement. Some students, however, can be trained to move themselves with minimal adult assistance or full independence. A goal of physical management procedures for some students is actually instructional in that the methods used to manage them should be selected to allow them to perform as many components of the task as are physically possible.

LIFTING AND TRANSFER

Lifting

There are many different times during a day when a student must be moved from one position or one situation to another. Students who are dependent physically, or who are young, may be unable to assist themselves and may need to be lifted. Every attempt should be made to design ways of moving a student from one position to another that allow him to participate actively in whatever ways possible—however limited. A student who is unable to stand independently may still be able to perform an assisted standing transfer where the feet become a point for pivoting the body from a wheelchair to a classroom chair or onto the toilet. Maintaining the head against gravity can be required, for example, through procedures used to lift a student with low tone.

Each student should be lifted or transferred from one position or situation to another using individually designed, maximally therapeutic methods. A number of essential factors are considered when determining methods for moving a student. These include (a) specific movements that the student is able to perform either independently or with assistance; (b) degree of discrepancy in postural tone and the specific factors that are related to increases in tone; (c) the positions (postures) that have been selected to be used in relation to instructional activities; (d) adaptive equipment that is being used for positioning the student; (e) the number, size, and strength of the adults who will be moving the student; and (f) the size and weight of the student. Lifting students from the floor is illustrated in Figure 7.1. Other examples can be found in Conner, Williamson, and Sieppe (1978), Finnie (1975), and Galka and Fraser, 1980.

Some standard procedures are incorporated into any method that is used to lift students in order to make the task physically easier for the adult. Adults who are involved in lifting students should incorporate these measures into all individually designed lifting programs, even those for infants and small children. In general, the rule is to lift with the legs rather than with the back. Lifting improperly may result in physical problems for the parent, teacher, or other adults involved in frequent lifting. Back pain and more serious complications are frequently the direct result of using incorrect lifting methods.

Transfer

Several methods are typically used to teach children and adults to move independently from one situation into another (from a chair to the floor, from chair to the toilet, from one chair to another). The specific methods of transfer directly depend on two factors: the transfer situation (the points between which the student will be moving) and the abilities of the student to maintain posture and to perform selected movements independently. Home, school, and typical community environments, in which transfer procedures will be used, must be analyzed to determine the most appropriate procedures for each environment. Methods for transferring students must also be individually designed in order to achieve biomechanical advantage for the student (making the task as motorically efficient as possible for the student). The two basic approaches to transfer frequently used are *standing* and *sliding* transfers. A physical or occupational therapist should be consulted to design methods that will assist a student to achieve transfer independently.

CARRYING

Many younger students may need to be carried within the home or classroom. Infants may be carried by parents and teachers more frequently than are preschool-aged students. Children with severe dysfunction in posture and movement can be difficult to carry for long distances, even when small in size. Equipment (strollers) can be selected, or specifically designed to limit the amount of carrying required. Wheelchairs or other types of adaptive seating can be designed for older or severely dependent children to be used primarily for transporting the child. The distance for which any student is carried should be as short as possible. It is important for students to learn to move themselves in whatever ways are possible because it is physically stressful for parents and teachers to carry them for long distances.

Carrying methods are designed, as are lifting and transfer procedures, to be maximally therapeutic for the student. The way(s) in which he is carried can normalize muscle tone, achieve body alignment, and allow for independent performance of selected movements. The specific methods used, however, include design factors (the size and strength of the adult). A parent who does not have good arm strength will probably not be able to use a carrying procedure that requires it. Nor will she use a two-handed carrying procedure if the second arm needs to be used for carrying other items (a diaper bag).

Many examples of ways in which students can be carried therapeutically can be found in reference texts (Finnie, 1975; Fraser & Hensinger, 1983).

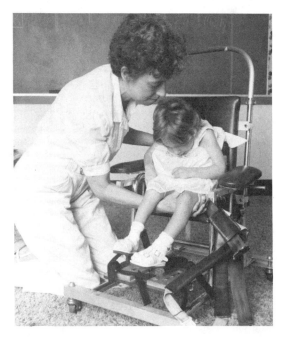

FIGURE 7.1 Small students can be lifted by one adult from floor by bending the knees and using the legs (not just the back) to assist in the lift.

POSITIONING

Well-aligned posture results from muscle contractions that maintain the body in positions against varying influences of gravity. Increased muscle tone frequently occurs in response to gravitational effects on the body. A student who is able to lie on the floor with normalized tone may become high toned when placed in sitting. These changes may result when the motor system is unable to coordinate tone and muscle contractions against the influences of gravity. Positioning a student can help to maintain both normalized muscle tone and body alignment by considering gravitational influences. Many students can be successfully positioned with adequate postural support and alignment without use of extensive adaptive equipment. Most students, however, require equipment to provide support necessary for maintaining body alignment (Bergen & Colangelo, 1982; Campbell & Hanna, in press; Trefler, 1984). Furthermore, many students can be positioned properly without use of extensive adaptive devices.

Several precautions must be taken when using adaptive equipment. First, equipment will not *produce* either normalized tone or body alignment. Well-selected and well-fitted equipment will only *maintain* normal tone if appropriate methods have first been used to increase or decrease tone. Second, equipment will only maintain body alignment if it fits well and if the student has been properly placed in it. Just because adaptive equipment is advertised to produce a specific effect does not mean that it will be successful with every user. The teacher, parent, or therapist must carefully observe the student using the equipment over time and in a variety of situations to see if it is performing the desired function (see Figure 7.2). A third precaution involves the length of time the student is placed in the equipment. Many students with dysfunction in posture and movement are relatively immobile and lack the postural adjustments necessary to remain in static positions for long periods of time. Restricting them to one position can produce secondary problems of poor circulation, skin ulcerations, muscle tightness, or contractures that can lead to deformity. Every student should have a minimum of two (and preferably more) ways of being positioned in the classroom. All equipment used should be comfortable and fit well. Teachers and parents should ask therapists to specify the length of time the student can be positioned in equipment. Some can stand or sit comfortably for long periods of time (2 to 3 hours). Other students should be repositioned as frequently as every 20 to 30 minutes.

Many types of equipment have been designed to be built or adapted. Other types of equipment are available ready-made from a wide variety of commercial sources. Despite the innumerable resources for procuring appropriate equipment, no one piece of equipment, whether homemade or commercially purchased, is appropriate for all students (Campbell, Green, & Carlsen, 1977; Trefler, 1984). Equipment varies in purpose, cost, and durability; and all these factors must be considered when making a selection. Some students require a device that is durable and will last for many years. Others need something that will be only used temporarily or until skills are acquired that will make another piece of equipment more appropriate. Because infants and young children are growing, their needs may be met most appropri-

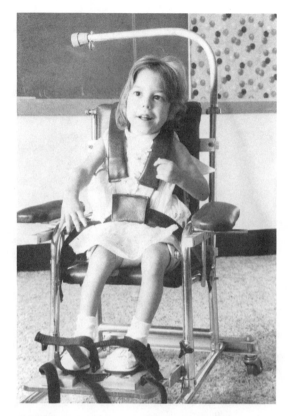

FIGURE 7.2 This photograph illustrates appropriate alignment attained through positioning equipment.

ately by equipment that is highly adjustable or low enough in cost to be replaced when outgrown.

Equipment must be appropriate and well-fitted but also should be appropriate for the student's chronological age and ability level. It should also be normalized in appearance to enhance the social integration of a student by not stigmatizing his appearance or physically isolating him. A student who is positioned on a prone board, illustrated in Figure 7.3 is likely to be unable to participate in group activities. Adaptive classroom chairs can provide an appropriate position at table height but prevent mobility due to lack of wheels. Table 7.1 lists some of the major equipment manufacturers and devices that are available.

Positioning equipment is typically designed or selected to place the student in one or more basic postures in as normal body alignment as possible. Sitting and standing postures are most frequently used in classrooms. Sidelying postures can also be used in a classroom if not age-inappropriate for a student; they may also be used at home for activ-

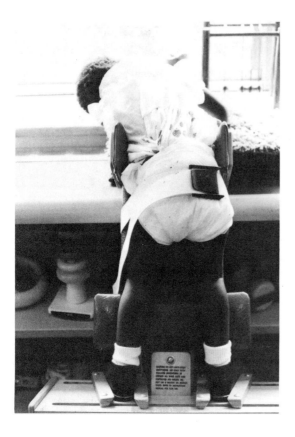 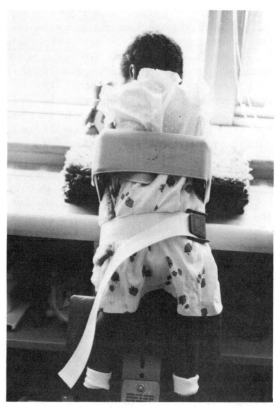

FIGURE 7.3   This prone board may position a student properly but can only be used for individual activities as the student is physically isolated from group participation.

ities such as sleeping or watching television. Adaptive devices used to maintain alignment in each of these postures are illustrated in Figure 7.4.

ENHANCING FUNCTIONAL ABILITIES IN CONJUNCTION WITH USE OF POSITIONING EQUIPMENT

Adaptive positioning equipment will not enhance functional abilities of students all by itself. Rather, teachers, therapists, and parents must select and use equipment that places a student in postures where functional movement abilities will be more easily performed. A student who is unable to attain sufficient trunk control to maintain an upright posture may automatically use his arms to help hold his trunk upright; however, using the arms for a postural support function prevents their use for reach or other types of directed arm movement.

Adaptive positioning equipment that provides support to the trunk can enable a student such as this one to use his arms for a more functional purpose than holding trunk musculature upright.

The ways that are selected for positioning must not only provide body alignment (to prevent orthopedic problems) but must also directly relate to the activity that will be performed while in the equipment. A student may be positioned in good alignment in a sidelyer but will be unable to eat, dress, or participate fully in group activities from this position. A student who is sitting in a wheelchair may be able to eat independently but may not be able to dress in it. Most students require a variety of positions and adaptive equipment, not simply to change positions but also to fit with their instructional needs.

The types of equipment that a student may need are best selected by a team of professionals and

TABLE 7.1 Major commercial equipment distributors

Company Name and Address	Types of Products
Achievement Products for Children P.O. Box 547 Mineola, NY 11501	Transporters Corner chairs; potty chairs Crawlers Self-feeding equipment Head pointers
Community Playthings Rifton, NY 12471	Corner, preschool/toddler chairs Standing boards Mobility tricycles; Kiddie car
Equipment Shop P.O. Box 33 Bedford, MA 01730	TrippTrapp chair with attachments Corner chairs Standing boards Scooter boards; tricycles Self-care equipment
Kaye Products, Inc. 1010 E. Pettigrew St. Durham, NC 27701	Seat inserts for strollers Booster; Corner chairs Standing boards Toilet aids
J.A. Preston Corporation 60 Page Road Clifton, NJ 07012	Wheelchairs/transporter chairs TumbleForms positioning aids/scooter Rehabilitation equipment Self-care aids Educational materials
Fred Sammons, Inc. Box 32 Brookfield, IL 60513	Self-care aids/Feeding & dressing Toileting aids Scooter boards Misc. rehabilitation devices/materials

parents. Both teachers and parents must be able to communicate his programming needs sufficiently to allow physical and occupational therapists to help identify the most appropriate devices. Only through team interaction and planning can physical and instructional needs be jointly met.

EATING AND DRINKING

Some students, unable to eat and drink independently, must be fed by an adult. Very few infants and some older children may have gastrostomies or nasogastric tubes that replace eating and drinking by mouth. These are typically provided for children who are ill, unable to take in sufficient food

or liquid by mouth, or are in severe medical jeopardy due to poor nutrition. Tube feedings can be administered in a classroom without too much difficulty to children with gastrostomies and/or nasogastric tubes that do not have to be inserted daily. The teacher should be individually trained to administer the feedings by the child's physician or by a nurse. Any individual precautions related to the feeding should be made known to classroom personnel. In addition, a system should be set up to provide daily communication about the feedings between school and home. Finally, attempts should be made to develop an individualized program to enable the child to eat and drink orally. Speech pathologists or occupational therapists and nutritionists, as well as the child's physician, should be consulted to develop and monitor the feeding program.

Many procedures have been suggested to help a student eat and drink using better patterns of movement in the oral/motor musculature (Alexander & Bigge, 1982; Campbell, in press; Morris, 1982b; Mueller, 1975; Sobsey & Orelove, 1984). These procedures may assist a child to acquire better patterns of eating and drinking and, in that sense, may be considered to be instructional. Poorly coordinated movements may result in gagging on the food, choking, or aspiration (see Chapter 8 for management procedures). Methods for teaching better muscular coordination for eating and drinking are included as physical management techniques. Use of these methods will not necessarily result in more independent performance but will make feeding easier and prevent choking or aspiration.

Well-coordinated contractions of muscles in the oral/motor area result in appropriate use of the lips, teeth, tongue, and jaw for eating and drinking (Campbell, 1979; Morris, 1978, 1982a). Contractions of these muscles depend on appropriate alignment of the spine. Most students will be fed in a seated position; therefore, alignment starts with the position of the pelvis and hips, which in a seated position, are the primary weight bearing surfaces of the body. The spine aligns from the supporting base of the pelvis and hips, allowing for alignment with the head on an erect spine. Proper alignment of the spine and head is illustrated in Figure 7.5. This alignment is the first step for implementing appropriate eating and drinking methods since the muscles in the oral/motor area

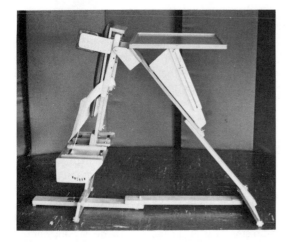

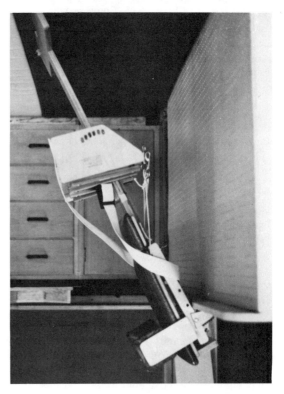

FIGURE 7.4 A wide variety of types of adaptive equipment can be fabricated or commercially purchased to properly position students.

will not be able to contract in coordinated ways if posture is misaligned.

Positioning for Proper Feeding

Good alignment is achieved through proper positioning of a student using specialized adaptive equipment, where necessary. Many students have low postural tone in the head/neck and trunk areas and may be unable to maintain the head in alignment on the spine. One method for assisting a student to do this is to tip the chair backwards approximately 10 to 20 degrees. This positioning takes the head out of an antigravity position and

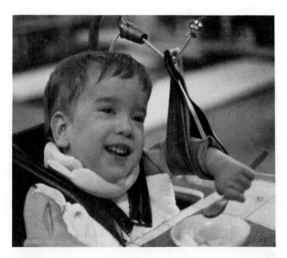

FIGURE 7.5 Proper alignment of the head and neck have been achieved with this student

prevents the use of neck hyperextension to keep the head upright. Another method is to provide additional head and trunk supports to help achieve alignment. Towel rolls or pieces of foam rubber can be used to provide sufficient temporary supports for the head and trunk. Most students should also have a support surface for their arms when being fed (the table at which he is seated or a tray placed at either lap or shoulder level on the chair). Some students may be more easily fed out of adaptive equipment, either held by the trainer or positioned on the floor. In general, however, these positions should be used only when others are ineffective (eating on the floor or while being held is not age-appropriate unless the student is still a very young infant).

Approaches to Eating and Drinking

Many students have difficulty with jaw, lip, tongue, and other movement necessary to take food or liquids into the body without difficulty. Other students may have acquired poor eating habits, in general, or may use mealtimes to manipulate adult behavior. Developing appropriate eating and drinking starts with an assessment that is performed *after* the best possible alignment has been achieved (Campbell, in press; Morris, 1982b). Assessment should not be completed until after positioning has been attained since many of the difficulties that occur in eating and drinking can be corrected through proper body alignment. If a student's head is positioned in hyperextension, it is apparent that

the jaw movements necessary to close the mouth or to bring the teeth together will be made more difficult. By achieving head alignment (see Figure 7.5), the position of the jaw and lips is also changed, thereby allowing for easier mouth closure, swallowing, and chewing. Speech pathologists and occupational therapists can help teachers and parents identify the primary problems that a student may be demonstrating when trying to eat. The most appropriate approach for the individual difficulties that a student demonstrates can then be selected.

Two general approaches can be taken to help a student eat and drink using more normal patterns of muscular coordination. The first is a behavioral approach where antecedents and consequences are structured to help him manage food more appropriately (see Jones, 1982; 1983; Palmer, Thompson, & Linscheid, 1975). This approach works effectively with students who may have poor eating habits or who may be exerting control over adults through mealtime activities. Generally, feeding behavior, such as pushing food out of the mouth with the tongue or refusing to eat solid foods, is viewed as noncompliant in a behavioral approach. Procedures are then established to ignore (or extinguish) inappropriate or resistant behavior and to reinforce appropriate movements. For example, Jones (1983) successfully taught students to eat solid foods by using jaw control procedures to physically guide students to open the mouth, chew, and swallow table foods. Students' attempts to resist physical guidance were ignored and guidance was removed as the students became less resistant. Students trained with this method accepted and chewed solid foods more quickly than did students who received physical guidance that was withdrawn if they resisted the control and foods that were graded from strained to regular texture.

A second approach incorporates neuromotor principles into methods used to develop oral/motor coordination (Alexander & Bigge, 1982; Morris, 1977). Problems with eating are viewed as resulting from dysfunction in the motor system. Movement patterns are carefully observed and classified in a detailed assessment that is completed by a therapist or trained teacher. Patterns that are associated with hypertonus (or spasticity), such as a tongue-thrust pattern, are classified as pathological. Other patterns, such as the forward-backward tongue movement associated with suckling, are labeled as primitive. Intervention methods, in this approach, are selected to normalize muscle tone, where necessary, and facilitate the use of coordinated patterns of movement in the jaw, lips, and tongue, and for chewing and swallowing.

Differentiation between eating disorders that are behavioral and those that originate from neuro-motor problems is not always clear-cut. Most often, children (and even infants) use atypical movement patterns, such as a tongue thrust, for behavioral purposes such as moving food out of the mouth (Campbell, in press). Observational assessment procedures can help distinguish interrelationships among neuromotor and behaviorally based eating problems and help parents, therapists, and teachers select the most appropriate combination of inter-vention procedures.

Methods to Normalize Tone

Normalization of muscle tone begins with proper preparation and positioning of the student. Thera-pists can assist teachers and parents to implement procedures that will prepare a student for more normalized tone before he is placed in the feeding position. Preparation procedures are only required for students with severe hypertonus (spasticity) and, realistically, are difficult to implement in a classroom where many may need to be fed in short periods of time. Proper positioning in a chair or another position will help maintain normalized tone and proper body alignment throughout the meal. Additional methods can then be used to normalize tone in specific areas of the body, such as the chest/upper back, head/neck, and mouth areas. Placing a hand below the sternum allows an adult to use small (subtle) weight shifts across the body midline to reduce muscle tone that is hypertonic. Slight downward pressure of the hand on the chest area can facilitate better alignment of the head.

Some students may hold the trunk in an upright position by supporting with the arms on the tray or table surface. Slowly bringing the arms down and out will help to decrease shoulder elevation, obtain head alignment, and allow the muscles in the neck (throat) area to be used for more coordinated swallowing.

Additional procedures have been developed to normalize tone in the muscles in the face, head, and neck. Speech pathologists and occupational therapists, who have completed specific training in working with feeding disorders, can demonstrate individual procedures that can be used to further normalize tone in a child with severe deviations in postural tone. These procedures can be easily used at home or in the classroom (Campbell, in press).

Coordinated Patterns of Movement

The muscles in the face and throat, used for eating, drinking, and intelligible speech, produce finely coordinated and highly complex patterns of move-ment. Normally coordinated patterns cannot be easily produced when deviations are present in the muscle groups of the head, neck, shoulder girdle, or trunk. These larger muscle groups provide both postural stability and the base against which the smaller and more finely coordinated muscles contract.

Procedures that can be used to facilitate desired movement patterns in the finer muscles are not designed to alter the postural base of support. These procedures are maximally effective as a means of teaching fine muscle coordination *only* when postural tone and alignment have been nor-malized in the larger postural muscle groups. Many procedures have been used to teach students to accept foods of varying textures, take food from a spoon or fork, use appropriate tongue movements for chewing, chew, and swallow foods and/or liquids (see Alexander & Bigge, 1982; Campbell, in press; Morris, 1977; Mueller, 1975). Each of the many procedures that are available must be selected for use with a given student on the basis of his eating or drinking difficulties. Occupational therapists and speech pathologists can provide individually designed programs for these students.

Nutrition

Many students have specific likes and dislikes in food. Others may resist specific foods due to sen-sory characteristics (temperature, taste, texture). Many students may lack sufficient intake of proper foods and liquids due to severe neuromuscular problems that make eating and drinking difficult and time consuming. These restricted food prefer-ences may lead to additional problems of poor nutrition which results in diminished growth, weight problems, and poor health (Sobsey, 1983). Nutri-tional factors should be included in eating pro-grams for all students but are of critical importance with all infants and with students who are highly medicated, difficult to feed, or showing poor rates of growth (height and weight).

Public education programs are not likely to employ nutritionists. Consultations can be obtained, however, through local hospitals and agencies such as visiting nurse or other home health providers. These types of consultations provide helpful information to increase the types or quantities of foods or liquids as well as ensure good nutrition during programming.

Independent Eating and Drinking

Students should receive instruction leading to independent eating and drinking skills when sufficient arm movement is present to bring the spoon to the mouth (Bigge, 1982; Campbell, in press). Special utensils (spoons, forks, and dishes) can be purchased to make eating and drinking easier for a student with movement dysfunction (see Figure 7.6). Arm slings and other adaptations can be fabricated to make the movement of the hand to the mouth easier for students who need these interventions. Special feeders can be used with students who lack sufficient arm movement. Devices can help make the required movement patterns easier to perform but will not teach student independence in eating. Systematic procedures (see Chapter 13) must be applied in order to teach students with movement disorders to eat and drink, using adaptive devices as necessary.

Oral motor competence is *not* a prerequisite for beginning to provide training in self-feeding skills. Coordination of certain oral movement patterns,

however, will enhance training in self-feeding. For example, a student who is unable to get food from a utensil using the lips and teeth will have difficulty getting food into the mouth even when the utensil can be brought to the mouth. Problems with tongue movement may make movement of food from the front of the mouth to the side, for chewing, and to the back, for swallowing, quite difficult. Some students compensate for poorly coordinated tongue movement by pushing the food around in the mouth with the fingers. Some students may undergo increases in muscle tone in the body and the mouth with the introduction of food. This situation has been labeled as anticipation (Mueller, 1975) and results in poorly coordinated oral movement patterns. For instance, with anticipation, increased tone may cause the student's body to move away from the food and spoon, the jaw to open widely, and the tongue to pull back in the mouth. Each of these patterns make removal of food from the spoon, chewing, and swallowing almost impossible to accomplish without choking.

Tone changes, postural stability, coordinated movement of the oral musculature, and hand-to-mouth movement patterns should be individually assessed in each student before a decision to teach self-feeding is made. Food is a reinforcer for many (but not all) students. Teaching a student to self-feed but to eat with poorly coordinated movements strengthens the behavior of poor oral motor coor-

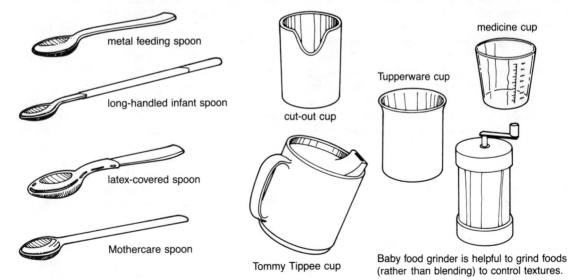

metal feeding spoon

long-handled infant spoon

latex-covered spoon

Mothercare spoon

cut-out cup

Tommy Tippee cup

medicine cup

Tupperware cup

Baby food grinder is helpful to grind foods (rather than blending) to control textures.

FIGURE 7.6 Examples of feeding equipment: cups and spoons

dination. However, preventing a student from acquiring independence may result in learned help-lessness. All factors should be carefully weighed by parents and professionals working with a student so that effective overall programming strategies can be designed for each situation.

TOILETING

Students with movement dysfunction can be toilet trained using standard procedures (such as those described in Chapter 13) with consideration of several additional factors (Bigge, 1982; Campbell, in press; Finnie, 1975). Positioning of the student with physical disabilities is an essential component in effective toileting. Of particular importance are muscle tone and alignment and postural control in the muscles of the pelvis, hips, and trunk. Reasonably normal degrees of tone must be attained in order for elimination to be possible. For example, students with hypertonus, particularly in the pelvis, hips, and legs, may have even greater increases of tone during toileting, thereby preventing elimination due to muscle "stiffness." A student with low tone may lack the muscle contractions necessary for effective bowel and bladder elimination. Proper positioning can, as with other management and instructional activities, normalize muscle tone and provide needed postural support. Many types of toileting equipment are commercially available (see Figure 7.7 for one example). Students may require additional modifications (towel roll supports or pads) to ensure proper support and alignment when using commercial equipment (Bergen & Colangelo, 1982).

Another factor that must be considered when designing toilet training programs is the nutritional intake of a student. The amount of liquid that is taken in during the day is of critical importance. Many students, particularly those with severe eating problems, may consume little liquid during a day. Elimination may be so infrequent as to make training difficult. Specific elimination patterns can be determined by taking baseline data to determine both the approximate time during the day and the frequency and type of elimination (see Chapter 13). Providing a student with liquids approximately every half hour during the day (and particularly in the morning) may be necessary in order to increase the number of opportunities per day for training (see Chapter 13).

Many students with severe movement disorders may have particular difficulty with bowel elimina-

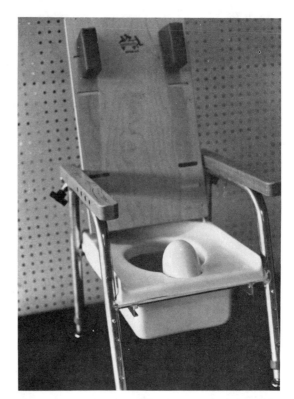

FIGURE 7.7 Adapted toilets can be used to position students for toilet training.

tion. These difficulties may be associated with poor nutritional intake, medication side-effects, physical immobility, poor muscle tone, or other factors (Batshaw & Perret, 1981; Sobsey, 1982). A student with chronic constipation will have great difficulty acquiring bowel continence. Problems with constipation can be managed through increased liquid intake, adding high fiber foods to the diet, and using mild natural laxatives, such as prune juice. Stool softeners can be used as a laxative, or stronger laxatives may be suggested by a doctor.

Teachers and parents may often not begin toilet training with a child because of difficulties encountered in positioning or underestimation of training potential. Fully independent toileting involves not only elimination on the toilet but also communication of toileting needs, mobility to the bathroom, independence in transfer onto the toilet, and management of clothing. Although many students with physical disabilities may only be able to partially complete the total sequence, successful elimination patterns can be trained using existing procedures with accommodation for individual positioning needs and nutritional considerations. Studies of toilet training procedures indicate that most students can be trained, regardless of cognitive level (Smith, 1979; Smith & Smith, 1977). The procedures developed by Foxx and Azrin appear to be the most effective across populations although individual student-timed procedures, such as a wet-alarm pants system, have also been attempted (Anderson, 1982).

Wet-alarm pants systems can also be used to manage the toileting needs of a student who is not on a toilet training program. Cooper, McInerney, and Macke (1983) used pants alerts in a classroom of six adolescent students with severe physical disabilities to indicate when each student needed to be changed. This application increased overall instructional time available for students by decreasing staff time spent transporting students to the bathroom, removing and putting them in adaptive equipment, and checking for wet pants. Activation of the pants alarm also allowed staff to collect accurate baseline data on elimination patterns that were later used to toilet students at individually scheduled times throughout the school day (Cooper, 1984).

DRESSING

Dressing and undressing without assistance are extremely complex movement tasks. Many of the required motor patterns involve wide movements of the extremities away from the trunk of the body. Managing fastenings, in contrast, requires very finely coordinated manipulation of the fingers. These gross and fine muscle movement patterns must be performed while moving from one posture into another. Shirts or jackets may be put on or removed while in a sitting position; however, in order to pull pants up or down, a student must be able to roll or stand.

Many students with severe movement disorders will never be able to dress and undress without assistance, due to the variety and complexity of required movement patterns; but, these activities can be accomplished by adults, using procedures to normalize muscle tone and facilitate partial acquisition of these tasks.

Positioning for Dressing and Undressing

Most students above the chronological age of 12 to 18 months should be dressed and undressed in sitting positions. Sitting is a chronologically age-appropriate position from which students can learn to use their arms and observe the dressing activity. Supported sitting positions, achieved either with equipment or adult support will be necessary for students who are unable to balance well using the trunk muscles. Students who need to use their arms to hold themselves upright in sitting will also be unable to use the arms for movements in and out of clothing. Barrel chairs and benches can be used to provide support for students with some sitting balance and arm and leg movements. Students who lack sitting balance or who will require considerable guidance of arm and leg movements by an adult can be provided with postural support through the adult's position and body (see Figure 7.8). Additional examples of alternate positions that can be used for dressing and undressing can be found in Campbell (in press), Conner, Williamson, and Sieppe (1978), or Finnie (1975).

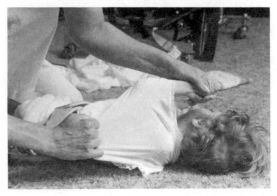

FIGURE 7.8 An adult can provide support in a variety of ways for a child during dressing.

Some activities, such as changing diapers or dressing and undressing infants, cannot be accomplished well with the child in a sitting position. Changing diapers with the child lying on the back is easiest. Increases in tone may occur with students who are in a supine position. Placing a small pillow under the head or applying pressure with the hands on the chest while rotating the student's hips toward his trunk may help to normalize tone. Students should then be moved into sitting positions to finish dressing or can be moved into sidelying to pull the pants up.

Facilitation Procedures

Physical guidance procedures are typically used to teach students to perform necessary movement patterns for dressing and undressing (Azrin, Schaeffer, & Weslowski, 1976; Campbell, 1977). Guidance is provided in ways that normalize tone and *promote* more normal movement patterns with students who have severe discrepancies in postural tone or a limited range of joint motion (Campbell, in press). This type of guidance, referred to as *facilitation*, results in two possible outcomes: (a) students whose movements are guided using facilitation methods will be physically managed in ways that will normalize tone and help prevent further problems, such as limitations in range of motion of the joints, (b) repetitive practice of the proper movement patterns may enable students to learn to perform the necessary movements as a component of acquiring partial or total independence in dressing. In this sense, use of facilitation procedures during dressing and undressing is both physical management and instruction.

Specific facilitation procedures are developed for individuals by physical or occupational therapists. Several general principles, however, can be incorporated into programs for all students. Most individuals are best guided by moving them from the shoulders or hips. An adult can guide a student's arm through a sleeve, for example, by moving his arm from shoulder, rather than by pulling his hand through the sleeve. Slow guidance of movement patterns will be less likely to result in tone increases. Adults should guide the extremities *slowly* through the clothing, rather than by quickly moving the arms or legs. Tone may also increase in some students when attempts are made to initiate movement. A student's efforts to produce the required movement may result in increases in arm and leg stiffness that prevent the movement from occurring. Adults can assist students who experience this difficulty by guiding the initiation but letting the student finish the movement pattern, without further assistance.

Use of these general management principles, in combination with individual facilitation procedures that may be suggested by therapists, may not be fully sufficient to teach dressing independence. These methods often must be combined with specific dressing training procedures, such as those described further in Chapter 13.

Managing Fastenings

Shoe laces, buttons, zippers, belts and other clothing fastenings require degrees of movement coordination that many students with severe handicaps may not be able to perform. These manipulation schemes, however, can be easily bypassed through clothing modifications (Campbell, in press). Using velcro in place of buttons and metal waistband fasteners, for example, may allow independence in dressing without performance of fine manipulation skills. Some examples of clothing modifications to make dressing easier are suggested in Table 7.2.

TABLE 7.2 Clothing modifications

Has trouble getting arms through sleeves.	Wear short-sleeve shirts. Wear shirts without tight sleeves (short or long)— raglan sleeves are good.
Has trouble buttoning shirt.	Wear shirts that zip part-way down front. Replace buttonholes with Velcro closings. Select shirts with large buttons.
Has trouble getting legs into pants.	Wear short-leg pants. Wear pants with wide legs.
Has trouble getting pants over braces.	Slit pants up inside of legs and insert snap-tapes or Velcro or zipper closings.
Has trouble with elastic waists.	Select pants with waistbands (not tight).
Has trouble fastening pants.	Replace button or hook fastening with Velcro.
Has trouble with belt.	Select belt with cinch-type fastening or with pull-through fastening.
Has trouble with zippers.	Only choose clothing which zips in front. Use ring attached to zipper for easier grasp and pulling.
Has trouble with buttons (on pants, shirts, jackets, sweaters).	Replace buttonholes with Velcro or select clothing without buttons.

PHYSICAL MANAGEMENT

In summary, managing the physical needs for children with severe movement dysfunction enables them to maintain normalized tone; prevents the development of changes in muscle length, bones, and joints; and can be combined with traditional instructional methods to enable acquisition of, at least, partial independence in self-care skills. Many students with severe movement handicaps may never be fully independent in all aspects of self-care; however, proper management procedures can enable partial independence, thereby reducing the levels of physical care required by these students.

REFERENCES

Alexander, R., & Bigge, J. (1982). Facilitation of language and speech. In J. L. Bigge (Ed.), *Teaching individuals with physical and multiple disabilities* (pp. 257–289). Columbus, OH: Charles E. Merrill.

Anderson, D. M. (1982). Ten years later: Training in the post-Azrin-and-Foxx era. *The Journal of the Association for the Severely Handicapped, 7,* 71–79.

Azrin, N. H., Schaeffer, R. M., & Weslowski, M. D. (1976). A rapid method of teaching profoundly retarded persons to dress. *Mental Retardation, 14,* 29–33.

Batshaw, M. L., & Perret, U. M. (1981). *Children with handicaps: A medical primer.* Baltimore: Paul H. Brookes.

Bergen, A. F. & Colangelo, C. (1982). *Positioning the client with central nervous system deficits: The wheelchair and other adapted equipment.* Valhalla, NY: Valhalla Rehabilitation Publications, Ltd.

Bigge, J. (1982). Self-care. In J. L. Bigge (Ed.), *Teaching individuals with physical and multiple disabilities* (2nd ed.). Columbus, OH: Charles E. Merrill.

Campbell, P. (1977). Self-care skills. In N. Haring (Ed.), *Developing effective individual educational programs for severely handicapped children and youth* (pp. 115–138). Columbus, OH: Specialized Press.

Campbell, P. H. (1979). Teaching oral-motor skills to severely handicapped children. In G. Edgar & R. York (Eds.), *Teaching the severely handicapped* (Vol. 4, pp. 39–63). Columbus, OH: Specialized Press.

Campbell, P. H. (in press). *Neurodevelopmental treatment methods for teaching self-care skills: A handbook for parents and professionals.* Baltimore: Paul H. Brookes.

Campbell, P. H., Green, K. M., & Carlsen, L. M. (1977). Approximating the norm through environmental and child-centered prosthetics and adaptive equipment. In E. Sontag (Ed.), *Educational programming for the severely and profoundly handicapped* (pp. 300–322). Reston, VA: Council for Exceptional Children.

Campbell, P. H., & Hanna, L. M. (in press). A comparison of two methods to train adult learners to properly position children with physical handicaps in adaptive seating devices. *American Physical Therapy Association.*

Conner, F. P., Williamson, G. C., & Sieppe, J. M. (1978) *Program guide for infants and toddlers with neuromotor and other developmental disabilities.* New York: Teachers College Press.

Cooper, M. (1984). *Toileting programming for students with severe and multiple handicaps.* Unpublished manuscript.

Cooper, M., McInerney, W., & Macke, P. (1983). *Use of simple electronic devices to improve educational programming and data collection procedures in classrooms for severely handicapped students.* Poster session presented at The Association for Persons with Severe Handicaps Convention, San Francisco.

Finnie, N. (Ed.). (1975). *Handling your young cerebral palsied child at home.* New York: Dutton.

Fraser, B. A., & Hensinger, R. N. (1983). *Managing physical handicaps.* Baltimore: Paul H. Brookes.

Galka, G., & Fraser, B. A. (1980). *Gross motor management of severely multiply impaired students* (Vol. 2). Baltimore: University Park Press.

Morris, S. E. (1977). *Program guidelines for children with feeding problems.* Edison, NJ: Childcraft Education.

Morris, S. E. (1978). Oral-motor movement in eating. In J. Wilson (Ed.), *Oral-motor function and dysfunction in children.* Chapel Hill: University of North Carolina.

Morris, S. E. (1982a). *The normal acquisition of oral feeding skills: Implications for assessment and treatment.* New York: Therapeutic Media, Inc.

Morris, S. E. (1982b). *Pre-speech assessment scale* (rev. ed.). Clifton, NJ: J. A. Preston.

Mueller, H. (1975). Feeding. In N. Finnie (Ed.), *Handling your young cerebral palsied child at home.* New York: Dutton.

Smith, P. S. (1979). A comparison of different methods of toilet training the mentally handicapped. *Behavior Research and Therapy, 17,* 33–43.

Smith, P. S., & Smith, L. J. (1977). Chronological age and social age as factors in intensive, daytime toilet training of institutionalized, mentally retarded individuals. *Journal of Behavior Therapy and Experimental Psychiatry, 8,* 269–273.

Sobsey, R. J. (1983). Nutrition of children with severely handicapping conditions. *The Journal of the Association for Persons with Severe Handicaps, 8,* 14–17.

Sobsey, R. J., & Orelove, F. (1984). Neurophysiological facilitation of eating skills in severely handicapped children. *The Journal of the Association for the Severely Handicapped, 9,* 111–122.

Trefler, E. (Ed.). (1984). *Seating for children with cerebral palsy.* Memphis: Rehabilitation Engineering Program.

8

Programming for Students with Dysfunction in Posture and Movement

Philippa H. Campbell
Director, Family Child Learning Center
Children's Hospital Medical Center of Akron
and Kent State University

Movement difficulties can result from genetic causes; damage to the infant before, during, or after birth; or various traumatic events such as gunshot wounds, automobile accidents, or child abuse. The conditions that produce movement problems can *generally* be classified into one of two basic origins. The first group includes disorders (such as polio) that originate from damage to the anterior horn cell and the nerves leading to the muscles. These conditions are lower motor neuron lesions. A second group, upper motor neuron lesions, derives from damage to the structures of the brain, including the cerebral cortex, the spinal cord, and the cerebellum. Cerebral palsy is the single largest category of diagnosed upper motor neuron problems in children. (See Bleck and Nagel (1982), Bigge (1982), or Umbreit (1983) for further discussion of conditions producing impaired motor functioning.)

Lower motor neuron problems typically involve weakened muscles with limited or no power to move. In contrast, the motor impairment in cerebral palsy is not initially characterized by weak muscles or decreased strength. Rather, the child's ability to move in response to events is limited by atypical muscle tone and poor coordination among muscle groups. The ways in which the environment is represented motorically to the infant or young child with motor dysfunction may include distortions characterized or defined by the limitations of the movement. For instance, a child with poorly coordinated movement patterns may develop a representation of shaking a rattle that is quite different from the representation of shaking produced by the infant with normal movement. Furthermore, the infant with severely limited movement may develop no representation of a rattle as a shakeable object simply because the limitation of movement prevents shaking actions.

Material supported in part by the U.S. Department Office of Education, Personnel Preparation, Special Projects awards to the Children's Hospital Medical Center of Akron (Training Physical and Occupational Therapy Personnel to Serve Severely/Multiply Handicapped Students, No. G008301649 and Innovative Programs for Severely Handicapped Children, No. G008302839).

In cerebral palsy as well as in other conditions involving disturbance to the central nervous system (CNS), all of the child's movements may be atypical. However, not all individuals with deviations in movement show overt CNS dysfunction. Students with Down syndrome frequently demonstrate deficient movement, as do students with labels of psychomotor retardation or developmental delay. Movement may also be atypical in children with genetic abnormalities or degenerative diseases or conditions of the central nervous system. Posture and movement may be atypical in children with genetic abnormalities or degenerative diseases or conditions of the central nervous system. Posture and movement may be atypical in terms of the quality (or pattern of movement). Delayed performance of skills may also be present. Both atypical patterns and delayed performance are related to deviations in postural or muscle tone, on which all movement is based.

MOVEMENT COMPETENCE

Coordinated movement depends on integrities of the neuromotor system as well as on an aligned posture (Bobath & Bobath, 1984; S. Campbell, 1984). Muscle tone, strength, endurance, flexibility, and range of motion at joints throughout the body influence the quality of movement patterns used to perform posture and coordinated movement (Campbell, in press–a). The quantity of movement produced is also important.

The most critical of these factors is postural tone or the degree of tension in the body musculature. Related to this very basic process are measures of the quality and the amount of movement performed in both structured and nonstructured situations. Each of these basic processes, as well as skills in mobility, hand transport, manipulation, oral-motor/eating, and oral-motor/vocalization, can be represented in a way that allows us to not only measure initial performance, but also to indicate methods of intervention.

The relationship among the various types of movement required for everyday living and the basic processes underlying movement production is outlined as a model for intervention with students with movement dysfunction in Figure 8.1. All movement can be classified as either posture, automatic, primary, or cognitively directed; however, neither posture or movement is produced without a stimulus. For this reason, movement difficulties are often described as sensorimotor disturbances to emphasize the relationship between the sensory and the motor systems in producing posture and movement. The function or purpose of each type of movement is unique. Posture (Function A) can be defined as the extent to which the body is maintained in alignment with a variety of positions such as prone (stomachlying), supine (backlying), sidelying, sitting, and standing. Automatic movements (Function B) result from disturbances to body alignment in relation to gravity. These movements automatically realign body parts and institute and maintain balance against gravity. Primary movements are the initial step in acquisition of cognitively directed (Function C) patterns (Piaget, 1952). These movements are very simple schemes involving a stimulus and a movement reponse that results in a consequence. More complex movement organization, in which simple movement schemes are uniquely grouped together to attain predetermined ends, results in functionally useful cognitively directed movement.

The basic motor processes of tone, movement quality, and movement quantity provide the basis on which posture and automatic, primary, and cognitively directed movement is produced. Disturbances in any of the three basic processes will cause all movements to be atypical. Complex cognitively directed movements are the result of intention (Bower, 1979) expressed in relation to people, events, and objects in the student's environment. *Intention* can be defined as the coordination of two existing schemes in order to obtain a pre-existing and desired goal (Bricker, Macke, Levin, & Campbell, 1981). Many students with dysfunction in tone and movement quality and quantity may use movement intentionally and to attain a goal; however, there are other students whose movement is not cognitively directed with or without disturbance in the basic underlying processes. This differentiation is critical when choosing intervention strategies since techniques designed to alter the underlying process of movement will not, in and of themselves, produce cognitively directed motor behavior.

UNDERLYING PROCESSES

Tone

Postural tone is a measure of the tension in the muscles throughout the body. It is the basis on which posture and automatic and goal-directed

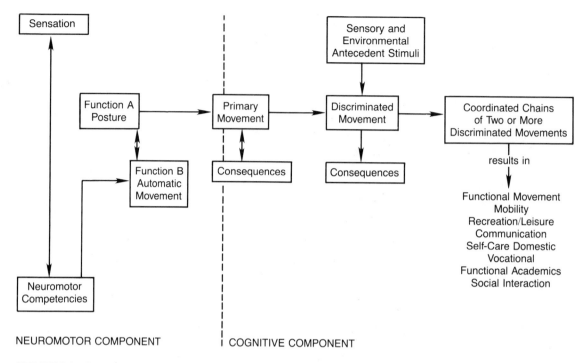

FIGURE 8.1 Expanded integrated programming model

movements are produced. Normal postural tone allows postural stability with mobility; that is, the head can remain stable when the arm moves forward or the wrist remains stable while the fingers move. Deviations in postural tone range from an absence or severe limitation in tone (hypotonia or too little tone) to too much postural tone (hypertonus or spasticity). An individual with hypertonus may have difficulty with motor skills because of stiffness in involved parts of the body. Adequate muscle tension to move against gravity is absent or limited in students with hypotonia.

Other children have unstable postural tone which fluctuates even when the child is not performing motor actions. These students may show relatively low postural tone at one moment and be severely hypertonic the next moment. Postural tone fluctuations from one extreme in the range to the other are the most dramatic, but fluctuations can occur anywhere on the continuum from hypotonic to hypertonic. Fluctuating tonicity inhibits movement in that muscle tone is not only atypical but also constantly changing. The student, therefore, has not only an atypical but also an unstable base from

which to generate motor patterns necessary to interact with the environment.

Tone can be represented on a continuum such as the scale illustrated in Figure 8.2 by using ratings of 1 for hypotonic students and 9 for those students who are so severely hypertonic as to be labeled *rigid*. These initial ratings reflect the *underlying tone* under conditions of rest.

Observations of the student when resting, lying down, or sitting quietly provide the necessary information. The measurement of *underlying tone* is essentially a rating of postural tone under conditions as inactive as possible. More critical to developing and implementing intervention methods to normalize postural tone are measurements of tone under varying conditions of stimulation or movement. The tone exhibited under more active conditions is labeled *predominant tone*.

Postural tone can be modified systematically by using intervention methods to increase tone (facilitation) or decrease tone (inhibition); however, it is more important to realize that postural tone can also be changed nonsystematically as a functional response to influences from the environment. A

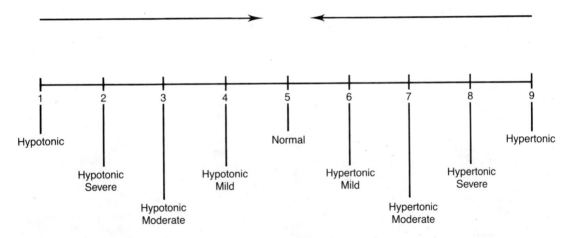

FIGURE 8.2 Two-dimensional representation of the domain of tonicity

severely hypertonic child may tighten up even more when someone speaks to him or attempts to pick him up, or simply because someone else in the classroom coughs or makes a sudden noise. Those children with fluctuating tone may show even greater fluctuations in response to a favorite toy or when attempting to vocalize or talk. Some children even show changes in postural tone in *anticipation* of something that is going to occur but has not yet actually happened. The point here is that postural tone is not fixed, but is changeable; tone changes in uncontrolled (or nonsystematic) situations as well as under the controlled and systematic conditions of intervention. Knowing how *underlying* and *predominant* differ is important information used to carry out appropriate intervention strategies. A complete assessment, however, will not just label the type of tone in each category. Structured observation of a student's behavior, in the classroom or at home, will produce information about the types of conditions that cause tone to change.

There are many situations that potentially can occur in the classroom to alter the postural tone of individual students. Some of these factors are outlined in Table 8.1. All of these factors may negatively influence the student's tone in the classroom, at home, or in community environments.

Influences of Position (Gravity)
The way in which a student is positioned influences both postural alignment (stability) and the extent to which normally coordinated movement patterns can be produced. Most often, students are posi-

tioned in some sort of seating equipment (although positioning in other types of postures, like standing, may also be used). Positioning equipment is designed to align the student in as normal posture as possible. Some students may not be properly aligned in the equipment. Negative tone changes may then occur automatically as the body musculature attempts to adjust to maintain an upright posture. Difficulty producing normally coordinated antigravity movement, may also result in further tonal changes, even when the student has been properly positioned. A student who tries to use her arms in sitting may demonstrate tone changes when initiating movement.

Influences of Sensory Stimuli
Sensory stimuli precede both posture and movement responses. These stimuli may be presented to the student through systematic educational instruction or may simply occur in the environment. A particular type of stimuli or the characteristics of a stimulus may negatively influence tone. Tactile or auditory stimuli, in particular, may cause the tone of some students to increase although visual stimuli also may produce the same result. Often, it is not the stimuli itself but its associated characteristics: the suddenness of noise or of being touched may result in tone changes. This information is critical to provide appropriate programming. Systematic *grading* of sensory stimuli can enable a student to develop control over tonal changes; therefore, it is important to understand the sensory stimuli that are associated with changes in posture tone.

TABLE 8.1 Examples of factors that may impact on muscle tone

Influences of Position (Gravity):
Pro (with) gravity
Anti (against) gravity
Gravity neutral

Influences of Sensory Stimuli:

Auditory:	*Visual:*	*Tactile:*
Tone	Size	Location
Loudness	Shape	Pressure
Timing in onset	Color	Type of Stimuli
Duration	Configuration	
	Movement of Stimuli	

Environmental Factors:	*Physical Management:*	*Child State:*
Object Placement	Carrying	Emotional (laughing; crying)
Time of Day	Lifting	Neurological (seizures, etc.)
Type of Instruction	Transfer	
Demands for Response	Positioning	
Task Difficulty	Care Activities such as	
Reinforcing Properties of Object or Person	Feeding, Changing	

Environmental Factors, Physical Management, and Child State

Activities routinely done with students with physical handicaps to move them from one instructional situation to another frequently alter tone (lifting, carrying, dressing, positioning, repositioning, transferring, toileting). Tonal changes can be dramatic if the student is not handled appropriately. Numerous environmental events may also change tone. Increased tone is predictable when the movement required is extremely difficult for the student. Tone may significantly increase in the left hand and arm when the student is required to use fine manipulation of the fingers in her right hand. Most environmental events, such as object placement, performance requirements or task difficulty, can be gradually increased in difficulty to teach students to move with more normalized tone. However, a few factors are not easily alterable by instructional and therapeutic personnel. Some students receive medication that may change postural tone (while controlling seizures). Or, a student who is crying or laughing may do so with increased tone.

All skills have some component of motor behavior regardless of whether required performances are classified as linguistic, social, or cognitive. The preverbal student has only movement as a means for responding to the environment. Postural tone must be as normalized as possible for her to acquire the functional movements necessary to perform developmental skills such as sitting, walking, and self-feeding and even problem-solving skills such as object permanence or means-end relationships. The results of programming for tone normalization provided through basic therapy alone, or without regard for the tone changes that occur in non-specific intervention situations, will not be as significant as when postural tone is viewed as an essential component of all of the student's activity. Teachers, therapists, and parents of students with postural tone deviations must not lose sight of the relationships between the motor system and environmental interaction. Intervention strategies can only be as effective as the assessment on which the selection of those strategies is based. If the teacher fails to identify that the tone of a particular student changes when the child is provided with a specific toy and therefore continues to provide the toy, the intervention might teach the student to be more hypertonic. No teacher, therapist, or parent would intentionally instruct a student that way. However, these instructional situations often occur when observational assessment has not been careful or precise or when postural tone is viewed as a fixed and unchangeable dimension of behavior.

Qualitative Movement

Most assessments or observations of motor skills focus on the number of motor milestone skills performed by a student (Campbell, Clegg, & McFarland, 1982); however, most physical and occupational therapists are also interested in determining the patterns of movement a student uses to perform posture and automatic and cognitively directed movements.

Historically, patterns of movement were described as normal, abnormal, primitive, or mixed (Bobath & Bobath, 1975). These categories have largely been abandoned in favor of a system that operationally describes the *form* of posture and movement patterns while also looking at the *function* or *purpose* of the movement (Campbell, 1985a; in press–a; Wilson, 1984). We want to know the *form* used to achieve posture and to move under varying conditions of gravity; however, we also need to know whether the *forms* used to achieve the *functions* of posture are automatic and cognitively-directed movement.

The purpose or function of posture and movement is to provide coordinated interaction with various aspects of the environment. Gravity is the primary factor with which the very young infant must learn to contend. Muscle activity provides the force necessary to enable the human body to move against gravity, to perform actions that resist the influence of the pull of gravity. For instance, lifting the head in a prone (stomach lying) position is an antigravity movement; the muscles of the head and neck must contract to provide the force necessary to move the head upward against the downward pull of gravity. This movement would be classified as an active motion, one performed through activation of the muscles of head extension. Once moved to this position, if the head is held upright, both the muscles that extend the head and those that bend the head must cocontract to provide stability against the gravitational pull. However, when the child then moves her head, for instance turns it to the side, the result is *activation* (mobility) of the neck rotator muscles against a background of postural stability achieved through cocontraction. All normal functional movement is the result of a coordinated relationship of muscle activity that allows for active movement (mobility) in combination with postural control (stability).

Postural tone provides the background for both active muscle contraction and cocontraction; however, postural tone is deficient or atypical in most types of movement disorders because of CNS damage. Therefore, the resultant movement, whether functional for stability or mobility, will also be atypical. In infancy, many variations in postural tone may be seen. The majority of infants are believed to have hypotonic (rather than hypertonic) tone variations. The infant's initial movements are likely to be those which gain some degree of stability against gravity (such as head control); but when postural tone is deficient, cocontraction for stability may not be possible. Postural stability, however, may still occur. This stability will be achieved through an atypical adjustment of body parts rather than through normal cocontraction of the muscles. These adjustments compensate for lack of cocontraction and insufficient tone artificially, allowing for the function, postural stability, to be achieved through atypical means.

Several examples may help to clarify the concept of postural adjustment of body parts to each other for biomechanical advantage. Students with low underlying tone in the musculature of the head/neck and trunk commonly turtle their heads (see Figure 8.3). The shoulders are elevated toward the ear lobes and the neck is subsequently "shortened." The result is a change in the relationship of gravity to movement. The amount of balance required to maintain the head in relationship to the shoulders is significantly decreased.

Many students may achieve upright posture in sitting through increased tone in the pelvis and the hips combined with flexion in the upper spine. This atypical postural adjustment allows the student to "sit" but inhibits use of the arms and legs for functional movement. The resultant movement patterns depend on and are restricted to postural stability rather than characterized by stability with mobility, as are normal movement patterns.

Atypical postural tone and biomechanical adjustment of body parts initiate a cycle that results in increasing impaired posture and movement

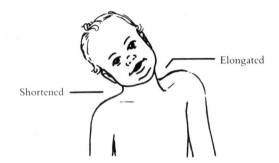

FIGURE 8.3 An example of postural misalignment where elevation of the shoulders shortens the neck, thereby allowing the head to be maintained against gravity

(see Figure 8.4). This progression is sequential. The atypically aligned posture (due to insufficient postural tone) severely limits the performance of both automatic and cognitively directed movement patterns.

Compensatory patterns that are not normal in form and are seldom efficient in function derive directly from atypical posture. If repeated or practiced, they become habitual; the student spontaneously produces these restricted patterns in a variety of conditions. The habitual patterns are frequently characterized by limited range of motion of involved joints. When untreated or unaltered, they can lead to secondary problems of muscle shortening or elongation. These problems with muscle length are sometimes referred to as *muscle tightness, muscle lengthening,* or *contractures.* Contractures must be stretched out through direct exercise to return muscles to their correct and optimal length. As shown in Figure 8.5, when unaltered, contractures become *deformities* that can only be changed through surgery. Thus, the atypical postural tone limits muscle cocontraction and results in atypical postural adjustments which, in turn, force the production of atypical compensatory movement patterns. Practiced or repeated patterns become habitual, produce secondary

muscle tightness due to movement being restricted, and result in the formation of deformities that are correctable only through surgery.

The greatest number of postural adjustments (normal or atypical) occur at the proximal joints—head/neck, scapula, shoulder, hip, and pelvis. These joints represent the areas of the body where the largest bulk muscles are placed and where motor actions require little fine coordination and control. Movement that occurs, for instance, at the head/neck or the shoulder is gross motor controlled in contrast to the finely coordinated movement performed by muscles in the hands or in the oral-motor region. The very young baby's first attempts to move against gravity involve the head/neck and the shoulders. Therefore, initial atypical postural adjustments are likely to occur in these proximal areas. For instance, in the head/neck movement described earlier, the turtling produces a compensatory pattern of neck extensor hyperextension. The neck hyperextension (without balanced flexion necessary for cocontraction) results in a limited function of prone head control that is restricted to an atypical movement form. In other words, the purpose of the activity is met with a qualitatively atypical movement form. As a result, the muscles of the head/neck may become short-

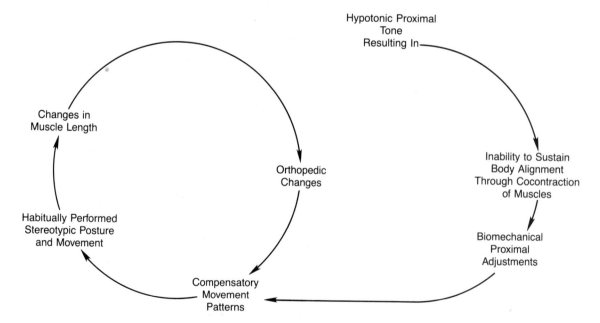

FIGURE 8.4 Cycle of development of abnormal movement

SPASM ──────▶ CONTRACTURE ──────▶ DEFORMITY

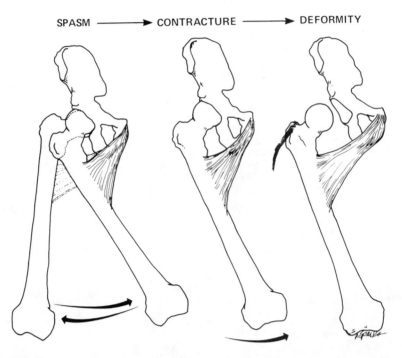

FIGURE 8.5   Progression from tightness to deformity in the hip joint with resultant deformity of dislocation of the hip

Source: From *Physically Handicapped Children: A Medical Atlas for Teachers* (p. 64) by Eugene Bleck and Donald Nagel, 1982, New York: Grune & Stratton. Reprinted by permission.

ened and elongated, and contractures may develop if this pattern is practiced and becomes habitual. Furthermore, though head control may seem to be present, the movement is restricted to only one *form*. The student may be prevented from using the neck extensors/flexors and rotators to flex the head laterally or to turn through rotation. Or flexion of the head forward (chin tucked toward neck) may be prevented through elongation of the neck flexor muscles. The full range of head movement is therefore prevented by a pattern of fixation that originally produced stability against gravity.

The quality of posture and movement is an essential component of an evaluation of the motor system. Physical and occupational therapists, especially those who are trained in Neurodevelopmental Treatment, carry out a task analysis of muscle coordination, in various postures and movements, that is referred to as a *kinesiological analysis*. This assessment process yields global information about posture and movement as well as specific muscle groups. Information derived from the analysis is then combined with information about other factors,

such as muscle strength or joint range of motion that underlie production of posture and movement. The therapist, then, uses this information as the basis for formulating treatment goals and objectives. The movement analysis and treatment goal plan described in Tables 8.2 and 8.3 were prepared for a child (with low underlying tone but predominantly increased tone in the arms and legs) who will serve as illustration of other concepts throughout this chapter.

Intervention provided by a physical or occupational therapist is typically directed at normalizing postural tone and simultaneously improving the quality of movements, particularly the automatic movements. Educational programming more often is aimed at primary or cognitively directed movements required for functional skills; however, in order for both the therapists and the teachers to be effective, postural tone must be normalized as part of all posture and movement training (whether automatic, primary, or goal-directed) and the student must be taught to perform each type of movement with patterns as normal as possible.

TABLE 8.2 Movement analysis for a child with low underlying tone but predominantly increased tone in arms and legs

Key Problem/Posture	Compensatory Movements	Implications
Low central tone, increasing to high tone in extremities, legs more than arms.	Increased tone in extremities limits antigravity use.	Development of tightness and overlengthening in specific muscle groups.
Hyperextension (active) in head/neck with elevation and forward tipping in scapula (bilaterally); thoracic flexion results in upper trunk falling into gravity.	Arm movements limited to extension with abduction—limits reach and grasp; tone increases for support produce alternate movement of internal rotation and flexion of humerus; arm patterns alternate between the two.	Overlengthening in thoracic spine; tightness in pectoralis muscles; overlengthening of scapular adductors.
Limited adduction of scapula for stability and movement of arm without scapular outward rotation; limited stability of upper back for reaching and arm use.	Biomechanical malalignment for extension rotation; limited arm use (see above).	Overlengthening of scapula adductors, thoracic extensors.
Malalignment of rib cage with flaring lower ribs; tendency to concavity in upper rib cage (sternum).	Poor coordination of respiration/phonation due to overlengthening of obliques.	Breathing difficulties; low volume on speech, short duration and low volume.
Anterior pelvic tilt in all positions with tendency to low back extension.	Hip flexion, abduction, external rotation and/or extension, internal rotation in hips with high tone.	Poor spinal mobility for rotation in lumbar spine; difficulty in shifting weight anteriorly; tightness in low back extensors and hamstrings.

Therefore, the teacher must be skillful in observing patterns of movement and determining whether they are normal or atypical in order to effectively train functional skills such as eating, toileting, communicating, and manipulating.

Movement Quantity

The amount of movement present is a dimension that is seldom evaluated by teachers or therapists; however, deviation on this dimension has significant implications for the intervention provided for individuals with motor dysfunction, particularly where the other movement processes of tone and movement quality are normal. Furthermore, movement quantity or rate acts to bridge the underlying processes with mobility, manipulation, and other movement-based functional skills.

Some students with relatively normal postural tone and patterns of movement are seldom observed to move. For instance, many severely handicapped students with long histories of institutionalization or lack of programming have not been placed in situations requiring movement. In fact, many custodial care environments inadvertently foster immobility since immobile people are easier to care for than mobile ones. These students often show a lack of movement quantity that we cannot account for on the basis of deviations in postural tone or movement quality. Seligman (1975) refers to this type of situation as *learned helplessness*—which implies not just that the student had not had the opportunity to learn to move, but rather that the opportunities provided for the student have taught *lack* of movement even when the motor capability for producing the movement was present. Students with long histories of no intervention are not the only ones who learn to be helpless when movement is required. Younger children can also inadvertently be taught not to move by receiving passive motor intervention (such as range of motion exercises) or by being prevented from performing movement activities through management routines such as carrying, dressing, or feeding.

All types of movement—automatic, primary, and cognitively directed—result in response to incoming stimuli and produce a consequence to the movement. However, each isolated movement pattern must occur often enough to be incorporated into the more complex organizations of movement

TABLE 8.3

Treatment Goal Plan (for child in Table 8.2)

Key Problems:	1. Inability to maintain alignment in antigravity postures —sitting, standing; can only lie supine (back) or prone (stomach) without assistance.
	2. Low tone centrally with increases in tone in arms and legs against gravity that limit functional use of extremities.
	3. Limited upper back (thoracic) stability for reaching and arm use; limited spinal rotation for full arm use.
	4. Development of tightness and overlengthening as future possible deformities.

General Plan

Direct Treatment:	1. Increase support and anti-gravity tone in spine (trunk).
	2. Weight shift in sitting—all planes.
	3. Facilitate thoracic and lumbosacral rotation for increased arm use.
Carryover Treatment:	1. Positioning in sitting and standing for alignment.
	2. Reaching—forward (flexion of humerus without internal rotation).

patterns, to be functional for the student, and to be practiced enough that the response is strengthened and maintained. For instance, the consequence of turning the head from midline to the side is viewing or listening to something. In other words, a child is not likely to turn her head from midline to the side for the sake of head turning alone. The movement is present for some purpose or function. If a student were able to turn her head from midline with balance between the neck flexors/extensors and with normal postural tone, a movement response of head turning to the side would be said to be present in the student's repertoire; however, if the student performed this movement only once per day or once per hour, the rate or the quantity of the movement would be insufficient for functional use without intervention. Furthermore, the movement of head turning would not be likely to be

strengthened or increased without intervention to provide repeated practice under functional and motivating conditions.

Assessments of movement quantity are most typically made in relation to primary or goal-directed movements and, therefore, are frequently confounded with other variables such as opportunity to perform or consequence preferences. When a student does not move her head from midline to the side more frequently than once per minute, the teacher can say that the rate of movement is atypical but cannot determine the reason for the low rate. This same student may motorically be able to perform at a higher rate, but not do so because she does not prefer the resultant consequence of looking or listening or does not see or hear well enough for the consequence to be relevant.

The relationship between consequences of performing a desired posture and the rate (quantity) of performance of that movement with an 18-month-old child with Down syndrome is illustrated in Figure 8.6. This student had achieved mobility by crawling; however, walking was inhibited by lack of weight bearing on the legs, regardless of the amount of support provided for weight bearing. When placed on a prone standing board, the child cried and withdrew the legs from the supporting surface unless well strapped. Baseline measurements of standing, in the initial segments of the graph, show that weight bearing on the legs was virtually absent; however, the staff judged that weight bearing was physically possible and not prevented by postural tone. Therefore, they instituted an intervention program that provided highly preferred consequences for weight bearing in a supported standing position. The student was given her favorite foods (which she fed herself) for increasingly long periods of weight bearing. The second segment of the graph illustrates the effectiveness of highly preferred foods in increasing the rate of weight bearing. To validate the effectiveness of this strategy, the highly preferred consequences for standing were eliminated and social praise was provided. The third section of the graph shows the *decrease* in rate of movement as a function of altering the consequences this way. The remaining sections document the progression from supported weight bearing to independent weight bearing once food reinforcement was reinstated.

This example emphasizes the importance of the consequences to movement, both in terms of

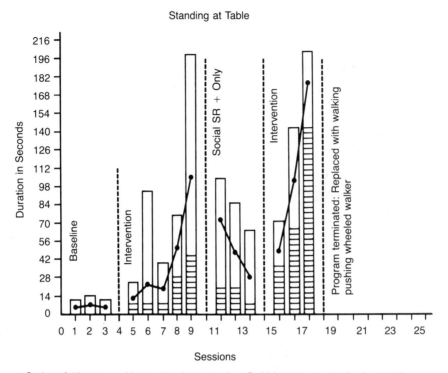

Series of 10 opportunities to stand per session. Solid bar represents the longest time in standing of any trial. Hatched bar represents the shortest time in standing of any trial. Solid line indicates the mean time in standing per session.

FIGURE 8.6   Relationship between motivation and length of standing

increasing and decreasing rate of movement; however, more important is the relationship of sufficient rate to the acquisition of additional, more complex movement patterns. The student in this illustration was prevented from acquiring the complex movement pattern required for walking, but not because of insufficient postural tone or inability to perform a specific movement pattern (weight bearing on the legs in standing). Rather, insufficient consequences for weight bearing in standing prevented him from developing the necessary *rate*—a critical component from which other, more complex movement patterns required for walking develop.

PROCESSES INVOLVED IN AUTOMATIC, PRIMARY, AND COGNITIVELY DIRECTED MOVEMENT

The general purpose of all intervention with students with movement impairment is to promote the acquisition of functional skills that will enable them to be as independent as possible in both current and future environments. Separate measurements of postural tone, movement quality, and movement quantity are essential to generate intervention strategies to both help students move (improve postural tone and movement quality) and teach both automatic and cognitively directed movement. Many parents and teachers of students with movement impairments who do not know that tone can be modified do not construct home or classroom environments that allow or systematically program for movement. These negative expectations can limit the quantity and type of movement of the severely involved student (because movement is not expected) or restrict available movement to atypical compensatory or abnormal patterns.

Each of the descriptors used to identify motor processes refers to the *function* of a particular behavior rather than to its specific *form*. The function of postural tone is to maintain sufficient muscle tension for a variety of movements against gravity; however, postural tone may take many forms, ranging from severely limited to severely excessive. Similarly, the purpose of movement quality is to allow for the performance of smooth, well-coordinated, efficient ways of moving in and around the environment. The forms of patterns of movement, however, can range from primitive to abnormal or from compensatory movements to movement abnormalities as a result of contractures or deformities.

Motor processes of mobility, manipulation, hand transport, and oral-motor proficiency are based on necessary and sufficient postural tone, movement quality, and movement quantity. The phrase *necessary and sufficient* is important; it does not imply "normality." For instance, hypotonia can in fact be sufficient for the production of certain motor patterns, even though it is not "normal." *Necessary and sufficient*, therefore, directly relates to the function of the dimension under consideration in certain circumstances. Hypotonia in the head/neck and shoulders may be sufficient to produce postural *fixes* that allow head control in a prone position but insufficient to allow head control in a standing position.

Further, the function of mobility is to go from place to place, but the form of that mobility can include many behaviors. Thus, forms of mobility include rolling, creeping, crawling, knee walking, walking, running, and jumping, or hopping on one foot. All these ways of moving would be present in the repertoires of most normal children; however, other mobility forms such as scooting on one's bottom in a sitting position, "frog leaping," or "bunny hopping" in a hand-knee position, or walking up on one's toes with the legs turned in and scissoring would be less likely to be observed in a normally developing child. Still others, such as moving a wheelchair by pushing the wheels or using a mouth stick to operate a switch to activate an electric wheelchair, would probably not be observed with normal children. Forms of mobility that are typically observed in developing children without movement disorders can be classified as normal in relation to particular chronological age ranges. Other mobility forms can be categorized as primitive in relation to chronological age ranges. For instance, a 5-year-old student who uses crawling as the primary form of mobility has a primitive form of mobility, since walking is the primary form of mobility of a typical 5-year-old. Still

other forms of mobility, such as walking up on the toes, might be described as atypical; where using a walker or crutches, or being mobile in a sitting position in a wheelchair, provide the function of mobility through unusual behavior forms.

Using the hand to interact with and manipulate objects in the environment with precise and controlled movements is one behavior that differentiates humans from lower animals (see Bower, 1979; Bruner, 1974; Piaget, 1952). The use of the hand as a tool for object manipulation precedes the normally developing infant's use of other tools in relation to objects. Within this context, upper extremity skills or arm movements have two primary functions in relation to movement. The first is to move the arms to bring the hand to a particular location to manipulate objects. This function is typically referred to as *reach* or *hand transport*. (Bower, 1979). The second function is *manipulation*, typically described as *grasp* or by Piaget (1952) and Uzgiris and Hunt (1975) as *schemes of prehension*. The forms of behavior that perform the functions of hand transport or manipulation are varied.

Using the oral musculature for eating and for vocalization are two separate behavioral functions that may be related. The forms of behavior used to perform these functions of eating and vocalizing (speech and nonspeech sounds) are differentiated in relation to purpose. Oral-motor movements to obtain liquid from a straw are different from those that produce sound or word production. The literature is confusing, and research is limited in documenting specific relationships between movement competence in eating functions and in speaking functions. One hypothesis holds that young children practice coordination of the oral musculature in eating and that coordination developed in relation to eating facilitates the coordination required for later sound, word, and sentence production (Campbell, 1979). These dimensions are represented as separate functions, since we cannot assume that programming in eating skills will, in fact, carry over to or influence oral motor coordination in relation to sound production.

Forms of behavior for each of these dimensions—hand transport, manipulation, oral-motor/feeding, and oral-motor/vocalization—are varied and show changes in organizational form during infancy. Specific forms of behavior demonstrated by older students will relate directly to necessary and sufficient basic motor processes as well as to movement forms used by the student (perhaps long before school age). As with mobility, the range of response forms in each of these behavioral functions can be defined as any motoric organization that allows the behavioral function to be realized. These forms subsequently can be judged in relation to chronological age range expectations. Behavioral forms for each of these dimensions can also be rated with older (noninfant) students in terms of functional competence. Unusual forms of behavior which allow for the function may well enable the handicapped student to perform competently. A student with severe motor impairment who is mobile with an electric wheelchair would be competent in mobility although the form is unusual Similarly, a student who is able to use a head wand or electronic switches to point would be using unusual forms of hand transport, but the forms allow the performance of certain manipulatory functions. Functional competence on each dimension is the end goal of programming, whether the chosen response form is normal or unusual.

IMPLICATIONS FOR PROGRAMMING

Each of the processes that underlie production of posture and the various types of movement can be represented in a two-dimensional scale form (Bricker & Campbell, 1980; Campbell, 1985c) as was previously illustrated for postural tone (See Figure 8.2). The initial information derived from using the scale across a number of dimensions, such as those illustrated in Table 8.4, defines the specialists who are necessary to ensure comprehensive programming. For instance, a student who is rated atypical on tone, movement quality and quantity, and other motoric dimensions would require services from a physical or occupational therapist. Students with atypical scores on oral-motor dimensions would also require speech and language services; however, a student without oral-motor difficulties or without atypical motor ratings would probably be provided with adequate programming by a teacher, alone.

Initial functional goals of programming as well as the class of intervention approaches needed to influence behavior on each dimension can also be determined. A student with a rating of 8 or 9 on postural tone would require programming to normalize tone and any intervention techniques that *reduce* tone would be effective. Similarly,

TABLE 8.4   Dimensions from index of qualification

Health

Sensory Abilities
Vision
Hearing
Tactile/Kinesthetic
    Proprioceptive (as related to movement)

Neuromotor Capabilities
Tone/Central
Tone/Distal
Movement Quality
    Head/Neck
    Shoulders
    Pelvis/Hips
Movement Quantity
Mobility
Oral-Motor/Eating
Oral-Motor/Drinking
Oral-Motor/Vocal
Respiration-Phonation
Hand Transport
Manipulation

Cognitive/Communication Abilities
Motivation
Primary Circular
Joint Reciprocity
Secondary Circular
Discrimination
Imitation
Preintentional
Intentionality
Vocabulary

Other Functional Areas
Self-Care/Personal Management
Vocational
Recreation/Leisure
Academics

normalization of postural tone would also be an appropriate goal for a student with a tonicity rating of 1 or 2; however, the intervention approaches required would be those that *increase* tone. A rating of 9 on mobility would signal intervention to reduce or structure mobility in the environment, where a rating of 1 would indicate approaches to produce some form of mobility.

There are many ways of intervening to improve the functioning of students with movement disorders. Primary among these approaches is *neurodevelopmental treatment* (or the Bobath approach). This approach focuses on changing tone and patterns of movement through use of *preparation* to attain body alignment (Smith, 1984) and *facilitation* and *inhibition* (see Bobath & Bobath, 1984) to obtain functionally useful ways of interacting with the environment using posture and movement. The integrated, interrelated approach used to provide intervention to enhance posture and movement is illustrated by Figure 8.7. Both posture and movement are *dynamic* and *active* processes; therefore, an active movement situation that can best be provided in one-on-one interaction between an adult and student is necessary. Active treatment uses procedures to attain as normal procedural alignment as is possible, instate normally coordinated patterns of movement, and train use of movement patterns for functional interaction with the environment. These movement patterns *must* be carried over through integrated physical management.

Attaining Postural Alignment

Normally coordinated movement cannot be instated if tone is severely atypical or changes in muscle length have occurred. Specific strategies are used to *prepare* the body so that more normally coordinated movement can be produced (Campbell, in press–a). These include normalization of tone in specific muscle groups or attaining lengthening in specific muscles. Preparation strategies are not used as the total basis for intervention with any student but as the initial step in an intervention process leading to functional use of posture and movement to interact with the environment.

Instating Normally Coordinated Movement Patterns

The automatic movement patterns that right the body in space, restore and maintain alignment when the body has been displaced in space. These movements can be *facilitated* when postural tone is not severely abnormal. Automatic movement patterns have been traced to specific areas of the brain through animal studies severing brain fibers at various CNS levels (Talbott & Humphrey, 1979). To a certain extent, automatic righting reactions can be considered reflexive behavior because they result from response to a specific set of stimulus conditions, are integrated at neurological levels lower than the cortex, and include patterns of movement that are typically very similar from person to person. Equilibrium (or balance) reactions are an elaboration of righting reactions because the body

must be righted in relation to gravity before the equilibrium reactions can function. These automatic movements also result from disturbances of body alignment in relation to gravity but are thought to be cortical functions and not the result of confining stimulus conditions. The resultant components of movement, however, are similar from person to person (Weisz, 1938).

The possibility of responding motorically (governed by postural tone and muscle action) in ways which right the body and keep it upright against gravity probably occurs as a function of genetic expression and, in infant development (under 6 months of age), of CNS maturation; however, the maintenance and elaboration of responses are probably a function of sensorimotor coordination. Head control provides a simple example. The very young infant may "discover" that if she keeps her head to the side of her body as opposed to downward in the pillow, the side position is more comfortable (and certainly relates to survival in that it is easier to breathe if her head is not held directly downward when she is on her stomach). The infant may happen to raise her head at a time when interesting events are occurring and "discover" a new relationship of "seeing" what is going on around her. The initial response of prone head raising is related to certain levels of motor competence present as a function of genetic expression. The initial movement is automatic and reflexive head righting; however, all subsequent responses, increase in the rate of head raising, and maintenance of the newly discovered relationship between seeing and head raising occur as a function of the consequences to that behavior (primary movement). The subsequent behavior, labeled a *head righting reaction*, actually is *strengthened and maintained* under the control of the consequences to the behavior—not because of genetic expression or maturation. In other words, as long as interesting and novel events are going on, the child will continue to produce temporary discoveries of the relationship between seeing and movement of the head. Head raising then comes under the control of antecedent conditions. When the child hears something interesting or someone visually stimulates her, she will raise her head in a goal-directed sense for the purpose of seeing or hearing something motivating.

Children can be placed in positions but, at young ages or with inexperience, may not be able to maintain balance in those positions. For instance,

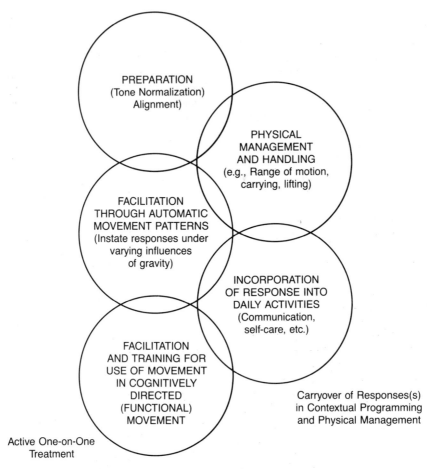

PREPARATION
(Tone Normalization)
Alignment)

PHYSICAL
MANAGEMENT
AND HANDLING
(e.g., Range of motion,
carrying, lifting)

FACILITATION
THROUGH AUTOMATIC
MOVEMENT PATTERNS
(Instate responses under
varying influences
of gravity)

INCORPORATION
OF RESPONSE INTO
DAILY ACTIVITIES
(Communication,
self-care, etc.)

FACILITATION
AND TRAINING FOR
USE OF MOVEMENT
IN COGNITIVELY
DIRECTED
(FUNCTIONAL)
MOVEMENT

Carryover of Responses(s)
in Contextual Programming
and Physical Management

Active One-on-One
Treatment

FIGURE 8.7   Intervention components needed for students with movement dysfunction

when the very young infant is placed in a sitting position and her balance is disturbed, she is likely to fall over (or to be caught by an adult!). Later, the child may catch herself with her arms with what has been described as protective responses of the arms (Milani-Comparetti & Gidoni, 1967). Using the arms for balancing allows the child to stay upright without having to use the muscles in the trunk and the legs (Figure 8.8); however, the function of the protective responses of the arms is the same as the function of equilibrium reactions in sitting, both movements allow the individual to remain upright when the body is displaced in relation to gravity. Using the arms for protection from falling also prevents use of the arms for reaching and manipulation. The arms are not released from protective functions until the child develops equilibrium

reactions that allow maintenance of balance without the arms.

Automatic movement patterns are *facilitated* following preparation strategies that have obtained as normalized tone as is possible. Performance of automatic movements (with facilitation) allows for demonstration of movements that might not be able to be independently performed by a student due to the influences of tone and gravity; however, these movements must be incorporated into functional use during one-on-one intervention for the movements to be useful. In essence, therapists use the automatic movement patterns, not as an end in themselves, but as a means to obtain desired movement patterns that are as normally coordinated as is possible. A student (or infant) does not have to be able to follow directions or perform any other

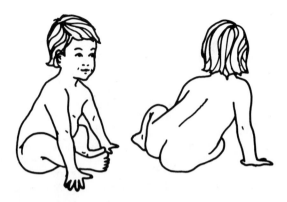

FIGURE 8.8 Protective reactions of the arms in sitting

cognitive actions for the programmer to be able to instate the movement pattern; therefore, facilitation procedures used in this context are particularly valuable in the treatment of infants and students with severe degrees of cognitive impairment.

Training Functionally Useful Movements

Movement must be used to interact with the environment to be functionally useful to the student. The degree of cognitive complexity required for functional use can vary from very simple movements to those that coordinate two or more movement patterns. Primary movements are demonstrated by babies soon after birth and consist of simple stimulus-response behaviors. The function of this type of movement is to receive interesting consequences; however, the child with atypical postural tone may not have enough basic competence to perform even the simplest form of primary movement. The child may find noise from a rattle interesting when the rattle is moved by somebody else, but may not subsequently shake the rattle because rate of arm movement is too low to produce sufficient noise. Other students with disturbances in the underlying processes of movement may generate interesting consequences with qualitatively deficient patterns of movement. Perhaps rather than shaking the rattle up and down, as most infants would, the student waves his arms back and forth with atypical patterns of movement; however, as long as the arm movements generate a reinforcing consequence, the student will increase those arm movements (along with the atypical patterns of movement). Even the simplest form of movement

must be viewed in relation to the sensorimotor processes involved and the environmental conditions under which the response is performed. If not, the student will acquire atypical postural tone, quantity of movement, and movement quality.

Primary movement is important because it is the most primitive form of movement organization in relation to environmental events and objects. Through this type of basic movement organization, the child has chances to practice various kinds of muscle coordinations. These coordinations are refined into more complex and goal-directed movement organizations. The very young infant, if properly positioned, is able to reach for an object within the visual field. In fact, the infant can anticipate the movement of the object and move the arm toward where the object will be at the end of the movement (VonHefstein & Lindahagen, 1979), but the quality of the movement's organization is poorly coordinated. The organization of this primary movement increases in precision and coordination with practice and precedes the organized control of the motor system required for adult reaching. The student with atypical underlying motor processes may not generate a reaching motion and therefore may lack practice in learning to organize primary motor behaviors into goal-directed movement. This lack of experience with normally organized patterns of movement will affect acquisition of goal-directed and intentional motor behavior.

The relationships between tone, movement quantity, and movement quality and primary and goal-directed movement are such that the basic processes are present or absent in varying degrees in relation to genetic expression and CNS functions. Only the initial and most primitively organized unit of motor behavior (whether head righting, sucking, arm movement, or grasping) is related to genetic expression. All responses which follow develop as a function of cognitive processes of assimilation and accommodation producing more elaborately organized and more precise forms of motor interaction with the environment. Basic therapeutic procedures that normalize tone and make some degree of movement organization possible can be effective in facilitating the initial production of the movement; however, once the movement has been initiated and produced, elaboration and maintenance of the response can be best facilitated by constructing and arranging the environment systematically.

INTERVENTION METHODS

Students with dysfunctional patterns of posture and movement require both active, one-on-one intervention *and* physical management and care to promote use of normalized posture and movement pattern across a wide variety of environments and people. Methods to manage the physical behavior of a student are typically noninstructional. Rather, techniques are used to maintain existing integrity of the motor system. Therapists, teachers, and parents may carry out range of motion procedures to maintain the range of movement in the wrist and fingers. Placing a student in a piece of equipment will help maintain body alignment but does not teach a student to perform movement skills. Lifting and carrying a student properly may help to normalize muscle tone and enable her to hold up her head. Although a student may be practicing (or learning) head control while being lifted and carried, the activity is not teaching her to use movement functionally to interact with objects in the environment. Approaches for physical management and care have already been discussed in Chapter 7. The information presented in this chapter emphasizes those *active intervention* methods that assist students with dysfunctional movement to acquire and use movement in interaction with the environment.

Programming for Normalized Tone and Coordinated Movement

Programming to normalize tone and patterns of movement begins with *preparation* techniques,

where necessary. Some students may not yet demonstrate changes in muscle length or atypical tone and may not need to have much preparation before active movement is *facilitated*. Activation of the automatic movement patterns is the primary mechanism used to instate movement patterns. These patterns must then be trained for the student to be able to use them functionally to interact with the physical and social environment.

Both *preparation* and *facilitation*, using automatic movement patterns, occur in one-on-one interaction with the student and are typically provided by trained physical and occupational therapists (see Campbell, in press-a; Scherzer & Tscharnuter, 1982; Wilson, 1984). The placement of the adult's hands on the student is specific to obtaining the desired contractions of muscles. Location, amount of pressure provided, and duration are all used to facilitate or inhibit tone and specific patterns of muscle contractions and cocontractions. Body weight is simultaneously shifted through specific planes of space by the direction(s) in which the adult moves the student. The student can be moved through lateral (sideways), anterior/posterior (front/back), diagonal, or rotational planes of movement for the purpose of facilitating specific movement patterns. The therapist designs a facilitation sequence that will allow production of a desired, coordinated movement pattern with tone as normalized as possible (Campbell & Forsyth, 1985). The facilitation sequence used to instate coordinated movement with the arms for the student whose assessment results are reported earlier in this chapter is written in Table 8.5. This

TABLE 8.5 Intervention sequence (classroom) for student with low underlying tone but increased tone in arms and legs

Child's Position	Teacher Does	Resultant Response
Sitting in chair with low back.	Sits behind child, places hands on rib cage, laterally.	Alignment of rib cage on spine.
	Shifts child's weight downward onto buttocks.	Extension in low back.
	Shifts child's weight forward.	Extension throughout spine.
	Shifts child's weight backward.	Flexor of the lumbar spine.
	Shifts child's weight laterally.	Activation of spinal muscles. Increase in tone in the trunk with spinal extension, pelvic mobility.
	Places left hand on left scapula of child with pressure inward.	Thoracic extension with scapular adduction for stability.
	Places right hand under right humerus, guides reaching movement forward to object.	Arm movement forward with contact to object.

intervention yields production of coordinated movement (or a specific desired movement) but does not necessarily result in patterns that will be functionally used. The patterns must then be trained for use ·in functional situations (Campbell, in press-a, in press-b).

Programming for Functional Use of Movement

Too often, students with dysfunctional posture and movement receive "motor programs" for part of the classroom day and other programs for the rest of the day. The basic motor processes affect every skill the child may be learning—regardless of whether that skill is classified as language, vocational, self-help, cognitive, leisure, or recreational. Before the student is asked to put the spoon in her mouth in self-feeding or to point to a symbol in nonverbal communication training, the teacher should be sure that the postural tone is as normal as possible and that appropriate facilitation/inhibition techniques have been used to allow the required cognitively directed behavior.

Ideally, the movement patterns that are being worked with in *active intervention* should be those that are being used in functional programming both in the classroom and at home. If active intervention is focused on instating forward reaching movements with the arm, the teacher and parent should incorporate this movement into as many classroom activities as possible (Campbell, McInerney, & Cooper, 1984). The following examples suggest ways in which a reaching movement might be practiced and used across a number of different situations: having the student reach to select objects, clothing to wear, or foods to eat, for the spoon during eating, for materials to be used in classroom activities (spoon and bowl during cooking), or to activate a control switch interface to hear music. Incorporating movement into functional use, *if practiced with as normal as possible tone and patterns of coordination*, will enable the student not just to perform movements but to use them for greater independence. General examples of treatment methods that can be used to influence posture and movement are listed on Table 8.6. Two methods are of particular importance when training use of movement for functional use: *control of environmental and sensory influences* and *facilitation of coordinated movement* (especially of the arms and hands).

Control of Environmental and Sensory Influences

The very factors that can cause tone to change (refer to Table 8.1), and that are identified as part of assessment, can be systematically manipulated in intervention. This method is referred to, by therapists, as *grading the stimulus*. Educators use similar methods to bring behavior under *stimulus control*. The important point to remember is that postural tone (and, therefore, movement patterns) can be different in relation to environmental and sensory stimuli. Therapists and teachers can gradually introduce stimuli known to be related to increased tone to teach the student to have normalized tone when a specifically identified stimulus condition is present. A student who always showed increased tone with objects that make noise could be gradually taught to maintain normalized tone as noisemaking objects were introduced. The programmer might initially introduce the object without noise, then with soft noise, and eventually with louder sound, each time using tone normalization procedures to help the student maintain normalized tone. Or, a student who always demonstrated increased tone when crying could be helped through programming to decrease the crying (where excessive) or by providing tone normalization procedures when the student was crying.

Facilitation of Coordinated Movement

Coordinated movement patterns are qualitatively related to postural tone and alignment. Upper extremity movement, for instance, depends on good postural alignment of the head and neck with the shoulders, of the shoulders with the trunk, and of the pelvis with the trunk. Positioning in adaptive equipment is used in the classroom and at home as a method to establish postural alignment in a variety of positions (sitting, standing, sidelying). Facilitation procedures can then be used to assist the student to perform coordinated movement with the arms and hands. Facilitation procedures, viewed from the standpoint of overall learning, are simply precise forms of physical guidance. The specific procedures used with a student should *carryover* those being used in active intervention to other environments. Therapists and teachers who are trained in neurodevelopmental treatment can train parents and teachers to perform the specific facilitation procedures that will be most helpful for a student. The carryover intervention plan that was

TABLE 8.6 Examples of treatment methods

Preparation to attain tone normalization and muscle lengthening for body alignment (active programming)	Deep pressure over selected muscle group(s)—applied with hands and/or through weight bearing on muscle group(s). Weight shifts on body surface in lateral or head to tail (cephalocaudal) directions.
Control of environmental and sensory influences related to tone increases	Materials adaptation to make task easier. Control of tone changes by physical manipulation while systematically grading sensory stimuli—holding the student in sitting to prevent tone increases while bringing in an object (or food) that typically is related to tone increases.
Facilitation of movement in or through space (active programming)	Hand placement over specific muscle group(s) to inhibit tone changes and maintain body alignment; in conjunction with weight shifts of the body through space in lateral, diagonal, anterior-posterior, or rotational planes of movement.
Functional use of movement for mobility, communication, self-care, academics, vocational, recreation leisure skills	Preparation of isolated muscle group(s) for tone normalization and/or lengthening. Hand placement over specific muscle group(s) to facilitate desired movement pattern. Carryover of active treatment goals into functional use.
Maintenance of body alignment and muscle length	Proper positioning in adaptive equipment. Proper use of therapeutic physical management techniques. Passive range of motion and/or therapeutic "stretching" of muscles.
Correction of muscle contractures, bone and joint deformities	Orthopedic surgery. Bracing and orthotic devices.

designed to carryover the movement being established through the intervention described previously (see Table 8.5) is illustrated on Table 8.7.

Adaptive Training Aids

Some students may have extreme difficulty learning to perform normally coordinated movement patterns. Other students may be unable to perform selected coordinated movement patterns due to the severity of postural tone discrepancies, changes in muscle length, or orthopedic problems. Adaptive training aids can be used with these students for two purposes. One is to assist them to perform a specific pattern in carryover situations. The second is to allow the performance of a functional activity that may never be possible with total independence. Aids such as walkers and crutches may enable ambulation. Special eating utensils and devices may allow for independent eating and drinking. Adapted toys, games, or sports equipment allow students to engage in recreational-leisure activities.

Special aids can be used for communication and for greater social interaction and independence.

Many aids are available through commercial sources. Some can easily be fabricated to meet individual student needs. Two points are important when selecting and using an aid: (a) an aid should not be operable with *abnormal movement* but should be designed to promote more coordinated patterns, and (b) an aid that is given to a student may be removed (or even systematically faded) when and if the student learns to perform the movement pattern independently. A student who is communicating by pointing to a communication board and simultaneously verbalizing may have the communication board taken away when speech alone is intelligible. An adaptive spoon may only be required until the time that grasping becomes independent.

Some types of adaptive training aids are electronically operable. The use of switch interface devices allows students with severe restrictions in movement quantity to perform a variety of func-

TABLE 8.7 Carryover plan—reach

Antecedent	Response	Consequence
Adult positions child with head at midline, presents object or person at child's midline, twelve inches away from child's face. Adult says, "Get the X " (or "Touch X ").	Arm/hand movement toward object/person within ten seconds.	Social interaction with object/person. Place object in child's hand and physically guide through appropriate actions.

tional skills (Campbell, Bricker, & Esposito, 1981, Esposito & Campbell, in press; York, Nietupski, and Hamre-Nietupski, 1985). Interfaces may be hooked to battery operated toys, electric appliances, environmental control devices, wheelchairs, communication aids, and computers. A number of different types of devices are illustrated in Figure 8.9. These devices are available through commercial sources or can be hand fabricated. See Burkhart (1980) or Campbell, McInerney, and Middleton (1983) for further discussion of types of interface devices.

While electronic interface devices successfully enable performance of functional skills without the required movement patterns, students with severe cognitive impairment may have difficulty using some devices without specific and systematic training. In general, once an appropriate device is selected for use and the student has demonstrated adequate rates of activation, motor behavior must be brought under stimulus control. In other words, the student must learn to activate the switch when specific consequences are produced and not activate the switch when inappropriate or no consequences result. A number of different approaches to training switch activation have been published and can be used by the teacher or therapist to train switch activation for specific functional purposes. See Brinker and Lewis (1982), Campbell (1985d), Campbell and Mulhauser (1984), or Inman (1984) for examples of successful training methods.

DETERMINING PROGRAM EFFECTIVENESS

The effectiveness of any instructional or therapeutic program must be judged on the basis of change in the student. Many techniques have been suggested as appropriate but have been only clinically judged as effective. Therefore, the teacher or therapist

must individually evaluate the effectiveness of the techniques with each student with whom they are used. Decisions on when to alter programming techniques can then be made objectively (Campbell, Clegg, & McFarland, 1982; Campbell & Steward, 1986).

As an example, the integrated therapy and education programming team, working with the student who has been described throughout this chapter, established increased reaching as his primary objective. Underlying tone was low, particularly in the head/neck and trunk (spine) but fluctuated to high tone when the student attempted to move his arms. Persistent high tone in the internal rotator muscles of the arm in combination with limited activation of the muscles in the upper back resulted in the following difficulties in the shoulder and arm area of the body:

1. Increased shoulder (scapular) elevation in combination with hyperextension of the head and neck musculature with tightness but no muscle shortening.
2. Increased forward tipping of the scapula with shortening in the internal rotators of the arm and overlengthening in the scapular stabilizers.
3. Shortening of the pectoralis muscles (underarm in front of body) and of trapezius (underarm in back of body) causing difficulty reaching in front of the body and with arm movement above shoulder level.
4. Tightness in the elbow flexors, forearm supinators, wrist and finger flexors with radial deviation of the wrists.

Tone was also increased in the legs and resulted in a pattern of posterior pelvic tilt with adduction, internal rotation at the hips. Mobility of the pelvis was poor. This student was unable to achieve a neutrally aligned pelvis in sitting due to poor cocontraction of the low back extensors/abdominals and tightness of the hamstring muscles.

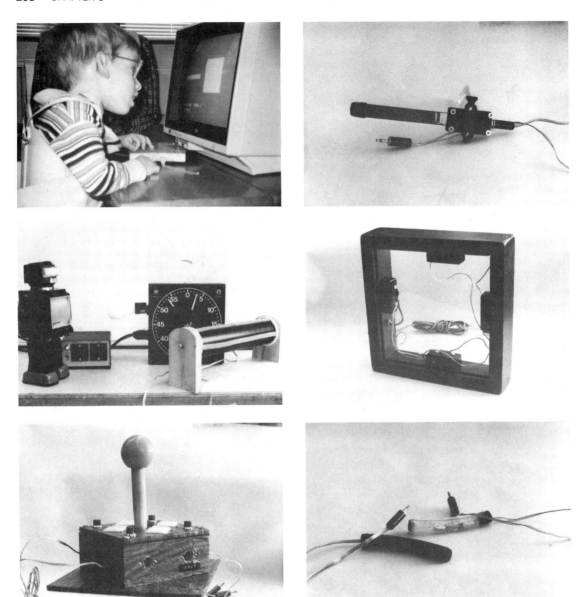

FIGURE 8.9 Various types of switch interfaces that can be used for mobility, communication, recreation-leisure, environmental control, and computer access. Switch interface devices allow students to interact with the environment in various ways even when motor control is poor.

Data on reaching were collected in three situations. Twenty trials of reaching were conducted with the student in his adaptive wheelchair following each active intervention session. These data were outcome measures on which the effectiveness of active intervention methods, as a group, were measured. Secondly, data on reach were collected with this student in the classroom and during communication programming where the reach response was incorporated into all aspects of programming using facilitation procedures described in the carryover intervention plan (refer to Table 8.7). These facilitation procedures included normalizing the tone in the pectoralis muscles and

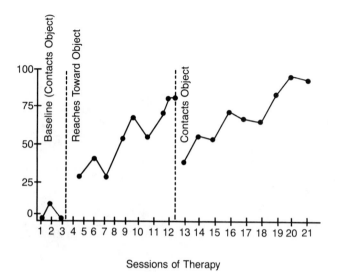

Sessions of Therapy

FIGURE 8.10   Percentage of correct reaching following active treatment

passively guiding the student through two reaching movements prior to each trial by cueing the movement pattern from the shoulder. These data, presented in Figures 8.10 and 8.11, indicate that procedures increased reaching both after active intervention had been provided and in carryover during classroom activities and communication programming.

INTEGRATING THERAPEUTIC AND INSTRUCTIONAL METHODS INTO FUNCTIONAL CURRICULUM

Effective programming for students with disorders of posture and movement depends on the integration of both therapeutic and instructional methods so that the student learns greater independence (Campbell, 1985b). Instructional domains may vary somewhat dependent on the chronological age of the student. Communication, mobility, self-care and personal management, social interaction, and recreation-leisure domains are important for all chronological ages while functional academics and vocational skills may be more appropriate for school-aged students. Instructional goals and objectives that are written on the individual education plan (IEP) for all students should be drawn from these curricular areas. Specific movement patterns, such as reach and grasp, are then programmed within identified instructional areas. A student might reach and touch a joystick to operate

a computer for instruction, recreation-leisure, or communication or to use an electric mobility device. Reach and grasp could be required as the initial component of self-feeding or reach, alone, used to nonverbally signal needs for adult assistance of object selection. Specifically incorporating desired movement responses into all areas of functional programming provides more practice of the movement pattern for students and allows for generalized use across a variety of situations.

The role of the team of professionals responsible for providing programming for a given student is to determine (a) the ways in which a specific movement pattern will be used across instructional domains and objectives, (b) integrated therapeutic and educational methods required to train the desired movement (carryover strategies), (c) locations for training, and (d) the data collection methods. The physical and occupational therapist must then train other team members to deliver the appropriate tone normalization and facilitation methods within each of the instructional domains.

Traditional approaches to motor programming have focused on the acquisition of motor milestone skills, often ignoring the modifiability of tone, patterns of movement, and movement quantity. The integrated programming system presented in this chapter facilitates acquisition of movement skills across all disciplines and all functional behavior domains. The motor system does not function in isolation but rather provides each of us with a

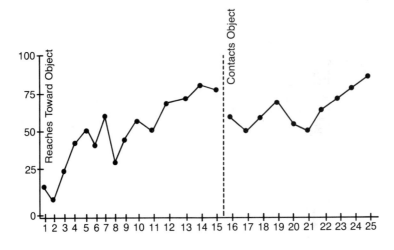

FIGURE 8.11 Percentage of opportunities where reaching was performed in communication sessions and in classroom programming

means of interacting with our environments. Neurodevelopmental treatment approaches, when combined with applied behavior analysis techniques and carefully evaluated through ongoing data collection, provide one approach to helping students with disordered movement to perform independently in areas critical for independence as adult members of society.

REFERENCES

Bleck, E., & Nagel, D. (1982). *Physically handicapped children: A medical atlas for teachers.* New York: Grune & Stratton.

Bigge, J. L. (1982). *Teaching individuals with physical and multiple disabilities* (2nd ed.). Columbus, OH: Charles E. Merrill.

Bobath, B., & Bobath, K. (1975). *Motor development in the different types of cerebral palsy.* London: William Heinemann.

Bobath, K., & Bobath, B. (1984). The neurodevelopmental treatment. In D. Stratton (Ed.), *Management of the motor disorders of children with cerebral palsy.* Philadelphia: J. B. Lippincott.

Bower, T. G. R. (1979). *Human development.* San Francisco: W. H. Freeman.

Bricker, W. A., & Campbell, P. H. (1980). Interdisciplinary programming. In W. Sailor, L. Browh, & B. Wilcox (Eds.), *Teaching the severely handicapped.* Baltimore: Paul H. Brookes

Bricker, W. A., Macke, P. R., Levin, J. A., & Campbell, P. H. (1981). The modifiability of intelligent behavior. *Journal of Special Education, 15*(2), 145–163.

Brinker, R. P., & Lewis, M. (1982). Making the world work with microcomputers: A learning prosthesis for handicapped infants. *Exceptional Children, 49,* 163–172.

Bruner, J. (1974). The organization of early skilled action. In M. Richards (Ed.), *The integrations of a child into a social world.* London: Cambridge University Press.

Burkhart, L. (1980). *Homemade battery-powered toys and educational devices for severely handicapped children.* (Available from Linda J. Burkhart, 8502 Rhode Island Ave., College Park, MD 20740).

Campbell, P. H. (1979). Assessing oral-motor skills in severely handicapped persons: An analysis of normal and abnormal patterns of movement. In R. L. York & E. Edgar (Eds.), *Teaching the severely handicapped* (Vol. 4). Seattle: American Association for the Education of the Severely/Profoundly Handicapped.

Campbell, P. H. (1982). Measuring motor behavior. In M. Stevens-Dominquez & K. Stremel-Campbell (Eds.), *Ongoing data collection for measuring child progress.* Monmouth, OR: WESTAR.

Campbell, P. H. (in press–a). The application of neurodevelopmental tratment with children with severe handicaps. In J. Miednar (Ed.), *Proceedings of the Northeastern Neurodevelopmental Treatment Association Workshop.*

Campbell, P. H. (in press–b). *Neurodevelopmental treatment methods for teaching self-care skills.* Baltimore: Paul H. Brookes.

Campbell, P. H. (1985a). *Assessment of posture and movement in students with multihandicaps.* Akron, OH: Children's Hospital Medical Center of Akron.

Campbell, P. H. (1985b). *Integrated therapy and educational programming for students with severe handicaps.* Akron, OH: Children's Hospital Medical Center of Akron.

Campbell, P. H. (1985c). *The index of qualification for specialized services.* Akron, OH: Children's Hospital Medical Center of Akron.

Campbell, P. H. (1985d). *Owner's manual for the TA-2 training aide.* (Available from Prentke Romich Company, 1022 Heyl Road Wooster, OH 44691).

Campbell, P. H., Bricker, W. A., & Esposito, L. (1981). Technology in the education of the severely handicapped. B. Wilcox & R. York (Eds.), *Quality education for the severely handicapped.* Washington, DC: U.S. Office of Special Education.

Campbell, P. H., Clegg. K., McFarland, L. (1982). Measuring motor behavior. In M. Meade, M. Stevens-Dominques, & K. Stremmel-Campbell (Eds.), *Ongoing data collection for measuring child progress.* (pp. 59-89). Monmouth, OR: WESTAR.

Campbell, P. H., & Forsyth, S. (1985). *Active mat treatment programs.* Akron, OH: Children's Hospital Medical Center of Akron.

Campbell, P. H., McInerney, W., & Cooper, M. A. (1984). Therapeutic programming for students with severe handicaps. *The American Journal of Occupational Therapy, 38*(9), 594-602.

Campbell, P. H., McInerney, W., & Middleton, M. Q. (1983). *A manual of augmented sensory feedback devices for teaching severely handicapped students.* Akron, OH: Children's Hospital Medical Center of Akron.

Campbell, P. H., & Mulhauser, M. B. (1984). *Use of electronic switch interface devices in discrimination training with severely handicapped students.* Manuscript submitted for publication.

Campbell, P. H., & Steward, B. (1986). *Measuring changes in movement skills in infants and young children with handicaps.* Manuscript submitted for publication.

Campbell, S. (1984). *Pediatric neurological physical therapy,* (Vol. 5), New York: Churchill Livingstone.

Esposito, L., & Campbell, P. H. (in press). Computers and the severely and physically handicapped. In J. Lindsey (Ed.), *Computers and exceptional individuals.* Columbus, OH: Charles E. Merrill.

Inman, D. (1984). *Functional assessment and neuromuscular education for children with physical handicaps.* TASH Presentation, Chicago, Illinois.

Milani-Comparetti A., & Gidoni, E. A. (1967). Routine developmental examination in normal and retarded children. *Developmental Medicine and Child Neurology, 9,* 631-638.

Piaget, J. (1952). *The origins of intelligence.* New York: W. W. Norton.

Scherzer, A., & Tscharnuter, I. (1982). *Early diagnosis and therapy in cerebral palsy.* New York: Marcel Decker.

Seligman, M. E. (1975). *Helplessness: On depression, death and development.* San Francisco: W. H. Freeman.

Smith, M. (Personal communication, 1984).

Talbott, R. E., & Humphrey, D. E. (1979). *Posture and movement.* New York: Raven Press.

Umbreit, J. (1983). *Physical disabilities and health impairments: An introduction.* Columbus, OH: Charles E. Merrill.

Uzgiris, I., & Hunt, J. McV. (1975). *Assessment in infancy: Ordinal scales of psychological development.* Chicago: University of Illinois Press.

VonHefstein, C., & Lindahagen, K. (1979). Observations on the development of reaching for moving objects. *Journal of Experimental Child Psychology, 28,* 158-173.

Weisz, S. (1938). Studies in equilibrium reaction. *Journal of Nervous and Mental Disease, 88,* 150-162.

Wilson, J. (1984). Cerebral palsy. In S. Campbell (Ed.), *Pediatric neurologic physical therapy* (Vol. 5, pp. 353-414). New York: Churchill Livingstone.

York, J., Nietupski, S., & Hamre-Nietupski, S. (1985). A decision-making process for using microswitches. *The Journal of the Association for Persons with Severe Handicaps, 10*(4), 214-223.

But she doesn't have anything to do when she gets home. I mean she doesn't know how to play with toys or with other kids. We've bought her toys but she really can't use them. Sometimes she seems interested in the musical toys, but she mostly spends a lot of time flipping her hands and staring at her fingers; other times she just follows me around the house or sits and rocks.

John is really out of shape. Even though he eats pretty well, he is still too heavy, somewhat flabby and pretty uncoordinated. We have tried to get him to exercise with us, but he gives up. I'm worried about what this means for his future, his appearance, and his health.

These examples are not unusual for students with severe handicaps. When their curriculum does not include objectives in the leisure or recreation domain, students are unlikely to acquire these skills. By contrast, those who are taught to enjoy their free time by engaging in recreational activities appropriate for the age, interests, family practices, and motoric capabilities will have multiple benefits. Researchers have demonstrated that leisure skills can replace maladaptive behaviors which formerly filled the functions of stimulation or getting attention from others. Other studies have shown how leisure skills can create opportunities for social interaction with peers who do not have handicaps, which in turn may impact positively on the peers' attitudes toward and expectations of the person with handicaps. Personal enjoyment and improvements in health are other clear benefits of having leisure skills.

In this next chapter, Sherril Moon and Linda Bunker describe how recreation and motor skill programs can be designed and monitored, and they also review instructional methods proven effective with students who have severe handicaps.

Introduction to Chapter 9

9

Recreation and Motor Skills Programming

M. Sherril Moon
Virginia Commonwealth University

Linda Bunker
University of Virginia

Leisure activities are an important aspect of everyone's life, but until recently recreational activities were not systematically taught to persons who have severe handicaps. However, as more individuals have moved from institutions into integrated community settings (schools, family homes, and regular job settings), the need for formal programs have emerged (Stanfield, 1973; Stein, 1977; Wehman, Renzaglia, & Bates, 1985). The beginning of recreation programming for persons with developmental disabilities can be traced to the late 1940s and 1950s and the advent of advocacy groups such as the National Association of Retarded Citizens (Bates & Renzaglia, 1979; Witt, 1977). In the 1960s recreational programming for all citizens evolved as a distinct discipline. By the mid 1970s with the enactment of P.L. 94-142 (The Education for All Handicapped Children Act of 1975), physical education instruction became a mandated part of the educational program for all children with handicapping conditions. Such instruction should include provision for acquiring recreational skills. During the past 10 years a number of papers have been published indicating the needs as well as the potential of individuals with severe handicaps in this domain (Nietupski, Hamre-Nietupski, & Ayers, 1984; Voeltz, Wuerch, & Wilcox, 1982).

Recreational programming is now recognized as one of three or four major curriculum domains for students with severe handicaps. Such leisure skills have gained an equal status with vocational, community, and domestic activities (Brown, Branston-McClean, Baumgart, Vincent, Falvey, & Schroeder, 1979; Wilcox & Bellamy, 1982). This chapter focuses on the rationale for the formal systematic training of recreation or leisure skills. Guidelines are provided for curriculum development, selection of appropriate activities, assessment techniques, and instruction in community and home settings.

A RATIONALE FOR TEACHING LEISURE ACTIVITIES

The Leisure Domain Defined

Throughout this chapter the words "leisure" and "recreation" will be used synonymously to refer to any number of activities that one would typically choose to engage in during "free time." Traditionally, engaging in recreational activities has been termed "playing," and this implies choosing particular activities based on preference and personal enjoyment (Wuerch & Voeltz, 1982). As Voeltz et al. (1982) pointed out, leisure time often becomes meaningless for an individual with a severe handicap because he lacks the skills needed to choose an appropriate free-time activity. Leisure activities have been classified in a variety of ways, typically according to behaviors required or environments in which the activities should occur (Wehman & Moon, 1965; Wuerch & Voeltz, 1982). Some of the categories that have most recently appeared in the literature include: physical, cultural, social, and mental; outdoor and indoor; spectators and participant; formal and informal events; passive and active; independent, cooperative, and competitive; community and home-based; and sports, games, hobbies, and toy play (Table 9.1). For descriptive purposes only, the last classification system will be elaborated because it encompasses many functional activities that have been successfully taught to individuals with severe handicaps and includes many of the other categories (Wehman & Moon, 1985). However, this system by no means includes all appropriate activities.

Each leisure program should be characterized by fun and enjoyment, purposeful behavior, some degree of participation, and an element of choice. Each of these characteristics is briefly described (Wehman & Moon, 1985).

1. *Fun and enjoyment*—This element differentiates the leisure domain from all others. If an activity is not naturally reinforcing or enjoyable, it cannot be considered recreational.
2. *Purposeful behavior*—One must evaluate why an activity is being engaged in and whether or not the activity is at all normalizing. The body rocking of an adult with profound retardation, who is left alone for long periods, cannot be considered a leisure activity.
3. *Participation*—Leisure is a domain in which maximum learning proficiency is not essential. If someone can enjoy an activity by partially participating through the use of rule or material adaptations, then the activity should be considered.
4. *Choice*—A person must want to participate in a leisure activity when it is provided along with

other options. The challenge for instructors is to provide a repertoire of appropriate options and to teach persons with handicaps to *self-initiate* these options at the appropriate times.

The Importance of Leisure Activities

As individuals with severe handicaps obtain the skills necessary to function in domestic, vocational, and community environments, they also must be taught how to spend the free time appropriately in each environment. Some of the reasons for the instruction of leisure activities across environments are provided below.

The Relationships between Normalization and Leisure Instruction

Leisure programs may be one of the easiest areas in which to integrate disabled and nondisabled citizens because proficiency and competence are not necessarily critical factors (Moon & Renzaglia, 1982; Wehman & Schleien, 1981; Wolfensberger, 1972). The increased availability of free time for all citizens and the disproportionately larger amount available to those who are handicapped emphasizes the importance of systematic training in this area. The normalization principle dictates that persons with severe handicaps learn leisure activities in community settings not only so the learning will generalize, but also so the general public can observe disabled persons participating in normal leisure pursuits (Wehman, Renzaglia, & Bates, 1985). This principle also suggests the selection of age-appropriate activities and materials (Brown et al., 1979); use of a variety of adaptations (Wehman & Schleien, 1981); and the grouping of persons with disabilities (Reynolds, 1981).

Prevention of Institutionalization

The instruction of leisure skills can have a direct bearing on the successful community integration of disabled persons (Gollay, Freedman, Wyngaarden, & Kurtz, 1978). In fact, one of the major reasons cited by researchers for the reinstitutionalization of disabled persons is the lack of appropriate skills to occupy free time without supervision (Novak & Heal, 1980; Wuerch & Voeltz, 1982). Most studies have shown that adults with disabilities residing in community settings participate primarily in passive leisure activities such as watching TV. They seldom ever interact with persons without disabilities while enjoying leisure activities, and they usually do not travel outside the immediate neighborhood (Bates

TABLE 9.1 Sample sports/fitness activities, hobbies, games, and toy play skills appropriate for severely handicapped citizens

Sports/Fitness Activities		
Independent or Individual Activities		
Yoga	Biking	Jumping rope
Walking	Putt-Putt	Horseshoes
Swimming	Aerobic exercise	Dancing
Tumbling	Weight training	Archery
Skating	Horseback riding	Jogging
Hiking	Using playground equipment	Climbing
Skiing	Baton twirling	*Fishing
Dual or Cooperative Activities		
*Boating	Horseshoes	Golf
Bowling	Martial arts	*Darts
Boxing	Gymnastics	Handball
*Croquet	*Shuffleboard	Tetherball
*Dancing	Racquet sports	Frisbee
Team Sports		
Hockey	Basketball	Dodgeball
Softball	Touch football	Soccer
Lacrosse	Volleyball	Baseball
Kickball	Water polo	*Stickball
Hobbies		
Plant care	Cooking, Dining out	Books and magazines
Pet care	Ceramics/Pottery	Collecting
Needlework/Sewing	Woodworking/Furniture refinishing	Fan Clubs
Painting/Coloring	Weaving	Movies/Cultural activities
Photography	Sports spectating	Organized clubs (4-H,
Music		Scouts, YMCA)
Games		
**Cootie	UNO	Shuffleboard
**Mr. Potato Head	Twister	Yard games
Perfection	**Candyland	War Slap/Jack
Trouble	Simon	Marbles
Checkers	Pinball	Ping Pong
Old Maid	Tick-Tac-Toe	Jacks
Pool	Foosball	Pick Up Sticks
**Hop Scotch	Charades	Bingo
Picture Lotto	Video games	Target Games
Concentration		
Toy Play/Object Manipulation		
Balls	**Lincoln Logs	Marbles
**Blocks	**Tricycle/Bicycle with training wheels	Yo-Yo
**Bucket and shovel	Needle/Sewing material	View Finder
Camera	Musical Toys/Instruments	Matchbox cars
Crayons	Puppets	**Big Wheel
**Dolls	**Rocking toys	Record player
Dice	Silly Putty	Scissors
Etch-a-Sketch	**Slinky	Telephone
Frisbee	Pinball/Video machine	Paints
**Hammer toys	Trucks/Trains	Plants
Hula Hoop	Magazines/Books	Vending machine
**Jack-in-the-Box	Pick Up Sticks	

Note: Many of the Sports/Fitness Activities can be included in more than one of the first three lists.

*May be considered game or hobby. **Appropriate only for younger students.

Source: Adapted from P. Wehman and M. S. Moon, Designing and Implementing Leisure Programs for Individuals with Severe Handicaps. In M. P. Brady and P. L. Gunter (Eds.), *Integrating Moderately and Severely Handicapped Learners*, 1985. Courtesy of Charles C Thomas, Publisher, Springfield, Illinois.

& Renzaglia, 1979; Moon & Snell, 1985). The provision for thorough training and participation opportunities would make increased participation more likely.

Reduction of Inappropriate Behaviors

Several studies have shown that the instruction of appropriate leisure activities can reduce inappropriate or excessive behaviors such as self-abuse, stereotypic body rocking or hand waving, property destruction, and pica (Favell, 1973; Wehman, Renzaglia, & Bates, 1985). Because children, especially, are going to do something active during free periods, it makes sense to train constructive leisure options that are incompatible with inappropriate social behaviors.

Increases in Other Skill Areas

Research, though sparse in this area, has shown a positive relationship between the instruction of certain leisure activities and the development of other academic, social, and communication capabilities (Wuerch & Voeltz, 1982). A positive correlation was indicated between learning a physical fitness activity and self-concept in students in a TMR class (Simpson & Meaney, 1979). Gross and fine motor skills are enhanced anytime one actively participates, no matter how proficiently, in a leisure activity such as a hobby or sport (Moon & Renzaglia, 1982). Finally, anyone who plays a game or sport with someone else must communicate successfully in some fashion (Cavallaro & Bambara, 1982).

SELECTING APPROPRIATE LEISURE ACTIVITIES

A number of factors will determine the type and the number of activities chosen for a particular student with severe handicaps. These factors include age, handicapping condition, home and neighborhood characteristics, and personal and family preferences. A preschool child may initially need to learn only two or three object manipulation or toy play activities. Perhaps all activities will involve cooperative play skills with other children of the same age. A middle school student will likely need to receive training on several activities from the four categories shown in Table 9.1. Some may involve learning to recreate with other *players*. The concept of competition can also be introduced to this student. With approaching adulthood, more emphasis would be placed on learning skills for hobbies and individual sports such as fitness

maintenance that one could enjoy alone and throughout life.

The following section provides guidelines for determining appropriate activities, prioritizing skills for instruction, and assessing an individual student's level of proficiency on a chosen activity.

Screening Home, Community, and Work Sites

The first step in deciding what leisure activities should be instructed is to find out what activities a student may be able to participate in when at home, at work, and in the community with family and friends (Wehman & Moon, 1985). It is important to identify activities that could be currently enjoyed within the student's present environments as well as future possibilities (Wuerch & Voeltz, 1982). The idea of surveying various environments through cataloging activities that would be appropriate for training is an accepted method for building a curriculum in all instructional areas (Brown et al., 1979; Bunker & Moon, 1983). Conducting surveys of home, community, and job sites involves asking significant persons, particularly parents or guardians, to provide information on what is or what could be available. The inventory questions provided in Table 9.2 show the types of information that can be gathered either through a formal interview, phone interview, or mail correspondence. Other examples of surveys that may be used for obtaining this kind of information may be found in Wehman et al. (1985) and Wuerch and Voeltz (1982).

It is particularly important to pay attention to parental or guardian needs and desires in choosing leisure activities since free time occurs when students are at home. One way or another, parental involvement has to be built into a training program (Stein, 1981). However, until recently home-based leisure programs have received no emphasis. An excellent source for incorporating parental input during the skills selection phase and throughout skill maintenance in the home is Wuerch and Voeltz (1982).

Cataloging Identified Activities

Once environments have been surveyed, a listing of possible activities can be compiled. An example of a "leisure catalog" compiled for one student is provided in Table 9.3. Note both the variety of activities and the parallel activities at home, school, and in the community.

TABLE 9.2 Questions appropriate for home and community leisure recreation surveys

Home Survey Questions

1. What leisure activities and materials are currently available in your home?
2. What materials or activities not currently available would you be willing to purchase?
3. What does your child do with his or her free time?
4. Do you think your child would enjoy the following leisure activities? (List several and ask about each one.)
5. What leisure activities do family members participate in out in community settings?
6. What are some activities in the community that you would like to see your child participate in?
7. Which family members are most likely to "play" with your child?
8. Would you be willing to transport your child to recreational activities that occur in community settings?
9. Would you be willing to help your child learn home and community leisure activities with our assistance?

Community Survey Questions

1. What are the major recreational facilities in the immediate neighborhood?
2. Are there other recreational facilities outside the immediate neighborhood but relatively accessible?
3. What activities occur in community facilities?
4. What are the transportation options for using community facilities?
5. Are community programs segregated, integrated, or both?
6. Are community recreation personnel receptive to integrated programming?
7. What are the attitudes of key personnel?
8. Can you use facilities during and after school hours for training purposes?
9. Are facilities adapted and accessible for persons with physical and sensory impairments?

Prioritizing Identified Activities for Instruction

After cataloging possible activities, one must decide which skills should be learned first. Some may be more appropriate than others according to several dimensions. A checklist can be used to select activities by comparing several possible choices according to their ratings on prespecified criteria. One example using 13 criteria and three broad cagetories was developed by Wuerch and Voeltz (1982) (see Table 9.4). However, any checklist must be interpreted in relation to individual and family preference.

Assessing Student Competence and Preference

Two types of behavioral assessments must be completed before instructional goals and objectives can be established. First, objective data concerning a student's preferences for activities must be collected. Second, a student's level of proficiency in a particular activity must be established.

Determining Preference

There are a variety of ways to determine individual preference. The first step is to analyze carefully what an individual does during free time (Reid, Willis, Jarman, & Brown, 1978). Parental surveys and informal observations will provide some answers. Formal assessment based on activities that are identified by parents and by informal observation should also be done. One way to assess preferences for known activities is to present several familiar activities at once and then record *duration* and *type of interaction* for each during a specified time period. A variety of activities within and across categories should be presented, and the student should have the opportunity to engage with others in the activity. A recording sheet such as that shown in Figure 9.1 can be used for this type of assessment.

The same type of assessment can be used to show preferences for nonfamiliar but appropriate activities. The combined information obtained from presenting both familiar and unfamiliar activities reveals activities most preferred, those which could be used as reinforcers, and gross information on proficiency.

Latency or the amount of time before one responds to an activity can also be used to determine preference. When an item is presented, simply record the time that passes between item presentation and a participant response. If multiple items are presented, the differences in latency represent the individual's preference. The same recording sheet described previously (in Figure 9.1) can be used for this purpose.

Regardless of whether latency, duration, or quality of interaction is being recorded, there are three general guidelines to follow in assessing preference: (1) each type of assessment, even when all are done simultaneously, should be done over a period of days; (2) all activities should be presented several times and always in different combinations; and (3) equal attention should be paid to duration and quality of interactions. If a student spends the

TABLE 9.3 Catalog of leisure activities for a 14-year-old student

Home	School	Community
Hobbies	*Hobbies*	*Hobbies*
Album collecting	School chorus	Attending semi-pro baseball games
Model car building	Photography club	Church choir
Comic book collecting		Local video club
Watching movies on VCR/TV		
Photography		
Sports	*Sports*	*Sports*
Horseshoes	All 9th grade PE units including	Aerobics classes
Croquet	golf, weight training, softball,	YMCA swimming class
Badminton	swimming, badminton, and	Local park fitness trail
Softball	dance	YMCA weight training
Basketball	Shuffleboard	Family bowling (once each month)
Touch football	Ping-Pong	Putt-Putt
Ping-Pong		Shuffleboard at church
Cycling		Ping-Pong at church
Games	*Games*	*Games*
Checkers	Checkers	Bingo at church
Twister	Twister	
Old Maid	Pick Up Sticks	
Rook	Jacks	
Life	Old Maid	
Pick Up Sticks	Concentration	
	Bingo	
Toy Play/Object Manipulation	*Toy Play/Object Manipulation*	*Toy Play/Object Manipulation*
Radio	Stereo	Vending machines at YMCA and church
Stereo	Radio	
TV/VCR	Frisbee	
Telephone	Camera	
Camera	Oil paints/watercolors	
Model cars	Vending machines	
Bicycle		
Frisbee		

most time with a frisbee but appears to know best what to do with a bowling ball and pins, perhaps both should be chosen at this time for instruction.

Determining Competence

The most commonly used means of measuring skill level on a recreational activity (or any other) before and during instruction is a task analytic assessment (Snell, 1983; Wehman, Renzaglia, & Bates, 1985). To use a task analysis, the sequence of behaviors (steps) in the task (activity) must be analyzed by either observing a competent person perform the activity and/or by actually performing it. The steps must be recorded in order of occurrence on a data sheet such as the one shown in Figure 9.2. The major advantage to using this method of assessment is that the same task analysis can be used for assessing learning before and during instruction

(probing) and for actual instruction of the activity. There are two ways of conducting a task analytic assessment: (1) single opportunity and (2) multiple opportunity, as described in Chapter 4.

The single-opportunity method for assessing recreation activities is the easiest to use. With this method, the instructor arranges the setting and materials and provides an instructional cue such as, "It's time for a break. Choose a game." The cue can be more specific at first, but should be as natural as possible. Then the instructor uses the recording sheet to enter a symbol by each step for either correct or incorrect performance. No instructional prompts or reinforcement are given for performance, but attending and effort can be rewarded. Testing is stopped after an error is made, when there is a sustained period of no response (5 or more seconds), or inappropriate behavior occurs. Multiple testing opportunities (at least three) over a

TABLE 9.4   Leisure activity selection checklist

Student: Pat Smith _____   Date: _____   Completed by: Terry Jones _____

	TV game Activity	Simon Activity	Bowling Activity

Normalization: A concern for selecting activities that have social validity and that will facilitate normalized play and leisure behaviors, as well as provide opportunities for movement toward increasingly complex interactions.

	TV game	Simon	Bowling
1. *Age Appropriateness.* Is this activity something a nonhandicapped peer would enjoy during free time?	**(yes)** no	**(yes)** no	**(yes)** no
2. *Attraction.* Is this activity likely to promote interest of others who frequently are found in the youth's leisure time settings?	**(yes)** no	**(yes)** no	**(yes)** no
3. *Environmental Flexibility.* Can this activity be used in a variety of potential leisure time situations on an individual and group basis?	**(yes)** no	**(yes)** no	**(yes)** no
4. *Degree of Supervision.* Can the activity be used under varying degrees of caregiver supervision without major modifications?	**(yes)** no	**(yes)** no	yes **(no)**
5. *Longitudinal Application.* Is use of the activity appropriate for both an adolescent and an adult?	**(yes)** no	**(yes)** no	**(yes)** no

Individualization: Concerns related to meeting the unique and ever-changing needs and skills of handicapped youth.

	TV game	Simon	Bowling
1. *Skill Level Flexibility.* Can the activity be adapted for low to high entry skill levels without major modifications?	**(yes)** no	**(yes)** no	**(yes)** no
2. *Prosthetic Capabilities.* Can the activity be adapted to varying handicapping conditions (sensory, motor, behavior)?	yes **(no)**	**(yes)** no	**(yes)** no
3. *Reinforcement Power.* Is the activity sufficiently novel or stimulating to maintain interest?	**(yes)** no	**(yes)** no	**(yes)** no

Environmental: Concerns related to logistical and physical demands of leisure activities on current and future environments and free time situations.

	TV game	Simon	Bowling
1. *Availability.* Is the activity available (or can it easily be made so) across the youth's leisure environments?	**(yes)** no	**(yes)** no	**(yes)** no
2. *Durability.* Is the activity likely to last without need for major repair or replacement of parts for at least a year?	**(yes)** no	**(yes)** no	**(yes)** no
3. *Safety.* Is the activity safe, i.e., would not pose a serious threat to or harm the handicapped youth, others, or the environment if abused or used inappropriately?	**(yes)** no	**(yes)** no	**(yes)** no
4. *Noxiousness.* Is the activity not likely to be overly noxious (noisy, space consuming, distracting) to others in the youth's leisure environments?	yes **(no)**	yes **(no)**	**(yes)** no
5. *Expense.* Is the cost of the activity reasonable? That is, is it likely to be used for multiple purposes?	yes **(no)**	**(yes)** no	**(yes)** no

Area of Concern Scores	TV game	Simon	Bowling
1. Normalization	5	5	4
2. Individualization	2	3	3
3. Environmental	3	4	5
Total Activity Score	10	12	12

Source: Reprinted with permission from Wuerch, Bonnie Biel and Voeltz, Luanna M. *Longitudinal Leisure Skills for Severely Handicapped Learners:* The Ho'onanea Curriculum Component. Baltimore: Paul H. Brookes Publishing Co. ©1982.

Name: _____

Prioritized activities: Camera, checkers, Frisbee, badminton, Twister, Pick Up Sticks
Familiar activities: Radio, stereo, Old Maid cards, basketball

Date of Baseline Period	Activity	(Latency) Time Before Responding[1]	(Duration) Time of Interaction[2]	(Quality of Interaction) Explain What the Child Does[3]
9/5	1. Camera	———	———	
	2. Frisbee	5 seconds	30 seconds (2 occasions)	Tried to toss twice
	3. Pick up sticks	1 minute	5 seconds	Threw on floor—did not attempt to pick up
9/5	1. Frisbee	10 seconds	1 minute	Tried to toss several times
	2. Basketball	2 minutes	5 minutes	Shot baskets, passed
	3. Twister	———	———	
	4. Old Maid	10 minutes	5 minutes	Played hand with me
9/6	1. Old Maid	3 seconds	10 minutes	Played hand with me
	2. Radio	———	———	
	3. Camera	12 minutes	5 seconds	Held to face and pretended to take picture
		[1]Indicate the item chosen first and the amount of time passed between presentation of items and participant response	[2]Indicate the number of minutes/seconds of each instance of interaction within the specific activities	[3]Provide a one- to two-word description of the student's behavior—Is it appropriate?

FIGURE 9.1 Assessment of leisure activity preference

period of at least 2 days should occur in order to obtain an accurate baseline of performance.

Figure 9.2 shows the baseline data obtained on a sample recreational activity. On three assessment trials, this student performed correctly on 45%, 27%, and 27% of the task steps which indicates that instruction is warranted.

Other Assessment Modes

Wehman, Renzaglia, and Bates (1985) provided five methods for answering different concerns that arise in the assessment of a student's competence and preferences. These concerns and corresponding methods of assessment are provided in Table 9.5; a description of each method can be found in Chapter 4.

DEVELOPING LEISURE TRAINING PROGRAMS

Establishing Goals and Objectives

The process recommended for selecting appropriate leisure activities, beginning with home and community screening and ending with behavioral assessment techniques such as a task analytic assessment, should lead directly to the development of several annual goals and related behavioral objectives in the leisure domain. The goals and objectives should then become an integral part of the student's IEP or IHP (individual habilitation plan) depending on the setting and age of the student.

Teacher: Moon Student's Name: Sandy Date: _____ Environment: YWCA Pool Instructional Cue: Swim with the Kickboard Program	8/13	8/14	8/15																					
1. Walk into waist-deep water with kickboard.	+	+	+																					
2. Extend arms straight out.	+	+	+																					
3. Grasp opposite sides of board with palmar grasp.	+	+	+																					
4. Push feet off pool bottom bringing entire body parallel to water surface.	+	–	–																					
5. Rest upper body from neck down on water surface.	+	–	–																					
6. Extend legs straight out with toes pointed.	–	–	–																					
7. Lower left leg 6" into water and bring right leg up to water surface with bended knee.	–	–	–																					
8. Lower right leg 6" into water and bring left leg up to water surface with bended knee.	–	–	–																					
9. Continue kicking motion to move two feet forward.	–	–	–																					
10. Continue to move 5 feet ahead.	–	–	–																					
11. Continue to move 10 feet ahead.	–	–	–																					

TASK COMPONENTS

% CORRECT RESPONSES   45 27 27

FIGURE 9.2 Task analytic data sheet for assessing swimming with a kickboard

An excellent guide for establishing goals and objectives that includes the recreation domain has been provided by Wilcox and Bellamy (1982). They point out that the goals should be very broad and relate directly to activities selected and prioritized from the catalog of leisure activities established earlier (see Table 9.3). Short-term objectives, on the other hand, are based on component tasks that are part of the whole leisure activity (annual goal). Each objective should be based on a specific, observable behavior, environmental conditions, and criteria for mastery of the behavior (Mager, 1976).

TABLE 9.5 Major assessment methods and corresponding training concerns

Mode of Assessment	Concern
Task analysis	Proficiency of an individual on primary skill steps
Frequency recording	1. Independent performance over a sustained time period
	2. Preference for activity
Social validation	Appropriate use of leisure materials and appropriate social interactions
Frequency or time-sample recording of social interactions	Interactions with others during leisure time
Latency recording	Preference for activities
Survey	1. Availability of activities in home and community settings
	2. Preference for activities

A sample set of goals and related objectives for the three students can be found in Table 9.6.

Initial Instruction (Skill Acquisition)

A behavioral approach to training leisure activities must be used for individuals with severe handicaps. The same systematic procedures that would be used for domestic or vocational training programs also apply to leisure program development. There are six components of a skill acquisition program: (1) goals and objectives; (2) the rationale for activity selection; (3) skill sequence and task analysis; (4) teaching techniques including shaping and chaining, prompting, reinforcement, and data collection procedures; (5) the instructional schedule; and (6) preliminary plans for maintenance and generalization training. The rationale for activity selection, the goals, and objectives is established according to the activity selection process described earlier in this chapter. The other components of program development are described briefly in this chapter and in Chapters 4 and 5 of this text. Further information on program development in the leisure domain is detailed in Wehman and Schleien (1981), Wuerch and Voeltz (1982).

Skill Sequencing and Task Analysis

During the assessment process, an activity must be broken into component parts. For example, the activity of cycling has a number of "skill sequences"

including riding a stationary bike, a three-wheeler, a two-wheeler on level terrain, and a two-wheeler on all surfaces. This cycling skill sequence indicates a number of smaller, sequenced activities of skills that can be taught. In some cases, the entire sequence must be taught so that the student can be an independent performer. In other situations, the instructor may choose one or two skills from a sequence so that the student can at least "partially participate." An IEP objective should, therefore, be based on one or several skills from within a total task analysis or skill sequence. For other examples of skill sequences refer to Table 9.7.

Once an activity has been sequenced into component skills, each skill must be task analyzed. This task analysis is then used to teach each part of a particular activity. For example, playing softball may have a sequence of 10 skills, all of which need to be taught if a student is going to play softball unassisted. Each of the 10 skills is to be task analyzed before instruction occurs. (See Table 9.8 for a sample task analysis of softball skills.)

As instruction progresses with the use of skill sequences and task analyses, each activity can be adapted to each student's needs for instruction, and individual steps of a particular task analysis may be modified. In some instances, an entire skill such as running the bases in softball may be eliminated or adapted: a peer may run the bases for a student who cannot effectively execute this aspect of the game.

Shaping and Chaining

Two specific methods, shaping and chaining, may be used to develop new behaviors. These methods are described in detail in Chapter 5. Response chaining is typically used to teach the steps of a leisure activity which were identified through a task analysis (Wehman & Schleien, 1981). Total task and single step (Snell, 1983; Wuerch & Voeltz, 1982) are two response chaining teaching methods that are used most often. "Total-task," or "simultaneous-task," training teaches each step of the task analysis regardless of the student's competence level on any single step. The second method, "single step," teaches an individual step of the task analysis until its performance criterion is met. After each criterion is met, the individual moves to the next step. Either forward or backward chaining would be used with single-step training so that the student could proceed with assistance through the entire skill.

TABLE 9.6 Sample IEP annual goals and instructional objectives in the leisure domain

Goal (Activity)	Objective (Skills)
1. Susan will become a member of the Jr. High Photography Club by Sept. 1986 (beginning of next school year)	1a. Given an instamatic camera and a roll of film, Susan will independently insert cartridge into the camera and take a clear photograph on 12 of the 15 cartridge spaces over a 2-week period during school hours. 1b. Given a photo album and 12 photographs, Susan will place 4 photographs on a page on three consecutive pages with 100% accuracy according to TA steps over four trials (one per week for a month).
2. Jim will work in the family greenhouse on Saturdays by June, 1986 (end of this school year)	2a. Given a 6" pot, soil, garden spoon, rocks and watering can, Jim will put rocks and soil in pot, scoop out area for plant, and plant bedding plant in center of pot correctly according to 100% correct performance on steps of TA on four consecutive trials (two per week for a 2-week period). 2b. Given three plants which have soil that is dry to touch and one that is damp, Jim will water the dry plants by pouring two cups of water into the soil on four consecutive trials over a 2-week period (two trials per week at beginning and end of week).
3 Amy will take a daily walk 30 minutes without stopping.	3a. Given a set wrist alarm watch and a 40-minute phys. ed. period, Amy will walk continuously around the school track until the alarm sounds over three consecutive trials (one trial at the end of each week for three weeks). 3b. Given a set wrist alarm watch and a 30-minute period on Saturdays and Sundays, Amy will walk on the town park fitness trail with her Mom until the alarm sounds on six consecutive trials (Sat. and Sun. for a 3-week period).

Total-task training should be used whenever possible because it is a more natural and reinforcing method (Snell, 1983). This method allows for practice on steps that the student has learned to criterion as well as instruction on those steps that are not yet learned.

Instructional Prompts

Ultimately the student must be able to respond to cues which occur in the natural environment. A particular time of the day designated by a wall chart and the sound of a buzzer ending a work period should be enough to prompt a student to choose a leisure activity. Similarly, a family member asking if anyone wants to play a particular game should also prompt a response. Such cues must be built into initial instruction and should always be used along with more artificial prompts. As a rule, the natural, environmental cue should be given as the discriminative stimulus (S^D) on all probe and training trials.

Other prompts may need to be provided to promote correct responses to individual steps in a task analysis. Commonly used prompts are verbal cues, gestural or model prompts, physical guidance, and stimulus prompts such as color or shape coding. One must be very cautious in using any of these artificial prompts because the student may become dependent on these rather than natural, environmental stimuli.

One prompting method that has been used successfully to teach leisure skills involves the use of verbal, model, and physical prompts (Moon & Renzaglia, 1982; Wehman, Renzaglia, & Bates, 1985). The prompts are arranged in the order of least-to-most intrusive (verbal-model-physical) and are applied in that order, one at a time, until a correct response occurs on each step of the task analysis. The advantage to this system is that prompts are faded naturally (Snell, 1983).

Some students, particularly those with sensory disabilities, may need a single, more intrusive prompt, such as physical guidance, that is gradually

TABLE 9.7 Sample skill sequence of cycling, swimming, softball, basketball, and walking to be considered as lead up activities

Swimming	Basketball
1. Water adjustment	1. Catch basketball
2. Putting face in water	2. Chest pass
3. Submerging entire body	3. Overhead pass
4. Submerging body and lifting legs from bottom	4. Bounce pass
5. Blowing bubbles	5. Dribble stationary
6. Prone float	6. Dribble and walk
7. Prone glide	7. Two-hand shot
8. Supine float	8. Dribble-pass-shoot on move
9. Supine glide	9. Play one-on-one half-court
10. Roll from prone to supine	10. Play three-on-three half-court
11. Kick with flotation device	11. Play five-on-five half-court
12. Prone/supine glides with kick	12. Play five-on-five full-court
13. Back kick and fin	
14. Treading water	Softball
15. Strokes:	
a. Kick and overhand stroke	1. Underhand throw
b. American crawl	2. Overhand throw
c. Elementary backstroke	3. Catch with glove
d. Side stroke	4. Batting ball from stationary tee
e. Breast stroke	5. Hitting pitched ball
	6. Running bases
Walking (On Track)	7. Throwing to person at base
	8. Tagging runner
1. Move with support 20 yards	9. Hitting pitched ball
2. Move with support 100 yards	10. Catching hit ball
3. Move alone 120 yards	11. Playing softball game
4. Move alone 220 yards	
5. Move alone 440 yards	
6. Move alone 880 yards	

Source: From "Physical Fitness and the Mentally Retarded: A Critical Review of the Literature" by M. S. Moon and A. Renzaglia, 1982, *Journal of Special Education*, 16, p. 280. Copyright 1982 by the Journal of Special Education. Adapted by permission.

faded. The various levels of physical prompting must be determined and standardized, with some criterion for changing levels, from most-to-least intrusive, and for fading all assistance, being established prior to instruction. Wuerch and Voeltz (1982) warn against using any particular prompt hierarchy and suggest that previous training data should dictate the amount of assistance needed on a day to day basis.

Reinforcers

Although leisure activities should be naturally reinforcing, the process of learning these activities may not be innately motivating; therefore, anything that is reinforcing to an individual can be used at first. More naturally occurring reinforcers such as praise, peer attention, or a physical sign of affection such as a pat on the back should be used, especially if these are equally as effective as food or activities. Reinforcers can be administered after each correct response, regardless of the level of prompt needed. As the student becomes more independent, reinforcers should be faded to occur only after several responses and/or only after responses occur independently or with less and less intrusive prompts.

Data Collection Procedures

The instructor must specify how probe and training data will be recorded. Typically, a task analytic data sheet will be used for probing performance (see task analytic assessment on page 222) on a daily or weekly basis. The same type of form can be used to record the types of prompts provided on training trials. If a particular prompt hierarchy or instructional design such as multi-element is being used, instructions for recording and graphing results must also be provided.

TABLE 9.8 Task analysis of underhand softball throw

1. Stand with foot opposite throwing hand forward.
2. Curl fingers around ball.
3. Wrap thumb around opposite side of ball.
4. Apply inward pressure between thumb and fingers to grasp ball firmly.
5. Bend elbow, bringing ball to waist level.
6. Extend elbow, bringing arm outward to dominant side of body.
7. Extend elbow, moving arm backward behind body, forming 45-degree angle with back of body.
8. Rotate wrist so that palm of hand is facing forward.
9. Extend elbow, swinging arm forward to front of body in a pendular motion, while shifting weight to forward foot (foot opposite the throwing hand).
10. When arm is extended forward, pointing at target, release ball in forward direction.

Schedule for Training

Leisure activities should be taught not only in conjunction with physical education, but also at times when they naturally occur such as before and after classes, during recess periods, during breaks at work, after school, and during weekends. There are times that are appropriate for more passive, quiet activities and other times that are suitable for active, group activities such as aerobic activities or team sports. Whenever possible, training should occur in distributed trials during naturally occurring leisure periods. Several short instructional periods (15 to 20 minutes) for each activity, is preferable. The total amount of time spent on leisure activity training will vary for each student, but should comprise at least an hour of each school day for everyone.

Skill Maintenance

After a student has reached performance criterion, conditions must be determined for maintaining continued performance under natural, environmental stimuli. Hopefully, the student will want to participate in the activity during specified leisure periods. If this occurs, probe data can be collected regularly during some of these periods. Maintenance probes are conducted as during the baseline and acquisition phases with a task analysis. These probes should be done infrequently but over a period of months after instruction stops.

Skill Generalization

When a training program is developed, the instructor knows where the activity should occur. Most likely this setting is a home or community setting, and training should be in this same setting. A plan for training activities in their natural settings should be outlined before instruction ever begins. This plan will allow family members and nondisabled peers to be involved in a total-community, recreation activity.

Community-Based Instruction

Community-based training of recreational skills will facilitate learning generalization (Bates & Renzaglia, 1979; Johnson & Bailey, 1977; Stokes & Baer, 1977). It is essential that the activity selection process identify settings, people, and materials that exist in community facilities and that these elements be used during training programs. If the goal for one student is to learn to bowl in a neighborhood bowling facility, then training and maintenance probes should occur in these facilities. If phonograph collecting is the chosen hobby of one student, then she must be shown how to interact with sales clerks in several record stores so that she may purchase her favorite albums. Involving the clerks during training will acquaint them with the student who may be alone or with a family member. This type of arrangement also allows the instructor to help business people, community recreation facility personnel, and the public in general to accept and integrate people with disabilities.

It is extremely important for school and community special education and recreation personnel to work jointly on programs for persons with severe handicaps (Stein, 1981; Witt, 1977). One of the first steps in this cooperative process is the use of community facilities such as YWCAs and YMCAs, city parks, recreation gyms, swimming pools, outdoor parks, and public golf and racquet clubs. It is usually feasible to gain access to these facilities during school hours because of a general lack of use during the day. The second step is to integrate nondisabled participants, involved in regular programs, at these facilities with your students. This process can be made easier by adherence to the guidelines in Table 9.9.

Parental Involvement

Because much of an individual's free time occurs in the home setting, family members or other significant persons living in the home must be involved in leisure activity programming (Stein, 1981). First, family members help decide which activities are

TABLE 9.9 Guidelines for enhancing integration of community leisure programs

1. Use community facilities for training skill acquisition, but in doing so, adhere to these rules:
   a. Do not take large groups (more than three) of students with handicaps into the community for training.
   b. Do not allow students to exhibit gross stereotypic or excessive behaviors repeatedly. Work on minimizing these behaviors before a great deal of training in the community is done.
   c. Provide positive feedback to the businesses, community facility personnel, and the general public for welcoming and accepting the person with a disability. Offer formal presentations to groups on the importance of integrating citizens with severe disabilities.
   d. Training for students in each facility should occur on a regular basis and at least twice each week.
2. Encourage parents or guardians to take their child who is severely handicapped to the same settings where you are providing training. This allows for more practice, more exposure, and parents can see what progress is being made. Explain the training program, and show parents how they can train also, if they want to participate in this way.
3. Provide inservice to community recreation personnel, and offer to "trade off" training responsibilities. For example, if a recreation specialist is willing to teach your students to swim at the YMCA, then perhaps you could volunteer to work one evening a week in one of their programs.
4. Participate with one or two of your students at a time in an integrated community program such as aerobics, arts and crafts, yoga, watching ballgames, concerts, and movies.
5. Teach related skills such as transportation, emergency identification procedures, and use of facility restrooms and snackbars while you are training the leisure activity.
6. Establish programs such as "Advocacy Clubs" in which nondisabled students or adults can accompany a "friend" who is handicapped to leisure events in the community.

most feasible for instruction by indicating what activities the family enjoys. Available materials in the home and in neighborhood programs are also identified. Finally, the willingness of the family to follow through on training in home and community settings must be established. All three types of information can be collected on the home screening inventory which is administered prior to program development (see Table 9.2). Instructors must also make an effort to invite family members to participate in classroom and community-based training. They should also visit the home to help family members learn how they can encourage individuals to pursue appropriate leisure activities. Unfortunately, there are very few reports in the literature of home-based leisure instruction (Hill, 1980; Johnson & Bailey, 1977; Wehman, Renzaglia, & Bates, 1985). One of the best sources of specific information on parent involvement in leisure programs is Wuerch and Voeltz (1982). They provide guidelines as well as forms that can be used for determining (a) needs and experiences in home leisure time planning, (b) selection of leisure time planning, (c) parent assessment of their child's leisure preferences, (d) consultation and home training needs, and (e) parent satisfaction with leisure programming.

Continuous parental input is necessary because as Wuerch and Voeltz (1982) emphasize:

In the final analysis, the true test of acquisition of a leisure repertoire is not the percentage of correct responses on steps in the task analysis of a leisure activity skill during instruction. If behavior in the home setting and other relevant community environments shows no improvement, the leisure education program cannot be considered a success. (p. 172)

The Involvement of Nondisabled Peers

Peer involvement in recreation programs can have a positive influence on both the individual with a handicapping condition and the nondisabled participant. Wehman and Hill (1980) found that gifted high school students were able to teach a group of students who had severe handicaps to play games such as pinball and darts. Moon (1983) found that during an integrated physical education class of high school sophomores and juniors and students with severe handicaps, who were the same age, the presence of the nondisabled students was as effective as tangible reinforcers or teacher praise in maintaining performance. In addition, the attitudes of the nondisabled students also significantly improved after participation in the class. Another study (Santomier & Kopczuk, 1981) indicated that integrated physical education classes can increase positive social interactions between students.

Peer involvement can also be encouraged by having students with severe handicaps join regular scout troups, 4-H clubs, and church youth organizations. Of course, this will involve some education and orientation of troop or club leaders and members. Advocacy clubs can be formed for junior and senior high school students in which each nondisabled member has a friend who is disabled. The pairs of students can attend school social functions, community sports, and cultural events together. Through the club framework, young people can receive information on handicapping conditions and learn about the importance of integrating persons with disabilities into the school and community. A teacher, aide, or interested parent can be a sponsor of a club to enhance interactions and assist whenever necessary.

ADAPTING LEISURE PROGRAMS

Often some component of a leisure activity will have to be adapted to allow an individual with severe handicaps to participate more fully. A well-designed adaptation will improve the level of participation of the handicapped individual and also enhance the attitude toward nondisabled citizens. Several guidelines should be followed when considering program adaptations. First, no special techniques should be tried until task analytic assessment and instruction indicate that an individual cannot learn the entire task or skill sequence through conventional teaching practices. Second, any adaptation should be considered temporary, and attempts at fading the adaptation should be systematically implemented. When someone needs a long-term adaptation, care must be taken in designing a *normalizing* alteration. A strange looking mechanical device or a complete rule change can be as disconcerting to others as the incompetence of the individual who is not assisted. Third, inexpensive and portable adaptations should be tried first. It may be frustrating to use an adaptation to learn a game at school but not at home. Some of the adaptations will be described later in this section.

The Principle of Partial Participation

Some individuals with severe handicaps will never be able to participate independently in a community-based leisure activity regardless of the adaptations; however, in this domain, independent participation need not be the ultimate goal for all activities. Because enjoyment of the activity is the primary objective, the principle of partial participation has special applicability to leisure programs. As this principle asserts, limited participation in an appro-priate, functional, community-based activity is more desirable than independent performance in an age-inappropriate, segregated one. The leisure domain is probably the easiest one in which to use this principle for program design.

Types of Adaptations

A number of different types of adaptations can be applied to leisure activities. These adaptations generally fall into one of the following categories: material changes, role or procedural alterations, environmental adaptations, modifications of skill sequences based on task analyses, or the addition of lead-up activities (Wehman & Moon, 1985). Each type of adaptation will be described briefly in this section. Examples of various types are provided in Table 9.10.

Material Changes

Material alterations can be as simple as computer-controlled levers or switches or special grips on equipment. Such adaptations are particularly bene-ficial to persons with sensory or physical impair-ments. The use of inexpensive electromechanical switches, for example, has proved very successful in enabling physically involved children to use toys and cassette or record players. Burkhart (1982) provides easy-to-use directions for building such switches. Other examples of material adaptations are provided by AAHPERD (1977), Wehman and Schleien (1981), Cowart (1979), Aharoni (1982), Bauer (1981), and Wuerch and Voeltz (1982).

Environmental Adaptations

Inaccessibility of facilities has kept many persons from participating in community-based programs. Narrow doors, lack of ramps or elevators, and poorly designed bathrooms are common problems along with the lack of equipment to assist persons who have special needs related to mobility and lifting. However, newer buildings are becoming more accessible due to federal and state mandates. Guidelines for making environmental adaptations and for purchasing special equipment are available from many sources, including the Virginia Com-mission (1976).

Rule or Procedural Alterations

Intricate rules can be big barriers to participation in some games and sports. In some cases rules can be changed or entirely dropped, so long as all participants agree. Some sources of information on

TABLE 9.10 Examples of adaptations applied to the four categories of leisure skills

Activity	Type of Adaptation
	Sports
Badminton	Material
	• Short-handled racket
	• Enlarged, foam rubber racket handle
	• Indoor play (eliminate wind factor)
	• Lowered net
	• Lightweight ball (or yarn or heavier weighted birdie)
	Procedural/Rule
	• Serve to any area
Basketball	Procedural/Rule
	• More than five players (increase court coverage and eliminate need for long passes)
	• Use of half a court
	• Allow two-handed dribbling
	• Allow two or more steps per dribble
Bowling	Skill Sequence
	• Start with plastic set in gym
	• One-step delivery to three and four step
	• Trainer picks up ball and gives to bowler to perform a two-handed bowl.
Baseball	Lead-Up Activity
	• Kickball to learn concepts of scoring runs, running bases, fielding
	• Punchball to develop gross motor coordination
	• Tee ball to practice batting swing and hitting any size ball
	• Suspend ball from ceiling for continuous batting practice
	• Whiffle ball: slower, safer version of baseball
	Hobbies
Photography	Material
	• Extend button with attachment
	• Color designated buttons
	• Polaroid camera
Plant care	• Use 1-cup measure to prevent overwatering
Cooking	• Color-coded dials and temperatures on stove
	• Picture recipes
Needlework	Lead Up Activity
	• Lacing board with plastic needle attached to nylon cord
	• Sewing cards to learn basic movements necessary for sewing
Collecting/Fan Club	• Cutting pictures from magazines (to be categorized by someone else)
	Games
Ping-Pong	Material
	• Nerf balls and paddles
	• Large paddle head
Pool	Procedural/Rule
	• Rather than designate striped or solid balls, shoot at any ball and record number of balls hit into pockets
	Skill Sequence
	• Game of 9-ball
Playing Cards	Skill Sequence
	• Pick up cards only after all have been dealt to all players
	• Allow some players to have "silent partner"
Darts	Lead Up Activities
	• Cricket requiring player to count number of darts thrown on board instead of adding numbers
	• Using numbers 1 through 6 as designated scoring numbers rather than 15 through 20 as usually done in Cricket, allowing for easier number identification
	Objective Manipulation
Telephone	Material
	• Use shoulder supporter to hold phone
	• Push buttons
Balls	• Start with large, light balls and progress to smaller, heavier ones
Viewfinder	• Skill Sequence
	• Have second person push button to change picture
Vending Machine	• Having picture cards denoting items and corresponding correct coins

Source: Adapted from P. Wehman and M. S. Moon, *Designing and Implementing Leisure Programs for Individuals with Severe Handicaps*. In M. P. Brady and P. L. Gunter (Eds.), *Integrating Moderately and Severely Handicapped Learners* 1985. Courtesy of Charles C Thomas, Publisher, Springfield, Illinois.

rule adaptations for particular games, sports, and hobbies include Adams, Daniel, and Pullman (1975); Groose (1971); Information and Research Utilization Center (1976); and Wehman and Schleien (1981).

Task Analytic and Skill Sequence Modifications

As pointed out earlier in this chapter, task analytical instruction should indicate which step(s), or series of steps, in an activity can and cannot be performed independently by a particular individual. Some steps may require assistance from others or may need to be done is an unusual order. See Table 9.10 for examples of this type of adaptation.

Lead-Up Activities

Wehman and Schleien (1981) described lead-up activities as a simplified form of an activity that allows for partial participation in some aspect. Lead-up activities can also be created by isolating one or more skills from an entire skill sequence such as hitting and pitching in softball or shooting baskets and passing in basketball (see Table 9.7). These activities can be taught separately and then linked together as part of a more complicated activity as an individual becomes more competent.

SPECIAL OLYMPICS

The Special Olympics program has become a major recreational activity for many severely retarded persons in this country. The program has provided both cooperative and competitive leisure opportunities for both participants, volunteers, and families since its inception in 1968. However, the program has been criticized on the basis of its lack of adherence to normalization theory and because of its emphasis on isolated, sometimes nonfunctional activities which are primarily track and field related (Orelove & Moon, 1984; Wehman & Moon, 1985). Unfortunately, for many school-aged, disabled individuals, Special Olympics has become their primary recreational experience.

Orelove and Moon (1984) offered several suggestions for modifying the Special Olympics format to permit nonhandicapped individuals to participate. These suggestions include:

1. Format changes could involve more nonhandicapped participants of the same chronological age as the athletes with handicaps to serve as coaches, "rabbits" (race pacers), timers, and trainers rather than as "huggers"; this type of more normalized interaction could eventually lead to open competitions.
2. Regional and national competitions could be replaced with local clinics in which volunteers learn how to communicate and recreate with participants who are handicapped.
3. Special efforts should be made to screen out exceptional athletes so that they can participate in integrated sports programs.
4. Competitors could focus on a variety of games and hobbies as well as sports to offer a more well-rounded preparation program and could include older and multihandicapped persons. The events included in each community could be based on what is actually available to all citizens in that particular area.

After the Special Olympic event, volunteers could pair up with participants to attend local events.

A REVIEW OF EXISTING LEISURE PROGRAMS AND RESEARCH STUDIES

The number of published reports on leisure skill development for persons who are severely disabled has increased dramatically over the past 10 years. Several reviews of the literature have indicated both strides made in this area as well as a number of problems with existing programs. (Moon & Renzaglia, 1981; Nietupski, Hamre-Nietupski, & Ayers, 1984; Wehman, Renzaglia, & Bates, 1985; Wuerch & Voeltz, 1982)

A variety of activities have been taught to individuals through the use of behavioral training techniques, and several validated skill sequences, task analyses, and instructional procedures now exist. Three of the most commonly referred to published leisure programs, each of which outlines a variety of activities, include: (a) *Longitudinal Leisure Skills for Severely Handicapped Learners* by Wuerch and Voeltz (1982); (b) *Leisure Programs for Handicapped Persons* by Wehman and Schleien (1981); and (c) *The "I Can" Curriculum* by Wessel (1976). Together these three programs contain procedures for teaching nearly 100 activities. We recommend that a teacher purchase all these materials if possible. Most students will have at least one identified activity that has already been analyzed by one of these programs; however, no student's entire leisure program needs will be covered by any existing curriculum.

Besides leisure programs that encompass a number of activities, there are several empirical reports of leisure training programs that have focused on a single activity category. Toy play involving the object manipulation of a variety of age-appropriate items has been successfully instructed (Gaylord-Ross, Haring, Breen, & Pitts-Conway, 1984; Hill, Wehman, & Horst, 1982; Hopper & Wambold, 1978; Horst, Wehman, Hill, & Bailey, 1981; Kissel & Whitman, 1977; Williams, Hamre-Nietupski, Pumpian, McDaniel-Marks, & Wheeler, 1978; Wuerch & Voeltz, 1982). Some of the materials involved in these instructional programs included a Viewmaster, Old Maid cards, balls, frisbee, electronic bowling, darts, pinball, remote control vehicle, gum, radio, Lego blocks, dolls, and several preschool toys.

Table games involving the use of rules and cooperative play with others such as bingo, lotto, video games, target games, card games, and others have been instructed to severely retarded individuals (Keogh, Faw, Whitman, & Reid, 1984; Nietupski, & Svoboda, 1982; Sedlack, Doyle, & Schloss, 1982; Williams et al., 1978; and Wuerch & Voeltz, 1982). Hobbies such as listening to records and tapes, photography, weaving, painting, and dining out have also been taught as leisure activities (Giangreco, 1983; Horst et al., 1981; Johnson & Bailey, 1977)

Some of the studies documenting the successful training of physical fitness activities have already been mentioned earlier in this chapter. Other recreation activities involving gross motor capabilities such as dancing, the use of playground equipment, and tricycle riding have also been taught to persons with severe handicaps (Lagomarcino, Reid, Ivancic, & Faw, 1984; Marchant & Wehman, 1979).

Implications for the Design of Future Recreation Programs

Several researchers have pointed out a number of issues that must be examined in future research studies and leisure skill training programs for persons having severe handicaps (Nietupski, Hamre-Nietupski, & Ayers, 1984; Wehman, Renzalia, & Bates, 1985; Wuerch & Voeltz, 1982). Some of the issues most commonly discussed in the literature reviews and empirical studies mentioned in this chapter are delineated next.

1. *Instruction of leisure skills must occur in integrated community environments.* If individuals are expected to practice leisure skills in their homes or community settings, then the skills must be taught in these settings. Wehman, Renzaglia, and Bates (1985) found in a review of 30 data-based studies that only 5 involved the home setting, and less than 10 utilized community-based recreation settings. Recommendations were made indicating the need for demonstrations on (a) ways to access integrated facilities, (b) effective administrative models for combining handicapped and non-handicapped persons in a variety of programs, and (c) methods for facilitating interactions among all persons participating in these programs (Nietupski et al., 1984).

2. *Instructional strategies must be documented and optional methods determined.* A number of traditional behavioral techniques have been used effectively in leisure programs; however, comparisons of different methods have not been made. It would be especially helpful to validate the effectiveness of peers as instructors in leisure programs.

3. *Methods for assuring maintenance and generalization of skill performance must be developed.* Only a few empirical studies have examined the generalization of skill performance, but those that have done so (Gaylord-Ross et al., 1984; Hill et al., 1982; Sedlack et al., 1982; Stainback et al., 1983) have provided some guidelines: (a) multiple training exemplars should be used during acquisition training (several trainers, settings, and materials), (b) subtle environmental factors such as distracting noises and presence or absence of people must be programmed, and (c) performance in the natural environment must be assessed. If the activity cannot be performed, it must be instructed again in that environment.

Skill maintenance has received less attention than generalization, but it is equally important. It is now thought that reducing the schedule of reinforcement and allowing extra time to build skill proficiency after acquisition may be effective ways of ensuring maintenance (Nietupski et al., 1984). Nonhandicapped peer participation in programs has also helped maintain the performance of individuals who have severe disabilities (Moon, 1983).

4. *Better programs must be developed for persons with multiple handicaps.* Most programs have been developed for individuals who possess basic gross, fine, and locomotor skills. These programs must be adapted for persons with physical handicaps by using the variety of adaptations discussed earlier in this chapter. There is little documentation existing which shows how rule, material, or facility modifications have been used, although as Nietupski et al. (1984) pointed out, the new electromechanical technology shows great promise.

TEACHING MOTOR SKILLS

Both fine and gross motor skills are involved in the accomplishment of almost all activities within every domain, particularly in recreation activities. However, little data-based information exists on the most efficient ways to train motor skills for individuals with severe handicaps (Bunker & Moon, 1983). The problem is compounded by the fact that motor development is highly sequential and interdependent and is influenced by an individual's physical fitness, body awareness, posture, and functioning level of the central nervous system. Nevertheless, there is ample evidence that even the most profoundly retarded person can be taught not only fundamental gross and fine motor activities, but also complicated fitness and sports skills (Haavik & Altman, 1977; Hardiman, Goetz, Reuter, & LeBlanc, 1975; Moon & Renzaglia, 1982; Wehman, Renzaglia, & Bates, 1985).

A general rule of thumb should be to train fine and gross motor skills within the context of a functional activity that requires that particular skill. Walking can be instructed during community activities such as learning to use the neighborhood grocery store or traveling independently to school or work. Other gross motor skills such as climbing, throwing, kicking, catching, running, and jumping can be learned within the context of a sport or individual physical fitness activity. It is important that fine motor skills including grasping, finger use, eye-hand coordination, and arm and hand use should te taught as part of some functional activity as exemplified in Table 9.11.

Chronological Age of the Student

A student's age will determine which motor skills are taught and the way they are instructed. For

TABLE 9.11 Fine motor skills and functional activities

Skill	Activity
1. Fingers move in any direction and with control	Turning book pages
2. Individual finger use	Dialing telephone
3. Individual thumb use	Clothes snaps
4. Coordinated finger use	Typing, playing musical instruments, shoe tying
5. Arm placement	Placing arm on small table or in water basin.
6. Placing objects in/on other objects	Jar lids, box tops, records/tapes
7. Using both arms for holding and carrying	Carrying cafeteria tray
8. One hand holding, one hand manipulating	Painting, stirring, gardening
9. Hook or shovel grasp	Tooth brushing, racquet sports
10. Pincer grasp	Buttoning, zipping, sewing
11. Lateral pincer grasp	Using scissors
12. Spherical grasp	Throwing and catching, eating/drinking

example, it may be appropriate to spend time teaching a preschooler to walk by working on the following skill sequence: (a) righting and equilibrium responses, (b) standing from a sitting position, (c) crawling, (d) creeping, (e) walking with support, (f) independent stepping, (g) walking with balance, and (h) maneuvering with obstacles, height barriers, etc. However, this same skill sequence would be inappropriate for a 16-year-old boy with profound retardation who prefers to crawl although he has no major physical disabilities. A more efficient program for this older student would be similar to that proposed by O'Brien, Azrin, and Bugle (1972), in which crawling is restrained and walking is primed by physical assistance to a standing position and then reinforced appropriately.

The student's age will also determine whether basic fine and gross motor and body management skills are taught in isolation or within the context of other activities. It is reasonable to work on advanced locomotor skills such as running, jumping, and climbing with preschool and early elementary aged children by task analyzing these skills and training them in a variety of settings. These same locomotor skills should be taught to adolescents and adults in the context of age-appropriate recreational, vocational, and community mobility activities. If certain skills, such as hopping, skipping, and galloping, are not necessary for adaptation to potential adult environments, they should not receive a large portion of attention within the curriculum.

Analyzing Motor Skills

Because so many recreation activities involve gross motor skills, it is important to understand how both locomotor and manipulative skills can be developed. The following section should be helpful in the task analysis of activities involving gross and fine motor skills and in the instruction of such activities. Remember that an individual need not be totally proficient in these motor aspects of an activity in order to participate.

Fundamental Motor Skills

The motor skills discussed in this chapter depend on the earlier, more fundamental motor responses that usually develop in nonhandicapped children before the age of one year. For example, each child must have adequate equilibrium and body control skills to progress to more advanced motor skills such as standing, walking, and manipulating objects. Many persons with motoric disorders do not have even the most fundamental motor functions. This may be further complicated by the presence of nonfunctional, primary reflexes. This group of people with motoric involvement also needs physical education experiences, as emphasized in Chapter 7.

Primitive reflexes generally persist for a number of weeks in all children, and then gradually disappear as corresponding functional voluntary reflexes appear; however, these primitive responses can interfere with normal movement, and the child needs programs to inhibit and integrate them. The most commonly seen reflexes in this category include the tonic labyrinthine reflex (TLR), asymmetrical tonic neck reflex (ATNR), the symmetrical tonic neck reflex (TNR), primitive neck righting reflex (PNRR), grasp reflex, and the Moro (head turn to startle) reflex. Whenever these reflexes persist, a program should be implemented in conjunction with occupational or physical therapy to modify them or accommodate their presence.

Righting and equilibrium responses are automatic responses that facilitate balance and support as the body moves from one position to another. Children need a wide variety of experiences to learn to control the head, arms, and total body as it moves from aligned to off-balance positions. For example, it must be possible to shift the head, trunk, or extremities from side to side, forward to backward, to create all forms of body positions (Johnson, 1978).

Head control is the first major accomplishment that ultimately contributes to total movement control. Normal development moves downward from the head (cephalocaudal) and outward from the center of the body (proximal-distal). Head control refers to the ability to stabilize the head in space. It is the alignment of the head with the rest of the body, without excessive sideward tilt, flexion forward, or extension backward.

Trunk control is the second ability necessary for independent movement. The ability to control the position and movement of the trunk in relation to the rest of the body is essential for sitting as well as all locomotor skills, including crawling, standing, and walking.

Trunk control can be assessed by observing the quality of alignment and trunk rotation. These questions may be asked: Can the student roll from side to side while lying on the ground? Does the whole trunk rotate when the shoulders turn from side to side in a seated position? With both trunk and head control while upright, the student should be ready to attain a sitting position.

Rolling is actually the first locomotor movement to develop. By 6 months, an infant should be able to roll from back to back or abdomen to abdomen without assistance (Sherrill, 1981). Mature rolling is segmental in nature and involves turning the head first, followed sequentially by the shoulders, pelvis, and legs.

Sitting is a total body response which requires not only trunk and head control, but also the ability to use the legs, feet, and arms for balance. Prerequisite skills for sitting can be tested by having the child sit on the floor, receiving support at the lower back; on a large beach ball while held at the thighs; or on a tilt board, as you observe the balance responses as the surface is slowly tilted from side to side (Finnie, 1975).

Locomotor Skills

Crawling and Creeping

The rudiments of all locomotor skills behavior can be observed in reflex form in neonatal crawling movements. These movements show that the basic movements necessary for locomotion are innate and are developed through normal maturation. The first volitional locomotor movement occurs as the child begins to crawl. Often the first movements are accidental, as the kneeling child tries to reach for a distant object. If the object is out of reach, the child's chest falls to the floor causing a forward slide as the arms attempt to pull. This early crawling behavior uses the arms exclusively. As the child learns to use both arms and legs, two forms of quadripedal locomotion may develop. The crawling pattern may show a well coordinated, oppositional action of the arms and legs (right arm and left leg move simultaneously). At approximately the same point in development, a hand-knee position and characteristic knee rock may be seen. In this position, the child may rock in a steady forward-backward sway. The hand-knee position represents a definite attempt to creep even though there is no actual motion through space.

Once the hand-knee position is attained, loco-motion is almost inevitable. Early creeping move-ment may vary markedly, with erratic arm and leg coordination, and unilateral, bilateral, and cross-lateral movements randomly interspersed. Although nonambulatory individuals with severe handicaps sometimes creep and crawl rather than walk, this is generally inappropriate and unnecessary in most older students since crawling can usually be replaced with walking through operant training (O'Brien et al., 1972).

The systematic teaching of creeping provides a good example of careful task analyses. For example, if creeping is to be targeted for a young child with severe handicaps, it must first be determined that the child has outgrown the symmetrical tonic neck reflex and can maintain balance on three body parts. At that point, crosslateral movement (right arm and left leg simultaneously) can be primed. Sherrill (1981) suggests that scooter boards, movement on mirrored surfaces, and creeping over and through hoops can promote this crosslateral patterning.

Walking

Most children's first locomotor patterns are crawling and creeping, though some do bypass these patterns in favor of seat sliding or scooting or moving directly from an upright posture. Attaining a standing position is a task worth noting because it depends upon a complex combination of basic physical abilities, including balance, strength, and flexibility. To reach a standing position, most children roll from their front and then rise to stand. Children first learn to sit and later to be pulled to standing either by being pulled by some other person or by pulling themselves up on a stable object. Once upright, they then walk with the assistance of a stable object such as a chair or an adult's hand. The importance of environmental support is critical at this stage.

Truly independent stepping develops after both an upright posture and initial bipedal locomotion requiring hand support are achieved. The first independent steps are hesitant, irregular in length and rate, and quite unstable. Early walking is generally characterized by a wide stance with knees flexed. The toes are usually turned out to increase the base of support. The initial, irregular steps sometimes appear to consist of a few running steps with arms held high, for safety or to counteract gravity. This arm action progresses through a series of developmental changes. During the inter-mediate stages, the arms may swing with the legs unilaterally, where in the mature walk the arms swing in opposition to the legs to help counterbalance hip rotation.

The walk of many people with severe handicaps is unnecessarily characterized by a shuffle step and somewhat stooped posture. In contrast, the well integrated, mature walk is characterized by a narrow and more rhythmic gait, with the feet pointed straight ahead and a heel-toe progression of weight bearing. The feet move as if the inner borders of each foot were placed on opposite sides of a line rather than directly in front of each other, as in the "model's walk." As the walk matures, arm-leg opposition becomes obvious and up-down motion decreases.

Applied behavior analysis can be used to develop independent walking in children and adolescents with sensory, motor, and mental handicaps. For example, positive reinforcement can be used to teach walking in the sequence of (a) cruising along a table, (b) walking around a table, (c) crossing a gradually increasing space, and (d) facing of the table by using other objects (broomsticks, a person's hand, tape, a piece of string) (Loynd & Barclay, 1970). Similar positive reinforcement and shaping procedures have been used with students having severe handicaps (Chandler & Adams, 1972; Horner, 1971; O'Brien et al., 1972; Westervelt & Luiselli, 1975). Haavik and Altman (1977) have also use positive reinforcement, a physical prompting-to-walk procedure to stop crawling, and a four-step sequence of skills to train independent walking.

Once independent walking is established, students must have opportunities to practice on a variety of surfaces because only through practice can proper balance and posture be refined. Teachers should also encourage increasing or decreasing speeds until the rate stabilizes at approximately 115 to 145 steps-per-minute (Sherril, 1981).

Stair Climbing

Once the initial walking pattern is developed, walking up and down stairs requires only a modification of the fundamental pattern. Stair walking demands the integration of sufficient strength, control, and balance to support the body weight on one foot while moving forward and either downward or upward. Most first attempts at stair climbing are a "marking time" movement, where one foot advances a step, the trailing foot comes to rest on that step, and then the lead foot again advances one step. The task analysis in Table 9.12 shows both this form and mature stair climbing. Either one may initially be appropriate for a student with severe handicaps who has no stair-climbing experiences.

When children are learning to negotiate stairs, it is common to have them climb up and then require help because they cannot descend. This is generally caused by the perceptual fear of looking down the flight of stairs. Other intermediate solutions for descending stairs may need to be provided for those who have not mastered climbing down such as either walking or crawling backward down the stairs or sitting down on the steps and scooting down.

Most studies investigating developmental sequences indicate that climbing up stairs develops before climbing down stairs, that shorter flights of stairs are negotiated before longer flights, and that stairs with lower risers are mastered before higher and deeper stairs (Bayley, 1935; Gesell & Thompson, 1929; Shirley, 1933; Wellman, 1937). Some variations have been reported, but the basic sequence remains consistent suggesting that stairs should be scaled to meet the child's physical abilities (Espenschade & Eckert, 1980).

Other climbing skills develop similarly. Ladder climbing is characterized by "marking time" fol-

TABLE 9.12 Task analysis for stair climbing

*Immature Pattern**
1. Stand at bottom of stairs.
2. Grasp handrail (hook grasp).
3. Lift one foot to first stair.
4. Transfer weight to foot on first stair.
5. Bring other foot to first stair.
6. Lift first foot to second stair.
7. Transfer weight to foot.
8. Bring other foot to second stair.
9. Continue lifting one foot and then the other to stair until all stairs are climbed.

Mature Pattern
1. Stand at bottom of stairs.
2. Grasp handrail.
3. Lift one foot to first stair.
4. Put weight on foot on first stair.
5. Bring other foot to second stair.
6. Put weight on foot on second stair.
7. Lift first foot to third stair.
8. Put weight on foot.
9. Lift other foot to fourth stair.
10. Continue lifting alternative feet to stairs until all steps are climbed.

*The immature pattern may be initially taught to individuals with little locomotor experience.

lowed by the more mature, alternate foot pattern. Many other activities require either the basic walking pattern or a modification. It is, therefore, particularly important that young children have a wide range of environmental stimuli, including stairs, ladders, lofts, and bridges, to climb. Ultimately, however, locomotor skills must be taught in the natural settings where the behavior will occur. It may not be adequate to train stair climbing on a simulated five-step staircase during physical education class if the student needs to negotiate the stairwell between the two floors of the school. In this case, it would be more efficient to train on the school stairwell whenever possible during the day, or at least regularly probe performance on the stairwell to check for generalization.

Running

Running is primarily an adaptation and extension of the basic walking movement. The basic walking pattern is modified to produce a run in which there is a period of nonsupport (a flight phase), in contrast to the walk, in which one foot is always in contact with the ground. Arm and leg opposition are critical in both the well-balanced, efficient walk and run.

A significant maturational step occurs in running as the arms are moved in opposition to the legs. In the early run, arms and legs move unilaterally (right arm and right leg forward simultaneously), causing a great deal of upper body rotation. During this stage, the arms are extended and swing through a very short arc, in a pattern similar to the leg action. As the knee and leg action increases, the arm swings more rapidly, often swinging across the middle of the body (Wickstrom, 1980). Finally, in the mature run, the arms are flexed to approximately 90 degrees at the elbow and swing up and down in the vertical plane, remaining synchronized in opposition to the legs (Corbin, 1980).

Other Advanced Locomotor Skills

A wide variety of upright locomotor skills develop from the basic walking pattern. There are eight basic upright locomotor movements, each of which can be identified by a specific sequence of foot movements and by the underlying rhythm of the movement. Of these eight locomotor patterns, there are five even locomotor patterns (2/4 or 4/4 time) that are all modifications of the walk.

1. *Walk*—The transfer of weight from one foot to the other while moving forward or backward with one foot always in contact with the floor.
2. *Run*—The transfer of weight from one foot to the other (as in the walk) but with a momentary loss of contact with the floor, providing a period of flight when neither foot is in contact with the ground.
3. *Leap*—The transfer of weight from one foot to the other foot as in the run, but with a more sustained period of flight and greater height and distance. In the mature leap, the toe of one foot is the last to leave the floor and the toe on the opposite foot is the first to land.
4. *Hop*—The transfer of weight from one foot to the same foot, with the opposite foot never touching the surface. In the mature form, the toe is the last to leave the floor and the first to contact again on the downward flight.
5. *Jump*—The transfer of weight from one or both feet, with a landing on both feet.

These five even locomotor patterns are combined with three uneven locomotor patterns (sometimes called two-part or long-short rhythms). These uneven locomotor skills develop later and provide fundamental skills for many recreational activities.

1. *Gallop*—Moving with the same foot in front, in a step-close sequence.
2. *Slide*—Moving sideward with the same foot always leading. The weight is sequentially transferred from the lead foot to the closing foot and back to the same lead foot.
3. *Skip*—Moving forward with a combination of long step-hop patterns during which the lead foot is alternated.

The skip and slide are both rather complex. The slide is quite difficult for some children since it requires moving in one direction while facing another; however, it is necessary for many functional behaviors, because it occurs in many recreational activities such as dancing and most sports such as tennis and basketball.

Gross Motor Manipulative Skills

Rolling and Pushing

Manipulating objects by rolling and pushing is often prerequisite to recreational skills, especially those requiring throwing and catching. Teaching these patterns can be particularly beneficial to very young children who are not physically ready to catch. Rolling and pushing balls are also good ways to encourage partner or group participation. In older students, these skills should be taught in the context of bowling or shuffle board or vocational activities such as pushing tables, carts, or brooms.

Throwing

The three basic throwing patterns—overhand, underhand, and sidearm—form the foundations for many functional skills. The overarm pattern is the basic movement in hammering, swimming, and throwing objects. It also occurs in nearly every sport involving ball playing.

The basic developmental sequence for overhand throwing progresses through four distinct phases of movement: monoplanar action, whole body rotation, unilateral action, and sequential, crosslateral movement (Bunker, 1975; Deach, 1950; Hanson, 1961; Halverson & Roberton, 1966; Jones, 1951; Wickstrom, 1980).

The development of the underarm pattern is very similar to that of the overarm throw. It typically progresses from a single plane action to crosslateral movement. A task analysis of an underhand softball throw which was shown in Table 9.8 illustrates how this pattern can be broken down for instruction.

Catching

Catching and throwing skills are sometimes thought to be linked; however, they are actually quite different. Throwing and catching develop independently, with throwing skills generally thought to precede catching by as much as 12 to 24 months (Gutteridge, 1939; Wickstrom, 1980).

Like throwing, catching can involve several different types of movements and can be affected by many external variables. Wickstrom (1980) and Ridenour (1975) have pointed out six major variables affecting both the performance and analysis of catching patterns: the size of the ball, the speed of the ball, the distance the ball travels before it is caught, the method of projecting the ball, the direction of the ball in relation to the catch, and the arm action of the catcher. The shape of the ball, the trajectory of the flight, and the position of the catcher (moving or stationary) should also be considered.

The three basic developmental stages of catching include (a) nesting, in which the ball is scooped or trapped against the body; (b) hands-only catch, in which arm flexion allows the hands to capture the ball; and (c) mature catching, in which upper body action joins hands and arms to absorb force to catch the ball. The sequence implies that shaping procedures may be needed to develop mature catching gradually from nesting and hands-only catching.

In the first stages of catching, the object is trapped against the chest, suggesting that large, soft objects are more likely to be caught successfully than small, hard objects. The importance of using large objects in learning to catch must not be confused with the need for smaller objects for early throwing experiences. The size of the object to be caught can affect the type of catching behavior that develops. The same person may catch a large ball by using an arm-trapping motion, but may use a hand clasp catch when a small ball is tossed (Halverson & Roberton, 1966). Similarly, during the initial attempts, catchers should be encouraged to "make a nest" for the ball and hold it close to their chest. During the later stages, they should be more successful at catching a ball which has been allowed to bounce first (Pedersen, 1973).

Striking

The developmental sequences for striking behaviors are similar in direction and rate to the progress of throwing skills. Part of this association is no doubt due to the similarity of overarm, sidearm, and underarm movement patterns. In addition, striking skills are affected by the same variables (the size of the object being struck, and speed of the object, the direction and trajectory of the object, the source of force for the object, anticipatory adjustments required (spatial and locomotor), and the weight of the object). In addition to these object-related considerations, other factors related to the implement and the performer must be considered. The striking surface may be part of the body (hand, foot, head) or an external object (bat, racket, paddle, stick) which contributes weight, size, and shape that must also be considered. A third consideration concerns the interaction of the object and implement. There are two basic combinations: (a) a resting object and the moving implement (croquet, hammering) or (b) a moving object and implement, which requires more complex visual-motor integration for coincident timing (batting, playing tennis). Striking skills therefore involve not only the physical skill of striking but also visual-motor integration.

Watching students' striking behavior provides a dramatic example of individual variability influenced by external factors. The weight and size of the striking implement may significantly affect the movement. When a student is given a large, heavy object, such as a wooden paddle, the movement patterns may regress from a more mature sidearm swing to a poking, overarm action (Halverson & Roberton, 1966; Seefeldt & Haubenstricker, 1974).

Leverage also affects striking. The shorter the lever, the easier it is to strike with accuracy and control. Therefore, striking with the hand in games like volleyball or with very short implements when learning softball or tennis can be helpful (Sherrill, 1981).

The basic developmental sequence for striking is similar for all children and all three striking patterns. The mature patterns of each skill contain three essential components: (a) the body weight shifts forward, usually onto the opposite foot; (b) the trunk rotates rapidly to add to the sequential force production; and (c) the arm action follows at the moment of maximum speed of rotation or force. The difference in the striking patterns is quite obvious, but these three underlying similarities will be critical in each pattern.

Kicking

The kick is a unique manipulative skill because it is a propulsive movement pattern requiring a sophisticated interaction of the visual system with the legs and feet. Because it is necessary to balance on one foot while striking an object, the individual must be able to run and balance effectively before being asked to kick.

In the early stages of kicking, balance may be a major problem. Children often merely push the ball forward to avoid losing their equilibrium. The first actual kicking consists of moving the leg forward only, as in pushing. Children appear to be able to execute this rudimentary kick soon after they are able to run effectively. The second stage merely adds some preliminary backward leg action in a pendular motion, to provide for a more powerful leg swing. It is later accompanied by a compensatory action of the opposite arm, a rather difficult skill. The mature kick is characterized by the addition of a sequence of preliminary hip extension and knee flexion, followed by forceful leg extension and a backward trunk lean (Dohrman, 1967; Wickstrom, 1980). This is often combined with a preparatory phase, including an approach to the ball while walking or running.

Fine Motor Skills

The most important fine motor skills involve different types of grasps. There are seven fundamental grasping patterns, each of which is used to accomplish specific types of tasks (see Figure 9.3). The *palmar grasp* is the most fundamental and primitive of all grasps. It involves raking objects into the palm without using the thumb. As soon as a student is able to reach, grasp, and release objects independently, this grasp should be discouraged and thumb use encouraged through shaping. *The cylindrical grasp* is usually the next to develop. It involves use of the thumb in wide opposition to the fingers. This kind of grasp is typically used by youngsters who are just beginning to spoon feed or for grasping wide objects that do not require much thumb usage.

The cylindrical grasp is usually replaced by the *spherical grasp*, in which the thumb is not in direct opposition to fingers, but in wide abduction. This is a functional grasp that can be used for handling (throwing and catching) recreational materials or for holding any two-dimensional objects such as a glass.

The *pincer grasp* is the most sophisticated and functional of all grasps. It involves using the thumb in abduction to the index finger. The *three-jaw chuck* is a more fundamental pincer grasp involving the thumb and first two fingers. It is usually used for grasping wide objects. The *lateral pincer* or scissors grasp involves the use of the thumb to the side of the index finger. It is necessary for actions such as using scissors or tongs and is best developed by practicing with these implements. The refined

ILLUSTRATION OF THE TYPICAL GRASPS

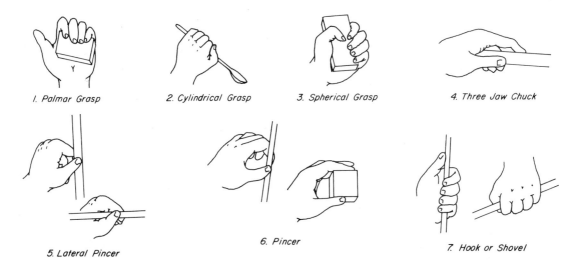

1. Palmar Grasp   2. Cylindrical Grasp   3. Spherical Grasp   4. Three Jaw Chuck

5. Lateral Pincer   6. Pincer   7. Hook or Shovel

FIGURE 9.3 Fundamental grasps

pincer involves use of thumb and index finger with the index finger exhibiting tip control. This grasp is necessary for writing, painting or drawing, zipping, sewing, and many vocational tasks.

The last type of grasp is the *hook or shovel,* in which the fingers serve as a hook to wrap around an object without involvement of the thumb. The thumb can serve as a lever or work with the fingers by wrapping over or under them. This type of grasp is used in toothbrushing, hammering, and most racquet sports. Whenever possible, the various grasps should always be developed within the context of functional skills. A teacher should be able to analyze the grasp involved in vocational, self-care, and recreational activities to determine which of the seven fundamental grasps is appropriate for a specific activity. Note the grasps used in the recreational activities listed in Table 9.11.

Physical Fitness

At least one and probably several physical fitness activities should be included in every student's recreation program (see Table 9.13 for examples). The training of physical fitness to persons who are disabled is important for a variety of reasons. Probably most important is the fact that basic fitness attributes including lean body weight, cardiovascular or respiratory efficiency, neuromuscular efficiency, strength, power, agility, flexibility, balance, speed, and general motor coordination are necessary prerequisites to complicated gross and fine motor skill development (Bunker, 1978; Corbin, Dowell, Lindsey, & Tolson, 1978; Digennaro, 1974). Another reason for training physical fitness skills to persons who are disabled is that such skills constitute normal leisure time activities in which many nonhandicapped citizens participate (Bates & Renzaglia, 1979). Moreover, these programs are excellent ways of integrating students with and without handicaps because skill deficits in fitness can be compensated for with adaptive rules or equipment (Polloway & Smith, 1979; Rarick, Widdop, & Broadhead, 1970; Wehman & Schleien, 1981). Finally, these activities typically are pleasurable to the learner and can be continued in a variety of settings on a lifelong basis (Moon & Renzaglia, 1982).

Most studies have shown that persons with severe handicapping conditions have deficits in all fitness attributes. Therefore, no single exercise or sports program can improve one's overall fitness level (Moon & Renzaglia, 1982; Cooper & Cooper, 1972). There is evidence now that the skills necessary to participate in fitness programs can be taught to persons with severe handicaps. For example, individual exercises such as sit-ups, toe touches, leg lifts, and push-ups have been successfully taught to students with moderate, severe, and profound mental retardation (Allen & Iwata, 1980; Coleman & Whitman, 1984; Moon, 1983; Stainback, Stainback, Wehman & Spangiers, 1983; Wehman, Renzaglia, Berry, Schutz, & Karan, 1978).

TABLE 9.13 Functional activities and exercises related to physical fitness components

	Preschool Elementary	Junior/Senior High	Adult	Individual Exercises
1. Strength	Building blocks climbing objects	Carrying objects	Moving objects Bowling	Flexed armhang
2. Flexibility	Tying shoes Tumbling activities	Swimming	Picking up objects/ yoga	Sit and reach Shoulder rotation
3. Agility	Tag games	Moving through crowds	Square dancing	Squat thrust Obstacle course
4. Balance	Walking on curbs Riding bicycle	Waiting on tables	Carrying supplies	Stork stand Stick balance test Balance beam walk
5. Cardiorespiratory endurance	Running	Jumping rope Bicycling	Aerobic dance Hiking Stair climbing Carrying objects	Running in place Run-walk
6. Power	Hammering skills	Baseball batting	Chopping wood	Softball throw Vertical jump
7. Speed	Games of chase	Discus	Assembly line work	50-yard dash
8. Coordination	Bouncing balls	Swimming	Bowling	Jumping jacks

More complex fitness activities such as swimming, jogging, weight lifting, and track events have also been successfully taught (Bundschuh, Williams, Hollingsworth, Gooch & Shirer,, 1972; Cuvo, Ellis, Wisotzek, Davis, Schilling, and Bechtal, 1983; Moon, 1983).

Posture

One of the most important body management abilities is the integration of body awareness and physical fitness to produce a pleasing functional posture. Posture refers to the manner in which you stand, sit, move, and perform daily activities. It is generally judged by the relationship of various body parts to one another. Posture may be affected by the relative strength and flexibility of various muscle groups and by visual and proprioceptive perception of verticality.

Body posture is a key in all motor skills, for it provides the basic starting position for all movement. Good body alignment is important not only for proper functioning of internal organs but also because it reflects the general health and psychological well-being (self-image) of the individual. It contributes not only to static, nonlocomotor behavior but also to dynamic, moving activities, which contribute to all aspects of daily living.

The functional posture of many people with handicaps is stereotyped by slumped shoulders and a downward gaze. This posture is not permanent and can be modified with careful teaching. A child's functional posture may be evaluated with respect to the relationship between the base of support and the five main weight centers of the body: head, chest, shoulders, pelvis, and knees and feet. The most typical posture problems involve misalignment of these weight centers. If you were to hold a plumb line next to a student, a good standing posture would be indicated by the line passing slightly behind the ear, through the shoulder, through the hip, behind the knee, and in front of the ankle (see Figure 9.4).

Two of the most common postural problems, *kyphosis* and *lordosis*, are illustrated in Figure 9.4.

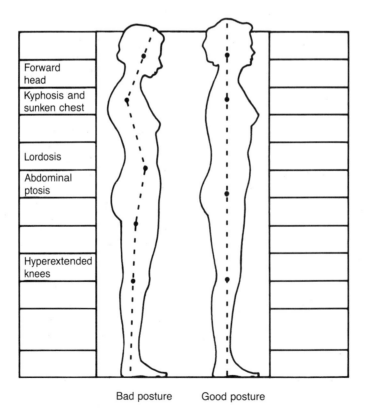

Forward head

Kyphosis and sunken chest

Lordosis

Abdominal ptosis

Hyperextended knees

Bad posture   Good posture

FIGURE 9.4 Erect standing posture should be characterized by well-balanced body centers. A plumb line hung along the body should fall slightly behind the ear, through the shoulder, through the hip, behind the knee, and in front of the ankle.

TABLE 9.14 Self-assessment of posture

Award 3 points if correct; 2 points if slight deviation; and 1 point if moderate to severe.
I. Side View: Partner Observing
  Hang a plumb line from ceiling or some object away from the wall.
  Place sideward-facing subject behind the plumb line and check the following points.

		Score
A. Head erect		A. _____
B. Shoulders		B. _____
C. Lumbar spine		C. _____
D. Pelvis		D. _____
E. Knees		E. _____
F. Ankles		F. _____
G. Body lean (Total body tilted forward or backward)		G. _____

II. Back View
  Subject bends forward and observer marks spineous process of each vertebrae with colored chalk or washable marker.
  Subject stands and is evaluated in an upright position. (It may be easier to do this with S facing a grid or wall which has horizontal markings).

H. Head square (versus tilted)		H. _____
I. Shoulders even		I. _____
J. Hips even		J. _____
K. Spine straight		K. _____
Check for simple or compound lateral curves.		

TOTAL: _____

Rating Scale

Total Score:	33	Excellent
	29–31	Very good
	26–28	Marginal
	23–25	Poor
	less than 22	Very poor

Kyphosis is a postural problem generally characterized by rounded shoulders and a somewhat forward head. This change in thoracic curvature of the spine may be caused by an imbalance of the musculature, with the anterior chest muscles too tight and the posterior (upper back muscles) too loose. To reduce the problem, it would be important to strengthen the muscles of the upper back and stretch the muscles on the front or chest side.

Lordosis is a very common problem in children, teenagers, and adult females. It is characterized by an increased forward curvature of the lumbar spine, often referred to as a *hollow back* and accompanied by a "protruding tummy." As in the case of kyphosis, it may be alleviated (in nonpathological cases) by a conscious effort to strengthen the abdominal muscles and stretch the muscles of the lower back.

Conditions such as lordosis and kyphosis often combine to produce a kind of zig-zag alignment that stretches certain muscles and ligaments while others must work constantly to maintain balance. In addition, these misalignments may also place undue stress on joint structures such as the hips and knees. For example, our students frequently stand with their toes pointed outward and their knees "locked" to maintain a counter-balanced position. The posture assessment in Table 9.14 can serve as a good check for potential postural problems.

It is especially critical that classroom teachers of students with severe handicaps screen for postural abnormalities. The awareness of the students' postural needs can provide important information about needed services and programming direction for specialists in physical education and therapy (Sherrill, 1980).

CONCLUSION

The development of recreational and functional motor skills is essential for all people. Each individual's unique home and community environment, as well as physical abilities and past experiences, must be considered in planning optimal learning programs. A well-rounded curriculum should be designed to train needed skills in the following diverse areas: recreational activities, locomotor abilities, fine motor skills, physical fitness, and posture. Such a curriculum should not only improve functional skills in other domains but should also have a positive impact upon an individual's self concept and increased capacity to enjoy life.

REFERENCES

Adams, R., Daniel, A., & Pullman, L. (1975). *Games, sports, and exercise for the physically handicapped.* Philadelphia: Lea and Febiger.

Aharoni, H. (1982). Games and activities for severely handicapped students utilizing small space and minimal equipment. *Practical Pointers, 5*(11), 1-27.

Allen, L. D., & Iwata, B. A. (1980). Reinforcing exercise maintenance using existing high rate activities. *Behavior Modification, 4,* 337-354.

American Alliance for Health, Physical Education and Recreation (1977). Adapted equipment for physical activities. *Practical Pointers, 1*(5).

Baumgart, D., Brown, L., Pumpian, I., Nisbet, J., Ford, A., Sweet, M., Messina, R., & Schroeder, J. (1982). Principle of partial participation and individualized adaptations in educational programs for severely handicapped students. *The Journal of the Association for the Severely Handicapped, 7,* 17-27.

Bates, P., & Renzaglia, A. (1979). Community-based recreation program. In P. Wehman (Ed.), *Recreation programming for developmentally disabled persons* (pp. 97-123). Baltimore: University Park Press, 1979.

Bauer, D. (1981). Aerobic fitness for the moderately retarded. *Practical Pointers, 5*(5), 1-32.

Bayley, N. (1935). The development of motor abilities during the first three years. *Monographs of the Society for Research in Child Development,* No. 1.

Brown, L., Branston-McLean, M., Baumgart, D., Vincent, B., Falvey, M,. & Schroeder, J. (1979). Using the characteristics of current and subsequent least restrictive environments in the development of curricular content for severely handicapped students. *AAESPH Review, 4*(4), 407-424.

Bundschuh, E. L., Williams, W. C., Hollingsworth, J. D., Gooch, S., & Shirer, C. (1972). Teaching the retarded to swim. *Mental Retardation, 10*(3), 14-17.

Bunker, L., & Moon, S. (1983). Motor skills. In M. E. Snell (Ed.), *Systematic instruction of the moderately and severely handicapped* (2nd ed.) (pp. 203-226). Columbus, OH: Charles E. Merrill.

Burkhart, L. J. (1982). *More home-made battery devices for severely handicapped children.* College Park, MD: Author.

Campbell, J. (1973). Physical fitness and the MR: A review of research. *Mental Retardation, 11*(5), 26-29.

Cavallaro, C., & Bambara, L. (1982). Two strategies for teaching language during free play. *The Journal of the Association for the Severely Handicapped, 7*(2), 80-92.

Chandler, L. S., & Adams, M. A. (1972). Multiple handicapped child motivated for ambulation through behavior modification. *Physical Therapy, 52,* 399-401.

Coleman, R. S., & Whitman, T. L. (1984). Developing, generalizing, and maintaining physical fitness in mentally retarded adults: Toward a self-directed program. *Analysis and Intervention in Developmental Disabilities, 4*(109-128).

Cooper, M., & Cooper, K. H. (1972). *Aerobics for Women.* New York: Bantam Books.

Corbin, C. B., Dowell, L. J., Lindsey, R., & Tolson, H. (1978). *Concepts of physical education with labora-tories and experiments.* Dubuque, IA: Wm. C. Brown Company.

Corbin, C. (1980). *A textbook of motor development.* Dubuque, IA: Wm. C. Brown.

Cowart, J. (1979). Instructional aids for adaptive physical education. Hayward, CA: Alameda County School Department. (ERIC Document Reproduction Service No. ED 106-341).

Cuvo, A. J., Ellis, P. J., Wisotzek, I. E., Davis, P. J., Schilling, D., & Bechtal, D. R. (1983). Teaching athletic skills to students who are mentally retarded. *The Journal of the Association for the Severely Handicapped, 8,* 72-81.

Deach, D. (1950). *Genetic development of motor skills in children two through six years of age.* Unpublished doctoral dissertation, University of Michigan.

Digennaro, J. (1974). *Individualized exercise and optimal physical fitness.* Philadelphia: Lea and Febiger.

Dohrman, P. (1967). Throwing and kicking ability of eight-year-old boys and girls. *Research Quarterly, 35,* 464-471.

Espenschade, A. S., & Eckert, H. M. (1980). *Motor development.* Columbus, OH: Charles E. Merrill.

Favell, J. (1973). Reduction of stereotypes by reinforcement of toy play. *Mental Retardation, 11,* 21-23.

Finnie, N. (1975). *Handling the upcoming cerebral palsied child at home.* New York: E. P. Hutton.

Gaylord-Ross, R. J., Haring, T. G., Breen, C., & Pitts-Conway, V. (1984). The training and generalization of social interaction skills with autistic youth. *Journal of Applied Behavior Analysis, 17,* 229-247.

Gesell, A., & Thompson, H. (1929). Learning and growth in identical twin infants. *Genetic Psychology Monographs, 6,* 1-24.

Giangreco, M. (1983). Teaching basic photography skills to a severely handicapped young adult using simulated materials. *The Journal of the Association for the Severely Handicapped, 8*(1), 43-49.

Gollay, E., Freedman, R., Wyngaarden, M., & Kurtz, N. R. (1978). *Coming back.* Cambridge, MA: Abt Books.

Groose, S. (1971). Indoor target gold. *Journal of Health, Physical Education, and Recreation, 42*(1).

Gutteridge, M. (1939). A study of motor achievements of young children. *Archives of Psychology, 34,* 1-244.

Haavik, S., & Altman, K. (1977). Establishing walking by severely retarded children. *Perceptual and Motor Skills, 44,* 1107-1114.

Halverson, L. E., & Roberton, M. A. (1966). *A study of motor pattern development in young children.* Paper presented at American Alliance of Health, Physical Education, and Recreation research conference, Chicago, March 1966.

Hanson, S. K. (1961). *A comparison of the overhand throw performance of instructed and non-instructed kindergarten boys and girls.* Unpublished master's thesis, University of Wisconsin.

Hardiman, S. A., Goetz, E. M., Reuter, K. E., & LeBlanc, J. M. (1975). Primes, contingent attention, and training: Effects on a child's motor behavior. *Journal of Applied Behavior Analysis, 8,* 399-409.

Hill, J., Wehman, P., & Horst, G. (1982). Toward generalization of appropriate leisure and social behavior in severely handicapped youth: Pinball machine use. *Journal of the Association for the Severely Handicapped, 6*(4), 34–44.

Hill, J. (1980). Use of an automated recreation device to facilitate independent leisure and motor behavior in a profoundly retarded male. In P. Wehman and J. Hill (Eds.), *Instructional programming for severely handicapped youth,* 101–103. Richmond: Virginia Commonwealth University.

Hopper, C., & Wambold, C. (1978). Improving the independent play of severely mentally retarded children. *Education and Training of the Mentally Retarded,* 4–7.

Horner, R. D. (1971). Establishing use of crutches by a mentally retarded spina bifida child. *Journal of Applied Behavior Analysis, 4,* 183–189.

Horst, G., Wehman, P., Hill, J., & Bailey, C. (1981). Developing age-appropriate leisure skills in severely handicapped adolescents. *Teaching Exceptional Children, 14,* 11–15.

Information and Research Utilization Center in Physical Education and Recreation for the Handicapped (1976). *Physical activities for impaired, disabled, and handicapped individuals.* Washington, DC: Author.

Johnson, J. L. (1978). Programming for early motor responses within the classroom. *AAESPH Review, 3,* 4–14.

Johnson, M., & Bailey, F. (1977). The modification of leisure behavior in a half-way house for retarded women. *Journal of Applied Behavior Analysis, 10*(1), 273–282.

Jones, R. A. (1951). *A descriptive and mechanical analysis of throwing skills of children.* Unpublished master's thesis, University of Wisconsin.

Keogh, D. A., Faw, G. D., Whitman, T. L., & Reid, D. H. (1984). Enhancing leisure skills in severely retarded adolescents through a self-instructional treatment package. *Analysis and Intervention in Developmental Disabilities, 4*(4), 333–352.

Kissel, R., & Whitman, T. (1977). An examination of direct and generalized effects of play-training and a correction procedure upon the self-stimulatory behavior of a profoundly retarded boy. *AAESPH Review,* 131–146.

Knowles, C., Vogel, P., & Wessel, J. (1976). Project I Can: Individualized curriculum designed for mentally retarded children and youth. *Education and Training of the Mentally Retarded, 10,* 155–180.

Lagomarcino, A., Reid, D. H., Ivanic, M. T., & Faw, G. D. (1984). Leisure-dance instruction for severely and profoundly retarded persons: Teaching an intermediate community-living skill. *Journal of Applied Behavior Analysis, 17,* 71–84.

Loynd, J., & Barclay, A. (1970). A case study in developing ambulation in a profoundly retarded child. *Behaviour Research and Therapy, 8,* 207.

Mager, R. (1976). *Preparing instructional objectives.* Belmont, CA: Fearon.

Marchant, J., & Wehman, P. (1979). Teaching table games to severely retarded children. *Mental Retardation, 17,* 150–151.

Moon, M. S., & Renzaglia, A. (1982). Physical fitness and the mentally retarded: A critical review of the literature. *The Journal of Special Education, 16,* 269–287.

Moon, M. S., & Snell, M. (1985). Deinstitutionalization of the severely and profoundly retarded: Facts, figures, and misconceptions. In F. Orelove, K. Inge, and P. Wehman (Eds.), *Issues related to community integration for people with severe handicaps* (pp. 22–59). Richmond: Virginia Commonwealth University.

Moon, M. S. (1983). *The effects of nonhandicapped peer participation and different reinforcement procedures on the maintenance of performance of fitness activities in severely handicapped adolescents.* Unpublished doctoral dissertation, University of Virginia.

Nietupski, J., & Svoboda, R. (1982). Teaching a cooperative leisure skill to severely handicapped adults. *Education and Training of the Mentally Retarded, 17*(1), 4–7.

Nietupski, J. A., Hamre-Nietupski, S., & Ayers, B. (1984). Review of task analytic leisure skill training efforts: Practioner implications and future research needs. *The Journal of the Association for Persons With Severe Handicaps, 9,* 88–97.

Novak, A. E., & Heal, L. W. (Eds.) (1980). *Integration of developmentally disabled individuals into the community.* Baltimore: Paul H. Brookes.

O'Brien, F., Azrin, N. H., & Bugle, C. (1972). Training profoundly retarded children to stop crawling. *Journal of Applied Behavior Analysis, 5,* 131–137.

Pedersen, E. J. (1973). *A study of ball catching abilities of first, third, and fifth grade children on twelve selected ball catching tasks.* Unpublished doctoral dissertation, Indiana University.

Polloway, E. A., & Smith, J. D. (1978). Special Olympics: A second look. *Education and Training of the Mentally Retarded, 13,* 432–433.

Rarick, G. L., Widdop, J. H., & Broadhead, G. D. (1970). The physical fitness and motor performance of educable mentally retarded children. *Exceptional Children, 35,* 509–519.

Reid, D., Willis, B., Jarman, P., & Brown, K. (1978). Increasing leisure activity of physically disabled retarded persons through modifying resource availability. *AAESPH Review, 3*(2), 78–93.

Reynolds, R. P. (1981). Normalization: A guideline to leisure skills programming for handicapped individuals. In P. Wehman & S. Schleien (Eds.), *Leisure programs for handicapped persons,* (pp. 1–13). Baltimore: University Park Press.

Reynolds, R. P. (1979). What is normalization and how can you do it? *Parks and Recreation, 14,* 33–34.

Ridenour, M. D. (1975). Bicycles and tricycles for pre-school children. *Physical Education, 32,* 71–73.

Santomier, J., & Kopczuk, W. (1981). Facilitation of interactions between retarded and nonretarded students in a physical education setting. *Education and Training of the Mentally Retarded, 3,* 20–23.

Sedlak, R., Doyle, M., & Schloss, P. (1982). Video games: A training and generalization demonstration with severely retarded adolescents. *Education and Training of the Mentally Retarded, 17*(4), 332–336.

Seefeldt, V., & Haubenstricker, J. (1974). *Developmental sequence of striking.* Unpublished material from Motor Development Conference, Michigan State University, July 1974.

Sherrill, C. (1981). *Adapted physical education and recreation: A multi-disciplinary approach.* Dubuque, IA: William C. Brown.

Shirley, M. M. (1933). *The first two years: A study of twenty-five babies (Vol. 2).* Minneapolis: University of Minnesota Press.

Simpson, H. M., & Meaney, C. (1979). Effects of learning to ski on the self-concept of mentally retarded children. *American Journal of Mental Deficiency, 84,* 25-29.

Snell, M. E. (1983). Implementing the IEP. In M. E. Snell (Ed.), *Systematic instruction of the moderately and severely handicapped,* (pp. 113-145). Columbus, OH: Charles E. Merrill.

Stainback, S., Stainback, W., Wehman, P., & Spangiers, L. (1983). Acquisition and generalization of physical fitness exercises in three profoundly retarded adults. *The Journal of the Association for the Severely Handicapped, 8,* 47-55.

Stanfield, J. S. (1973). What happens to the retarded child when he grows up? *Exceptional Children, 39,* 550-552.

Stein, J. U. (1981). Physical education, recreation, and sports for special populations. *Education and Training of the Mentally Retarded, 12*(1), 4-13.

Stokes, T., & Baer, D. (1977). An implicit technology of generalization. *Journal of Applied Behavior Analysis, 10,* 341-367.

Virginia Commission of Outdoor Recreation-Recreation Services Section (1976). *Architectural accessibility for the disabled in park and recreation facilities.* Richmond, VA: Author.

Voeltz, L. M., Wuerch, B. B., & Wilcox, B. (1982). Leisure and recreation: Preparation for independence, integration, and self-fulfillment. In B. Wilcox & G. T. Bellamy (Eds.), *Design of high school programs for severely handicapped students* (pp. 175-210). Baltimore: Paul H. Brookes.

Wehman, P. (1977). Research and leisure time and the severely developmentally disabled. *Rehabilitation Literature, 38*(4), 98-105.

Wehman, P., & Hill, J. (Eds.), (1980). *Instructional programming for severely handicapped youth.* Richmond: Virginia Commonwealth University.

Wehman, P., & Moon, M. S. (1985). Designing and implementing leisure programs for individuals with severe handicaps. In M. P. Brady & P. L. Gunter (Eds.), *Integrating moderately and severely handicapped learners,* (pp. 214-237). Springfield, IL: Charles C. Thomas.

Wehman, P. Renzaglia. A., & Bates, P. (1985). Leisure skill instruction. In P. Wehman, A. Renzaglia, and P. Bates, (Eds.), *Functional living skills for moderately and severely handicapped individuals,* (pp. 123-154). Austin, TX: Pro-Ed.

Wehman, P., Renzaglia, A., Berry, G., Schutz, R., & Karan, O. (1978). Developing a leisure skill repertoire in severely profoundly handicapped persons. *American Association for the Education of the Severely/Profoundly Handicapped Review, 3,* 162-172.

Wehman, P., & Schleien, S. (1981). Leisure programs for handicapped persons. Baltimore: University Park Press.

Wellman, B. L. (1937). Motor achievements of preschool children. *Childhood Education,* 311-316.

Westervelt, J. D., & Luiselli, J. K. (1975). Establishing standing and walking behavior in a physically handicapped, retarded child. *Physical Therapy, 55,* 761-765.

Wickstrom, R. L. (1980). *Fundamental motor patterns.* Philadelphia: Lea and Febiger.

Wilcox, B., & Bellamy, G. T. (1982). *Design of high school programs for severely handicapped students.* Baltimore: Paul H. Brookes.

Williams, W., Hamre-Nietupski, S., Pumpian, I., McDaniel-Marks, J., & Wheeler, J. (1978). Teaching social skills. In M. Snell (Ed.), *Systematic instruction of the moderately and severely handicapped,* (pp. 281-300). Columbus, OH: Charles E. Merrill.

Witt, P. A. (1979). Therapeutic recreation: The outmoded label. *Therapeutic Recreation Journal,* (2nd Quarter), 39-41.

Wolfensberger, W. (1972). *Principles of normalization.* Toronto: National Institute of Mental Retardation.

Wuerch, B., & Voeltz, L. (1982). *Longitudinal leisure skills for severely handicapped learners.* Baltimore: Paul H. Brookes.

In programs for students with severe handicaps, there is often a "language training period" scheduled for 30 minutes. During this time the teacher might gather part or all of the students together and, using picture cards or a box of objects, present one request after another in order to prompt and motivate students to use their communication system. Ironically, during the remainder of the day, students may not be expected to communicate although plenty of natural opportunities exist to sign, speak, nod, or to point to a picture.

More often than not our students do not have a useful means of communicating their wants, needs, or feelings. We tend to talk *for* them instead. Despite this prevalent absence of communication skills, our goal is to teach all of our students to communicate, if not by voice, then by manual sign, symbol, pictures, gaze or a combination of methods.

When students exhibit deficiencies in the so-called prerequisites for communication, it often is not clear what approach to take. How can teachers facilitate the emergence of functional speech in a young child who appears lethargic, seems to take no interest in toys or people, and seldom makes any noise at all except to cry? If allowed, this child would spend most of her time sleeping. How can someone teach an adolescent who speaks in phrases but primarily echoes others and does not follow most directions? What about the students whose tone and movement limitations prevent controlled speech and controlled hand motions?

While most special educators feel that all handicapped persons can learn some form of communication, however simple, it is the teacher on the front lines who must determine when and how to start teaching communication. There are procedures for making these complex decisions. Some of these choices include (a) whether to focus upon language prerequisites (attending, imitation) or to begin with expression of wants; (b) whether to teach a vocal or nonvocal system of communication; (c) what nonvocal system or systems to select if this route is chosen; and (d) what vocabulary to teach. Two important factors in making each of these decisions are the number of years of school remaining and what communication capabilities, if any, the student reliably performs.

In the first chapter of this section of the book, Ann Kaiser, Cathy Alpert and Steve Warren address milieu techniques for building functional communi-

Introduction to Chapters 10 and 11

cation skills. These techniques are so named because they fit into the natural routine of the day and thus are used whenever communication opportunities arise. Because teaching is done incidentally or during naturalistic moments, students experience fewer problems with transferring their skills from "communication group time" to the real times they need to communicate. Furthermore, the procedures described in this chapter are applicable to teaching any system of communication.

In the second chapter of this section, Joan Miller and Jan Allaire describe the augmentative systems for communication. These systems which include sign, symbols, pictures, and visual gaze offer alternatives to the speech mode of communication. Augmentative communication systems vary widely. The obvious variations of vocabulary and length of utterance are accompanied by differences in the speed of transmission, the topography and duration of the communicative response, the skills required to listen as well as to express, the portability of the system, the ability of a system to change and expand, and the equipment or materials required. Besides surveying the range of nonvocal systems suitable for students with severe handicaps and the selection rules, this chapter also addresses proven methods for teaching students how to use the chosen system.

Ann P. Kaiser
Cathy L. Alpert
Steven F. Warren

George Peabody College of
Vanderbilt University

10

Teaching Functional Language: Strategies for Language Intervention

Kristi is a nine-year-old student with multiple handicaps and limited social and academic skills. Kristi has learned six signs in one-to-one training with her speech therapist but rarely signs at home or in the classroom. Her teacher is interested in teaching Kristi communication skills that will be functional for her in communicating with her parents, sibling, and classmates. Where does she begin?

The last 5 years have brought noticeable changes in language intervention for persons with severe handicaps. Significant shifts have occurred in both the content and the strategy of intervention. These shifts have resulted from changes in guiding assumptions regarding the nature of language and communication, and from our experiences in working with persons with severely handicapping conditions.

Currently, language is viewed not just as a formal linguistic system, but as a social communication medium closely linked to an individual's cognitive and social skills. The behavioral technology developed during the 1970s to teach specific skills to persons with language deficiencies has not been discarded; rather, the application of this technology has been extended to teaching functional skills in more natural settings. Our experiences working with persons with severe handicaps have led to identifying both the critical needs of this population and the limits of existing language intervention technology. Increasingly, we have recognized that teaching functional communication skills may require a different approach to intervention than teaching the rudiments of a formal linguistic repertoire. An emphasis on functional skills has important implications for both intervention strategy and curriculum content.

Recent research has provided data supporting this shift in emphasis. Generalization and maintenance of newly trained communication skills have been shown to require specific planning (Rogers-Warren & Warren, 1985). Both longitudinal (Warren & Rogers-Warren, 1983) and specific experimental analyses (c.f. Anderson & Spradlin, 1980) have demonstrated that limited generalization of newly trained language skills by persons having handicaps is a typical training outcome. Clearly, limited generalization is a major barrier to acquisition of a functional communication repertoire, and our teaching strategies must include plans to surmount this barrier.

For students like Kristi, the difference in emphasis translates into selecting an alternative mode of communication (signing) that is likely to be acquired most easily, focusing on teaching responses that have an immediate function in indicating needs and wants, and providing specific training to promote generalized use of the new skills. To ensure that skills are functional and generalized, training must occur in the settings where communication is needed. Dinner at home, recess on the play ground, lunch in the cafeteria, and bus rides to school are settings for training, not just the classroom or speech therapy room. Teaching Kristi new skills requires assessment that is focused not just on her existing skills, but on her needs for communication and the environmental demands for communication. The new emphasis on generalized functional skills requires the use of instructional strategies that take advantage of the naturally occurring opportunities to teach language and to promote generalization.

OVERVIEW

This chapter focuses on milieu strategies for language intervention with persons with severe handicaps. We assume that most readers already will have knowledge of basic direct instructional techniques. Thus, those techniques are not described in detail when they are referred to in the text. Our perspective is largely behavioral with a strong functional orientation; however, many of the principles of effective communication and naturalistic teaching derive from an eclectic theoretical base. The chapter primarily addresses teaching verbal skills; however, we realize that many persons with severe handicaps will not use the verbal modality as their primary means of communication. In most cases, the principles outlined here can be applied to teaching alternate communication modes. The chapter is organized into five sections: (1) goals of language intervention; (2) milieu teaching techniques; (3) assessment, planning, and implementation strategies; (4) teaching generalized

skills; and (5) a case study illustrating applications of milieu teaching.

GOALS OF LANGUAGE INTERVENTION

Teaching Functional Skills

The overriding goal of language intervention always is to increase the student's functional communication. As obvious as this goal is, functional communication is easily forgotten when there are many students to be trained and teaching requires many, many trials before acquisition of even a simple labeling response is assured. Faced with the many needs and modest skill repertoires of persons with severe handicaps, teachers easily lose sight of the function of language intervention while focusing on the long list of forms that must be taught.

Selecting Short-Term Targets That Are Functional

There is a particular need to consider functional communication as a *short-term* training objective as well as a long-term goal. Target forms should be immediately usable by the student. Selecting functional targets is based on both the student's needs and the characteristics of the environments in which the student will be expected to communicate. It is easy to identify specific targets that are logical in terms of the student's skills but which are not particularly functional in terms of immediate usefulness in social interaction. Training Kristi to articulate early phonemes such as /ba/ and /ma/ will do very little to increase her functional communication skills. Given limited instructional time, focusing on signs that can be used immediately seems to be a much more appropriate choice.

It is important to remember that it is not the specific form that renders training dysfunctional. The response of the environment determines the function of a specific form. Emerging phonemes such as /ba/ and /ma/ are highly functional communication forms for very young normally developing children because their caretakers attend to the appearance of new phonemic forms and are willing to interpret them *as if* they had communicative intent. For Kristi, training vocal imitation of phonemes will be a functional communication goal only if persons in the environment respond to particular vocalizations in functional and systematic ways.

Making Training Functional

Three steps can be taken to increase the functionality of short-term training targets: (1) selecting forms known to be functional in a particular setting frequented by the child, (2) teaching the child to use the form in a functional manner by training specific intent such as greeting and requesting in conjunction with training the form, and (3) preparing persons in the environment to respond to new forms in a functional manner.

Functional forms for training can be determined by observing the settings in which students spend time and noting the types of interaction in which they engage and the communication required to participate in those interactions. By observing Kristi throughout her day, a list of communication opportunities can be compiled. Certainly, she needs greeting skills as she gets on the bus and as she enters the classroom; she needs simple requests to obtain classroom materials and to ask for assistance; she needs to be able to indicate her food preferences at lunch; and it would be enjoyable for her to be able to indicate to a peer that she would like to play. From the list of opportunities, a set of potential target forms can be generated that takes into account Kristi's preferences. It makes sense to teach generic forms, such as "Help," but forms that allow the student to acquire preferred reinforcers, such as hugs and tickles or a favorite toy, also should be trained.

Functional forms become useful only when the environment responds to their use in particular ways. Teaching a form in its functional communicative context literally gives meaning to an otherwise artibrary sign. That is, meaning derives from the consequences of attempted communication. When Kristi signs, "Julie come," and her friend joins her at the lunch table, she has controlled her environment and demonstrated that she can express her communicative intent. Her signs have meaning and function for her.

Ensuring functional use may require intervention in the environment to make people responsive to a student's emerging communication skills. This is particularly true when the student is using an alternative communication mode, has unclear articulation, or has a history of very limited language use. In Kristi's case, signing her request for a friend to come will not be a functional response unless her friend responds to the request. Her friend may need support from a teacher (such as a prompt to respond or a verbal interpretation of Kristi's sign) in order to understand and respond to Kristi's attempt to communicate. Training parents, classroom aides, community service providers (such as the bus driver), and peers to pay attention and respond to such communication attempts often is a critical part of functional language intervention.

Teaching Interactional Strategies to Facilitate Language Learning

Functional language training should include the teaching of *strategies* for learning language. "Strategy," in this instance, refers to a broad class of behaviors that supports the student in practicing language forms, in interacting with others so as to increase the opportunity for language use, or in soliciting new linguistic or conceptual information. In normal children, skills and strategies for acquiring new skills emerge concurrently probably because skill acquisition is the result of effective behavioral strategies. When language is taught through traditional, didactic procedures, trials are presented so that the student needs to exhibit minimal active learning strategies to produce correct responses. In the short term, direct instruction is an excellent intervention because information is acquired more rapidly than when students are left to their own devices for learning. However, direct instruction may not provide students with opportunities to develop strategies for acquiring new language skills in unstructured, naturally occurring interactions.

Three specific classes of behavior have been shown to facilitate language learning in language deficient children. Those strategies are (1) generalized imitation, (2) frequent communication attempts, and (3) actively seeking new information.

To date, the strongest support for teaching behavioral strategies as a means of facilitating language learning comes from Leonard's (1981) review of studies with language-delayed children. Leonard's review suggests that broad-based interventions that target both skills and strategies for learning are more likely to result in accelerated, generalized learning. It is not clear how accurately his findings with these children apply to children with more severe handicaps. Experimental studies are needed that demonstrate the generalized effects of interventions which target both strategy and specific skills of students with severe handicaps.

For a student like Kristi, generalized imitation of signs may be an essential skill for expanding her sign repertoire. Kristi's spontaneous imitation of signs used by peers could be especially valuable in adding to her sign vocabulary. Even if generalized imitation alone is insufficient for new learning, imitation does provide an opportunity for reinforcement and for shaping more complex responses. There are several experimental studies (Lovaas, 1977) that have demonstrated the positive effects of generalized imitation on increasing language learning in one-to-one instruction, but no studies have examined the effects of training generalized imitation during naturalistic interactions.

Increasing students' communicative initiations to persons in the environment is another means of promoting social interaction and arranging for opportunities to prompt more complex responses. In addition, studies with language delayed (Rogers-Warren & Warren, 1980), low socioeconomic status (Hart & Risley, 1968), and normal children (Nelson, 1973) have shown a direct relationship between frequency of verbal responding and complexity of children's language. The correlations between rate of initiating and developing language reported in these diverse studies suggests that both practice and consequences for language may play a role. Adolescents with severe retardation generalized newly trained language skills more frequently in settings where they talked more often, apparently because of the more frequent positive consequences for language (Warren & Rogers-Warren, 1983). In Kristi's case, increasing the frequency of her initiations to her parents may be a particularly effective way to prompt them to teach her new signs as well as to provide functional reinforcers for her communicative behavior.

As Kristi's signing skills develop, she also may benefit from being taught a third strategy, soliciting specific information about language forms. A study of adolescents with severe retardation, (Warren, Baxter, Anderson, Marshall, & Baer, 1981) showed that training students to ask, "What's that?" when a paper bag containing an unknown object was brought into the room, was an effective means of increasing both question asking and vocabulary. Training involved teaching the questioning form and then prompting use of the newly provided label.

Teaching these three strategies might be combined and extended to coincide with Leonard's (1981) recommendation to increase general interactive skills as a means of increasing the student's overall responsiveness in communicative interactions. In Table 10.1, a number of specific child-response strategies are shown to illustrate different targets for interactional training. For students like Kristi, one or more skills (turntaking or indicating interest through visual attention) might be trained concurrently with new signs in naturalistic interactions.

OVERVIEW

When functional use and concurrent training of language learning strategies are considered as the primary goals of language intervention, the intervention must occur in naturalistic settings, address the student's immediate communication needs, and enhance her interactional skills. Traditional didactic instruction, designed to teach specific forms under a carefully controlled set of instructional conditions, is unlikely to be sufficient for meeting these two goals. Alternative teaching formats, such as milieu (incidental) teaching described in the next section, may be more compatible with these goals.

MILIEU TEACHING TECHNIQUES

"Milieu language training" refers to language and communication training procedures that are brief and positive in nature, carried out in the natural environment as opportunities for teaching functional communication naturally occur, and occasioned by child interest in the topic to which training will relate. Milieu teaching procedures, which often are called "incidental teaching" after Hart and Risley (1968) or naturalistic teaching procedures, provide specific instruction for the three aspects of the language system that have been emphasized in this chapter: linguistic forms, pragmatic function, and strategy for learning additional language.

Summary of Research Findings

The first milieu language-training study was published by Hart and Risley (1968) and described the application of an incidental language-training technique to establish the use of descriptive adjectives in the spontaneous speech of disadvantaged preschool children. Since then, a number of studies have documented the effects of incidental teaching (Hart & Risley, 1974, 1975, 1980; McGee, Krantz,

TABLE 10.1 Interactional and conversational strategies for language learning

Nonverbal Interactional Strategies
Directed attention to the conversational partner
Joint attention on the environmental topic of interest
Joint activity focused on the environmental topic of interest
   Responsiveness during joint activity as demonstrated by:
     Nonverbal turntaking
     Generalized nonverbal imitation
     Generalized instruction following
   Initiating nonverbal interaction
   Topic maintenance through sustained joint attention and joint activity

Conversational Strategies
Verbal responsiveness to initiations of the conversational partner as demonstrated by:
   Verbal turntaking
   Generalized verbal imitation
   Acknowledgments
   Adding information
Initiating conversation
Maintaining conversation through, for example:
   Seeking clarification of ambiguous information
   Adding topic relevant information
   Seeking new information
   Building upon the topic (topic expansion)

Mason & McClannahon, 1983) and two other techniques: mand-model (Rogers-Warren & Warren, 1980; Warren, McQuarter, & Rogers-Warren, 1984) and time-delay (Halle, Marshall, & Spradlin, 1979; Halle, Baer, & Spradlin, 1981). Other studies recently have investigated a combination of these techniques (Alpert & Rogers-Warren, 1983; Cavallaro & Bambara 1982; Oliver & Halle, 1982).

The effects of milieu teaching techniques have been investigated with young disadvantaged children (Hart & Risley, 1975), young language-delayed children (Rogers-Warren & Warren, 1980), institutionalized adolescents with severe retardation (Halle et al., 1979), and children with autism (McGee et al., 1983). These techniques have been used to teach adjectives, requests, social initiations, labels, two- and three-word sentences, and compound sentences. In many cases, the generalized results of training have included: (a) greatly increased frequency of talking, (b) increased child responsiveness to adult and peer speech, (c) elaborated vocabulary and sentence usage repertoires, (d) significant increases in overall mean length of utterance, (e) enhanced generalization from one-to-one training when milieu training was used adjunctively with it, and (f) generalization of these effects to other nontraining settings. These results suggest that milieu training techniques have general effects on the child's language system

and actually stimulate the broad development of the entire response class of language in addition to teaching specific forms (Hart, 1981; Hart & Risley, 1980). Except for the studies by Halle and his colleagues, the experimental applications of incidental teaching of persons with severe handicaps have been somewhat limited. Given this limited research base, care should be taken to monitor the application and effects of incidental teaching, particularly when it is the primary form of language intervention.

Using Milieu Teaching with a Severely Handicapped Student

Milieu teaching procedures are ideally suited to training functional language skills to older students with severe handicaps. Michael, for example, is a 15-year-old student with severe mental retardation and a moderate hearing loss. He uses a wheelchair for ambulation. Michael is enrolled in a multi-ability prevocational high school program. Much of the instruction in this program takes place in community settings. Michael is socially responsive and enjoys participating in a variety of activities with peers. When teaching Michael new language skills, his teachers match his intentions (greeting, answering, requesting, commenting) and his linguistic level (single words with some simple two-word requests). They model appropriate words and short phrases when his attention is focused on something of interest to him in the environment (a favorite material, an activity, or a peer). The teachers attempt to fit their requests for language and their models as closely as possible to Michael's emerging skills. They teach target forms that are just slightly more advanced than his current spontaneous language. Since Michael uses a few two-word utterances, such as "want" plus a noun ("want cookie") to make requests, teachers work to expand his requesting repertoire by modeling a variety of new nouns in combination with the verb "want." Modeling of new forms occurs *as* Michael attends to the specific aspect of the environment that the new label describes. Thus, environmental stimuli and language are contiguous with one another.

Successful milieu teaching occurs only when language is functional, that is, when the student's language works to control the immediate environment. For Michael, teaching new requesting forms is most effective when he has indicated his desire for a specific object (his favorite record, his new baseball cap, or another sandwich) or a specific activity (to get a soft drink or to have assistance in putting on his sweater). Initiations to the adult, signal that students have specific communicative intentions; they already have made discriminations among many aspects of the communication context (what they want, the presence of cooperative adult, that language is needed to request). When the teacher prompts or models language that matches the student's intentions it helps the student learn how language functions to control the environment. Furthermore, a teacher who requires elaborated language (a specific two-word request) is also teaching students, such as Michael, that specific forms work more effectively than general or incomplete ones.

Milieu teaching also may assist students in developing strategies that will increase their naturally occurring language learning. In the example of requesting above, Michael is being taught to attend to two kinds of stimuli for talking: listeners and environment. His verbal initiations are reinforced with consequences he has specified. Thus, frequent milieu teaching should be effective in increasing Michael's rate of social-verbal initiations as well as establishing interactions with adults as positive events. When elaborated language is requested through a sequence of teacher prompts, Michael has an opportunity to practice verbal turntaking within a conversational framework.

Milieu teaching also encourages Michael to learn from naturally occurring language models. Repeated presentation of linguistically appropriate models, when Michael's attention is focused on the immediate context, teaches him to attend to the specific words teachers use to describe objects and events and, hopefully, increases his observational learning. Repeated responding to formal models in naturalistic interactions may facilitate attention to and learning from models presented informally.

Milieu teaching also may promote establishment of functional response classes composed of functionally equivalent utterances. In every incidental teaching episode, Michael hears at least two utterances that serve the same purpose: the original form he produced and the elaborated form modeled or prompted by the teacher. When Michael requests more milk at lunch by saying, "milk," and his mother models a slightly more elaborate request, "Milk, please," he has an opportunity to equate his single word request with a more polite form of requesting. When teachers and parents accompany their delivery of child-requested consequences (providing Michael with another container of milk) with additional descriptive talk ("It's *chocolate milk*"; "Yes, you can have *more* milk"), several equivalent forms may be paired with the same function during a very brief interaction.

Finally, because teaching occurs in communicative contexts, generalization to other conversational interactions is facilitated. Teaching incorporates a variety of stimuli that occur in naturalistic contexts. Thus, it is unlikely that students will become "stimulus-bound" to the same extent that is observed after traditional one-to-one training. Teaching that responds to Michael's attention to a specific object or event increases the likelihood that he will learn new labels and simple request forms without the use of massed trials and intensive practice (which might mitigate against generalization).

The Procedures

Four milieu teaching procedures—"Child-directed modeling," the "mand-model," "time-delay," and "incidental teaching procedures,"—will be described. Table 10.2 summarizes the teaching techniques used in each of these procedures.

Child-Directed Modeling

Child-directed modeling may be considered the most fundamental milieu teaching process. The

TABLE 10.2   A summary of milieu language teaching techniques

Child-Directed Modeling Procedure	*Mand-Model Procedure*
Note focus of child's interest.	Note focus of child's interest.
Establish joint attention.	Establish joint attention.
Present verbal model related to focus of child's interest.	Present verbal mand related to focus of child's interest.
Correct child response receives immediate praise, verbal expansion, and (when material is being withheld) access to material.	Correct child response receives immediate praise, verbal expansion, and (when material is being withheld) access to material.
Incorrect child response is followed by a corrective model.	Incorrect child response is followed by a second mand (when child's attention is high and when she is likely to know the answer) or a model (when child's interest is waning she is unlikely to know the answer).
Correct child response receives immediate praise, verbal expansion, and access to material.	Correct response to mand or model is followed by immediate praise, verbal expansion, and access to material.
Incorrect response to corrective model is followed by corrective feedback plus access to material.	Steps involved in the Model Procedure follow incorrect child response to corrective mand or model.
Time-Delay Procedure	*Incidental Teaching Procedure*
Identify occasions when child is likely to need materials or assistance.	Identify occasions when child is verbally or nonverbally requesting materials or assistance.
Establish joint attention.	Establish joint attention.
Introduce Time Delay.	Use occasion to teach more intelligible, complex, or elaborated language/communication skills by applying steps of the:
Correct child response (child communicates what she needs) receives immediate praise, verbal expansion, and materials or assistance.	a. Model Procedure (use to train new or difficult forms or structures or to improve intelligibility), or the
Incorrect child response is followed by application of the Mand-Model Procedure (if child interest is high and she is likely to know the answer) or application of the Model Procedure (if child interest is waning and she is unlikely to know the answer).	b. Mand-Model Procedure (use to train complexity and conversational skills), or the
	c. Time-Delay Procedure (use to train the child to initiate verbal or nonverbal communicative behavior about environmental stimuli)

four primary goals of child-directed modeling are: (a) building turntaking skills, (b) training generalized imitation skills, (c) establishing a basic vocabulary, and (d) participating in conversations that occur outside the training context.

Child-directed modeling can be used in environments that are arranged to facilitate communication by the student. The teacher first establishes joint attention by focusing her attention on what the student is interested in or by getting the student to attend to something the teacher wants to discuss. Next, the teacher presents a model for the student to imitate that is related to the topic material. The model is presented when the teacher has control over the object and can manipulate the object being discussed. If the student imitates the model correctly, immediate verbal praise (which includes an expansion of the student's response) and the requested material are offered to her. The student's verbal response is expanded in order to present a model of more complex language for future responses. If she doesn't respond to the initial model

or responds with an unintelligible, partial, incorrect, or unrelated response, the teacher establishes joint attention again and presents the model a second time (corrective model). A correct response should result in immediate acknowledgment and expansion of the student's utterance as well as access to the topic material. If an incorrect response follows the corrective model, the teacher simply will provide corrective feedback by stating the desired response and giving the topic material to the student. All milieu procedures have a modeling component which includes the steps described here.

The following example illustrates how child-directed modeling might be used to increase the complexity of Michael's requesting.

Context: *Michael and two peers are taking records from the shelf to play on the record player. Michael looks at his friend holding a favorite album and gestures to request his friend to give it to him.*

Teacher: *Say, "Play record." (MODEL)*
Michael: *Record. (PARTIAL STUDENT RESPONSE)*
Teacher: Play *record. (CORRECTIVE MODEL)*

Michael: *Play record. (CORRECT STUDENT RESPONSE)*

Teacher: *Right, you want Jamie to play the record for you. Let's help him put it on the turntable. (ACKNOWLEDGEMENT + EXPANSION + NATURAL CONSEQUENCES)*

The Mand-Model Procedure

The mand-model procedure was developed by Rogers-Warren and Warren (1980) to program for generalization of language skills from one-to-one training sessions to the classroom. Generalization was programmed by training the classroom teacher to increase the number of opportunities for students to display trained language in the classroom. During the mand-model procedure, a variety of interesting materials were provided. When a student approached a material, the teacher manded (verbally instructed) the student to describe the material ("Tell me what this is"). If the student gave an appropriate response, the teacher praised her descriptively for talking ("Okay, you want the red truck") and provided the material. If she did not respond or gave an incorrect response, the teacher provided a model to imitate. The teacher also could prompt within this step, by manding her to give a more complex response ("Tell me in a whole sentence"), and then modeling if she failed to respond appropriately. Verbal responses to models and elaborated mands also resulted in praise and immediate presentation of the material.

Use of the mand-model procedure is arranged and initiated by the adult. Ideally, the adult is responsive to the student's interest and presents mands related to that topic. The procedure also may be used effectively when the adult directs the student's attention to a particular stimulus, and once joint attention is established, presents a mand related to it. The particular goals toward which the mand-model process is directed are establishing joint attention (topic selection) as a cue for verbalization, training turntaking skills, training the student to provide information upon verbal request or instruction, and training the student to respond to a variety of adult-presented verbal cues.

In the same context described above, Michael's teacher might use the mand-model technique in this way:

Context: *Michael and two peers are taking records from the shelf to play on the record player. Michael looks at his friend holding a favorite album and gestures to request his friend to give it to him.*

Teacher: *Tell Jamie what you want. (MAND)*
Michael: *(No response)*
Teacher: *Say, "Play record, please." (MODEL)*
Michael: *Play record. (PARTIAL RESPONSE)*
Teacher: *Play record, please. (CORRECTIVE MODEL)*
Michael: *Play record, please. (CORRECT RESPONSE)*
Teacher: *That was nice asking, Michael. Let's help Jamie play the record. (ACKNOWLEDGEMENT + NATURAL CONSEQUENCES)*

The Time-Delay Procedure

Communication involves not only responding to another person's models and mands for verbalization, but also involves initiating conversation about various aspects of the environment. The time-delay procedure was developed to establish environmental stimuli other than verbally presented models and mands as cues for verbalization. The effects of the time-delay procedure were experimentally demonstrated in two studies by Halle and his colleagues (Halle et al., 1979; Halle et al., 1981). Adults in these studies (caretaking staff and teachers) were instructed to attend to individual students by introducing a time delay in situations where the students were likely to need assistance or materials. Elements of the time-delay procedure include: (a) the adult (in proximity to, and looking at, the student) delays following student attention to the material, (b) praise and immediate offering of the material or assistance follow appropriate student verbalizations, or (c) verbal prompts follow incorrect student responses.

The time-delay procedure might be used effectively in prompting Michael's language interactions with persons in the community. The bus driver might wait to open the door to the bus until Michael verbalizes. The cafeteria worker might hold on to Michael's tray until he requests it ("Tray, please"). Any regular routing, such as entering and leaving a workshop might be interrupted by pausing between routine steps, focusing attention on the student as a prompt to verbalize, then waiting for a verbal request, and finally providing the requested action.

Context: *Michael is assembling a bicycle gear by taking parts from each of the six containers and fitting them together.*

Teacher: *Places her hand over the second container (DELAY) Focuses her visual attention on Michael and waits for him to verbalize.*

Michael: *Washer (PARTIAL RESPONSE)*
Teacher: *Want washer (CORRECTIVE MODEL)*
Michael: *Want washer (CORRECT RESPONSE)*
Teacher: *Yes, Michael, you want a washer. Help yourself. (ACKNOWLEDGEMENT + EX-PANSION + NATURAL CONSEQUENCE)*

The Incidental Teaching Procedure

In addition to intervention strategies that teach students to "respond" to models and mands and "initiate" about environmental stimuli, a fourth strategy has been developed for the purpose of teaching more "elaborate language" and for "improving conversational skills" about particular topics. Incidental teaching is used to elicit language about some reinforcer specified by the student. The first step in the incidental teaching procedure is arranging the environment in ways that will encourage student requests for materials and assistance. This can be achieved by attractively displaying potential reinforcers within the student's view but out of reach. The student verbally or nonverbally requests materials or assistance to identify what is of prepotent interest (a reinforcer) at that moment. The adult responds by modeling, manding, or delaying for a more sophisticated response or for additional information about the reinforcer. When the student responds appropriately, the adult gives the reinforcer while affirming and repeating the answer in an expanded fashion thereby presenting a model of more complex language for future student responses. If the student does not respond appropriately to the adult's prompts, the adult instructs the student to imitate a model of an appropriate elaboration, confirms the accuracy of the imitation, repeats what the student said, and gives the student whatever he initiated about. Because the adult can teach relative to the reinforcer only so long as it remains a reinforcer, teaching episodes are brief and positive in nature. Imitation is the only prerequisite student skill for incidental teaching.

Context: *Michael and a peer have been taken to a variety store to purchase a birthday present for a classmate. They are looking at a rack of baseball caps.*

Michael: *(Points to a blue cap) One (INITIATION)*
Teacher: *Tell me which one you like. (MAND)*
Michael: *(Continues to point)*
Teacher: *Say, "Blue one." (CORRECTIVE MODEL)*
Michael: *Blue one. (CORRECT RESPONSE)*
Teacher: *Here you go. You like the blue one. I'm glad you told me. Do you think Jimmy will like this one? (NATURAL CONSEQUENCE + EXPANSION + ACKNOWLEDGEMENT)*
Michael: *(Nods head yes)*

How to Implement a Milieu Language Training Program

There are a number of important issues that must be addressed when planning and implementing a milieu language teaching program. These include arrangement of the environment, prerequisite teaching skills, and data collection and evaluation. These issues are discussed below.

Arranging the Environment

A critical part of milieu teaching is arranging the environment to set up student requests and to apply specific teaching procedures. Simply arranging the environment may be sufficient to increase the rate of requests and other communicative initiations by the student. A stimulating environment that contains objects and events of interest to the student may encourage language use or communicative gestures to make needs known. Environments that contain few reinforcers or meet the student's every need are not functional for teaching language (Hart & Rogers-Warren, 1978). Classrooms can be designed to elicit many requests by placing needed or desirable materials in sight but out of reach of the student, or by establishing a rule which says she must communicate before receiving a desired material. Snack and dining situations can be arranged by providing food and drink only upon a communicative request or attempt and then in relatively small portions so that further requests are likely. Milieu teaching also can occur in play situations. For a more advanced student, for example, requests and initiations can be elicited if the teacher takes possession of part of the material the student is using (puzzle pieces, Lego pieces, crayons) and keeps it in sight (so that the student can indicate what she wants) but out of reach so that she must ask the teacher for it. For the student who is functioning at a developmentally lower level, the teacher may engage her in an enjoyable activity suitable for her age (rocking or bouncing, listening to music), periodically stop the activity, and encourage her to use a nonverbal procedure (touching the adult, clapping) to indicate the desire for the activity to continue. Routine situations such as transitions, going to the bathroom, or getting dressed or undressed are excellent times to teach communicative responses incidentally. The environment must require that the student use language in order to have her needs met. Anticipating needs and meeting them in advance reduces her need to learn language and wastes excellent teaching opportunities that occur throughout the day.

Critical Teaching Skills

There are certain skills that an adult needs to be an effective milieu language teacher. Many parents and teachers naturally have these skills and only need to learn to use them systematically. Others do not have these skills or do not use them. Milieu teaching procedures include standard behavioral techniques such as shaping, fading, and differential reinforcement combined in various ways to create a teaching process. But some additional skills typically not taught in teacher education programs are crucial for effective teaching.

Probably the most important skill teachers must learn is to identify what the student is attending to, follow this attentional lead, establish joint attention, and then use this student-identified topic as the focus of teaching. This requires giving up some control of the interactional situation and following the student's lead. When the student focuses her attention on an object, event, or notion, she has indicated a topic of interest. By also focusing on this topic, the adult creates joint attention. An excellent teaching situation has been established because the adult knows that he has the student's attention, that he has a topic to teach about, and that he has a strong student-selected reinforcer (the topic) to use in the teaching situation. When a student initiates a request, the object of the request becomes the topic of the ensuing conversation and the reinforcer.

Data Collection and Evaluation

Effective milieu language teaching must be data based. Many aspects of the process may be monitored. At a minimum it is recommended that data be kept on the following dimensions:

1. The number of incidental teaching episodes per day and the targets taught in these episodes. A total of 10 to 20 episodes per day is a reasonable teaching base.
2. The number of student initiations per day. An increase in number of student initiations is often one of the primary effects of milieu teaching. Initiations typically are defined as

directed speech that occurs in the absence of an adult verbal stimulus (such as a request).
3. The responsiveness of the student in obligatory speech situations. This can be measured by counting the number of appropriate student responses to questions, mands and models, and delays. For example, a teacher could determine the number of times a student responded to 10 different questions across the day. Normal students typically respond 65 to 75% of the time.
4. Initiations of the target skills. This indicates a level of unprompted generalization that can be assessed across forms of the target skill as well as people and settings.

Each of these measures is easy to monitor, requiring only a clip board and tally sheet. Daily monitoring is recommended. Non-data-based milieu teaching is likely to be highly erratic and, like any non-data-based approach, may prolong the use of ineffective strategies, depriving the student of critical learning time. Figure 10.1 shows a sample data sheet that can be used to collect data for three students across a school day's varied activities.

How to Use Milieu Language Teaching

Milieu language teaching can be used either as a primary language intervention approach or in combination with didactic teaching to facilitate generalization and promote further acquisition. When used as a primary intervention approach, it should be applied systematically in routine interaction situations, in small groups, and any other time a need for language use can be specified. One of the best strategies may be to combine milieu teaching with an individualized curriculum sequencing approach (Mulligan & Guess, 1984). Individual curriculum sequencing (ICS) is a dispersed trial teaching process in which target skills are clustered into functional sequences. Milieu teaching shares many common assumptions with this approach, including the notion that communication training should be overlaid with the teaching of other skills and never taught in isolation of its natural functions.

Figure 10.2 shows a cluster of skills being taught in the ICS model. In this example, a student, Kelly, is being taught to sign. In the grooming sequence, Kelly practices washing her face and combing her hair. The teacher uses time delay to prompt Kelly to sign for soap, towel, comb, and if needed, help

Student _____			Student _____			Student _____		
Target 1 _____			Target 1 _____			Target 1 _____		
Setting	Times	Prompts/ Conseq.	Setting	Times	Prompts/ Conseq.	Setting	Times	Prompts/ Conseq.
____	___	_____	____	___	_____	____	___	_____
____	___	_____	____	___	_____	____	___	_____
____	___	_____	____	___	_____	____	___	_____
____	___	_____	____	___	_____	____	___	_____
____	___	_____	____	___	_____	____	___	_____
Target 2 _____			Target 2 _____			Target 2 _____		
____	___	_____	____	___	_____	____	___	_____
____	___	_____	____	___	_____	____	___	_____
____	___	_____	____	___	_____	____	___	_____
____	___	_____	____	___	_____	____	___	_____
____	___	_____	____	___	_____	____	___	_____
Target 3 _____			Target 3 _____			Target 3 _____		
____	___	_____	____	___	_____	____	___	_____
____	___	_____	____	___	_____	____	___	_____
____	___	_____	____	___	_____	____	___	_____
____	___	_____	____	___	_____	____	___	_____
____	___	_____	____	___	_____	____	___	_____

Setting: Specify activity when response occurred
Times: Use slash for each occurrence
Prompts: (Record one symbol for each occurrence) M = Model   S = Spontaneous   T = Acknowledged by adult or peer   MQ = Question or Mand   TD = Time delay
FIGURE 10.1 Milieu training data

from the teacher. Initially, the teacher modeled these signs and prompted Kelly to imitate, but now she focuses her attention on Kelly and awaits her request for the needed objects. The teaching of labels and requesting fits well with the grooming task and helps the student acquire appropriate and situation-specific language.

ASSESSMENT, PLANNING AND IMPLEMENTATION

The general purposes of assessment are to *describe* the student's existing language skills and to construct a data base for *prescribing* a set of treatment goals and strategies for intervention. When milieu teaching is proposed as an intervention strategy, both student skills and environmental demands for language must be assessed in formulating a func-

tional intervention plan. In the following section, a three-part assessment strategy is outlined that involves performing an ecological inventory, assessing student skills, and combining the results of the student and environment assessments in order to prescribe training targets and settings.

Ecological Inventory

The purpose of an ecological inventory is to identify the environments in which students need communication skills. Since almost every setting requires such skills, the first step of an ecological inventory is listing the settings where a student spends the majority of her time. Settings are physically defined (home, school, church, transportation vehicles) and activity defined (transitions at schools, eating, helping with chores at home,

Student: Kelly

Kelly walks to sink—(Gross Motor)
Turns water on—(Fine motor)
*Signs "soap"—(Communication)
*Signs "towel"—(Communication)
Washes and dries hands—(Self-help)
Turns water off—(Fine motor)
*Signs "comb"—(Communication)
Combs hair—(Self-help)

*Language-teaching opportunities

FIGURE 10.2 ICS Sequence (Individual curriculum sequencing, Mulligan & Guess, 1984) including opportunities to train communication skills

ordering and paying in a restaurant). After the general physical setting is identified, specific activities within each setting can be listed and particular communication demands identified.

Figure 10.3 shows a sample inventory describing communication opportunities arising during a student's ride to school each morning. The setting (bus to school) is identified and five discrete activities during the ride are indicated. For each activity, general communication opportunities are listed, and a potential trainer is identified. To plan an intervention, specific forms and functions of language would be delineated, and a training plan would be specified along with a potential trainer. This inventory gives a very general picture of the opportunities for training. A more detailed analysis, such as the one outlined in Table 10.3, could be used to describe the specific types of communication demands and supports that each activity such as the bus ride offers.

Completion of the environmental inventory and the specific assessment of the language environment should be based on direct observation of the student in the potential teaching settings plus informal interviews with significant others. Informal interviews will be especially helpful in selecting settings for training and in clarifying whether information gained during direct observation is representative of both the student and the environment.

Figure 10.4 summarizes a plan for intervening to teach a student to greet the driver and peers when getting on the bus each morning.

Assessing Student Skills

Two general classes of information are needed to assess student skills. The first is a comprehensive overview of student skills that describes cognitive functioning, social skills, motor skills, and communication abilities. Obtaining this type of information is not described in detail in this chapter.

Setting	Activities	Communication Demands	Possible Training Site	Trainer	Comments
Bus to School	Getting on bus	Greet driver	Yes	Mother or sibling	Mother willing/ Sibling maybe
	Paying driver	May ask social questions, inquire about exact change	No	No trainer, driver too busy	Check for generalization from other social talk training
	Greeting riders	Greet friends, ask social questions			
	Riding to school	Varied questions, can comment on environment	Yes	Normal peer or sibling	Sibling willing
	Getting off bus	Thank driver, say goodbye to driver, passengers	Maybe	Teacher who greets students at bus stop	Could coordinate with Mother on greeting

FIGURE 10.3 Environment inventory

TABLE 10.3   Guidelines for assessing the language environment

1. *What type(s) of student responses are elicited?*
   _____ Questions and instructions requiring a verbal response.
   _____ Instructions requiring a nonverbal response.
   _____ Conversational or commentary requiring no response.

2. *What type(s) of language models are presented?*
   _____ Conversation occurs in the language environment, but it is not directed toward the student.
   _____ Language is directed toward the student, but it generally is not matched to her level of functioning and appears not to serve a teaching purpose.
   _____ Language is directed toward the student that is matched to her level of functioning. Imitative responses generally are not elicited from the student.
   _____ Particular language forms that are appropriate for the student's level of functioning are presented and imitative responses are required

3. *What kind(s) of consequences are presented for language use?*
   _____ Positive feedback for using any language.
   _____ Positive feedback for using specific language forms.
   _____ No feedback for language usage.
   _____ Negative feedback or constraints on language usage.
   _____ Natural consequences for language usage such as _____ materials,
   _____ social interaction, _____ attention from conversational partner.

4. *What opportunities exist for language usage?*
   _____ Obligatory response occasions: questions, mands for verbalization.
   _____ Social response occasions: greetings, conversation opportunities.
   _____ Functional response occasions: requests for materials, indicating preferences.
   _____ Descriptive response occasions: an event and a listener.
   _____ Imitative response occasions: prompted or unprompted opportunities to repeat verbal forms modeled in the environment.

5. *Description of nonverbal environment:*
   _____ A variety of toys and materials are accessible to the student.
   _____ Toys and materials are present but are inaccessible to the student.
   _____ Few or no toys or materials are available.
   _____ Television is watched _____ little _____ some _____ much of the time.
   _____ Other _____
   _____
   _____
   _____

Schiefelbusch and Bricker (1981) and McLean and Snyder-McLean (1978) offer excellent strategies for comprehensive assessments related to language intervention. The second type of assessment focuses on the student's performance of communicative behaviors in the settings identified through the ecological inventory. We will focus primarily on the second type of assessment information.

Before we turn to assessing students' functional skills, one comment is in order. Individuals often are assessed many times in the course of a few years of intervention. Existing information should be reviewed to determine where new information is needed and to glean information about intervention strategies that have been used successfully in the past. Test results are useful, but past training data may yield even more useful information about the types of training that have been effective, the expected duration of training for new skills, and the specific skills that have been taught. If it exists, information about the student's ability to generalize new information would be especially valuable. New assessments should provide new or more specific information about the student's skills. Unless there

Student Tommy   DATE: January 10-30 TRAINER RESPONSIBLE: Cathy

New Training   Generalization Training   XX

Setting	Activity	Trainer	Language Targets	Procedure	Data/Monitoring
Bus to School	Greeting Driver	Sibling	"Good Morning" (plus eye contact, smile)	Sibling *Models*, verbal praise for success, one corrective model; driver responds positively	Sibling records on note card for teacher. Teacher summarizes and gives sibling feedback
	Responding to Driver	Sibling	"Fine" in response to "How are you?"	Sibling *Models*; prompts if needed, acknowledges	Same
	Greeting Friends	Sibling	"Hello and name"	Sibling *Mands* (say hello to your friend); *Models if needed*; expansion and acknowledgment	Same
	Responding to Friends	Sibling	Varies: a) reply "hello" b) answer "fine" c) answer "yes/no"	Sibling *Models* appropriate reply; use delayed Modeling; expansion and praise	Same

FIGURE 10.4 Milieu intervention plan

is a reason for repeating an entire assessment, it may be more parsimonious to repeat only the portions where new learning is likely to have occurred.

Assessing students' functional communication skills involves observing them in the previously identified activities and answering the following five questions.

1. *What does the student find interesting in this setting?* To answer this question, observe the student and note the people, objects and events to which she attends. Determine if and how the student initiates socially to the people in the setting and if she is responsive to particular people. Note the objects or aspects of the environment that engage her attention.

2. *What communication functions does the student exhibit in this setting?* Seven basic communication functions should be considered: greetings, protests, requests for objects, requests for assistance, commenting, and answering. Some settings where there are infrequent adult-initiated interactions may offer few opportunities for answering and commenting, and thus, it will be important to notice if opportunities occurred and how the student responded to them.

3. *What forms does the student use to express these functions?* Communication functions can be expressed verbally and nonverbally. Some examples of the varied ways of expressing these seven functions are noted in Table 10.4. Students with severe handicaps often have idio-

TABLE 10.4 Basic communication functions

Functions	Possible Forms
Greetings	Waves Eye contact "Hello" "Name"
Requests for Assistance	Gesture to come Giving object for which assistance is needed Taking the adult hand and directing them to the task Crying "Help" Use of the adult's name
Requests for Object	Pointing Attempting to grab object Taking adult's hand and directing it to object Verbal requests: "Give me," "Want that" Naming object
Requests for Information	Echoic imitation "What?" Eye contact plus quizzical look Showing object (requesting name or function of object)
Protests	"No" Pushing adult away Crying Turning away from adult or peer Throwing objects
Comments	Echoic imitation Pointing to object Showing object to adult

syncratic ways of expressing functions. For example, a student may tantrum or throw objects in protest rather than nod or say "no." A student such as Kristi who has a limited sign repertoire may use a single gesture to indicate requests for help, for objects, or to invite joint play. Understanding a student's idiosyncratic communication forms is sometimes difficult but always worth the time invested in observation and analysis because current communication forms are the beginning point for teaching more elaborated language.

4. *What skills in the student's repertoire can be the base for building new language skills?* At this point, the general information gleaned from the review of existing language assess-

ments (the outcomes of criterion-referenced assessment of all of Kristi's signs or of Michael's single-word vocabulary and two-word phrases) should be integrated with the assessment of communication performance in natural settings. Discrepancies between tested performance and naturalistic performance are ideal beginning points for milieu teaching interventions. Milieu teaching focuses on training skills slightly in advance of the student's current functional repertoire. Often this will mean generalization training focusing on transfer of already learned forms into use in their functional contexts. Enlarging vocabulary, extending the number of different forms used to express an already mastered function such as greetings, and teaching new responses in familiar social routines are other logical ways to build on the student's existing skills. Language targets that already have been acquired receptively but are not yet in the student's productive repertoire are potentially excellent targets.

5. *What communication strategies are used by the student?* To answer this question, the student must be observed interacting in the setting. The purpose of this observation is to determine if he is socially responsive and which basic interactional skills he already exhibits. Milieu teaching strategies will be used to strengthen and train interactional skills as well as to train communication skills. A checklist of basic communication strategies is found in Table 10.5. Basic strategies include attention to persons and objects in the environment, responsiveness to adult and peer verbalizations, and initiating communicative interactions.

Combining Ecological Information and Student Assessments

The final step in assessment is to combine information gathered about the environment and the student's skills in order to make a plan for training. The training plan should specify

1. The mode for training (verbal, sign, symbol system),
2. Specific training targets described in terms of both linguistic form and communicative function,
3. Where intervention will occur,

TABLE 10.5 Communication strategies checklist

Attention

_____ Student visually attends to adults when they talk

_____ Student visually attends to peers when they talk

_____ Student visually attends to a referent (object of person) named by an adult or peer

_____ Student visually attends to novel or changing aspects of the environment

_____ Student attends when instructed to do so

List the objects or activities you have seen the student attending to:

Responsiveness

_____ Student is socially responsive to adults (smiles, greets, acknowledges, approaches them)

_____ Student is socially responsive to peers

_____ Student complies with instructions

_____ Student responds verbally (any mode) to simple greetings, questions

_____ Students responds verbally (any mode) to comments

_____ Student accepts invitations to join activities (play together, share material, sit next to peer)

_____ Student can take turns nonverbally (in games, or routines)

_____ Student imitates motor behaviors spontaneously

_____ Student imitates verbal behavior spontaneously

_____ Student imitates motor behavior when prompted

_____ Student imitates verbal behavior when prompted

Initiative

_____ Student greets others spontaneously

_____ Student nonverbally initiates play or activity

_____ Student verbally (any mode) initiates (other than greetings)

_____ Student shares materials without prompting from adult or peer

Other Observations

---

4. How the training environment needs to be restructured to include milieu teaching interactions,
5. Who will do the training,
6. What assistance the trainer may need to apply milieu teaching strategies, and
7. If supplemental didactic instruction will be needed in addition to milieu training.

Selection of student communication mode and specific training targets derives primarily from student assessment, but should also be determined by the characteristics of the settings. If no one in the student's most frequented settings knows about communication boards, and if her significant others are unwilling to learn this symbol system, the choice of mode may be different than when parents, teachers, and siblings are knowledgeable or willing to learn.

The first training setting should be one in which the target skills will be most functional, but it should also be one in which it will be relatively easy to begin a milieu intervention. Identification of a trainer who can apply the milieu techniques is essential to selecting a setting. Often trainers will need support to begin the intervention. Assistance in identifying interactions training specific language targets; using modeling, manding, and time delay; and providing feedback should be a planned part of the trainer's preparation. Continued feedback to the trainer also will be needed if the intervention is to be effective.

Finally, some skills may need supplemental didactic instruction. For example, when teaching a student an initial set of signs, massed-trial practice may be very useful in learning the basic motor skills involved in producing the sign. Didactic instruction and milieu teaching can proceed concurrently. Noting the actual number of incidental teaching trials the student is receiving and her progress toward criterion performance is one way to determine if more intensive teaching may be needed. If the number of trials is low, or if the student is not acquiring the target form after a reasonable length of time (3 weeks of six trials each day), then didactic instruction might be added to facilitate acquisition with milieu teaching continued as a means of insuring generalization to functional use.

To meet the goal of teaching functional language, the effectiveness of the intervention must be assessed at frequent intervals. If the child's functional communication repertoire is not expanding during the intervention, adjustments in teaching tactics and target skills should be made. A sort of bottom line question might be posed at 3 month intervals: What does this child communicate effectively now that she was unable to communicate three months ago? Assuming regular teaching sessions, even the student with the most severe handicaps should show some progress toward more functional skills after 3 months of training.

TEACHING GENERALIZED SKILLS

One of the strengths of a milieu training approach is that it is designed to facilitate generalization. The use of multiple exemplars in functional communication contexts and naturally occurring reinforcers makes it likely that newly trained forms will be generalized; however, it is still important to consider the issues surrounding generalization of language training when planning a milieu intervention.

Language generalization occurs at several levels. Using a specific communication function (requests) or form (adjective-noun combinations, "red ball") across individuals and settings is an important but relatively simple form of generalization. Formation of a generalized concept, such as "ball," "cup," or "go," so that the student neither over- or undergeneralizes the word representing the concept, is a more difficult level of generalization. Generative language use (spontaneously initiating novel, meaningful word combinations in varied communication situations) is the most complex form of generalization.

Generalization is an aspect of the learning process, which may be characterized as consisting of three overlapping levels. First, during the *acquisition level*, the student learns the basic response or skill (the word *ball* is associated with a spherical object). Language intervention typically has concentrated on this level by teaching simple form-object and form-event relationships and teaching

new skills as soon as the student shows evidence of associative learning. When the *generalization level* is reached the student has begun to use the trained response under a variety of conditions. She may overgeneralize or undergeneralize use of the response as she explores its potential functions and discovers its essential attributes and delimiters. This level of language learning frequently has been ignored in language intervention. Finally, the third level of learning is achieved when the student attains *competence* in using the trained response. At this level, the student may approximate adult competence in use of the response. She knows when to use the response and when not to use it. She also uses the response generatively, integrating it with other communicative responses in her repertoire. This level of language learning, which is the desired outcome of intervention, has been overlooked completely in training.

The three levels of learning are interrelated. If teaching at the basic acquisition level produces a very well-discriminated response (the student learns to associate the word *ball* with only one or two particular balls), then generalization is unlikely unless it subsequently is programmed. If generalization is restricted or fails to occur, she will have no basis for attaining competence. An effective language remediation approach must ensure that learning occurs across all three levels.

Initial acquisition, generalization, and generative use may be influenced by a number of variables related to the nature of training, environmental support for trained language, and criteria for mastery of trained responses. Eight variables that are related specifically to training outcomes are

1. What is taught,
2. Who teaches,
3. How skills are taught,
4. How the student is reinforced,
5. Where teaching occurs,
6. How the content of training is organized,
7. What criteria for learning are applied, and
8. How responsive and supportive the student's environments are to new learning.

What Is Taught?

Both the forms of language (words, sentences, signs) and their functions (greetings, commenting, questioning, requesting) must be learned if new skills are to be used. Simply put, the content of training must be functional for the student and she must have experience using the content in a functional manner during training.

New forms should map pragmatic functions the student already has acquired. For Michael who already requests objects, a new form of requesting ("give me" + noun label) could be taught easily. New forms selected for teaching should be only slightly more complex than the forms the student currently uses to express a particular function. Conversely, when teaching a new function, such as requesting information, it is easiest to begin with a form already known or to teach the function with a single, simple form ("What?").

Who Teaches?

The simple answer to this question is "everyone." As many people as possible who come in contact with the student regularly and are willing to be either a *spontaneous* teacher or a *trained* teacher should be involved in the student's language learning. Learning to use specific incidental teaching techniques can enhance the natural abilities of teachers and parents. Milieu teaching is a particularly feasible approach because training can be incorporated easily into other routine activities throughout the day. Parents and significant others are likely to be more effective in facilitating generalization through their incidental teaching although some families are willing to take on primary training responsibilities.

How Is the Student Reinforced?

For language to generalize, it must come under the control of a breadth and range of naturally occurring consequences. When possible, only student-selected, naturally occurring reinforcers should be used in training. If this is not initially possible with some training targets, then the systematic introduction of naturally occurring consequences must be a central part of the training process.

Where Does Teaching Occur?

Language should be taught in those settings where communication naturally occurs. Teaching should be done at home, on the playground, in the lunch room, in the community, during all academic activities, in the hallway, on the bus, during family outings, and in all the daily routines where language is functional. With normally developing children, parents and teachers rarely set aside particular time for specifically teaching language or other skills. There are too many other things to be done. Language is taught informally in the course of typical activities such as eating, dressing, toileting, bathing, and transitions between activities. In general, the same model should apply with students who have severe handicaps. In the classroom and in community instruction, it is important to integrate language training with training of other skills with which the use of language normally occurs (e.g., fine and gross motor skills, self-help skills).

How Is the Content of Training Organized?

One implicit goal of language training is efficiency: maximum learning from minimum input. Some ways of organizing and presenting the content of training are more efficient than others. If a training goal is to teach a set of verb-noun combinations, a method that works through the possible combinations in steps (two nouns get trained with each verb and one of these nouns is trained with another verb in an overlapping fashion), will allow the student to abstract the rule for verb-noun combinations with less training (Goldstein, 1985). An example of stepwise training is shown in Figure 10.5.

Taking advantage of the "stimulus-equivalent" nature of many words is another means of enhancing training efficiency. Equivalent implies that one stimulus can be substituted for another. Different referents, symbols, and linguistic responses can be substitutable members of a stimulus class. Many types of cars, as well as pictures, emblems, trademarks, and model names all denote "car." The systematic use of carefully selected multiple training exemplars can be one of the most efficient ways to promote generalization (Stremel-Campbell & Campbell, 1985). For example, when teaching Kristi to sign "drink," it is important to first provide her with many different examples of drinks (milk, apple juice, soft drinks, milkshakes, water) in order for her to learn that "drinking" applies across many different liquids. Subsequently, she might be taught the specific names of drinks and the two-sign combination "drink" + label in addition to the two-sign combination "pour" + label using

Nouns*

	Water	Milk	Juice	Soft Drink
Give	1a	2a	3a	4d
Drink	4b	1b	2b	3b
Pour	4c	3c	1c	2c
Want	2d	4d	3d	1d

Verbs (label on left side)

Key:
1—Train first; Begin with 1a, then 1b, etc.
2—Train second if generalization does not occur spontaneously (2a, 2b, 2c, 2d)
3—Train third if generalization does not occur spontaneously
4—Train last, if necessary
*Already learned individually

FIGURE 10.5 Matrix training

the stepwise training progression described in Figure 10.5

What Criteria for Learning Are Applied?

One frequent error in language training is to claim success prematurely. Often, it is assumed that students have learned a language structure or function because they can accurately display the response on 80% of the posttraining probe trials. Demonstration by the student of the trained language response under the conditions imposed by the everyday environment is critical to its mastery (Warren & Rogers-Warren, 1983). Applying more stringent criteria, particularly including evidence of generalization as a condition for completing training, may be one of the most straightforward ways of increasing the impact of training. In the example of teaching Kristi to sign "drink" discussed above, generalization to five novel "drinkable" liquids not used in training but presented at appropriate times during the day (meals and snacks) would be a stringent but appropriate criterion for generalization. Anderson and Spradlin (1980) found that some learners with severe handicaps needed more than 10 training examples before they showed generalization to all appropriate exemplars of a label. Successful performance on probes for generalization across objects, setting, and people has also been shown to be prerequisite for generaliza-

tion to spontaneous usage by students with severe handicaps (Warren & Rogers-Warren, 1983).

How Responsive Is the Student's Environment to New Learning?

One way to program for generalization is to introduce a new skill to its natural community of reinforcement (Stokes & Baer, 1977). As students acquire new skills and their behavior changes, the natural environment must respond in ways that support those changes. During normal development, adaptation naturally occurs in mother-child interaction. Mothers are aware of their children's improved skills because they are in close contact with the children and "expect" them to change (Newport, 1976). With handicapped students, adults sometimes lose the expectation that the students will change and, thus, fail to respond differentially when change and growth do occur. If peers, teachers, and parents are made aware of changes in students' skill repertoire, they can be responsive to those changes by both requiring them and providing consequences for their use. For example, in both Michael and Kristi's cases, their parents should be provided regular updates on newly learned words and signs. In classrooms, demonstration of new skills during group times can be a way of helping peers attend to new communication forms. Kristi might be given the opportunity to show the new signs she has learned in a large group activity. Michael might be invited to show his friends pictures or objects and label them with his newly learned words.

DESIGNING AN OPTIMAL TRAINING APPROACH

Each of these variables should be directly addressed in designing an individualized communication training program for a student. Generalization to probes and to the student's spontaneous repertoire should be assessed on a weekly basis. Parents should be asked to note the use of new forms, and their help in promoting generalization should be sought. A simple report form, such as the one shown in Figure 10.6, can be used to both assess generalization and prompt adults to facilitate language use.

Teachers need to be familiar with the specific training approaches outlined by Stokes and Baer

Student   Kristi M   Date   March 3, 1987

Person Reporting   Sharon M (Mom)   Mode   Signs

Target*	Use in School*	When and How Often Used*	Opportunities Missed*
1. Help	Kristi does this one really well at school	Opening jar—1 Trying to get toys from Sibling—3	Trying to get arm in coat
2. Candy	Kristi's favorite	Lots of times! She really likes to try this request	None
3. Potty		About 5 times (always appropriate)	Yes—several
4. Hug	Just started training this	Not seen	
5.			

Comments and Suggestions:
I think "hug" will need my prompting. Kristi doesn't know how to ask for hugs yet. I may be missing some signs, they're "sloppy."

*Columns 1 and 2 filled out by teacher; columns 3 and 4 filled out by parent.

FIGURE 10.6   Language use report

(1977) and more recent generalization facilitating techniques such as case programming (Horner & McDonald, 1982). More thorough discussions of the uses of these generalization facilitation strategies applied in language training can be found in McCormick and Schiefelbusch (1984), Warren and Rogers-Warren (1985), Schiefelbusch (1978), Schiefelbusch and Bricker (1981), and McLean and Snyder-McLean (1978).

Figure 10.7 is a generalization planning worksheet developed to assist teachers in monitoring and planning for generalization. The basic strategy is to plan training to include multiple, functional exemplars; to probe for simple generalization across persons, settings and objects; to report observation in functional contexts; and to remediate observed deficits in generalization as soon as they are detected. A generalization report is updated on a weekly basis and is shared with all persons involved the student's training.

Case Study

Jordon is 4 years, 3 months old. His mother's pregnancy and his birth were normal. When he was 4 months old, Jordon contracted cerebrospinal meningitis and was hospitalized for a period of 5 weeks. As a result of the meningitis, Jordon suffered significant brain damage which resulted in hemiplegia of the left side and severe mental retardation. Jordon currently lives at home with his mother, 12-year-old sister, and maternal grandmother. He attends an early intervention program from 9:00 A.M. to 1:00 P.M. on Monday through Thursday. His afternoons are spent at home with his grandmother and, when she arrives home from school, his sister. Jordon's mother comes home from work around 6:00 P.M. On Fridays, Jordon attends a neighborhood daycare center (primarily for children without handicaps) from 8:30 A.M. to 6:00 P.M. Weekends are generally less structured, and Jordon tends to spend his time in activities such as going to the grocery with his mother, going to the playground with his sister, and accompanying his grandmother as she does chores around the house.

The teachers at the early intervention program followed a series of steps in developing a functional language-training program for Jordon that used milieu language-teaching strategies. First, func-

Student _____ Trainer _____ Date _____

Form	Training Criterion Met (Date & %)	Generalization Probed			Spontaneous Use Observed		Further Training Needed? (Date, plan, person responsible)
		Setting (%)	Trainer (%)	Stimulus (%)	Prompted (# & occasion)	Unprompted (# & occasion)	

FIGURE 10.7 Generalization worksheet

tional communication skills that would give Jordon more control over the physical and social environment were identified by conducting an ecological inventory of the environments in which he spent the majority of his time. For each of these environments (preschool, home, daycare, playground), the following information was determined:

1. The major activities that occurred within the environment, for example:
   Preschool
      large group
      small group
      snack/lunch
      gym/recess
   Playground
      swings
      merry-go-round
      slide;

2. Basic communication skills that would help Jordon function more independently and which would facilitate increased participation in activities;

3. The person in each environment/activity who was the logical candidate for milieu language trainer and his or her current proficiency at conducting naturalistic language training; and,

4. Whether the materials available and arrangement of the environment were optimal for promoting initiations and choice making by Jordon and facilitating the application of milieu teaching procedures by adults.

Information needed to complete the ecological inventories for activities occurring in the preschool environment was readily available to the teachers. Completing the inventories for activities occurring in nonpreschool environments, however, required direct observation of Jordon (and the significant others) in those environments. The teachers divided the responsibility of observing Jordon at home after school, at daycare, and at a sampling of representative times during the weekend. In each environment, the teachers completed "Guidelines for Assessing the Language Environment" (see Table 10.3) as an aid to obtaining information about existing strategies used to teach language, the responsiveness of adults to Jordon when he showed interest in something or made attempts to communicate, and opportunities for Jordon to contact the physical and social environment.

In addition to conducting the ecological observations, the teachers also "informally" interviewed one or more significant others in each environment. The interviews were designed to obtain specific information about existing environmental demands for Jordon to communicate, social and communicative behaviors exhibited by Jordon in each setting, and the minimal skills considered to be needed by Jordon to improve his ability to interact and communicate with others in the environment. The teachers used the interview data to verify, clarify, and augment their observational data, and to determine the ability of the significant other to identify and foster communicative behavior by Jordon.

In addition to taking into account environmental characteristics and demands, the teachers also specified student characteristics that were essential to consider in developing an individualized, functional, communication training program for Jordon. Test results (including the results of diagnostic testing), training data, reports by significant others, and informal observation by the teachers were the primary sources used to obtain relevant information about Jordon's receptive and expressive language skills, social interaction strategies, motor development, sensory abilities, and engagement with the physical environment. General findings related to each area are summarized below:

1. *Receptive language skills*—Jordan was able to do picture-to-object and object-to-picture matching. Jordon's teacher currently was working on a program to teach Jordon to point to an object following presentation of its verbal label. He also was able to imitate a variety of motor gestures with his right hand (touch his head, tap his leg, wave "hi") and responded to the word "no" by stopping whatever he was doing.

2. *Expressive communication skills*—Jordon spontaneously produced a variety of one-syllable sounds (/ma/, /ba/, /ha/, /ee/, /oh/). He used these sounds to engage in turntaking and initiated interactions as well as responding to the initiations of others. The teachers were in the process of informally training vocal imitation skills, but Jordon was not making much progress in that area. Jordon indicated a desire for objects by reaching toward them, looking at an adult, and vocalizing. He also protested vocally when he did not want to do something he was instructed to do.

3. *Social interaction strategies*—Jordon spent much of his time attempting to get an adult's attention. He typically did this by visually following the person until eye contact was established. Upon making eye contact, he would smile at the person and produce a string of sound but showed little interest in interacting with other children.

4. *Motor development*—Jordon basically did not use the left side of his body: he kept his left hand tightly clenched and his arm was drawn upward. He could sit independently for long periods of time, was able to pivot around in a circle, and was able to roll from one place to another, but typically relied on prompting to do so.

5. *Sensory abilities*—Jordon showed mild inward positioning (esotropia) of the left eye, but professional testing indicated good visual and auditory functioning.

6. *Engagement with the physical environment*—Jordon showed little interest in toys or other types of objects. He would, however, watch the Playskool TV for up to 10 minutes, independently looked at pictures in books, liked most foods, and finger fed himself as well as scooping food with a spoon.

Jordon's teachers planned his functional communication program by considering the data on child performance, deficiencies, and learning characteristics in light of the data obtained from the ecological inventories. They began by determining target responses that were slightly above Jordon's current level of functioning and that were functional across the environments and activities identified in the ecological inventories. Selected training targets included the words "more," "help," and pointing to one of two pictures as a means of choosing one of the two represented objects (choice making). The teachers felt that many natural opportunities to teach each of these responses would occur across the primary activities and environments. The teachers next considered the communication mode to be used in teaching each response. A review of Jordon's expressive modalities indicated that he spontaneously produced a variety of one-word sounds, but he did not imitate vocal stimuli. He used his right hand for pointing to things that he wanted and also for picture-object and object-picture matching. He had virtually no use of his left hand. Because this disability would place limitations on the repertoire of signs he ultimately could produce, and because he already showed some degree of skill using pictures, Jordon's teachers decided that his primary communication system would involve a picture communication board. Appropriate vocal stimuli would be paired with pictorial stimuli and vocal imitation training would occur with the nonvocal communication training. Teachers felt that, at least initially, iconic or concrete pictorial stimuli should be used. This posed a problem for training the more abstract concepts of "help" and "more." They decided to teach Jordon to express these notions by producing signs that were modified to accommodate his physical disability. Verbal imitation training of "help" and "more" would accompany the respective sign training. The third goal, involving choice making, would utilize the communication board. Initially, two choice pictures would be presented. As Jordon became more proficient in using the communication board, additional pictures gradually would be added. The pictures on the communication board would vary and be functionally related to the activity at hand. Once Jordon indicated his choice, he would be given access to that material.

The teachers next discussed the techniques that would be used to train the target responses. Milieu language training procedures were selected. Initially, the model procedure would be used to train "help" and "more" at times when Jordon appeared to need help or want more of something. The teachers agreed that they would attempt to give Jordon the opportunity to express each function himself before modeling the appropriate (modified)

sign. When Jordon correctly imitated each sign at 80% correct, the teachers would interchange use of the mand-model and time-delay procedures to elicit the response. (Note: Attempts by Jordon to indicate "help" or "more" that are followed by the model, mand-model, or time-delay procedure technically represent applications of the incidental teaching procedure—a student request followed by the model, mand-model, or time-delay procedure.) In addition to collecting performance data on sign production, data also would be collected on vocal imitation training that accompanied each nonvocal training trial. Three milieu teaching techniques, the mand-model, time-delay, and incidental teaching procedures, would be used to teach Jordon to make choices using the communication board. An example of how each of these techniques would be applied for this purpose follows.

Mand-Model Procedure

When it was Jordon's turn during music group, the teacher would show him the bells and the tambourine. She then would place his communication board showing a picture of each of these objects and ask, "Which musical instrument do you want?" If Jordon did not respond or if he made an incomplete or unclear response, the teacher could prompt by presenting a model of the correct response (demonstrate a clear pointing response to the picture that Jordon appeared to favor) or she would physically prompt him to make a clear response. The teacher then would "verbally expand" his nonvocal response ("You want the bells.") and provide a verbal model that was appropriate for the situation and Jordon's level of functioning such as the verbal model, "Be." Following use of the model procedure to train "be," Jordan would be given the bells to shake.

Delay Procedure

In free play, when Jordon visually expressed interest in a toy, the teacher would present his communication board displaying pictures of the toy of interest and another toy. The teacher would look at Jordon but say nothing (delay). If Jordon pointed to either picture, he would receive the corresponding object. Pointing to the "wrong" picture ("wrong" being determined if Jordon showed displeasure upon receiving the object) or an incomplete or unclear response would result in a mand or model prompt with or without a physical prompt, as necessary. An appropriate vocal model would be presented prior to delivering the chosen toy.

Incidental Teaching Procedure

The incidental teaching procedure would be used on occasions when Jordon requested a material or activity. If he pointed to the record player, the teacher would present his communication board displaying pictures of the record player and something else. She would then use the mand-model or delay procedure to elicit a pointing response. Verbal and physical prompts would be presented as necessary. Before giving Jordon access to the record player, the model procedure would be applied to elicit an appropriate vocal response.

Several additional tasks were completed in developing Jordon's communication training programs. Task-analyzed instructional programs (including levels of prompts, vocal imitation training procedures, and criterion performance levels) were written for each communication objective. Procedures for data collection and data sheets also were developed. The teachers agreed to do milieu language training whenever naturalistic opportunities occurred, especially in the context of other kinds of skill training. Data would be collected daily on a minimum of 10 trials for each objective; however, training was to occur during naturalistic teaching opportunities that present themselves throughout the day. The teachers decided to use certain situations as training settings and other situations as generalization settings. In school, Jordon's communication goals would be trained formally during small group, snack, and recess. Probes for generalization would be conducted during large group, lunch, and gym. The teachers also determined that communication training should occur in the nonschool settings of Jordon's daycare and home. Information obtained during the ecological inventories indicated that training in environmental arrangement and use of milieu language techniques was in order for Jordon's mother, grandmother, and workers at his daycare. The teachers decided to prepare and conduct such training within the next 2 months. (Participation in the training also would be offered to Jordon's sister.) Periodic posttraining visits would be made to each nonschool training setting to access the milieu teaching and to provide feedback and additional training as necessary. Finally, the teachers considered whether didactic communication training should be conducted in conjunction with the naturalistic communication training. The consensus was to implement just the naturalistic training procedures initially. Jordon's vocal imitation skills would be monitored carefully and, if the anticipated rate of acquisition was not achieved within four months time, the issue of concomitant didactic training on vocal imitation skills again would be considered.

CONCLUSION

This chapter has focused on applying milieu teaching strategies in training functional language skills to persons with severe handicaps. Choosing milieu strategies requires consideration of the larger system in which language instruction will occur. Thus, this conclusion focuses on changes that the choice to teach functional language may require from the student's environment if the goal of useable skills, generalized across appropriate settings and events is to be realized.

Teaching functional language is a curriculum goal that requires support from a variety of persons in the larger ecosystem in which instruction occurs. In a very real sense, teaching functional language will require a larger number of persons sharing the responsibility for training than simple didactic intervention. A functional approach to language increases the number of settings in which training occurs to include all those in which functional skills are needed. Functional teaching cannot be limited to classrooms; lunch rooms, playgrounds, vocational settings, homes, transportation vehicles, and the community all may be necessary training sites. Functional language training occurs within the context of other activities; it is not separate from social interaction or from learning and application of cognitive skills. The choice to teach functional language implies that training will be more frequent and more dispersed than easily can be managed by the speech clinician when she sees a student for two or three sessions each week. Significant others in the student's life must be involved in training new language. The first significant other trainer for the child with severe handicaps is likely to be a teacher; the second significant trainer is usually the student's parent or primary caregiver. Classroom aids, siblings, other therapists, and possibly classmates may also serve as trainers.

Planning begins by gaining consensus that teaching functional language is a priority. Speech clinicians, teachers, parents, and program administrators must agree that language teaching will be a shared responsibility and that language cannot be taught separately from other skills if the new language is to be functional. Planning is realized when plans for teaching functional language are embedded in the other aspects of the curriculum for each student. A truly critical step in planning is allocation of resources for training. Assigning responsibility, providing necessary training and access to appropriate training settings, and sharing information are essential aspects of allocating resources for functional language training. Finally, the development of problem-solving strategies must be part of the planning effort because problems will undoubtedly arise when such broad-based instruction is undertaken.

Not surprisingly, the teacher who chooses the goal of teaching functional language must often advocate to build a system in which meeting this goal is possible. Functional language teachers must enlist the cooperation and support of colleagues in other disciplines who work with their students. Functional language teachers may find it necessary to provide training for willing colleagues and to negotiate compromises with less willing ones. Data on a student's progress may be used for a new purpose: to demonstrate that a functional approach produces the desired changes in a student's communication. Choosing to implement a functional teaching approach may require improving one's own skills, learning new ways to teach and to promote environmental support for language. To paraphrase a familiar poster, "No one ever said 'functional' teaching would be easy!"

REFERENCES

Alpert, C. L., & Rogers-Warren, A. K. (1983, March). Mothers as incidental language trainers of their language disordered children. Paper presented at the Gatlinburg Conference on Mental Retardation, Gatlinburg, TN.

Anderson, S. R., & Spradlin, J. E. (1980). The generalized effects of productive labeling training involving comment object classes. *Journal of the Association of the Severely Handicapped, 5,* 143–157.

Cavallaro, C. C., & Bambara, L. M. (1982). Two strategies for teaching language during free play. *The Journal of the Association for Persons with Severe Handicaps, 7,* 80–92.

Goldstein, H. (1985). Enhancing language generalization using matrix and stimulus equivalence training. In S. F. Warren and A. K. Rogers-Warren (Eds.), *Teaching functional language.* Austin, TX: Pro-Ed.

Halle, J. W., Baer, D. M., & Spradlin, J. E. (1981). Teacher's generalized use of delay as a stimulus control procedure to increase language use in handicapped children. *Journal of Applied Behavior Analysis, 14,* 4.

Halle, J. W., Marshall, A. M., & Spradlin, J. E. (1979). Time delay: A technique to increase language use and facilitate generalization in retarded children. *Journal of Applied Behavior Analysis, 12,* 431–440.

Hart, B. (1981). Pragmatics and language development. In B. B. Lahey and A. E. Kazdin (Eds.), *Advances in clinical child psychology,* Vol. 3. New York: Plenum Press.

Hart, B., & Risley, T. R. (1980). *In vivo* language intervention: Unanticipated general effects. *Journal of Applied Behavior Analysis, 13,* 407–432.

Hart, B., & Risley, T. R. (1974). Using preschool materials to modify the language of disadvantaged children. *Journal of Applied Behavior Analysis, 7,* 243–256.

Hart, B., & Risley, T. R. (1975). Incidental teaching of language in the preschool. *Journal of Applied Behavior Analysis, 8,* 411–420.

Hart, B. M., & Risley, T. R. (1968). Establishing use of descriptive adjectives in the spontaneous speech of disadvantaged preschool children. *Journal of Applied Behavior Analysis, 1,* 109–120.

Hart, B. M., and Rogers-Warren, A. (1978). Milieu teaching approaches. In R. L. Schiefelbusch (Ed.) *Bases of language intervention,* Vol. 2. Baltimore: University Park Press.

Horner, R. H., & McDonald, R. S. (1982). Comparison of single instance and general case instruction in teaching a generalized vocational skills. *Journal of the Association for the Severely Handicapped, 7(3),* 7–20.

Leonard, L. B. (1981). An invited article facilitating linguistic skills in children with specific language impairment. *Applied Psycholinguistics, 1,* 89–118.

Lovaas, I. O. (1977). Chapter Two: Building the first words and labels. In *The Autistic Child: Language Development Through Behavior Modification* (pp. 35–55). New York: John Wiley and Sons.

McCormick, L., & Schiefelbusch, R. L. (Eds.). (1984). *Early language intervention: An introduction.* Columbus, OH: Charles E. Merrill.

McGee, G. G., Krantz, P. J., Mason, D., & McClannahan, L. E. (1983). A modified incidental-teaching procedure for autistic youth: Acquisition and generalization of receptive object labels. *Journal of Applied Behavior Analysis, 16,* 329–338.

McLean, J. E., & Snyder-McLean, L. K. (1978). *A transactional approach to early language training.* Columbus, OH: Charles E. Merrill.

Mulligan, M., & Guess, D. (1984). Using an individualized curriculum sequencing model. In L. McCormick & R. L. Schiefelbusch (Eds.), *Early language intervention: An introduction* (pp. 299–323). Columbus, OH: Charles E. Merrill.

Nelson, K. (1973). Early speech in its communicative context in F. D. Minifie and L. L. Lloyd (Eds.), *Communicative and cognitive abilities—Early behavioral assessment.* Baltimore: University Park Press.

Newport, E. L. (1976). The speech of mothers to young children. In N. J. Castellan, D. B. Pisoni, & G. R. Potts (Eds.), *Cognitive theory,* Vol. 2. Hillsdale, NJ: Lawrence Erlbaum Associates.

Oliver, C. B., & Halle, J. W. (1982). Language training in the everyday environment: Teaching functional sign use to a retarded child. *The Journal of the Association for the Severely Handicapped, 8,* 3.

Rogers-Warren, A., & Warren, S. F. (1980). Mands for verbalization: Facilitating the display of newly taught language. *Behavior Modification, 4,* 361–382.

Schiefelbusch, R. L. (1978). *Bases of language intervention.* Baltimore: University Park Press.

Schiefelbusch, R. L., & Bricker, D. D. (1981). *Early language: Acquisition and intervention.* Baltimore: University Park Press.

Stokes, T. F., & Baer, D. M. (1977). An implicit technology of generalization. *Journal of Applied Behavior Analysis, 10,* 349–367.

Stremel-Campbell, K., & Campbell, C. R. (1985). Training techniques that may facilitate generalization. In S. F. Warren & A. K. Rogers-Warren (Eds.), *Teaching functional language.* Austin, TX: Pro-Ed.

Warren, S. F., McQuarter, R. J., & Rogers-Warren, A. K. (1984). The effects of mands and models on the speech of unresponsive socially isolate children. *Journal of Speech and Hearing Disorders, 47,* 42–52.

Warren, S. F., Baxter, D., Anderson, S., Marshall, A., & Baer, D. (1981). Generalization and maintenance of question asking by severely retarded individuals. *Journal of the Association of the Severely Handicapped, 6,* 15–22.

Warren, S. F., & Rogers-Warren, A. K. (1985). Teaching functional language: An introduction. In Warren, S. F. and Rogers-Warren, A. K. (Eds.), *Teaching functional language.* Baltimore: University Park Press.

Warren, S. F., & Rogers-Warren, A. K. (1983). A longitudinal analysis of language generalization among adolescents with severely handicapping conditions. *The Journal of the Association for Persons with Severe Handicaps, 8,* 18–31.

Joan Miller
Mount St. Mary's College

Jan Allaire
University of Virginia

11

Augmentative Communication

The American Speech, Language and Hearing Association (1981) has estimated that more than 1½ million adults and children are unable to use speech effectively. Among the school-aged population, the largest categories of nonspeaking individuals are students classified as having multiple handicaps, severe or profound mental retardation, and/or autism (Bryen & Joyce, 1985; Matas, Mathy-Laikko, Beukelman, & Legresley, 1985).

When speech is not functional for such individuals, it becomes necessary to augment it or to provide an alternative means of expression. More than 100 different systems are available for this purpose (Silverman, 1980), known as augmentative, alternative, nonvocal, or nonspeech systems of communication. The first section of this chapter describes various types of augmentative systems commonly used with persons having severe and profound handicaps (SPH). The second section addresses issues related to selecting systems based on a goal of functional communication. The final section describes teaching approaches that are most suitable for training the student to a system within functional, daily activities.

TYPES OF AUGMENTATIVE COMMUNICATION

Augmentative systems fall into two major categories (Lloyd, 1985). Unaided systems are those in which the person uses some system of hand motions such as sign language or gestures, without using any sort of adaptive communication aid. Aided systems, the second category, are those in which the individual uses some sort of picture or word board, a notebook, or a computerized aid. Because unaided systems require no equipment other than the user's body, they are always available. In contrast, the user of an aided system depends on having the aid available in order to communicate.

Unaided Systems

Natural Gestures
Commonly understood gestures constitute one viable mode through which a student with severe

handicaps may communicate. Hamre-Nietupski and her colleagues (1977) have listed more than 160 natural gestures that are understandable to untrained persons, such as shaking a fist to express anger, shivering and rubbing crossed arms to indicate being cold, or pointing to an object to request or comment about it. These gestures are commonly used by people, with or without handicaps, to supplement speech.

Bryen and Joyce (1985) found general confusion between the terms "gestures" and "sign language" among individuals reporting the use of unaided systems with persons having severe handicaps. These two terms are not interchangeable. Natural gestures are not language per se; rather, they are pre- or extra-linguistic signals (Bryen & Joyce, 1985) that can be used to convey a particular, usually concrete (Lloyd, 1985), message in a particular context. In contrast, sign language is a *language* in which various grammatical and semantic rules govern the sequence and form in which its abstract symbols are produced. This distinction between natural gestures and sign language is an important one. Because sign language is symbolic and rule-based, a signer's messages will be understood only by others who have been trained in the same symbols and rules. Therefore, the target audience will be restricted in number. In contrast, untrained "listeners" can usually guess the meaning of gestures (Lloyd, 1985). Thus, the student with severe handicaps who gestures a given message may be more successful than a signer in having that message understood in community or vocational settings.

A second distinction between sign language and natural gestures is that signs tend to require a higher degree of fine motor control than do gestures (Hamre-Nietupski et al., 1977; Sailor et al., 1980). Limitations in the ability to manipulate one's hands and fingers independently may restrict the number and/or intelligibility of signs that an individual may be able to produce and therefore may lead to "sign articulation" problems that could impair successful communication (Dennis, Reichle, Williams, & Vogelsburg, 1982).

Despite their relative advantages in intelligibility and motor requirements, gestures have a serious disadvantage compared with sign language. While the latter has an unrestricted vocabulary that can be combined to express any idea, the number of messages that can be expressed through gestures is limited (Nietupski & Hamre-Nietupski, 1979).

Thus, a student would be able to convey fewer messages through gestures than through signs.

Signing Systems

Just as there are differences between natural gestures and sign language, there are differences among signing systems that have been used with persons who do not speak, particularly in their relationship to the English language. We will describe each briefly.*

Amer-Ind Amer-Ind is a manual system developed by Skelly (1979) for clinical use with people having communicative handicaps. Derived from American Indian Hand Talk, Amer-Ind is a manual code that has no grammatical or structural rules and, thus, is not a language (Kirschner, Algozzine, & Abbott, 1979; Skelly, 1979). Amer-Ind signals are based on general concepts rather than words. Thus, each signal has several related meanings. For example, the signal that represents the action "throw" also conveys the concepts *ball, game, play,* and *projectile* (Skelly, 1979). Particular advantages of Ameri-Ind are that 80% of its signals can be performed with only one hand (Musselwhite & St. Louis, 1982), and its signals tend to be highly concrete. They have been found to be more understandable to untrained observers than signs from American Sign Language (Kirschner et al., 1979).

American Sign Language Also known as ASL and Ameslan, American Sign Language was derived from a sign language developed in France and then brought to this country (Musselwhite & St. Louis, 1982). ASL is *not* a manual version of the English language, nor is it a worldwide sign language. It is a separate, self-contained language that differs from English and other languages in many significant ways: (a) it does not use English word order (the English statement "There is food in the store" would be expressed in ASL as "It store have food" [Shroyer, 1982, p., 4]; (b) it has no form of the verb *to be;* (c) it has no passive voice; (d) it uses no articles; (e) it marks verb tense for a whole conversation or segment of conversation, not for individual verbs; (f) it does not have signs for pronouns, but establishes the intended referent(s) in space; and (g) it can use movement in space to convey in one sign a subject + verb + object statement that would require three words in English (Fristoe & Lloyd,

---

*For more complete descriptions, see Mayberry (1976), Musselwhite and St. Louis (1982), and Wilbur (1979).

1977; Mayberry, 1976; Moores, 1974). Thus, the syntactic and semantic rules of ASL differ greatly from those of English.

Systems That Parallel English Several signing systems were specifically developed to parallel the English language. Referred to as systems of manually coded English (Lloyd, 1985), these alternatives include Signed English (Bornstein, Saulnier, & Hamilton,1983); Seeing Essential English, referred to as SEE[1], (Anthony, 1971); and Signing Exact English, referred to as SEE[2] (Gustason, Pfetzing, & Zawolkow, 1972). Often drawing their basic signs from those used in ASL, these systems differ significantly from ASL in that they use English word order and reflect English syntax and morphology (Musselwhite & St. Louis, 1982; Shroyer, 1982). Thus, these systems incorporate signs for affixes such as "–s" and "–ed," pronouns, and usually articles; however, these systems differ from each other in the rules used to reflect English structure and morphology. Other differences include rules for forming past particles, contractions, and plurals; the number of signs borrowed from ASL; the extent to which fingerspelling is allowed; the number of affixes included; and the rules for choosing or creating signs (Fristoe & Lloyd, 1977; Mayberry, 1976; Wilbur, 1979). See Figure 11.1 for an example of the word *eat* in various signing systems.

Given the many differences among these systems, Musselwhite and St. Louis (1982) have argued that signed English may be particularly suitable for individuals with severe handicaps because of its relative simplicity.

Research on Using Unaided Systems with Learners Having Severe and Profound Handicaps

Unaided nonspeech systems have been used extensively with persons having handicaps. Sign language, spoken language, and combined sign and speech were the most frequently reported types of unaided systems employed in language intervention research with this population during the 1970s (Bryen & Joyce, 1985); whereas sign language and gestural/emotional reactions were the most frequently used nonspeech systems reported by special education teachers and speech/language pathologists in a recent survey of one western state (Matas et al., 1985). Unaided systems have been taught to a variety of individuals with severe handicaps, preschoolers through adolescents having autism (Barrera, Lobato-Barrera, & Sulzer-Azaroff, 1980; Cohen, 1981; Remington & Clarke, 1983; Schepis et al., 1982); preschoolers and children classified as having developmental disabilities (Jago, Jago, & Hart, 1984; Willems, Lombardino, MacDonald, & Owens, 1982); and

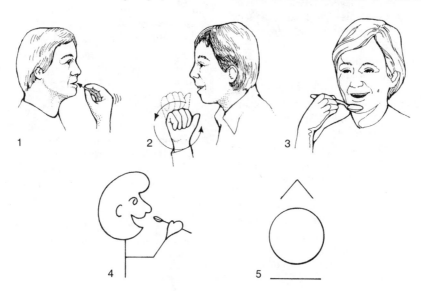

FIGURE 11.1 The word *eat* is shown in (1) American sign language (the Amer-Ind sign for *eat* is similar), (2) Signing Exact English (SEE[2]), (3) a line drawing, (4) rebus, and (5) Blissymbols.

Source: Illustration by John Owen.

preschoolers through adults with mild through profound retardation and/or individuals with multiple handicaps (Browder, Morris, & Snell, 1981; Daniloff & Schafer, 1981; Duker & Morsink, 1984; Duker & vanGrinsven, 1983; Faw, Reid, Schepis, Fitzgerald, & Welty, 1981; Kleinert & Gast, 1982; Oliver & Halle, 1982; Reichle, Rogers, & Barrett, 1984; Schepis et al., 1982; Sisson & Barrett, 1984; Weller & Mahoney, 1983). The majority of these studies have focused on single-word responses, usually in the form of labeling common objects of food items in response to "What is this?" or "What is the sign for—?" (Barrera et al., 1980; Browder et al., 1981; Daniloff & Schafer, 1981; Duker & Morsink, 1984; Faw et al., 1981; Kleinart & Gast, 1982; Reichle et al., 1984; Remington & Clarke, 1983; Schepis et al., 1982). Others have targeted two-word chains such as "doll sleep" or "ball throw" (Cohen, 1981; Duker & vanGrinsven, 1983), imitation of four-word sentences such as "The shirt is blue" (Sisson & Barrett, 1984), or general forms of *expressive* language (Jago et al., 1984; Willems et al., 1982). Vocabulary has been drawn from ASL (Barrera et al., 1980; Cohen, 1981; Reichle et al., 1984), Signed English (Browder et al., 1981), SEE$_1$, (Willems et al., 1982), See$_2$ (Oliver & Halle, 1982; Weller & Mahoney, 1983), Amer-Ind (Daniloff & Schafer, 1981), and gestures (Duker & vanGrinsven, 1983). However, because so many of the studies using sign language focused on one- or two-word responses from subjects, it appears that only single signs were selected and taught rather than syntactically correct combinations of signs or the linguistic rules governing each system. Thus, it is unclear whether persons with severe handicaps have acquired a sign language system per se. As noted by Bryen and Joyce (1985) and Fristoe and Lloyd (1978), it may be that there is still a good deal of confusion among practitioners regarding differences among signing systems and the need to make a judicious selection of the system to be used. Furthermore, there is considerable evidence that although persons with severe and profound handicaps have learned signs to label or request objects or events, there is far less evidence that they use these signs spontaneously in natural contexts (Bryen & Joyce, 1985).

Aided Systems

Aided systems vary tremendously in the type of motor response required to use the device (pointing to a symbol or pressing a switch until a marker arrives at the desired symbol) and in the type of messages displayed on the device (pictures, special symbols, or printed words). Because a practitioner needs to make separate but interrelated decisions for the three aspects of type of aid, response mode, and symbol system, each will be discussed in turn.

Types of Aids

Boards and Similar Aids* Basically, a communication board is any type of flat surface on which written or drawn symbols are displayed so that the user may choose among them, using a predetermined method of responding in order to communicate a specific message. Communication boards may take many forms. For the student who is just beginning communication training or who has a limited vocabulary, a single sheet may be used to display all symbols used by the student, as shown in Figure 11.2. According to Vicker (1974), the single-sheet display is easiest for the student to use and easiest for the practitioner to make and mount within a frame. Single-sheet displays may be fitted beneath plexiglass on the student's lap tray (Silverman, 1980), folded in half and equipped with handles for carrying (Detamore & Lippke, 1980), or reproduced several times so that one copy may be kept in each location frequented by the student, such as the home, classroom, cafeteria, or workshop.

Another option is to use "miniboards" (Bottorf & DePape, 1982), which are smaller, single-sheet displays of vocabulary pertinent to a specific environment or activity. One mini-board used by a 7-year-old girl with cerebral palsy was constructed for use during lunch. It contained symbols for "I'm full," "I need my washcloth," and "thank you," and allowed her to communicate what she wanted to eat (O'Brien & Andresen, 1983). Another miniboard used by five adolescents with moderate retardation was a 3- by 6-inch laminated card containing pictures of seven food items purchasable at a fast-food counter. Within 5 weeks, four of the five subjects met criterion on a task analysis that included steps for removing the card from a pocket, wallet, or purse; presenting the card at the fast food

---

*For more complete descriptions of display format and construction, see Mirenda (1985), Vicker (1974), and Waldo, Barnes, and Berry (1981).

FIGURE 11.2 A single-sheet design illustrates the learner's wants and needs. This board combines line drawings, Blissymbols, and a photograph.

counter; and pointing to the desired item to place the order (Christoph, Nietupski, & Pumpian, 1980).

Alternatives to single-sheet displays are possible for students whose vocabulary is large and who are able to turn pages or cards in some way. Multiple displays may be combined into one unit, such as a flip chart (Vicker, 1974), notebook (Detamore & Lippke, 1980), or set of wallet-sized cards attached to a key chain or metal ring (Silverman, 1980). Each sheet may be tabbed to help turn the pages or cards. Using a similar arrangement, Karel and her associates (1981) developed a wallet-sized set of flipcards for one student, grouping them in categories such as recreation activities and vocational items. The student was required to scan the tabs separating the categories, select the correct one, and then point to the desired drawing. Mirenda (1985) has reported a different variation of the tabbed communication notebook. For one adolescent, each category of pictures was placed on different colored pages (food on blue sheets, leisure/recreation on pink sheets). Corresponding color tabs containing a representative picture of each category (a blue tab with a picture of a meal on it) were used to mark the various

sections of the notebook. According to Mirenda (1985), the use of color-coded sheets and corresponding tabs decreased search time (the time it takes the user to locate a specific symbol) by nearly one third and encouraged the student to use the notebook more frequently.

The arrangement of symbols on either single-sheet or multiple displays will depend, in part, on the motor response to be used. If there are no constraints, symbols may be grouped according to syntactic function (subjects, verbs, prepositions, modifiers, objects) or so that frequently used words are most easily indicated. For the student who has developed sufficient skill to communicate two or more word messages and who is using a notebook or other multipage aid, the most frequently used symbols can be reproduced on each page or reproduced on the first page of each section (Mirenda, 1985). This type of arrangement can reduce search time by decreasing the need to flip back and forth among pages of the notebook. For example, people symbols (photos of the student, his parents, a classmate) and/or action symbols (eat, go, play) included in each section would enable the user to express agent-object ("Dad I ballgame"), action-object ("eat sandwich" or "play cards"), or more complex messages ("Dad and I go ballgame" or "Mom eat sandwich" [Mirenda, 1985]).

For the student with more restricted motor or perceptual skills, symbols can be arranged to accommodate particular needs. If a single-sheet display is used, the most frequently used symbols can be placed on the most easily reached part of the board to increase response speed (Waldo et al., 1981) and to decrease fatigue. If a notebook is used and if the student has difficulty crossing midline, symbols may be placed only on the front (for a right-handed student) or only on the back (for a left-handed student) of notebook sheets (Mirenda, 1985). Likewise, if a notebook is used and if the student has limited visual scanning skills, symbols can be displayed one-to-a-page or can be arranged in a top-to-bottom or a left-to-right format, depending on the arrangement that is more successful for the student (Mirenda, 1985).

A final point regarding boards or similar devices is in order. When a student uses the aid routinely, chances are that it will become worn, damaged, or misplaced. Therefore, the ease of replacing the board should be considered (Waldo et al., 1981), both in terms of materials used (light-weight plastic or laminated heavy paper) and the types of symbols displayed (photographs and magazine cutouts can be more difficult to replace than drawings, Bliss-symbols, or printed words). Although the student's learning needs must have priority over device-replacement needs when a system is being planned, a practitioner may consider ease of replacement in those situations in which other variables are equal. At the least, the planning sheet used to create the device should be kept in a permanent place so the aid can be reconstructed quickly if necessary (Waldo et al., 1981).

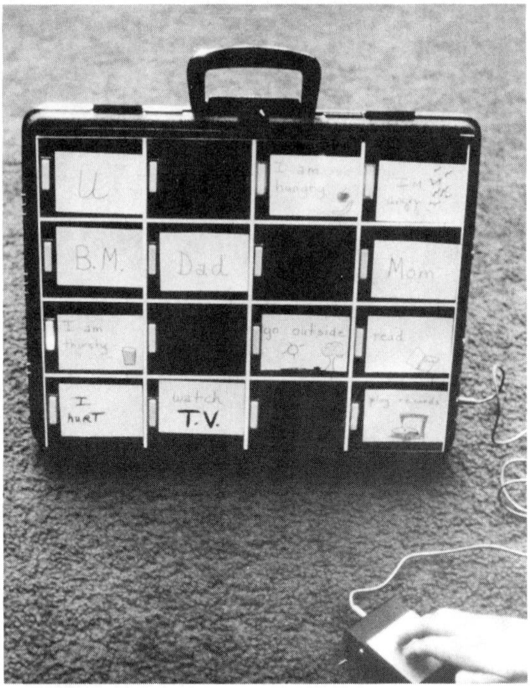

Electronic Aids* Including relatively simple home-made devices, commercially available "dedicated" aids, and personal computers, electronic aids are available for individuals who have severe motor impairments or who need to convey lengthy complex messages. Some electronic aids produce temporary visual output such as a movable light or pointer directed toward a specific symbol (see Figure 11.3). Others produce auditory output through artificial speech. Referred to as voice

FIGURE 11.3 When simple electronic scanning is used, as in the Zygo Communicator Model 16, a light moves serially across the squares until the user selects one by activating a switch.

output communication aids or VOCAs (Musselwhite & St. Louis, 1982), these devices may offer stored speech, reproduced from recordings of actual human speech. The Texas Instruments Vocaid (Eulenberg & Rosenfeld, 1982) is one example of this type. VOCAs may also produce synthesized speech, which is completely machine-generated, such as the Handivoice (Goodrich, 1979)*.

Other communication aids can produce both visual and auditory output such as the Words + Portable Voice II (News on aids, 1985). The micro-computer also falls into this category. It can use visual graphic or speech as an output mode and with various adaptations, can incorporate many of the switch options that would allow the person with motoric problems to use it easily. The computer offers numerous formats for not only communication purposes but instructional use as well. A computer can also be used by a person with motor

---

*For more complete descriptions, see *Communication Outlook*, Silverman (1980), and Taber (1983).

*For further explanations of artificial voice see Fons and Gargagliano (1981) and Miller (1985).

impairment to control the environment, performing such activities as turning lamps on and off, playing the radio, or answering a telephone (Taber, 1983). The myriad of uses of the computer offers versatility to such a student that was not possible in the past.

Response Modes

Just as there are many types of communication aids, there are many variations in the way the person without speech can use them. Methods of responding fall into three categories: direct selection, scanning, and encoding.

Direct Selection   Vanderheiden and Grilley (1976) describe this response as one in which the user directly indicates the message, usually by moving one body part, such as a fist or arm, in a pointing motion. For those students with adequate motor control, it offers the important advantage of being efficient and rapid; however, direct selection may not be possible for some persons with severe motor impairment.

Pointing with the index finger to a symbol or object is the most common way to select a bit of information. However, variations in pointing can be achieved using certain electronic systems or other body parts. Pressing a key on a typewriter, computer keyboard, or special communication aid such as a Handivoice allows the user to select a specific message directly. A student could also use an optical headpointer which, by using a small light and a specialized light-sensitive board, allows for efficient direct selection by lateral and vertical head movement (Vanderheiden, 1982a, b). Another possibility is for the student to use the eyes to focus on the symbol that needs to be communicated. This type of eyepointing (Connor, 1978) works when a clear piece of plexiglass is placed vertically before the student with various symbols around its outside border. (See Figure 11.4 for a variation of eyepointing.) This simple response can be used when motor deficits prevent valid and reliable pointing with the hands or arms.

Scanning   Scanning systems, which are quite common, may or may not be electronic. In its simplest form, scanning consists of a "listener's" asking the student a series of yes/no questions to which he makes some sort of predetermined response, such as head nodding, or eye movement (Musselwhite & St. Louis, 1982). Using scanning during a recreational activity, a teacher might ask "Do you want to listen to this record?" "Do you

FIGURE 11.4   Using dots of various colors around the periphery of a plexiglass sheet, a student learns to use eyepointing to encode a given message, matching the colored dot to the color outlining each picture.

want to play cards?" pausing after each question until the student shakes or nods his head, or blinks once (for yes) or twice (for no). This form of human-aided scanning or communication code (Nietupski & Hamre-Nietupski, 1979) can be used by almost any student with severe handicaps because it requires only one reliable motor response. However, the "20 questions" variety of scanning can be very trying for both the nonspeaking person and the "listener" until the latter hits upon the right question.

A second variety of scanning, in which electronic or computerized devices are used, provides greater independence for the student compared with human-aided scanning. Electronic scanning systems usually involve a light or marker of some sort that systematically scans through rows and columns of vocabulary when the user activates a switch. The speed and direction of the scanner can often be adapted to reduce search (see Musselwhite & St. Louis, 1982, and Vanderheiden, 1981).

Even with techniques for reducing search time, scanning still tends to require more time than direct selection; however, like human-aided scanning, electronic scanning requires only one reliable motor response. Thus, it can provide almost any person with severe handicaps some degree of independence during communication. Usually, the motor response required for electronic scanning entails activating a switch of some sort, such as pressing a lever with one's hand or arm, moving one's head to activate a tilt switch or to lean against a pressure-sensitive pillow, or pushing a foot pedal (see Figure 11.5. Also see Silverman [1980] for a more complete description.)*

Encoding   The third general category of response mode is encoding, a system that uses a response panel of some sort and a separate list of coded vocabulary. The coded vocabulary may be memorized or placed on a chart that is visible to both parties. The response panel may be a flat board of some sort partitioned into color and/or number-coded squares large enough to accommodate a fistpoint or other gross pointing action. In ETRAN, with which the student uses eye gaze, the response panel is a large square of clear plexiglass mounted vertically at the student's eye level with a code system of colors, numbers, or letters displayed around the edge.

To use encoding, the student chooses a message, looks up or remembers the code for the message, and then communicates that code using the response panel. If a student is using a symbol board with 100 vocabulary items, each item could be coded with a color and number. If the student looks at number *5* and *red,* he would be communicating symbol 5-red. The listener would then consult the vocabulary chart to find that *5-red* means "thirsty."

A strategic advantage of encoding is that it allows for a much larger vocabulary than do most direct-selection or scanning systems, inasmuch as a set of 10 numbers, letters, and colors may be used to code many different words or messages. However, encoding requires a multistep response with rather complex representational

---

*Switches can be used not only to control scanning devices, voice synthesizers, and environmental control units, but also tape recorders, (May, 1983), video games (Powers & Ball, 1983), and a variety of mechanical toys as well (Meehan, Mineo & Lyon, 1985; Wacker, Berg, Wiggins, Muldoon, & Cavanaugh, 1985). Thus, switch-based activities can become an essential component of individualized educational programs (IEPs) for many multihandicapped students, particularly because there are now several resources available on how to construct switches and connect them to adaptive equipment or toys. Two such resources, directed toward people who do not know much about soldering and wiring, are Burkhart's books (1980, 1984) on battery-powered toys and equipment and a set of illustrated manuals on how to make microlever, pneumatic, and momentary pull switches as well as a tone generator that signals when a switch has been activated (Artificial Language Laboratory, 1985).

and sequencing skills that would make it inappropriate for many students.

Symbol Systems

Symbols (or objects) of some sort must be displayed on a communication device so that the user can select or compose the message he wishes to convey. We will describe options more commonly used with students having severe handicaps.

Objects   Some students may not yet understand that pictures can be used to refer to objects or events. For students such as this, it is possible to use objects as part of the array to teach a generalized "I want that" message. Objects cannot be the sole source of communication stimuli in this case because the student must use a different type of symbol for "want," such as an index card containing the Blissymbol (Keogh & Reichle, 1985) or the manual sign (Reichle, Rogers, & Barrett, 1984) for "want." However, when the "want" symbol is combined with a cafeteria tray of preferred items, the objects become communicative stimuli as well as enabling the student to use direct selection of the desired item to complete the "I want that" message. As described later, objects and events can often be manipulated in their natural contexts to elicit similar types of communication.

Photographs   Photographs of a student's cup, a preferred game, or a favorite snack may be useful as communication "symbols." To help a student realize the relationship between the photograph and its physical referent, Dixon (1981) found that cutting out the figure of the photograph and training cutout-to-object matching was highly effective for three out of four adolescents with severe retardation. She also found that the three subjects generalized this skill rather quickly to matching whole photographs with objects. Thus, photo cutouts may be a useful transition for some students between objects and photographs.

Pictures   Pictures are one of the most commonly used symbol systems. They may be drawn by hand, cut out of magazines, or purchased expressly for use on a communication aid*.

Some students may need to use exact-match pictures (a picture of a cup to represent the one the student routinely uses for juice). Others may be

---

*See Mirenda (1985) for a listing of commercially available line drawings.

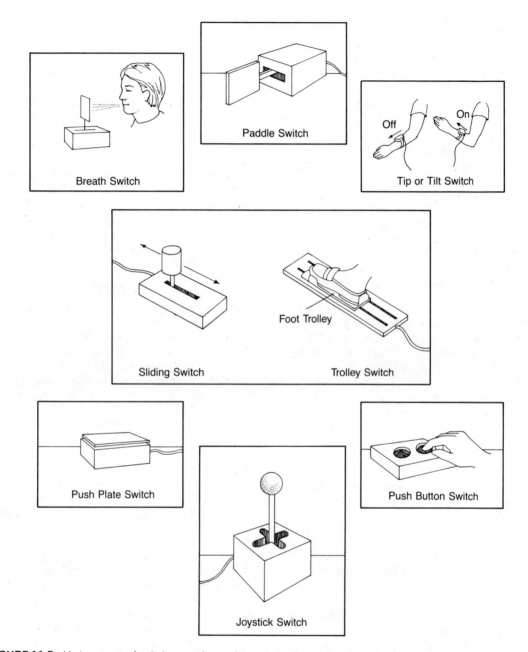

FIGURE 11.5 Various types of switches may be used to activate electronic communication systems or battery-powered leisure materials such as toys or tape recorders. If a student has a reliable motor response, a switch may be found.

Source: From "Interface Switch Profile and Annotated List of Commercial Switches," by C. Holt, D. Buelow, & G. Vanderheiden, 1978. In G. Vanderheiden (Ed.), *Nonvocal communication resource book.* Baltimore: University Park Press. Reprinted with permission.

able to use nonidentical-match pictures (a picture of a cup to represent any liquid refreshment). In either case, many drawings have the inherent advantage of being iconic: they tend to resemble their referent. If a drawing is not iconic, it should be labeled with its corresponding word to enable the "listener" to interpret the message (Musselwhite & St. Louis, 1982).

Rebus Symbols Often iconic in nature (Hurlbut, Iwata, & Green, 1982), rebus symbols are used to represent entire words or parts of words. They may be *concrete*, such as the picture of a girl's face to mean "girl"; *relational*, such as a ball on top of a box to mean "on"; or *abstract*, such as a dash (-) to mean "is." Suffixes, such as "-ing" and "-s," are written out in traditional orthography with this system. Clark, Davies, and Woodcock (1974) have published a standardized set of more than 800 rebuses.

Blissymbolics This concept-based system uses standardized symbols that, in some cases, are similar to the objects or events they represent. Such standardized line drawings as a house, a chair, and a heart are used. However, many other symbols are not immediately guessable but are *translucent:* they make sense once the untrained observer has been told the meaning (Luftig & Bersani, 1985). Other Blissymbols are *opaque,* bearing no resemblance to their referents. Individual symbols may be combined to denote specific states of other symbols. For example, a wheel placed under a chair conveys "wheelchair"; a verb marker placed over a circle conveys "to eat" rather than the noun "food" (see Figure 11.1, illustration 5). In general, Blissymbols are not guessable to untrained people and are only moderately *translucent* (Luftig & Bersani, 1985). This attribute may affect the willingness of people in community and vocational settings to interact with the student who uses Blissymbols, though the written word always accompanies the symbol.

Although easier to learn than printed words, Blissymbols were more difficult to learn than rebus symbols for preschool children without handicaps (Clark, 1981). With three adolescents having severe retardation and cerebral palsy, Hurlbut et al. (1982) found that faster learning, less retraining, greater generalization, and more spontaneous usage occurred for line drawings compared with Blissymbols. (See Clark [1984] for a comparison between rebus and Blissymbols.)

Traditional Orthography For students who can read, the printed word can be used to express any message. Traditional orthography may be used as the primary symbol system, particularly with computers and/or voice output devices. Some children with severe physical disabilities are being taught to read using this type of equipment (Bruno & Goodman, 1983; Coon & Lambert, 1985), whereas others have used traditional orthography and computers for highly sophisticated purposes (Eulenberg, 1985). However, traditional orthography can also be used to supplement other symbol systems or to replace other symbols once the student has become adept at using them. Mithaug and Liberty (1980) demonstrated this type of approach with one 20-year-old woman with Down syndrome and severe retardation. The woman had been using a ring-held set of cards as her communication system. Seven of the cards contained pictures of relevant vocabulary for her prevocational classroom (record player, lunchbox, and hammer). Another three cards contained hand-printed words for messages not easily conveyed through pictures, such as "P.E." (physical education), "help," and "good morning." Because the woman was adept at using both the pictures and words within natural contexts, Mithaug and Liberty (1980) taught her to recognize lower case, primary-sizes, typed sight words for all of her cards, using a "Show me (the word for . . .)" training task. The woman learned all 10 words, generalized seven of them to upper case, pica-sized type and used the printed word cards in natural contexts with the same accuracy she had shown previously with the picture system. Thus, this woman acquired a more "normative" symbol system.

Research on Using Aided Systems with Learners Having Severe and Profound Handicaps

Communication boards and similar devices appear to be used more frequently than electronic devices (Matas et al., 1985) and have been used predominantly with direct selection through (a) finger- or thumb-pointing (Hurlbut et al., 1982; Kohl & Stettner-Eaton, 1985; Light, Collier, & Parnes, 1985a, b; Oliver, 1983; Reichle & Yoder, 1985; Romski, Sevcik, & Rumbaugh, 1985; Song, 1979); (b) using a head pointer or head-held lightbeam (Hurlbut et al,. 1982; Reid and Hurlbut, 1977); (c) using eyepointing (Elder & Bergman, 1978; Light et al., 1985a); or (d) finding the right card in a set or the right page in a notebook (Breen, Haring, Pitts-Conway, & Gaylord-Ross, 1985; Goetz, Gee, & Sailor, 1985; Mithaug & Liberty, 1980; Murphy, Steele, Gilligan, Yeow, & Spars, 1977). Direct selection with boards or similar devices has been used by persons with moderate or severe retardation (Goetz et al., 1985; Kohl & Stettner-Eaton, 1985; Mithaug & Liberty, 1980; Oliver, 1983; Reichle & Yoder, 1985; Romski et al., 1985); autism (Breen et al., 1985); retardation and autism (Murphy et al., 1977); cerebral palsy (Light et al., 1985a); or cerebral palsy and mental retardation (Elder & Bergman, 1978; Hurlbut et al., 1982; Reid & Hurlbut, 1977; Song, 1979). A color- or number-encoding system was used with fist- or eye-pointing by some of the 4-to-6-year-olds with cerebral palsy but no mental retardation in one study (Light et al., 1985a).

Although cited less frequently, electronic aids have been used with individuals having cerebral palsy and mental retardation (Beukelman, Yorkston, & Dowden, 1985; Kucherawy & Kucherawy, 1978) or who were functioning within a normal cognitive range (Harris, 1982; O'Brien & Andresen, 1983). Devices used with these individuals include (a) a pressure-sensitive, enlarged keyboard connected to an Apple computer with a voice synthesizer for vocal output of the picture or photograph pressed by the user (Beukelman et al., 1985)' (b) a home-made rotary scanner mounted on the bed of a nonambulatory woman who used pictures and printed words as well as an "I want" card to convey her needs (Kucherawy & Kucherawy, 1978); and (c) commercially available communication aids such as the Auto-Com (Harris, 1982) and the Zygo (O'Brien & Andresen, 1983). Thus, individuals using electronic aids have used either direct selection (Beukelman et al., 1985; Harris, 1982) or scanning (Kucherawy & Kucherawy, 1978; O'Brien & Andresen, 1983). However, all of the individuals who used electronic aids were also reported to use other nonspeech systems to supplement their aids, including eyepointing (Kucherawy & Kucherawy, 1978); human-aided scanning, limited signing, and typing (Beukelman et al., 1985); and gestures, gross pointing, and some vocalizations (Harris, 1982; O'Brien & Andresen, 1983).

A variety of symbol systems have been used including (a) photographs (Reid & Hurlbut, 1977); (b) line drawings (Goetz et al., 1985; Kohl & Stettner-Eaton, 1985; Murphy et al., 1977; Reichle & Yoder, 1985); (c) Blissymbols (Elder & Bergman, 1978; Kohl & Stettner-Eaton, 1985; O'Brien & Andresen, 1983; Oliver, 1983; Song, 1979); (d) combinations of photographs, words, and drawings (Beukelman et al., 1985) or combinations of drawings and Blissymbols (Hurlbut et al., 1982; Light et al., 1985a); (e) abstract, rule-based symbols such as Non-Slip (Hodges & Deich, 1978; Porter & Schroeder, 1980) and yerkish lexigrams (Romski et al., 1985)*; and (f) traditional orthography used for complete statements (Breen et al., 1985) or for single words to replace pictures or to represent abstract ideas (Kucherawy & Kucherawy, 1978; Mithaug & Liberty, 1980). Target skills included (a) "Show me (the symbol for this object)" or *receptive* labeling (Elder & Bergman, 1978; Oliver, 1983); (b) "What is this (object)" or *expressive* labeling, requiring selection of the correct symbol (Hurlbut et al., 1982; Kucherawy & Kucherawy, 1978; Reid & Hurlbut, 1977); (c) "What do you want" or *requesting*, labeling requiring selection of an appropriate symbol (Goetz et al., 1985; Reichle & Yoder, 1985); and (d) general language usage in natural contexts (Harris, 1982; Light et al., 1985a,b; Mithaug & Liberty, 1980; Romski et al., 1985). Within natural contexts young children with severe and profound handicaps have been observed to use their aids with or without other nonspeech modes to request objects or actions, to answer questions, and to clarify their own statements when asked. In more structured social interactions, they have also been observed to greet and/or say good-bye to others, and to request information; however, observers have also noted that the children initiated interactions infrequently, made few social comments, rarely asked for information or clarification, and/or rarely interacted with each other. Parents and teachers tended to control interactions and to engage in question asking, thus placing the children in a passive, respondent role (Harris, 1982; Light et al., 1985a,b). With older children and adults having moderate to profound retardation, a similar pattern of aid user as respondent rather than initiator was found (Calculator & Dollaghen, 1982). In addition, when these individuals did use their boards to initiate, their messages tended to be just as ambiguous as when they used nonboard modes (yes/no head movements or vocalizations).

---

*See Musselwhite and St. Louis (1982) for descriptions of these less commonly used systems.

CHOOSING NONSPEECH SYSTEMS

Given the many augmentative systems available, choosing appropriate communication modes for a student can be a complex and long-range process. Major components of this process will be discussed from a perspective of setting a clearly fixed goal and then making all decisions in relationship to this goal.

The Goal of Communication Training

In recent years, the focus of language and communication intervention has shifted from teaching specific language content within one-to-one, isolated settings to training everyday language usage within natural settings. (Campbell, Stremel-Campbell, & Rogers-Warren, 1985; Warren & Rogers-Warren, 1985b). A major reason for this shift has been increasing evidence that nonfunctional communication skills or skills acquired under isolated conditions do not generalize to natural settings (Campbell et al., 1985). During specially designated "communication training," for instance, students may learn to label common objects using a picture communication board while not using these same labels to request desired objects throughout the rest of the day (Reichle & Yoder, 1985).

In view of accumulated evidence that many students with severe handicaps fail to generalize newly acquired communication skills on their own, Warren and Rogers-Warren (1985a) have stated the case succinctly: "At this point in the development of intervention strategies, teaching procedures that do not produce generalized use in natural settings can no longer be considered effective" (pp. xi–xii).

A variety of teaching techniques (to be discussed later) have emerged as effective means of teaching a student to generalize communication skills to the natural environment (see Figure 11.6). These techniques share the goal of developing "functional language," that is, language used in everyday settings to communicate with and influence the behavior of other people in those settings (Schiefelbusch, 1985; Warren & Rogers-Warren, 1985a). This goal of teaching functional language must be the underpinning for all programming decisions, including what will be taught, where it will be taught, and who will teach it (Reichle & Keogh, 1985). For students who do not speak, the goal of

functional language must also guide the selection of augmentation systems.

Assessing Communication Needs

To enable a student with severe handicaps to develop functional language, it is essential that the teacher first identify his specific communication needs. These will include the settings in which, people with whom, and purposes for which he will need to communicate.

Beukelman, Yorkston, and Dowden (1985) have developed a needs assessment guide to be used during an interview with the person without speech, his family, and other important communication partners. The guide addresses several facets of particular needs such as positioning factors, communication partners, location, message needs, and modality of communication. During the interview, each "needs statement" is assessed for whether the person currently has a means of satisfying the need and whether the need is mandatory, desirable, unimportant, or potentially mandatory in the future. These data are then used to match the individual's needs to available augmentative systems, with mandatory needs receiving highest priority.

A top-down curriculum approach (Brown et al., 1979), as described in Chapter 4, provides another framework for assessing communication needs. Beginning with an inventory of students' homes, schools, and communities, Hamre-Nietupski et al. (1977) identified important activities as well as words frequently used by others within those contexts. Based on this information, Hamre-Nietupski et al., selected the most appropriate communication content for each student and targeted naturally occurring opportunities for training. Thus, if the survey revealed that people frequently made requests during mealtimes, the student would be taught this skill by the trainer's placing a preferred food within sight but out of reach and then prompting the student to convey "I want" using a gesture, sign, or communication board. (See Table 11.1 for another application of the top-down curriculum approach to assessing communication needs.)

For students who are "difficult to teach" (those who have failed to learn from previous training, have severe motor impairments, or are passive toward the environment), communication may need to begin at the level of expressing wants and needs (Keogh & Reichle, 1985). Two methods

FIGURE 11.6 Using an augmentative system, a severely handicapped child can "ham it up" as well as the next person. In this case, a pocket chart used in the home provides an easy means of altering vocabulary as needs dictate.

of assessing communication needs for these students have been demonstrated. In the first, a reinforcer-preference task is used systematically to identify motivating objects or events that can be used later to train as "I want that" type of response. The reinforcer preference task may consist of (a) presenting a cafeteria tray containing assorted edibles, leisure materials, fashion accessories or other objects, and recording the item selected within 10 seconds for each trial, with objects rearranged and/or replaced before the next trial (Keogh & Reichle, 1985; Reichle & Yoder, 1985); (b) presenting a series of events or objects such as hearing a watch beep, lying on a heating pad, looking in a mirror, or having some coffee, and recording for each whether the subject reached or moved toward the stimulus within 5 (or 10) seconds (Pace, Ivancic, Edwards, Iwata, & Page, 1985); or (c) placing a mercury tilt switch on a student's arm

or hand, correcting it to a variety of battery-powered or electrical games and toys, and recording the frequency and total duration of switch activation per game/toy (Wacker et al., 1985). In all three versions of the reinforcer preference task, blocks of trials are conducted across days to identify several consistently chosen objects of events.

A second method of assessing communication needs by using a motivational framework was demonstrated wtih two students having severe retardation. Goetz, Gee, and Sailor (1985) focused on eliciting communication behaviors within daily routines by assessing the students' motivation to engage in those routines. After selecting tasks in which the students engaged each day, each student was interrupted at predetermined points in the sequence of task steps by physically stopping the student or removing a needed material. A student was judged to be motivated toward a task if he

TABLE 11.1 A partial top-down curriculum

Domain:	Community
Environment:	School
Subenvironment:	1. Cafeteria
Activity:	1.1 Getting lunch
Skills:	a. Get a tray of food
	b. Put napkin, utensils, straw, and milk on tray
	c. Present meal card
Activity:	1.2 Eating
Skills:	a. Find a place to sit
	b. Open milk carton
	c. Eat with fork and spoon
	d. Use napkin
	e. Clean up
Subenvironment:	2. Playground Area
Activity:	2.1 Playing group games
Skills:	a. Catch/throw a ball
	b. Play adapted volleyball
Activity:	2.2 Playing alone
Skills:	a. Move wheelchair over grass
	b. Take pictures with a camera
Domain:	Domestic
Environment:	Home
Subenvironment:	1. Kitchen
Activity:	1.1 Eating with family
Skills:	a. Pass food to others
	b. Cut meat
Activity:	1.2 Cleaning
	a. Assist in clearing table
	b. Dry and store dinner utensils
Subenvironment:	2. Bedroom
Activity:	2.1 Getting dressed/undressed
Skills:	a. Take off slacks
	b. Take off pullover shirt
	c. Put on pullover shirt
	d. Put on slip-on shoes

consistently attempted to complete it (by reaching around the observer or by taking the material back) and if he displayed a moderate degree of distress. Three different tasks per student were identified using this approach and then they were taught communication board or notebook responses to "What do you want?" during daily task performance.

Approaches to Choosing Systems

Once the teacher has generated a list of specific communication needs, he is in a position to consider ways of meeting them. Three different approaches to selecting appropriate augmentative systems are available.

The first approach to choosing systems is to use "decision rules" (Chapman & Miller, 1977; Shane & Bashir, 1980). Besides addressing the question of whether a student is cognitively or linguistically ready to begin augmentative communication, decision rules have traditionally recommended signing over aid usage if possible (Nietupski & Hamre-Nietupski, 1979; Sailor et al., 1980).

The second approach is to use "mixed-mode communication," selecting an aided or unaided mode depending on the specific communication need and the iconicity of available symbols or signs. After extensively reviewing various decision rules and concluding that using such rules can lead to faulty decisions, Reichle and Karlan (1985) have recommended mixed-mode communication as a means of preventing serious communication deficits from developing and of taking advantage of the relative benefits of various systems while avoiding some of their limitations. Hamre-Nietupski et al. (1977) have advocated use of mixed-mode communication to allow for a wider range of communication partners, including individuals who do not understand signing or the written word. Simultaneous training in more than one system can also provide an objective basis for selecting one system over another if one proves to be more efficient for a student (Hamre-Nietupski, Nietupski, & Rathe, 1986).

The third approach is to use aided systems rather than signing whenever possible. Reversing their previous "decision rule" (Sailor et al., 1980) for choosing signing over communication boards, Sailor and Guess (1983) now advise that signing seriously impairs both integration and functional communication in natural settings because most people do not understand signs. Sailor and Guess strongly recommend the use of boards and notebooks, both because they can be used in natural settings and because they appear to motivate students with severe handicaps to develop functional and complex language skills. Communication boards have also been cited as the system of choice for certain groups of these students. In particular, addressing the more concrete pictorial systems, Mirenda (1985) has pointed out that pictorial aids are more suitable for students who have better visual than auditory processing skills, who need a longer lasting stimulus than that provided through speech or signing, and who understand concrete images more easily than symbolic representations. Taking this perspective one step further, Keogh and Reichle (1985) have recommended picture boards for students who are just beginning communication instruction. According to Keogh and Reichle, students who are difficult to teach can use picture boards to acquire functional requesting ("want" + object) and describing skills (responding to "What's this?") without needing to produce, or even understand, labels for common environmental stimuli.

Making Data-Based Decisions

In light of the ultimate goal of enabling the student to use functional communication in everyday situations, we believe that mixed mode communication, probably with greater reliance on aided systems, is the most promising approach. However, we are also convinced that the only way to be sure that an augmentative system is appropriate is to measure the student's acquisition and daily use of that system.

An appropriate beginning point is to select from the list of a student's communication needs those that are mandatory (Beukelman et al., 1985) and/or frequently used (Hamre-Nietupski et al., 1977); or, for students who are difficult to teach, those that are most likely to reinforce requesting and describing behaviors (Keogh & Reichle, 1985; Goetz et al., 1985). The next step is to ". . . eliminate from consideration approaches that clearly do not meet the specific needs of the nonspeaking individual, even though that individual may have the capability to use the approach" (Beukelman et al., 1985, p. 10). Thus, if a student's daily routine requires moving from setting to setting, a table-top computer would not be an efficient choice with which to begin instruction. Similarly, if a student needs to interact with peers who are not handicapped in a structured leisure activity or to place an order at a fast-food restaurant, signing can be eliminated as an effective way to meet these needs.

Once the practitioner has narrowed the choices to systems that would be viable for a given set of needs, he must consider the student's cognitive, language, motor, and visual capabilities. Assessment conducted for this purpose need not be exhaustive. Instead of assessing the student's maximum level of performance in each of these areas, testing should focus on whether he has *enough* ability to use a particular system according to Beukelman et al., 1985. These researchers have honed their user assessment process so they now

use the display of the actual system they are considering to determine how large the display needs to be or where the symbols might best be placed to accommodate visual and motoric needs.

Screening Tasks

Systematic screening tasks can be designed to determine the student's ability to use a particular system and/or how best to design the system for particular needs. For example, if a single-sheet display for a lapboard would satisfy initial needs using changeable overlays of setting-specific vocabulary, the practitioner might (a) prepare a pointing board by dividing a rectangular surface into 10 spaces and numbering each (Waldo et al., 1981); (b) test the student's ability to touch each area by indicating a square and saying, "Touch here" (Reid & Hurlbut, 1977) or placing a small reinforcer in the square and saying, "Get the _____" (Sailor et al., 1980); (c) recording the number of seconds required for a correct response and whether the student maintained the response for 2 seconds without tremors or extraneous movements (Waldo et al., 1981); and (d) conducting repeated trials across all 10 squares in random order. This last step is necessary to determine whether fatigue sets in (as reflected through increasing extraneous movements and/or increased response latency) and to identify those areas of the board that are fastest for the student to access and therefore are suitable for most frequently needed vocabulary items. Based on data collected through this task, the practitioner can then divide the board into a larger or smaller number of cells and repeat the screening to determine the number of vocabulary items that could be included. If fingerpointing had been too limited, the practitioner could also retest for a different type of pointing response such as fistpointing, thumbpointing, sliding a pointer of some sort across the board using an upright dowel secured to the pointer, using a head-held lightbeam, using the other hand, or even eye gaze.

Although this example pertains just to single board displays, it illustrates some key elements necessary for systematic screening of other systems as well. These elements include focusing on a system that would fulfill practical needs; breaking down the response into small, observable parts; conducting an initial screening; and using the data generated by the initial task to vary and re-test those components that are not yet satisfactory.

Symbol Selection

The same data-based procedures may be used to select the specific symbols needed by the subject. Suppose that a target skill for a young student is to be able to convey whether he is full at mealtimes or whether he wants more food. Because this child eats the vast majority of meals at home or in school, and because his family has expressed a willingness to learn some signing, signing may be an efficient mode for this particular communication need. To test this possibility, the practitioner may choose a few messages that would serve this need such as "more," "please," or "give me" and then survey available signing systems to identify signs for these messages. The practitioner would then need to select those which research has suggested are most easily learnable. These would include signs that are iconic or at least translucent, involve contact between the hand and another body part, do not involve a series of movements, and are motorically dissimilar to other signs the student may use (Dennis et al., 1982; Doherty, 1985). Once potentially useful signs have been identified, the practitioner can systematically test them to see which one the student produces most clearly and efficiently across 2 or 3 days of repeated trials. Thus, the practitioner could model the various signs in random order while saying, "Do this" for each and then record the response latency and a clarity rating for the student's imitation. Once the most useful sign has been identified, the practitioner can begin to teach it within the context of mealtimes, perhaps adding the gesture of head shaking for "no" to teach the equivalent of "no more."

Selection of graphic symbols may proceed in a similar fashion although probably for several vocabulary items at a time. Suppose, for instance, that a tabbed notebook, organized into categories of vocabulary, might serve a student's needs during leisure training at a video arcade, community training at a mall, and while having lunch at school with nonhandicapped peers. Also suppose that a single-board display would be practical if posted on the refrigerator of the group home where the student receives domestic training. After having listed messages the student will need in these settings, the practitioner can use a procedure similar to that developed by Beukelman et al. (1985) for symbol selection. Using a hierarchy of symbol abstractness, each target message is systematically tested to see whether the student can recognize it when depicted as a printed word, Blissymbol, line drawing, or photograph. Then the most abstract image recognized by the subject is selected. However, because the notebook would be used heavily in integrated community settings, the practitioner should include Blissymbols during assessment only if they are clearly iconic. In contrast, we would include Blissymbols during evaluation of messages for the refrigerator board in the group home because there would be few communication partners in this setting, and they would be more likely to know Blissymbols.

Thus far, the outcome of the selection process has been described as if results will be clearcut. For many students, this will not be the case, as when a student does not imitate any signs correctly or does not readily recognize any of the graphic symbols for a given message. In such instances, the practitioner may need to consider another system that would be functional for the target communication needs; however, it may be more efficient to train the student in the target response for a fixed amount of time before making such a decision. The data generated through such training can be used to determine whether the student can develop a sufficient response and whether he has sufficient cognition to acquire the system, whatever the cognitive requirements may be (cf. Reichle & Karlan, 1985).

When screening indicates that two or three response or symbol options are equally viable but insufficient for daily use, a multielement design is especially useful (See Chapter 4. Also see Hamre-Nietupski et al. [1986] for a detailed application of this design.)

Consider the example in which a student does not recognize pictures or photographs of objects he will need in daily settings. In this case, the practitioner could prepare both a picture and a photograph of each object and then, during separate, randomly sequenced training sessions each day, train both the set of pictures and the set of photographs. By collecting probe data each day on the number of correct independent responses per set, the practitioner will be able to select one type of symbol over the other for further training, once a clear pattern of responding emerges. A similar procedure could be used to select printed words versus Blissymbols for messages that cannot be represented through pictures ("give me" or "help") or to choose which sign to select if a student approximates more than one with equal efficiency.

Selecting Systems: An Example

To illustrate the selection process, let us look at one student. This example focuses on the *types* of factors and decisions involved; it is in no way intended to represent the "right" answers for all severely handicapped students.

Susan, a 12-year-old girl, has cerebral palsy and retardation. She is not ambulatory and has better use of her arms and hands than her legs. She uses a wheelchair, a standing table, and an adapted chair during her school day in a classroom for students with severe and profound handicaps in a regular public school. Susan's class is self-contained but is integrated with 6th grade for lunch and recess. She lives with her parents and two siblings (ages 10 and 4) in a suburb.

Table 11.1, a partial, top-down curriculum for Susan, shows several natural contexts for communication. In the cafeteria, Susan might ask for help in opening her milk carton or cutting her meat. On the playground, she might ask school mates to play catch or push her over a bump in the grass. Susan would not only need to respond if asked to join in a game, but she would also need to ask for assistance. At home, Susan will at least need to understand directions for wiping the table, drying dinner utensils, and getting dressed or undressed. She will need to ask for food to be passed to her and might want to tell her family about children at school or in the neighborhood. She might also need to tell her brother to stop teasing her or might want to ask to listen to the stereo in the evening. Thus, Susan will require a system available in her kitchen and bedroom at home and in the cafeteria and playground area at school. Were Susan's complete curriculum presented in Table 11.1 it would indicate that she will need to communicate in many other areas as well, such as her living room and backyard at home; the classroom, school bus, and gymnasium at school; her grandparents' home; a neighbor's swimming pool; and a restaurant frequented by her family. Thus, Susan needs a highly portable means of communicating. Because she needs to communicate with her family, classmates, and neighborhood peers every day her method of communicating must be understandable to many others, at least some of whom will not know sign language or how to read.

It is also apparent that Susan needs an expandable system. Examination of Susan's completed top-down curriculum would show many words and word chains she will need. Because she will not learn all of these words at once, her communication system must allow for expansion of vocabulary as she acquires trained items and as additional sub-environments, activities, and skills become relevant.

Given Susan's needs for a portable system that would be understandable to a variety of people, the speech/language therapist, teacher, and physical therapist eliminated signing and electronic aids from initial consideration. They then agreed that a notebook system would satisfy most of her immediate needs.

In screening for a symbol system, the teacher found that 1-inch square images would be appropriate. Line drawings were chosen because Susan could associate at least some with their referents, because they were easily produced, and because most peers and family members would be able to recognize them. Each picture would be labeled with its word underneath. Because screening revealed that Susan could use direct selection using thumbpointing, these pictures could be placed in a small notebook under sheets of clear plastic. The notebook could be placed in a side pocket on her wheelchair to move from place to place, but would be on her lap tray at other times (see Figure 11.7).

In addition, a wallet-sized packet of the same line drawings would be given to Susan's parents for use at home or in the community. Information on frequency of use, need for expandability, and feasibility of the symbol system would be gathered while Susan used this initial system. Later, Susan might be considered a likely candidate for an electronic system using synthesized speech to communicate in her classroom, home, grandparents' home, and community.

However, because of the limitations imposed by her pictorial system (it must be immediately available, other people must be able to interpret pictures, and it must be as acceptable as possible in various settings), a second form of communication, such as natural gestures, would accompany it. Thus, Susan could learn the gestures for "stop," "give me," and "come here" (described by Hamre-Nietupski et al., 1977). Therefore, she would have a second way to make her needs known when her communication book was unavailable. Finally, Susan would be trained to say "ah" to signal people to come over and interact with her. Had she not been able to vocalize one sound reliably, we would have targeted hitting a bell on her

FIGURE 11.7 Susan might use a conversation notebook like this, although probably smaller.

lapboard as a signal, inasmuch as users of aided systems are seriously limited unless they can gain the attention of others (Light et al., 1985a,b; Reichle et al., 1984).

Thus, Susan's initial modes of communication would include a picture conversation book, natural gestures, and vocalizing. These systems may be temporary and only give her instructors data about other plausible systems. Nevertheless, they allow her an immediate and effective means of communicating within her daily routine.

TEACHING FUNCTIONAL COMMUNICATION

Because the goal of intervention is to enable the student to communicate effectively in everyday situations and because research results have repeatedly demonstrated that students with severe and profound handicaps do not generalize acquired skills unless taught to do so, communication training must be included within naturally occurring contexts. A set of teaching techniques for this

purpose has been developed originally for use with language-delayed children who use spoken language. Recently, an empirical basis has begun to emerge for using these techniques with users (with severe handicaps) of augmentative systems (Klein et al., 1981; Oliver & Halle, 1982). Within each description, therefore, we have inserted, in brackets, adaptations that would be appropriate for augmentative communication training.

Types of Naturalistic Teaching

Incidental Teaching
According to this strategy, the student initiates an interaction, which the teacher then uses as an occasion for training. When the student somehow conveys a need for help or an object at some point during the day, the teacher focuses on the student and requires a communicative behavior. The teacher's directions generally take one of these forms: (a) providing the cue, "What do you want?"; (b) giving a direct command, "You need to tell me what you want"; (c) partially modeling the desired

response [by saying "I want" while pointing toward the student's hands or communication aid]; or (d) modeling the entire desired response (Halle, 1982). As soon as the student has responded correctly, the teacher says "That's right" to confirm the appropriateness of the response, repeats the student's response (through signing or using the student's device while verbalizing the message), and then presents the object or event the student has requested (Hart, 1985).

Mand-Model Techniques

This strategy also makes use of naturally occurring situations but does not require the student to initiate a request. Instead, having placed several highly attractive materials in the learning environment, the teacher waits until the student approaches one. Then the teacher approaches the student, focuses on the material, and presents the instruction "Tell me what this is" or "Tell me what you want." If the student fails to respond or responds incompletely, the teacher either requests a fuller response, "Tell me a whole sentence" or models the target response (using signing or the device). After the student responds correctly, the teacher praises the student for appropriate communication and allows him to use the material (Halle, 1982; Hart, 1985).

Delay Procedure

The first component of this strategy is to increase the number of occasions requiring communication, either by placing high-demand items within sight, but out of reach, or by withholding objects or assistance needed for a particular task (Halle, 1982). At lunch, for instance, the student's tray could be presented without an eating utensil; likewise, if a teacher routinely helps the student unfasten his pants for toileting, she could place his hands near the snap on his pants, but then not provide the needed help (Oliver & Halle, 1982).

The second component of this strategy involves systematically delaying any cues or prompts used by the teacher. In the example of the lunch tray with no utensil, then, the teacher would initially present the lunch tray without saying anything and then wait expectantly for 5 seconds (Halle, 1982) or 10 seconds (Oliver & Halle, 1982). If the student makes no response, the teacher provides a prompt only after the delay has elapsed. For example, depending on the length of previous training, Oliver and Halle (1982) used (a) a full degree prompt

consisting of a model of the target sign, followed by physical guidance to form the sign, then a request for imitation; (b) a medium degree prompt consisting of a model to the target sign followed by a request for imitation; and (c) a minimal degree prompt consisting just of saying "You need to show me the sign for _____." As soon as the student responded correctly, the teacher confirmed appropriate communication by saying "Yes, that is the sign for _____" or "Nice signing _____," executed the sign, and then provided the desired object or event.

Integrating Naturalistic Techniques

Because incidental teaching, mand-model, and delay each focus on different aspects of the communicative situation, they lend themselves to sequential use (Halle, 1982). Initial instruction would commence with the mand-model technique, which elicits a communicative behavior under control of the teacher's demand. Once the student reliably responds to the teacher's demand, time delay would be implemented in order to shift control from the teacher's cue to the stimulus of needing an object or help. Thus, time delay focuses on the student's initiation of a response. Finally, incidental teaching can be used to elicit a more elaborate response such as a word chain or an added piece of information about the stimulus (Halle, 1982; Hart, 1985).

Let us take a target skill for Susan (pp. 289–290) to illustrate integrated use of the three naturalistic strategies. We want Susan to ask for help in opening her milk, so we have included a picture of a milk carton in her notebook. We would begin instruction using the mand-model technique. Once she is seated at the lunch table, we would present the closed milk carton and say "Tell me what you want." If Susan does not respond, we would say "Tell me you want me to open your milk like this" while simultaneously opening her notebook to the correct page and pointing to the picture of the milk carton. We would then close the book and say "Now you do it," providing physical guidance if necessary. When Susan has completed the correct response, we would praise her with "Good; you told me what you wanted" or a similar statement and then immediately open her milk carton.

Once Susan has met a predetermined criterion (such as three consecutive lunch periods) of correct responses to the cue "Tell me what you want," we would implement a delay procedure. Therefore, we would present the closed milk carton as before, but now we would wait 5 seconds without saying anything. If, after 5 seconds, Susan does not respond, we would say "You need to tell me to open your milk" and, if necessary, would model the response as before. As soon as Susan completes the response, we would praise her as before and comply with her request.

Finally, when Susan independently initiates her request within 5 seconds of presentation of the milk carton for three consecutive lunch periods, we would begin an incidental teaching procedure to elicit "Help milk" as an elaborated response. Therefore, we would add a symbol for "help" to Susan's notebook and would respond to Susan's self-initiated point to the milk carton picture by saying "Tell me more." We would then model the elaborated target response by pointing first to the help symbol and then to the milk carton symbol and would instruct Susan, "Now you do it." We would praise her with "Good, you told me more," and then would comply with her request.

Variations of Naturalistic Training

Naturalistic teaching techniques need not be limited to the context in which the student already knows how to perform the ongoing activity. They may also be embedded within training or other functional skills. As described earlier (see Assessing Communication Needs), Goetz et al. (1985) used an "interruption strategy" to identify tasks that were motivating to the students and subsequently to teach communication behaviors during training on these tasks. For example, since one student responded positively to learning to make toast, Goetz et al., created an opportunity for communication training by interrupting the student before he pushed down the lever on the toaster. Just before the student initiated this step, the trainer said, "Wait," blocked the student from continuing, and said, "What do you want." The expected response for this student was to point to the card containing a line drawing of a piece of toast when presented in a random position with two blank cards. If the student pointed to the correct card, the teacher delivered praise and a cue to continue making toast. If the student gave no response or an incorrect one, the teacher gave a model and then a physical prompt to elicit the correct response. In the latter case, however, the teacher neither praised the student nor allowed him to continue making toast until 20 to 40 seconds later when a new trial

was initiated. Using a multiple baseline design, Goetz et al., demonstrated that interrupting the student and making continued access to a preferred task contingent on a communicative behavior was more effective than training him to display the same communication behavior prior to task commencement. It must be noted, however, that toast-making training had been started before communication interruption was used. Thus, it is likely that the student had already partially acquired the chain of behaviors involved in the food preparation task. This would have put him less at risk for becoming confused about steps in the original task once communication training was incorporated.

Breen et al. (1985) also embedded communication skills within training on another task but did so by including communication steps at natural points within a task analysis. The target skill for four young men with autism was not communication per se, but social interaction with colleagues without handicaps in the breakrooms of the students' vocational training sites. Three of the students used spoken language, but the fourth used a card system of written statements. Breen et al., developed a 13-step task analysis for getting a cup of coffee, initiating interaction with people having no handicaps—a high school student during training and a co-worker during generalization probes—then closing the conversation to return to work. Five of the steps directly involved communication, including asking "How are you," "Would you like a cup of coffee," and "What's new"; and responding to a question like "What have you been doing?" or to the closing, "Take it easy." Systematic training on the task analysis resulted in acquisition and generalization to nonhandicapped co-workers for all four students, including the student who used the printed statement card system. Unfortunately, Breen et al., did not describe any adaptations that may have been necessary for the nonspeaking student; nevertheless, their results clearly indicated that this student succeeded in acquiring and generalizing communication behaviors within the context of social skills training.

Reducing Aberrant Behavior

Just as communication training within natural contexts can be used to increase adaptive functioning, it may also be used to reduce maladaptive behavior. When viewed through a perspective of the pragmatic aspects of language, instances of self-injurious behavior (SIB) and aggression can be interpreted as the messages "Pay attention to me" or "I don't want to do this" (Donnellan, Mirenda, Mesaros, & Fassbender, 1984). Thus, they may serve social functions of obtaining attention or escape (Carr & Durand, 1985).

Once the message value of a particular aberrant behavior has been determined through an ABC analysis (Donnellan et al., 1984; see Chapters 4, 5) or through systematic manipulation of teacher attention and task difficulty (Carr & Durand, 1985), a specific communication skill can be taught as a more efficient alternative for conveying the same message. Carr and Durand did this by teaching four youths having autism, brain-damage, or developmental disabilities to say "Am I doing good work?" as a means of gaining the teacher's attention or to say "I don't understand," in order to seek help and thus to avoid the need to escape from the task at hand. The trainer first taught simple imitation of these statements ("Say 'Am I doing good work?' "). Next, the trainer taught the students to use these messages during training on other tasks, using a mand-model variation with the instructional cue, "Do you have any questions?" This training procedure proved to be highly effective in reducing the incidence of aggression, SIB, tantrums, stripping, and oppositional behavior.

While Carr and Durand's study focused on training a vocal alternative to aberrant behavior, two other applications have indicated that this strategy can be equally effective with augmentative communication. In the first, a young man, with severe retardation, who engaged in severe SIB was taught to approach and signal the teacher, to sign "help," and to return to the work area and point to the task he was having difficulty with, in order to secure both attention and assistance. Adapting the first component of the delay technique for creating opportunities to communicate, Donnellan et al. (1984) purposefully assigned difficult tasks to the student during initial training and then responded immediately at the first indication of SIB by physically guiding the student through the three-step sequence for requesting help. According to this case description, the student used his new communication skill routinely within 6 weeks, thereby replacing the SIB almost completely.

The second application also involved signing, this time with an 11-year-old boy with autism and retardation who engaged in high rates of yelling and grabbing (Horner & Budd, 1985). A systematic ABC analysis revealed that this child's disruptive

behavior served to convey "I want _____" during five daily activities. Therefore, the student was taught to sign the label for each of the four objects he consistently grabbed, including "juice" and "timer," and to sign "choose" for the context in which he tended to grab for available reinforcers. Using a multiple baseline design, Horner and Budd demonstrated that the child continued to use grabbing and yelling rather than the signs he had mastered during isolated training until training was transferred to the daily routine activities.

Isolated Training

While naturalistic training techniques have much greater potential for ensuring functional language, separate communication lessons may be more effective for some students for establishing a beginning communication response. Keogh and Reichle (1985) have developed a procedure of this sort for use with students who are difficult to teach. After a set of desirable objects has been identified through a reinforcer preference task (see Assessing Communication Needs), the student is taught a requesting skill. Using a "communication card" that is essentially an index card with a Blissymbol for "want," the student learns to point to the message "want" in order to gain access to the tray of objects for making a selection. Once the student has mastered this skill, training is initiated to teach labels for the objects themselves.

We strongly recommend Keogh and Reichle's chapter for structuring lessons for students who are difficult to teach, as well as programs and strategies described by Klein et al. (1981); Waldo, Barnes, and Berry (1981); and Waldo, Riggs et al. (no date). For students who are extremely non-responsive, strategies described by Sternberg (1982) and Sternberg, Pegnatore, and Hill (1983) may be a useful beginning point. Ultimately, however, the advisability of using these or any other strategies must be confirmed through careful monitoring of the student's daily usage.

CONCLUSION

Developing appropriate communication systems for people with severe handicaps is a dynamic and demanding process. The teacher carrying out this process must focus as much on the purposes and circumstances under which the student communicates as on the mode or modes of expression. Success can be measured against only one criterion—the extent to which the person with disabilities is able to and does communicate within his unique environment.

REFERENCES

American Speech, Language and Hearing ad hoc Committee on Communication Processes and Nonspeaking Persons. (1981). Position statement on nonspeech communication. *ASHA, 23,* 577–581.

Anthony, D. (1971). *Seeing essential English.* Anaheim, CA: Educational Services Division, Anaheim Union School District.

Artificial Language Laboratory. (1985). 405 Computer Center, Michigan State University, East Lansing, MI 48825.

Barrera, R. D., Lobato-Barrera, D., & Sulzer-Azaroff, B. (1980). A simultaneous treatment comparison of three expressive language training programs with a mute autistic child. *Journal of Autism and Developmental Disorders, 10*(1), 21–37.

Beukelman, D. R., Yorkston, K. M., & Dowden, P. A. (1985). *Communication augmentation: A casebook of clinical management.* San Diego, CA: College-Hill Press.

Bornstein, H. Saulnier, K. L., & Hamilton, L. B. (1983). *The comprehensive signed English dictionary.* Washington, DC: Gallaudet College Press.

Bottorf, L., & DePape, D. (1982). Initiating communication systems for severely speech-impaired persons. *Topics in Language Disorders, 2,* 55–71.

Breen, C., Haring, T., Pitts-Conway, V., & Gaylord-Ross, R. (1985). The training and generalization of social interaction during breaktime at two job sites in the natural environment. *Journal of the Association for Persons with Severe Handicaps, 10,* 41–50.

Browder, D. M., Morris, W. W., & Snell, M. E. (1981). Using time delay to teach manual signs to a severely retarded student. Education and Training of the Mentally Retarded, 16, 252–258.

Brown, L., Branston, M., Hamre-Nietupski, S., Pumpian, I., Certo, N., & Gruenewald, L. (1979). A strategy for developing chronological-age-appropriate and functional curricular content for severely handicapped adolescents and young adults. *Journal of Special Education, 13,* 81–90.

Bruno, J., & Goodman, J. (1983). Computer aided development of phonetic skills in non-vocal pre-reading children. *Journal of Special Education Technology, 6*(4), 39–45.

Bryen, D. N., & Joyce, D. G. (1985). Language intervention with the severely handicapped: A decade of research. *Journal of Special Education, 19,* 7–39.

Burkhart, L. J. (1980). *Homemade battery-powered toys and educational devices for severely handicapped children.* 8503 Rhode Island Avenue, College Park, MD 20740.

Burkhart, L. J. (1984). *More homemade battery devices for severely handicapped children—with suggested activities.* 8503 Rhode Island Avenue, College Park, MD 20740.

Calculator, S., & Bollaghen, C. (1982). The use of communication boards in a residential setting: An evaluation. *Journal of Speech and Hearing Disorders, 47,* 281–287.

Campbell, C. R., Stremel-Campbell, K., & Rogers-Warren, A. K. (1985). Programming teacher support for functional language. In S. F. Warren & A. K. Rogers-Warren (Eds.), *Teaching functional language: Generalization and maintenance of language skills* (pp. 309–339). Baltimore: University Park Press.

Carr, E. G., & Durand, V. M. (1985). Reducing behavior problems through functional communication training. *Journal of Applied Behavior Analysis, 18,* 111–126.

Chapman, R., & Miller, J. (1977). *Analyzing language and communication in the child.* Paper presented at the Conference on Nonspeech Language Intervention, Gulf State Park, Alabama.

Christoph, D., Nietupski, J., & Pumpian, I. (1980). Teaching severely handicapped adolescents and young adults to use *communication cards* to make purchases at a fast-food counter. In L. Brown, M. Falvey, D. Baumgart, I. Pumpian, J. Schroeder, & L. Gruenewald (Eds.), *Strategies for teaching chronological, age-appropriate functional skills to adolescent and young adult severely handicapped students* (Vol. 9, Part 1). Madison: University of Wisconsin Madison Metropolitan School District.

Clark, C. R. (1981). Learning words using traditional orthography and the symbols of Rebus, Bliss, and Carrier. *Journal of Speech and Hearing Disorders, 46,* 191–196.

Clark, C. R. (1984). A close look at the Standard Rebus system and Blissymbolics. *Journal of the Association for Persons with Severe Handicaps, 9,* 37–48.

Clark, C. R., Davies, C. O., & Woodcock, R. W. (1974). *Standard rebus glossary.* Minnesota: American Guidance Service.

Cohen, M. (1981). Development of language behavior in an autistic child using total communication. *Exceptional Children, 47,* 374–379.

Communication Outlook. Artificial Language Laboratory, Michigan State University, 405 Computer Center, East Lansing, MI 48824–1042.

Connor, P. (1978). Appendix II: Eyepointing. In H. Silverman, S. McNaughton, & B. Kates, *Handbook of Blissymbolics.* Ontario, CN: Blissymbolics Communication Institute.

Coon, C., & Lambert, H. (1985). A communication skills learning and improvement program. *Communication Outlook, 7*(2), 5–6.

Daniloff, J. K., & Schafer, A. (1981). A gestural communication program for severely and profoundly handicapped children. *Language, Speech, and Hearing Services in Schools, 12,* 258–267.

Dennis, R., Reichle, J., Williams, W., & Vogelsberg, R. T. (1982). Motoric factors influencing the selection of vocabulary for sign production programs. *Journal of the Association for Persons with Severe Handicaps, 7*(1), 20–32.

Detamore, K., & Lippke, B. (1980). Handicapped students learn language skills with communication boards. *Teaching Exceptional Children, 12,* 104–106.

Dixon, L. S. (1981). A functional analysis of photo-object matching skills of severely retarded adolescents. *Journal of Applied Behavior Analysis, 14,* 465–478.

Doherty, J. E. (1985). The effects of sign characteristics on sign acquisition and retention: An integrative review of the literature. *Augmentative and Alternative Communication, 1*, 108–121.

Donnellan, A. M., Mirenda, P. L., Mesaros, R. A., & Fassbender, L. L. (1984). Analyzing the communicative functions of aberrant behavior. *Journal of the Association for Persons with Severe Handicaps, 9*, 201–212.

Duker, P. C., & Morsink, H. (1984). Acquisition and cross-setting generalization of manual signs with severely retarded individuals. *Journal of Applied Behavior Analysis, 17*, 93–103.

Duker, P. C., & vanGrinsven, D. (1983). The effect of gestural facilitation on the acquisition of noun-verb labeling responses with severely retarded individuals. *Journal of Special Education Technology, 6*(4), 20–27.

Elder, P. S., & Bergman, J. S. (1978). Visual symbol communication instruction with nonverbal, multiply handicapped individuals. *Mental Retardation, 16*, 107–112.

Eulenberg, J. B. (1985). Coming of age in the age of computers. *Communication Outlook, 7*(2), 14–15.

Eulenberg, J. B., & Rosenfeld, J. (1982). Vocaid—A new product from Texas Instruments. *Communication Outlook, 3*(3), 1–3.

Faw, G., Reid, D., Schepis, M., Fitzgerald, J., & Welty, P. (1981). Involving institutional staff in the development and maintenance of sign language skills with profoundly retarded persons. *Journal of Applied Behavior Analysis, 14*, 411–423.

Fons, K., & Gargagliano, T. (1981). Articulate automata: An overview of voice synthesis. *Byte, 6*(2), 164–187.

Fristoe, M., & Lloyd, L. L. (1977). *The use of manual communication with the retarded.* Paper presented at the Gatlinburg Conference on Mental Retardation.

Fristoe, M., & Lloyd, L. L. (1978). A survey of the use of non-speech systems with the severely communication impaired. *Mental Retardation, 16*, 99–103.

Goetz, L., Gee, K., & Sailor, W. (1985). Using a behavior chain interruption strategy to teach communication skills to students with severe disabilities. *Journal of the Association for Persons with Severe Handicaps, 10*, 21–30.

Goodrich, E. (1979). Modern voice generation techniques. *Communication Outlook, 2*(1), 6.

Gustason, G., Pfetzing, D., & Zawolkow, E. (1972). *Signing exact English.* Rossmoor, CA: Modern Signs Press.

Halle, J. W. (1982). Teaching functional language to the handicapped: An integrative model of natural environment teaching techniques. *Journal of the Association for Persons with Severe Handicaps, 7*(4), 29–37.

Hamre-Nietupski, S., Nietupski, J., & Rathe, T. (1986). Letting the data do the talking: Selecting the appropriate nonverbal communication system for severely handicapped students. *Teaching Exceptional Children, 18*, 130–134.

Hamre-Nietupski, S., Stoll, A., Holtz, K., Fullerton, P., Ryan-Flottum, M., & Brown, L. (1977). Curricular strategies for teaching selected non-verbal communication skills to non-verbal and verbal severely handicapped students. In L. Brown, J. Nietupski, S. Lyon, S. Hamre-Nietupski, T. Crowner, & L. Gruenewald (Eds.), *Curricular strategies for teaching functional object use, nonverbal communication, problem solving, and mealtime skills to severely handicapped students* (Vol. 7, Part 1). Madison: University of Wisconsin and Madison Metropolitan School District.

Harris, D. (1982). Communicative interaction processes involving nonvocal physically handicapped children. *Topics in Language Disorders, 2*, 21–37.

Hart, B. (1985). Naturalistic language training techniques. In S. F. Warren and A. K. Rogers-Warren (Eds.), *Teaching functional language: Generalization and maintenance of language skills* (pp. 63–88). Baltimore: University Park Press.

Hodges, P. M., & Deich, R. F. (1978). Teaching an artificial language to nonverbal retardates. *Behavior Modification, 2*, 489–509.

Horner, R. H., & Budd, C. M. (1985). Acquisition of manual sign use: Collateral reduction of maladaptive behavior and factors limiting generalization. *Education and Training of the Mentally Retarded, 20*, 39–47.

Hurlbut, B., Iwata, B., & Green, J. (1982). Nonvocal language acquisition in adolescents with severe physical disabilities: Blissymbol versus iconic stimulus formats. *Journal of Applied Behavior Analysis, 15*, 241–258.

Jago, J. L., Jago, A. G., & Hart, M. (1984). An evaluation of the total communication approach for teaching language skills to developmentally delayed preschool children. *Education and Training of the Mentally Retarded, 19*, 175–182.

Karel, P., Galloway, A. Brankin, G., Pajor, M., & Freagon, S. (1981). Alternate forms of communication to increase successful interactions. In S. Freagon, M. Pajor, G. Brankin, A. Galloway, D. Rich, P. Karel, M. Wilson, D. Costello, W. Peters, and D. Hurd, *Teaching severely handicapped students in the community: Processes and procedures.* DeKalb: Northern Illinois University and DeKalb County Special Education Association.

Keogh, W. J., & Reichle, J. (1985). Communication intervention for the "difficult-to-teach" severely handicapped. In S. F. Warren & A. K. Rogers-Warren (Eds.), *Teaching functional language: Generalization and maintenance of language skills* (pp. 157–194). Baltimore: University Park Press.

Kirschner, A., Algozzine, B., & Abbott, T. (1979). Manual communication systems: A comparison and its implications. *Education and Training of the Mentally Retarded, 14*, 5–10.

Klein, M. D., Wulz, S. V., Hall, M. K., Waldo, L. J., Carpenter, S. A., Lathan, D. A., Myers, S. P., Fox, T., & Marshall, A. M. (1981). *Comprehensive communication curriculum guide.* Lawrence, KS: Early Childhood Institute, Haworth Hall, University of Kansas.

Kleinert, H. L., & Gast, D. L. (1982). Teaching a multihandicapped adult manual signs using a constant time-delay procedure. *Journal of the Association for Persons with Severe Handicaps, 6*(4), 25–32.

Kohl, F. L., & Stettner-Eaton, B. A. (1985). Fourth graders as trainers of cafeteria skills to severely handicapped students. *Education and Training of the Mentally Retarded, 20*, 60–68.

Kucherawy, D. A., & Kucherawy, J. M. (1978). An electrical communication system for a nonverbal, profoundly retarded, spastic quadriplegic. *Education and Training of the Mentally Retarded, 13*, 342–344.

Light, L., Collier, B., & Parnes, P. (1985a). Communicative interaction between young, nonspeaking, physically disabled children and their primary caregivers: Part I—Discourse patterns. *Augmentative and Alternative Communication, 1,* 74–83.

Light, J., Collier, B., & Parnes, P. (1985b). Communicative interaction between young, nonspeaking, physically disabled children and their primary caregivers: Part II—Communicative function. *Augmentative and Alternative Communication, 1,* 98–107.

Lloyd, L. L. (1985). Comments on terminology. *Augmentative and Alternative Communication, 1,* 95–97.

Luftig, R. L., & Bersani, H. A. (1985). An initial investigation of translucency, transparency, and component complexity of Blissymbolics. *Journal of Childhood Communication Disorders, 8*(2), 191–209.

Matas, J. A. Mathy-Laikko, P., Beukelman, D. R., & Legresley, K. (1985). Identifying the nonspeaking population: A demographic study. *Augmentative and Alternative Communication, 1,* 17–31.

May, D. C. (1983). The use of an electronic switch to increase independent head control in a severely handicapped student. *Journal of Special Education Technology, 6*(4), 14–19.

Mayberry, R. (1976). If a chimp can learn sign language, surely my nonverbal client can too. *ASHA, 18,* 223–228.

Meehan, D. M., Mineo, B. A., & Lyon, S. R. (1985). Use of systematic prompting and prompt withdrawal to establish and maintain switch activation in a severely handicapped student. *Journal of Special Education Technology, 7*(1), 5–11.

Miller, J. M. (1985). *The effects of voice synthesis on the acquisition of Blissymbols by nonvocal, motorically impaired, and intact mentally retarded persons.* Doctoral dissertation, University of Virginia, Charlottesville.

Mirenda, P. (1985). Designing pictorial communication systems for physically able-bodied students with severe handicaps. *Augmentative and Alternative Communication, 1,* 58–64.

Mithaug, D. E., & Liberty, S. (1980). Word discrimination training to improve the communication skills of a severely retarded, non-vocal woman: A case study. *Education and Treatment of Children, 3,* 1–12.

Moores, D. (1974). Nonvocal systems of verbal behavior. In R. L. Schiefelbusch and L. L. Lloyd (Eds.), *Language perspectives: Acquisition, retardation, and intervention.* Baltimore: University Park Press.

Murphy, G., Steele, K., Gilligan, T., Yeow, J., & Spars, D. (1977). Teaching a picture language to a non-speaking retarded boy. *Behavior Research and Therapy, 15,* 198–201.

Musselwhite, C. R., & St. Louis, K. W. (1982). *Communication programming for the severely handicapped: Vocal and non-vocal strategies.* Houston, TX: College-Hill Press.

News on aids. (1985). *Communication Outlook, 6*(3), 19.

Nietupski, J., & Hamre-Nietupski, S. (1979). Teaching auxillary communication skills to severely handicapped students. *AAESPH Review, 4*(2), 107–123.

O'Brien, L., & Andresen, J. (1983). A family matter: Stimulating communication in the young cerebral-palsied child. *Teaching Exceptional Children, 16,* 47–50.

Oliver, P. R. (1983). Effects of teaching different tasks in group versus individual training formats with severely handicapped individuals. *Journal of the Association for Persons with Severe Handicaps, 8*(2), 79–91.

Oliver, C. B., & Halle, J. W. (1982). Language training in the everyday environment: Teaching functional sign use to a retarded child. *Journal of the Association for Persons with Severe Handicaps, 7*(3), 50–62.

Pace, G. M., Ivancic, M. T., Edwards, G. L., Iwata, B. A., & Page, T. J. (1985). Assessment of stimulus preference and reinforcer value with profoundly retarded individuals. *Journal of Applied Behavior Analysis, 18,* 249–255.

Porter, P. B., & Schroeder, S. R. (1980). Generalization and maintenance of skills acquired in Non-speech Language Initiation Program training. *Applied Research in Mental Retardation, 1,* 71–84.

Powers, J., & Ball, T. S. (1983). Video games to augment leisure programming in a state hospital residence for developmentally disabled clients. *Journal of Special Education Technology, 6*(1), 48–57.

Reichle, J., & Karlan, G. (1985). The selection of an augmentative system in communication intervention: A critique of decision rules. *Journal of the Association for Persons with Severe Handicaps, 10,* 146–156.

Reichle, J., & Keogh, W. J. (1985). Communication intervention: A selective review of what, when, and how to teach. In S. F. Warren & A. K. Rogers-Warren (Eds.), *Teaching functional language: Generalization and maintenance of language skills* (pp. 25–59). Baltimore: University Park Press.

Reichle, J., Rogers, N., & Barrett, C. (1984). Establishing pragmatic discrimination among the communicative functions of requesting, rejecting, and commenting in an adolescent. *Journal of the Association for Persons with Severe Handicaps, 9*(1), 31–36.

Reichle, J., & Yoder, D. E. (1985). Communication board use in severely handicapped learners. *Language, Speech, and Hearing Services in Schools, 16,* 146–157.

Reid, D. H., & Hurlbut, B. (1977). Teaching nonvocal communication skills to multihandicapped adults. *Journal of Applied Behavior Analysis, 10,* 591–603.

Remington, B., & Clarke, S. (1983). Acquisition of expressive signing by autistic children: An evaluation of the relative results of simultaneous communication and sign-alone training. *Journal of Applied Behavior Analysis, 16,* 315–328.

Romski, M. A., Sevcik, R. A., & Rumbaugh, D. M. (1985). Retention of symbolic communication skills by severely mentally retarded persons. *American Journal of Mental Deficiency, 89,* 441–444.

Sailor, W., & Guess, D. (1983). *Severely handicapped students: An instructional design.* Boston: Houghton Mifflin.

Sailor, W., Guess, D., Goetz, L., Schuler, A., Utley, B., & Baldwin, M. (1980). Language and severely handicapped persons: Deciding what to teach to whom. In W. Sailor, B. Wilcox, & L. Brown (Eds.), *Methods of instruction for severely handicapped students.* Baltimore: Paul H. Brookes Publishers.

Schepis, M., Reid, D., Fitzgerald, J., Faw, G., vanderPol, R., & Welty, P. (1982). A program for increasing manual signing by autistic and profoundly retarded youth within the daily environment. *Journal of Applied Behavior Analysis, 15,* 363–379.

Schiefelbusch, R. L. (1985). Foreword. In S. F. Warren & A. K. Rogers-Warren (Eds.), *Teaching functional language: Generalization and maintenance of language skills* (pp. xiii–xiv). Baltimore: University Park Press.

Shane, H. C., & Bashir, A. S. (1980). Election criteria for the adoption of an augmentative communication system: Preliminary considerations. *Journal of Speech and Hearing Disorders, 45,* 408–414.

Shroyer, E. H. (1982). *Signs of the times.* Washington, DC: Gallaudet College Press.

Silverman, F. H. (1980). *Communication for the speechless.* Englewood Cliffs, NJ: Prentice-Hall.

Sisson, L. A., & Barrett, R. P. (1984). An alternating treatments comparison of oral and total communication training with minimally verbal, retarded children. *Journal of Applied Behavior Analysis, 17,* 559–566.

Skelly, M. (1979). *Amerind gestural code based on universal American Indian hand talk.* New York: Elsevier North Holland, Inc.

Song, A. Y. (1979). Acquisition and use of Blissymbols by severely mentally retarded adolescents. *Mental Retardation, 17,* 253–255.

Sternberg, L. (1982). Communication instruction. In L. Sternberg & G. L. Adams, *Educating severely and profoundly handicapped students* (pp. 209–241). Rockville, MD: Aspen Systems Corp.

Sternberg, L., Pegnatore, L., & Hill, C. (1983). Establishing interactive communication behaviors with profoundly mentally handicapped students. *Journal of the Association for Persons with Severe Handicaps, 8*(2), 39–46.

Taber, F. M. (1983). *Microcomputers in special education: Selection and decision making process.* Reston, VA: Council for Exceptional Children.

Vanderheiden, G. C. (1981). Technically speaking. *Communication Outlook, 3*(2), 15.

Vanderheiden, G. C. (1982a). Trace-hybrid lightbeam/sensor technique. *Communication Outlook, 3*(3), 6–7.

Vanderheiden, G. C. (1982b). Lightbeam headpointer research. *Communication Outlook, 3*(4), 11.

Vanderheiden, G. C., & Grilley, K. (eds.). (1976). *Nonvocal communication techniques and aids for the severely physically handicapped.* Baltimore: University Park Press.

Vicker, B. (1974). *Nonoral communication system project 1964/1973.* Iowa City: Campus Stores, The University of Iowa.

Wacker, D. P., Berg, W. K., Wiggins, B., Muldoon, M., & Cavanaugh, J. (1985). Evaluation of reinforcer preference for profoundly handicapped students. *Journal of Applied Behavior Analysis, 18,* 173–178.

Waldo, L. J., Barnes, K. J., & Berry, G. W. (1981). *Total communication checklist.* Topeka: Kansas Neurological Institute.

Waldo, L., Riggs, P., Davez, K., Hirsch, M., Eye, R., & Marshall, A. (no date). Functional communication board training for the severely multiply handicapped. Lawrence, KS: Haworth Hall, University of Kansas. Lawrence, KS 66045.

Warren, S. F., & Rogers-Warren, A. K. (1985a). Preface. In S. F. Warren & A. K. Rogers-Warren (Eds.), *Teaching functional language: Generalization and maintenance of language skills* (pp. xi–xii). Baltimore: University Park Press.

Warren, S. F., & Rogers-Warren, A. K. (1985b). Teaching functional language: An introduction. In S. F. Warren and A. K. Rogers-Warren (Eds.), *Teaching functional language: Generalization and maintenance of language skills* (pp. 3–23). Baltimore: University Park Press.

Weller, E. L., & Mahoney, G. J. (1983). A comparison of oral and total communication modalities on the language training of young, mentally handicapped children. *Education and Training of the Mentally Retarded, 18,* 103–110.

Wilbur, R. B. (1979). *American sign language and sign systems.* Baltimore: University Park Press.

Willems, S. G., Lombardino, L. J., MacDonald, J. D., & Owens, R. E. (1982). Total communication: Clinical report on a parent-based, language training program. *Education and Training of the Mentally Retarded, 17,* 293–298.

Perhaps the most difficult aspect of teaching individuals who have severe handicaps is the replacement of maladaptive behaviors with appropriate and functional social interaction skills. Until students' aberrant behaviors are controlled, they may be prevented from spending time in the community learning other important skills. Without time in the community, the mastery of additional useful skills is less likely; thus, a vicious cycle is created: inappropriate behavior keeps students from being in situations where they can learn appropriate behavior. It is easy for teachers to become discouraged and angry when students frequently display whining, tantrums, and aggressive and stereotypic behaviors. When the maladaptive behaviors are life-threatening, interventionists intently feel the "need to do something now."

Intervention research on the control of maladaptive behavior is plentiful and numerous procedures exist. Some of these intervention procedures are much more intrusive than others. All of them require careful implementation; some involve application of painful stimuli; some are time consuming; and some may be repulsive to staff, family members, and bystanders. It is the responsibility of intervention teams to select procedures that are minimally intrusive, yet effective. To achieve our goal of facilitating students' access to less restrictive environments, interventionists must balance the intrusiveness and effectiveness of the procedures.

One of the most hopeful aspects of the current literature on maladaptive behavior is the revival of functional analysis. In this next chapter, David Gast and Mark Wolery describe this practice and illustrate its application to typical examples of the serious maladaptive behaviors that may dominate our students' repertoires. They also address the debate that has developed among professionals serving students with severe handicaps. Two questions raised in this debate are: (a) Do intrusive and aversive interventions that are meant to eliminate serious maladaptive behaviors violate students' basic rights to liberty and the pursuit of happiness? and (b) Should interventions be selected for their effectiveness, intrusiveness, restrictiveness, social acceptability, or some combination of these characteristics? This debate involves all of us and is one that requires careful thought.

Introduction to Chapter 12

12

Severe Maladaptive Behaviors

David L. Gast
University of Kentucky

Mark Wolery
University of Kentucky

The trend toward educating students with moderate, severe, and multiple handicaps in less restrictive environments has recently gained considerable momentum in special education (cf. Certo, Haring, & York, 1984; Novak & Heal, 1980). A decade ago when Brown, Nietupski, and Hamre-Nietupski (1976) introduced the concept of the "criterion of ultimate functioning," few professionals questioned its intent, although many questioned whether its realization was practical or affordable in the foreseeable future. This straightforward and simply stated principle has resulted in a new direction in the education of students with severe handicaps, a direction welcomed and advocated by most parents, professionals, and service providers. Its adoption has influenced *what* special educators teach (functional, chronologically age-appropriate skills), *where* they teach (integrated schools and community environments), and *how* they teach (group arrangements, distributed trial formats, and least intrusive prompting procedures). The current trend in serving children with moderate to severe developmental disabilities is clearly founded on the criterion of ultimate functioning.

The adoption of this basic principle has greatly influenced the way special educators manage disruptive, aggressive, and potentially dangerous behaviors. The movement from serving students with severe learning and behavior problems in restricted, isolated, segregated settings (cluster special education schools, residential institutions) to less restrictive, integrated settings (neighborhood elementary, middle, and secondary schools; community-based apartments and group homes) has prompted special educators, behavioral psychologists, and other behavior management specialists to reevaluate the methods used to bring about positive behavior change. In years past, students exhibiting an excess behavior, such as stereotypic head weaving, may have found themselves as participants in an overcorrection program involving "functional movement training" (Axelrod, Brantner, & Meddock, 1978). Operationalizing this procedure may have required the teacher to restrain the student's weaving head, followed by 5 minutes of repeatedly instructing and physically guiding the student's head in an up, down, or straight position (Foxx & Azrin, 1973). This punishment procedure may have been the intervention of first choice because of its effectiveness with various forms of stereotypic behaviors.

Today, the behavior management specialist would approach this behavior differently. First, he is apt to conduct a functional or ABC analysis of the behavior (Kerr & Nelson, 1983). That is, a thorough investigation of antecedent conditions (activity, teacher demands, setting, time of day, etc.), behavior (topography, frequency, duration) and consequent events (teacher attention, termination of activity, peer response) would be undertaken. He would also determine whether there may be a medical basis for the head weaving (inner ear infection), particularly if the behavior had a short history. If a medical basis were ruled out, he would analyze the data generated by the functional analysis and identify antecedent and consequent events that positively correlate with the emission of the behavior. Such information may indicate altering some antecedent or setting event (changing the size of the group or the group composition, reducing task demands, introducing a rest period prior to the instructional activity) which sets the occasion for the behavior. Alternatively, the data may indicate a need to change the consequent event (terminating the instructional activity, making teacher attention contingent upon the nonoccurrence of the behavior, varying the reinforcer).

A second difference in today's approach to behavior management would be the concerted effort made to modify head weaving by means of an ecological, reinforcement, or curriculum manipulation before designing and implementing a punishment program (Evans & Meyer, 1985; Gaylord-Ross, 1980). This would be in accordance with the principle of using the least intrusive behavior management strategy that may prove effective before employing more intrusive or aversive intervention strategies. Even within the punishment component the behavior management specialist would adhere to this principle, with only few exceptions (life-threatening behaviors such as head banging, rumination, pica). That is, punishment procedures, which withdraw a positive reinforcer or the opportunity to earn a positive reinforcer contingent upon a behavior (systematic ignoring, timeout from positive reinforcement, response cost) would be attempted before using

punishment procedures, which deliver an aversive stimulus contingent upon a behavior (overcorrection, contingent restraint, contingent slaps). This principle is advocated throughout the behavior management literature regardless of the age or functioning level of the target student (Bailey, Wolery, & Sugai, in press; Gaylord-Ross, 1980; Nelson & Rutherford, in press; Polsgrove & Reith, 1983).

A third difference between today's behavior analyst and the one of a decade ago is found in the practice of targeting a socially appropriate behavior to increase in frequency while attempting to decrease the frequency of a "socially inappropriate" behavior (the "fair pair" rule). This dual focus of a behavior management plan is firmly imbedded in ethical behavior modification practice. To accomplish both objectives, the special educator may use one of the positive reductive procedures discussed by Dietz and Repp (1983) alone or in combination with a punishment procedure. Particularly appropriate for use is the differential reinforcement of incompatible behavior procedure (DRI) or the differential reinforcement of alternative behavior procedure (DRA), both which require pinpointing a social (DRI) or "academic" (DRA) behavior to increase in frequency while attempting to decelerate the socially inappropriate behavior.

This change in approach to managing aberrant behavior has been brought about largely by the change in settings for students with moderate and severe handicaps. Movement to integrated environments has resulted in public scrutiny of the way special educators attempt to modify problem behaviors. With more children with severe handicaps remaining at home and attending neighborhood schools, parents, peers, professionals from other disciplines, and lay persons are afforded the opportunity to observe and comment on behavior management practices. Parents have increasingly become active participants in the decision-making process. They are better informed about their rights and those of their children, as well as procedural alternatives for managing behavior. The time has passed when special educators can act autocratically; input from and consideration of parents' perceptions, and those of others who come in contact with moderately and severely handicapped students, must be taken into account regardless of the proven effectiveness of a given behavior management strategy. In recent years, the social acceptability (appearance) of a method of intervention has come to be viewed as important as its effectiveness. Such social validation (Wolf, 1978) of what practitioners do is welcomed by most, but it cannot be forgotten that the primary goal of any educational, clinical, or behavior management program is to ready the student for as productive and independent a life as possible in community environments (Brown et al., 1976). To achieve this goal, practitioners may ultimately have to select a procedure for its effectiveness, rather than for its appearance, if more socially acceptable, less intrusive, and more naturalistic strategies have failed. This we believe to be a critical point if special educators are to achieve the criterion of ultimate functioning with their students.

SEVERE MALADAPTIVE BEHAVIOR

Definition

What distinguishes a severe behavior problem from a moderate or mild behavior problem is, for the most part, a subjective determination. There is, of course, agreement by professionals and lay persons alike that behaviors which are life-threatening, to self or others, constitute severe problems that need immediate intervention. With classes of behaviors that do not affect the physical well-being of self or others, there is a greater likelihood that two persons will disagree on the severity of the problem. For example, parents and teachers may disagree among themselves, or between each other, over the relative importance of teaching compliant behavior, decelerating the frequency of a stereotypic behavior, managing behavior that results in property damage, modifying a behavior that competes with instructional activities, or increasing the time a child spends socially interacting with peers. There are inherent problems associated with classification systems that are based on "degrees of deviancy" (including levels of mental retardation designated as mild, moderate, severe, or profound) because such classification systems provide little useful information to the special educator responsible for designing behavior management and instructional programs. The term "severe" is used here to identify those maladaptive behaviors that, because of their form, frequency, or resultant effect, interfere with a student's achieving the criterion of ultimate functioning (maximum independence and productivity in community environments). We adopt the defini-

tion of severe behavior disorders forwarded by Nelson and Rutherford (in press) for defining the focus and scope of our discussion.

Moderate to severe behavior disorders are defined as behaviors occurring with sufficient frequency, intensity, or chronicity across settings so as to be intolerable to educators, parents, or others; that are incompatible with school progress; and/or that threaten the safety or well-being of the student or others. (p. 3)

The classification of a maladaptive behavior as severe is determined in conference by parents and professionals. Special educators should view those identified behaviors as priority targets for behavior management and social skill training that need their immediate attention.

Explanatory Models

It is not uncommon to hear the cause of a particular class of maladaptive behaviors (self-injury, social isolation, stereotypy) attributed to a particular diagnostic classification (autism) or to assign a particular diagnostic classification to an individual who exhibits an aberrant behavior. Such circular explanations are simplistic and misleading and serve no useful purpose in treatment. A more accurate statement might be that certain classes of behavior are associated with individuals who carry a particular diagnostic label. Whereas, such explanations attempt to explain the cause of a behavior problem, no cause has in fact been pinpointed.

Biological factors may be responsible for some forms of aberrant behavior (Cataldo & Harris, 1982). Persons who experience psychomotor seizures (Bigge, 1982), exhibit an increase in activity level that often takes the form of aggressive or stereotypic behavior. Such episodes are usually of short duration (2 to 5 minutes). It is important for teachers to understand that students who experience psychomotor seizures · have no volitional control over their behavior. The teacher's immediate responsibility is to protect the student and others from physical harm, and to report the episode to the appropriate school officials, parents, and possibly the student's physician. A second biological disorder that appears to have a causal relationship to severe maladaptive behavior is Lesch-Nyhan syndrome (Russo, Carr, & Lovaas, 1980). This genetic anomaly, which affects males, is the result of a metabolic dysfunction that is associated with self-injurious behavior (biting lips, fingers, and hands). It is a rare disorder, which is present at birth, but seldom shows its behavioral and neurological manifestations until age 2 and requires immediate medical intervention (Carter, 1975). The responsibility of the teacher is to protect the student from further physical harm, possibly through the use of protective gloves or arm restraints. Other biological factors have also been reported to be closely associated with various types of excess behaviors (Evans & Meyer, 1985).

Closely linked to the biological model for explaining some forms of aberrant behavior, is the *arousal* or *self-regulatory model*. This model focuses on the importance of sensory systems of the body to maintain a state of equilibrium. Evans and Meyer (1985) summarize the basic tenet of the self-regulatory model when they state: "Organisms attempt to maintain optimal levels of arousal and will make efforts to increase stimulation in monotonous situations and will try to decrease sensory input in overstimulating situations" (p. 36). Arousal theory has frequently been used to explain the behavior of children diagnosed as autistic. Although there is disagreement over whether an autistic child's behavior is a function of being underaroused (Rimland, 1964) or overaroused (Hutt & Hutt, 1968), attention to the concept of arousal is warranted because it may lead to an environmental solution to a behavior problem (Baker, 1980). It has been demonstrated that altering the level of activity (Rogers-Warren & Baer, 1976), availability of social and nonsocial stimuli (Hollis, 1965a, 1965b), schedule of reinforcement (Carr & Durand, 1985), and task difficulty (Durand, 1982) can dramatically affect both the form and frequency of behavior emitted by individuals with severe handicaps. It is important to note that different students may respond differently to the same level of stimulation. A novel situation or difficult task may heighten the activity level of one student (increase the frequency of stereotypic behavior) and lower the activity level of another (promote social withdrawal). It is, therefore, important for the teacher to individualize an intervention and continuously monitor its effect and side effects until an acceptable solution to the problem has been found.

A third model for explaining maladaptive behavior is the *operant* or *behavioral model*. This model explains maladaptive behavior by focusing on the consequences derived from the behavior. The two principles proposed to explain excessive behaviors are positive reinforcement and negative reinforcement. Positive reinforcement of a maladaptive behavior may be a direct consequence of the behavior itself (intrinsic), as in the case of a stereotypic behavior, or it may be a consequence delivered by someone in the environment (extrinsic), as when social attention is delivered contingent upon an inappropriate behavior. Closely related to the principle of positive reinforcement is that of negative reinforcement. Like positive reinforcement, it can maintain a high frequency of a maladaptive behavior if that behavior terminates an ongoing aversive stimulus or situations. The research conducted by Carr, Newsom, and Binkoff (1976) and replicated by Weeks and Gaylord-Ross (1981) have clearly shown how situations viewed as aversive (demand versus no-demand activities, difficult versus easy tasks) can maintain high rates of maladaptive behavior.

The behavioral model has particular utility for the teacher, psychologist, or behavior management specialist interested in both the cause and solution to a behavior problem. By conducting a functional analysis, a practitioner can identify antecedent and consequent events that positively correlate with the emission of an aberrant behavior. This information can then be used to manipulate environmental variables (task demands, instructional materials, physical arrangement of the setting, teacher response patterns) in a least-to-most intrusive hierarchy to bring about change. As part of this analysis process, it is important for the teacher to analyze the behavioral repertoire of the student and the possible communicative purpose of the problem behavior (Donnellan, 1984; Iwata, Dorsey, Slifer, Bauman, & Richman, 1982). In recent years, there has been a resurgence of the position that all behavior, verbal and nonverbal, has a communicative function (Carr, 1977; Schuler & Goetz, 1981; Watzlawick, Beavin, & Jackson, 1967). It has greatly influenced the way special educators approach maladaptive behavior. By identifying the motivational or communicative intent of a problem behavior, behavior analysts have been able to pinpoint and teach an adaptive replacement behavior that serves the same communicative function when no such adaptive behavior has formerly been available to the student. Through the use of errorless instructional methods (Weeks & Gaylord-Ross, 1981) and other behavioral procedures (Favell, McGimsey, & Schell, 1982; Horner & Budd, 1985) behavior analysts have been able to teach severely handicapped students socially appropriate behaviors to express their needs and wants.

Each of the three explanatory models merits consideration when attempting to identify the underlying cause of a maladaptive behavior. Though few maladaptive behaviors have been identified as having a biological basis, a teacher should never discount the possibility. The prudent first step is to refer the student to a physician for a thorough medical examination. This can identify chronic as well as acute medical conditions that may explain the student's behavior. The self-regulatory (arousal) model and behavioral model direct the behavior analyst's attention to the interaction that takes place between an organism and its environment. In combination they focus attention on individual differences and the importance of individualized interventions. For the practitioner, the behavioral model will give direction as to how to proceed: it can identify which antecedent or consequent events can be manipulated to facilitate positive behavior change. The behavioral analytic approach is a low inference model that, in our opinion, is the explanatory model presenting the least numerous and dangerous assumptions (to paraphrase Donnellan). We believe the operant model will continue to be the most effective and socially responsible approach to understanding and modifying severe maladaptive behavior.

BEHAVIORAL-EDUCATIONAL APPROACH TO MANAGING MALADAPTIVE BEHAVIOR

Any decision model designed to reduce the occurrence of inappropriate, socially maladaptive behavior must meet certain criteria. First, it must address all types of behavior problems regardless of topography, severity, and frequency. Second, it must incorporate formative evaluation (the repeated measurement of a behavior within the context of an experimental design). Included under formative evaluation is the reliable measurement of the behavior (dependent variable) and the consistency with which the intervention (independent variable) is implemented. Third, to be useful to the teacher, a behavior management model must emphasize an ecobehavioral approach to modifying a behavior problem. That is, the model should present intervention alternatives that are based on reinforcement, environmental, and curricular manipulations.

Fourth, it should be educational in that it addresses deceleration of the maladaptive behavior while *concurrently* teaching functional/adaptive replacement behaviors. Fifth, and finally, the model must permit input from significant others, including parents, professionals from related disciplines, and administrators. Decisions should be made in a democratic, rather than an autocratic manner; informed consent must be obtained.

Three such decision models have recently appeared in the applied behavior analysis/special education literature (Bailey et al., in press; Evans & Meyer, 1985; Gaylord-Ross, 1980). Each model may be characterized as a "behavioral-educational" decision model for managing aberrant behavior. Although they vary in the extent to which they meet the above criteria, each incorporates the basic tenets of applied behavior analysis (formative evaluation, environmental/curricular analysis and intervention) and "state of the art" special education practice (functional skill training, social validation). Although each model has a different number of components, levels, or steps, they are similar in their recommendations for assessing and intervening with problem behaviors. Rather than operationalize each model, behavioral assessment and intervention guidelines common to these models are discussed next.

Behavioral Assessment

The purpose of the assessment component of a behavior management model is to obtain as much information about students and their environments prior to designing a social behavior change program. Common questions asked include:

- What are the behavioral expectations of current and probable future environments?
- What behaviors must students learn to function more independently in current and future environments?
- Does a behavior problem really exist?
- Does the behavior endanger the safety or physical well-being of the student or others?
- Do medical explanations exist for the behavior?
- Do motivational explanations exist for the behavior?
- How is the student's behavior perceived by those in his current environment?

Answers to these questions will assist the teacher in establishing priority behavioral objectives, designing intervention programs, and establishing criteria for evaluating the effectiveness and social acceptability of a program.

Environmental Analysis

Environmental analysis entails systematically surveying a student's current environment and potential future environments. Brown, Branston-McClean, Baumgart, Vincent, Falvey, and Schroeder (1979) have referred to this as an ecological inventory (see Chapter 4 for a detailed discussion). In the design of behavior management programs, the importance of this analysis rests with the identification of functional, chronologically age-appropriate skills that can be taught as replacement behaviors for maladaptive behaviors. An environmental analysis should be undertaken immediately upon placement of a student in a special education unit, regardless of whether or not the student exhibits behavior problems. Although Bailey et al. (in press) and Gaylord-Ross (1980) do not explicitly describe environmental analysis in their decision models, as do Evans and Meyer (1985), it is implied to be an important part of the assessment process when targeting alternative replacement behaviors.

Discrepancy Analysis

A discrepancy analysis has two purposes: (1) to identify functional behaviors that will permit a student greater independence and entry into less restrictive environments and (2) to determine whether there is, in fact, a behavior problem. The first purpose pertains to identifying adaptive behaviors that are not currently in a student's repertoire but are expected by persons in the immediate environment. A discrepancy analysis based on findings from an environmental analysis assists in identifying behaviors that must be taught to enable a student to achieve the criterion of ultimate functioning. These target behaviors may be in any or all functional curriculum domains (domestic, leisure/recreational, community, vocational/educational). When conducting discrepancy analyses of this type, teachers observe students performing activities under natural conditions while recording skill deficits that preclude independence. These behaviors are then targeted for instruction and may be used as replacement responses for maladaptive behaviors.

The second purpose of a discrepancy analysis is to determine objectively whether a problem exists by observing whether others, who function in the same environments, behave differently from the target student. In order to make this determination, the teacher defines the behavior in observable terms and collects baseline data over several days on both the target student *and* peers who are not perceived as exhibiting the maladaptive behavior. By comparing the topography, frequency, and duration of the behavior for "deviant" and "nondeviant" students, it is possible to determine whether there is a behavior problem. Theoretically, if a teacher focuses his intervention efforts on those behaviors, or behavior attributes, which differentiate the deviant student from her "nondeviant" counterpart, she will come to be viewed as nondeviant. This analysis can prove useful to the classroom teacher who believes there is a problem; however, if it is only the parents who perceive a problem, then the teacher must address their concerns regardless of the ways the child compares to her peers.

Functional Analysis of Behavior

If the occurrence of a problem behavior has been substantiated through baseline assessment, the next step is to determine whether there is a medical explanation for the behavior. This entails recommending to the parents or guardian that the student undergo a thorough medical examination. This is particularly important if the student is nonverbal and the behavior in question has only recently appeared. It may be that the student is experiencing physical discomfort due to an acute illness (flu, ear infection, toothache) or a medication side effect. By objectively describing the behavior, the teacher may be able to provide valuable information to the student's physician. In addition to identifying an acute condition that may be responsible for the student's behavior, a medical examination may detect a previously unidentified chronic condition (psychomotor seizure, food allergy). If the cause of the behavior problem is found to be biological, a medical intervention alone may be indicated. If, however, no biological explanation is evident, the teacher should undertake a functional analysis.

A functional analysis entails systematically observing the student in the natural environment and recording over several days the events preceding and following each occurrence of the behavior. Such analyses should be conducted as part of the baseline assessment. Antecedent and consequent variables that should be assessed may be divided into four categories: instructional dimensions of

TABLE 12.1 Variables to consider when assessing the relationship between maladaptive behavior and setting events

Type of Variable to Consider *Specific Variables*	*Sample Questions about Variables*
Instructional Dimensions of the Environment	
Nature of Materials	Are materials/activities perceived by students as too immature ("This is baby stuff" or
Nature of Activity	"This is first grade work")?
Nature of Instruction	Are materials/activities perceived by students as too gender specific ("This is boys/
Sequence of Activities	girls' work")?
	Have the same materials/activities been used for several days in a row?
	Do materials/activities require skills the student cannot perform?
	Are materials/activities too easy/difficult for student?
	Are directions for activity clearly understood by student?
	Is the pace of instruction rapid?
	Does student always have some activity to do?
	Does student receive a high rate of reinforcement or other positive feedback for correct
	responses to instructional activities?
	What activity immediately preceded the activity where the problem behavior is
	displayed?
	What activity immediately follows the activity where the problem behavior is
	displayed?
Physical Dimensions of the Environment: Noninstructional Variables	
Nature of Lighting	Is the student's area well lighted?
Noise	Is there a glare from the sun or other lighting?
Heat	Is student able to see instructional materials (blackboard)?
Physical Arrangement	Does student appear to be bothered by too much noise?
Time of Day	Is student facing stimuli that may be distracting (Corridor, window, or other students)
	Does student appear to react to temperature of the room?
	Does student appear to react to noise in room?
	Is the student seated too near other students?
	Do particular odors appear to affect the student's behavior?
	Does behavior occur at a specific time of day (just after gym, just before lunch)?
Social Dimensions of the Environment	
Number of Other Students	Do changes in the number of students in the room/area affect student's behavior?
Number of Adults	Do changes in the number of adults affect student's behavior?
Behavior of Others Towards	Does inappropriate behavior occur only in the presence of specific students?
Student	Does inappropriate behavior occur only in the presence of specific adults?
Proximity of Others	Does inappropriate behavior occur only when others have performed a specific
	behavior?
	Does inappropriate behavior occur only when close to, away from, specific students?
	Does student behave more/less appropriately when given persons are present/absent?
	Does behavior appear to increase/decrease when other students or adults respond in
	a specific manner?
Changes in the Environment	
Changes in Schedule	Are transition times correlated with the occurrence of the behavior?
Changes in Physical	Do disruptions to the schedule appear to increase/decrease the behavior?
Arrangement	Do changes in the physical arrangement appear to increase/decrease the inappro-
Changes at Home	priate behavior?
	Do specific changes in the student's living environment appear to increase/decrease
	the occurrence of the inappropriate behavior?

Source: From *Effective Teaching: Principles and Procedures of Applied Behavior Analysis with Exceptional Children* by D.B. Bailey, M. Wolery, and G.M. Sugai (in press), Boston: Allyn & Bacon. Copyright by Allyn & Bacon. Reprinted by permission.

the setting, physical dimensions, social dimensions, and changes in the environment. Specific variables to be considered under each category and a list of sample questions that should be asked are described in Table 12.1.

Traditionally, behavior analysts have focused their attention on events that have immediately preceded and followed an occurrence of a behavior undergoing functional analysis. With few exceptions, attention has not been given to more distal events and their influence on behavior (cf. Krantz & Risley, 1977). Wahler and Fox (1981) in their discussion of "setting events," articulate the shortcoming of restricting one's analysis to "temporally proximate" stimulus events and those which relate only to principles of reinforcement. They advocate a more global focus that includes an analysis of "temporally distant behavior-environment interactions" (p. 328). The inclusion of setting events, as outlined in Table 12.1, may reveal environmental variables that correlate with the emission of a target behavior and indicate an ecological or curricular intervention rather than a reinforcement or punishment intervention. In keeping with the "principle of least intrusive alternative," the prudent behavior analyst will expand the functional analysis process to include setting events.

The inclusion of these temporally distant variables into the functional analysis should not be misconstrued to mean that it is acceptable to ignore motivational or reinforcement principles to explain the occurrence of a behavior. Motivational analysis continues to be the primary focus when assessing the relationship between behavior and environmental events. Although not new, there is increasing interest by behavior analysts and communication specialists in the communicative function of maladaptive behavior (Watzlawick et al., 1967; Carr, 1977; Carr & Durand, 1985). Donnellan (1984) advocates assessing the possible communicative intent of a problem behavior as part of a functional analysis. Motivational sources and possible communicative messages associated with each source are listed in Table 12.2. This focus on the importance of function rather than form is compatible with the behavioral analytic approach. From an educational perspective, understanding the communicative function of a maladaptive behavior and teaching an adaptive form that fulfills the same message function has been an effective means of reducing the occurrence of a problem behavior while simultaneously teaching a functional skill (Carr & Durand, 1985; Durand, 1982; Horner & Budd, 1985).

Social Validation Survey

Since Wolf (1978) introduced the concept of social validity, behavior analysts, including special educators, have increasingly solicited input from individuals regarding the social importance of behavior management and educational programs. Wolf (1978) recommends that behavior analysts validate their work on at least three levels:

1. The social significance of the *goals*. Are the specific behavioral goals really what society wants?
2. The social appropriateness of the *procedures*. Do the ends justify the means? That is, do the participants, caregivers and other consumers consider the treatment procedures acceptable?
3. The social importance of the *effects*. Are consumers satisfied with the results? All the results, including any unpredicted ones? (p. 207)

Social validation procedures are firmly embedded into special education practice. Parents and significant others are repeatedly asked to judge the social significance of educational goals, the acceptability of a particular instructional or behavioral management procedure, and the importance of the resultant behavior change. Translated into educational practice, special educators include parents (and others) at *every* step of the decision-making process, from identifying target behaviors or skills to be included in the IEP to evaluating the practical significance of behavior gains. Input from parents can be obtained by regularly scheduled conferences, weekly progress reports, and questionnaires. It is important to point out that social validation procedures and measures were not intended to replace more objective, empirically based identification and evaluation procedures. Social validity measures should be viewed as important supplementary measures of consumer satisfaction and used in combination with more objective measures generated through formative evaluation.

Behavioral-Educational Interventions

Prior to the design and implementation of a behavior change program the behavior analyst will have:

TABLE 12.2 Summary of motivational sources, possible communicative messages, and related interventions

Motivational Source	Possible Communicative Message(s)	Intervention Procedures		
		Teach Replacement Communicative Response	Functionally Related Alt-R Procedures	Manipulation of Antecedent Conditions
I. Positive Reinforcement:[a, b.] *Attention* maintains behavior (Lovaas, Freitag, Gold, & Kassorla, 1965)	"Pay attention to me" (general) "Hello!" (greeting) "Look at me, I'm silly" (humor) "Play with me" "Look at _____" (comment) "Help me"	Teach a variety of means for requesting/soliciting attention, depending on context (e.g., tap on arm, greeting sign, "Play," "Help," etc.; discussed by Carr, 1981; Durand, 1982)	Use attention to reinforce already-occurring alternative responses (Hall, Lund, & Jackson, 1968; Lovaas et al., 1965) Direct instruction + social reinforcement of new alternative responses (Russo, Cataldo, & Cushing 1981)	Alter environment to provide non-contingent attention
Material reinforcers (e.g., food, objects) maintain behavior (Lovaas & Simmons, (1969)	"I want _____"	Teach manual sign for desired object/food (Carr, 1979; Horner & Budd, 1983)	Use desired materials to reinforce already-occurring alternative responses Direct instruction + material reinforcement of new, alternative responses (Favell, McGimsey, & Jones, 1978)	Alter environment to provide non-contingent access to material reinforcers (stimulus satiation, Aylion, 1963)
II. Negative reinforcement:[a, b] *Termination* of an aversive stimulus or situation maintains behavior (Carr, Newsom, & Binkoff, 1976)	"I don't want to do this anymore" "Stop!" "No!" "I don't understand; I want out!"	Teach manual/gestural sign to terminate activity/escape (Carr, Newsom, & Binkoff, 1980; discussed by Durand, 1982)	Reinforce already-occurring alternative responses with escape	Alter context to decrease/eliminate aversiveness: *simplify tasks* (Weeks & Gaylord-Ross, 1981); *Increase preference value of tasks* (Carr et al., 1980; Gaylord-Ross, Weeks, & Lipner, 1980); *decrease or alter instructional demands* Carr et al., 1976; Gaylord-Ross et al., 1980); *alter instructional procedures* (Weeks & Gaylord-Ross, 1981)

TABLE 12.2 (continued)

		Intervention Procedures		
Motivational Source	Possible Communicative Message(s)	Teach Replacement Communicative Response	Functionally Related Alt-R Procedures	Manipulation of Antecedent Conditions
III. Extinction/Frustration:[b] Previously available reinforcers are no longer available (Baumeister & Forehand, 1971)	"Help me" "I'm frustrated" "Why can't I have . . . ?" "You used to give ___ to me; I want it now"	Teach communicative means for obtaining desired reinforcers and/or for enlisting aid to obtain reinforcers	Reinstate previously available reinforcers contingent on occurrence of alternative response	Alter environment to provide previously available reinforcers: alter instructional procedures, provide richer reinforcement schedule, etc.
IV. Arousal induction/sensory reinforcement:[a, b] Behavior provides sensory stimulation that is intrinsically reinforcing (Berkson, 1967)	"I'm not getting the input I want" "I'm bored"	Teach communicative means to obtain sensory input, e.g., request for sensory activity (discussed by Durand, 1982)	Provide reinforcing sensory input through alternative activities (Eason, White, & Newsom, 1982; Favell, McGimsey, & Schell, 1982) Direct instruction + reinforcement of alternative behaviors (Mullick, Hoyt, Rojahn, & Schroeder, 1978)	Alter environment to provide more sensory input and stimulation: enrich environment and curriculum (Gaylord-Ross, 1980)
V. Arousal Reduction:[b] Behavior maintained by termination of aversive overstimulation—i.e., behavior "blocks out" excess sensory input (Hutt & Hutt, 1965)	"I'm anxious/tense/excited/nervous/overwhelmed, etc." "Help me"	Teach alternative communicative means for expressing distress/enlisting aid	Provide and reinforce alternative means of removing the aversive effects of overstimulation: *vigorous exercise* (Ohlsen, 1978; Kern, Koegel, Dyer, Blew, & Fenton, 1982); *relaxation response* (Graziano & Kean, 1971)	Alter environment to decrease environmental stimulation and demands (Weeks & Gaylord-Ross, 1981)
VI. Respondent Conditioning:[b] Behavior originated from association with a traumatic event (eg., loud noise, pain) that triggers the behavior (Wolpe, 1973). Behavior is then maintained by positive or negative reinforcement.	"I'm scared/afraid" "This is a bad habit that I can't control" "I want _____ to stop" "Help!"	Teach communicative means to express distress or enlist assistance	Reinforce gradual tolerance of trigger stimulus: systematic desensitization (Wolpe, 1973; see Miranda, in press, for a review) Direct instruction + reinforcement of alternative responses to trigger stimulus	Alter environment to preclude occurrence of the trigger stimulus

Table 12.2 (continued)

Motivational Source	Possible Communicative Message(s)	Intervention Procedures		
		Teach Replacement Communicative Response	Functionally Related Alt-R Procedures	Manipulation of Antecedent Conditions
VII. Physiological:[a, b] Behavior is the product of an aberrant physiological process (Cataldo & Harris, 1982)	"I hurt" "I'm tired"	Teach communicative means to express distress	Not applicable	Not applicable

a—discussed by Carr, 1977
b—discussed by Romanczyk, Kistner, & Shakelford, 1982

Source: From "Analyzing the Communicative Functions of Aberrant Behavior" by A.M. Donellan, P.L. Mirenda, R.A. Mesaros and L.L. Fassbender, 1984, *Journal of the Association for Persons with Severe Handicaps, 9*(3), pp. 206–207. Copyright 1984 by The Association for Persons with Severe Handicaps. Reprinted by permission.

1. Verified that there is a problem (environmental analysis, discrepancy analysis, baseline assessment, social validation),
2. Identified the conditions under which the behavior is emitted (functional analysis),
3. Referred the child to a physician to obviate the possibility of there being a biological/medical basis for the maladaptive behavior (medical assessment),
4. Pinpointed a replacement behavior that has the same communicative function (environmental analysis, motivational analysis), and
5. Informed parents and significant others of the potential long-term effect that not intervening might have on the child attaining maximum independence and productivity in current and future environments (environmental analysis, social validation).

The end result of the behavioral assessment process should be consensus among teachers, parents, and significant others as to the need to intervene. Questions that should be answered to arrive at a decision include:

- Does the behavior cause injury to the student or others?
- Does the behavior present a safety risk to the student or others?
- Does the behavior interfere with the student's or another's learning?
- Does the behavior cause others to avoid interacting with the student? (Gaylord-Ross, 1980).

If the answer to any one of these questions is "yes," the next step is to develop an intervention plan. The first step of any intervention plan is to write a behavioral objective for both the replacement behavior and the maladaptive behavior. Two objectives are recommended to accentuate the importance of monitoring the effects and side effects of an intervention. Each of these objectives should identify that characteristic of the behavior to be changed (frequency, duration, magnitude), specify the conditions under which the replacement behavior is to occur (and maladaptive behavior is not to occur), and specify the criterion level for evaluating the effectiveness of the program. Each of these components of the behavioral objectives require input from parents and significant others.

As described in the Bailey et al. (in press), Evans and Meyer (1985), and Gaylord-Ross (1980) models for approaching behavior problems, a behavior management plan should adhere to the "criterion of the least dangerous assumption," "principle of least intrusive alternative," and "fair pair" rule and include both formative evaluation and social validation procedures. Adherence to these principles and procedures ensures that the behavior management plan is designed and implemented following ethical guidelines, state-of-the-art educational practices, and a data-based approach for objectively evaluating the effectiveness of the plan. When developing an intervention plan it is important to realize that the plan is not "etched in stone." Based on the data that are collected on the target behaviors (maladaptive and adaptive), as well as any other behavior that may be influenced by the intervention strategy (negative and positive side effects), the practitioner may decide to modify the plan. For this reason it is important to formatively evaluate and socially validate the effectiveness of the behavior change on a regular basis.

Criterion of the Least Dangerous Assumption

The criterion of the least dangerous assumption was introduced into the behavior management literature by Donnellan (1984). She writes: "This criterion or standard asserts that in the absence of conclusive data, educational decisions should be based on assumptions which if incorrect, will have the least dangerous effect on the students" (p. 142). It is clear from this statement that the criterion of the least dangerous assumption is an interim standard to be used only when data supporting a particular strategy or method of intervention are not available. If an intervention has supporting data as to its effectiveness, and it is the least intrusive intervention with such support data, it is appropriate to select this intervention over less intrusive alternatives that have no data base documenting their effectiveness with the target behavior. As with any method used to reduce the occurrence of an excess behavior, an appropriate replacement behavior should be taught concurrently. In addition to having implications in the design of behavior intervention plans, Donnellan recommends its use in making decisions regarding a special needs student's opportunity to interact with non-handicapped peers, placement, instructional locations and arrangements, curriculum, instructional methods and parents' involvement in the educational program. When objectively collected and empirically valid data are not available, it is both ethical and logical to adhere to the criterion of the least dangerous assumption.

Principle of Least Intrusive Alternative

The principle of least intrusive alternative has become a "yardstick" for selecting one intervention over another. This principle is an extension of the "principle of parsimony," which is used by educators when selecting instructional procedures for "difficult-to-teach" children (Etzel & LeBlanc, 1979). Simply stated, both principles advocate the use of the simplest, *yet effective*, intervention when changing behavior.

A difference of approach appears in the literature regarding the use of intrusive (aversive) procedures. One position is stated in the standards put forth by the Association for the Advancement of Behavior Therapy (AABT) (Favell et al., 1982a) regarding the treatment of self-injury. The AABT recommendations are listed in Table 12.3. These guidelines are arranged in a least intrusive (or punitive) hierarchy and reflect the task force's understanding of the life-threatening nature of some self-injurious behavior. We believe these recommendations may extend to other aberrant behaviors including severe physical aggression directed at peers. Essentially these recommendations suggest that medical/biological and ecological variables should be thoroughly and competently assessed, and the results should be actively used in planning treatment programs. Further, they clearly stipulate that the selection of treatments adhere to the principle of least intrusive but effective intervention. If the choice of treatments is between procedures that are equally effective, then the least aversive (intrusive) should be selected. If the choice is between a less intrusive but *in*effective procedure and a more aversive but effective procedure, then the effective procedure should be selected.

The second position is similar and is reflected in The Association for Persons with Severe Handicaps (TASH) resolution shown in Table 12.4. According to Evans and Meyer (1985), the resolution specifies that students "have a right to effective interventions that do not inflict pain, tissue damage, humiliation, discomfort, and stigma as expected side effects accompanying behavior change" (p. 48). They further discuss the AABT standards and make the following points:

While these standards do represent a valuable advance in decision making, we disagree that the failure of other methods should be part of the judgment as one cannot determine whether such failure reflects an incorrect functional analysis, poor treatment planning, or a history of repeated failure to provide a comprehensive state-of-the-art remedial educational program and habilitative living environment. In contrast, this text supports the TASH resolution in asserting the general principle that handicapped individuals have a right to effective interventions that do not inflict pain, tissue damage, humiliation, discomfort, and stigma as expected side effects accompanying behavior change. (p. 48)

TABLE 12.3 Association for Advancement of Behavior Therapy (AABT) recommendations for the treatment of self-injury

- The identification of biological and environmental conditions which may maintain the client's self-injury and the explicit inclusion of that information in the design of treatment. Such an analysis should include identification of medical conditions which may contribute to the problem, environmental situations which regularly evoke the behavior, and the consequences of self-injury which may be reinforcing it.
- The deliberate teaching and reinforcement of noninjurious, appropriate behavior. Such behavioral alternatives to self-injury may include communication, cooperation with tasks, independent leisure, and social skills.
- The identification and discontinuation of reinforcers for the self-injurious behavior, typically by arranging conditions so that caretakers can safely and consistently minimize reactions to the behavior which might be inadvertently reinforcing it.
- The establishment and provision of overall stimulus conditions which are associated with noninjurious behavior (such as through environmental enrichment), and the alteration or elimination of environmental conditions which are regularly associated with self-injury (such as situations which are unnecessarily frustrating or nonreinforcing).
- In cases where the behavior is dangerous, interferes excessively with habilitative or humanizing activities, or has failed to improve when treated with the less intrusive procedures outlined above, a punishing consequence such as overcorrection, or in extremely severe cases, shock for self-injury may also be necessary.
- The provision for generalizing improvement into all environments in which the individual lives and for maintaining improvement over time.

Source: From "The Treatment of Self-injurious Behavior" by J.E. Favell, N.H. Azrin, A.A. Baumeister, E.G. Carr, M.F. Dorsey, R. Forehand, R.M. Foxx, O.I. Lovaas, A. Rincover, T.R. Risley, R.G. Romanczyk, D.C. Russo, S.R. Schroeder, and J.V. Solnick, 1982, *Behavior Therapy, 13*, p. 545. Copyright 1982 by the Association for Advancement of Behavior Therapy. Reprinted by permission of the publisher and the author.

The two positions appear to agree on three points:

1. Both positions assume that professionals are under an obligation to assess thoroughly and competently medical/biological and ecological variables that may be related to students' severe behavior problems.
2. Both positions assume that professionals are under an obligation to provide adequate and appropriate interventions that accelerate functional, adaptive behaviors.
3. Both positions assume that professionals are under an obligation to use effective procedures for treating severe aberrant behavior.

The dilemma and potential disagreement arise in the following situation: A self-injurious behavior or severe aggression exists and has been thoroughly and competently assessed; extensive attempts have been made to develop adaptive replacement and communicative behaviors, and to treat it competently with nonaversive procedures, and yet the aberrant behavior continues at a high rate. The question is, "Should aversive procedures that have been shown to be effective in the past be used even if they inflict pain and discomfort?" If the answer is no, the professional assumes that some nonpunitive alternative is available and will be successful. In all honesty, we cannot accept this assumption although it has great appeal and is desirable. It simply does not reflect the field's current level of knowledge. Research focusing on the development

of such interventions is badly needed, and we support it. If on the other hand, one answers, "Yes, aversives can be used," then the professional should use the least aversive but effective procedure responsibly.

The principle of least intrusive alternative should be used in making at least two decisions when designing a behavior management plan. First, it should be used in deciding whether to implement a reinforcement, ecological, curriculum, punishment, or some combination intervention (Gaylord-Ross, 1980). Assuming these categories of interventions are listed in a least intrusive hierarchy, the behavior analyst will implement a reinforcement plan (differential reinforcement of other behavior) before a punishment program. Even if there are no data supporting the effectiveness of a reinforcement intervention with a class of behaviors similar to that of the target behavior, the behavior management specialist must attempt to document the effects (and side effects) of such a plan. In reality, the practitioner is likely to combine reinforcement, ecological, and curricular interventions prior to resorting to the use of a punishment procedure. This is both a logical and an ethical decision on the part of the behavior analyst before recommending, designing, and implementing a punitive intervention. *The exception to this fundamental standard operates when no data are available to support a less intrusive intervention and the target behavior is an immediate (moment to moment) threat to the*

TABLE 12.4 The Association for Persons with Severe Handicaps (TASH) resolution on intrusive interventions (passed, October 1981)

WHEREAS, in order to realize the goals and objectives of The Association for Persons with Severe Handicaps, including the right of each severely handicapped person to grow, develop, and enjoy life in integrated and normalized community environments, the following resolution is adopted:

WHEREAS, educational and other habilitative services must employ instructional and management strategies which are consistent with the right of each individual with severe handicaps to an effective treatment which does not compromise the equal important right to freedom from harm. This requires educational and habilitative procedures free from indiscriminant use of drugs, aversive stimuli, environmental deprivation, or exclusion from services; and

WHEREAS, TASH supports a cessation of the use of any treatment option which exhibits some or all of the following characteristics: (1) obvious signs of physical pain experienced by the individual; (2) potential or actual physical side effects, including tissue damage, physical illness, severe stress, and/or death, that would properly require the involvement of medical personnel; (3) dehumanization of persons with severe handicaps because the procedures are normally unacceptable for nonhandicapped persons in community environment; (4) extreme ambivalence and discomfort by family, staff, and/or caregivers regarding the necessity of such extreme strategies or their own involvement in such interventions; and (5) obvious repulsion and/or stress felt by nonhandicapped peers and community members who cannot reconcile extreme procedures with acceptable standard practice;

RESOLVED, that The Association for Persons with Severe Handicaps' resources and expertise be dedicated to the development, implementation, evaluation, dissemination, and advocacy of educational and management practices which are appropriate for use in integrated environments and which are consistent with the commitment to a high quality of life for individuals with severe handicaps.

Source: From "Resolution on Intrusive Interventions" by The Association for Persons with Severe Handicaps (TASH), 1985, *TASH Newsletter, 11* (November), p. 3. Copyright 1985 by the Association for Persons with Severe Handicaps. Reprinted by permission.

life, safety, or physical well-being of the student or others. In such rare cases, a punishment intervention, in combination with reinforcement, ecological, and curricular interventions may be indicated from the start.

The second time the special educator should adhere to the principle of least intrusive alternative is when selecting the specific punishment procedure to be implemented. Less aversive procedures should be tried before more aversive procedures: punishment procedures that remove positive reinforcers that maintain a behavior (Type 2 punishment) should be attempted before punishment procedures that present an aversive stimulus contingent upon an occurrence of a behavior (Type 1 punishment). Within each type of punishment, it is prudent first to select those methods of intervention that are believed to be least intrusive and that have a data base supporting their effectiveness with topographically similar behaviors. The exception to this recommendation operates when there is reason to believe, based on the applied research literature, that the child will come to tolerate or habituate to a "mild" aversive consequence, forcing the use of a more aversive procedure that may not have been necessary if an "intermediate" punishment procedure had been selected initially. Unfortunately, there are no clear-cut guidelines for evaluating the aversiveness of most punishment

procedures. However, through logical analysis, formative evaluation, and social validation efforts, behavior analysts, in concert with parents and significant others, should be able to select effective methods of intervention that are least intrusive. A review of commonly used intervention techniques, including those addressing reinforcement, ecological, and curriculum strategies, are presented in Chapter 5.

"Fair Pair" Rule

The "fair pair" rule (White & Haring, 1976), as discussed in Chapter 5, states that "when it is necessary to decrease an undesirable behavior, you should select one or more desirable behaviors to increase at the same time." This rule is fundamental to ethical behavior management practice. It calls attention to the fact that behavior deceleration programs are not education: alone they do not teach adaptive behaviors that can replace the maladaptive behavior. If a special educator or behavior analyst has conducted a behavioral assessment as previously described, then the teacher should pinpoint and teach an *appropriate alternative behavior* having the same communicative function. This can be accomplished through the use of any one of the differential reinforcement procedures discussed in Chapter 5 or by a more complex social skills training program. Under no circumstances is it appropriate to design a behavior intervention plan for decreasing the frequency of an excess behavior without giving equal attention and effort to increasing the frequency of a socially appropriate alternative behavior.

Formative Evaluation

In keeping with AABT standards for the treatment of self-injurious behavior and sound educational practice, all behavior intervention plans should include the repeated measurement of behavior within the context of a single-subject research design (formative evaluation). Tawney and Gast (1984) describe formative evaluation as a dynamic or ongoing process that "emphasizes the frequent and repeated measurement of student performance on functional and age-appropriate tasks, assessed under natural conditions, over time" (p. 81). Unlike summative evaluation, which incorporates infrequent or periodic measures of student behavior, formative evaluation permits teachers and applied researchers to make data-based decisions about the effectiveness of an instructional or behavior management program achieving its intended objective. Through constant daily feedback on where a student is relative to his instructional/behavior management objective, the teacher can make an objective decision whether to maintain, modify, or completely change the intervention strategy. With no class of behaviors is it more important to monitor directly and continuously the effects and side effects (positive and negative) of an intervention plan than it is with a plan that is aimed at modifying the frequency of a maladaptive behavior. If clinicians are to be effective in their implementation of interventions they must make objective decisions, that is, decisions that are both logically and empirically based and in accordance with the agreed-upon plan. To deviate from an intervention plan that was developed with parents and other professionals could jeopardize the clinician's credibility and result in student regression.

All moment-to-moment decisions made in response to a student's behavior should be consistent with the filed plan and document the effect the program change has on the student's behavior. It is the era of accountability in special education, and there is no more appropriate way for a special educator to be accountable than to evaluate formatively the effects and side effects of a prescribed intervention. Therefore, it is imperative that teachers be thoroughly familiar with and competent in the use of the direct observational measurement procedures and single-subject research designs discussed in Chapter 4. Competence in these components of formative evaluation is important not only from the standpoint of a consumer of applied research, but also as a developer and implementor of effective instructional and behavior management programs.

The remainder of this chapter reviews five different classes of severe aberrant behavior: self-injurious, stereotypic, aggressive/disruptive, social withdrawal, and noncompliant behavior. We are not suggesting that students with any of the behaviors will automatically require treatment, nor do these five classes constitute all of the potentially severe, aberrant behavior that will require intervention. These are included because they are sufficiently frequent and sufficiently aberrant. Two notes of caution are pertinent. First, we assume that intervention will be conducted by a team of competent professionals that includes the parents. Second, we assume consideration will be given to the issues discussed earlier when decisions about treatment are made.

DESCRIPTION AND MANAGEMENT OF SELF-INJURIOUS BEHAVIOR

Individuals with moderate and severe handicaps may display behaviors that are disturbing to others; but no behavior probably is more disturbing than self-injurious behavior (SIB). Consider the following example: Lisa is a 6-year-old girl with autism. She is a beautiful child with small features, blond hair, large brown eyes, and an interesting, quizzical smile. She speaks with one- and two-word phrases; can feed, dress, and bathe herself; has learned to play with certain toys for as much as 15 minutes; and can swim and ride a tricycle. However, in certain situations she clenches her fist and hits her head sharply and repeatedly. The noise from the blows is startling and indicates their force is considerable. She also strikes her head against the floor or furniture. How can such behavior be explained? Why does she do it? What can be done about the behavior? Will she always be like this? The following sections explore these questions further.

Self-injurious behavior (SIB) refers "to a broad array of responses which result in physical damage to the individual displaying the behavior" (Favell et al., 1982a, p. 531); frequently they are stereotypic and repetitious. Common examples are hitting one's head or banging it on objects, biting various parts of the body, pulling hair, scratching, and poking eyes. Head banging, hand biting, and eye poking are the most frequent (Whitman & Scibak, 1979). Other less common SIBs (some of which may be life-threatening) include repeated vomiting, rumination (vomiting and swallowing vomitus), pica (eating inedible objects), coprophagia (eating feces), and self-induced seizures (Favell et al., 1982a; Johnson & Baumeister, 1978). Many terms have been used to describe such behavior, but self-injurious behavior is preferred because it is descriptive and does not imply a specific motivation on the part of the performer (Corbett, 1975).

Nonhandicapped children may engage in SIB, but it is "usually mild and transient" (Corbett, 1975, p. 79). SIB is most common in infants under 18 months (11–17%), less common at two years (9%), and nearly nonexistent by 5 years. Although estimates of the incidence of SIB vary with developmentally disabled populations (5–15%), self-injury is more common and more severe in students with autism and retardation than in nonhandicapped and mildly handicapped populations (Corbett, 1975; Favell et al., 1982a).

Proposed Explanations for Self-Injurious Behavior

At least four general types of explanations for SIB have been postulated. The least accepted and most difficult to document scientifically is the *psychoanalytic explanation*. This position proposes that students engage in SIB to reduce guilt by inflicting pain on themselves, to distinguish their "self" from the external world, and to "invert" their aggression (Corbett, 1975). Another explanation is the *neurophysiological* or sensory stimulation hypothesis; this explanation suggests that the self-injury stimulates a given portion of the brain or that it is related to a level or type of sensory stimulation that has reinforcing properties (Corbett, 1975; Rincover & Devany, 1982). A related explanation is the *organic or biological approach*, where the SIB is thought to be a result of some physiological disorder (Carr, 1977; Demchak & Halle, 1985). One reason for this explanation is that students with Cornelia de Lange syndrome and Lesch-Nyhan syndrome often engage in self-injury. Further, some medical conditions such as otitis media (middle ear infection)

may result in SIB (Demchak & Halle, 1985; Favell et al., 1982a). The final explanation is that *environmental contingencies* may be causing the child to engage in self-injury, because it is positively or negatively reinforced (Carr, 1977; Demchak & Halle, 1985).

With the exception of the psychoanalytic position, most researchers agree that SIB may be caused and maintained by any of the explanations listed above; that is, one individual's SIB may be due to one cause and another's related to a different cause (Carr, 1977). It is also clear that some SIB may be caused by one explanation (organic as in the case of otitis media) and then maintained by another (environmental contingencies) (Demchak & Halle, 1985). Further, an organic and neurophysiological disorder may explain the cause of SIB, but the SIB can be treated with behavioral procedures (Favell et al., 1982a). Although more research is needed, medical treatments currently are not the "treatments of choice" (Favell et al., 1982a). Finally, identifying the factors that maintain SIB allows more appropriate intervention planning, especially if the cause is related to environmental contingencies (Demchak & Halle, 1975; Durand & Carr, 1985).

Management of Self-Injurious Behavior

Assessment

Because of the nature of SIB, most professionals would agree that intervention should be implemented to reduce it (Hollis, 1982). However, deciding to intervene may be much easier than selecting an appropriate intervention procedure. Once the team, including the parents, have decided to treat the SIB, an assessment of variables that maintain it should be conducted. This assessment should include a functional analysis of the SIB in the natural environment. However, if the self-injury is frequent and severe, a functional analysis in the natural setting may not be practical. An alternative is to assess the effects of specific environmental conditions in isolated, short duration, artificial situations. For example, Iwata et al. (1982) analyzed the SIB of 9 students under four specific conditions. In the first condition, *social disapproval*, the student and experimenter were in a room together, toys were available, and the experimenter pretended to read a book. For each episode of SIB, the experimenter told the student to stop being self-injurious and provided brief (nonpunitive) physical contact.

This was done to stimulate the type of adult attention that may unintentionally positively reinforce students for SIB in the natural environment. The second condition, *academic demand,* involved the experimenter and child in a structured instructional task. Contingent upon each SIB, the experimenter turned away for 30 seconds. This allowed the experimenters to determine whether the SIB was being maintained by escape or avoidance of the task (negative reinforcement). The third condition, *unstructured play,* involved the experimenter and child in a room with a variety of toys. No demands were placed on student, praise and physical contact were provided for appropriate responses, and self-injury was ignored. This condition served as an "enriched" environment for purposes of control. The final condition, *alone,* involved only the child in the room with no materials available. This represented an impoverished environment with minimal stimulation. By systematically observing students' levels of SIB under these conditions, the experimenters established hypotheses about factors maintaining the behavior for 6 of the 9 students. One hypothesis was that students sought sensory stimulation by their SIB (high rates in the "alone" condition); this is consistent with previous research (cf. Durand, 1982; Rincover & Devany, 1982). Another hypothesis proposed that students escaped the demands of tasks; thus, they were negatively reinforced, (high rates in the "academic demand" condition). This hypothesis is also consistent with considerable research showing students are more apt to display inappropriate behavior, including SIB, in difficult rather than easy instructional situations (cf. Carr & Durand, 1985; Carr, et al., 1976; Durand, 1982). Another hypothesis was that adult social attention maintained the SIB (high rates in the "social disapproval" condition). This hypothesis is also supported by previous research (cf. Lovaas, Freitag, Gold, & Kassorla, 1965). Durand and Carr (1985) suggest a variation of this hypothesis: students receive tangible objects that have reinforcing value contingent upon SIB. The practical value of the study by Iwata et al. (1982) is that it provides a model for designing artificial assessment situations that allow teachers to identify the factors maintaining SIB. By conducting functional analyses or short assessment sessions as described by Iwata et al. (1982), the factors that appear to maintain the SIB can be identified. This information can be used to plan treatments (Carr & Durand, 1985; Demchak &

Halle, 1985; Durand, 1982); see the guidelines section below.

Treatment

In the past 20 years, SIB has been a focus of considerable applied research, and a number of different intervention procedures that span the range of intrusiveness have been used (Favell et al., 1982a). The methodological adequacy of much of this research has been analyzed by Johnson and Baumeister (1978). However, since the late 1970s a significant shift has occurred in the treatment of SIB. This shift is a result of the failure of otherwise effective procedures with some students, and the convincing case developed by Carr (1977) showing that SIB is potentially caused and clearly maintained by multiple factors.

Curricular modifications and *environmental enrichment* have been used to treat SIB. An enriched environment, one characterized by increases in the density of differential reinforcement and the amount and type of toys or materials, may be associated with decreased levels of SIB (Horner, 1980); however, some SIB may occur under such conditions (Iwata et al., 1982). For some students, the probability of SIB is higher during instructional sessions where tasks are difficult as compared to those that are easy (Carr et al., 1976; Durand, 1982). The use of errorless learning procedures may result in decreases in errors and SIB (Weeks & Gaylord-Ross, 1981). Further, teaching students to manipulate materials that result in similar sensory stimulation as their SIB may be a reductive procedure (Favell et al., 1982b; Lockwood & Bourland, 1982). Some data suggest that providing sensory integrative therapy may result in decreases in SIB (Wells & Smith, 1983).

Modification of reinforcement contingencies, including differential reinforcement, extinction, and timeout, have been used. Differential reinforcement of other behaviors (DRO) and differential reinforcement of incompatible behaviors (DRI) have been used alone (Repp, Deitz, & Deitz, 1976; Weiher & Harman, 1975) and in combination with other procedures such as a verbal reprimand (Repp & Deitz, 1974), contingent restraint (Favell, McGimsey, & Jones, 1978), interruption of the SIB (Azrin, Besalel, & Wigotzek, 1982), and (as noted earlier) in combination with curricular modifications. However, DRO alone is not always effective (Corte, Wolfe, & Locke, 1971), but when more intrusive procedures are used, reinforcement of incompatible adaptive responses should occur. Extinction has been effective in some cases (Lovaas & Simmons, 1969), but also has been ineffective (Bucher & Lovaas, 1968). It presents problems because of the potential "extinction burst," the gradual change that may occur, considerable damage that may be possible during the course of intervention, and the ethical ramifications. Timeout from positive reinforcement has also been used to reduce self-injury. Its effectiveness is clearly related to the conditions of the time-in environment; if the time-in environment is enriched with materials and reinforcement for adaptive behaviors, then timeout is likely to be more effective (Solnick, Rincover, & Peterson, 1977).

A wide variety of *Type 1 punishment procedures* has been used to control SIB. Examples include contingent use of aromatic ammonia (Altman, Haavik, & Cook, 1978; Baumeister & Baumeister, 1978), facial screening (Barmann & Vitali, 1982; Lutzker, 1978), physical exercise (Borreson, 1980), water mist (Bailey, Pokrzywinski, & Bryant, 1983), and substances with aversive tastes (Becker, Turner, & Sajwaj, 1978; Mayhew & Harris, 1979). A great many studies have investigated the use of contingent electric shock; for reviews see Corbett (1975), Frankel and Simmons (1976), and Lichstein and Schreibman (1976). Overcorrection has also been used extensively (Azrin, Gottlieb, Hughart, Wesolowski, & Rahn, 1975; Harris & Romanczyk, 1976; Kelly & Drabman, 1977). In almost all of these cases, the punishment procedures have been used concomitantly with reinforcement of adaptive responses. Restraint has been used to prevent SIB, and applied contingently when self-injury occurs (Dorsey, Iwata, Reid, & Davis, 1982); however, in some cases it can serve as a reinforcer (Favell et al., 1978). Recently, flexible arm splints that allow sufficient range of motion for functional tasks have been used with a student who has Lesch-Nyhan syndrome to reduce finger biting (Ball, Datta, Rios, & Constantine, 1985). Such restraints hold advantages over nonflexible restraints.

Guidelines for Reducing Self-Injurious Behavior

Despite the fact that many procedures have been effective, examples exist where each procedure has been ineffective or has had limited effectiveness. As a whole, the treatment literature related to SIB suggests several general guidelines that are listed below. These guidelines are similar to those suggested by the Association for Advancement of Behavior Therapy (AABT) task force on SIB (Favell et al., 1982a); however, attempts have been made to integrate information related to the maintaining factors of SIB. In addition to these guidelines, the procedures described by the AABT task force for implementation of reduction programs should be followed.

1. Assessment of factors that appear to be controlling the response should be made, and a motivational hypothesis should be generated prior to the initiation of intervention (Durand & Carr, 1985; Iwata et al., 1982).
2. Intervention should include differential reinforcement of adaptive, incompatible responses and enrichment of treatment and nontreatment environments (Favell et al., 1982a; Horner, 1980).
3. Based on the motivational hypothesis, the intervention should attempt to minimize or eliminate the influence of the motivational factors that appear to be maintaining the SIB (Durand & Carr, 1985). When the hypothesis suggests social attention or receipt of tangibles function as positive reinforcers, then social attention or tangibles should be removed (extinction) for the SIB. When escape (negative reinforcement) is the hypothesis, then the child should *not* be allowed to escape from social contact or the instructional task by engaging in SIB. If the hypothesis suggests the SIB is for sensory stimulation, then sensory extinction should be used or the child should be taught to receive similar sensory stimulation through more appropriate responses (toy play or self-stimulatory behavior) (Durand & Carr, 1985; Rincover & Devany, 1982).
4. Based on the motivational hypothesis, the intervention should involve attempts to teach the child more appropriate alternative responses (Durand & Carr, 1985). If the hypothesis suggests the SIB is maintained by social attention or receipt of tangibles, the child should be taught more adaptive communicative responses for requesting attention and/or objects. If the hypothesis suggests the SIB is controlled by escape, the student should be taught more appropriate responses for requesting assistance and protesting. Reinforcement for correct responses and task completion should be increased, instructional task should be revised, or

errorless learning procedures should be used (Durand & Carr, 1985; Weeks & Gaylord-Ross, 1981). If the hypothesis suggests the function of SIB is sensory stimulation, then the child should be taught to request more appropriate sensory stimulation or to play with appropriate toys that provide similar sensory stimulation (Favell et al., 1982b). Use of sensory integrative therapy may also be considered (Wells & Smith, 1983).

5. When environmental enrichment, DRO or DRI, and attempts to minimize the influence of motivational factors have been adequately implemented, but the SIB has not been reduced, the treatment team should continue these procedures and select a more intrusive intervention procedure. When judged appropriate by the treatment team and reviewed by competent behavior analysts, Type 1 and 2 punishment procedures should be considered (Favell et al., 1982a).

6. All intervention attempts should plan for the maintenance of desirable treatment effects, generalization of those effects, and detection of undesirable "side" or multiple effects (Baumeister & Rollings, 1976; Johnson & Baumeister, 1978).

DESCRIPTION AND MANAGEMENT OF STEREOTYPIC BEHAVIOR

Stereotypic responses, commonly called self-stimulatory behaviors, are idiosyncratic, highly consistent, repetitive, rhythmic movements of the body or body parts (Baumeister, 1978). Examples include head weaving, rocking, arm and finger flapping, posturing, and mouthing hands or objects. The term *stereotypy* is preferred over *self-stimulation* because it is descriptive and does not imply that the child is stimulating herself. The origins of stereotypy are unclear (Baumeister, 1978; Baumeister & Forehand, 1973). Although they appear to provide sensory input that has reinforcing properties (Rincover, 1978), their functions are also unclear. This has led some authors to conclude that stereotypy has no obvious social consequences (Koegel, Firestone, Kramme, & Dunlap, 1974).

The occurrence of stereotypic behavior is affected by a number of variables, some of which are environmental. Stereotypic behaviors are cyclic and may increase and decrease in rate on daily,

monthly, and perhaps yearly cycles (Brusca, 1985). As students grow older, the frequency of stereotypy appears to increase (Thompson, & Berkson, 1985). When students are in high demand situations ("frustrating" ones), they are more apt to engage in stereotypy (Baumeister, 1978). After a stereotypic response has been treated with a punishment procedure, the proximity of the teacher is related to the rate of the response; the farther away the teacher is from the student, the greater the likelihood of stereotypic behavior (Rollings, Baumeister, & Baumeister, 1977). When toys are accessible, a decrease in the rate of stereotypic behavior may occur, although habituation is possible; students may be more apt to engage in stereotypy when they are alone than when they are with other people (Baumeister, 1978). Thus, being meaningfully engaged will likely result in less stereotypic behavior.

Management of Stereotypic Responses

Assessment

Stereotypic behaviors have been considered pathological, and Baumeister (1978), while observing how little is known about the origins and functions of stereotypy, states, "What I do know is that they are not normal" (p. 354). Stereotypic behaviors may be bizarre, they may call attention to the performer, and may result in nonhandicapped persons avoiding the students; thus, less interaction may occur between the two populations. When this scenario is true, sufficient reason may exist for treating such behaviors. Another reason for treating stereotypic behavior is its relationship to learning. When some students engage in stereotypy, they do not learn; however, when their stereotypy is suppressed, learning increases (Koegel & Covert, 1972; Koegel et al., 1974; Risley, 1968.

In recent years, however, stereotypic behaviors are being viewed more favorably. Nearly everyone engages in stereotypic behavior: we stroke our beards, twirl our hair, swing our feet, tap our fingers, or repetitively play with objects. Rago and Case (1978) found that college students during a lecture spend similar amounts of time in stereotypic behaviors as do persons with mental retardation. However, college students are engaged in a larger *variety* of stereotypic behaviors whereas students with retardation tend to engage in a limited number. Such data and our inability to identify the functions of these behaviors suggest that automatically making the decision to reduce or eliminate these responses may be premature. Further, some students learn despite engaging in stereotypic behaviors (Klier & Harris, 1977; Wolery, 1978). In fact, Hargrave and Swisher (1975) described a student who actually learned better in a condition where he engaged in stereotypic responding. Chock and Glahn (1983) found that higher functioning echolalic children with autism learned while also engaging in stereotypic responding, but children with autism who were classified as mute and low functioning did not. LaGrow and Repp (1984) raise two questions: "The first is whether researchers and practitioners should attempt to eliminate stereotypic responding for all persons or whether, instead, they should teach these individuals to discriminate between free periods, learning periods, and social periods, with stereotypy considered inappropriate only in the latter two" (p. 607). It is our position that teams should approach cautiously the use of reductive procedures for stereotypy. If the response interferes with instruction or calls undue notice to the student, then perhaps the behavior should become a target for deceleration.

Treatment

The following paragraphs briefly identify and discuss procedures for reducing the occurrence of stereotypic behaviors. This section relies heavily on a review by LaGrow and Repp (1984). A review of the methodological adequacy of the research literature on stereotypic responses is provided by Schrader, Shaull, and Elmore (1983).

As would be expected from the factors that influence the rate of stereotypy, *curricular modifications and environmental enrichment* may decrease the behavior. Increased manipulation of objects, increased teacher-initiated social interactions, specific directions not to engage in stereotypy, and increased reinforcement for adaptive responses may result in decreased stereotypic responding (LaGrow & Repp, 1984). Thus, facilitating active engagement in adaptive behaviors is a legitimate intervention for decreasing the rate of stereotypic behavior. Simply providing increased materials and enrichment of the environment may not eliminate the behavior, but are prerequisite conditions for using more intrusive procedures.

Modification of reinforcement contingencies including differential reinforcement, timeout, and sensory extinction have been used. DRO and DRI have been used alone and in combination with other procedures. When used alone, both may reduce the frequency of stereotypic responding; however, they may be more effective when used in combination with other procedures such as a contingent "no," physical restraint, or interrupting the behavior (LaGrow & Repp, 1984). DRI may be preferred over DRO because the increases in compatible behavior may result in more generalized reduction. Timeout from positive reinforcement has been used with some effectiveness. However, when the student's stereotypic behavior can be performed during timeout, social isolation (as is commonly done with timeout procedures) may not be warranted.

In a unique investigation into reinforcement contingencies, Neisworth, Hunt, Gallop, & Madle (1985) reinforced students with edibles *for* engaging in stereotypic behaviors. After several sessions of continuous reinforcement of the stereotypy, they stopped reinforcing them. As a result, the rate of stereotypic responding dropped considerably. The reduced rates maintained for one of the students. It would appear that the edible reinforcer had acquired control over the stereotypic behavior; thus, when it was removed the behavior was essentially put on extinction.

Rincover, Cook, Peoples, and Packard (1979) attempted to remove the sensory reinforcers students received during stereotypic responding. They determined that the stereotypic behavior produced three types of sensory feedback: proprioceptive, visual, and auditory. Different types of feedback held reinforcing properties for different students. They then eliminated or masked the reinforcing feedback: a table was carpeted to eliminate the auditory feedback a student received when he spun a plate on it, and a small vibrator was put on the student's hand to mask the proprioceptive feedback from finger movements. These attempts resulted in substantial decreases in the rate of stereotypic behaviors. Provision of toys that produced similar sensory feedback resulted in increased use of those toys. Clearly sensory extinction should be used when the elimination or masking of the feedback reduces the stereotypic responding and concomitantly allows students to acquire adaptive responses.

Numerous Type 1 punishment procedures have been used to treat stereotypic responding. Overcorrection (Foxx & Azrin, 1973) is one of the most commonly used procedures. Generally, overcorrection produces decreases in the target stereotypic responses and has done so when other procedures were ineffective (LaGrow & Repp, 1984). However, overcorrection may have multiple effects: it has produced increases in nontargeted stereotypic behaviors and SIB (LaGrow & Repp, 1984). Not all effects are negative; increases in adaptive responses (appropriate toy play) have been observed (cf. Epstein, Doke, Sajwaj, Sorrell & Rimmer, 1974). With stereotypy, overcorrection does not appear to be "educative": it does not teach the behaviors students are required to perform during its application (LaGrow & Repp, 1984). Other aversive stimuli such as contingent electric shock, physical restraint, and aversive physical stimuli (slaps) have produced consistent reductions in stereotypic responding; verbal reprimands have also been used, but less effectively (LaGrow & Repp, 1984). Although a broad array of procedures have been successful in reducing stereotypic behaviors, generalization and maintenance of these effects needs additional study (Schrader et al., 1983). Additional research is also needed that investigates the effects of reducing one stereotypic response on other nontargeted stereotypic behaviors (Rollings & Baumeister, 1981).

As noted above, the primary issue is *whether* to target stereotypic responses for reduction, rather than *how* to reduce them. LaGrow and Repp's (1984) suggestion appears appropriate: we should teach students when and when not to engage in stereotypic responding. Some information related to this issue exists. Students in a laboratory investigation learned that when certain lights were illuminated, the punishment contingencies were in effect; but when others were lit, it was "safe" to engage in stereotypy (Rollings & Baumeister, 1981). In more applied studies, reduction has occurred in punishment settings but not in others; it has also occurred in the presence of the person providing the punishment but not in the presence of persons who had not administered it (Matson & Stephens, 1981). Thus, it is clear that some students can discriminate when punishment contingencies are in effect and, with minimal instruction, may be able to discriminate settings and times when stereotypic responding would and would not be acceptable.

Not all of the research has attempted to reduce stereotypic responding. Hung (1978) allowed students to exchange tokens for time to engage in stereotypic behaviors; as a result, the students' behaviors that earned tokens increased. Wolery

(1978) attempted to duplicate the sensory stimulation students received during stereotypic responding and then provided this stimulation to students contingent upon correct responses. This contingency produced increases in the percent of correct responses. Devany (1979) provided students with the object they used in their stereotypic behaviors contingent upon correct responses, and the percentage of correct responses increased. During extra-therapy sessions, the student appeared to engage in less stereotypic behavior after such use. Wolery, Kirk, and Gast (1985) measured stereotypic behavior in extra-therapy sessions occurring immediately before and after training sessions. They taught students to engage in stereotypic behavior when cued, and used it as a reinforcer. Although the stereotypic behavior functioned as a reinforcer, such use did not result in systematic decreases in the behavior during extra-therapy settings. Based on these studies, it is clear that teachers can use the stereotypic responding as a reinforcer. Such use does not appear to increase students' rate of the response in other situations and, in at least one case, has resulted in a decrease in rate.

Guidelines for Managing Stereotypic Behavior

Stereotypy is common across human beings, but students with developmental disabilities appear to engage in a limited number of these behaviors at high rates. Although these responses are influenced by a variety of environmental stimuli, being engaged with materials and activities decreases their occurrence. The following guidelines should be used when treating stereotypic behaviors.

1. Stereotypic behavior should be assessed to determine whether it interferes with learning and causes other persons to avoid interacting with the student. Only when these conditions are shown should the behavior be targeted for reduction.

2. Environmental enrichment in terms of providing appropriate toys and materials, differential reinforcement for engagement with materials, and instructions not to engage in stereotypy should be prerequisites to more intrusive procedures.

3. Consideration should be given to teaching students when and when not to engage in stereotypic behavior.

4. DRO, DRI, and sensory extinction appear to be treatments of choice. However, when they

have been consistently and appropriately implemented, and shown to be ineffective, then Type 1 punishers should be used. In general, timeout and verbal reprimands should be avoided with stereotypic behaviors.

5. For students where deliverable reinforcers cannot be identified, their stereotypic behavior can be used as reinforcers. The effects of such use should be monitored in extra-therapy settings to ensure that it does not produce increases in the behavior.

DESCRIPTION AND MANAGEMENT OF AGGRESSIVE AND DISRUPTIVE BEHAVIORS

Aggressive and disruptive behaviors of students with moderate and severe handicaps have been widely studied (Bates & Wehman, 1977) and are some of the most frequently cited problems by teachers serving this population (Wehman & McLaughlin, 1979). *Aggression* has many definitions with none being acceptable to everyone (Kerr & Nelson, 1983); In general, it is behavior that results in harm or injury to another individual. Examples include hitting, kicking, biting, pinching, choking, hair pulling, and throwing objects that hit another person. Some authors include property damage and threats (verbal aggression) as aggressive behaviors. *Disruption* presents similar definitional problems; obviously, it is behavior that interferes with (disrupts) something. It may interfere with instruction, others' freedoms, or others' comforts; examples are crying, running about the room, yelling, arguing, temper tantrums, and talking to peers (Kerr & Nelson, 1983). Many disruptive behaviors (running, talking to peers) are appropriate behaviors in some situations such as the playground, but are inappropriate in others.

Explanations for Aggressive and Disruptive Behaviors

Many explanations concerning the cause of these behaviors exist. Evidence suggests that certain *environmental conditions* (noise, temperature, crowding) influence the occurrence of aggressive and disruptive behaviors. For example, aggressive behaviors increase as space allotments decrease, aggressive and disruptive behaviors become more frequent as the availability of materials decreases,

aggression increases when the temperature in the room increases (Nordquist, 1978). Whereas these types of environmental conditions influence aggression and disruption, effective teaching may mediate their effects (Kerr & Nelson, 1983). However, some students are more apt to be disruptive and aggressive in difficult, as compared to easy, instructional sessions (Carr & Durand, 1985; Weeks & Gaylord-Ross, 1981). Another explanation for these behaviors is that *students have not learned which behaviors are acceptable and expected.* Young children and students who transfer into existing programs may have never learned that certain disruptive behaviors should not be displayed. Similarly, some students may not have learned under which conditions certain behaviors should be performed. For example, yelling is acceptable on many playgrounds but would be considered disruptive in most classrooms. Another explanation for aggressive and disruptive behaviors is that *students have observed models perform these behaviors.* Obviously, this explanation only applies to students who are imitative. When students see persons similar to them display behaviors that are reinforced, the likelihood of the observer imitating the model is increased (Hartup, 1978). In other cases, disruptive and aggressive behavior may occur because they *have been positively or negatively reinforced.* For example, a student who is attempting to get a peer's toy and is successful when he hits the peer will likely use aggression in similar situations in the future. Similarly, if adult attention is a positive reinforcer for a student, and disruptive behavior results in adult attention, then disruption is apt to increase. If on the other hand, aggressive or disruptive behavior results in escape form an aversive situation (a difficult task), then the aggression or disruption is apt to be negatively reinforced (Carr et al., 1980). Closely related to this explanation is the notion that *aberrant behaviors may serve communicative functions.* Horner and Budd (1985) described a student with limited expressive language skills who engaged in disruptive yelling and materials grabbing. He was taught to produce the manual sign for the desired object in situations where he displayed these behaviors; as a result, the frequency of the yelling and grabbing decreased. Similarly, Carr and Durand (1985) taught four developmentally disabled students to request assistance and/or attention from adults and produced decreases in aggressive and disruptive behaviors for each student.

Management of Aggressive and Disruptive Behavior

Assessment

The explanations described above should be considered prior to planning intervention programs. Carr and Durand (1985) describe a method for assessing the effects of the amount of adult attention (in the form of commands, praise, and incidental comments) and task difficulty (easy versus difficult). They used short, artificial sessions similar to those used by Iwata et al. (1982). Three conditions were systematically compared: easy tasks plus a lot of adult attention (easy 100%), easy tasks with less adult attention (easy 33%), and difficult tasks with a lot of adult attention (difficult 100%). The easy 100% attention and the easy 33% conditions allowed them to determine whether the aggression or disruption was related to the amount of teacher attention. The easy 100% and difficult 100% conditions allowed them to determine whether the aggression or disruption was due to the difficulty of the task. The results of their assessment are shown in Figure 12.1. Two of the children were most disruptive during the "difficult 100%" condition. Their disruptive and aggressive behavior appeared to be related to escape from difficult situations, thus, possibly maintained by negative reinforcement. Another student displayed maladaptive behavior in the "easy 33%" condition indicating his behavior may have been controlled by adult attention (positive reinforcement). The fourth student displayed increases in aggressive and disruptive behavior in the "difficult 100%" and "easy 33%" conditions indicating her behavior may have been both positively and negatively reinforced. This study has two important implications: first, aggressive and disruptive behaviors may be maintained by different factors for different students; second, the factors that appear to maintain the aggression/disruption can be used to plan the treatment program. For example, if a student's aggression appears to be related to the difficulty of the tasks (higher during the difficult 100% sessions), then errorless learning procedures should be considered; if the student's aggression appears to be related to adult attention, then attention should be provided only for adaptive responses. Many times teachers will have a guess as to what is maintaining a response. When they design short assessment sessions to test that "guess," they can determine whether it is supported and should be

incorporated into the intervention plan, or whether it was incorrect.

Treatment

If aggressive behavior is frequent, intense, and directed at peers, then, in most cases, it should be targeted for deceleration. This decision is a bit more problematic with disruptive behavior. The decision to treat disruptive behavior should be based on the extent to which it interferes with the student's and others' learning and well-being rather than on the extent to which it is annoying. With both types of behaviors, selection of the most appropriate intervention strategy can also be difficult. *Curricular modifications* for aggressive and disruptive behaviors take various forms. Russo, Cataldo, and Cushing (1981) decreased both aggressive and disruptive behaviors by reinforcing children for complying with adult requests. Thus, by teaching a new adaptive behavior, the maladaptive behaviors decreased. When the aggressive or disruptive behaviors are related to task difficulty, using different instructional strategies such as errorless learning procedures is appropriate (Weeks & Gaylord-Ross, 1981). Another method involves teaching children signed or verbal responses that serve the same communicative function as the maladaptive behavior (Carr & Durand, 1985; Horner & Budd, 1985). Modification of *reinforcement contingencies* have also been used to control these behaviors. DRO, DRI, and DRL have a long history of successful use, and probably should always be used (Deitz & Repp, 1974; Deitz, Repp, & Deitz, 1976; Repp, Barton, Brulle, 1983; Repp & Deitz, 1974). Carr et al. (1980) found that using highly preferred reinforcers could reduce the number and possibly the intensity of aggressive responses. With another student whose aggression appeared to be negatively reinforced by escape, allowing him to escape contingent upon a more adaptive communicative response resulted in a decrease in aggression (Carr et al., 1980).

Timeout has been effective when it was used as contingent observation (Porterfield, Herbert-Jackson, & Risley, 1976), and when students remained in the activity but lost opportunities for reinforcement (Foxx & Shapiro, 1978). However, its effectiveness is tied to the density of reinforcement in the time-in environment (Solnick et al., 1978). A number of punishment procedures have been used to decrease disruptive and aggressive behaviors including contingent exercise (Luce, Del-

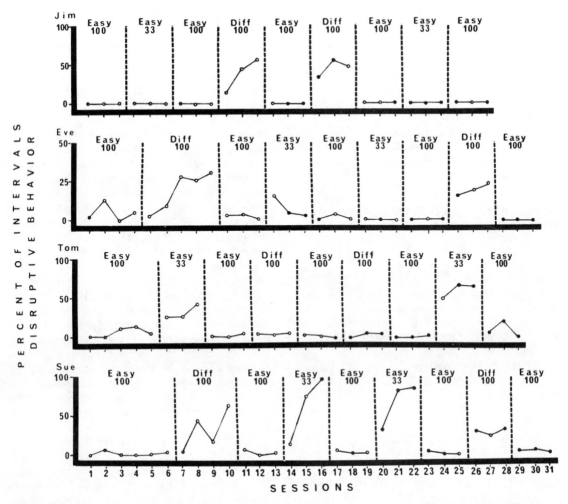

FIGURE 12.1 Percent of intervals of disruptive behavior as a function of level of task difficulty (easy vs. difficult) and overall level of adult attention (100% vs. 33% of total intervals). Open circles depict sessions conducted by an informed experimenter; filled circles, sessions conducted by naive experimenters.

Source: From "Reducing Behavior Problems Through Functional Communication Training" by E.G. Carr and V.M. Durand, 1985, *Journal of Applied Behavior Analysis (JABA), 18*(2), p. 117. Copyright 1985 by Journal of Applied Behavior Analysis. Reprinted by permission.

quadri, & Hall, 1980), water spray (Gross, Berler, & Drabman, 1982), aromatic ammonia (Doke, Wolery, & Sumberg, 1983), and overcorrection (Matson & Stephens, 1977; Shapiro, 1979).

Guidelines for Managing Aggressive and Disruptive Behaviors

1. An assessment of the factors that appear to be maintaining the aggressive or disruptive behaviors should be conducted, and the results should be integrated into intervention plans.

High rates of these behaviors may indicate the curriculum is inadequate. This issue also should be assessed.

2. Intervention should include differential reinforcement of adaptive, incompatible responses; in addition, specific instruction in social skills may be appropriate.

3. Based on the maintaining factors, the intervention should attempt to minimize or eliminate the influence of those variables. When the hypothesis suggests positive reinforcement is maintaining the behavior, the reinforcement should

be removed for that behavior if possible. When escape from aversive situations (negative reinforcement) is the hypothesis, then the student should not be allowed to escape by being disruptive or aggressive. In some cases, if other procedures are not effective, negative reinforcement could be used to increase adaptive behaviors.

4. If the disruptive or aggressive behavior appears to fulfill specific communicative functions, then a more acceptable communicative form should be taught.

DESCRIPTION AND MANAGEMENT OF SOCIAL WITHDRAWAL

"Social withdrawal refers to a cluster of behaviors that result in an individual escaping or avoiding social contact" (Kerr & Nelson, 1983, p. 177). Unlike self-injurious, stereotypic, and disruptive/aggressive behavior, social withdrawal may go undetected by teachers because it does not "call attention" to its performer. This may be particularly true in special schools and self-contained classrooms where teachers' perceptions of "normal social behavior" become skewed because of lack of contact with nonhandicapped students. Social withdrawal may take specific forms such as elective mutism or can be conceptualized as a general deficit in social competence (Kerr & Nelson, 1983). Although social competence is an illusive hypothetical construct, functional and performance-based models have recently appeared (Bailey & Simeonsson, 1985; Odom & McConnell, 1985). Essentially, social withdrawal is the failure to engage in pro-social behaviors that are situation appropriate such as initiating social interactions, responding to others' social initiations, engaging in conversations, playing with age-appropriate toys, and engaging in adaptive leisure activities. Pervasive social withdrawal has been used as a diagnostic characteristic for children with autism (Johnson & Koegel, 1982).

Explanations for Social Withdrawal

The origins of social withdrawal have been hypothesized as a failure to form attachment relationships with parents, specific emotional disorders, and biochemical disorders. In this section, however, we discuss some low-inference explanations that appear, in some cases, to maintain social withdrawal regardless of its origins.

One explanation for social withdrawal is *lack of prerequisite behaviors*. To initiate, respond, and maintain interactions, students can use a number of behaviors (Neel et al., 1983). Examples of common behaviors used to initiate social interactions include eye contact, vocalizations with the face directed toward the responder, giving affection, using "play organizers," physical contact, and giving a toy or material (Strain, 1985). If the student does not perform such behaviors, social isolation is likely. Another explanation for social withdrawal is that *the environment may inhibit social interactions*. The physical arrangement of the environment may be designed to minimize contact between students. Likewise, the human aspects of the environment may include peers who are not competent interactors. A third explanation for social withdrawal is that *social initiations and responses may be punished*. For example, if students initiating responses are difficult for caregivers to "read" or detect, then those behaviors may not be responded to as an initiation. Further, if the form of students' initiating responses are inappropriate, then responses they receive may function as punishers. Social withdrawal may also be *negatively reinforced*. If a student can avoid aversive interactions or situations by not initiating or not responding to others' initiations, then they may well be reinforced for not engaging in further interactions. *Performance of behaviors that access more reinforcing stimuli than social interactions may occur* and, thus, maintain social withdrawal (Kerr & Nelson, 1983). Stereotypic behavior may provide more reinforcing stimuli than do social interactions, or teachers may unwittingly reinforce interactions with adults that preclude interactions with peers. Finally, students may be *taught to engage in socially isolating behaviors*. In school, students may unintentionally, yet systematically, be taught to be quiet, not to engage in interactions with peers, and to interact with teachers rather than peers (Winett & Winkler, 1972). These are desirable school behaviors, but may be overgeneralized and result in isolation.

Management of Social Withdrawal

Assessment

As noted above, social withdrawal may be maintained by a number of environmental conditions, and careful assessment of those conditions is an important step in planning interventions. Two issues that generally need assessment are play or leisure skills and the amount of social contact. A variety of means exist for assessing these issues, but the most accepted method is the use of direct observation in low structure situations (Bailey & Wolery, 1984; Kerr & Nelson, 1983).

Treatment

In almost all cases, treatment of social withdrawal involves acceleration of interactive responses rather than punishment of social withdrawal. Numerous *environmental and curricular modifications* should be used to facilitate social interactions. Teachers should ensure that students have regular times during the day (free play or free time) for interacting with peers, ideally nonhandicapped peers. Snack, break, lunch, and some transition times are ideal opportunities for facilitating these interactions. During such times, the toys and materials should be carefully selected. Examples of toys and materials that appear to facilitate social interactions include dress-up clothes, balls, blocks, "don't break the ice," and parallel bars. Toys and materials that increase the probability of isolate behaviors include paper and pencils, crayons, beads, puzzles, and clay, (Kerr & Nelson, 1983). Another environmental modification is to ensure that contact with competent interactors is available. Such students provide opportunities for social interactions and models for appropriate social exchanges.

Beyond structuring opportunities, providing specific materials, and ensuring the availability of competent interactors, *teacher-mediated strategies* can facilitate social interactions. A number of curricula exist for teaching social skills to students (cf. Hoyson, Jamieson, & Strain, 1984; Nelson & Rutherford, in press) as do a number of descriptions for teaching play skills (Bailey & Wolery, 1984; Wehman, 1976; 1977). Teacher prompting and reinforcement can be used to teach prerequisite skills and social interactions (Strain, Shores, & Kerr, 1976). Prompting takes the form of encouraging competent interactors to play with the socially withdrawn student, encouraging sharing, and assisting students who cannot independently participate in the activity (helping a student catch a playground ball and roll it back to a peer) (Kerr & Nelson, 1983). When reinforcing interactions, the teacher must be careful not to interrupt the interaction. Provision of additional materials or brief physical contact (pats on the back) are appropriate ways of reinforcing interactions without stopping them. Another teacher-mediated strategy for facilitating social interactions is known as "affection training." Affection training involves short sessions (10–15 minutes) of game playing with intense social and physical contact between the target student and four to six students with appropriate social skills (usually nonhandicapped students). The interactions are directly controlled by the teacher who provides frequent prompts and reinforcement for engaging in the activities. Preschool, socially isolated children (Twardosz, Nordquist, Simon, & Botkin, 1983) and early elementary students with autism (McEvoy, 1985) have participated in the studies on affection training. The studies produced increases in social interactions, peer social approaches, number of peers contacted, smiling, and duration of interactions during free play generalization periods. These increases appear to be separate from changes in teacher attention during generalization sessions (Twardosz et al., 1983).

In addition to environmental structuring and teacher-mediated strategies, *peer-mediated* strategies are appropriate for reducing social withdrawal (Strain, 1981). To train the peer confederates, direct instruction, role playing with an adult, and reinforcement have been used (Kerr & Strain, 1979). During this training the peer confederate learns to initiate social interactions persistently, prompt interactions, model appropriate interactions and play, and reinforce the target student for engaging in social interactions. Another strategy is to teach the socially withdrawn child to imitate a competent peer (Apolloni, Cooke, & Cooke, 1977; Cooke, Apolloni, & Cooke, 1977; Peck, Apolloni, Cooke, & Raver, 1978). Peer imitation training involves prompting and reinforcing socially withdrawn students to imitate the appropriate play or social behaviors of their peers. Although it may be conducted within structured one-to-one sessions, generalization of the imitative repertoire appears to occur more readily if training occurs in free play sessions. The peer-mediated strategies require contact with socially competent peers. Much of this research was conducted with nonhandicapped peers in integrated preschool classrooms.

Guidelines for Managing Social Withdrawal

1. Planning interventions for reducing social withdrawal should begin with an assessment of the factors that appear to be maintaining the behavior.

2. Intervention plans should focus on facilitating the acquisition of adaptive social skills (play, leisure recreation, and social interactions) rather than elimination of social withdrawal behavior through the use of Type 1 and Type 2 punishment procedures.

3. Educational environments should be designed to facilitate acquisition of social interaction skills by structuring opportunities for interaction, using materials that facilitate interaction, and providing peers who are competent social interactors.

4. When possible, peer-mediated procedures for teaching social interaction should be used. When these strategies are employed, the peer confederate should receive specific instructions about what to do, and then reinforcement for doing it.

DESCRIPTION AND MANAGEMENT OF NONCOMPLIANT BEHAVIOR

Noncompliant responses are particularly disturbing because they interfere with social interactions and instruction. Noncompliance refers to the failure to respond correctly and within a reasonable latency to a request, direction, command, or instruction. It has been rated by teachers of students having severe and profound handicaps as the most frequent behavior problem they face (Wehman & McLaughlin, 1979).

Explanations for Noncompliant Behavior

Several explanations can be proposed to account for the occurrence of noncompliance. First, noncompliant behavior may occur because of *receptive language deficits*. Obviously, not understanding the nature of the request or command will undoubtedly result in failure to perform the correct response. In such cases, the noncompliance is a result of inappropriate verbal behavior on the part of the caregiver rather than a behavior problem displayed by the student. Second, noncompliant behavior may occur because students have received *positive reinforcement for not following requests and commands*. For example, if social attention is a powerful reinforcer for a student and attention is provided for noncompliant behaviors (being disruptive) but not for compliant behaviors (attending to

and completing tasks), then it is probable that noncompliance will increase (Becker, Madsen, Arnold, & Thomas, 1967). Third, noncompliant behavior may occur because *compliant behavior is on extinction*. When students are asked to do a task and comply with it but no reinforcement for participation occurs, then the compliance would probably decrease over time due to the lack of reinforcement. Fourth, noncompliance may increase because *compliance results in punishment*. Many times, when students comply with a request, they are faced with aversive consequences such as expending effort or stopping activities (play) that allow them access to reinforcers. Such results may well function as punishing stimuli and produce decreases in compliant behavior. Finally, *noncompliance may occur as a form of protest*. Students with communication deficits may not have a standard means of communicating that they want to stop an activity, do not want an object, or do not want to participate in an activity (Donnellan, Mirenda, Mesaros, & Fassbender, 1984). Because they have no standard means of communicating, they simply do not comply with the request or direction. Thus, as with other maladaptive behaviors, the explanations (causes and maintaining factors) of noncompliant behavior appear to be multiple.

Management of Noncompliant Behavior

Assessment

Noncompliance can be identified in two ways. An adult may realize that a student does not do what is asked. Another means of identifying noncompliance is to analyze the data patterns from students' instructional programs (Haring, White, & Liberty, 1978). Patterns characterized by high variability are indicative of noncompliance as are patterns where steady progress is followed by a sharp drop in the rate of correct responses. Because multiple factors can cause or maintain noncompliance, the team should attempt to determine what function the noncompliant behavior serves for each student. This information should be used in developing intervention plans.

Treatment

Bates and Wehman (1977) analyzed the behavioral literature related to treating maladaptive behavior and found that instruction, DRO, timeout, and response cost have been studied with noncompliant behavior. Instruction was the most frequently used procedure. Clearly, *curricular modification* strategies should be used when students have not learned the "meaning" of given commands or have not learned that they should do what the teacher says. Effective procedures for teaching generalized instruction following include: providing students with controlled commands that involve a $noun_1$ + $verb_1$ and then $noun_1$ + $verb_2$ and continuing by mixing known and unknown words, modeling or physically prompting students to comply with the commands, reinforcing them for compliance, and transferring stimulus control from the prompts to the commands (Striefel, Wetherby, & Karlan, 1978). When noncompliant behaviors appear to serve communicative functions (protesting), then students should be taught a communicative form that will allow them to express the function efficiently without being noncompliant (Carr & Durand, 1985). When this is done, the student will then need to be taught when it is appropriate to protest. Another curricular modification is illustrated by Rusch and Menchetti (1981). They provided a noncompliant student with verbal practice in being compliant at the beginning of a work day and stated a contingency that he would be sent home from work if he was not compliant. This procedure was effective in reducing the frequency of noncompliant responses. *Manipulation of reinforcement contingencies* has been used alone and in combination with curricular modifications. Wahler and Fox (1980) used reinforcement for solitary play and timeout for noncompliance and aggression to treat successfully children with severe oppositional behavior in home environments. Russo et al. (1981) found using reinforcement for compliance with adult requests increased compliance and decreased other aberrant behaviors such as crying, SIB, and aggression. Some data indicate that if reinforcement is delivered for a specific type of request ("Do" or "Don't"), then generalized compliance should be expected for only that type of request (Neef, Shafer, Egel, Cataldo, & Parrish, 1983). Further, compliance may be increased when eye contact is established prior to the presentation of the request (Hamlet, Axelrod, & Kuershner, 1984). More intrusive procedures have also been used to establish noncompliant behaviors. Perhaps the least intrusive Type 1 punisher is the use of "mandating" (Liberty, 1977). Mandating involves physically prompting the student to comply with the request contingent upon noncompliance.

Guidelines for Managing Noncompliant Behavior

1. Intervention for noncompliance should be based on an assessment of the factors that appear to control it. The intervention should be planned as a result of the assessment information.
2. Instructions, directions, requests, or commands should be administered in language that is clearly understood by students receiving them. Eye contact should precede presentation of the request.
3. When students do not have the receptive language behaviors for complying with high priority requests, then they should receive instruction relative to those requests. This instruction should include presentation of controlled requests, prompting, reinforcement for compliance, and transferring stimulus control from the prompts to the requests.
4. When students understand the nature of the request, the factors maintaining noncompliance should be removed or reversed. This practice plus differential reinforcement of compliance are the treatments of choice.
5. When noncompliance appears to serve the communicative function of protesting, an adaptive form of expressing that function should be taught. After the form is established, the student should be taught when that function may and may not be used.

SUMMARY: SEVERE ABERRANT BEHAVIORS

This chapter has emphasized a number of recurring issues relative to the control of severe maladaptive behaviors:

1. Severe maladaptive behaviors appear to be caused and/or maintained by one or more relationship(s) with environmental stimuli and in some cases possibly physiological/biological factors.
2. Treatment of severe maladaptive behavior should involve the application of a systematic process characterized by thorough assessment; formative measurement; careful selection and use of intervention strategies; and determination of the social validity of goals, procedures, and effects.
3. Assessment and identification of the functional relationships between environmental stimuli and

the behavior (including communicative functions) should occur prior to planning treatment programs.

4. Teams should clearly identify the target behaviors, define those behaviors, collect data relative to their occurrence in important contexts, and continue to monitor those behaviors until significant others in the student's environment determine the behaviors are no longer a problem. Likewise, they should monitor the effects of interventions with experimental designs that address the questions being asked. Finally, the team should monitor multiple behaviors to determine the side effects of the treatments.

5. Selection of treatment procedures for severe maladaptive behaviors should be made on a number of principles, including the least intrusive, most natural, and most acceptable *yet* effective strategy available. However, when these principles are in conflict with one another, the effectiveness should take precedent over the others. Treatment procedures that are more intrusive than curricular modifications, environmental enhancement, and manipulations of reinforcement contingencies should be approved prior to their use by the appropriate review and administrative groups. Implementation of treatment should be monitored as should the effects.

6. The social validity of the goals, procedures, and effects should be assessed at multiple points in the process of attempting to treat severe maladaptive behaviors. This assessment should involve relevant members of the team, the student's parents and/or other caregivers, and, when appropriate, the student.

7. Development of adaptive behavior, including but not limited to communicative and social skills, should accompany all attempts to reduce the occurrence of severe maladaptive behavior.

8. When specific types of aberrant behavior such as self-injury, stereotypy, aggression/disruption, social withdrawal, or noncompliance are present and targeted for intervention, then the guidelines discussed for each class of behavior should be considered.

REFERENCES

Altman, K., Haavik, S., & Cook, J. (1978). Punishment of self-injurious behavior in natural settings using contingent aromatic ammonia. *Behaviour Research and Therapy, 16,* 85–96.

Apolloni, T., Cooke, S. A., & Cooke, T. P. (1977). Establishing a normal peer as a behavioral model for delayed toddlers. *Perceptual and Motor Skills, 44,* 231–241.

Axelrod, S., Brantner, J. P., & Meddock, T. D. (1978). Overcorrection: A review and critical analysis. *Journal of Special Education, 12,* 367–391.

Azrin, N. H., Besalel, V. A., Wigotzek, I. E. (1982). Treatment of self-injury by a reinforcement plus interruption procedure. *Analysis and Intervention in Developmental Disabilities, 2,* 105–113.

Azrin, N. H., Gottlieb, L., Hughart, L., Wesolowski, M. D., & Rahn, T. (1974). Eliminating self-injurious behavior by educative procedures. *Behaviour Research and Therapy, 13,* 101–111.

Bailey, D. B., & Simeonsson, R. J. (1985). A functional model of social competence. *Topics in Early Childhood Special Education, 4*(4), 20–31.

Bailey, D. B., & Wolery, M. (1984). *Teaching infants and preschoolers with handicaps.* Columbus, OH: Charles E. Merrill.

Bailey, D. B., Wolery, M., & Sugai, G. M. (in press). *Effective teaching: Principles and procedures of applied behavior analysis with exceptional children.* Boston: Allyn and Bacon.

Bailey, S. L., Pokrzywinski, J., & Bryant, L. E. (1983). Using water mist to reduce self-injurious and stereotypic behavior. *Applied Research in Mental Retardation, 4,* 229–241.

Baker, D. B. (1980). Applications of environmental psychology in programming for severely handicapped persons. *Journal of the Association for the Severely Handicapped, 5,* 234–249.

Ball, T. S., Datta, P. C., Rios, M., & Constantine, C. (1985). Flexible arm splints in the control of a Lesch-Nyhan victim's finger biting and a profoundly retarded client's finger sucking. *Journal of Autism and Developmental Disorders, 15,* 177–184.

Barmann, B. C., & Vitali, D. L. (1982). Facial screening to eliminate trichotillomania in developmentally disabled persons. *Behavior Therapy, 13,* 735–742.

Bates, P., & Wehman, P. (1977). Behavior management with the mentally retarded: An empirical analysis of the research. *Mental Retardation, 15*(6), 9–12.

Baumeister, A. A., Sr. (1978). Origins and control of stereotyped movements. In C. E. Meyers (Ed.), *Quality of life in severely and profoundly mentally retarded people: Research foundations for improvement.* (pp. 353–384). Washington, DC: American Association on Mental Deficiency.

Baumeister, A. A., Sr., & Baumeister, A. A., Jr. (1978). Suppression of repetitive self-injurious behavior by contingent inhalation of aromatic ammonia. *Journal of Autism and Childhood Schizophrenia, 8,* 71–77.

Baumeister, A. A., Sr., & Forehand, R. (1973). Stereotyped acts. In N. R. Ellis (Ed.), *International review of research in mental retardation.* (Vol. 6, pp. 55–96). New York: Academic Press.

Baumeister, A. A., Sr., & Rollings, J. P. (1976). Self-injurious behavior. In N. R. Ellis (Ed.), *International review of research in mental retardation.* (Vol. 8, pp. 1–34). New York: Academic Press.

Becker, J. V., Turner, S. M., & Sajwaj, T. E. (1978). Multiple behavioral effects of the use of lemon juice with a ruminating toddler-age child. *Behavior Modification, 2,* 267–278.

Becker, W. C., Madsen, C. H., Arnold, C. R., & Thomas, D. R. (1967). The contingent use of teacher attention and praise in reducing classroom behavior problems. *Journal of Special Education, 1,* 287–307.

Bigge, J. L. (1982). *Teaching individuals with physical and multiple disabilities* (2nd ed.). Columbus, OH: Charles E. Merrill.

Borreson, P. M. (1980). Elimination of a self-injurious avoidance response through a forced running consequence. *Mental Retardation, 18,* 73–77.

Brown, L., Branston-McClean, M., Baumgart, D., Vincent, L., Falvey, M., & Schroeder, J. (1979). Using the characteristics of current and subsequent least restrictive environments as factors in development of curricular content for severely handicapped students. *TASH Review, 4,* 407–424.

Brown, L., Nietupski, J., & Hamre-Nietupski, S. (1976). Criterion of ultimate functioning. In M. A. Thomas (Ed.), *Hey don't forget about me,* (pp. 2–15), Reston, VA: Council for Exceptional Children.

Brusca, R. (1985). Chronobiological aspects of stereotypy. *American Journal of Mental Deficiency, 89,* 650–652.

Bucher, B., & Lovaas, O. I. (1968). Use of aversive stimulation in behavior modification. In M. Jones (Ed.), *Miami symposium on the prediction of behavior, 1967: Aversive stimulation.* (pp. 77–147). Coral Gables, FL: University of Miami Press.

Carr, E. G. (1977). The motivation of self-injurious behavior: A review of some hypotheses. *Psychological Bulletin, 84,* 800–816.

Carr, E. G., & Durand, V. M. (1985). Reducing behavior problems through functional communication training. *Journal of Applied Behavior Analysis, 18,* 111–126.

Carr, E. G., Newsom, C. D., & Binkoff, J. A. (1976). Stimulus control of self-destructive behavior in a psychotic child. *Journal of Abnormal Child Psychology, 4,* 139–153.

Carr, E. G., Newsom, C. D., & Binkoff, J. A. (1980). Escape as a factor in the aggressive behavior of two retarded children. *Journal of Applied Behavior Analysis, 13,* 101–117.

Carter, C. H. (1975). *Handbook of mental retardation syndromes.* (3rd ed.), Springfield, IL: Thomas.

Cataldo, M. F., & Harris, J. (1982). The biological basis for self-injury in the mentally retarded. *Analysis and Intervention in Developmental Disabilities, 2,* 21–39.

Certo, N., Haring, N. G., & York, R. (1984). *Public school integration of severely handicapped students.* Baltimore: Paul Brookes.

Chock, P. M., & Glahn, T. J. (1983). Learning and self-stimulation in mute and echolalic children. *Journal of Autism and Developmental Disorders, 14*(4), 365–381.

Cooke, T. P., Apolloni, T., & Cooke, S. A. (1977). Normal preschool children as behavioral models for retarded peers. *Exceptional Children, 43,* 531–532.

Corbett, J. (1975). Aversion for the treatment of self-injurious behaviour. *Journal of Mental Deficiency Research, 19,* 79–95.

Corte, H. E., Wolf, M. M., & Locke, B. J. (1971). A comparison of procedures for eliminating self-injurious behavior of retarded adolescents. *Journal of Applied Behavior Analysis, 4,* 201–213.

Deitz, D. E., & Repp, A. C. (1983). Reducing behavior through reinforcement. *Exceptional Education Quarterly, 3,* 34–46.

Deitz, S. M., & Repp, A. C. (1974). Differentially reinforcing low rates of misbehavior with normal elementary school children. *Journal of Applied Behavior Analysis, 7,* 622. (Abstract).

Deitz, S. M., Repp, A. C., & Deitz, D. E. D. (1976). Reducing inappropriate classroom behavior of retarded students through three procedures of differential reinforcement. *Journal of Mental Deficiency Research, 20,* 155–170.

Demchak, M. A., & Halle, J. W. (1985). Motivational assessment: A potential means of enhancing treatment success of self-injurious individuals. *Education and Training of the Mentally Retarded, 20*(1), 25–38.

Devany, J. (1979, December). *Assessment of the effects of using self-stimulation as a reinforcer.* Paper presented at the 13th Annual Convention of the Association for the Advancement of Behavior Therapy, San Francisco.

Doke, L. A., Wolery, M., & Sumberg, C. (1983). Effects and side-effects of response contingent, ammonia spirits in treating chronic aggression. *Behavior Modification, 7*(4), 531–556.

Donnellan, A. M. (1984). The criterion of the least dangerous assumption. *Behavior Disorders, 9,* 141–150.

Donnellan, A. M., Mirenda, P. L., Mesaros, R. A., & Fassbender, L. L. (1984). Analyzing the communicative functions of aberrant behavior. *Journal of the Association for Persons with Severe Handicaps, 9*(3), 201–212.

Dorsey, M. F., Iwata, B. A., Reid, D. H., & Davis, P. A. (1982). Protective equipment: Continuous and contingent application in the treatment of self-injurious behavior. *Journal of Applied Behavior Analysis, 15,* 217–230.

Durand, V. M. (1982). Analysis and intervention of self-injurious behavior. *Journal of the Association for the Severely Handicapped, 7,* 44–53.

Durand, V. M., & Carr, E. G. (1985). Self-injurious behavior: Motivating conditions and guidelines for treatment. *School Psychology Review, 14*(2), 171–176.

Epstein, L. H., Doke. L A., Sajwaj, T. E., Sorrell, S., & Rimmer, B. (1974). Generality and side effects of overcorrection. *Journal of Applied Behavior Analysis, 7*(3), 385–390.

Etzel, B. C., & LeBlanc, J. M. (1979). The simplest treatment alternative: appropriate instructional control and errorless learning procedures for the difficult-to-teach child. *Journal of Autism and Developmental Disorders, 9,* 361–382.

Evans, I., & Meyer, L. H. (1985). *An educative approach to behavior problems: A practical decision model for interventions with severely handicapped learners.* Baltimore: Paul Brookes.

Favell, J. E., Azrin, N. H., Baumeister, A. A., Sr., Carr, E. G., Dorsey, M. F., Forehand, R., Foxx, R. M., Lovaas, O. I., Rincover, A., Risley, T. R., Romanczyk, R. G., Russo, D. C., Schroeder, S. R., & Solnick, J. V. (1981a). The treatment of self-injurious behavior. *Behavior Therapy, 13,* 529–554.

Favell, J. E., McGimsey, J. F., & Jones, M. L. (1978). The use of physical restraint in the treatment of self-injury and as positive reinforcement. *Journal of Applied Behavior Analysis, 11*, 225–241.

Favell, J. E., McGimsey, J. F., & Schell, R. M. (1982b). Treatment of self-injury by providing alternate sensory activities. *Analysis and Intervention in Developmental Disabilities, 2*(3), 83–104.

Foxx, R. M., & Azrin, N. H. (1973). The elimination of autistic self-stimulatory behavior by overcorrection. *Journal of Applied Behavior Analysis, 6*(1), 1–14.

Foxx, R. M., & Shapiro, S. T. (1978). The timeout ribbon: A nonexclusionary timeout procedure. *Journal of Applied Behavior Analysis, 11*(1), 125–136.

Frankel, F., & Simmons, J. Q. (1976). Self-injurious behavior in schizophrenic and retarded children. *American Journal of Mental Deficiency, 80*, 512–522.

Gaylord-Ross, R. (1980). A decision model for the treatment of aberrant behavior in applied settings. In W. Sailor, B. Wilcox, & L. Brown (Eds.), *Methods of instruction for severely handicapped students* (pp. 135–158). Baltimore: Paul Brookes.

Gross, A. M., Berler, E. S., & Drabman, R. S. (1982). Reduction of aggressive behavior in a retarded boy using a water squirt. *Journal of Behavior Therapy and Experimental Psychiatry, 13*, 95–98.

Hamlet, C. C., Axelrod, S., & Kuerschner, S. (1984). Eye contact as an antecedent to compliant behavior. *Journal of Applied Behavior Analysis, 17*, 553–557.

Hargrave, E., & Swisher, L. (1975). Modifying the verbal expression of a child with autistic behaviors. *Journal of Autism and Childhood Schizophrenia, 5*, 147–154.

Haring, N. G., White, O. R., & Liberty, K. A. (1978). *An investigation of phases of learning and facilitating instructional events for the severely handicapped: Annual progress report 1977–1978.* (Bureau of Education for the Handicapped, Project No. 443CH70564). Seattle: University of Washington.

Harris, S. L., & Romanczyk, R. G. (1976). Treating self-injurious behavior of a retarded child by overcorrection. *Behavior therapy, 7*, 235–239.

Hartup, W. W. (1978). Peer interaction and the processes of socialization. In M. Guralnick (Ed.), *Early intervention and the integration of handicapped and nonhandicapped children* (pp. 27–51). Baltimore: University Park Press.

Hollis, J. H. (1965a). The effects of social and nonsocial stimuli on the behavior of profoundly retarded children: Part I. *American Journal of Mental Deficiency, 69*, 755–771.

Hollis, J. H. (1965b). The effects of social and nonsocial stimuli on the behavior of profoundly retarded children: Part II. *American Journal of Mental Deficiency, 69*, 772–789.

Hollis, J. H. (1982). Summary and discussion of special issues. In J. H. Hollis & C. E. Meyers (Eds.), *Life-threatening behavior: Analysis and intervention* (pp. 331–342), Washington, DC: American Association on Mental Deficiency.

Horner, R. D. (1980). The effects of an environmental "enrichment" program on the behavior of institutionalized profoundly retarded children. *Journal of Applied Behavior Analysis, 13*, 473–491.

Horner, R. H., & Budd, C. M. (1985). Acquisition of manual sign use: Collateral reduction of maladaptive behavior and factors limiting generalization. *Education and Training of the Mentally Retarded, 20*(1), 39–47.

Hoyson, M., Jamieson, B., & Strain, P. S. (1984). Individualized group instruction of normally developing and autistic-like children: The LEAP curriculum model. *Journal of the Division for Early Childhood, 8*(2), 157–172.

Hung, D. W. (1978). Using self-stimulation as reinforcement for autistic children. *Journal of Autism and Developmental Disorders, 8*(3), 355–366.

Hutt, S., & Hutt, C. (1968). Stereotypy, arousal, and autism. *Human Development, 11*, 277–286.

Iwata, B. A., Dorsey, M. F., Slifer, K. J., Bauman, K. E., & Richman, G. S. (1982). Toward a functional analysis of self-injury. *Analysis and Intervention in Developmental Disabilities, 2*(3), 3–20.

Johnson, J., & Koegel, R. L. (1982). Behavioral assessment and curriculum development. In R. L. Koegel, A. Rincover, & A. L. Egel (Eds.), *Educating and understanding autistic children.* (pp. 1–32). San Diego, CA: College Hill.

Johnson, W. L., & Baumeister, A. A., Sr. (1978). Self-injurious behavior: A review and analysis of methodological details of published studies. *Behavior Modification, 2*(4), 465–487.

Kelly, J. A., & Drabman, R. S. (1977). Generalizing response suppression of self-injurious behavior through an overcorrection punishment procedure: A case study. *Behavior Therapy, 8*, 468–472.

Kerr, M. M., & Nelson, C. M. (1983). *Strategies for managing behavior problems in the classroom.* Columbus, OH: Charles E. Merrill.

Kerr, M. M., & Strain, P. S. (1979). The use of peer social initiation strategies to improve the social skills of withdrawn children. In A. H. Fink (Ed.), *International perspectives on future special education.* Reston, VA: Council for Exceptional Children.

Klier, J., & Harris, S. L. (1977). Self-stimulation and learning in autistic children: Physical or functional incompatibility? *Journal of Applied Behavior Analysis, 10*, 311. (Abstract).

Koegel, R. L., & Covert, A. (1972). The relationship of self-stimulation to learning in autistic children. *Journal of Applied Behavior Analysis, 5*, 391–387.

Koegel, R. L., Firestone, P. B., Kramme, K. W., & Dunlap, G. (1974). Increasing spontaneous play by suppressing self-stimulation in autistic children. *Journal of Applied Behavior Analysis, 7*(4), 521–528.

Krantz, P., & Risley, T. R. (1977). Behavior ecology in the classroom. In K. D. O'Leary and S. O'Leary (Eds.), *Classroom management: The successful use of behavior modification.* New York: Pergamon.

LaGrow, S. J., & Repp, A. C. (1984). Stereotypic responding: A review of intervention research. *American Journal of Mental Deficiency, 88*, 595–609.

Liberty, K. A. (1977). *An investigation of two methods of achieving compliance with the severely handicapped in a classroom setting.* Unpublished doctoral dissertation, University of Washington, Seattle.

Lichstein, K. L., & Schreibman, L. (1976). Employing electric shock with autistic children: A review of the side effects. *Journal of Autism and Childhood Schizophrenia,* *6,* 163–173.

Lockwood, K., & Bourland, G. (1982). Reduction of self-injurious behaviors by reinforcement and toy use. *Mental Retardation, 20,* 169–173.

Lovaas, O. I., Freitag, G., Gold, V. J., & Kassorla, I. C. (1965). Experimental studies in childhood schizophrenia: Analysis of self-destructive behavior. *Journal of Experimental Child Psychology, 2,* 67–84.

Lovaas, O I., & Simmons, J. Q. (1969). Manipulation of self-destruction in three retarded children. *Journal of Applied Behavior Analysis, 2,* 143–157.

Luce, S. C., Delquadri, J., Hall, R. V. (1980). Contingent exercise: A mild but powerful procedure for suppressing inappropriate verbal and aggressive behavior. *Journal of Applied Behavior Analysis, 13.* 583–594.

Lutzker, J. R. (1978). Reducing self-injurious behavior by facial screening. *American Journal of Mental Deficiency, 82,* 510–513.

Matson, J. L., & Stephens, R. M. (1977). Overcorrection of aggressive behavior in a chronic psychiatric patient. *Behavior Modification, 1,* 559–564.

Matson, J. L., & Stephens, R. M. (1981). Overcorrection treatment of stereotyped behaviors. *Behavior Modification, 5,* 491–502.

Mayhew, G., & Harris, F. (1979). Decreasing self-injurious behavior: Punishment with citric acid and reinforcement of alternative behavior. *Behavior Modification, 3,* 322–336.

McEvoy, M. E. (1985). *Use of affection activities for increasing the social interaction skills of autistic children in an integrated kindergarten setting.* Paper presented at the National Early Childhood Conference on Children with Special Needs, Denver, CO.

Neef, N. A., Shafer, M S., Egel, A. L., Cataldo, M., & Parrish, J. M. (1983). The class specific effect of compliance training with "do" and "don't" requests: Analogue analysis and classroom applications. *Journal of Applied Behavior Analysis, 16,* 81–99.

Neel, R. S., Billingsley, F. F., McCarty, F., Symonds, D., Lambert, C., Lewis-Smith, N., & Hanashiro, R. (1983). *Innovative model program for autistic children and their teachers.* Unpublished manuscript, University of Washintgon, Seattle.

Neisworth, J. T., Hunt, F. M., Gallop, H. R., & Madle, R. A. (1985). Reinforcer displacement: A preliminary study of the clinical application of the CRF/EXT effect. *Behavior Modification, 9*(1), 103–115.

Nelson, C. M., & Rutherford, R. B. (in press). Behavioral interventions with behaviorally disordered students. In M. C. Wang, H. J. Walberg, & M. C. Reynolds (Eds.), *Handbook of Special Education: Research and Practice.* (Vol. 1–3). Oxford, England: Pergamon Press.

Nordquist, V. M. (1978). A behavioral approach to the analysis of peer interactions. In M. Guralnick (Ed.), *Early intervention and the integration of handicapped and nonhandicapped children.* (pp. 53–84). Baltimore: University Park Press.

Novak, A. R., & Heal, L. W. (1980). *Integration of developmentally disabled individuals into the community.* Baltimore: Paul Brookes.

Odom, S. L., & McConnell, S. R. (1985). A performance-based conceptualization of social competence of handicapped preschool children: Implications for assessment. *Topics in Early Childhood Special Education, 4*(4), 1–19.

Peck, C. A., Apolloni, T., Cooke, T. P., & Raver, S. (1978). Teaching retarded preschoolers to imitate the free-play behavior of nonretarded classmates: Trained and generalized effects. *Journal of Special Education, 12,* 195–207.

Polsgrove, L., & Reith, H. J. (1983). Procedures for reducing children's inappropriate behavior in special education settings. *Exceptional Education Quarterly, 3,* 20–33.

Porterfield, J. K., Herbert-Jackson, E., & Risley, T. R. (1976). Contingent observation: An effective and acceptable procedure for reducing disruptive behavior of young children in a group setting, *Journal of Applied Behavior Analysis, 9,* 55–64.

Rago, W. V., & Case, J. C. (1978). Stereotyped behavior in special education teachers, *Exceptional Children, 44*(5), 342–344.

Repp, A. C., Barton, L. E., Brulle, A. R. (1983). A comparison of two procedures for programming the differential reinforcement of other behaviors. *Journal of Applied Behavior Analysis, 16,* 435–445.

Repp, A. C., & Deitz, S. M. (1974). Reducing aggressive and self-injurious behavior of institutionalized retarded children through reinforcement of other behaviors. *Journal of Applied Behavior Analysis, 7,* 313–325.

Repp, A. C., Deitz, S. M., & Deitz, D. E. D. (1976). Reducing inappropriate behaviors. *Mental Retardation, 14*(1), 11–15.

Rimland, B. (1964). *Infantile autism: The syndrome and its implications for a neural theory of behavior.* New York: Appleton-Century-Crofts.

Rincover, A. (1978). Sensory extinction: A procedure for eliminating self-stimulatory behaviors in psychotic children. *Journal of Abnormal Child Psychology, 6,* 299–310.

Rincover, A., Cook, R., Peoples, A., & Packard, D. (1979). Sensory extinction and sensory reinforcement principles for programming multiple adaptive behavior change. *Journal of Applied Behavior Analysis, 12,* 221–233.

Rincover, A., & Devany, J. (1982). The application of sensory extinction procedures to self-injury. *Analysis and Intervention in Developmental Disabilities, 2*(3), 67–81.

Risley, T. R. (1968). The effects and side effects of punishing the autistic behaviors of a deviant child. *Journal of Applied Behavior Analysis, 1,* 21–34.

Rogers-Warren, A., & Baer, D. M. (1976). *An analysis of two naturally covarying behaviors: Activity level and inappropriateness.* Lawrence, KS: Department of Human Development. (ERIC Document Reproduction Service No. ED 136 473).

Rollings, J. P., & Baumeister, A. A., Sr. (1981). Stimulus control of stereotypic responding: Effects on target and collateral behavior. *American Journal of Mental Deficiency, 86*(1), 67–77.

Rollings, J. P., Baumeister, A. A., Sr., & Baumeister, A. A., Jr. (1977). The use of overcorrection procedures to eliminate the stereotyped behaviors of retarded individuals: An analysis of collateral behaviors and generalization of suppressive effects. *Behavior Modification, 1,* 29–46.

Rusch, F. R., & Menchetti, B. M. (1981). Increasing compliant work behaviors in a non-sheltered work setting. *Mental Retardation, 19*, 107–111.

Russo, D. C., Carr, E. G., & Lovaas, O. I. (1980). Self-injury in pediatric populations. In J. M. Ferguson & C. B. Taylor (Ed.), *The comprehensive handbook of behavioral medicine* (pp. 183–201). New York: Spectrum.

Russo, D. C., Cataldo, M. F., & Cushing, P. J. (1981). Compliance training and behavioral covariation in the treatment of multiple behavior problems. *Journal of Applied Behavior Analysis, 14*, 209–222.

Schrader, C., Shaull, J., & Elmore, B. (1983). Behavioral treatment of self-stimulation in the developmentally disabled: A methodological review. *Behavior Modification, 7*(2), 267–294.

Schuler, A. L., & Goetz, C. (1981). The assessment of severe language disabilities: Communicative and cognitive considerations. *Analysis and Intervention in Developmental Disabilities, 1*, 333–346.

Shapiro, E. S. (1979). Restitution and positive practice overcorrection in reducing aggressive-disruptive behavior: A long-term follow-up. *Journal of Behavior Therapy and Experimental Psychiatry, 10*, 131–134.

Solnick, J. V., Rincover, A., & Peterson, C. R., (1977). Some determinants of reinforcing and punishing effects of timeout. *Journal of Applied Behavior Analysis, 10*, 415–424.

Strain, P. S. (1981). *The utilization of classroom peers as behavior change agents.* New York: Plenum Press.

Strain, P. S. (1985). Preschool children's social competence. *Topics in Early Childhood Special Education, 4*(4), 47–58.

Strain, P. S., Shores, R. E., & Kerr, M. M. (1976). An experimental analysis of "spillover" effects on the social interaction of behaviorally handicapped preschool children. *Journal of Applied Behavior Analysis, 9*, 31–40.

Striefel, S., Wetherby, B., & Karlan, G. (1978). Developing generalized instruction-following behavior in severely retarded people. In C. E. Meyers (Ed.), *Quality of life in severely and profoundly mentally retarded people: Research foundations for improvement* (pp. 267–326). Washington, DC: American Association on Mental Deficiency.

Tawney, J. W., & Gast, D. L., (1984). *Single subject research designs in special education.* Columbus, OH: Charles E. Merrill.

Thompson, T. J., & Berkson, G. (1985). Stereotyped behavior of severely disabled children in classroom and free-play settings. *American Journal of Mental Deficiency, 89*, 580–586.

Twardosz, S., Nordquist, V. M., Simon, R., & Botkin, D. (1983). The effect of group affection activities on the interaction of socially isolate children. *Analysis and Intervention in Developmental Disabilities, 3*(4), 311–338.

Wahler, R. G., & Fox, J. J. (1980). Solitary toy play and time-out: A family treatment package for aggressive and oppositional children. *Journal of Applied Behavior Analysis, 13*(1), 23–39.

Wahler, R. G., & Fox, J. J., (1981). Setting events in applied behavior analysis: Toward a conceptual and methodological expansion. *Journal of Applied Behavior Analysis, 14*(3), 327–338.

Watzlawick, P., Beavin, J. H., & Jackson, D. D. (1967). *Pragmatics of human communication.* New York: W. W. Norton.

Weeks, M., & Gaylord-Ross, R. (1981). Task difficulty and aberrant behavior in severely handicapped students. *Journal of Applied Behavior Analysis, 14*(4), 449–463.

Wehman, P. (1976). Selection of play materials for the severely handicapped: A continuing dilemma. *Education and Training of the Mentally Retarded, 11*, 46–50.

Wehman, P. (1977). *Helping the mentally retarded acquire play skills.* Springfield, IL: Charles C. Thomas.

Wehman, P., & McLaughlin, P. J. (1979). Teachers' perceptions of behavior problems with severely and profoundly handicapped students. *Mental Retardation, 17*, 20–21.

Weiher, R. H., & Harman, R. E. (1975). The use of omission training to reduce self-injurious behavior in a retarded child. *Behavior Therapy, 6*, 261–268.

Wells, M. E., & Smith, D. W. (1983). Reduction of self-injurious behavior of mentally retarded persons using sensory integrative techniques. *American Journal of Mental Deficiency, 87*, 664–666.

Whitman, T. L., & Scibak, J. W. (1979). Behavior modification research with the severely and profoundly retarded. In N. R. Ellis (Ed.), *Handbook of mental deficiency, psychological theory and research* (2nd ed.) (pp. 289–340). Hillsdale, NJ: Lawrence Erlbaum Associates.

White, O. R., & Haring, N. G. (1976). *Exceptional teaching* (1st ed.). Columbus, OH: Charles E. Merrill.

Winett, R. A., & Winkler, R. C. (1972). Current behavior modification in the classroom: Be still, be quiet, be docile. *Journal of Applied Behavior Analysis, 5*, 499–504.

Wolery, M. (1978). Self-stimulatory behavior as a basis for devising reinforcers. *AAESPH Review, 3*, 23–29.

Wolery, M., Kirk, K., & Gast, D. L. (1985). Stereotypic behavior as a reinforcer: Effects and side effects. *Journal of Autism and Developmental Disorders, 15*(2), 145–157.

Wolf, M. M. (1978). Social validity: The case for subjective measurement or how applied behavior analysis is finding its heart. *Journal of Applied Behavior Analysis, 11*(2), 203–214.

From the beginning of each day to the end, everyone has personal, basic needs that must be dealt with, if not by ourselves, by someone else. We clean, dress, and prepare ourselves; we eliminate, we blow our noses, perform straightening and tidying tasks routinely, without much thought. On a daily basis, we must eat and care for our health. Beyond these tasks come those involved with our living places—cleanliness, repair, organization, restocking, and enjoyment. This rather vast domain of domestic activities will be relevant for our students throughout their school years and beyond. Younger students will focus on partial and full participation in their self-care and will add aspects of housekeeping, cooking, and home and yard care when they are targeted as being important to a particular person's current or future life.

Use of the surrounding community likewise constitutes a vast division of abilities. Community skills together with those in the domestic domain make up half or more of the curricular content for our students. It also is true that some of the skills in these two domains will influence success in other curriculum domains. For example, in order to prepare a snack one must have food supplies, which requires a store visit and purchase. To use a restaurant or a movie theater one will be expected to make choices, to eat, to behave appropriately, to use restroom facilities and to sit quietly. To hold a job, one must get to work, maintain a physical appearance suited to the job, and manage one's hygiene and health.

Diane Browder and I speak to these curricular domains in the next two chapters. As you read, topics addressed earlier in this text reappear: the importance of the ecological inventory to the selection of functional skills, the regular observation of behavior as the method for monitoring learning, and the central importance of promoting skill generalization. Two other themes are evident. First, research has more often excluded students with significant motor problems, thus teachers must devise and adapt procedures. Pip Campbell's earlier chapters will help in this task. Second, the students' ongoing social and communicative behavior accompany their performance of domestic and community skills. Thus, as will also be the case when teaching leisure and vocational skills, the teacher is advised to teach appropriate behavior and communication concurrently.

Introduction to Chapters 13 and 14

13

Basic Self-Care Instruction for Students Without Motor Impairments

Martha E. Snell
University of Virginia

The development of self-care skills that begin early in the normal child's life represents a beginning of independence from parents. For children and young adults with handicaps, this independence is of equal significance, although mental, physical, or behavioral deficiencies, as well as environmental expectations, may slow, limit, or indefinitely postpone the development of these basic adaptive skills. Feeding, dressing, and toileting are the most basic self-care skills. Early grooming skills supplement these basic abilities. They include handwashing, facewashing, toothbrushing, nasal hygiene, and later bathing and showering, haircombing, and washing. Although most of these tasks are performed daily, all involve complex arrays of subskills learned in a highly organized sequence along with early cognitive, social, and motor abilities.

This chapter focuses on basic self-care—feeding, dressing, toileting, and early grooming skills—and how to measure and teach performance in these areas. Chapter 7 addresses these same basic skills as they are performed for, and taught to, students with movement difficulties. Then, in Chapter 14 the focus is upon more advanced personal maintenance, including showering, grooming habits, clothing combination, and clothing care along with other skills in the domestic domain.

BEHAVIORS INFLUENCING SELF-CARE SKILL LEARNING

Most children with severe handicaps show delays in the mastery of self-care skills. Many causes beyond mental retardation may account for or contribute to this delay. The fine motor skills needed for self-care may be inadequate, or physical handicaps (visual, motoric) may aggravate the retardation or emotional disturbance. If a student's manipulative motor abilities are weak, reaching, grasping, and eye-hand coordination may need careful examination. Physical handicaps such as cerebral palsy (CP) require close guidance in assessment and training by a physical or occupational therapist to set realistic targets rather than encouraging dependency. (see Figure 13.1.) The student with athetoid CP has problems of muscle control that are vastly different from the individual with severe spastic CP; these differences mandate procedural prescriptions for positioning, transporting, and specific movement requirements

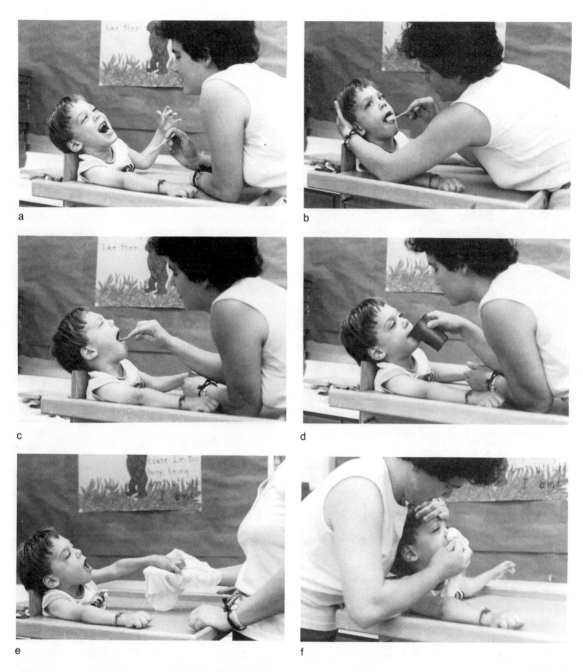

FIGURE 13.1 Tom learns to help during toothbrushing by holding his mouth open (a–c) as each quadrant is brushed and by rinsing out the toothpaste (d). During handwashing (e), Tom assists his teacher by extending his arm and wiping each hand across a wet washcloth. In facewashing (f), he participates by turning his head from side to side as his teacher holds the cloth against his mouth. Grooming tasks are a lot easier and more enjoyable for everyone when Tom actively participates.

Credit must be given to Carolyn Haykin and the Community-Based Instructional Program of Albermarle County Public Schools in Charlottesville, Virginia.

for eating, toileting, and dressing. Chapters 7 and 8 address programming adaptations necessary for teaching basic self-care skills to students with movement limitations.

For most students having no limitations in their movement skills, but needing instruction in self-care, comprehension of simple commands and possibly motor imitation and visual attending skills are likely to be minimal. Most researchers have not chosen to view these latter skills as prerequisites. Instead, gains in self-care skills have been accompanied by increased comprehension of verbal requests to perform these skills (Bensberg, Colwell, & Cassel, 1965; Minge & Ball, 1967). This same logic may also apply when the learner has extensive disruptive behaviors that result in inattention or aggressive behavior (repetitious hand staring, throwing objects, hitting others, running away from the task). Therefore, a teacher may elect to deal directly with the disruptive behaviors while reinforcing any improvements or even cooperation in self-care, but not to teach new skills until self-control is more predictable. More often, training in self-care and behavior management will proceed simultaneously. Because of the differential reinforcement of self-help behaviors along with ignoring or timing-out of misbehaviors, the incidence of disruptive behavior will decrease (Azrin & Armstrong, 1973; Christian, Hollomon, & Lanier, 1973; Minge & Ball, 1967; O'Brien & Azrin, 1972; Song & Gandhi, 1974).

An additional class of behavior—noncompliance—may falsify assessment results and confuse teaching techniques. *Noncompliance* is the habitual tendency to refuse to perform skills or portions of skills that actually are in the individual's repertoire. This behavior is often inadvertently maintained by teachers who provide help at the least refusal to perform or complete a task or who inconsistently require the learner to perform self-care behaviors, and alternate between firmness in task completion and "giving in" to extreme refusals or time constraints. For example, dressing training can be done at relevant times (right before dismissal) but enough time must be available to ignore refusals to perform without necessitating the teacher's dressing the student.

The informal assessment should not only allow measurement of self-care skills but also estimate additional behaviors influencing training: physical handicaps and their effect on self-care behavior, level of fine motor development, attending, motor imitation, comprehension of simple commands ("Look here," "Eat with your spoon," "No," "Do this"), and disruptive or noncompliant behaviors that occur during meals, dressing periods, and toileting. In some cases a teacher can observe another teacher (parent or aide) working with a learner on self-care. These observations enable one to observe the student's response to commands, various prompts and reinforcement procedures, the learning situation, and so on, and to predict the success of changes in current antecedent or consequent events. Whenever possible, interviews with or observations of the parents' interaction with their child during self-care times are recommended. The teacher should gather information on the parents' expectations for performance, their understanding of analyzing tasks into small steps and reinforcing successive approximations, their consistency in approach, the use of imitative models, the appropriateness of the teaching materials (texture, flavor of food, level of toilet seat, size and complexity of clothing), and their feelings about the teaching program. All of this information, along with the self-care skill data, will be valuable in creating and monitoring an individualized instructional program.

Summary of Self-Care Instructional Decisions

Chapters 4 and 5 discussed the steps involved in systematic instruction. The list below summarizes the instructional decisions involved in teaching feeding, toileting, dressing, and basic grooming skills.

1. What foods, toys, activities, and types of social attention and praise that are reinforcing to the learner and appropriate to his chronological and social age may be efficiently used in teaching?
2. How will undesirable behaviors that interfere with learning be handled?
3. What self-help training objectives will be set?
   A. What skills are of most immediate importance to the individual, the home, or the school: what self-care behaviors are frequently performed in part or in total for the individual?
   B. What skills will be required in the future?
   C. What is the student's current or baseline performance on these skills?

4. What instructional methods will be used to achieve the set objectives?
   A. Teacher instructions and requests,
   B. Effective prompts,
   C. Training setting and instructional materials,
   D. Teaching times and frequency,
   E. Task analysis of behavior,
   F. Specific teaching techniques (shaping, backward chaining, dry pants check, positive practice, etc.).
5. How will changes in performance be monitored?
6. How will skill gains be maintained?
7. How will skill gains be generalized to other teachers, materials, and settings?

TOILET TRAINING

Independent toileting skills are all too often an unattained goal for students with severe disabilities. This failure often leads to exclusion from social and recreational programs and public schooling. It reduces teaching time between parent or ward attendant and the "accident prone" student, causes serious health hazards in the form of inadequate residential hygiene, dysentery, and intestinal infection, and makes the student less pleasant to be around. The high prevalence of daytime incontinence in this population is surpassed by nighttime incontinence or enuresis. While some have estimated that 40% of the institutionalized retarded adult population are enuretic at night (Smith, 1981), others (Azrin, Sneed, & Foxx, 1973; Sugaya, 1967) place this figure at 70%. Both estimates are in stark contrast to those reported for nonhandicapped 5-year-olds (17%), 11-year-olds (11%), and 15-year-olds (2%) (Kolvin, 1975).

In a 5-year survey of the toileting skill changes in a group of 3,427 institutionalized individuals with retardation, Lohman, Eyman, and Lask (1967) discovered that 63% of the sample—those with the highest functioning capabilities (IQ 20)—were, or became, toilet trained during the 5 years rather easily by traditional methods without any special equipment or systematic operant techniques; however, 31% made no progress or regressed. Most members of this group had one or more of the following characteristics: IQ 10 or under, severely disturbed behavior, medically significant physical problems. The remaining 6.2% had an IQ between 10 and 20 and made progress during the 5 years

toward daytime regulation (eliminated on toilet when taken but no self-initiation) with traditional methods of toilet training. The authors hypothesized that the unsuccessful group with "complex custodial problems" would probably never improve, whereas the smaller group of 6.2% would respond to intensive operant training.

Motivated by these statistics and their negative effect on development of independence in persons with handicaps, teachers and applied behavior analysts have in the past 20 years created, tested, and improved treatment procedures for incontinence. This section sets forth the basic elements of successfully documented toilet training procedures, drawing heavily upon recent research and curricular applications in this area.

Entry Skills for Toilet Training

As with other tasks, toileting is learned in a logical developmental sequence building upon certain prerequisite behaviors. Developmental sequences reveal a number of important points.

1. Daytime regulation and training precedes nighttime training.
2. Bowel movements are regulated before urination, but toileting independence in both is generally learned at the same time.
3. The additional skills of undressing, dressing, and wiping "slow down" total independence in the normal child.
4. Nighttime bladder control is acquired only after daytime control.

Some entry behaviors, such as bladder and bowel regulation, are directly requisite to independent elimination. However, other entry skills such as walking, vision, comprehension of simple verbal commands, though not mandatory, will facilitate learning greatly.

Essential Entry Criteria

There are probably three essential characteristics of readiness for toilet training. They are interdependent and relate to physiological development—specifically the maturity of the central nervous system and the elimination sphincters.

1. The student should have a rather stable pattern of elimination. That is, urination and bowel responses occur within certain daily time periods (as illustrated in Figure 13.2) rather

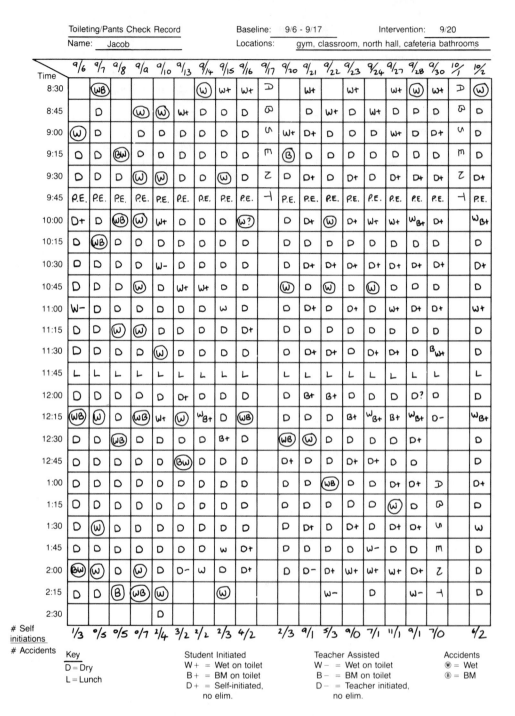

FIGURE 13.2 In this actual toileting/pants check record, 8-year-old Jacob was checked every 15 minutes. Records taken the first two weeks (9/6 to 9/17) before intervention was begun, indicated (a) stable dry periods (early A.M., though he usually arrived wet, and between 12:45 and 1:45); and (b) regular elimination times (before or after P.E., after lunch, around 2:00). His teachers continued his other programs while starting toileting intervention on 9/20 with 15-minute toiletings except during his dry periods and then administered 15-minute dry pants checks. Self-initiations increased rapidly during intervention and accidents began to decline. Intervention continued until accidents were eliminated; then, a maintenance program was begun.

than "dribbling" throughout the day or having bowel movements at random times.

2. The student should have daily stable periods of dryness—the ability to withhold eliminations extending from 1 to 2 hours (as illustrated in Figure 13.2).

3. The student should be 2½-years-old or older. With persons having mental retardation, there appears to be a positive relationship between progress in training and chronological age (CA) relating to central nervous system (CNS) maturity; however, research results are somewhat inconsistent (Osarchuk, 1973). Hundziak, Maurer, and Watson (1965) noted that CA is less important because of the indirect relationship between CA and the ability of the CNS to exert sphincter control. The relationship of mental age and success in toilet training is even less clear but recommendations reflect the rule: the greater the retardation, the longer you should wait before initiating training (Foxx & Azrin, 1974). The rationale for this rule concerns inadequate physiological readiness. For students with milder handicaps, little or no delay appears necessary (Bensberg et al., 1965). Foxx and Azrin (1973a) recommend that children with moderate retardation be at least 2½ years, while training may proceed best after a CA of 5 with students having severe or profound disability; however, *in practice, if a student who is not toilet-trained meets the three criteria described, instruction should be provided anyway, regardless of the level of measured retardation.*

Additional Entry Skills

Although these skills are *not* essential indicators of readiness, they will facilitate learning. Their absence, in part or total, will mean the teacher must make special additions to the instructional procedure (instruction in wheelchair mobility and transfer; modification in wheelchair design; instruction in attending and sitting, sign language, or simple gestures; mobility training).

1. The student is ambulatory and can walk to and from the bathroom independently.

2. The student has the manipulative skills to learn the basic undressing and dressing tasks needed for independent toileting.

3. The student indicates a need to eliminate by facial expression or posture.

4. The student dislikes being wet or soiled and shows displeasure.

5. The student will remain seated for at least 5 minutes.

6. The student *understands* some simple commands ("Look at me," "Come here," "Sit," "Eat this").

7. The absence of behavior problems: aggressiveness, self-destructive behavior, withdrawal from social contact (Lohman et al., 1967).

Measurement of Entry Skills

Daytime regulation and dryness may be measured with the same elimination chart. The many toilet-training programs available for students with disabilities provide a range of recommendations about how to record these baseline data with many consistencies.

Data Recording Form Using a data collection form similar to that in Figure 13.2, check the student at the beginning of every half-hour from waking to bedtime and record whether he is wet (W or B) or dry (D or blank); if wet, is it due to bowel movement (B), urination (W), or both (WB)? Furthermore, record whether the elimination occurred off the toilet (Ⓦ Ⓑ Ⓦ/Ⓑ) or on the toilet (W, B, W/B). As shown in Figure 13.2, accidents are indicated by circling the appropriate symbol. Additional symbols may indicate whether the toileting behavior was student-initiated (W+). If the student was placed on the toilet and no elimination occurred, an X could be recorded; whereas, self-initiated toileting which resulted in no elimination would be recorded as X+.

Depending upon the student and the method of training, Fredericks, Baldwin, Grove, and Moore (1975) suggest additional codes: a small dot would indicate liquids were given to the student, M would be placed in those intervals where meals occurred, and naps would be marked on the chart with arrows extending from beginning to end. As long as the essential information is recorded in the appropriate time interval, any symbols may be used.

During the collection of these data it is essential to change the student into dry clothing immediately after each accident with neutral teacher-student interaction (neither punishing or reinforcing) so that each accident will not be confused with earlier accidents. Clothing students in training pants rather than diapers will facilitate changing and detection of accidents. Although it is easier to train students when they do not wear outer pants or clothing over their underpants, the student's chronological age may make this practice inappropriate.

Length of Data Collection While some programs recommend a minimum of 3 (Foxx & Azrin, 1973b) to 7 days of baseline records, others use at least 15 days with a possible extension to 30 days if necessary to discover whether reliable toileting patterns exist (Fredericks et al., 1975; Giles & Wolf, 1966).*

Task Analysis of Toileting Skills

In 1963, Ellis proposed an analytical model of the stimuli and responses involved in toilet training which was the first task analysis. He reasoned that before toilet training, the elimination response (R_E) occurs in the presence of unpleasant bladder and rectal tension which act as discriminative stimuli (S^D) for these initially reflexive responses. R_E results in immediate reduction of the unpleasant tension, a process of negative reinforcement; however, as the child matures, the unpleasantness of wet and soiled clothes and parental disapproval are added. Ellis represented this as:

$$S^D \longrightarrow R_E \longrightarrow \text{Consequences}$$

Tension in bladder and rectum

Eliminatory response

1. Reduction of unpleasant tension (+)
2. Wet clothing (−)
3. Adult disapproval (−)

During toilet training a child is taught a variety of responses that precede elimination (R_A, approach

to the toilet, preparation for toileting) and result in additional intermediate discriminative stimuli (S_A, cues generated by approach response; S_T, cues associated with toilet) in the presence of which the elimination occurs.

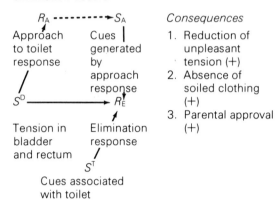

This model not only stimulated toilet-training research but also served as the first task analysis of elimination as a "conditionable" behavior.

A more detailed task analysis of the approach and the behaviors that immediately follow elimination (wiping, pants up and fastened) identifies the teachable steps and serves as a checklist assessment of baseline skill. Figure 13.3 provides a sequenced breakdown of the behavior chains before and after elimination. As with all task analyses, the number and order of the behaviors as well as the actual behaviors themselves will vary if one teacher's task analysis is compared to another's. With younger children, a better method of teaching wiping requires that the child stand up and then wipe rather than remain seated. If shirts or dresses are worn, the pants down and up sequence will change. Some teachers will prefer to teach boys to stand and face the toilet bowl rather than sit during urination. Although this task analysis has eight behavior chains, some of which are subdivided, the number of components and their subdivisions depends upon the method selected to perform the task and the amount of detail imposed.

Multiple baseline observations should be made to obtain more accurate measurement. The teacher may also wish to use a more or less rigorous testing method than that described in Figure 13.3. The more rigorous method, referred to as the *single opportunity method* (see Chapter 4), entails giving the student a single S^D or instructional cue ("Go to the bathroom"). The resultant performance would be scored without providing further assistance. Any

---

*The purposes of baseline charting vary depending upon the method of toilet training. While all programs may use a 3- to 30-day baseline as a standard to evaluate the effectiveness of an intervention, some methods (referred to here as *the improved traditional methods*) rely upon baseline records to determine the expected time of elimination for each student. These expected times for urination and bowel movement become the training periods; however, in methods which use additional fluids and mechanical signaling devices (Azrin & Foxx, 1971; Foxx & Azrin, 1973b; Mahoney, Van Wagenen, & Meyerson, 1971), pretraining accident and success records are kept as "an objective means of evaluating the seriousness of the incontinence problem and the need for the program" (Foxx & Azrin, 1973b, p. 25). Longer baselines revealing more accurate elimination schedules are probably most important for use with the improved traditional methods.

Individual: _____ Date(s): _____

Directions: Test the student at least 3 times over a period of 2 or 3 days. Try to select a time when bladder or bowel tension is most likely. Give the first cue, observe and score the performance; give successive cues only if student hesitates for more than 5 seconds or omits a behavior after completion of the entire preceding behavior. Score as incorrect the first behavior in every chain you must cue. Use a + if behavior is performed without help, a − if attempted but imperfect or incomplete, and a 0 if not tried.

Final Internal Cue (S^D) after Training	Intermediate Training Cues (S^D)	Behavior		Date					
Bladder and/ or Bowel Tension	1. "Go to the bathroom" (gesture)	1. Walks directly to bathroom without more than a 3-second delay in initiating the response	1.						
	2. "Pull your pants down" (gesture)	2a. Unfasten buttons, zippers	2a.						
		b. Hooks thumbs into tops of underpants	b.						
		c. Removes underwear and outerwear to at least mid-thigh	c.						
	3. "Sit on the toilet" (gesture)	3. Sits appropriately	3.						
	4. "Pee"*	4. Eliminates	4.						
	5. "Wipe yourself" (gesture)	5a. Stands	5a.						
		b. Reaches and grasps toilet paper	b.						
		c. Pulls out and tears off an appropriate amount	c.						
		d. Bends and wipes self	d.						
		e. Drops paper into toilet	e.						
	6. "Flush the toilet" (gesture)	6a. Places hand on top of flusher	6a.						
		b. Pushes down until toilet flushes	b.						
	7. "Pull your pants up" (gesture)	7a. Grasps top band of underwear with both hands	7a.						
		b. Pulls underpants up and into place	b.						
		c. Grasps top band of outer pants with both hands	c.						
		d. Pulls pants up and into place	d.						
		e. Fastens buttons and zippers	e.						
	8. "Wash your hands" (gesture)	8a. Approaches sink	8a.						
		b. Turns water on	b.						
		c. Wets hands	c.						
		d. Picks up soap and rubs hands	d.						
		e. Replaces soap	e.						
		f. Lathers hands	f.						
		g. Rinses hands	g.						
		h. Turns water off	h.						
		i. Reaches for towel and dries hands	i.						
	9. Gesture	9. Leaves bathroom	9.						

FIGURE 13.3   Toileting skill checklist

*Use language suited to the student's chronological age and the family's practice.

errors or hesitations of more than 5 seconds would cause all remaining steps to be scored as errors. The less rigorous method, the *multiple opportunity* assessment procedure (see Chapter 4), allows each erred or omitted response to be scored accordingly, then performed for the student by the teacher. This prepares the student to perform the next step in the chain and allows an observation of all steps. This method takes longer but often is more informative.

An assessment checklist, like this, should be used before toilet training and readministered regularly during training, where the toileting behavior chart (Figure 13.2) should be used before and *throughout* training. The information obtained from these two measurements is needed to set training objectives and evaluate progress during teaching.

General Elements of Toilet Training

After determining the learner's readiness for training, baseline elimination schedule, and current skills in the task analysis, the teacher must make instructional decisions about effective reinforcers and punishers as well as set instructional targets and specify methods to teach.

1. *What Training Objectives Will Be Set?*
   A. *Elimination.* Will bladder control and *bowel* control be taught together or separately? If separately, which will be taught first? Although teaching may proceed either way, the learner must have a stable pattern of elimination (in urination or bowel movement) in the areas selected for training. If only one area is selected, accidents in the other area must *not* be punished, though success certainly would be treated with the same reinforcing consequences as the targeted behavior.
   B. *Daytime or Night Training.* Only after the student has mastered daytime toileting skills (eliminations on toilet most of the time when taken, and has few or no daytime accidents) should night training begin (Azrin & Foxx, 1974; Baller, 1975; Finnie, 1975; Foxx & Azrin, 1973b; Linford et al., 1972). Fredericks et al. (1975) suggest that night training begin at this time regardless of whether the child has begun to express a need to go to the toilet or to initiate toileting.
   C. *Related Toileting Skills.* What deficiencies are potential teaching targets? Does the learner need prodding to walk to the bath-

room or restraining to remain seated on the toilet? Is he unable to manipulate his belt, snaps, and zippers? Does the child perform four of the nine steps in handwashing but hesitate or fail on the remaining five? Choosing additional training targets beyond the elimination target relates partly to the teacher's time but primarily to the learner's deviation from performance expected at his age and with his mental and physical ability. Because elimination training requires at least five additional chains of behavior (toilet approach, pants removal, sitting, pants replacement, and leaving the bathroom), a teacher should identify how many of these behaviors a learner is capable of and, at the very minimum, require that level of performance while reinforcing any improvements.

Some orthopedically impaired students may focus on the portions of these skills they are physically capable of performing, while the teacher, a peer, or other care provider performs the remaining parts. This practice, referred to by Baumgart and her colleagues as *partial participation*, allows the student to attain dignity and profit from some independence in self-care rather than to remain totally dependent. (Refer to Chapter 4 and to Baumgart et al., 1982, for more on partial participation).

2. *What Instructional Methods Will Be Selected?* As discussed in the next section, there are two major daytime training methods: improved traditional training and rapid training procedures with intentionally increased elimination with or without the use of mechanical signals. Variations of both methods may be used for night training as well. Because teaching procedures should complement an individual learner's entry skills and learning characteristics, the teacher should specify the following elements of the teaching program. (Some of these will be determined by the method employed.)
   A. *Instructions.* Verbal and gestural directions must be matched to the student's comprehension skills. Assessment of language skills will aid appropriate selection of meaningful instructions. For some, one-word commands accompanied by gestures are necessary; others may be able to follow more lengthy verbal instructions. With both extremes, consistency is of utmost importance. Instruc-

tions must be selected and standardized for each training objective.

B. *Effective Prompts.* At times a teacher will simply reinforce improvements in the toileting performance (shaping); but more often the need arises to prompt a nonoccurring behavior. Prompts may range from additional verbal directions ("Flush the toilet"), to demonstrations (by a teacher or peer models), to pointing and various amounts of physical assistance. Good instruction generally means providing the *least* assistance necessary to get the learner to perform. This allows the learner to perform more of the behavior and makes the eventual removal of assistance easier.

C. *Training Setting and Materials.* When a child is beginning to learn toileting skills, one bathroom area as close to the classroom as possible should be used. If the bathroom is too far away and if some students have difficulty walking, the teacher should consider moving portable toilets or potty chairs into a screened portion of the classroom. Some rapid methods involving signaling equipment (Azrin & Foxx, 1971; Foxx & Azrin, 1973a, 1973b) suggest moving the classroom into the bathroom. (This will be explained in more detail later.) Because there should be as many toilets as there are learners in a toileting program, the purchase of additional portable toilets may be necessary.

Once a student has learned to use one toilet and sink reliably, the training setting should be expanded to include other bathrooms. Although the need for adapted equipment may complicate this stage of teaching, it is essential that skill generalization be taught.

Reinforcers must be individually determined and their effectiveness tested before training begins. This determination may also include what *quantity* will be effective with different individuals (Osarchuk, 1973).

D. *Teaching Times and Frequency.* With the improved traditional method, toilet training will occur just before *every* normally expected time for urination and bowel movements (or one type of elimination, depending upon the objectives). With the rapid methods, additional fluids are given, creating the need

for more elimination and more training sessions; however, with both methods, students may be taught various aspects of the toileting chains (pants up and down, toilet approach, handwashing at times other than when bowel and bladder tension exist or are believed to exist). This extra training must only supplement that which is done in association with the internal bladder and bowel stimuli.

E. *Task Analysis.* The task analysis provided earlier may be used during assessment and as a teaching guide. Teachers will need to modify it to suit the particular needs and additional handicaps of their students (shorten, lengthen, use entirely different behavior chains) as well as the training setting.

F. *Specific Training Techniques.* Although some techniques were developed as part of a larger toileting program, many can be used in the original or a modified form to create another program. The "dry pants inspection," first described by Azrin and Foxx (1971), was one of the many techniques in their rapid toilet-training method. Linford et al. (1972) include a less frequent dry pants inspection in their programs. Generally these *new* toilet-training "packages" have not been experimentally tested; however, if a teacher clearly understands the learning outcome of a particular procedure, can adjust the elements of that procedure to suit a specific student, and uses a data system of program evaluation, new combinations of techniques are justified.

Dry Pants Inspection

This technique (Azrin & Foxx, 1971; Foxx & Azrin, 1973b) consists of three steps.

1. Question the individual about dryness, using simple phrases and gestures ("Are you dry?").
2. Prompt the person to look at and feel the crotch area of the pants.
3. A. If the pants are dry, reinforce with praise for dryness ("Good, you have dry pants!") and an edible.

   B. If pants are wet, verbally chastise and withhold the edible ("No, you have wet pants, no candy!").

In a rapid training program where extra fluids are given, dry pants inspections are carried out every 5 minutes unless an accident occurs to delay the next inspection (Foxx & Azrin, 1973b). If dry pants inspection is part of a more traditional program, it would be less frequent.

Accident Treatment

Many accidents will be prevented by adhering strictly to a toileting schedule, maintaining a standardized eating and drinking pattern, and strongly reinforcing correct toileting behavior. However, not *all* accidents will be prevented, so a regular procedure for responding to accidents should be determined. The consequences may range from ignoring or extinction to punishment. Unless mandated by the program, select an accident treatment that best suits the learner. If, under the traditional method, daytime accidents continue after 2 months, a mild punishing accident consequence may be appropriate. Instead, the teacher may wish to change systematically some single element of the program at a time: reinforcers, toileting schedule, change to a more rapid method, addition of signaling equipment.

1. *Extinction.* Without talking to the student, change his pants and clean him, using lukewarm water. Be careful not to provide any reinforcing activity too soon after an accident.
2. *Mild Punishment.* As soon as an accident is discovered, approach the learner, have him feel and look at his pants, and provide verbal disapproval ("You wet your pants" or "No, you have wet pants"). The student may be left wet for a few minutes to experience the discomfort. The teacher then changes the student, using the extinction procedure. Smith (1979) successfully used a verbal reprimand and a 10-minute timeout from reinforcement in place of the Azrin and Foxx (1971) overcorrection procedures which he and others have found to be overly aversive.
   A. *Cleanliness Training.* As soon as the accident is signaled, the student is grasped and told, "No, you wet your pants!" Next he is told to undress and given a tepid shower. Then he is expected to dress in clean clothing, place his clothes in a sink, immerse them in water, wring out the water, spread them to dry, and clean the floor or chair where the accident occurred with a mop or cloth. Students resisting cleanliness training are physically assisted through every step. No reinforcers,

social or edible, are given for an hour after an accident. A shortened version, which excludes clothing change and washing, is suggested for use during initial bladder training (Foxx & Azrin, 1973b). The expanded version just described is used once the student begins to toilet himself without a prompt (self-initiation stage). If the student is verbal, this overcorrection procedure may be enhanced by requiring him to verbalize the relationship between the overcorrection procedure and soiling with a statement such as "I am cleaning my pants because I soiled them and will have to do this each time it happens" (Doleys & Arnold, 1975, p. 16).
   B. *Positive Practice.* Immediately after cleanliness training for an accident, Foxx and Azrin (1973b) use positive practice—the continuous repetition of movements related to toileting: toilet approach, pants down, sit for a few moments, rise, pants up, leave toilet area. Positive practice is continued, with prompting as needed, for the remainder of the half-hour cycle. If shortened cleanliness training is used, the student still has his wet pants on and a dry pants inspection follows at the end of every positive practice cycle. This means he feels his wet pants and is verbally chastised.
   C. *Other Punishment Procedures.* Although toileting accidents have been reduced by fairly extreme punishment procedures such as spanking, termination of meals, and restraining jackets, these extreme methods are not necessary. Less punitive methods have been used with success (Barmann, Katz, O'Brien, & Beauchamp, 1981) and are characterized by immediate and consistent application after each accident and with strong positive reinforcement for appropriate behavior. The immediacy problem—discovering accidents as soon as they occur—is best solved by urine signaling equipment, but also may be decreased with frequent dry pants inspections.

Instruction of Related Behaviors

Most toilet training involves early shaping of behaviors preceding and following toilet elimination—walking to the toilet, pulling pants down, sitting on the toilet. Although this training would naturally occur with every scheduled toileting, extra training also may be needed so the individual masters these skills before elimination control.

Using forward chaining in combination with prompting, fading, and shaping, Mahoney and colleagues (1971) taught normal and retarded youngsters first to approach the toilet when they heard an auditory signaling device. Next, reinforcement was made contingent upon toilet approach and pulling pants down; *then* approach, pants down and sitting (or standing). At this point fluid intake was increased and the signaling device modified so that each inpants urination produced the auditory signal. Individuals who did not then go to the toilet were prompted by the experimenter, "No! Go potty!" If some urine was deposited in the toilet, the child was reinforced.

Giles and Wolf (1966) initially fed their students, who had severe retardation, their meals contingent upon sitting on the toilet. Next, after suppositories and milk of magnesia were given to increase the probability of bowel movements, the students were reinforced only for sitting and eliminating on the toilet. Similarly, Marshall (1966) shaped the behavior of a boy with autism by reinforcing correct performance of each successive component of the chain. Even in an institution where the attendant-resident ratio often was 1 to 10, this forward chaining to build the chain of responses was successful (Levine & Elliot, 1970).

Moisture-Signaling Devices

Regardless of whether extra fluids or moisture-signaling pants are used in a training program, reinforcement may be given more quickly if the moment of sphincter relaxation and elimination is known. Because training consists primarily of associating reinforcing consequences with sphincter control leading to elimination on the toilet, urine-signaling devices for the toilet let the teacher provide reinforcement without delay. Listening or looking for the movement of urination or defecation (even with aluminum foil placed on the potty to magnify the sound) are inaccurate and time consuming in comparison to moisture-detecting equipment.

Moisture-detecting devices may be built into a potty chair or into a plastic bowl which fits inside the regular toilet bowl (Figure 13.4). One way to build such a device involves fastening two snap studs about ½-inch apart to the bottom center of

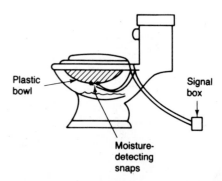

FIGURE 13.4 The urine alert. The plastic bowl fits into normal toilet bowl and rests on its top edge. The detachable wires connect the moisture-detecting snaps to the signal box, which can rest on the floor or top of the toilet. The signal box sounds a tone when urine or feces touches the snaps.

Source: From *Toilet Training the Retarded: A Rapid Program for Day and Nighttime Independent Toileting* (p. 30) by R.M. Foxx and N.H. Azrin, 1973b, Champaign, IL: Research Press. Reprinted with permission.

the plastic bowl. Next, following the circuit schematic pictured in the lower half of Figure 13.5, detachable insulated wires are connected to the studs and run to a circuit box with batteries. Urine or feces falling into the potty bowl complete a low voltage circuit between the two metal studs, which in turn produces a sound from a small speaker in the circuit box. Herreshoff (1973) describes two wiring plans for sensing devices connecting to a record player or a light. Sensing plates have also been used in place of snap studs (Training Resource Center, 1973). As soon as the signal sounds, the teacher reinforces the student for a successful elimination and detaches the wires from the bottom of the bowl so that it may be emptied into the toilet, rinsed, dried, and reconnected in preparation for the next use.

Whereas a moisture-detecting potty chair signals the moment for positive reinforcement, moisture-detecting underpants (one design is pictured in Figure 13.6) signal the moment an accident occurs. Thus, accident procedures can be implemented without delay. Wet pants are disconnected from the circuit box by unsnapping the wires. Dry pants are placed on the individual and reconnected. If both moisture-detecting pants and potties are part of the toileting program, as in Azrin and Foxx (1971) and Foxx and Azrin (1973b), two different signals need to be used so that the associated

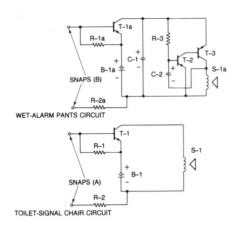

WET-ALARM PANTS CIRCUIT

TOILET-SIGNAL CHAIR CIRCUIT

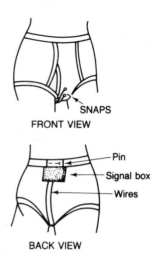

SNAPS
FRONT VIEW

Pin
Signal box
Wires

BACK VIEW

FIGURE 13.5 Schematic of wet-alarm pants circuit (top) and toilet-signal chair circuit (bottom). Component identifications are as follow: R-1 and R-1a, 100 ohm, ⅛ watt resistor; R-2 and R-2a, 15,000 ohm, ⅛ watt resistor; R-3, 22,000 ohm, ⅛ watt resistor; C-1, 100 mfd capacitor, 15 volts; C-2, 22 mfd capacitor, 15 volt; T-1, T-1a, and T-3; transitor #GE-2; T-2, transitor #GE-7; S-1, "Bleep-tone" signal tone device available from C. A. Briggs Co., Glenside, PA.; S-1a, speaker, 1.5 inch, 0.1 watt, 8 ohm, B-1 and B-1a battery, Eveready #216, 9 volt, or equivalent; snaps, Nu-Way, available from Burstein-Applebee Co., Kansas City, MO. The A-snaps attach to matching snaps on the training pants; the B-snaps attach to matching studs on the toilet chair.

Source: "Behavioral Engineering: Two Apparatuses for Toilet Training Retarded Children" by N.H. Azrin, C. Bugle, and F. O'Brien, 1971, *Journal of Applied Behavior Analysis, 4,* p. 251. Reprinted with permission.

responses will not be confused. The wiring schematic for underpants, pictured in the upper portion of Figure 13.5 involves a somewhat similar circuit plan to the potty signal with the alarm box attached to the back of the pants or worn in a pocketed vest or chest harness.* Other designs (Van Wagenen & Murdock, 1966; Training Resource Center, 1973) use cloth-encapsulated parallel wires running along the crotch of the pants and up the back to a circuit-box connection.

Mahoney et al. (1971) used more elaborate auditory signaling devices in combination with urine-detecting pants (Van Wagenen & Murdock,

---

*Urine-detecting training pants may be obtained commercially, already built or ready to assemble. Information on company, addresses, prices, and references is provided at the end of this chapter.

FIGURE 13.6 The pants alarm. The front view shows the moisture-detecting snaps fastened to the briefs. The back view shows the two flexible wires which lead from the snaps to the signal box. The snaps on the end of the wire are manually removable from the snaps on the clothing. The signal box is pinned to the back of the briefs (back view). A tone is sounded by the signal box when urine or feces moistens the area between the snaps.

Source: From *Toilet Training the Retarded: A Rapid Program for Day and Nighttime Independent Toileting* (p. 32) by R.M Foxx and N.H. Azrin, 1973b, Champaign, IL: Research Press. Reprinted with permission.

1966). The experimenter in the study operated an FM radio transmitter while the child wore urine-detecting pants, an FM receiver, and an earphone. By pushing a button on the transmitter, a signal was generated in the child's receiver and sound transmitted through the earphone. In addition, the same signal could be triggered by urination. Training involved forward chaining; each step in the toilet approach chain was shaped, using prompts as needed, in response to the signal triggered from the transmitter. Once this chain was learned, elimination training began. Children were given extra fluids, radio devices were removed, and urination alone produced the signal. The child was reinforced for quickly going to and sitting on the toilet as long as some urine was deposited in the toilet. Although Mahoney et al. (1971) did not use toilet signaling devices or punishment for inappropriate eliminations, as was done by Azrin and Foxx (1971) and Azrin, Bugle, and O'Brien (1971), they were successful in training people with severe and profound handicaps.

Improved Traditional Methods

A primary assumption of the more traditional methods of toilet training is that training proceeds best if one can accurately cue performance at the times when bladder and bowel tension are greatest. Various researchers have successfully used operant reinforcement principles combined with a regular elimination schedule with learners having retardation (Baumeister & Klosowski, 1965; Bensberg et al., 1965; Dayan, 1964; Giles & Wolf, 1966; Hundziak et al., 1965; Kimbell, Luckey, Barberto, & Love, 1967; Levine & Elliot, 1970; Marshall, 1966; Smith, 1979).

Toileting records are kept for 15 or more days to identify these times, generally once daily for bowel movements and 3 to 5 times daily for urination. The learner is then cued to sit on the toilet and praised for any successful elimination. In a review of research on toileting with the severely retarded, Osarchuck (1973) stated that, at best, such records provide only "a very rough estimate of elimination probability" (p. 432); however, a number of toileting programs used with students having handicaps describe additional techniques that may be added to this traditional method to increase its success rate (Bensberg et al., 1965; Fredericks et al., 1975; Gilies & Wolf, 1966; Hundziak et al., 1965; Levine & Elliot, 1970; Linford et al., 1972; Marshall, 1966). These techniques include dry pants check; teaching related responses such as approach, sitting, and pants down and up, before teaching elimination control or more intensively than simply preceding each elimination; use of urine-detection devices; specific accident procedures; consistent instructions and reinforcement for correct responses; and self-control training.

Linford et al. (1972) view toilet training as consisting of three stages: baseline (14 to 28 days), initial implementation, and development of self-control. During the second stage, after obtaining an accurate record of the child's eliminations, the trainer decides whether there is a consistent toileting pattern in urinations or bowel and selects the area(s) and times for instruction. Fredericks et al. (1975) recommend that the trainer choose only two times during the day during which to begin training. After the learner eliminates 75% of the time when taken at the two selected periods, another time period is added until the same 75% success rate is achieved. This practice continues until the entire day is covered. The rationale for the gradual expansion is the time commitment involved in each toileting (approximately 20 minutes).

Actual training proceeds according to the following steps:

1. Approximately 10 minutes before an elimination typically will occur, the student is asked in simple terms to go to the bathroom. (The child charted in Figure 13.2 would be taken at 7:30 A.M., 8:50 A.M., 12:15 P.M., 3:50 P.M., 6:15 P.M., and 8:50 P.M., if both bowel and urine control were being taught for the entire day.)

2. If the student has not eliminated after sitting for 10 minutes, he may be asked to replace his clothes and continue his other activities for 5 minutes, without any criticism or praise. Next, he is asked to go to the toilet; an interval of 5 minutes is allowed for elimination. If the learner is successful, he is immediately reinforced; if not, he is neutrally requested to leave the bathroom and return to his activities.

3. All eliminations (accidents, correct urinations, and bowel movements) are recorded on a chart posted in the bathroom. Symbols may record those times when no elimination occurred on the toilet.

4. Whenever the student is taken to the toilet, the trainer should teach the related skills (approach, pants down), providing, only when necessary, a minimum of prompts beginning with verbal instructions and proceeding to demonstration, then physical assistance as needed.

5. Because all correct elimination and related toileting behaviors must be reinforced immediately, the teacher needs to monitor the child's performance closely. Simple, specific praise throughout performance may be accompanied by activity or food reinforcers.

6. The routine is repeated for all the times selected for training.

The accident treatment procedure chosen should be used only during training periods. Simple extinction should be applied as a consequence for accidents at other times. Dry pants checks may be added to the routine, as may the other techniques described earlier.

In the third stage of training, the student is taught to develop self-control. The teacher gradually fades out all prompts (physical assistance, demonstrations, and verbal instructions) used during the second stage to teach related skills and to take the individual to the toilet at the scheduled times. Linford et al. (1972) suggest that the teacher ask the student if he needs to go to the bathroom and prompt a headshake or a yes or no response. Additionally all spontaneous indications to self-toilet must be reinforced vigorously, while the trainer should decrease the amount of time spent in the bathroom.

Rapid Toilet-Training Methods

Although toilet-training procedures have been used with individuals having severe handicaps (Fredericks et al., 1975; Linford et al., 1972), no results have been reported by which to evaluate their effectiveness. The research cited earlier, which involved somewhat loosely described variations of traditional methods, generally has been poorly designed, inadequately described, or has reported incomplete results. However, various rapid methods have extensive research supporting their application with persons having severe handicaps.

"Rapid" toilet-training methods that involve intake to increase elimination do not rely upon baseline schedules because the extra fluids or suppositories change the normal elimination pattern. Although rapid methods were originally developed for use with mechanical signaling equipment (Azrin & Foxx, 1971; Mahoney et al., 1971), these methods may be used with students having handicaps regardless of whether or not moisture-detecting devices are employed (Williams & Sloop, 1978).

Azrin and Foxx Procedure

Foxx and Azrin (1973b) describe four stages in their daytime rapid method: baseline, initial bladder training, self-initiation, and maintenance. After a 3-day minimum baseline period, the trainer may begin initial bladder training, which should last a minimum of 4 consecutive hours per day. The teaching ratio may vary from one trainer per student to one to three. The *average* time to achieve toileting independence for ambulatory, institutionalized individuals having retardation with this rapid method is 4 days (8 hours per day), with faster learning related to higher intellectual functioning. All training during the initial bladder stage takes place in the bathroom. Two chairs and liquid and food reinforcers must be available. The student should be wearing the urine-alert pants, and the moisture-detecting toilet bowl insets must be in place. An hour before training, fluids are given so the urination might occur during the first half-hour. As described in Table 13.1 and illustrated in Figure 13.7, there is a sequence of nine steps to follow every half-hour. A prompting-fading procedure is used to guide the learner through the sequence, but once he independently carries out part of the chain (approaches the toilet, pulls pants down), no additional prompts are provided. Trainer-student interaction is kept to a minimum, until successful voiding occurs or the student is off the toilet seat. Accidents, of course, are signaled by the pants alarm and, after disconnecting the alarm, are followed by the brief cleanliness training and positive practice. Clean pants are provided and reconnected to the alarm at the end of the next scheduled toilet-approach trial.

TABLE 13.1 Sequence of steps in the bladder training procedure. (Step 1 in the sequence is begun exactly on the half-hour)

1. Give as much fluid to the student as he will drink while seated in his chair.
   A. Wait about 1 minute.
2. Direct student to sit on toilet seat using the minimal possible prompt.
3. Direct student to pull his pants down using the minimal possible prompt.
   A. When student voids, give edibles and praise while seated, then direct him to stand.
   B. If student does not void within 20 minutes after drinking the fluids, direct him to stand.
4. Direct student to pull up his pants using the minimal possible prompt.
   A. If student voided, direct him to flush the toilet using the minimal possible prompt.
5. Direct student to his chair using the minimal possible prompt.
6. After student has been sitting for 5 minutes, inspect him for dry pants.
   A. If pants are dry, give edible and praise.
   B. If pants are wet, only show him the edible and admonish him.
7. Check student for dry pants every 5 minutes.
8. At the end of 30 minutes, begin the sequence of steps again.

Source: Adapted from *Toilet Training the Retarded* (p. 45) by R.M. Foxx and N.H. Azrin, 1973b, Champaign, IL: Research Press. Reprinted with permission.

Note: If self-initiation occurs at any time, start the self-initiation procedure. Continuously praise for being dry while he is seated in his chair.

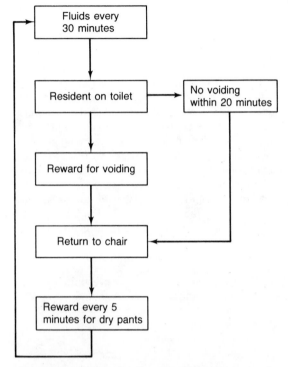

FIGURE 13.7 Flow chart of the bladder-training sequence (The specific steps involved in this flow chart are listed in Table 13.1.)
Source: Adapted from *Toilet Training the Retarded* (p. 47) by R.M. Foxx and N.H. Azrin, 1973b, Champaign, IL: Research Press. Reprinted with permission.

Self-initiation training begins once the learner tries to toilet himself totally unprompted. This stage involves the following instructional modifications:

1. Give fluids immediately following an elimination.
2. No further toilet-approach prompts.
3. Continue to provide guidance and prompts for dressing and undressing and for flushing the toilet, if necessary, but never at a level greater than that needed on previous toiletings.
4. Move chair farther from toilet on each successful self-initiation.
5. Gradually lengthen the time between dry pants inspections.
6. Intermittently reward correct toileting.
7. When learner is self-initiating from the area where he spend most of his time, remove urine alert from the toilet bowl, pants alarm from briefs and the chair.

8. Require learner to show you that he can find the toilet from various other places.
9. Include learner on the maintenance program after nine self-initiations (Foxx & Azrin, 1973b, p. 54).

Reinforcement for dry pants and correct elimination is faded to an intermittent schedule, prompts are systematically faded, and the toilet approach distance is gradually increased, then varied to yield more generalized behavior. The brief cleanliness training consequence for accidents is replaced by full cleanliness training, and continues to be accompanied by positive practice.

A maintenance program is begun once the learner achieves nine self-initiated toiletings. In this stage of learning, six dry pants inspections are provided daily: before every meal and snack, before going to bed, and spontaneously, so that one occurs every 2 hours. While dry pants are praised, wet pants are followed by the full cleanliness procedure and positive practice; accidents detected before meals, snacks, and bedtime also result in a 1-hour delay of eating and sleeping. Maintenance training is terminated when no accidents have been recorded for 2 weeks.

Mahoney, Van Wagenen, and Meyerson (1971) Procedure
This rapid procedure, also used successfully with people having profound retardation, differs from the Azrin and Foxx procedure in a variety of ways. The toilet-approach responses are taught before elimination training in response to an auditory signal sounded by the trainer over an FM transmitter into an earphone worn by the subjects. A gradual prompting-fading process was used to teach these first three prerequisite phases.

1. The student learns to walk to the toilet in response to an auditory signal.
2. The student learns to walk to the toilet and lower his pants in response to an auditory signal.
3. The student learns to walk to the toilet, lower pants, and take male stance or sit on the toilet.

Next, extra fluids were given and the moisture-detecting pants signal connected for automatic triggering of the auditory signal. Students were both signaled by the experimenter for practice (sat on the toilet for 30 seconds) and by their own urinations. In the latter situation, the child who did not immediately go sit on the toilet was approached quickly and told, "No, go potty," and assisted if necessary. In either case, reinforcement was contingent upon the presence of *some* urine in the toilet. No toilet signaling devices were used nor were accidents followed by punishment.

At this phase, students were taught to pull up their pants after urinating or sitting on the toilet. By this time, trainers recognized behaviors preceding elimination (increase in movements, tugging at genitals) and, at first, signaled toilet approach with the transmitted signal when it was not self-initiated. Next, all signaling equipment was removed, and reinforcement was contingent upon unsignaled correct elimination. In the last phase, verbal students were taught to answer "potty" in response to the question "Where are you going?" Parents were taught to continue the training in the home.

In this study four of the five children (having moderate to profound retardation and being primarily preschoolers) and all three normal preschoolers acquired toileting skills and attained bladder control with very few accidents over a 6-month period. An average of 29 hours of training and 262 training trials were required for the retarded children to reach criterion. Teaching the related toileting behaviors—walk to the toilet, lower pants, etc.—before teaching elimination training seems to be a good alternative to teaching related behavior at the same time as bladder control.

Lancioni and Ceccarani (1981)

Lancioni and Ceccarani (1981) used a variation of the Azrin and Foxx toileting procedure successfully with nine institutionalized adolescents having profound retardation. In the first of two studies, the researchers were interested in discovering whether students with a history of toileting accidents could attain bladder independence with "a procedure that would not imply drastic changes in their daily programs or in the program of their trainers" (p. 80).

First they asked whether hourly toiletings, 6 days per week, increased liquids intake (0 to 14 glasses per day), toileting cues, success reinforcement, and accident punishment would constitute a successful intervention package. Toiletings took roughly 30 to 45 minutes daily, depending upon accidents and the use of an accident procedure. Students spent the remainder of the day in other scheduled instructional activities (unlike other intensive toileting programs that occupy the entire day). During the first study, all accidents were punished by 90-second exercises (knee walking or deep knee bends), during which students were prompted repeatedly to look at and touch their wet clothes. In addition, 25 toilet insert seats (equipped with urine-sensitive alarms) were scattered in conspicuous places in and outside the classroom and play area where the students spent their time. The first step in the hourly toileting chain was to get a toilet seat before going to the bathroom. Thus, the toilet seats served as a visible reminder (discriminative stimulus) for toileting.

With this intervention, the accidents of five students were rapidly reduced (in roughly 10 to 12 days) and independent toileting appeared 7 to 10 days after baseline. Intervention procedures were gradually phased out over six successive phases:

1. Increased liquid, toilet seats present, increased assisted toileting, and punishments.
2. Assisted toileting reduced.
3. Assisted toileting discontinued.
4. Reinforcement reduced.
5. Gradual removal of toilet seats.
6. Reduction of liquids.

These changes let students acquire independence in toileting and return gradually to a normal routine with reduced assistance, fluids, and reinforcement; toileting was performed without insert toilet seats. Generally, students completed phase 3 (toileting assistance discontinued) after 20 days and phase 6 (reduction of liquids) after 40 days. A 60-day follow-up revealed that maintenance was good, with few or no accidents.

A second study with four similar students investigated whether the intervention would be effective if the accident punishment procedure were omitted. In particular, Lancioni and Ceccarani were interested in using this punishment-free procedure with students who were "regulated" and had very infrequent accidents (urinated at scheduled times of assisted toileting but never performed independently). Their reasoning was as follows:

Reduction in the rate of accidents increases the opportunities for pairing toileting activities and reinforcement. Even if punishment plays a role in the training of subjects who have a history of accidents, it could be superfluous in the training of subjects who have learned to urinate according to a schedule of assisted toileting, but who normally have no accidents. These subjects might display sporadic accidents at the beginning of the intervention when the amount of liquid increases, but they may then reacquire urinary control spontaneously (p. 89).

All procedures and phases were identical except that the few accidents that occurred with the initial liquid increases were ignored. As in the first study, the end of phase 3 (the elimination of toileting assistance) occurred after roughly 16 to 20 days of intervention, with phase 6 (elimination of fluids) occurring in somewhat less than 40 days and only one accident during the 60-day maintenance period. For these students, punishment did not seem to have a direct effect on the acquisition of independent toileting; however, the authors concluded that students with a history of extensive accidents need the punishment to reduce the accident rate and provide more opportunity to associate toileting cues, toileting, and reinforcement.

Although independence in toileting took longer with Lancioni and Ceccarani's modified approach than it takes with the original Azrin and Foxx version, the approach worked and was reported as being "less stressful" for both students and personnel, because entire days were not spent in the bathroom and other instructional programs could continue uninterrupted.

Bettison (1982)

Bettison's (1982) manual on toilet training is based upon several research studies that tested the procedures described (Bettison, Davidson, Taylor, & Fox, 1976). The program is an intensive one during which students' regular activities and/or training are reduced to enable three practice trials every half-hour across a 6-hour school day. As in other rapid methods, extra fluids are provided to increase the number of urinations.

First, students are taught the last step—pulling up their pants—and then are taught in seven additional training phases to: stand up from toilet and pull pants up (phase 2); sit on the toilet, void, stand, pull pants up (phase 3); sit and hold urine briefly, then void, stand, and pull up pants (phase 4); pull pants down, hold urine, void, stand, pull pants up (phase 5); move to toilet and complete chain (phase 6); use toilet without accidents over increasing distances (phase 7); and maintenance phase, during which the student returns to normal daily activities and intensive training ends with toileting skills being generalized. The program specifies a training criteria for movement from one

phase to the next, usually stated in terms of so many consecutive correct trials.

Bettison provides a checklist procedure to determine who is eligible for training. Also, baseline assessment procedures are described both for recording all eliminations during each half-hour and for measuring the student's entry performance in related toileting skills.

During the third through the seventh phases, moisture-sensitive underpants and toilet bowl insets are used with students. During these phases, accidents are treated by saying "No," loudly to the student, taking him immediately to the toilet, and prompting the student to sit and eliminate. Tangible reinforcements determined as being suitable to the individual student are provided at the end of each trial, though reinforcement guidelines differ somewhat from phase to phase. Praise is provided to shape performance throughout each trial. Prompts are given to promote correct responding and are faded by omitting the least intrusive prompts (verbal) before the more intrusive prompts (gestures, touch cues). Graduated guidance is used only as needed, with fading proceeding from full guidance to light touch to shadowing. Procedural guides for each phase are provided to record student performance and guide training procedures as in Foxx and Azrin (1973b).

While Bettison's (1981) program appears to be both well described for teachers and based on empirical data, there are some features (as in other rapid programs) which, if modified, would improve the "normalized" characteristics of the training. These modifications, however, have not been tested and might increase the training time and influence the effectiveness. These modifications include: (a) teaching the related skills of toilet tissue use, flushing, and hand washing; (b) teaching boys to stand to urinate rather than teaching students of both sexes to sit; (c) reducing the intensity of training so that more instruction is allowed in other skill areas while also teaching toileting; (d) requiring the student to assist in cleanup after accidents; and (e) allowing students to remain dressed normally during all phases of instruction, rather than removing outer pants and pinning up dresses or shirts. Without these modifications and using the program as described, Bettison indicates that the shortest time to the mastery of the first seven phases, excluding maintenance, has been 3 weeks, with most students having handicaps taking two or more months. Meeting criteria for the maintenance phase (the transfer of toileting skills to all other routine situations) is reported to vary considerably as well, from 3 weeks to 6 months or more.

Richmond (1983)

Perhaps the simplest and least intrusive variation of rapid daytime bladder training methods was that used by Richmond (1983) with preschoolers having profound retardation. The four children, between 3 and 4 years, were without sensory or motor impairment and did not take any medications. Richmond wished to test a method that used "regular potting" but avoided (a) the need for special trainers or equipment, (b) spending all day in the bathroom, (c) excessive punishment procedures for accidents, and (d) termination of all other programming. Using a multiple baseline-across-students design to test the effect of the intervention, students were toileted hourly during baseline while the schedule for the morning preschool remained unaffected. Social praise was given for successful toiletings and no comment made when accidents occurred. Intervention consisted of four training phases spread across four weeks followed by a posttraining or maintenance phase. While the daily classroom schedule remained the same, the frequency of trips to the toilet was increased during the first week to once every 15 minutes; during the following weeks this frequency was gradually reduced to one toileting every 30 minutes (second week), one every hour (third week), and one every 2 hours (fourth week). A simple version of Foxx and Azrin's procedures was applied during these four weeks.

Each trip was preceded by a dry and clean pants check. If no accident was detected, the child was praised for having dry and clean pants ("Good for you, Danny, your pants are dry and clean"). The teacher then asked the child, "Do you need to use the toilet?" The child was then prompted to respond and go to the bathroom. In the bathroom, the child was praised for engaging in the behaviors in preparation for and following toilet use (pulling pants down and up). If necessary, graduated guidance (Foxx & Azrin, 1972) was used for these behaviors. Using the toilet appropriately was reinforced with social praise and a preferred liquid. Liquids were used as reinforcement and to increase the frequency of urinations. An accident that was detected resulted in a brief reprimand and simple correction (the child was responsible for getting a clean set of clothes, removing the dirty clothes, washing necessary body areas, disposing of dirty clothes, and dressing). (p. 200)

During posttraining, students still were taken to the toilet once every 2 hours and were allowed extra trips when they indicated a need. Consequences for correct toileting and accidents were faded to those used during baseline—praise for correct use of the toilet and no consequence for accidents. All the students reduced their baseline accident rate from five per week or more to two or fewer per week during training. During the posttraining phase, all students further reduced their accident rates to zero.

Richmond's results offer encouraging news to teachers in that simple toileting methods applied in a consistent manner were found to be effective over a 9-to-15-week period without requiring extreme techniques or schedule changes. Richmond suggests that teachers may shorten the week-long phases for students demonstrating faster progress; likewise, the phases may be lengthened for others not progressing as quickly. Further, when toilet facilities are easily accessible, students should be taught during the later training phases to signal the need to use the toilet or simply to self-initiate approach and use of the toilet. The parents of Richmond's subjects indicated positive reports on toileting behavior at home.

A Comparison of Daytime Toileting Procedures

The success of either rapid methods or the traditional procedures will depend on the teacher's skills and the learner's handicapping conditions; however, there has not been any methodologically sound test of the traditional methods with students having severe handicaps. Thus, teachers or parents have little assurance that traditional methods will be successful with these students no matter how carefully they are applied. Currently, it appears that Richmond's simple variation of rapid procedures provides the least intrusive, but still effective, method to teach students with severe handicaps daytime bladder control. If faster learning is important, a more intensive procedure such as those previously reviewed may be used.

There has been little comparison research on toilet training methods. The single exception is Smith's (1979) study with 15 institutionalized students (ages 5 to 18) having severe to profound retardation. Three rapid methods were compared across groups of five students: the Azrin-Foxx procedure, the Mahoney et al. (1971) method, and a rapid group version of Azrin-Foxx. A few modifications were made in the rapid procedure, including the omission of overcorrection and positive practice for accidents, which have been reported to cause resistance and tantrums (Butler, 1976; Matson, 1975; Smith, Britton, Johnson, & Thomas, 1975). Instead, a sharp reprimand and timeout from reinforcement for 10 minutes was substituted. Second, rather than terminating prompts after the student made the first initiation, prompts were faded more gradually once self-initiations were reliable.

All three procedures used increased fluid intake and urine-sensing equipment. In the group procedure, one nurse worked with a group of five students and applied a version of Azrin-Foxx. These students were prompted to the toilet from the dayroom at regular 45-minute intervals, prompted individually to handle clothing and sit, immediately reinforced for correct eliminations, and given frequent dry pants checks; however, no pants alarms were used. Accidents resulted in 5 minutes of extinction and sitting in wet pants.

After 12 weeks of training, all five students on the Azrin-Foxx method were independent, whereas, four using the Mahoney et al. (1971) method and one receiving group rapid training were independent. Independence meant both no wet pants and the ability to handle clothing and the tasks of approaching and leaving the bathroom. Thus, both individualized intensive methods were more effective than the group version of Azrin-Foxx. In terms of staff hours required, the Azrin-Foxx method took the most staff time (2,330 hours), with the Mahoney method requiring almost as many hours (2,079 hours) and the group method roughly half the longest time (1,260 hours). Whereas the most effective method took almost twice as long as the group method, *it was* the most effective and thus the time was well spent in terms of outcome. Not only was the Mahoney method transistor equipment expensive, the staff members found the equipment difficult to maintain and use. Although the Mahoney method was effective, because of these problems Smith concluded that the time savings and results would need to be substantially better before the Mahoney method would be recommended over the Azrin-Foxx individualized method.

While the rapid methods require equipment and more staff time, they have been shown to be more effective with learners having severe disabilities; however, unmodified rapid methods eliminate time for instruction in anything else. These methods

seem to take more time in most cases than that originally reported by Azrin-Foxx (1971), which means more staff time and even less variety in programming (Bettison, Davidson, Taylor, & Fox, 1976; Smith, 1981). Thus, when choosing a procedure, a number of factors must be considered. First are the student's age and his toilet-training history. Generally with younger students (2 to 5 years), toilet training is a lower priority than at older ages, and thus, training time need not be so rapid. Most preschoolers do not have any history of failure in toilet training, which may mean that less intrusive procedures such as an improved traditional procedure should be tried before a rapid method.

However, students over 5 who appear physically capable of bladder control but are incontinent are likely to be excluded from programs, unpopular among their peers, and dependent upon teachers and parents. In these cases, toilet training should proceed rapidly. Thus, the programming and parental priorities must be considered for each student. If, for example, admission to a vocational or leisure program is denied due to incontinence, daytime control becomes more important. In these cases, time cannot be lost in achieving continence, and a more structured rapid procedure would be appropriate. Azrin-Foxx procedures have been implemented successfully by public school teachers of students having retardation (Trott, 1977), with individuals having deafness and blindness (Lancioni, 1980), and, in shortened form, with the elimination of the urine-sensing equipment (Williams & Sloop, 1978). The modified versions of Azrin and Foxx (Lancioni & Ceccarari, 1981; Smith, 1979) appear to be viable alternatives as well. Although independence is likely to take longer with these alternatives—7 to 12 weeks versus 4 days—the benefits may include less disruption of other instructional programs, a reduction in punishment, and possibly less stress for students and staff.

Irregular Enuresis

Far less research has dealt with the problem of partial bladder control or intermittent wetting or enuresis. Barmann et al. (1981) used a shortened version of the Azrin-Foxx procedures with three young boys having moderate to severe retardation using a multiple baseline design across subjects. They recorded toileting accidents in both the home and school during baseline, intervention, and follow-up for all three subjects. Because all the boys had self-initiated toileting in the past, initial bladder training procedures were unnecessary. Instead, the boys' pants were inspected hourly. If dry, they were praised verbally; when wet, *restitutional overcorrection* was employed. The child (a) obtained a towel, (b) cleaned up all traces of urine or feces, (c) went to his bedroom and obtained clean pants, and (d) placed the wet pants in a diaper pail. Immediately after these steps, *positive practice overcorrection* was required. The child (a) walked to the toilet, (b) lowered his pants, (c) sat for 3 to 5 seconds, (d) arose, (e) pulled up his pants, and (f) returned to the location of the accident. This sequence was repeated 10 times rapidly. Both forms of overcorrection together occupied roughly 20 minutes. The pants check and praise for dry pants was used in both the home and the school, while positive practice was required only at home to test whether its effects generalized into the classroom. Only the teacher and the boys' parents carried out the intervention.

The criterion for success was set at 13 of 14 consecutive days of no accident at home and in school. For all three subjects, the overcorrection led to substantial improvement over baseline accident levels (approximately 3¼ accidents daily). Once overcorrection was instituted, there was an immediate decline in accidents, followed by complete elimination. For all three boys, these results generalized from the home to the classroom and were maintained throughout a 2-month follow-up period. Thus, it appears that irregular enuresis can be eliminated in the home and school by parents using Azrin-Foxx accident treatment overcorrection procedures in the home and the teacher using only pants checks and verbal praise for dry pants. Because others have reported problems with the Azrin-Foxx overcorrection methods (see the Smith study reviewed above), it would be interesting to see whether a less aversive and time-consuming treatment would be as effective. For example, Smith (1979) effectively used a verbal correction during an application of Azrin-Foxx initial bladder training methods.

Continuity of treatment across the settings a person uses daily has been found to be important in the elimination of toileting accidents. Dunlap, Koegel, and Koegel (1984) found that when rapid procedures (with the exception of increased fluids) were employed either at the school or the homes of three young students with autism, learning showed no clear trends toward mastery. Only when training was consistently and simultaneously implemented across these and the other community settings that the students visited daily, were steady gains made in successful toileting. Furthermore, their version of rapid training did not require that other training programs be replaced with toileting training; instead, training was conducted within the context of other scheduled programs and across as many as six environments daily. The continuity-of-treatment method required that one individual per child be designated as the coordinator and that the child carry written instructions to facilitate consistent use of procedures. The coordinator made regular telephone contact with the additional trainers in the other settings to check on their use of procedures and the student's progress.

Precautions with Increased Fluid Intake

The use of increased fluids as a means of promoting urination and, thus, the conditions for bladder training must be accompanied by certain precautions. When the intake of water or other liquids is forced or encouraged over an extended period, as is the case with many of the rapid toileting methods, the balance of electrolytes in the body may be seriously endangered. Hyponatremia, or low serum sodium, may result, which is associated with nausea, emesis, muscular twitching, *grand mal* seizures, and coma (Thompson & Hanson, 1983). This condition requires immediate emergency medical combination of increased fluids over an extended period. Because teachers or other careproviders are unaware of the dangers of overhydration and students may be unable to report the early symptoms of hyponatremia, certain precautions must be taken whenever increased fluid intake is part of a bladder treatment program. Thompson and Hanson (1983) suggest several precautions.

1. All students being considered for a toilet training program that employs hydration should be medically evaluated for hypertension, as well as for normal heart, liver, and kidney function.
2. Increased fluid intake procedures should never be used with individuals having seizure disorders, hydrocephaly, or prior spinal injuries.
3. Once a student passes these two criteria, liquid intake should be limited per unit of time according to the student's weight and age: "85–125 ml [1/3–1/2 cup] per hour for children weighing 60–100 lbs and 165ml [3/4 cup] per hour for adolescents and adults weighing 100–150

lbs (for a maximum of 12 hours per 24 hours)"
(p. 141).

Although most researchers have failed to advise practitioners on the appropriate amount of fluids to use safely during a period of increased fluid intake, Bettison (1982) did address the amount of fluid needed to obtain frequent voiding and to avoid discomfort and vomiting (p. 28). Whereas her recommended fluid limits were slightly greater than those of Thompson and Hanson (1983), she did not give any breakdown by varying student weights or ages. Thus, this writer endorses the guidelines for limiting fluids that Thompson and Hanson set forth.

Nighttime Toilet Training

After a student has achieved reliable toileting during 75% or more of the day, training may be extended to develop nighttime bladder control. As with daytime training, various methods have been successful with nonhandicapped enuretic children and adolescents, while these other methods have been effective with students having severe handicaps. These methods include traditional procedures, the use of bed-wetting signaling equipment, and rapid methods.

Traditional Procedures

Linford et al. (1972) and Fredericks et al. (1975) described variations in traditional procedures found successful with individuals having severe handicaps, but unfortunately did not report any outcome data. Specific accident treatment procedures described earlier and urine-signaling devices for the bed and toilet may be added to improve these traditional methods. The parent follows the general steps listed below, taking special care to continue the daytime schedule, *reduce* fluids prior to bedtime, and keep accurate accident and toileting records so that a schedule may be prepared for parent-initiated toiletings at night.

1. Decrease the amount of liquids in the evening and give none within 1½ to 2 hours of bedtime. (Extra fluids may be provided during the day.)
2. Ask the person to go to the toilet just prior to a fixed bedtime.
3. Depending upon the parents' time, check the person as often as possible (every hour) to obtain a night schedule. Most parents will find this convenient only during their waking hours.

4. If the person understands, instruct him in simple language (perhaps showing him the reward) that a dry bed in the morning will be rewarded (special toy, activity). Check the bed in the morning to reinforce him if it is dry. Ignore wet beds.
5. About 1½ hours after the person has been in bed, awaken him and check for accidents or dryness, recording this on a nighttime chart.
   A. If dry, reinforce the person (dry pants inspection procedure may be used).
   B. If wet, either neutrally change the pants, pajamas, and sheets (extinction for accidents) or request his assistance. (A variation of the cleanliness training procedure may be used alone or accompanied by positive practice trips from the wet bed to the bathroom.)
6. Awaken the student before his usual accident time and direct him to go to the toilet. Require that the person sit on the toilet without sleeping for 5 minutes, or less if he urinates. Praise and chart successes; neutrally return the unsuccessful learner to bed, charting his failure to eliminate.
7. If the person is wet when awakened, chart the accident and awaken the child earlier the following night. Fredericks et al. (1975) provide an example to clarify this step.

Take the case of Jane, who went through the procedure of being told about a reinforcer, reduced her fluid intake, was awakened before the parents' bedtime, but was still wetting during the night. The parents usually retired at 11:00; Jane usually wakened in the morning at 7:00; thus there was an 8-hour period of sleep. The parents divided the night in half (4 hours), set their alarm at 3:00 and woke Jane at that time. Jane was wet for the first 5 nights that they awoke her. The parents then decided to awaken Jane at 1:00; half way between 11:00 and 3:00. Awaking her at that time, they found that Jane was dry. If she had been wet, they would have awakened her at 12:00. However, since she was dry they had her go to the bathroom and eliminate. This procedure succeeded in keeping her dry for the entire evening. (p. 13)

8. When the wake-up time that allows the person to be toileted once and remain dry has been identified, the person's ability to withhold urine

for longer periods each night should be strengthened by gradually moving back the wake-up time in intervals of 10 minutes, with continued charting to monitor accidents. Jane, for example, would be awakened at 12:50, then 12:40, then 12:30.

9. The parents should continue to provide powerful reinforcers in the morning for dry beds while giving social praise, at the least, during the night for correct elimination or dry bed checks.

Simple Fading Procedure

Currently there has been only one reported test of traditional nighttime training procedures with students having severe handicaps (Egan, Gruber, Hook, & Luce, 1984). Through individual baseline-intervention (AB) records were reported across five students with autism, who ranged in age from 9 to 13, more rigorous replication would add confidence to these important findings. Egan et al.'s methods employed 1 to 2 weeks of baseline during which time the students were checked hourly for accidents. This procedure was more easily implemented because the students resided in a residential program with night staff. Records were made of each student's wet and dry periods in order to identify the times when accidents were occurring ("wet hours"). When students were found to be wet, they were awakened and minimally prompted through a simple correction procedure (Foxx & Azrin, 1973b) to remove wet sheets and blankets, take them to the laundry, use the toilet, change their pajamas, and make the bed.

For each student one to two "wet hours" were identified from baseline data. Intervention consisted of prompting students to the toilet one hour before each "wet hour" with the goal being to fade scheduled prompting times as close as possible to the student's regular bedtime and waking time. Once a student had five or more consecutive dry nights, the scheduled awakening time has faded by a 15- or 30-minute increment. If the student's "wet time" was closer to his awake time, then the scheduled toileting time was faded earlier and earlier or toward the morning. For other students whose "wet times" occurred closer to bedtime, fading moved the toileting time closer to bedtime. This strategy is the same as that recommended by Fredericks et al. (1975), though the initial "wet times" were more precisely defined by Egan et al., and no students were awakened at the parent's normal bedtime or one and one-half hours after

they went to bed, unless that had been identified as a "wet time." Also, during the intervention, when students had 3 or more consecutive "wet nights" (nights in which the bed was wet at least once), the scheduled awakening time for toileting was faded in the opposite direction by 15 or 30 minutes, depending on the student. Only after 5 consecutive "dry nights" was the scheduled nighttime toileting again faded closer to normal bedtime or awakening time.

Other procedures employed included toileting just before bedtime, minimal prompting to get the student to make correct toileting responses, social praise for correct responses and all self-initiations, and simple corrections for all accidents. Trainers continued to check students hourly during intervention to record the state of their beds; however, students were awakened only at the one or two targeted "wet times" and whenever a wet bed was discovered on an hourly check.

Results indicated that all five students achieved nighttime control using these rather traditional methods after 7 to 38 weeks of intervention; and, in two cases, where maintenance data were reported, control was still present 10 months later. Although no extra equipment nor intensive overcorrection procedures were required, these procedures did involve hourly checks (and changes when wet) throughout intervention. If future research indicates this latter requirement is unnecessary, these simple fading procedures would be realistic methods for parents to employ.

Bedwetting Signaling Equipment

Several signaling devices have been developed to treat enuretic individuals with or without the additional handicaps of deafness, blindness, retardation, or behavior disorders (Coote, 1965; Lovibond, 1963, 1964; Mowrer & Mowrer, 1938; Seiger, 1952). There are two general designs.[*] The "sandwich" pad uses two pieces of screen or foil separated by fabric. Wet fabric results in contact between the positive and negative layers, completing an electric circuit. As with signaling underpants, this sounds a buzzer alarm and an optional light to wake the bedwetter. More expensive designs employ a one-piece pad that can be wiped dry after

---

[*]Commercially available bed-wetting signal devices are listed at the end of this chapter.

accidents, eliminating the need to replace the wet separating fabric.

The treatment procedure, which does not involve a reduction of fluid intake, tends to take several weeks or months to establish initial control but does so in about 80% to 90% of enuretics, though relapse is common (Lovibond, 1964; Sloop & Kennedy, 1972; Smith, 1981). Although the exact training procedure varies, a few similarities may be outlined (Baller, 1975). First, the student and parent should thoroughly understand the functioning of the equipment; "dry runs," especially important for the individual with handicaps, will aid this process. This familiarization includes correct placement on the bed, turning off the signal once activated, and the steps followed by the parent and learner once urination is signaled (turn off alarm, go to the bathroom to complete or practice voiding, change sheets and pajamas, and reconnect signaling wires). A positive attitude should accompany the treatment, with social praise and perhaps more powerful reinforcers for dry beds. Records should be kept for accidents and successful urinations including the date, time, and perhaps size of the wet spot. Finally, criterion for dryness before discontinuation of the equipment is 10 to 14 dry nights (Baller, 1975). Apparatus can be reinstated if later accidents occur.

During an 11-week treatment period in an institutional ward, Sloop and Kennedy (1973) reported success with 52% of the residents with moderate and severe retardation, who were taught using bed-wetting signaling equipment; however, the relapse rate of 36% indicated a need for modification, perhaps of the type tested by Azrin et al. (1973) with institutionalized people having profound retardation, which will be summarized in the next section.

If a traditional method (no extra fluids) is adopted, signaling equipment can simplify the task of obtaining a baseline nighttime elimination schedule. After explaining the equipment to the learner, the parent, house parent, or ward attendant would simply record whenever the signal sounds, turn off the signal, wipe the pads dry, and return the dry learner to bed. Thus, hourly bedchecks are not needed. After a stable schedule is obtained, a reinforcement plan and possible accident treatment could be instituted, along with a wake-up procedure and continued use of the urine-sensing equipment. Like the traditional method, this particular combination of traditional method plus urine-sensing equipment

has not been tested and thus may or may not prove effective.

Rapid Bedtime Training Procedures

Using methods similar to their rapid daytime bladder training program, Azrin et al. (1973) were able to reduce nighttime accidents by 85% in individuals having profound retardation during the first week after a single night of intensive training and then to 95% by the fifth week. Unlike other nighttime procedures, there was no relapse during a 3-month follow-up.

Because the procedure outlined in Table 13.2 was developed for institutional use, trainers were readily available on the midnight shift. Parents using this rapid procedure at home would need to modify it, as described in a later study (Azrin et al., 1974) with normal enuretic children. With further modifications, Bollard and Woodroffe (1977) found that parents of children with mild retardation or without handicaps could apply these (Azrin et al., 1974) steps and obtained more success with their bed-wetting children when signaling equipment was used.

A Variation of Azrin's Rapid Bedtime Procedure

Smith (1981) modified the nighttime training program used by Azrin and his colleagues, making it less intensive and thus more practical for most settings. All five institutionalized clients had severe or profound retardation, and three had serious behavior problems as well. Like Azrin, Smith used the enuresis alarm, increased fluids, and rewarded subjects for dryness; but also she reduced the punishment for accidents. Agreeing with other critics about the overcorrection accident treatment used by Azrin, Smith instead gave a sharp verbal reprimand for accidents and required the residents to feel the wet bed and use the toilet to finish urinating. Dry sheets were labeled ("nice clean dry sheets") and felt by the subjects to help them learn the difference between staying dry and having accidents. Wet sheets were left by the bed until the morning, to emphasize the accident, when the subject placed them in the laundry. In addition, those who had accidents the night before were mildly reprimanded by the day staff and "rewards were withdrawn" (Smith, 1981, p. 69). Although this treatment was not clearly defined, it was clear that positive reinforcement was emphasized both during the night and the following morning for those who had dry beds.

TABLE 13.2 Dry-bed procedures

I. Intensive training
  A. Before bedtime
    1. Student drinks fluids
    2. Urine alarm placed on the bed
    3. Potty-alert placed in toilet bowl
  B. Hourly awakenings
    1. Minimal prompt given for awakening the student
    2. Student instructed or guided to the toilet
    3. Student seated on toilet bowl
      a. If urination does not occur within 5 minutes
        (i) return student to bed
        (ii) at bedside give fluids and praise as reinforcers
      b. If urination does occur within 5 minutes
        (i) give student praise, snacks, and fluids as reinforcers
        (ii) return student to bed
    4. Praise student for having dry bed (require student to touch the dry sheets)
    5. Student returns to bed
  C. When accident occurs—45 minutes of cleanliness training and positive practice
    1. Disconnect the sound of the urine-alarm
    2. Awaken student
    3. Reprimand student for wetting and direct him to the toilet to finish urination
    4. Cleanliness training
      a. Bedwetter changes wet linen
      b. Teacher reactivates urine-alarm
    5. Positive practice in toileting
      a. Student lies down in bed for 3 minutes
      b. Student awakened with minimal prompt after 3 minutes
      c. Student directed to toilet
      d. Repeat steps a, b, c about 9 times
    6. Student returns to sleep when 45 minutes have elapsed since accident was detected

II. Monitored posttraining phase
  A. Initiation of monitored posttraining
    1. When student has no more than one accident during a training night
    2. When the student correctly toilets on at least 50% of all opportunities during a training night
  B. Procedure
    1. Urine-alarm on bed
    2. Whenever accident occurs, reprimand, cleanliness training, and positive practice follow for 45 minutes
    3. No fluids, no hourly awakenings, no reinforcers
  C. Termination of monitored posttraining
    1. Terminated 7 nights after last accident

III. Normal procedure
  A. Initiated after student goes 7 nights without accident
  B. No urine-alarm, no reinforcers, no positive practice
  C. Bed inspected each morning
    1. If bed wet, remakes and cleans bed (cleanliness training)
    2. If two accidents occur within a given week, the monitored phase is reinstated

Source: From "Dry-bed: A rapid method of eliminating bedwetting (enuresis) of the retarded" by N.H. Azrin, T.J. Sneed, and R.M. Foxx, 1973, *Behaviour Research and Therapy, 11,* p. 430, Pergamon Press, Ltd. Reprinted with permission.

All five subjects attained the criterion of 4 consecutive dry weeks after 18 weeks (4½ months) to 92 weeks (1.7 years) of training, with a mean length of 47.6 weeks. Among the five subjects there was great variability and frequent 2- to 3-week periods of dryness followed by several relapse weeks of wetness. Thus, a long criterion (4 or more weeks) was essential for obtaining long-term nighttime dryness. Follow-up checks on all five subjects at the same time revealed that all had remained dry without any relapses for 9 months to 2 years. Although Smith's successes were obtained after a much longer training period, a few comments can be offered. First, it is questionable how many parents or staff members in residential programs can carry out the intensive all-night training used by Azrin et al. (1973). Second, Smith and others who have replicated the Azrin and Foxx day and night training procedures (Bettison et al., 1976; Smith, 1979; Williams, Doleys, & Ciminero, 1978) have questioned the failure to replicate the rapid results of Azrin and his colleagues. Third, is the interest of all researchers in long-term retention of bowel and bladder control and the absence in many studies of follow-up data. Thus, although Smith's variation of nighttime training did not yield rapid results, the results appeared very resistant to relapse over time and the procedures were acceptable to those who had to implement them.

Given the success of repeated practice error

correction in contrast to other, simpler correction procedures (Close, Irvin, Prehm, & Taylor, 1978), it would be particularly interesting to know whether a *shorter* period of repeated practice overcorrection for bed-wetting accidents would be as effective as the longer period used by Azrin (2 to 5 trials of step I.C.5 in Table 13.2 rather than 9). If this were so, many trainers might be less critical of repeated practice correction procedures; with their use, results might be obtained more rapidly.

EATING SKILLS

Individuals with severe disabilities may learn to feed themselves without complication and with only slight delay when the environment is supportive and any additional handicaps (behavioral, movement, or sensory) are minimal or nonexistent. However, motor or neurological handicaps, structural abnormalities in the oral cavity and musculature, attention problems, extreme disruptive behaviors, special dietary needs, sensory deficiencies, or inadequate learning environments (overprotective or uninterested parents, uninformed teachers, poor teacher-child ratio) may lead to delayed, incomplete, or abnormal development of eating skills. Eating is perhaps the ideal skill for training because food is already a primary reinforcer. Related to this "built-in" reinforcement is the natural punishment of inappropriate eating—the interruption or delay of eating (O'Brien, Bugle, & Azrin, 1972).

To promote independence in eating and related table skills, the teacher will make the instructional decisions listed earlier, individualizing the answers to suit the specific needs of each learner. Often assistance must be sought from physicians and physical and occupational therapists during observation and assessment, selection of adapted eating equipment, program development, and implementation.

This next section provides basic assessment and teaching techniques that have been successful with students having severe handicaps that do not include movement difficulties.

Assessment of Eating Skills

Although there are several published assessment procedures for measuring eating abilities (Balthazar Scales of Functional Independence, 1976), direct observation of the particular eating behaviors of concern probably will provide the most useful

evaluation for the teacher (Wallander, Hubert, & Schroeder, 1983). As with toileting skills, the eating tasks—using a spoon, getting lunch from the cafeteria line, or clean-up—can be analyzed into steps suited to the situation and the student and used as the guide for instruction and evaluation. At times it will be more accurate to count and/or time the behavior rather than to rely on a task analysis of the steps involved because the student moves quickly through the steps and because the behavior is repeated many times during a meal. When teaching a student to use a spoon properly without spilling, the teacher might define "correct spoon use responses" as follows: "Moving appropriate food from the container (e.g., pudding, soup) with the spoon held in one hand, by the handle, right side up and without spilling, except back into the container from which the food was taken" (O'Brien & Azrin, 1972, p. 391).

The teacher would observe the student during a regular meal for either a set number of trials (the first 10 opportunities to use the spoon successfully or not) or for a set time period (the first 3 minutes of a meal), and count the number of correct responses and errors. In the first case, frequency data could be graphed in one of two ways: *number* of correct or *percentage* of correct spoon use responses. In the second case, when responses are counted for a fixed time period, data may be graphed in one of three ways as shown in Figure 13.8: rate for the entire fixed interval (number correct per 3 minutes), *or* average rate for a minute, *or* as the percentage of correct or error responses in the fixed time period. Semilogarithmic scale graphs may be used to display more accurately rate per minute data, as illustrated for dressing skills in Figure 13.17.

For students just learning to use the spoon, frequency- or rate-correct data will provide an accurate means to monitor progress. A limited number of targeted inappropriate behaviors could be counted as well for the same time period (food stealing, leaves table) if their rate or frequency will be directly or indirectly influenced by instruction in spoon usage. If the student's major eating problems are due to speed—either too slow or too fast—then rate data will be more informative than data taken for a fixed number of trials. Some students will not only have rate problems but also use the spoon incorrectly; in these cases, the teacher may use rate to monitor correct responses and speed.

To equip students with useful eating skills, it is advisable to teach related meal skills along with the

Name: Ray   Observer: Frank
Behavior: Correct & Error Spoon Use
Measurement: Frequency/10 trials   Data Collection Schedule: daily, 1st 10 trials during lunch

Date	Data Collection Time Start	Stop	Total Time/Trials	Frequency Correct	Error	Total Freq. Correct	Freq. Correct per min.	% Correct
2/7	11:45	11:47	2 1/2 m./10	II	卌 III	2/10	1.7	20
2/8	11:46	11:48	2 m./10	I	卌 IIII	1/10	2.3	10
2/9	11:49	11:51	3 m./10	III	卌 II	3/10	1.7	30
2/10	11:46	11:49	3 m./10		卌 卌	0/10	.7	0
2/11	11:45	11:48	3 m./10	I	卌 IIII	1/10	1.7	10

Name: Estelle   Observer: Janice
Behavior: Correct & Error Spoon Use
Measurement: Frequency/3 min.   Data Collection Schedule: daily, 1st 3 min. during lunch

Date	Data Collection Time Start	Stop	Total Time/Trials	Frequency Correct	Error	Total Freq. 3 min.	Total Freq. Correct	% Correct
2/7	11:47	11:50	3 m./12	卌	卌 II	5	5/12	42
2/8	11:45	11:48	3 m./15	卌 II	卌 III	7	7/15	47
2/9	11:50	11:53	3 m./15	卌	卌 卌	5	5/15	33
2/10	11:51	11:54	3 m./11	II	卌 IIII	2	2/11	18
2/11	11:46	11:49	3 m./15	卌	卌 卌	5	5/15	33

FIGURE 13.8 Two different procedures to observe the frequency rate of correct (or incorrect) spoon usage during lunch; frequency for a fixed number of eating opportunities or trials that may be graphed as frequency correct/error responses per fixed number of trials or per minute *or* as a percentage correct/error responses per fixed number of trials; frequency for a fixed time period (3 min.) which may be graphed as rate for an entire fixed interval, *or* as average rate for 1 minute (not shown), *or* as percentage or correct/error responses in a fixed time period.

basics of utensil use, drinking from a glass, and mealtime behavior. These skills usually consist of multiple steps that, unlike utensil use, are performed only once per meal, and are best measured through task analytic assessment (Chapter 4). For example, Matson, Ollendick, and Adkins (1980) used task analytic assessment to measure 26 mealtime behaviors involved in a family-style dining room program for 80 adults with moderate retardation. Table 13.3 lists these target behaviors: the skills directed toward orderliness or preparation and termination of the meal illustrate behaviors lending themselves to task analysis. Table 13.4 sets forth task analyses of some potential behaviors involved in using the cafeteria line, eating, and clean-up.

Depending upon what the student can do successfully during a baseline observation of some behaviors, targets will be identified and measurement procedures selected that give the most information about student performance. If, for example, the student has little success with opening the milk carton, this skill would be analyzed into steps for further measurement and instruction. In addition, this same student could be taught the steps involved in using the cafeteria line, although no further analysis of these steps might be necessary. (However, it is unlikely that all the steps will be suitable in most cafeterias; instead, task steps must be specified for the particular setting in which instruction will occur.)

TABLE 13.3 Hierarchical classification of the 26 mealtime target behaviors

Table Level	Target Behavior
Table Level 1: Orderliness	1. Picks up all utensils
	2. Appropriate noise level
	3. Appropriate line behavior
	4. Stays seated during meals
	5. Finishes eating before leaving table
	6. Returns tray and utensils properly
	7. Leaves dining room when finished eating
Table Level 2: Eating	8. Chews food before swallowing
	9. Takes small bites
	10. Swallows before next bite
	11. Drinks properly—glass in one hand
	12. Eats at normal pace—not too fast
Table Level 3: Utensil Use	13. Uses spoon appropriately
	14. Uses fork appropriately
	15. Uses knife appropriately
	16. Holds utensils properly
Table Level 4: Neatness	17. Eats neatly
	18. Wipes up spilled food
	19. Uses napkin
	20. Talks with mouth empty
	21. Has good posture
	22. Eats at normal pace
Table Level 5: Table Manners	23. Chews with mouth closed
	24. Elbows off table
	25. Hands in lap
	26. Pushes chair in

Source: From "A Comprehensive Dining Program for Mentally Retarded Adults" by J.L. Matson, T.H. Ollendick, & J. Adkins, 1981, *Behaviour Research and Therapy, 18.* p. 109. Pergamon Press, Ltd. Reprinted with permission.

Nutrition and Measurement of Food Intake

It is more often the case when students have severe handicaps that there will be threats to adequate nutrition. These threats may be the result of the particular handicap or due to the side effects of medications, to special diets, or to behavioral influences (Sobsey, 1983). For example, when students are taking drugs prescribed to control seizures, their tendency to excrete ascorbic acid (vitamin C) is likely to increase. Other students kept on pureed foods will lack fiber, protein, ascorbic acid, and B vitamins. Sosbey (1983) provides some general guidelines to ensure improved nutrition, while specific dietary recommendations must be made on an individual basis:

1. Whenever possible, efforts should be made to normalize the texture of students' diets.
2. When restrictive food preferences exist, teachers should work with parents and nutritionists to expand the variety in diet.

3. The nutritional effects of medications, in particular those that are given for long periods, should be evaluated and considered.
4. If foods must be removed from a student's diet due to allergy or metabolism problems, professionals with expertise in nutrition should be consulted to develop a plan for compensating the diet; in turn, the plan should be implemented.

For some students the quantity of food eaten may need to be modified. Any extreme can be a difficulty. The obese student who eats excessively may develop related social and health problems that can adversely affect vocational opportunities, leisure-recreational skills, physical fitness, and community integration. The underweight student who eats very little, either because of extreme motor impairment or behavior problems, is threatened by reduced energy and related health complications. In both cases, careful baseline records should be kept to quantify and define the extent of the problem

TABLE 13.4 School cafeteria skills

I. Cafeteria Line	II. Eating	III. Clean Up
1. Walks to appropriate lunchroom table	1. Initiates eating within 10 minutes	1. Initiates clean up within 5 seconds of cue
2. Puts down communication book	2. Opens milk	2. Picks up food, milk carton, and paper near tray
3. Greets peers	3. Removes wrapper from straw	3. Puts food, milk carton, and paper on tray
4. Walks to end of cafeteria line	4. Puts straw in milk	4. Stands up
5. Waits quietly in line	5. Replaces carton on tray after a few swallows	5. Steps over bench
6. Holds ticket in hand	6. Sucks liquid through straw	6. Picks up utensils and holds in one hand
7. Walks forward when line advances	7. Picks up finger foods	7. Grasps tray with both hands
8. Takes one plastic spoon from container	8. Brings finger foods to mouth	8. Walks to nearest trash can
9. Takes one plastic fork from container	9. Bites off appropriate size piece	9. Waits in line at trash can
10. Takes one plastic knife from container	10. Returns finger foods to tray	10. Turns tray over and dumps disposable items into trash
11. Walks into kitchen	11. Chews and swallows bite before bringing more food to mouth	11. Scrapes excess food from tray with utensils
12. Takes one milk from refrigerator	12. Chews with lips closed	12. Turns tray right side up
13. Greets cafeteria worker	13. Cuts food using side of fork/spoon	13. Walks to clean up window
14. Takes food tray when available	14. Cuts food using knife (for sandwich)	14. Puts tray on coutner
15. Places milk on tray	15. Cuts food using knife and fork	15. Puts utensils in tub of water
16. Places utensils on slot on tray	16. Uses adult grasp with utensils	16. Walks back to table
17. Places ticket in slot on tray	17. Uses fork for solid foods	17. Sits at table
18. Slides tray to the right	18. Spears food with fork	18. Initiates goodbye to peers
19. Takes one napkin from dispenser	19. Brings spoon/fork to mouth without spilling	
20. Places napkin on tray under milk carton	20. Keeps elbow close to body while using utensils	
21. Takes one straw	21. Holds utensil over tray	
22. Places straw in slot on tray	22. Eats dessert last	
23. Moves right when line moves	23. Uses napkin to wipe hands and mouth during meal	
24. Greets ticker taker	24. Uses napkin to wipe hands and mouth at the end of the meal	
25. Removes ticket from tray	25. Finishes entire lunch in 30 minutes	
26. Hands ticket to ticket taker		
27. Thanks ticket taker		
28. Lifts tray		
29. Walks to lunch table where communication book is located		
30. Puts tray down on table		
31. Steps over bench		
32. Sits down		

before setting instructional objectives. Consultation with a school nurse, nutritionist, or the student's physician should help verify whether intervention is necessary and may lead to more efficient ways to measure the weight problem initially. Although there are no published applications with students having severe handicaps, Rietz's (1984) research with adults having borderline or mild handicaps validates methods to teach consumption and self-monitoring of nutritionally balanced diets.

Pipes (1976) suggests a procedure for taking a 7-day food record (Figure 13.9) with cooperation from the parents. Beverages and foods are measured before and after a meal to determine the actual amount consumed, which is then recorded. With some severely involved students who are fed and have extremely poor oral-motor ability, excessive spillage will confuse these measurements. In these cases a dry washcloth or damp sponge, weighed before feeding, can be held under the cup

INSTRUCTIONS

1. Record *all* food or beverages immediately *after* they are eaten or drunk.

2. Measure the amounts of each food carefully in terms of standard measuring cups and spoons. Record meat portions in ounces or as fractions of pounds, for example: 8 ounces of milk; one medium egg; $\frac{1}{4}$ pound of hamburger; one slice of bread, white; $\frac{1}{2}$ small banana.

3. Indicate method of preparation, for example: medium egg, fried; $\frac{1}{2}$ cup baked beans with two-inch slice salt pork; four ounces steak, broiled.

4. Be sure to include any condiments, gravies, salad dressings, butter, marga-rine, whipped cream, relishes, etc., for example: $\frac{1}{4}$ cup mashed potatoes with 3 table-spoons brown gravy; $\frac{1}{4}$ cup cottage cheese salad with two olives; $\frac{1}{2}$ cup cornflakes with 1 teaspoon sugar and $\frac{1}{3}$ cup 2% milk.

5. Be sure to include all between meal foods and drinks, for example: coffee with 1 ounce of cream; 12 ounces of coke; four sugar cookies; one 10¢ candy bar (list brand).

6. If you eat away from home, please put a little symbol* beside the foods.

Date _____ Day of week _____

Weight _____

Time	Food	Amount	How prepared

FIGURE 13.9 Seven-day food record

Source: From "Assessing Food and Nutrient Intake" by P.L. Pipes. In M.L. Erickson (Ed.), 1976, *Assessment and Management of Developmental Changes in Children* (p. 140) St. Louis: C.V. Mosby. Taken from Nutrition Department, Child Development and Mental Retardation Center, University of Washington, Seattle, 1975. Reprinted by permission.

to catch spills. This amount is subtracted from the original quantity of liquid. Similarly, food that drops onto the table, place, or bib may be weighed and thus separated from the quantity actually eaten.

Selection of Teaching Targets

Eating skills are learned in a general order, begin-ning with various aspects of dependent feeding (anticipates spoon, uses lips to remove food) to eating finger foods, to spoon and cup use, followed by fork use, then knife spreading and cutting, food serving, condiment usage, and table manners. Some of these skills are shown in Figure 13.10.

In general, selected targets should be both realistic in relation to the student's current perfor-mance and also immediately or subsequently relevant (prioritized by the parent or teacher as being needed on a regular basis). Thus, although it would be of immediate value to teach Mary to cut with a knife, she still has not mastered independent spoon use, and should master this easier skill first; however, because she is mobile with a walker, it is not too early to teach her to use a napkin or to go through the lunch line and choose her food. Con-current objectives and training may occur for fine motor skills (grasp, object manipulation) that may improve utensil and food manipulation. Banerdt

a

b

c

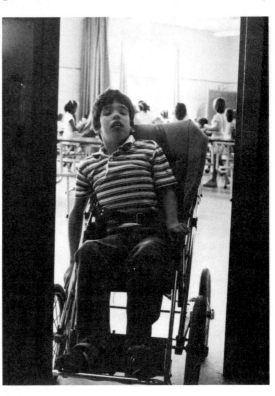

d

FIGURE 13.10 Learning to eat neatly in a noisy elementary school cafeteria presents many challenges to these two students. Aaron and Rick have made great gains in mastering the skills of using the cafeteria. While Aaron is learning to negotiate the cafeteria line to purchase his lunch and to eat without stuffing (a), Rick is almost completely independent in eating (b, c) and in maneuvering his wheelchair up the hall to and from lunch (d).

and Bricker (1978) identified a number of inter-mediate manual dexterity abilities relevant to inde-pendent feeding skills (Figure 13.11).

General Elements of Instruction

Teaching Times and Place

Depending upon the particular objectives, most instruction should occur before, during, and after eating in the school or home dining area. Azrin and Armstrong (1973) increased the number of daily training sessions by dividing meals into smaller portions or "mini-meals" served hourly. This allowed more intensive instruction for the students who all had profound retardation and resulted in appro-priate, independent eating after an average of 12 days on instruction. Others have replicated the effectiveness of mini-meals (Richman, Sonderby, & Kahn, 1980; Stimbert, Minor, & McCoy, 1977).

The literature on the best place to train basic eating skills is somewhat inconsistent. Azrin and Armstrong (1973) and Richman et al. (1980) found that eating instruction in a nondistracting setting produced a higher frequency of correct responses in less time than did instruction in the lunchroom; however, a study by Song and Gandhi (1974) supported the position that self-feeding skills learned in the natural setting are less likely to be forgotten or lost over time. Design and method-ological problems in these and other feeding studies prevent us from drawing clear-cut conclu-sions about the relationship of training setting to skill acquisition and maintenance.

Certainly, the ultimate goal is for the student with handicaps to be able to eat alongside others at home, at friends' homes, in the school cafeteria, and in public restaurants. At the same time, we know that they have difficulty generalizing learned skills from one setting to another. Both of these facts support instruction in the natural setting. A third related fact concerns those students with excessive behavior problems or movement diffi-culties due to upper motor neuron damage, pri-marily cerebral palsy. Two reasons are commonly cited to justify initial mealtime isolation of severely involved students. First is poor oral control, which results in excessive spillage even when the student is fed by a teacher. The second reason is the increased muscle tone that may result from cafeteria noise and distraction and, thus, may interfere with controlled movement, increase primitive reflexes, and reduce the amount actually eaten. In addition,

many students' extreme behavior problems will increase with outside distraction. In spite of these problems, the decision to teach feeding skills in isolation must be made cautiously, inasmuch as segregation eliminates social interaction, reduces the probability of skill generalization, and may mean less efficient use of staff time. In a few cases, either excessive meal-time behavior problems or extreme motor involvement may dictate temporary or partial isolation from the school cafeteria. For example, after conferring with the occupational therapist, a teacher decides to feed a student in a quiet corner of the classroom in two smaller meals before and after the noon meal, to facilitate greater food intake and more progress on cooperative feeding objectives; however, the same student would accompany the class to the school cafeteria at lunchtime, primarily for social interaction. A second student, who steals and throws food, has little or no utensil use and has frequent tantrums, may eat in the classroom initially with one or two other students (who are more independent and are rotated so they do not always eat in isolation). Once some of the inappropriate behavior is under control, the student might eat in the cafeteria when only one or two classmates are present. Later, this would be adjusted so the student would eat at the scheduled lunchtime.

Thus, although temporary mealtime isolation may be justified in special cases for a small number of students, the primary training setting for eating skills will be the school cafeteria, the student's home kitchen or dining room, or a local restaurant. In addition, using mini-meals may add more trips to these lunch areas.

Teaching Materials

When the learner does not have extensive move-ment limitations, adaptive eating equipment and therapeutic positioning are not complex issues; however, there still are several important considera-tions that the teacher must make concerning instructional materials and conditions. The chair and table height should match the learner's size and allow his feet to rest firmly on the floor or a foot block; utensil and cup size should fit the child, the food must be appealing, nourishing, and suited to the teaching goals (finger foods if this skill is targeted; slightly sticky foods when spoon instruc-tion begins). For many beginning learners, placing a wet washcloth, suction cup, or rubber mat

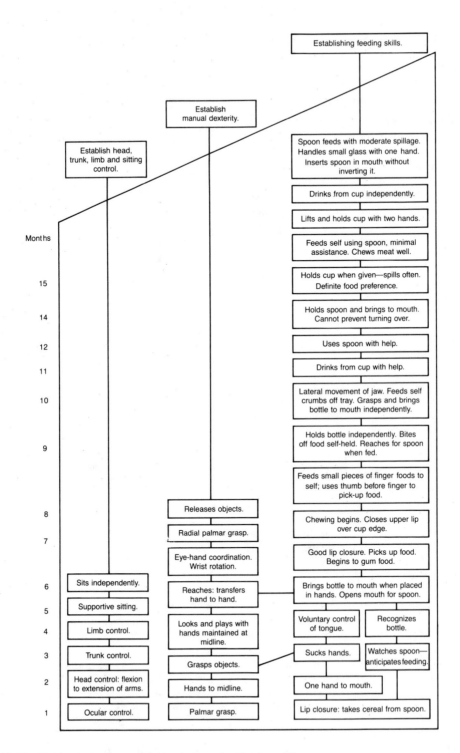

FIGURE 13.11 Training lattice for establishing independent feeding skills

Source: "A Training Program for Selected Self-Feeding Skills for the Moderately Impaired" by B. Banerdt and D. Bricker, 1978, *AAESPH Review, 3,* p. 224. Reprinted with permission.

beneath plates and bowls will prevent slipping and allow easier spoon filling. After basic eating skills are mastered, other teaching materials will be added. These may include forks and knives, paper napkins, salt and pepper shakers, serving bowls and spoons, milk cartons, cafeteria trays, straws, and specific types of food (thin soup, butter to spread, gravy to dip or pour, thermoses to pour from, spaghetti to eat, meat to cut). Finally, to facilitate generalization, a variety of materials and settings should be used. If a child has learned to use paper napkins, will he balk at the use of a cloth napkin? If a young man performs very well in the small school cafeteria where there are no food choices, how will he fare in the average cafeteria restaurant with many menu choices? This instructional concern moves beyond the mere learning of a skill (napkin usage); the generalization criterion deals with the successful use of the skill in realistic situations.

Basic Methods to Teach Self-Feeding

The primary procedures to teach basic eating skills and self-feeding include prompting targeted behaviors followed by fading or delay of prompts and shaping. Because many of the terminal goals actually involve chains of behavior (such as using utensils and going through a cafeteria line), the teacher will use both forward and backward chaining separately and in combination to "string together" the portions of these lengthy targeted skills. (See Chapter 5 for clarification.)

Finger Foods

The first sign of independence in self-feeding is the predictably messy stage of eating finger foods. At this early stage, a student practices the pincer grasp to pick up food and refines hand-to-mouth movements (which already have been used extensively to explore objects by mouthing) in combination with the sucking, gumming, chewing, and swallowing of many soft foods such as bananas and saliva-softened toast. Finger feeding provides an essential opportunity to improve the movements necessary for learning utensil use later.

If baseline assessment reveals deficiencies in utensil use as well as poor coordination of grasp, lift, and placement of finger foods in the mouth, then finger food instruction should have priority. The teacher must specify those particular portion(s) of the finger food chain that are missing or weak: food location, grasp, lift from table to mouth,

opening of mouth at appropriate time, putting food into open mouth, leaving food in mouth (releasing grasp or biting off a portion), chewing food, or swallowing food. In addition, the student's ability to deal with large pieces of food should be noted. Does he tear food into smaller pieces or does he gum or bite off smaller pieces from what he holds to the mouth (the more advanced method). Finally, if sloppiness is the primary problem, then its cause should be determined and targeted for instruction. For example, sloppiness may be caused by placing too much food in the mouth. Beginners should not be punished for sloppiness until they have developed the motor coordination needed for neatness.

Finger food self-feeding should be taught at the beginning of the meal when the student is hungry. Food consistency will depend on the presence or absence of teeth and the ability the student already has: bananas and breads will be more easily placed in the mouth, chewed, and swallowed than will partially cooked vegetables and hot dog bits or raw vegetables. Guided assistance may be the most useful prompt inasmuch as demonstrations require good attending and imitation skills (Nelson, Cone, & Hanson, 1975); however, this physical prompting should be provided from behind while sitting beside the learner so that the teacher's movements follow the natural pattern. The use of simple, consistent instructions ("Open;" "Chew, chew, chew") may be helpful when paired with teacher modeling and gestures during the early stages of learning. Later, after prompts are faded, the simple instructions could be used to remind the learner.

Drinking from a Cup or Glass

Initially students will help the parent or teacher hold the cup or glass and lift it to the mouth. At this early stage and when an individual first drinks from a cup independently, both hands will be used. When the student has the potential to master drinking from a cup without assistance, straw use is not taught until after this is learned. For students who cannot acquire independence in cup drinking, drinking liquids from stabilized cups through straws is a good alternative means to independence. Also, as with finger feeding, the learning process will be messy.

Prerequisite skills include upright or supported sitting, adequate head control, ability to grasp and lift a partially filled cup, and, perhaps most important, the ability to take sips of liquid from a cup with proper swallowing and without choking (Stainback & Healy, 1982).

As with all the self-care skills, a task analysis of the steps involved in drinking from a glass or cup may be used to guide assessment but certainly will be used to guide teaching so that a consistent approach is taken from trial to trial and across various teachers. Some teachers will elect to measure the student's progress by counting the number of correct cup drinking responses rather than using a task analytic assessment because the fast-paced nature of the response, even with students who have not mastered the skill, may threaten the accuracy of the data collected. As with the spoon feeding example given earlier, the accuracy of a frequency count depends upon a good or observable definition and also upon reliable observation.

The type of cup chosen for training may have an influence upon the student's initial success. Stainback and Healy (1982) suggest that short, squat cups that do not turn over easily and can be held without difficulty are best to begin with. With preschool-aged students, a weighted cup might be appropriate, although most cups of this style have a clear association with infants and would be age inappropriate. Similarly, whereas double-handled cups may be easier to hold, they also may be age inappropriate in design. Durable plastic cups are obviously safer to use than are containers made of glass, brittle plastic, or paper. Spouted or nipple cups should never be used because they stimulate abnormal sucking and do not allow the student to master the correct drinking response (Mueller, 1975). The amount of liquid in the cup should not be excessive (to reduce spilling) but also must not be too little or the student will need to tilt the head too much to obtain a drink, increasing the difficulty of the task. Finally, if the surface of the table where training is given is initially made less slippery, errors will be less frequent. Nonslip placemats or a damp terry towel may eliminate slipping; however, eventually, the student will need to use a glass or cup at a variety of tables without special modification of the surface.

For students with limited self-drinking abilities, manual guidance through the entire chain will be necessary, with fading proceeding backwards and forwards from points of successful performance in the chain. It is often easier to begin fading assistance at the point after the glass is rested on the lower lip and before any liquid is tipped into the mouth. Especially if the student is thirsty and likes the liquid, success will be immediately reinforced. Assistance may be needed to complete the chain. Manual guidance would gradually be faded backward first and then forward to the last step in the chain (glass is placed back on table). The teacher's manual guidance is most effectively provided when the student sits on the teacher's dominant side: a right-handed teacher would sit on the student's right side.

Only after the student learns to drink holding the handled cup or small glass with both hands should the teacher begin to emphasize a reduction of spilling. Spilling will occur while drinking but may also happen as the glass is grasped, lifted, or replaced on the table. Eventually, as drinking and other self-feeding skills improve, the student should be reminded to lift the glass with only the dominant hand.

Stimbert et al. (1977) used six daily mini-meals and graduated guidance to teach six students with moderate to profound retardation to drink from a glass and to use correctly the hands and spoon to eat. The graduated guidance (described in Chapter 5) was physical assistance through the chain of drinking from a cup. Initially, the trainer's hands were placed directly over the learner's hands, until pressure cues indicated that the student needed less than total assistance. Then the trainer's hands were shifted to the student's wrists to provide some, but not total, guidance. Over successive trials, the trainer rotated the manual assistance to the forearm, the elbow, the upper arm, and finally the shoulders, giving at any point only as much guidance as was necessary to complete the task. Generally, graduated guidance resulted in very few errors; however, when errors did occur the authors loudly reprimanded the student, stating specifically what was to be stopped ("No spilling"). As done by Azrin and Armstrong (1973), any spill or throwing of food was followed with guided clean-up (restitutional overcorrection) and three practice trials of lifting the glass with guidance (positive practice overcorrection). All correct responses initially, whether prompted or not, were praised. Results indicated that the students learned independent drinking from a glass along with spoon use and eliminated inappropriate mealtime behavior rather rapidly in (5 to 8 weeks). The new skills were still used after a 1-year follow-up.

Eating with a Spoon

Spoon use is the simplest of the utensil skills, followed in difficulty by eating with a fork, transferring spreads with a knife, spreading with a knife, cutting finger-grasped bread with a knife, and cutting meat with a fork and knife. When a learner has learned to grasp objects and demonstrates some success in manipulating finger foods, an assessment should be made of the ability to pick up and eat with a spoon.

Albin's (1977) rather simple task analysis of spoon use may be useful for assessment and later teaching. (Refer to Chapters 4 and 5 for more detail on these procedures.)

1. Pick up the spoon,
2. Scoop,
3. Raise spoon to mouth,
4. Remove food,
5. Return spoon to bowl.

For other students, a slightly more detailed task analysis may be more suitable.

1. Pick up the spoon.
2. Move the spoon to the bowl,
3. Scoop some food with the spoon,
4. Take the spoon to your mouth,
5. Open your mouth,
6. Put the food in your mouth (Eat),
7. Remove the food with your lips,
8. Return the spoon to the bowl,
9. Chew and swallow,
10. Repeat steps 3–9 until done.

In this example, the specific verbal prompts, which are simplified versions of some of the steps, are underlined. In other words, the student will be trained on each step but verbally prompted only with the underlined phrases in steps 1, 3, 5, 6, and 9. (See Chapter 4 for more information on task analysis.)

After field-testing a task analysis, the more difficult steps may need to be simplified; for example, food scooping has been identified as the most difficult step to teach persons with severe handicaps (Song & Gandhi, 1974). In addition, it is important to note how often the spoon is abandoned in favor of the fingers, how much spilling occurs and why (on the way to the mouth due to poor wrist rotation), and how the spoon is grasped. Younger children with immature grasps will hold the spoon in a palm-down finger or fist position, while the more mature palm-up position will be learned only after the child makes gains in fine motor development.

Looking at and reaching for the spoon is best taught while the student is still in the dependent feeding stage—being spoon-fed by the parent or teacher. To do this, the adult calls the student's name and, when he looks, places the spoon on the table within reach. The spoon may be gently tapped to cue attention. The food is presented as a consequence for looking at the spoon. Later the student will be expected to reach toward the spoon. Other guidelines for encouraging more active participation during dependent feeding may be found in the next chapter.

Progressing from dependent feeding to initial stages of teaching spoon use should be gradual, after the learner demonstrates some skill in eating finger foods, reaches for and holds the spoon, and can drink from a cup but not without spilling. Once baseline performance has been measured and an intervention plan initiated, instructional time should fill at least the initial part of most meals (if not the whole meal) when the student is hungry and should progress to the entire mealtime. That is, the teacher may choose to feed the student during the final third of a meal only after working on self-feeding. Eventually all dependent feeding should be replaced by instruction in self-feeding.

Several shaping and prompt-fade methods have been described to teach spoon use to individuals with severe handicaps. O'Brien et al. (1972) divided spoon use into six steps and manually guided the child's hand through all the steps, fading the guidance backward systematically. Their task analysis of the steps and the teacher guidance included:

1. Place the spoon handle in the student's dominant hand while holding the same hand over the student's grasp.
2. Guide the spoon into the food, scoop food, and lift the spoon 1 inch above the bowl.
3. Guide the spoon to a point 2 inches from the student's mouth.
4. Open the student's mouth by applying gentle pressure on the chin.
5. Guide the spoon into the student's mouth.
6. Guide the student's hand upward and outward to remove the food against the student's upper teeth or lips.

An interruption-extinction procedure was used whenever an incorrect response occurred or when the student resorted to eating with his hands. That is, he was not allowed to put food into his mouth if he made an error while getting the food (used his hand, did not complete the step from which assistance had been faded). Instead, the teacher emptied the food from his spoon or hand, cleaning the boy if necessary, and began the six-step sequence again.

The systematic fading of manual guidance proceeded as follows:

When training by manual guidance was first introduced, the teacher guided the child through all six of the steps. Whenever the sequence was completed correctly on three successive assisted trials, the child's hand was guided through one less step on the next assisted trial. Whenever an assisted trial was not completed correctly, it was interrupted and another guided trial was begun, which included one additional [guided] step. Whenever a step was eliminated [not guided], added [guided], eliminated, and added on three consecutive trials, the child's hand was guided through a point between that step and the next lower step (e.g., if step three was being added and eliminated, on the following trial the child's hand was guided to a point halfway between the bowl and her mouth). (p. 69)

Totally unguided trials were used after correct completions to probe independent performance.

This combination of manual guidance and interruption-extinction led to almost perfect independent performance after nine meals; however, O'Brien and his colleagues found that maintenance training consisting of interruption-extinction was essential to keep the student from reverting to eating without a spoon.

Azrin and Armstrong (1973) used a slightly different physical assistance (graduated guidance) and fading procedure called "hand-to-shoulder fading with constant contact." Napkin, glass, spoon, fork, and knife use were taught with this method, though one at a time and in this simple-to-complex order. To apply this method, a teacher would:

Begin guidance by having the trainer mold his hand around the student's and guide an entire response. As the student grasps the utensil himself, guidance is progressively reduced at the hand with a gentle touch. The locus of guidance is then faded up the arm to the forearm, elbow, upper arm then shoulder and upper back, always maintaining light touch

unless more guidance is required. This constant contact serves as a reminder to the student that inappropriate responses will be prevented. (p. 11)

During this prompt-fade procedure, the trainer applied only enough movement assistance "to get a response going" and only enough restraint to stop an error. Verbal praise, specific to what the student was doing, was given throughout each trial. Mini-meals were served hourly. Initially, if needed, two trainers worked with a single learner— one to guide the utensil hand while the other guided the student's "lap hand" and head to prevent errors. In combination with these intensive training methods, Azrin and Armstrong (1973) applied overcorrective maintenance for errors made once a student learned to spoon-feed (or fork). For example, after a student was able to eat with a particular utensil, he cleaned up spills made with that implement. These restitutions were followed by a few positive practice trials. Therefore, spills from an overfilled spoon were first cleaned up and then the student was expected to practice scooping very small amounts of food into his spoon. With this intensive procedure, most of the 11 students learned correct utensil use in 5 days, with a few requiring 12 days of training.

The study on utensil use by Stimbert et al. (1977) replicated Azrin and Armstrong's procedures, using a single subject experimental design and a similar population. Although a similar frequency of daily training sessions was used, the subjects appeared to need an average of 29 training days (versus the 5- to 12-day range reported by Azrin and Armstrong, 1973). While the reason for these deficiencies is not clear, the trainer using these procedures should not modify the procedures, but continue their use if the skills are not mastered as rapidly as Azrin and Armstrong report.

Like Azrin and Armstrong (1973) and Stimbert et al. (1977), Albin (1977) used forward chaining on all the spoon-feeding steps; but he taught only one step at a time while totally assisting the student through the unlearned steps. With three students having profound retardation, he successfully used a variation of graduated guidance to teach spoon use and later finger foods, fork, and bread plate use. First, verbal cues plus firm hand control were used; they gradually were reduced to gentle hand control. Next, verbal cues and firm wrist control were used and then replaced by gentle wrist control. After this, manual assistance was faded altogether, followed next by the discontinuation of verbal cues. Whenever the student failed to respond after 2 seconds with the level of assistance provided on a given step, a complete prompt was given. Continuous tactual reinforcement and praise was given for correctly performed steps, whether assisted or not.

At this point it should be clear that a rather wide variety of systematic procedures have been used to teach spoon usage as well as other self-feeding skills, including physical guidance (Albin, 1977; Azrin & Armstrong, 1973; Berkowitz, Sherry, & Davis, 1971; O'Brien et al., 1972), forward or backward chaining, praise and tactual reinforcement, and punishment of inappropriate behavior (which will be discussed in detail later). The more rapid and intensive procedures (e.g., Azrin & Armstrong, 1973; O'Brien et al., 1972; Stimbert et al., 1977) actually consist of a complex combination of precise techniques to schedule sessions; to shape, prompt, fade, and maintain correct responses; and to punish, ignore, and prevent errors. Most teachers may not be able to use such intensive interventions without additional help; however, simpler combinations of procedures have been effective when applied systematically (Berkowitz et al., 1971; Christian et al., 1973; Song & Gandhi, 1974). Informal applications of a physical prompt with time delay fading (see Chapter 5) indicate that this procedure may be particularly useful in place of graduated guidance. On the other hand, a system of least intrusive prompts incorporating verbal, model, and physical prompts has had only limited success with basic feeding skills (Kissel, Johnson, & Whitman, 1980), despite its documented success with more advanced daily living skills (putting on a hearing aid, housekeeping tasks, vocational assembly tasks, cooking, sewing, etc.) As discussed in Chapter 5, prompting procedures must be matched to the learner's ability to respond to them. As is often the case with people needing instruction in basic feeding skills, the more sophisticated prompts of modeling or verbal instructions *without physical assistance* are not as effective as some form of physical assistance (Nelson et al., 1975).

Eating with a Fork

Although the fork grasp may be modified and its use to pick up food is different from spoon scooping, the procedures for teaching fork use are essentially identical to those for spoon use (Azrin & Armstrong, 1973; Nelson et al., 1975). Fork use should not be taught until after the student has mastered the spoon. The finger-hold, palm-up grip pictured at the top of Figure 13.12 is probably the best to teach for spearing and lifting food. Later, when fork cutting is taught, the grip will be modified and held sideways against the food (Nelson et al., 1975). To teach spearing and lifting, precut chunks or cubes of food will be needed, avoiding soupy food more appropriate for eating with a spoon. Azrin and Armstrong (1973) taught the use of one utensil at a time and did not present combinations of utensils until each utensil was learned.

Knife Usage

Table knives may be used (a) to transport a spread, such as butter, from one place to another, (b) to spread a substance on food, (c) to cut breads while holding the food with one hand, (d) to push foods onto a fork, and (e), with a fork, to cut. These skills are taught and learned in this order.

As with spoon and fork use, Nelson et al. (1975) found that modeling was less effective than physical guidance during both instruction and correction of errors. O'Brien and Azrin (1972) and Ferneti, Lent, and Stevens (1974) used three types of assistance from manual guidance and instruction backward to modeling and instruction, to instruction only, and finally to no verbal reminders. If modeling is to be successful, the learner must be attentive and ready to imitate. The effectiveness of modeling is increased with imitative learners if they have already learned the behavior through shaping and physical guidance.

To simplify knife and fork cutting, a teacher may want to teach the continental style, which does *not* require switching the fork to the nondominant hand. To teach students with severe retardation this method, Azrin and Armstrong (1973) first provided precut meat chunks and directed students to hold their forks in the dominant hand with tines pointed down to spear the food. Then they were instructed to pick up the knife in the other hand and use a sawing motion while stabilizing the meat with the fork. The Project MORE program for eating (Ferneti et al., 1974) suggests teaching the learner to switch the implement from hand to hand; however, they do not provide performance data to support this recommendation with students having severe handicaps.

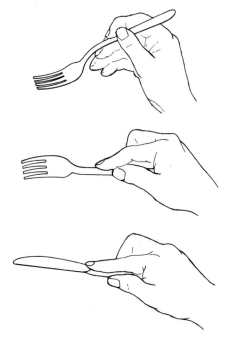

FIGURE 13.12 Correct grips for holding a fork to eat (top: palm-up finger grip) and to cut (center), and for spreading with a knife (bottom)

Source: From "Training Correct Utensil Use in Retarded Children: Modeling vs. Physical Guidance" by G.L. Nelson, J.D. Cone, and C.R. Hanson, 1975, *American Journal of Mental Deficiency, 80,* p. 115. Reprinted by permission.

Table Manners and Related Skills

Sloppiness

Many inappropriate behaviors that prevent or interfere with self-feeding may occur during mealtime. If a student is allowed to steal food or eat with his hands, he has little reason to learn or use the more difficult skills of utensil usage. Timeout from eating contingent upon inappropriate table behavior has been effective in improving mealtime behavior in retarded individuals (Barton, Guess, Garcia, & Baer, 1970; Christian et al., 1973; O'Brien & Azrin, 1972; Song & Gandhi, 1974). For some students a 30-second removal of the food tray is an aversive consequence strong enough to eliminate food stealing, food throwing, "pigging" or mouth stuffing, eating with hands, and inappropriately using utensils. With certain behaviors (food stealing), as with some students, tray removal is ineffective.

Instead, the individual is removed from the room for a time or for the remainder of the meal.

While Barton et al. (1970) found that these procedures quickly eliminated stealing, treatment guidelines may prevent the elimination of an individual's meals, as a violation of basic rights. A more positive alternative for eliminating food stealing and scavenging behavior was demonstrated as being successful by Smith, Piersel, Filbeck, and Gross (1983) with a young woman having severe retardation. Intervention initially required seating at a table away from others and involved frequent reinforcement with favorite edibles for periods of no stealing along with response cost (removal of accumulated edibles) for stealing. Over successive treatment phases, the woman was seated by other peers and reinforcement was reduced.

A successful method to reduce eating with fingers is to stop or interrupt the behavior before the individual can eat, remove the food from his hands, clean his hands, and manually guide correct spoon use (Azrin & Armstrong, 1973; O'Brien & Azrin, 1972). This interruption-extinction procedure prevents the student from reinforcing his own inappropriate responses. Finally, overcorrection and positive practice have been used to eliminate spilling and food and utensil throwing (Azrin & Armstrong, 1973).

Because of a high level of inappropriate mealtime behavior during baseline, Albin (1977) treated mealtime errors with a correction, a mild punishment, or both. For example, when a student's face came within 6 inches of the tray, the teacher said "NO!" and returned the head to an upright position. Eating with fingers was followed by a reprimand and 3 minutes in a timeout area, while spilling food, rubbing it on oneself, or pushing food off a utensil was reprimanded and the tray removed for 30 seconds. Additional instances of these behaviors during the same meal resulted in 3 minutes in timeout. A repeat of stealing terminated the meal. Once all three students acquired basic eating skills and appropriate mealtime behavior, a maintenance plan was instituted. Initially staff left the eating area for 30-second intervals. Next, they left for intervals of a few minutes. Then they stationed themselves in the back of the room, moved outside an open door, and finally outside a closed door. This gradual fading of supervision enabled the students to maintain their improved mealtime behavior even under minimal supervision.

Excessively Rapid Eating

Excessively rapid eating can be a serious problem for some students because of social acceptability and potential health problems (vomiting, aspiration, and poor digestion). A survey of persons with severe and profound retardation living in institutions (McGimsey, Note 2) cited by Favell, McGimsey, and Jones (1980) defined "normal" eating rates as approximately eight bites per minute with total meal consumed in 15 to 20 minutes. "Rapid" eaters, however, "consumed food at rates sometimes exceeding 20 bites per minute, and finished their entire meal within 1 to 3 minutes" (p. 482).

Using a nonpunishing intervention, Favell et al. (1980) successfully reduced the eating rates of four persons with profound retardation from an average of 10.5 bites per 30 seconds to 3 bites per 30 seconds. Other procedures such as increased meal portions, tray timeout, and removal from the dining area had failed to reduce eating rate. The successful intervention relied on two primary procedures: (a) social and edible reinforcement for increasingly longer unprompted pauses (up to 5 seconds) between bites; and (b) gradual reduction of physical prompts for pausing, contingent on instances of rapid eating. Once the goal was attained, a maintenance program of reinforcement and prompts for pausing was carried out by regular institutional staff. Side benefits of the training included a reduction in vomiting by one subject and sloppiness by another, appropriate weight gains in all, and an absence of misbehavior or undesirable alternatives to fast eating, such as the slower consumption of larger bites of food.

Knapczyk (1983) also addressed the problem of rapid and sloppy eating. The student was diagnosed as having severe retardation and moderate cerebral palsy with poor arm and hand coordination and no walking ability. The student used a spoon but ate only pureed foods and without any pause between bites. Frequently he performed the eating cycle but did not put food on his spoon. Finally, excessive spillage occurred during every meal. Using a withdrawal design, Knapczyk found that teacher-paced instructions in combination with removal from the group were effective in reducing the student's level of repetitive eating behavior and in increasing the frequency of pausing between each bite. Teacher-paced instruction consisted of beginning with an empty bowl into which the teacher placed one spoonful of food; whereupon, verbal instruction followed by manual guidance was given to eat the spoonful and lay down the spoon. This was repeated until the student followed the request without help. Next the amount was increased, but only as the student was able to pause between bites. Later the amount was increased gradually over a period of nine days so that the student was able to consume his entire meal and still pause between bites. During follow-up pureed food was changed to solid food without any disruption of pausing between bites.

Related Mealtime Skills

The preparatory and clean-up tasks may more naturally be taught prior to and after each meal, while instruction in the basics of self-feeding might occupy part of or all of a meal depending upon the availability of teachers. Kohl and Stettner-Eaton (1985) trained fourth grade peers to teach cafeteria, eating, and clean-up skills to three students with severe handicaps of the same age, thereby increasing effectively the number of trainers. Sailor and his colleagues (1986) suggest that speech and occupational therapists be recruited to provide their therapy during lunch time in community restaurants or in the school cafeteria, a strategy that not only increases the number of instructors but also facilitates the realism, and thus the generalizability, of therapy gains.

The exemplary research of Wilson, Reid, Phillips, and Burgio (1984) with four young adults having profound retardation validated a program for teaching family-style dining. Ecological inventories of the skills required by the targeted students in future less restrictive, though still institutional, settings identified table setting, food passing and self-serving, and table clearing as being important. Students were taught one at a time using a system of least intrusive prompts and a 3-second response latency: verbal prompt, verbal plus physical guidance. Initially, model prompts were provided by the trainer on a second trainer at the second prompt level; however, because these demonstrations proved counterproductive to learning by the first two subjects, in addition to requiring two trainers, they were dropped. The three skill clusters (table setting, food passing and self-serving, and table clearing) were taught in smaller subcomponents, with each successive subcomponent added once the preceeding subcomponent was mastered. Reinforcement consisted of praise and small snacks given contingent upon the first successful prompted performance of each step; additional food reinforcers for the same step were given contingent upon improvements in performance—with a lesser prompt or no prompt. When students required more intrusive prompts to complete the same step, no snacks or praise were given. After each training session, students went for brief walks with the trainer.

Whenever a student made two consecutive unprompted correct responses on a training step, training was introduced on the next subcomponent step while requiring continued performance of all preceding mastered steps. Whenever a learned step was forgotten or performed incorrectly, the prompting sequence was conducted with that step until it was performed correctly in sequence.

Although not intervened with directly, observations were made throughout baseline and intervention of students' rate of eating, mealtime messiness, use of 17 mealtime manual signs, and body weight in order to document any indirect effects of training in these areas. Results indicated that all four subjects mastered the skills they had been taught (table setting, food passing, and self-serving), while only one student made gains in the untaught skills of table clearing. All students demonstrated good skill maintenance throughout the 16-week follow-up period; however, students made no changes in the four areas of related behavior—mealtime communication, messiness, eating rate, or weight—with weight monitored only as a check on the amount of food consumed. Earlier research with students having fewer handicaps had indicated that mealtime conversation between peers had increased when family-style eating replaced cafeteria style. Wilson et al.'s research supports the use of systematic instruction to teach family-style eating skills and also seems to indicate that related mealtime behaviors—specifically communication, messiness, and eating rate—will remain unchanged unless the teacher directly intervenes.

DRESSING SKILLS

Just like eating with utensils, buttoning, snapping, buckling, zipping, lacing, and shoe tying involve refined eye-hand coordination and precise finger dexterity with controlled finger-thumb opposition. Dressing is more difficult than undressing for

normal children as well as for individuals with handicaps (Minge & Ball, 1967), as are buttoning, tying, snapping, in contrast with unbuttoning, untying, and unsnapping.

Programs to teach dressing skills to people with severe handicaps have involved prompting combined with shaping, backward chaining, and praise and food reinforcers. During short, daily training sessions, undressing usually has been taught before dressing. One garment is instructed at a time, beginning with loose-fitting socks, shirts, and pants and, if part of the program, proceeding to buttons, laces, snaps, zippers, and belts (Ball, Seric, & Payne, 1971; Bensberg et al., 1965; Colwell, Richards, McCarver, & Ellis, 1973; Martin, Kehoe, Bird, Jensen, & Darbyshire, 1971; Minge & Ball, 1967). Although these combinations of training methods have been successful with students having moderate and severe retardation, improvement in the dressing skills of institutionalized individuals with profound retardation taught by these traditional operant methods has been gradual. Learning is time-consuming and often temporary (Ball et al., 1971; Minge & Ball, 1967). Unfortunately, in contrast to eating and toileting skill instruction, less attention has been given in the research to study of dressing skill training for persons with severe handicaps (Konarski & Diorio, 1985).

This final section of the chapter describes dressing skill assessment and training procedures, with suggestions for improving instruction so that learning may be optimized for even those with extensive handicaps.

Assessment

Dressing assessment involves observing a student's performance with a variety of garments, with or without increasing assistance whenever a failure is observed. Regardless of whether the assessment device allows the teacher to evaluate the effect of prompts upon performance, it is essential that each task be stated in observable terms with specific directions so that with repeated application the teacher giving the same test and results are comparable. Teacher-made assessment devices are frequently used to measure entry skills and monitor learning, though some criterion-referenced, informal tests and checklists may be of use when initially selecting teaching targets (Ball et al., 1971; Balthazar, 1976; Hardy, Martin, Yu, Leader, & Quinn, 1981; Henderson & McDonald, 1973;

Popovich & Laham, 1981; Tawney, 1979). Two of these are reviewed briefly, along with other informal methods, described earlier in Chapter 4.

The dressing subscale of the *Balthazar Scales of Adaptive Behavior* (Balthazar, 1976) illustrated in Figure 13.13 uses a seven-point scoring system. Points earned are proportionate to independence in dressing and undressing. For each item, the learner is initially instructed by words and gestures to remove or put on, to fasten or unfasten, each article of clothing or fastening. If the student does not begin or complete the task, a demonstration is given. Additional assistance is provided step-by-step whenever performance stops or errors occur. Therefore, the learner is given credit for imitating a demonstration, for performing more than or less than half the task, and even for cooperating simply by positioning his limbs. The time allowed for performance at each level of prompt is specified in Table 13.5, as is the score awarded for various

performances. The ability to remove and put on pants, shoes, and shirts is evaluated separately from skills in buttoning, zipping, buckling, lacing, and tying. To increase its usefulness, the teacher could extend the Balthazar score sheet to include coats, hats, mittens, boots, bras, pantyhose, ties, etc. Although it may take some practice to obtain reliable results, such a score sheet provides information relevant to selecting effective teaching strategies for each individual assessed.

Hardy et al. (1980) provide a task-analyzed assessment procedure for the basic dressing and undressing tasks involving underpants, T-shirt, socks, open-front garment, shoes, headwear, and mittens. In addition, the opening and closing of various fasteners are included: zippers (closed and opened end), snaps, buttons, inserting belt into belt loops, belt buckle, lacing and tying shoes. As shown in Figure 13.14 the assessment procedure permits multiple opportunities for the student to try

---

DRESSING SCALES   Date: _____

DRESSING TALLY SHEET

	MALE			FEMALE		
Total Score	**ARTICLE/ACTIVITY**	**SCORE**		**ARTICLE/ACTIVITY**	**SCORE**	
		Right	Left		Right	Left
	Shoes			**Shoes**		
	PUT ON Shoes	1____	2____	PUT ON Shoes	1____	2____
	Tighten Laces	3____	4____	Tighten Laces	3____	4____
	Tie—single bow	5____	6____	Tie—single bow	5____	6____
	TAKE OFF Shoes	7____	8____	TAKE OFF Shoes	7____	8____
	Untie—start with a single bow	9____	10____	Untie—start with a single bow	9____	10____
	Socks			**Socks**		
	PUT ON Socks	11____	12____	PUT ON Socks	11____	12____
	TAKE OFF Socks	13____	14____	TAKE OFF Socks	13____	14____
	Pants			**Pants or Skirt**		
	PUT ON Pants	15____		PUT ON Pants or Skirt	15____	
	Fasten	16____		TAKE OFF Pants or Skirt	16____	
	Zip Up	17____		**Briefs**		
	Put Belt On	18____		PUT ON Briefs	17____	
	Fasten Belt	19____		TAKE OFF Briefs	18____	
	TAKE OFF Pants	20____		**T-Shirt/Undershirt**		
	Unfasten	21____		PUT ON T-Shirt	19____	
	Unzip	22____		TAKE OFF T-Shirt	20____	
	Take Belt Off	23____		**Blouse**		
	Unfasten Belt	24____		PUT ON Blouse	21____	
	Briefs			Button	22____	
	PUT ON Briefs	25____		TAKE OFF Blouse	23____	
	TAKE OFF Briefs	26____		Unbutton	24____	
	Shirt			**Dress**		
	PUT ON Shirt	27____		PUT ON Dress	25____	
	Button	28____		Zip Up	26____	
	TAKE OFF Shirt	29____		TAKE OFF Dress	27____	
	Unbutton	30____		Unzip	28____	
	T-Shirt/Undershirt			**Other:**		
	PUT ON T-Shirt	31____		**Brassiere**		
	TAKE OFF T-Shirt	32____		PUT ON Brassiere	29____	
				TAKE OFF Brassiere	30____	
	TOTAL SCORE _____			TOTAL SCORE _____		

FIGURE 13.13   A Balthazar scale for adaptive behavior in dressing

Source: From *Balthazar Scales of Adaptive Behavior for the Profoundly and Severely Mentally Retarded, Section 1* by E.E. Balthazar, 1971, Palo Alto, CA: Consulting Psychologists Press Inc. Copyright 1971 by Consulting Psychologists Press Inc. Reproduced by special permission.

TABLE 13.5   Scoring procedure for the dressing-undressing scale of the Balthazar Scales of Adaptive Behavior

Score	Dressing/Undressing Performance	Testing Procedure
6	Perfect and independent	Give command and gesture, then wait 10 seconds for student to initiate. After student *finishes*, score and record time needed to complete task.
5	Imperfect but independent (e.g., shirt on backwards)	
4	Demonstration provided	If no progress is made for a second period and task still is incomplete, repeat command and gesture accompanied by a demonstration (put shirt on student, then remove). Repeat command and allow 1 minute to complete first step before giving any physical assistance.
3	Partially assisted (less than half of steps)	
2	Primarily assisted (more than half of steps)	
1	Cooperative (e.g., holds arm out for shirt sleeve)	In subsequent steps, if needed give command and allow 10 seconds for progress to begin. If no progress or if student stops, help student through that step. Remember to give student an opportunity to perform each step in every sequence listed in the manual.
0	No participation	

the task-analyzed steps of each dressing skill using a standard response latency. This test procedure enables a teacher to determine whether the student can perform each step independently or with increasing amounts of assistance (verbal prompt, verbal plus model prompt). Such information is valuable both in planning an effective teaching approach and in obtaining a more accurate picture of the student's baseline and emerging skills.

Assessment may include the related skills of discriminating front from back and inside-out from right-side-out; hanging up clothes; putting away clean and dirty clothing; using a mirror to check appearance and adjust clothing; selecting clothes suitable to various occasions, seasons, and weather conditions; and discriminating between clean and dirty (ripped, wrinkled) clothing. Although these skills will be taught only after an individual acquires the basics of dressing and undressing, each ability represents more advanced independence in self-care and may constitute a relevant goal for the older student with handicaps. Assessment procedures also should include measuring skill maintenance and generalization (in various settings—in the school locker room, at home, and during summer camp—and under changing conditions—lacing boots as opposed to shoes, buttoning side and back buttons).

Teaching the student to look at his hands when he tries to remove, put on, or fasten clothing is another important area that may need instruction. To obtain baseline performance, students may

simply be asked to follow the cue "Look at this," while the teacher touches a garment, button, or zipper. If attending is deficient, contingent praise, pats, and possibly small food reinforcers on a more continuous schedule initially will be necessary to improve a student's visual attention to the task.

With the exception of awarding points for performance, the testing procedure used with the Balthazar dressing scale and with Hardy et al.'s (1980) assessment is similar to a multiple opportunity assessment with analyses of dressing tasks. (This procedure and others are described in Chapter 4.) If the teacher wants to individualize dressing task analyses to suit particular students and clothing rather than using prewritten ones like Balthazar's or Hardy's, it is best to avoid published assessment procedures. Instead, she would write task analyses to suit the student and situation, perhaps field-test or validate the task analyses for accuracy, select the method of assessment to be used (refer to Chapter 4), and proceed accordingly. Task analytic assessments, when consciensciously applied, yield the most useful information possible.

Figure 13.15 illustrates an intentionally simple task analysis for removing and hanging up an already unzipped jacket. In this example, the teacher chose to use a single opportunity task analysis as she plans to assess daily before instruction and knows this is faster than a multiple opportunity procedure, yet is still accurate. She will begin teaching immediately after the first error occurs, and, thus, testing ends. Assessment occurs in the

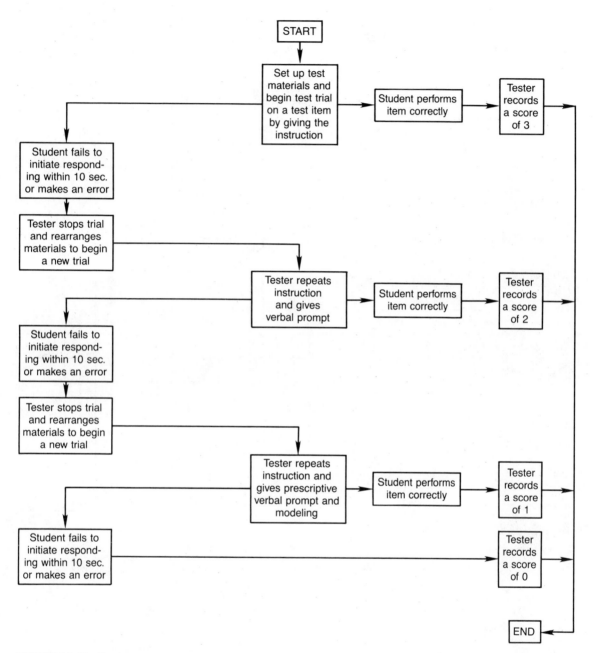

FIGURE 13.14 Testing procedure used with dressing/undressing tasks (and other self care skills) on the Objective Behavioral Assessment

Source: *Objective Behavioral Assessment of the Severely and Moderately Handicapped: The OBA* (p. 16) by L. Hardy, C. Martin, D. Yu, C. Leader, & G. Quinn, 1981. Springfield, IL: Charles C Thomas. Reprinted by permission.

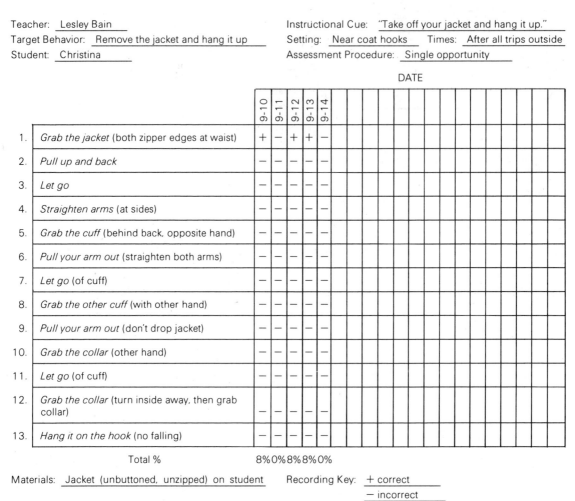

Teacher: _Lesley Bain_
Target Behavior: _Remove the jacket and hang it up_
Student: _Christina_

Instructional Cue: _"Take off your jacket and hang it up."_
Setting: _Near coat hooks_   Times: _After all trips outside_
Assessment Procedure: _Single opportunity_

DATE

		9-10	9-11	9-12	9-13	9-14																		
1.	_Grab the jacket_ (both zipper edges at waist)	+	–	+	+	–																		
2.	_Pull up and back_	–	–	–	–	–																		
3.	_Let go_	–	–	–	–	–																		
4.	_Straighten arms_ (at sides)	–	–	–	–	–																		
5.	_Grab the cuff_ (behind back, opposite hand)	–	–	–	–	–																		
6.	_Pull your arm out_ (straighten both arms)	–	–	–	–	–																		
7.	_Let go_ (of cuff)	–	–	–	–	–																		
8.	_Grab the other cuff_ (with other hand)	–	–	–	–	–																		
9.	_Pull your arm out_ (don't drop jacket)	–	–	–	–	–																		
10.	_Grab the collar_ (other hand)	–	–	–	–	–																		
11.	_Let go_ (of cuff)	–	–	–	–	–																		
12.	_Grab the collar_ (turn inside away, then grab collar)	–	–	–	–	–																		
13.	_Hang it on the hook_ (no falling)	–	–	–	–	–																		

Total %   8% 0% 8% 8% 0%

Materials: _Jacket (unbuttoned, unzipped) on student_

Response Latency: _3 seconds_

Recording Key: _+ correct_
– incorrect

Criterion: _3 consecutive days 100% performance_

FIGURE 13.15 Teacher-written task analysis for removal and hanging of a jacket

actual setting in which it will occur, by the coat hooks in the school hall. The teacher could also use a multiple opportunity method. In the multiple opportunity method, the instructional cue is given once when the student is attending, and he has 3 seconds to perform the first step. If no response is made during this period or if an error occurs, the assessment ends and all unperformed steps are scored as errors; however, the student is allowed to respond as long as no errors are made or no pauses longer than 3 seconds occur. If a multiple opportunity assessment had been chosen, the teacher would quickly perform each step not carried out or performed incorrectly. To avoid teaching

during assessment, in neither procedure is the student's specific performance commented upon, however, the teacher would simply thank the student at the end of each assessment.

Selecting Teaching Targets

After examining the baseline performance, the teacher will choose instructional targets. The teacher should consult parents and others to determine any dressing priorities in the home or in other relevant settings. If consistent with priorities, easier skills should be targeted and taught before more difficult dependent skills. Therefore, instruction in removing a garment will precede instruction in putting on that same garment. Depending upon the amount of time allowed for instruction, a student may be trained on a variety of targets simultaneously. When students must change their clothes to participate in swimming or gym, a teacher and parent might determine undressing and dressing performance targets for underware, pants, shirts, shoes, and socks as well as jackets or sweaters.

Freagon and her colleagues describe their use of domestic training environments to teach routine performance of daily living skills, including the complete sequence of dressing, undressing, clothing selection, and clothing care, skills that often present no natural training opportunities during the regular school schedule. The participating school program purchased a normalized home setting that was used to teach these skill clusters to small groups of students (Freagon et al., 1983).

General Elements of Instruction

Teaching Times and Place

As illustrated in Figure 13.16, to maximize positive transfer and maintenance of dressing and other grooming skills, it is best to teach in the places (bathroom, bedroom, locker room, coat area) and at least at the times when they are needed (Freagon & Rotatori, 1982). However, to guarantee an unhurried training session, the teacher must schedule sufficient time before the activity for which dressing and undressing are being carried out. If adequate time is allotted, she will not be tempted to overprompt to avoid being late.

Shorter training sessions of 10 to 20 minutes should be scheduled at various times throughout each day, rather than longer single sessions or sporadic training less than daily. However, Azrin, Schaeffer, and Wesolowski (1976) successfully used 3-hour sessions with students having profound retardation where attention was prolonged by intensive reinforcement and prompting procedures, though all other scheduled instruction was stopped.

Teaching Materials

When working with the beginning self-dresser, success is more attainable with modified clothing. For example, some studies have used simple clothing two sizes larger than the student's usual size and without zippers and buttons (elastic waist bands, pull-over shirts) (Azrin et al., 1976; Minge & Ball, 1967). Others suggest color coding or marking clothes: the outside or front of the shirt is marked with colored tape, the right side of both shoestrings is red and the left is white (1 red and 1 white shoestring is cut in half; each red half is joined with a white half to make the coded shoestrings).

If large buttons and buttonholes (snaps, zippers with large tabs) are taught first, the use of smaller fasteners will be learned more quickly. Kramer and Whitehurst (1981) found that students with handicaps could button larger buttons (38mm) located at the top of a garment significantly more easily than smaller buttons (22 and 19 mm) in the middle or bottom of a garment. Some teachers have attached strings to front and back zippers to make pulling easier.

For some students who lack the necessary muscle control, more long-term clothing adaptations may be necessary—a commonly used variation of partial participation (Baumgart et al., 1982). Velcro fasteners might replace buttons or simply be sewn beneath nonworking buttons; loose raglan sleeves, knitted fabrics, loafers, Velcro tennis shoes, elastic waistbands, and tubular socks without heels will present fewer dressing problems (Finnie, 1975).

While button, snap, and zipper boards or dolls with clothing seem to be useful, skill generalization may be a problem for the learner with severe handicaps. The buttoning task is quite different when buttoning another's buttons, and zipping up a zipper attached to a horizontal board is not the same as looking down on a zipper. These materials should be replaced with regular clothes with normal or enlarged fasteners. As long as a training wooden shoe is positioned normally with the shoe facing away from the student, lacing and tying practice with it may not result in transfer problems; however, in the interest of generalization, it makes the most sense simply to use the student's own shoe.

Basic Methods to Teach Self-Dressing

Encouraging Active Involvement

Before teaching the learner the first independent steps in self-dressing, the teacher should encourage active participation when she or the parent is dressing or undressing the learner. Active participation means extending hands, arms, or feet in anticipation of being dressed or undressed, looking at or reaching for garments and body parts that are

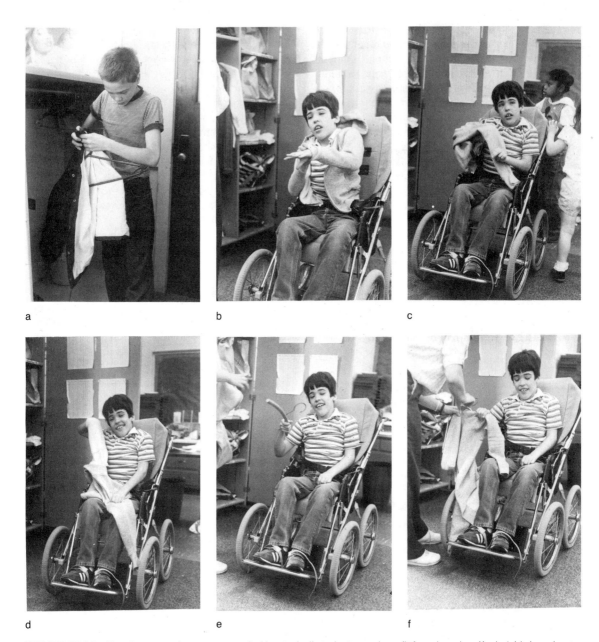

a

b

c

d

e

f

FIGURE 13.16 Hanging up one's coat upon arrival is a task all students can benefit from learning. Kevin (a) is learning to hang his coat using a standard method and hanger. Rick (b–f) has learned a special way to remove his jacket and to help the teacher place it on the hanger. Both methods get the job done.

Credit must be given to Paula Norton and Carolyn Haykin and to the Community-Based Instructional Program of Albermarle County Public Schools in Charlottesville, Virginia.

named and gestured toward by the teacher, and cooperating by moving limbs into or out of garments, as well as not resisting limb movement during dressing.

To teach these beginning dressing skills, the teacher must create an unhurried, positive atmosphere during dressing times. Clothes should be pointed to and labeled with simple phrases used to describe the activity ("Put on your shirt"). If the student's attention is not directed toward a particular garment before it is put on or removed, prompt attention by turning the student's head, moving the garment into view, or shaking it. At this time, the garment should be labeled and the looking behavior reinforced with approval, praise, hugs, or bits of food if necessary, making sure that reinforcers are suitable for the student's chronological age.

Once the learner demonstrates more visual attending to the teacher and garment, the teacher could prompt him to move his limbs appropriately. During dressing this is done by holding the garment next to the corresponding limb (sock by foot) when the student is attending, and physically prompting movement of that limb in the direction of the garment. Getting the learner to push limbs into garments (or pull out of) is done by pushing the garment onto the extended limb in short, gentle but abrupt movements, allowing the student opportunity to push (or pull away from) between movements. Any beginning efforts should be encouraged.

Sequenced Steps for Instruction

Generally the dressing or undressing steps are taught in one of two sequences: backward chaining, or whole task training. In *both* procedures the task is first analyzed into small steps using a dressing method suited to the specific learner, garment, and setting as illustrated in Figure 13.15. In *backward chaining* the student learns the last step first with each successive step added once the preceding step or combination of steps is learned. If backward chaining is used to teach jacket removal (Figure 13.15 & 13.16), the student, wearing an unzipped jacket, is asked to remove the coat and hang it up, and is physically assisted through all the steps except the last step. At this point the teacher waits the designated latency (3 seconds) and then encourages the learner to perform the last step by one or more of the following procedures: giving a direction while gesturing or touching the garment,

demonstrating the last step and allowing the learner to imitate, or applying varying amounts of physical assistance. Praise and tangible reinforcers are given after completion. Training continues until the learner carries out the last step without any assistance. Then training is directed toward the next-to-last step by providing assistance and gradually fading it over trials. The learner is expected to continue to perform learned steps without help. Reinforcement is provided after the chain is completed. Gradually, the student learns each successive step until a single garment can be removed when requested. These general backward chaining methods have been used to teach individuals with moderate and severe retardation to undress as well as to dress (Baldwin, Fredericks, & Brodsky, 1973; Ball et al., 1971; Bensberg et al., 1965; Colwell et al., 1973; Martin et al., 1971; Minge & Ball, 1967).

The chain may be divided into more steps if a student has difficulty when prompts are faded on any single step. At this early stage of dressing instruction, loose, simple clothing can be used, preferably without zippers, hooks, or buttons. If fasteners are present, they can be opened and closed for the student, because training at this stage focuses on the less complicated skills of clothing removal and replacement.

Whole task training (Spooner, Weber, & Spooner, 1984), which appears to lead to faster acquisition of the entire task, has been used more recently to teach dressing and undressing tasks (Azrin et al., 1976; Diorio & Konarski, 1984; Young, West, Howard, & Whitney, 1986). In this procedure, the student is taught each step in the chain as the task is performed in its natural sequence. Prompts, error corrections, and reinforcement are applied as planned by the teacher throughout the responses in the chain. Although mastery of each step *may* be slower, it seems that the entire sequence or chain of steps is mastered more quickly than in backward chaining. In any case, time is not wasted in whole task training by putting the student passively through the nontraining steps as occurs in backward chaining. Some teachers, however, still prefer backward chaining to teach students who have such movement difficulties as cerebral palsy. More research is needed to compare these sequencing procedures for different learners and tasks.

Azrin's "Rapid" Method

Azrin et al. (1976) developed a concentrated method for rapidly teaching dressing skills to students with profound retardation. Dressing skills were taught after undressing skills had been mastered; however, each student learned to remove (and put on) five garments, from outerwear to underwear, as an entire sequence (shoes, socks, pants, underpants, and shirt), rather than learning to remove one garment at a time. If a student had difficulty with one or two of the five garments, intensive training centered primarily on these garments. Seven students taught by this method learned to put on and remove all five garments after a median training time of 10 hours or over 2 days.

This rapid success resulted from a combination of intense training techniques: long instructional sessions (3 hours); the instruction of all steps simultaneously in a forward progression; extensive use of manual guidance early in learning, which was graduated in intensity to match the student's responsiveness; systematic application and fading of prompts; continuous use of praise and stroking contingent upon any effort to follow instructions or guidance; the requirement of visual attention to the task; and the initial involvement of two trainers so that praise, stroking, and manual guidance could be provided. Azrin and his co-workers used slip-on clothing without fasteners, which initially was two sizes larger than the student's regular clothes. After only touch assistance was needed to begin performance of the chain, clothing one size smaller was substituted. Students were taught to dress and undress while seated and to use both hands for all movements. Prompts were gradually increased until successful performance occurred.

The first instruction for each garment was simply verbal. If a few seconds passed with no action, the trainer pointed at or touched the garment. After a few seconds, the instruction was repeated and the trainer molded the student's hands around the garment. If a student still was not participating, the trainer then described each movement the student was to make as he guided the hands through the necessary motion. The instructions were very specific. This procedure provided multisensory information: verbal, visual, auditory, and tactual. (p. 30)

After manual guidance was faded for a garment, another student was encouraged to perform with pointing and instructional cues provided every 10 seconds as needed. If the response was not completed in 1 minute, manual guidance was reapplied. Some students, especially during early acquisition, resisted manual guidance. Although the trainer's hands were cupped around the student's, who in turn held the garment, the student was not forced to respond. After the student relaxed his resistance, manual graduated guidance was gently reinstated. As with methods to teach toileting and eating, Azrin and his co-workers have combined some of the best elements from the teaching technology to produce an instructional procedure that has yielded successful and swift results with learners having profound retardation. Although this method was not tested with learners having retardation and physical handicaps, such a rich combination of instructional elements applied under the direction of a physical or occupational therapist has potential for producing some skill development (Azrin et al., 1976, p. 33).

In a recent replication of Azrin et al.'s rapid procedures, Diorio and Konarski (1984) were unable to obtain the same success with three similar adults having profound retardation. After 32 and 41 hours of intensive training, two of the three subjects mastered undressing, but the third subject still had not met criterion after 150 hours of training. None of the three adults reached criterion on dressing after 108 hours of intensive training. Although these resarch findings do not invalidate the rapid techniques of Azrin et al., since gains were made, teachers using these techniques should not expect the speed or extensive progress reported originally.

A Method to Promote Learning Beyond Acquisition

Recently, Young, West, Howard, and Whitney (1986) demonstrated teaching methods that not only addressed acquisition and fluency of dressing tasks, but also resulted in skill generalization and maintenance without further training. Two preschool boys with moderate retardation, frequent noncompliant behavior, and no communication skills received instruction in this study. Training was given daily, but only in a single 20-minute session, rather than intensively as "rapid" methods advocate, thus allowing time for instruction in other skills. Three skills were taught one at a time (putting on a pullover shirt, taking it off, and putting on pants) using 9- to 10-step task analyses and whole task training.

During acquisition, prompts were applied only when the student did not respond or made an error.

The prompt procedure consisted of a two-step hierarchy with verbal-gestural prompts given first, followed by graduated physical guidance when verbal or gestural prompts were not successful. Intermittent praise was given to the child during the task for success, while praise, hugs, pats, and stickers were given at the end of the task whenever performance was improved over the previous session. Finally, inappropriate behavior such as noncompliance was interrupted during training with a stern "No," and a 30-second timeout involving the teacher merely turning away from the student.

Once the students could perform a task correctly in a consistent and unprompted manner, the training procedure was changed to improve fluency or rate of responding. Difficult steps, which were characterized by hesitation, more frequent errors, or self-correcting were identified and given repeated practice. Thus, if a student usually hesitated and sometimes erred only when pulling the shirt off his head, he was given 10 consecutive trials on this step alone. In order to set a realistic dressing speed, the authors recorded the dressing rate of skilled peers with and without handicaps; then they calculated a goal rate for each task which was an average of these times.

Each skill was learned after 32 days of instruction or less (20 minutes per day). As shown for one of the students in Figure 13.17, low baseline performances (both in terms of percentages of steps performed correctly and rate) were followed by steady improvements once acquisition training was implemented. Generalization performance (shown as solid squares in Figure 13.17), which was only assessed in three other school settings and not trained, improved only slightly during the acquisition phase. Likewise, the student's speed or rate of correct responses was influenced minimally during acquisition training; however, after fluency training began, both students reached or surpassed the goal rates and generalized their skills to other settings and retained them a month later.

The addition of fluency training proved to be important for two reasons. First, by improving their speed of dressing, it was more likely that the boys' parents and teachers would encourage their daily use. Second, fluency training seemed to have an indirect impact upon skill generalization by resulting in more social reinforcement for independent performance and more opportunities to perform in the natural environment.

Fasteners

Skills in unfastening should be mastered before fastening. When oversized fasteners, visible to the learner, are used as the teaching materials, fastener instruction probably increases in complexity across the following skills: zipping (with front-opening zipper already securely attached at bottom), snapping (large, plastic snaps), buttoning, hooking, buckling. Learning to align the zipper tab with the zipper end on a front-opening jacket and to fasten buttons, snaps, or hooks located out of direct view is difficult for students with handicaps (as well as for normal learners) and will be taught after the simple fasteners are mastered. Hardy et al. (1981) and Tawney (1979) provide useful task analyses of these skills with suggestions for teaching. For example, zipping unconnected, front-opening jackets may be divided into seven steps, which could be taught either with forward chaining or whole-task training.

1. First the learner grasps zipper tab and moves the slider with the dominant hand to the bottom of the track.
2. Then the pin is grasped between nondominant finger and thumb and is inserted into the slider (while holding onto both sides of the closure at the bottom).
3. The pin is pushed firmly into the slider box.
4. Nondominant hand grasps both sides of closure at bottom with thumb placed across zipper box (held through step 6).
5. With dominant hand the zipper tab is grasped.
6. Zipper tab is pulled up to top stop.
7. Zipper tab released and pushed with index finger to lock into position.

Some teachers will prefer subdividing the first two steps, whereas others may not teach the last step of locking the zipper. If a pull string is added to the zipper tab, the task is somewhat easier, and the steps are modified slightly.

As illustrated by this example, hand dominance influences the teaching procedure. Hand dominance, if unknown, can be determined by simple observation during eating and play. Or, the learner may be handed objects at midline while noting how often right- and left-hand grasps are used. To illustrate the importance of hand dominance, belt-buckling is easier if the learner is taught to grasp the buckle with the dominant hand and the strap with his other hand; however, with the changing

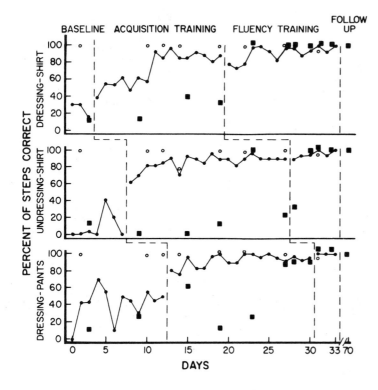

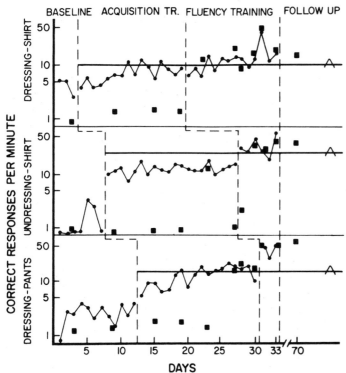

FIGURE 13.17 In the top graph the percentage of correctly and independently performed dressing steps of one child is graphed across time. Performance on generalization probes is indicated by solid squares, while open circles represent interobserver reliability scores. In the bottom graph the same child's performance is graphed on a semilogarithmic scale as the number of steps in the dressing or undressing task correctly completed per minute across conditions. Again, performance on generalization probes is indicated by solid squares, while goal or aim response rates are indicated by "A."

Source: From "Acquisition, Fluency Training, Generalization, and Maintenance of Dressing Skills of Two Developmentally Disabled Children" by K.R. Young, R.P. West, V.F. Harward, & R. Whitney, 1986. *Education and Treatment of Children, 9,* pp. 23, 25. Reprinted by permission.

position of buttons and snaps, the matching of dominant hand to the logically dominant side of the task may create a problem. The position of buttons and buttonholes as well as bottom-fitting (under snap) and top-fitting snaps (over snap) is one way on boys' clothing and the opposite for girls. In boys' clothing, buttons are on the right edge and holes on the left, while bottom snaps are on the right and the top half is positioned on the left edge. The opposite arrangement occurs with girls' clothing. Because it may be easier to teach a child to grasp buttons as well as bottom snaps in the dominant hand, boys' clothing would provide the appropriate arrangement for right handers while girls' clothing would be more suited to left handers; however, each sex must learn to fasten the corresponding clothing and perhaps learning both arrangements is best. Because the research is scanty in this area, girls and boys should begin on their own clothing, regardless of dominance and fastener arrangement. All beginning learning should involve the same arrangement of buttons, holes, and snaps. Once one arrangement is mastered, training could be provided with the opposite arrangement; however, if a student appears to be making slow progress during early learning and his hand dominance is not matched to the position of buttons on his clothing, the teacher may want to try the opposite arrangement.

Shoe Tying

Baldwin et al. (1973, Hardy et al. (1981), and Martin et. al (1971) describe two nontraditional methods of teaching shoe tying to learners with handicaps. The "rabbit ear" method involves tying a single knot, then forming two loops that are then tied together in another single knot (Figure 13.18). Martin and his co-workers used another procedure to teach the same skill: (a) tying a single knot, (b) tying a second knot that is not pulled tight, (c) making one loop by inserting one lace end into the hole between the knots, (d) pulling it to form a small loop, repeating steps (c) and (d) with the second lace end, and (e) grasping both loops and pulling the bow tight. (Refer to Figure 13.19.) Although there are data supporting the use of this method with students having severe retardation (Martin et al., 1971), the "rabbit ear" method, although reportedly used with the same population (Baldwin et al., 1973), lacks such data.

The traditional method (single knot, form loop

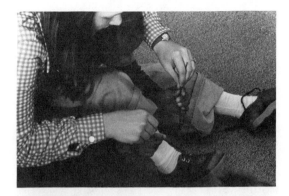

FIGURE 13.18 This teacher is using a backward chaining procedure to teach her student the traditional method of shoe tying. Jayne verbally instructs and manually helps Maude as needed with each step: tying a simple knot, making a loop with one lace, wrapping the free lace around the loop, switching position of fingers, pulling the second loop out through the opening, and pulling both loops tight. In the bottom picture which illustrates the last step, Jayne has faded out her manual assistance by letting Maude tighten the bow on her own.

with one lace, wrap free lace around loop) is recommended less often for learners with handicaps. This could be the case because of its nonsymmetrical formation as compared with the two nontraditional methods—each lace is manipulated in a different way. Regardless of the method selected, the learner should be taught to untie bows and single knots first, then to tie single knots and finally bows.

Because of the complexity of shoe tying and the necessity of precise finger control, some learners with handicaps probably should wear nontying or Velcro fastener shoes (especially if age and style-appropriate) and learning time should be directed to skills of a higher priority with a greater likelihood for success.

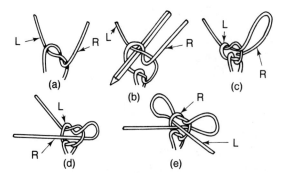

FIGURE 13.19 Diagram of steps for tying a bow. The letters "L" and "R" indicate the hands (left or right) of the subject that are holding the laces at the head of the arrows.

Source: From "Operant Conditioning in Dressing Behavior of Severely Retarded Girls" by G.L. Martin, B. Keogh, E. Bird, V. Jensen, and M. Darbyshire, 1971, *Mental Retardation, 9*(3). p. 29. Copyright 1971 by the American Association on Mental Deficiency. Reprinted by permission.

SUMMARY

This chapter describes procedures to assess and teach the basic self-care skills of independent toileting, eating, and dressing. It comments extensively on instructional prompts, shaping procedures, and materials, with a review of the research on teaching self-care skills to people with severe handicaps but without extensive motor impairments.

The extent to which an individual attains independence in basic self-care clearly will influence his inclusion in educational programs, social activities, and vocational opportunities and certainly will affect the amount of time available to the parent and teacher as well as the self-esteem of the individual. The volume of research directed toward self-care instruction has been productive in providing methodological guidelines for parents and teachers. If educational programs individualize this information and successfully implement this technology, independence in basic self-care abilities will be maximized in learners with severe handicaps.

REFERENCES

Albin, J. B. (1977). Some variables influencing the maintenance of acquired self-feeding behavior in profoundly retarded children. *Mental Retardation, 15*(5), 49–52.

Azrin, N. H., & Armstrong, P. M. (1973) The "mini-meal"—A method for teaching eating skills to the profoundly retarded. *Mental Retardation, 11*(1), 9–11.

Azrin, N. H., Bugle, C., & O'Brien, F. (1971). Behavioral engineering: Two apparatuses for toilet training retarded children. *Journal of Applied Behavioral Analysis, 4,* 249–253.

Azrin, N. H., & Foxx, R. M. (1971). A rapid method of toilet training the institutionalized retarded. *Journal of Applied Behavior Analysis, 4,* 89–99.

Azrin, N. H., Schaeffer, R. M., & Wesolowski, M. D. (1976). A rapid method of teaching profoundly retarded persons to dress by a reinforcement-guidance method. *Mental Retardation, 14*(6), 29–33.

Azrin, N. H., Sneed, T. J., & Foxx, R. M. (1973). Dry bed: A rapid method of eliminating bedwetting (enuresis) of the retarded. *Behaviour Research and Therapy, 11,* 427–434.

Baldwin, V. L., Fredericks, H. D. B., & Brodsky, G. (1973). *Isn't it time he outgrew this? or, A training program for parents of retarded children.* Springfield, IL: Charles C Thomas.

Ball, T. S., Seric, K., & Payne, L. E. (1971). Long-term retention of self-help skill training in the profoundly retarded. *American Journal of Mental Deficiency, 76,* 378–382.

Baller, W. R. (1975). *Bed-wetting: Origins and treatment.* New York: Pergamon Press.

Balthazar, E. E. (1976). *Balthazar scales of adaptive behavior.* Palo Alto, CA: Consulting Psychologist Press, Inc.

Banerdt, B., & Bricker, D. (1978). A training program for selected self-feeding skills for the motorically impaired. *AAESPH Review, 3,* 222–229.

Barmann, B. C., Katz, R. C., O'Brien, F., & Beauchamp, K. L. (1981). Treating irregular enuresis in developmentally disabled persons. *Behavior Modification, 5,* 336–346.

Barton, E. S., Guess, D., Garcia, E., & Baer, D. M. (1970). Improvement of retardates' mealtime behaviors by timeout procedures using multiple baseline techniques. *Journal of Applied Behavior Analysis, 3,* 77–84.

Baumeister, A., & Klosowski, R. (1965). An attempt to group train severely retarded patients. *Mental Retardation, 3,* 24–26.

Baumgart, D., Brown, L., Pumpian, I., Nisbet, J., Ford, A., Sweet, M., Messina, R., & Schroeder, J. (1982). Principle of partial participation and individualized adaptations in educational programs for severely handicapped students. *Journal of the Association for the Severely Handicapped, 7,* 17–27.

Bensberg, G. J., Colwell, C. N., & Cassel, R. H. (1965). Teaching the profoundly retarded self-help activities by behavior shaping techniques. *American Journal of Mental Deficiency, 69,* 674–679.

Berkowitz, S., Sherry, P. J., & Davis, B. A. (1971). Teaching self-feeding skills to profound retardates using reinforcement and fading procedures. *Behavior Therapy, 2,* 62–67.

Bettison, S. (1982). *Toileting training to independence for the handicapped. A manual for trainers.* Springfield, IL: Charles C Thomas.

Bettison, S., Davidson, D., Taylor, P., & Fox, B. (1976). The long-term effects of a toilet training programme for the retarded: A pilot study. *Australian Journal of Mental Deficiency, 4,* 28–35.

Bollard, R. J., & Woodroffe, P. (1977). The effect of parent-administration dry-bed training on nocturnal enuresis in children. *Behaviour Research and Therapy. 15*, 159-165.

Butler, J. F. (1976). The toilet training success of parents after reading 'Toilet training in less than a day," *Behavior Therapy, 1*, 185-191.

Christian, W. P., Hollomon, S. W., & Lanier, C. L. (1973). An attendant operated feeding program for severely and profoundly retarded females. *Mental Retardation, 11*(5), 35-37.

Close, D. W., Irvin, L. K., Prehm, H. J., & Taylor, V. E. (1978). Systematic correction procedures in vocational-skill training of severely retarded individuals. *American Journal of Mental Deficiency, 83*, 270-275.

Colwell, C. N., Richards, E., McCarver, R. B., & Ellis, N. R. (1973). Evaluation of self-help habit training of the profoundly retarded. *Mental Retardation, 11*(3), 14-18.

Coote, M. A. (1965). Apparatus for conditioning treatment of enuresis. *Behaviour Research and Therapy, 2*, 233-238.

Dayan, M. (1964). Toilet training retarded children in a state residential institution. *Mental Retardation, 2*, 116-117.

Diorio, M. A., & Konarski, E. A., Jr. (1984). Evaluation of a method for teaching dressing skills to profoundly mentally retarded persons. *American Journal of Mental Deficiency, 89*, 307-309.

Doleys, D. M., & Arnold, S. (1975). Treatment of childhood encopresis: Full cleanliness training. *Mental Retardation, 13*(6), 14-16.

Dunlap, G., Koegel, R. L., & Koegel, R. K. (1984). Continuity of treatment: Toilet training in multiple community settings. *Journal of the Association for Persons with Severe Handicaps, 9*, 134-141.

Egan, P., Gruber, B. K., Hook, R. J., & Luce, S. C. (1984, May). *A simple fading procedure for the treatment of nighttime enuresis.* Paper presented at the meeting of the Association for Behavior Analysis, Nashville, TN.

Ellis, N. R. (1963). Toilet training the severely defective patient: An S-R reinforcement analysis. *American Journal of Mental Deficiency, 68*, 98-103.

Favell, J. E., McGimsey, J. F., & Jones, M. L. (1980). Rapid eating in the retarded: Reduction by nonaversive procedures. *Behavior Modification, 4*, 481-492.

Ferneti, C. L., Lent, J. R., & Stevens, C. J. (1974). *Project MORE: Eating.* Bellevue, WA: Edmark.

Finnie, N. R. (Ed.). (1975). *Handling the young cerebral palsied child at home* (2nd ed.). New York: E. P. Dutton.

Foxx, R. M., & Azrin, N. H. (1973a). Dry pants: A rapid method of toilet training children. *Behaviour Research and Therapy, 11*, 435-422.

Foxx, R. M., & Azrin, N. H. (1974). *Toilet training in less than a day.* New York: Simon & Schuster.

Foxx, R. M., & Azrin, N. H. (1973b). *Toilet training the retarded: A rapid program for day and nighttime independent toileting.* Champaign, IL: Research Press.

Freagon, S., & Rotatori, A. F. (1982). Comparing natural and artificial environments in training self-care skills to group home residents. *Journal of the Association for the Severely Handicapped, 7*, 73-86.

Freagon, S., Wheeler, J., Hill, L., Brankin, G., Costello, D., & Peters, W. M. (1983). A domestic training environment for students who are severely handicapped. *The Journal of the Association for Persons with Severe Handicaps, 8*(4), 49-61.

Fredericks, H. D. B., Baldwin, V. L., Grove, D. N., & Moore, W. G. (1975). *Toilet training the handicapped child.* Monmouth, OR: Instructional Development Corporation.

Giles, D. K., & Wolf, M. M. (1966). Toilet training institutionalized severe retardates: An application of operant behavior modification techniques. *American Journal of Mental Deficiency, 70*, 766-780.

Hardy, L., Martin, G., Yu, D., Leader, C., & Quinn, G. (1981). *Objective behavioral assessment of the severely and moderately mentally retarded: The OBA.* Springfield, IL: Charles C Thomas.

Henderson, S., & McDonald, M. (1973). *Step-by-step dressing.* Champaign, IL: Suburban Publications.

Herreshoff, J. K. (1973). Two electronic devices for toilet training. *Mental Retardation, 11*(6), 54-55.

Hundziak, M., Maurer, R. A., & Watson, L. S. (1965). Operant conditioning in toilet training of severely retarded boys. *American Journal of Mental Deficiency, 70*, 120-124.

Kimbell, D. L., Luckey, R. E., Barberto, P. F., & Love, J. G. (1967). Operation dry pants: An intensive habit-training program for the severely and profoundly retarded. *Mental Retardation, 5*(2), 32-36.

Kissel, R. C., Johnson, M. R., & Whitman, T. L. (1980). Training a retarded client's mother and teacher through sequenced instructions to establish self-feeding. *Journal of the Association for the Severely Handicapped, 5*, 382-394.

Knapczyk, D. R. (1983). Use of teacher-paced instruction in developing and mainstreaming independent self-feeding. *The Journal of the Association for the Severely Handicapped, 8*(3), 10-16.

Kohl, F. L., & Stettner-Eaton, B. A. (1985). Fourth graders as trainers of cafeteria skills to severely handicapped students. *Education and Training of the Mentally Retarded, 20*, 60-68.

Kolvin, I. (1975). Enuresis in childhood. *Practitioner, 214*, 33-45.

Konarski, E. A., Jr., & Diorio, M. S. (1985). A quantitative review of self-help research with the severely and profoundly mentally retarded. *Applied Research in Mental Retardation, 6*, 229-245.

Kramer, L., & Whitehurst, C. (1981). Effects of button features on self-dressing in young retarded children. *Education and Training of the Mentally Retarded, 16*, 277-283.

Lancioni, G. E. (1980). Teaching independent toileting to profoundly retarded deaf-blind children. *Behavior Therapy, 11*, 234-244.

Lancioni, G. E., & Ceccarani, P. S. (1981). Teaching independent toileting within the normal daily program: Two studies with profoundly retarded children. *Behavior Research of Severe Development Disabilities, 2*, 79-96.

Levine, M. N., & Elliot, C. B. (1970). Toilet training for profoundly retarded with a limited staff. *Mental Retardation, 8*(3), 48-50.

Linford, M. D., Hipsher, L. W., & Silikovitz, R. G. (1972). *Systematic instruction for retarded children: The Illinois program, Part III: Self-help instruction.* Danville, IL: Interstate.

Lohman, W., Eyman, R., & Lask, E. (1967). Toilet training. *American Journal of Mental Deficiency, 71,* 551–557.

Lovibond, S. H. (1963). The mechanism of conditioning treatment of enuresis. *Behaviour Research and Therapy, 1,* 17–21.

Lovibond, S. H. (1964). *Conditioning and enuresis.* New York: Macmillan.

Mahoney, K., Van Wagenen, R. K., & Meyerson, L. (1971). Toilet training of normal and retarded children. *Journal of Applied Behavior Analysis, 4,* 173–181.

Marshall, G. R. (1966). Toilet training of an autistic eight-year-old through conditioning therapy: A case report. *Behaviour Research and Therapy, 4,* 242–245.

Martin, G. L., Kehoe, B., Bird, E., Jensen, V., & Darbyshire, M. (1971). Operant conditioning in dressing behavior of severely retarded girls. *Mental Retardation, 9*(3), 27–30.

Matson, J. L. (1975). Some practical considerations for using the Foxx and Azrin method of toilet training. *Psychological Reports, 37,* 350.

Matson, J. L., Ollendick, T. H., & Adkins, J. (1980). A comprehensive dining program for mentally retarded adults. *Behaviour Research and Therapy, 18,* 107–112.

McGimsey, J. F. (1977). *A brief survey of eating behaviors of 60 severe/profoundly retarded individuals.* Unpublished manuscript. Morganton, NC: Western Carolina Center.

Minge, M. R., & Ball, T. S. (1967). Teaching of self-help skills to profoundly retarded patients. *American Journal of Mental Deficiency, 71,* 864–868.

Mowrer, O. H., & Mowrer, W. M. (1938). Enuresis: A method for its study and treatment. *American Journal of Orthopsychiatry, 8,* 436–459.

Mueller, H. (1975). Feeding. In N. R. Finne (Ed.), *Handling the young cerebral palsied child at home* (pp. 113–132). New York: E. P. Dutton.

Nelson, G. L., Cone, J. D., & Hanson, C. R. (1975). Training correct utensil use in retarded children: Modeling vs. physical guidance. *American Journal of Mental Deficiency, 80,* 114–122.

O'Brien, F., & Azrin, N. H. (1972). Developing proper mealtime behaviors of the institutionalized retarded. *Journal of Applied Behavior Analysis, 5,* 389–399.

O'Brien, F., Bugle, C., & Azrin, N. H. (1972). Training and maintaining a retarded child's proper eating. *Journal of Applied Behavior Analysis, 5,* 67–73.

Osarchuk, M. (1973). Operant methods of toilet behavior training of the severely and profoundly retarded: A review. *Journal of Special Education, 7,* 423–437.

Pipes, P. L. (1976). Assessing food and nutrient in-take. In M. L. Erickson (Ed.), *Assessment and management of developmental changes in children* (pp. 137–151). St. Louis: C. V. Mosby.

Popovich, D., & Laham, S. L. (1981). *The adaptive behavior curriculum, Vol. 1.* Baltimore: Paul H. Brookes.

Richman, J. S., Sonderby, T., & Kahn, J. V. (1980). Prerequisite vs. *in vivo* acquisition of self-feeding skill.

Behaviour Research and Therapy, 18, 327–332.

Richmond, G. (1983). Shaping bladder and bowel continence in developmentally retarded preschool children. *Journal of Autism and Developmental Disorders, 13,* 197–205.

Rietz, A. L. (1984). Teaching community skills to formerly institutionalized adults: Eating nutritionally balanced diets. *Analysis and Intervention in Developmental Disabilities, 4,* 299–312.

Sailor, W., Halvorsen, A., Anderson, J., Goetz, L., Gee, K., Doering, K., & Hunt, P. (1986). Community intensive instruction. In R. Horner, L. Voeltz, & B. Fredericks (Eds.), *Education of learners with severe handicaps: Exemplary service strategies* (pp. 251–288). Baltimore: Paul H. Brookes.

Seiger, H. W. (1952). Treatment of essential nocturnal enuresis. *Journal of Pediatrics, 40,* 738–749.

Sloop, W. E., & Kennedy, W. A. (1973). Institutionalized retarded nocturnal enuretics treated by a conditioning technique. *American Journal of Mental Deficiency, 77,* 712–717.

Smith, A. L., Piersel, W. C., Filbeck, R. W., & Gross, E. J. (1983). The elimination of mealtime food stealing and scavenging behavior in an institutionalized severely mentally retarded adult. *Mental Retardation, 21,* 255–259.

Smith, L. J. (1981). Training severely and profoundly mentally handicapped nocturnal enuretics. *Behaviour Research and Therapy, 19,* 67–74.

Smith, P. S. (1979). A comparison of different methods of toilet training the mentally handicapped. *Behaviour Research and Therapy, 17,* 33–34.

Smith, P. S., Britton, P. G., Johnson, M., & Thomas, D. A. (1975). Problems involved in toilet training profoundly mentally handicapped adults. *Behaviour Research and Therapy, 15,* 301–307.

Sobsey, R. J. (1983). Nutrition of children with severely handicapping conditions. *Journal for the Association of the Severely Handicapped, 8,* 14–17.

Song, A. Y., & Gandhi, R. (1974). An analysis of behavior during the acquisition and maintenance phases of self-spoon feeding skills of profound retardates. *Mental Retardation, 12*(1), 25–28.

Spooner, F., Weber, L. H., & Spooner, D. (1984). The effects of backward chaining and total task presentation on the acquisition of complex tasks by severely retarded adolescents and adults. *Education and Treatment of Children, 6,* 401–420.

Stainback, S. S., & Healy, H. A. (1982). *Teaching eating skills: A handbook for teachers.* Springfield, IL: Charles C Thomas.

Stimbert, V. E., Minor, J. W., & McCoy, J. F. (1977). Intensive feeding training with retarded children. *Behavior Modification, 1,* 517–530.

Sugaya, K. (1967). Survey of the enuresis problem in an institution for the mentally retarded with emphasis on the clinical psychological aspects. *Japanese Journal of Child Psychiatry, 8,* 142–150.

Tawney, J. W. (1979). *Programmed environmental curriculum.* Columbus, OH: Charles E. Merrill.

Thompson, T., & Hanson, R. (1983). Overhydration:

Precautions when treating urinary incontinence. *Mental Retardation, 21,* 139–143.

Training Resource Center (1973). *Toilet training equipment.* Unpublished manuscript. Mansfield Depot, CT: Longley School, Mansfield Training School.

Trott, M. C. (1977). Application of Foxx and Azrin toilet training for the retarded in a school program. *Education and Training of the Mentally Retarded, 12,* 336–339.

Van Wagenen, R. K., & Murdock, E. E. (1966). A transistorized signal-package for toilet training of infants. *Journal of Experimental Child Psychology, 3,* 312–314.

Wallander, J. L., Hubert, N. S., & Schroeder, C. S. (1983). Self care skills. In J. L. Matson, & S. E. Bruening (Eds.), *Assessing the mentally retarded,* (pp. 209–246). New York: Grune & Stratton.

Williams, C. L., Doleys, D. D., & Ciminero, A. R. (1978). A two-year follow-up of enuretic children treated with Dry Bed Training. *Journal of Behavior Therapy and Experimental Psychiatry, 9,* 285–286.

Williams, F. E., & Sloop, W. E. (1978). Success with a shortened Foxx-Azrin toilet training program. *Education and Training of the Mentally Retarded, 4,* 399–402.

Wilson, P. G., Reid, D. H., Phillips, J. F., & Burgio, L. D. (1984). Normalization of institutional mealtimes for profoundly retarded persons. *Journal of Applied Behavior Analysis, 17,* 189–202.

Young, K. R., West, R. P., Howard, V. F., & Whitney, R. (1986). Acquisition, fluency training generalization, and maintenance or dressing skills of two developmentally disabled children. *Education and Treatment of Children, 9,* 16–29.

TOILET-TRAINING SIGNALING EQUIPMENT

Signaling Pants, Potty Chairs, and Instructions for Building

1. BRS/LVE
   9381-D Davis Ave.
   Laurel, MD. 20707
   301-474-3400
   A. Potty Alert (#552-08)—$77.00 plus shipping
   B. Pants Alert (#552-09)—$77.00 plus shipping

2. Dr. A. Yonovitz
   Speech, Language and Learning Center
   12777 Jones Rd., Suite 196
   Houston, TX 77070
   713-469-7811
   Construction Manual for Toilet Alarm and Body-Worn Alerting Unit—$7.50

3. Mr. Gil Langley
   Northern Virginia Training Center
   9901 Braddock Rd.
   Fairfax, VA 22030
   703-323-4045
   Diagram sheet for building the toilet alarm with easily obtained parts; free *but* you *must send a prestamped, preaddressed envelope* with your request.

4. Warrick Control, Inc.
   1964 W. Eleven Mile Rd.
   P.O. Box 1128
   Berkley, MI 48072
   313-545-2512
   Bleeptone audible signalling device—$17.00 plus shipping (for use with a body-worn alert or as part of a toilet alarm); Mini-Bleeptone-smaller, requires less current but produces some volume.

Bed-Signaling Equipment

Sears and Roebuck Co.
Catalogue Sales
A. Lite-Alert Alarm (#8G-1303)—$69.99 plus shipping
B. Wee Alarm (#8G-1302)—$46.99 plus shipping.
C. Extra Bedding Set (#8G-1172)—$8.99 plus shipping

14

Domestic and Community Skills

Martha E. Snell
University of Virginia

Diane M. Browder
Lehigh University

The domestic and community domains include all the competencies required to maintain one's personal appearance and residence and to use the surrounding community. Freagon and her colleagues (1983) list such domestic and community areas as self-care and personal health, housekeeping, clothing care, meal preparation, walking and transportation, various types of shopping, and the use of laundromats, restaurants, post offices, doctors, dentists, and banks. This chapter addresses these skills. Inasmuch as this list could be continued at great length and should also include the related social and communication abilities, teachers must have a method to determine which skills will both match actual student needs and may be reasonably mastered, whether through partial or full participation. The ecological inventory procedures described in Chapter 4 enable educators to assess which present and future community living skills are most important to a particular student.

Relevant ecological inventories include a visit to the student's current domestic environments (family home, grandparents, babysitter) and future domestic environments (group home, apartment), as well as to parts of the nearby community to determine what skills appear to be required. Home visits might reveal that one student has a washer and dryer while another must use a public laundromat. Each student will require slightly different instruction. The student who must use a laundromat will need to get there somehow, may need to wait for an available appliance, and also must select and insert the correct coins.

Also relevant will be inventories of the student's current and potential future communities to determine the type of street crossing that will be encountered, the travel skills needed to use the public health clinic, and the directions for operating public phones (cost, insertion of coin before or after dialing). Comparing the student's current skills with the skills needed in a future setting will suggest numerous targets. Both the number of years left in a student's schooling and the presence of physical handicaps will further influence which skills are targeted and whether a student will be taught independent or partial performance of the targeted skills.

SKILLS REQUIRED FOR COMMUNITY SUCCESS

Follow-up surveys of persons deinstitutionalized into the community underscore the critical relationship between basic competence in the domestic and community domains and success in the community placement. Schalock and Harper (1978) monitored 131 persons with borderline to severe retardation who had moved from the institution into the community. Of these 131 clients, 13% "failed" (had to return to the institution) because they lacked skills in money management, meal preparation, and housekeeping. In a follow-up of 80% of the original clients, Schalock and colleagues (1981) found that success predictors still included personal maintenance, clothing care and use, and food preparation, as well as communication and community use, whereas failure was often associated with inadequate home maintenance, bizarre behavior, and nutritional problems.

In a similar follow-up study of 400 deinstitutionalized retarded adults and children, Gollay, Freedman, Wyngaarden, and Kurtz (1978) noted that skills trained by the staff of community residences included housekeeping, meal preparation, shopping, money management, traveling, using the telephone, handling emergencies, and using community agencies. Although these skills were cited by community resident staff as being the most important, less than half of the clients studied received instruction in these skills because the caretakers either were not prepared to teach the skills or felt the students were not ready for the skills.

These findings should not be interpreted to mean that there is a standard set of critical skills nor that the community and domestic skills deemed important must be mastered *before* deinstitutionalization or *before* being placed in a community facility. First, a specific environmental inventory followed by a prioritization process is the most accurate means of selecting which skills are important. Furthermore, making placement in a community residence contingent upon complete attainment of needed skills would delay, or perhaps negate, the benefits that appear predictably to accompany movement into the community from large institutions. Follow-up comparison research of clients deinstitutionalized in New York and in Pennsylvania, demonstrated significant improvement in adaptive behavior by the "movers" over the "stayers" (Jones,

Conroy, Feinstein, & Lemanowicz, 1984), and showed significant progress toward normalized daily activity patterns accompanied by some skill gains, without any specific training (O'Neill, Brown, Gordon, & Schonhorn, 1985). Life in the community clearly appears to promote more learning than does life in a restricted living setting, regardless of specific training in either setting. For those people who have always lived with their parents, increased independence in domestic and community skills will assure that their future continues to be in the community.

Planning Domestic and Community Skills

Like all programs for students with severe handicaps, daily living skill programs should be individualized and systematically taught. We will review a few of the principles that guide all programs for this population as they relate to domestic and community skills: training setting and schedule, partial and full participation, self-management, validating procedures and results, and minimizing program expense.

Training Setting and Schedule

Consistent with the follow-up findings of Jones et al. (1984) on deinstitutionalized persons, there is growing support for the learning benefits promoted by instruction in realistic surroundings over settings bearing little resemblance to those in which the skill will be needed (Martin, Rusch, & Heal, 1982). The rationale for training students in settings which are natural to the skill being taught concerns skill generalization. When students learn to perform skills in the presence of stimuli naturally associated with that skill, their performance is more likely to occur when they actually need the skill. There are numerous published studies supporting this basic tenet. Goetz, Gee, and Sailor (1985) found that two students learned to associate picture communication cards more quickly with the respective task (making toast, washing dishes, emptying trash) when they were *interrupted during* the task rather than asked to locate the correct picture before performing the task. Students enjoyed the tasks and could complete the interrupted task only if they found the correct picture; thus, task completion served as a positive reinforcer and motivated learning. In addition, the motor and material stimulus cues were likely to be more evident *during* the task rather than *before* the task. *In vivo* instruction takes advantage of both facilitative features. Researchers teaching pedestrian skills to adults with moderate retardation found that community sidewalk settings yielded better learning than did a 4′ by 4′ model of a street (Marchetti, McCartney, Drain, Hooper, & Dix, 1983). Community sidewalks and all the surrounding setting stimuli were not represented by the 4′ by 4′ street models. Similarly, Coon and his co-workers (1981) could not effectively replicate buses and curbs in the classroom in order to teach bus use skills that would generalize. Livi and Ford (1985) found that younger students with moderate retardation transferred skills into their own home best when there was a close match between the two sets of stimuli involved in tasks like making a sack lunch, folding laundry, preparing toast, and putting tableware away.

These results and other research on daily living skill instruction with adolescents and adults having severe handicaps (Aeschleman & Schladenhauffen, 1984; Browder, Snell, & Ambrogio, 1984; Coon, Vogelsberg, & Williams, 1981; Freagon & Rotatori, 1982; Sprague & Horner, 1984) should *not* be interpreted to mean that *all training* has to take place in the very setting in which the skill will be used. Although the practice of natural setting training clearly will promote students' actual use of the skill in that same setting and may maximize transfer to other natural settings, daily instruction in natural settings may not be feasible or necessary for *all* skills. Travel time and costs, and *sometimes* the student's safety or social stigma, *may be* greater when a community-based program is used. On the other hand, simulation of task stimuli may be expensive and time consuming. The key factor is not cost or even safety alone, but it is the amount of useful learning that results, which appears related to the match in relevant stimuli between training time and setting and the actual time(s) and setting(s) for the skill to be used.

Thus, teachers should not merely "train and hope" that the skill taught will be used when and where it ultimately is needed. Teachers should take a more difficult but certain approach and use community-based instruction whenever it is feasible. Feasibility rests upon the answers to a series of questions, some of which include the following:

1. What are the criterion places and times for the target skill?

2. What considerations are involved if a given skill or cluster of skills is to be taught to a particular student under the critical criterion conditions?
   (a) What other students would benefit from learning the same skill or another skill that could be taught in that same setting?
   (b) What other needed skills could be taught on the same trip away from the classroom to increase efficiency (related social behavior, communication skills, ambulation as well as *other* community skill targets)?
   (c) How will the other students be "covered" by staff? Can related services staff provide their scheduled therapy in the community? Can nonhandicapped peers assist?
   (d) Can transportation be arranged?
   (e) Is safety or public embarrassment a problem if *in vivo* training is used? Can these problems be eliminated?
   (f) Is the skill really needed? Can a substitute skill be taught, which does not need training in that setting?
   (g) Are parents or students opposed to or supportive of community-based teaching?

3. What about classroom or simulated training of part of the skill, is it really more practical? Should it be used to supplement *in vivo* training or probes?
   (a) Can the relevant stimuli be easily replicated in the classroom or school? Can this be done for the entire task (use of school vending machines) or for just part of the task (selecting the correct coins to operate machines at a laundromat) to enable effective instruction and possibly faster learning since repeated trials may be easier?
   (b) Has the student shown successful previous generalization of skills trained in the classroom?
   (c) Are parents or students opposed to or supportive of classroom teaching?

This decision process may be extensive, but the initial conversion of classroom-based instruction to the community is indeed a complex process and, thus, requires development of a convincing rationale and good planning. Daily scheduling, transportation routes, adequate staff coverage, resolution of liability and school policy issues, and support from students' families are all potential areas of frustration. [Table 14.1 illustrates the way

TABLE 14.1 Community-based schedule for middle school students (M, W, F, 1:00 to 2:45 P.M.)

Time	Teacher	Physical Therapist	Graduate Student
1:00	*Activity:* With peer tutor walk to laundromat *Systematic programs:* —*Tan*—1) Street crossing, 2) walking on sidewalks without eating garbage, 3) walking by peer tutor —*David*—1) Use walker on sidewalks, 2) step off curbs with assistance	—Meet students in class *Activity:* Walk to nearby restaurant *Systematic programs:* —*Carey*—Using electric wheelchair in the community —*Janet*—Assist by *grasping* purse as P.T. pushes her	*Activity:* Take city bus to business district with peer tutors *Systematic programs:* —*Felicia*—1) Bus riding sequence with assistance, 2) socially acceptable behavior (no self-abusive behavior) —*Lamonte*—1) Climb stairs of bus, take transfer with assistance, 2) sit down with assistance, 3) no rocking behavior on bus, 4) give piece of gum to peer tutor
1:10	*Activity:* Use of laundromat and stores *Systematic programs:* —*Tan*—1) Laundry sequence—partial participation on money and sorting, 2) coin-operated soap machine programs, 3) money changer, 4) video game play with peer tutor, 5) shop for items at produce market nearby using precounted money, uses picture list with assistance to communicate in store, 6) maintain (no screaming or climbing) socially appropriate behavior, 7) folding clothes	*Activity:* Use restaurant *Systematic programs:* —*Carey*—1) Use communications board to indicate choice, use order card; 2) smile at waitress, listen; 3) open purse, get money out, hand precounted money to hostess when leaving; 4) use wheelchair in restaurant —*Janet*—1) chew food with assistance, 2) swallow liquids through straw, 3) use communication card to give order to waitress by grasping it and looking up when she arrives, 4) keep glasses on while in restaurant	*Activity:* Play cards and basketball in nearby park —*Felicia*—1) Throw, catch, and shoot with partial assistance (with peer tutor), 2) behavior (same) —*Lamonte*—1) Play modified card game with peer tutor with assistance, 2) same behavior program —*Felicia*—1) Do part of shopping sequence independently with supervision and assistance with money handling, 2) choose drink using communication booklet, remember to find same drink in store, 3) walk with peer tutor. —*Lamonte*—1) Carry drink to store counter, give money, put change in bag, 2) offer cookies out of backpack to peers with prompt from teacher, 3) eat with moderate speed
2:15	—*David*—1) Open washer, put soap and clothes in and out with assistance; open dryer and put in and out with assistance, 2) push money changer in and vending machine selector button in 3) keep hearing aids in while in laundromat, 4) use walker to enter corner market to buy juice for tomorrow's lunch, 5) hand store clerk money and receive change, place in pocket, 6) fold clothes with assistance *Activity:* Greet friends when they arrive: —*Tan*—smile, wave; *Carey*—smile, sounds (switch with P.T.)	*Activity:* Walk to nearby laundromat, meet teacher and other students, switch for the return to school *Systematic programs:* Same mobility programs, and: —*Carey*—1) greet friends using communication board and answer questions using known pictures —*Janet*—smile at friends and look at them while talking (switch with teacher)	
2:30	*Activity:* Return to school *Systematic programs:* —*Carey*—use electric wheelchair —*Janet*—hold purse	*Activity:* Return to school *Systematic programs:* —*Tan*—Street crossing —*David*—Use walker	*Activity:* Return on bus to school—same as above

Source: From "Community Intensive Instruction" by W. Sailor, A. Halvorson, J. Anderson, L. Goetz, K. Gee, K. Doering, & P. Hunt. In Robert H. Horner, Luanna H. Meyer, H.D. Bud Fredericks (Eds.). (1986). *Education of Learners with Severe Handicaps: Exemplary Service Strategies* (pp. 251–288). Baltimore, Paul H. Brookes Publishing Co. (P.O. Box 10624, Baltimore, MD 21285-0624). © 1986. Reprinted by permission.

the first three problems were resolved by a teacher and the related staff serving a group of middle school students with severe handicaps in San Francisco (Sailor et al., 1986).] Even if little community instruction is employed, *teachers are obligated, at the very minimum, to test* in vivo *for skill generalization*, because the research proves that there is need for concern. We feel it is best to assume that some (if not a lot of) community-based instruction is warranted for students having severe handicaps. Further, the initial conversion frustrations appear both to be worth the efforts and to lessen over time. Finally, there are adequate demonstrations of community-based teaching (both in urban and less populated areas) to indicate it is feasible as well as desirable (Freagon et al., 1983; Hamre-Nietupski, Nietupski, Bates, & Maurer, 1982; Sailor et al., 1986; Quirk & Janssen, 1984).

Partial and Full Participation

The teacher must decide with input from the ecological inventory, student, the parents, and related school personnel whether the goal will be independent performance of a skill or activity or partial performance. At times, students will not have enough time left in their school program to learn a skill in an unadapted form, or the skill will be too difficult in its academic demands or its movement or sensory skill requirements. If such a difficult skill has been designated as being "highly needed and age-appropriate," then the teacher will adapt or simplify the skill in some way so that it can be taught. This practice of teaching partial participation (addressed more fully in Chapter 4) will affect most domestic and community skills, although in varying degrees.

The most extensive degree of partial participation involving *personal assistance* is illustrated by teaching a child with extensive cerebral palsy to raise and hold out her arm during tub bathing and again during drying and dressing. The task may be completed more efficiently and the student has a role more active than simply being passively washed, dried, and dressed. In a similar way, Snell, Houghton, and Lewis (1985) adapted toothbrushing, rinsing, and face wiping tasks, and introduced personal assistance on some steps so that three students with movement difficulty could partially participate. The task analyses for the skills (Table 14.2) were developed with input from students' therapists and others familiar with the students and practices of partial participation. Once the targeted

TABLE 14.2 Task analyses of partial participation in toothbrushing

Toothbrushing

1. Open your mouth wide.
2. Keep it open (5 seconds).
   Teacher: a. Brushes outside of upper left teeth back to front.
   b. Brushes cutting edge of upper left teeth back to front.
3. Close your mouth (lips touch).
4. Open your mouth wide.
5. Keep it open (5 seconds).
   Teacher: a. Brushes outside of lower left teeth back to front.
   b. Brushes cutting edge of lower left teeth back to front.
6. Close your mouth (lips touch).
7. Open your mouth wide.
8. Keep it open (5 seconds).
   Teacher: a. Brushes outside of upper right teeth back to front.
   b. Brushes cutting edge of upper right teeth back to front.
9. Close your mouth (lips touch).
10. Open your mouth wide.
11. Keep it open (5 seconds).
    Teacher: a. Brushes outside of lower right teeth back to front.
    b. Brushes cutting edge of lower right teeth back to front.
12. Close your mouth (lips touch).

Rinsing

Teacher: Squirts water into the student's mouth.
1. Drop your head (chin to chest, until student spits).
2. Spit (drops water into the bowl).
3. Lift your head up.

Wiping

Teacher: Holds paper towel at the middle of the student's mouth.
1. Turn your head to the right (midline to cheek and back to midline).
2. Turn your head to the left (midline to cheek and back to midline).

Source: From *Teaching Students with Severe Handicaps to Partially Participate in Toothbrushing* by M.E. Snell, A. Houghton, and A.P. Lewis, 1986. Manuscript submitted for publication.

skill steps were learned, the student was expected to perform those steps alone but continued to receive assistance on the steps designated as "teacher steps." During a school year, two students mastered all three skills, while the other student learned the toothbrushing skill and made some progress on face wiping.

Other versions of partial participation simplify the skill by including changes in the manner or order in which a task is performed or the materials or methods that are used. If students require extra time to change into their gym clothes or bathing suits or need to lie on a mat to change clothes, they might change before going to the beach or be allowed extra time in the locker room. Numerous examples of materials modification exist, which allow partial or even full participation in the domestic and community domains. Frozen, fried chicken is easier and faster to prepare than a whole uncooked chicken; bus passes or tokens avoid having to count money. Many of these materials or methods simplifications are referred to as *prosthetic devices* that either help by-pass altogether, or reduce, the amount of reading or math skills needed to participate in a task. Although examples of such prosthetic devices are described later in this chapter, the following chapter more fully addresses the selection of prosthetic aids to avoid or limit academic skill instruction.

Full or independent participation of a domestic or community "skill" invariably requires the interrelated performance of *many* skills, not just the independent performance of a single skill. Whereas it is true that many of these skills may be simplified as just described, skilled performance ultimately means the student must "put it all together" and sequence many skills to complete an entire activity. Restaurant use includes many separate skills or skill chains that vary depending upon the restaurant chosen: initiates, selects restaurant, uses transportation, enters restaurant, selects food, orders, makes monetary transactions, seats self, eats, disposes of trash, uses bathroom as needed, uses proper social behavior, performs at appropriate speed, engages in problem solving, leaves restaurant, uses return transportation. Even if all or most of these separate skills or skill chains are performed in an adapted manner (personal assistance, use of prosthetic device), the student must finally learn to sequence the related parts of the activity. Regardless of the targeted level of independence, when instruction stops before students can combine the component skills in an activity, the value the isolated skills will have for the student may be questioned.

Self-Management and Maintenance

Domestic and community skills share several characteristics that make them especially appropriate for self-management strategies. Most nonhandicapped adults manage their daily routines through various self-management procedures (making lists and checking off completed tasks, scheduling leisure activities after chores are completed, taking a few minutes to observe and evaluate the results of cleaning a room). The self-management research literature provides examples of ways in which independent performance, generalization, and maintenance have been enhanced by these techniques (Bates, Renzaglia, & Clees, 1980; Baer, Holman, Stokes, Fowler, & Rowbury, 1981; Fantuzzo & Clement, 1981). Whereas this research has often been focused upon people who are nonhandicapped or mildly handicapped, applications to people with severe handicaps can be made (Browder & Shapiro, 1986). It is unnecessary to wait for skill mastery or for an individual to reach some "prerequisite" level of generalized skills to introduced self-management. Rather, these procedures may be introduced at various stages of instruction to enhance the learning and performance of daily living skills. Whenever introduced, self-management strategies invite the learner to have more control over her own daily routine.

Independent or self-managed performance of a skill is critical when the activity is typically performed alone. Often in early acquisition, a person with severe handicaps is given extensive teacher-provided help that later is faded. Several systematic prompting techniques with built-in fading rules have been used in teaching daily living skills, including a least-to-most intrusive prompt system (Johnson & Cuvo, 1981; Williams & Cuvo, 1986), a most-to-least intrusive prompt system (Cuvo, Jacobi, & Sipko, 1981), time-delay fading of a single prompt (Snell, 1982), and a less specific confirmation prompt for maintenance training (Cuvo, et al., 1981; Johnson & Cuvo, 1981). (Chapter 5 describes these procedures.) The choice of prompting and fading techniques will depend on the learner and the task to be taught. The teacher should select a technique that provides *no more help than is essential* to correct performance. To accomplish this end may mean that several instructional procedures are used, such as those implemented by Cuvo et al. (1981), in which the least intrusive prompt is provided for less difficult steps of a task, the most intrusive prompt is introduced only for steps with high error potential or dangerous steps (use of a butcher knife), and *nonspecific* prompts ("What's next?") are used for review. When a prompt is introduced before the student's response for the purpose of reducing errors, it may be faded using time delay or through a prompt hierarchy (Chapter 5).

While these teacher-delivered prompting procedures have been used effectively across many skills, the teacher may also wish to consider two alternatives that may minimize his assistance in early learning. One way is to build prompts into the naturally occurring cues in the environment. The other way is to involve the learner in her own instruction. Rusch and his colleagues successfully taught two young women to first ask themselves questions about which table bussing tasks needed completion, then to answer the questions, and quietly self-instruct as a means of monitoring their own work performance (Rusch, Morgan, Martin, Riva, & Agran, 1985). Ford and Mirenda (1984) recommend building prompts into the naturally occurring cues by emphasizing the salient features of natural cues (pointing to the wrinkles in made bed rather than physically prompting the student to smooth them out), and by using nonspecific prompts ("What's next?"). Some ideas for emphasizing natural cues are (a) color-coding possessions, thermostats, oven knobs; (b) using material placement as a cue, such as hanging together a complete, matching outfit of clothes; (c) amplifying natural auditory cues, such as traffic sounds, by use of a tape recorder during simulated practice sessions; and (d) using unrelated, naturally occurring events as cues (a reminder that the evening television news has begun in order to prompt dinner preparation).

Sometimes generalization and maintenance demands may be minimized through giving careful attention to natural cues and corrections (Falvey, Brown, Lyon, Baumgart, & Schroeder, 1980). Livi and Ford (1985) demonstrated that the transfer of domestic skills from a nonschool training site to the student's home was best when the teacher replicated natural home cues in the training site. One student, who had been trained to toast bread, failed to locate the bread when tested on the skill at home; however, when the training site replicated the family's practice of keeping the bread in the refrigerator instead of the breadbox, he transferred the skill to his home without any training in the home. Thus, when a teacher both notes the natural task cues and teaches students to use them, long-term skill use is facilitated.

Independence may also be fostered early in learning through self-instruction. Many adults use written aids to assist their daily routines (telephone directory, recipe books, package instructions, clothing care labels, clocks, calendars). Picture instruc-

tions provide an excellent tool for learners with severe handicaps to assist themselves in learning their routines (see Figure 14.1). Pictures may be used to follow the steps to perform a task such as food preparation (Martin, Rusch, James, Decker, & Trytol, 1982; Schleien, Ash, Kiernan, & Wehman, 1981), to set up a job (Wacker & Berg, 1984), or to manage daily or weekly schedules for work, housekeeping, or grooming (Connis, 1979; Sowers, Rusch, Connis, & Cummings, 1980; Spellman, DeBriere, Jarboe, Campbell, & Harris, 1978; Thinesen & Bryan, 1981). Whenever prosthetic aids, such as picture recipes or schedules, are considered for a teaching program, the disadvantages (their preparation, loss, size, and obstrusiveness) must be compared to their advantages for promoting self-management.

Self-management may also be introduced for generalization and maintenance of learned tasks. Browder, Hines, McCarthy, and Fees (1984) found that instruction booklets assisted generalization to new materials. Bauman and Iwata (1977) used self-scheduling to enhance long-term maintenance of housekeeping by two adults with mild handicaps. Self-reinforcement, self-recording, and self-evaluation are other strategies that may enhance generalization across time (Shapiro, 1981).

Validating Procedures and Results

Planning daily living skill instruction and writing task analyses may require more knowledge of community or domestic skills than the teacher has. In planning food preparation programs, the teacher needs to consider each student's medical dietary restrictions, if any, and be able to plan nutritionally balanced, economical meals. Consultation with a home economics teacher can help in developing the content of instruction. For example, Johnson and Cuvo (1981), Cuvo et al. (1981), and Cronin and Cuvo (1979) asked a professor of home economics, who had experience with developmentally disabled clients, to review task analyses for mending, washing, cooking, and some finished products (food) of their programs. Snell (1982) checked bed-making procedures and the completed bed with ward staff to be sure they would find the quality of bed-making worthy of praise after training. Consultation with experts (home economists, veteran bed-makers on housekeeping staff or fire fighters) is one way to validate the *procedures* socially (examining the task analyses for accuracy) and the *results* of the program (judging the quality of a

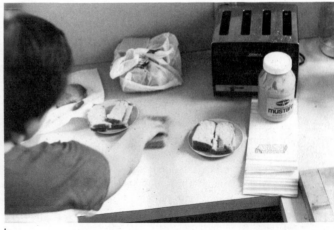

b

a

FIGURE 14.1 Cindy makes two meat sandwiches, one for her lunch and one for a classmate, which allows her twice the practice. She uses the pictures as a reminder for each step. Here she is shown as she cuts the sandwich in half (a) and later (b) during clean-up.

Credit must be given to Carolyn Warren, Bonnie Ruth and the Community Based Instructional Program of the Albemarle County Public Schools of Charlottesville, Virginia.

sandwich, a made bed, or the adequacy of fire escape performance) (Cuvo, 1978; Kazdin, 1977; Williams & Cuvo, 1986).

Another technique of social validation, *normative comparisons*, also can be useful (Kazdin, 1977). For example, before teaching clothing matching to women with severe and profound retardation, Nutter and Reid (1978) observed women in public settings to determine the most popular color combinations. This permitted them to teach color combinations that actually were popular in that area. Norm comparison is useful when defining specific grooming tasks (hair styling), household chores (identifying chores performed by the same age group), and use of community resources (popular restaurants or leisure settings for young adults). Also, an evaluation of the student's mastery might be based, in part, on comparison with nonhandicapped peers for skills such as restaurant manners and bus riding.

Program Expense

Domestic and community skill programs can be especially expensive because of the materials required. Several program variations can cut expenses without threatening quality. The most obvious way to minimize program expense is to select the most economical (though still *nonsimulated*) materials available (generic laundry detergent, economical menus). Savings also can result from reuse of materials with stimulus properties that are *not* changed by performance of a task. Johnson and Cuvo (1981) reused eggs to teach boiling over several sessions. The clients of Schleien, et al. (1981) practiced baking a foil-covered, but empty, TV dinner tray.

Further savings may be realized when the teacher uses real or nonsimulated training equipment already present in the community, instead of requesting new school purchases or constructing costly simulations. Using laundromats provides obvious initial savings, although transportation costs and the expense of their repeated use may gradually offset these savings. Transportation costs may be kept low by careful scheduling, use of public transportation, school bus drop off and pick up at community sites, and training multiple skills at fewer sites (Hamre-Nietupski, et al., 1982). Other costs can be offset by using funds normally budgeted for text book and teaching materials by recruiting donation of materials, and purchasing materials in bulk. By using small group as well as one-to-one instruction, the teacher can use time and available staff more efficiently. Small group instruction also may increase motivation, provide peer models, and enhance generalization (Brown, Holvoet, Guess, & Mulligan, 1980). The effectiveness of group instruction appears to depend on the task and group arrangement (Alberto, Jobes, Sizemore, & Doran, 1980; Brown et al., 1980). Whereas most published research on domestic and community skills has not involved group instruction, there are some successful demonstrations of group instruction in vending machine use (Browder et al., 1984), grocery shopping (Matson, 1981), accident prevention (Matson, 1980), and showering (Matson, DiLorenzo, & Esveldt-Dawson, 1981).

Smith and Meyers (1979) found small group instruction (five students with severe retardation) more effective than one-to-one instruction in teaching telephone skills. In contrast, Alberto et al. (1980) found group instruction less effective than one-to-one in teaching dressing, but equally effective for tasks taught at a table. Most domestic and community skills do not lend themselves to tabletop instruction; thus, when using group instruction, the teacher will need to organize the students and materials to ensure that all can observe each action clearly. Involving students in the presentations of instructional requests, prompts, and even dispensing reinforcers to peers in the group, will facilitate learning (Matson, 1980, 1981; Matson et al., 1981).

DOMESTIC DOMAIN

Domestic skill instruction is discussed in five categories: food preparation, personal maintenance, housekeeping, telephone use, and handling and preventing home accidents. Because the steps in program development and implementation in these skill categories (as well as in community skill categories) will have many similarities, the first section

(on food preparation) will address program planning in more detail in order to illustrate the preinstruction steps to take. For the remaining categories of domestic skills, the focus is limited to the instructional implications of existing research.

Food Preparation Skills

Some food preparation skills will be a priority for many daily-living-skills programs for several reasons (Johnson & Cuvo, 1981). First, being able to prepare snacks, sack lunches, and even meals enhances independent living (Crnic & Pym, 1979; Schalock & Harper, 1978). The alternatives to cooking—eating in restaurants or hiring a cook—can be quite expensive. Also, meal preparation provides survival, as well as social, benefits if the student cooks for family and friends; for some students, cooking might provide an employment alternative.

The development of a food preparation program is similar to other daily-living-skills programs (see Table 14.3). The teacher must ensure that the product is nutritious, is edible, does not violate any dietary restrictions, and is liked by the student. Also, kitchen utensils and appliances must be used both skillfully and safely. Related skills such as hand washing, food storage, and trash disposal are also necessary for healthy food preparation. The discussion below addresses these unique needs but also provides a general example of the planning and implementation process for any daily living skills program.

Ecological Inventory for Food Preparation

To determine what food preparation skills a student requires, the teacher must obtain information on the student and her environment. Table 14.4 illustrates an inventory completed for John, an 18-year-old student who lives with his parents. John's teacher surveyed his current and future environments to determine what food preparation skills were required in each setting and those he could not perform. Table 14.4 is the inventory for John's current home environment. The teacher also completed an inventory for a future group home and a convenience store. These inventories were used to make a curriculum chart. The curriculum chart is shown in Table 14.5

As the curriculum chart indicates, the two group homes for which he was eligible and on the waiting lists *did* require some basic skills in meal prepara-

TABLE 14.3 An outline for planning, implementing, and evaluating a food preparation program

1. Ecological Inventories for Task Selection
   a. Parents, practices and preferences
   b. Skills performed for or required of the student currently and in future
   c. Student's current skills and preferences
   d. Medical/diet considerations (doctor, dietician)

2. Scheduling
   a. Group and/or individual
   b. Prior to meals or as a snack
   c. Clean up time is included

3. Instructional Program
   A. Preparation Phase
      1. Task analyze skill and obtain a validation from a home economist (or other expert) and those who will require skill (group home)
      2. Secure materials, ready appliances (adapt as needed)
      3. Select recipe (make cards)
      4. Outline prompting technique
      5. Outline consequences and preparation (make histograms, secure tokens, etc.)
      6. Make data sheets with TA, scoring, and graphs
   B. Baseline Assessment
      1. Procedure specified
      2. Stable performance obtained
   C. Acquisition/Generalization
      1. Individual or group using procedures planned
      2. Daily data/update graph
      3. Teacher-delivered reinforcement thinned
      4. Self-reinforcement introduced
      5. Less specific prompts used in review sessions
      6. Self-cuing (pictures) introduced now or earlier
      7. Generalization probed now or earlier
      8. A new setting used (group home)
      9. Similar skills (new recipe cards with same words) are probed and taught as needed
   D. Program Evaluation
      1. Did learning occur? how efficiently?
      2. Cost?
      3. Social validation of learner's terminal performance?
      4. Generalization/maintenance probes?

tion (as shown with asteriks in Table 14.5). In addition, group home staff listed other more advanced skills (not marked with an asterisk) which would be needed, but which could be taught after entry into the home. The teacher had easy access to a nearby convenience store where food purchasing could be taught during the school day. Next, the teacher interviewed the clerk at the 7-Eleven store and watched other shoppers to find out what skills were required there. Subsequently, she watched John at the store and noted in Table 14.4 that he could

only consume purchased items (though he did so *in* the store), and carry purchases back to his dorm, but he could not perform any of the other listed skills. The teacher also talked to John's parents. Although they did not let him help prepare food because of his lack of skills, they were eager for him to learn these tasks. So the teacher noted various family food preparation activities.

The teacher repeated this ecological inventory for each of the students in her class. Before selecting which skills would be taught, she obtained other information on the students, summarized in Table 14.5. She consulted the students' records, their parents, and the institution's dietitian to determine dietary restrictions. She observed the clients at mealtime and talked to their parents to ascertain food preferences. She listed this information along with the student's current skills on the same chart (Table 14.4). She then identified three or four skills as priorities for instruction. The criteria used for establishing priorities included (a) student, parent, and staff preference (for John these were cleaning up and making things to eat); (b) skills that would be used in the future as well as at present (preparation of bag lunch, snacks, and clean up); (c) the student's chronological age (most nonhandicapped 13-year-olds prepare snacks, though not all prepare entire meals); (d) the importance (and comparable ease) of maintenance training as well as acquisition of new skills (independent sweeping); (e) skills that several students needed to enable the teacher to use group instruction (make drinks); (f) tasks that included other target skills for the student (fine motor, counting, matching); (g) good items that were economical and met diet restrictions (use of low-salt crackers and peanut butter, diet drink mix); and (h) skills that could be taught in the current environment (bag lunch and snack preparation being more feasible than meal cooking). These priority skills are noted in Table 14.6.

Scheduling

The next step in developing the program is to schedule time for teaching. To promote generalization, the teacher planned to teach the skills in the settings in which they would be used; however, the cafeteria was often confusing and noisy. The teacher decided to leave the classroom early at the end of each day and use the cafeteria when it was fairly quiet. An afternoon snack would be prepared and eaten there, allowing instruction in a realistic setting. Two students (Harold and Betty) capable of

TABLE 14.4 Ecological inventory of food preparation

Student: John   Date Began: 9/15/85

Current Environment ___✓___   Future Environment _____

1. *Description of Environment:*
   John lives in a ranch-style home with his parents and an older sister. The kitchen has a table that is at the correct height for John's wheelchair. The counters and sink are not within his reach. The refrigerator door handle is within reach.

2. *Activities of Nonhandicapped peers:*
   John's sister (Carla) is 15. Carla can make most breakfast or lunch menus the famiy typically has. She usually prepares the afternoon and evening snacks for John and the family which include peanut butter and crackers, popcorn, sliced apples, juice, or granola bars. Although it is her chore, Carla does not usually clean up after preparing the snack. She does wash the dinner dishes with her father.

3. *Behaviors Which Cannot be Tolerated in the Setting:*
   John's mother does not want John to use a sharp knife or glass container because of his lack of skill with utensils and throwing objects. John's mother and father emphasize *clean hands* and do not want a messy kitchen.

4. *Student and Family Preferences and Customs:*
   John loves popcorn and dislikes apples. He is allergic to chocolate. John's parents limit sweets and desserts to special occasions.

5. *Ideas for Instruction:*
   —Using the hot air pumper on the table to make popcorn for the family or class at school.
   —Spreading skills with dull knife. Begin with peanut butter on hard crackers and progress to crackers that crumble more easily.
   —Deceleration of throwing through frequent, social attention by teacher, family, and peers for incompatible, alternative behavior of making a snack.
   —Pouring. Begin with small pitcher and small amount of liquid. Fade in pitcher size and volume of liquid.

---

sweeping and table washing, but who needed regular practice to become more efficient, helped the cafeteria staff clean up after the noon meal.

Instructional Program

Writing Task Analyses The next step in the process is to plan an instructional program. First, each skill needs to be analyzed (refer to Chapter 4). Johnson and Cuvo (1981) developed a task analysis using comprehensive validation. To determine what foods to teach and how to prepare them, they consulted cookbooks, people in the community with cooking skills, the students' parents, a professor of home economics who had experience with the developmentally disabled, and the students themselves. In addition, the range of convenience foods available commercially (frozen, pre-made foods and mixes) was investigated so that simple options could be considered. Next, they gathered the necessary materials and watched three people perform the food preparation tasks. Written task analyses were developed and reviewed by the group-home staff and the home economics professor. Their feedback was used to further refine the tasks. Although these steps may seem rather involved, the quality of the task analysis is important because it determines exactly what will be taught and evaluated.

Task analyses may be further modified at this point to suit particular students, then validated again through actual field testing. For example, if the teacher plans to use a recipe, it should be selected and perhaps adapted for the student's picture or reading skills, motor skills (use of jig to open lid by physically handicapped student), and dietary restrictions (substitute another seasoning for salt). The practice of teaching students to perform portions or adapted versions of tasks will allow more students to gain some level of task independence and participation. (Chapter 4 elaborates upon this concept of partial participation.) For example, Aaron who is now 12, is being taught to accompany an

TABLE 14.5 Curriculum chart for food preparation

Student: __John__   Date Began: __9/15/85__

I. Current Environment
Place: Classroom/Cafeteria of school

Activity 1. Meal Clean Up

Performance	Skills
Partial	1. Dispose of trash, garbage, and dirty dishes
Partial	2. Wipe table

Activity 2. Snack Preparation

Performance	Skills
?	1. Pour drink (juice, ice tea)
?	2. Select snack materials (popcorn, peanut butter sandwich, cheese toast, peanut butter and crackers)
?	3. Make snack: popcorn
?	4. Make snack: peanut butter sandwich
No	5. Make snack: peanut butter and crackers
Partial	6. Serve snack
No	7. Wipe table

II. Current and Future Environment
Place: 7-Eleven Convenience Store

Activity 1. Buy Drink and Snack

Performance	Skills
Partial	1. Enter/leave store
No	2. Select drink
No	3. Select snack
No	4. Pay for items at counter

Activity 2. Buy Food to Fix Snacks

Performance	Skills
Partial	1. Enter store
?	2. Use picture list
No	3. Select drink mix
No	4. Select snack materials
No	5. Pay for items at counter

III. Current and Future Environment
Place: Parent's Home

Activity 1. Snack Preparation

Performance	Skills
No	1. Pour drink
No	2. Fix popcorn
No	3. Fix peanut butter and crackers
No	4. Serve snack
No	5. Clean up table
Partial	6. Wash hands
No	7. Decelerate throwing

Activity 2. Mealtime

Performance	Skills
?	1. Set table
No	2. Pour beverages
No	3. Wipe table

IV. Future Environment
Place: Group Homes

Activity 1. * *Snack Preparation*

Performance	Skills
?	*1. Make drink
?	*2. Fix popcorn
?	*3. Fix cheese and crackers
?	*4. Fix instant pudding
?	*5. Serve snack
?	*6. Clean up counter

Activity 2. ** *Prepare Sack Lunch*

Performance	Skills
?	**1. Gets sandwich materials
?	**2. Makes sandwich
?	**3. Puts materials away
?	**4. Packages and bags sandwich
?	**5. Selects fruit
?	**6. Selects prewrapped item (chips, granola bar, etc.)
?	**7. Cleans up counter

Activity 3. Meal Preparation

Performance	Skills
?	1. Make drink
?	2. Fix simple main course
?	3. Set table
?	4. Pour drinks
?	5. Serve food
?	6. Clear table
?	7. Wash table
?	8. Clean up leftovers

Activity 4. Grocery Shopping

Performance	Skills
?	1. Enter store
?	2. Use picture list
?	3. Select listed items
?	4. Pay at checkout

Key:
*Entry skill for one group home
**Entry skill for both group homes
Partial: observed to perform part of skill; training needed
?: probably cannot perform, unknown
No: cannot perform in that setting

TABLE 14.6 Task selection worksheet for planning group instruction in food preparation

Client's Name	John	Harold	Betty	Dale
1. Dietary Restrictions	chocolate sweets	calories (weight) problem)	low salt	none
2. Food Preferences	popcorn	sweets and all foods	pudding peanut butter apples	chocolate
3. Current Food Preparation Skills	none	1. Open food containers 2. Sweep floor (but needs reminders to finish) 3. Serve food	1. Clean table 2. Sweep floor 3. Pour drinks 4. Serve food	1. Serve food 2. Open food containers 3. Set snack table
4. Skills Needed (based on ecological inventory)	1. Make popcorn 2. Spread peanut butter to participate in lunch preparation 3. Select fruit 4. Clean up	1. Make drink from mix 2. Fix various snacks 3. Pour drinks 4. Clean up	1. Make and bag sandwich 2. Select and bag fruit 3. Select and bag other lunch items 4. Make drink from mix 5. Fix various snacks 6. Open food containers 7. Set table	1. Make drink from mix 2. Fix various snacks 3. Clean up

adult into a 7-Eleven by pushing open the door, not bumping into others, selecting a bag of chips, laying it on the counter, waiting for the parent or teacher to pay, and then leaving the store with them. The store-use task analysis reflects partial rather than full participation. Independence in paying is *not* an objective, but competence in quietly accompanying an adult or peer is a realistic objective for Aaron.* The task has been simplified through partial participation.

Eileen is 15 and is very restricted in voluntary movements. She has a reliable means of communicating "yes" and "no" to questions, though a more efficient electronic communication board is not usable outside the home or school building. One of her targeted community skills includes participation in developing a picture shopping list and in selecting the needed items from the store. Although her parents hope that a group home setting will one day make use of this skill, they plan to have Eileen assist in family grocery planning and shopping. In total time, shopping and menu planning takes somewhat longer when Eileen participates, but she eats much better because she has helped select the food, and she eagerly and happily goes shopping because she has a role in the activity and does not have to be left at home due to excessive whining in the store. As with Aaron, the task analyses developed to teach Eileen to help develop a picture menu and to select needed items in the grocery are personalized to suit: (a) her motor limitations (no reach or grasp, use of a wheelchair); (b) her communication mode in the school or at home (use of electronic board) and at the store (yes/no); (c) her and her family's food tastes, budget, and manner of shopping. Thus, to develop the task analyses, the teacher consulted Eileen's parents, spoke with her speech and physical therapists, and surveyed the grocery stores near the school and home. The draft versions of the task analyses were tried out and revised until they seemed satisfactory to all involved.

*The 7-Eleven task analyses were developed by Shara Walters and Trice Lewis for students served by the Community Integration Project (under the direction of Arlene Aveno), University of Virginia and Albemarle County Public Schools, Charlottesville, Va.

Cookbooks and Recipe Pictures Due to the requirements of measuring skills and reading on at least a third grade level, the use of children's cookbooks with students having severe handicaps generally is ineffective. Some cookbooks have been written specifically for students with moderate handicaps (Kahn, 1974; Staples, 1975; Steed, 1974; Yates, 1972). As Robinson-Wilson (1977) noted, these cookbooks may also be too difficult for some handicapped students because they require number recognition and a sight-word vocabulary and because they sometimes require several steps in response to one picture.

For many students, simplified teacher-made picture recipes might be the best alternative to cookbooks, though neither is essential for effective instruction. An advantage of using picture cards might be that students could recall more recipes without total reliance on memory, as we do when using a cookbook. Disadvantages include possible loss of skills if the picture cards are damaged or misplaced. Robinson-Wilson (1977) used teacher-made picture recipes to teach the preparation of gelatin, hot dogs, and hot chocolate to three adults with severe retardation. The pictures were drawn on 5″ × 8″ cards joined with two rings at the top. The first card contained a large color picture of the product; the next illustrated the equipment and food items to be set out; later ones illustrated the recipe, with three steps per card. Color-coding was used for the stove burners and measuring utensils to simplify appliance use and measurement skills. The cards were plastic-coated and displayed on a wooden stand. Although Robinson-Wilson's (1977) findings suggested the effectiveness of this system, the results were inconclusive due to a lack of experimental control (no baseline). Johnson and Cuvo (1981) and Martin et al. (1982) did establish experimental control in demonstrating the effectiveness of picture recipes for teaching food preparation to adults with mild-to-moderate retardation. Their studies suggested both effective materials and teaching techniques.

Teaching Procedures Using a single subject design, Johnson and Cuvo (1981) taught several cooking skills to four adults with moderate and mild handicaps in a sheltered workshop. The recipe cards had both written instructions and equivalent illustrations. The cooking skills taught were boiling eggs and vegetables, baking cornbread and biscuits, and broiling hot dogs and English muffins.

Before each training session, the teacher readied the necessary materials and appliances (moving oven rack for broiling). During the session the teacher gave the participant the recipe and asked her to prepare that food item ("Using this recipe, bake the cornbread"). The student was permitted to initiate each step of the recipe independently. If the step was not begun, the teacher prompted the cooking behavior, using the least intrusive prompt necessary in the following order:

1. *Verbal Instruction*—The teacher verbalized the step ("Set the timer for 5 minutes");
2. *Verbal Instruction + Visual Cue*—The teacher repeated the verbal cue with a visual cue, such as pointing to the equipment used or simulating the stimulus property for step completion (blowing through a straw in a pan of water to simulate boiling);
3. *Verbal Instruction + Modeling*—The teacher performed the step while verbalizing it;
4. *Verbal Instruction + Physical Guidance*—The teacher physically guided the student while repeating the step ("See how we pull out the oven rack").

In addition to praise during training, after a session students received verbal and graphic feedback by filling in a bar graph that displayed the number of steps completed without prompting.

Maintenance was provided through review sessions. During review, additional *confirmation* (the subject stated what came next and the trainer confirmed it) and a *nonspecific prompt* ("What's next?") were given. The consequences and materials used were the same as in acquisition training.

The study's results supported this procedure; the students improved in their performance of each subtask only after training. All four students reached the criterion of independent performance of all steps in each task. Generalization to untrained tasks occurred for three of the four students for both similar cooking processes (boiling eggs transferred to boiling vegetables) as well as for dissimilar cooking processes (improved performance on biscuit baking after mastering hot dog broiling). Only one or two review sessions were required for skill maintenance. The foods prepared by the students were rated by the home economist as being edible, and the cost of the program was fairly modest: including the materials and trainer wages, the cost for each student ranged from $36.63 to $60.06, and testing cost an additional $30.00 per student.

Further support for the benefit of using a recipe was found by Martin et al. (1982). They compared cooking performance with verbal instruction and feedback to performance with this help plus picture recipe cards to assess the effectiveness of the recipe cards themselves. In contrast to Johnson and Cuvo (1981), who recruited adults with mild-to-moderate retardation, Martin et al.'s students had severe handicaps. Target skills included preparing five nutritional meals (broiled fish, beans, and pudding). Training was conducted in the natural setting, the students' apartments. Black-and-white photographs bound in order were used in place of line drawings for the recipe cards, thus avoiding a lot of material preparation time. Each picture had a typed statement of the step and its number in the task analysis for the benefit of the teacher. Yellow stickers cued the student to recipes that required preparation the evening before the meal. During Martin's baseline phase, simple instruction and feedback were provided each student so that during the next phase, intervention, the added effects of the recipe cards could be compared with teacher instruction (verbal, modeling, or physical assistance) and feedback alone. Once the pictures were introduced, all subjects immediately performed a higher percentage of steps independently. The results of this study are noteworthy for several reasons. First, they demonstrated that picture-card instruction may speed learning of cooking tasks in contrast to trainer instruction and feedback alone. Second, this study taught complex meals, not just one cooking skill. Unfortunately, this study did not measure generalization or maintenance, and no social validation was reported.

In contrast, Schleien et al. (1981) did *not* use picture cards to cue cooking responses and still were successful in teaching three cooking tasks to a woman with profound retardation. The woman, who lived at home, had no past training in cooking but reportedly enjoyed watching others cook. In a multiple baseline design across skills, she learned to boil an egg, broil an English muffin with cheese, and bake a TV dinner (Table 14.7). As in earlier cooking studies, a system of least intrusive prompts was used to teach the 10 to 14 steps in each of the three task analyses. The subject not only mastered the three skills but also generalized performance to her own home and to another community day facility. When asked to bake and boil other foods, she generalized adequately on most of the steps, although she was unable to generalize the broiling

skill to another food. Schleien et al. (1981) demonstrated that pictures were not essential in teaching cooking skills, though systematic teaching certainly was.

Personal Maintenance

A second area of domestic skills is personal maintenance. Maintenance of personal health and appearance is critical to securing a job and being accepted in the community. A training program here will incorporate the principles we have already discussed. One unique concern to grooming is the consideration of personal preferences as well as peer norms in determining what to teach. Non-handicapped persons vary greatly in their clothing and hair styles, and the person with handicaps should also have choices in these areas and usually will have preferences. However, certain jobs and communities may have a low tolerance for some styles. If the student prefers or must secure a job that has dress guidelines, these norms will need to be taught.

Acquisition of Grooming

Hairwashing Grooming skills are an extension of basic self-help skills. Usually nonhandicapped persons learn grooming later than basic self-help skills, sometime between the ages 6 and 16 depending upon the skill. One example of a grooming program was described by Hamre (1974). She taught hairwashing to 39 adolescents with moderate retardation, some of whom had been labeled *aphasic, autistic,* and *cerebral palsied.* The students were grouped in classes of 11, 13, and 15 students with a teacher, student teacher, and aide. Only two students actually received instruction during each session because of the length of the task and the limited number of sinks. The teacher conducted a baseline assessment once for each student before training. In training, the teacher first modeled the entire procedure on herself, while describing it verbally. Then a student was asked to wash her hair. Each step performed correctly was praised; each error was corrected with modeling or physical assistance. By the end of the school year, 32 of 39 students met criterion (3 consecutive errorless trials) on the hairwashing task. In discussing the results, Hamre noted that this important skill required extensive teaching time to attain mastery and thus recommended that instruction begin during the preteen years.

TABLE 14.7   Task analyses for three cooking skills

I. Boiling Egg
Performance Objective: Given the appropriate cooking materials and kitchen stove (top burner), the participant will boil
                the egg until hardboiled with 100% proficiency on two consecutive days.
Verbal Cue: "Heidi, boil the egg."
  1. Place egg in saucepan without breaking it.
  2. Lift saucepan off stove with nondominant hand, using palmar grasp, and position directly under water faucet.
  3. Turn water on with dominant hand to fill sauce pan one-half full and turn water off.
  4. Place saucepan onto the top stove burner.
  5. Turn burner on underneath saucepan.
  6. Set electric timer for 15 minutes.
  7. Wait for timer to ring.
  8. Turn burner off.
  9. Remove egg from saucepan using slotted spoon.
 10. Place egg in bowl.

II. Broiling English Muffin and Cheese
Performance Objective: Given the appropriate cooking materials and kitchen stove (broiler), the participant will broil the
                English muffin and cheese with 100% proficiency on two consecutive days.
Verbal Cue: "Heidi, broil the English muffin and cheese."
  1. Place slice of cheese on English muffin half.
  2. Place prepared muffin onto oven tray.
  3. Open broiler door.
  4. Place tray on top rack in oven.
  5. Close broiler door three-quarters way to first stop position.
  6. Turn oven knob all the way to "broil."
  7. Set electric timer for five mintues.
  8. Wait for timer to ring.
  9. Turn broiler off.
 10. Place gloved pot holder on each hand.
 11. Open broiler door.
 12. Pull oven rack out half-way exposing oven tray.
 13. Remove tray from broiler (with palm facing upward) and place on stove top.
 14. Close broiler door.

III. Baking TV Dinner
Performance Objective: Given the appropriate cooking materials and kitchen stove (oven), the participant will bake the TV
                dinner with 100% proficiency on two consecutive days.
Verbal Cue: "Heidi, bake the TV dinner."
  1. Remove dinner from carton.
  2. Open oven door using nondominant hand and place TV dinner on bottom rack.
  3. Close oven door all the way.
  4. Turn oven temperature knob to "425°."
  5. Set electric timer for 40 minutes.
  6. Wait for timer to ring (participant should leave kitchen and resume other activity during this time).
  7. When timer rings, turn oven temperature knob to "off" position.
  8. Place gloved pot holder on each hand.
  9. Open oven door.
 10. Pull oven rack out half-way exposing TV dinner.
 11. Remove TV dinner from oven and place on stove top.
 12. Close oven door.

Source: From "Developing Independent Cooking Skills in a Profoundly Retarded Woman" by S. J. Schleien, T. Ash, J. Kiernan, and P. Wehman, 1981, *Journal of the Association for the Severely Handicapped, 6,* p. 26. Copyright 1981 by the Journal of the Association for the Severely Handicapped. Reprinted by permission.

Showering   The task of showering or bathing is central to routine hygiene, regardless of how handicapped an individual is. How the skill can be taught while still respecting instructor and student privacy is an issue teachers must be concerned with if showering skills are of priority.

Matson et al. (1981) worked on showering with 36 adult residents of a state institution scheduled for placement in the community. After analyzing the tasks of showering, drying, and applying deodorant into a 27-step chain, students *who elected to participate* were assessed and matched by their baseline skills with control group students. All of the students had been previously assigned at random to a treatment or no-treatment condition so that the effects of the instruction could be objectively evaluated at the conclusion of the study. Next, while the no-treatment group continued to be assisted through showering by staff as usual, the treatment group received independence training from one trainer in groups of five.

The procedure involved the residents in the teaching process; they were asked to praise other's successes, to prompt others verbally on steps they knew, and to evaluate their own performance routinely. In addition, the trainer commented on or corrected the accuracy of all self-evaluations. Finally, at the beginning of each training session, the trainer modeled all the steps, although the water was not turned on and the trainer remained dressed. After 4 months of hourly group training sessions 5 days a week, the treatment group clearly demonstrated more gains on the posttest and on a follow-up measure 3 months later. Average time required to master showering was 15 weeks, but varied across students from 3 to 16 weeks. Both the independence methods and the efficient group training format were responsible for the rapid success.

Menstrual Hygiene   Several authors have addressed the problems that develop when women are physically unable to care for themselves during menstruation or are not taught to do so (Kreutner, 1981; Richman, Reiss, Bauman, & Bailey, 1984; Vitello, 1978). Richman and her colleagues who have researched menstrual hygiene intervention procedures comment on two typical difficulties:

Two such difficulties are that the burden of responsibility often falls on family members or residential personnel who may find this duty aversive; and, because of the potential for soiling and resulting odor due to inappropriate menstrual care, outings in the community may be limited during this time. These problems have often resulted in caregivers, parents, and sometimes the handicapped individual herself requesting that menses be terminated via hysterectomy. (Richman et al., 1984, p. 441)

To avoid intrusive surgical solutions, systematic instruction of menstrual care has been recommended and described, but not fully tested until recently. Richman and her colleagues reported successful intervention with five institutionalized women, four of whom had severe retardation and

one who had mild retardation. The women were ambulatory and able to toilet themselves but were reliant on others for proper menstrual care. The three skills of changing stained underwear, changing a stained sanitary napkin, and changing both were task analyzed and taught one at a time in a forward sequence. (The task analysis for changing underwear is located in Table 14.8). Because the goal was to teach the women to respond to the natural cues of blood-stained underwear or sanitary napkins, food coloring was used on napkins and underpants during training and probes to simulate these conditions more frequently than would normally occur.

Verbal prompts were given only after the client failed to respond within 5 seconds or made an error. None of the clients required more than a verbal prompt to evoke a correct response, so modeling and physical guidance was not necessary. Once a client made an error she was verbally prompted on that step, and then she was expected to *begin the task over again and perform the sequence correctly up to and including the steps she had missed.* Once this forward chaining remedial procedure resulted in success without prompting on the difficult step, then she could progress to the next step. This approach involved forward chaining in place of the more typical teaching of all steps simultaneously as the task is performed. Although it is not evident that forward chaining was a faster method because no comparisons were made with other methods, the technique was successful and should be regarded as an alternative to whole-task instruction.

All five women learned to perform the three tasks independently after these intervention procedures were applied. Probes taken under natural conditions during their actual menstrual cycle indicated that they cared for themselves skillfully, even during a follow-up five months after training had terminated. Also, because the three tasks had many overlapping steps, the woman required very little training on skills 2 (changing stained napkin) and 3 (changing stained napkin and underwear) once they had mastered skill 1 (changing stained underwear).

Grooming Skill Maintenance

Once students learn one or two grooming skills, the focus of teaching should shift from acquisition to maintenance. Maintenance concerns include continued performance despite a reduction in rein-

TABLE 14.8 Task analysis for changing soiled underwear

1. Client walks into bathroom and closes the door.
2. Pulls down underwear below knees and sits on toilet.
3. Pulls up underwear and outerclothes.
4. Walks out of bathroom.
5. Obtains box containing underwear, sanitary napkin, plastic bag, and paper bag.
6. Walks into bathroom and closes door.
7. Washes complete surface of hands and fingers with soap and water so no dirt or residue remains visible on area, dries, throws paper towel in trash.
8. Brings box to stall, pulls down underwear below knees and sits on toilet.
9. Removes soiled underwear.
10. Places soiled underwear in plastic bag.
11. Wipes vaginal area at least once to remove residual blood and drops paper in toilet.
12. Puts on clean pair of underwear.
13. Pulls tab off clean sanitary napkin.
14. Disposes of strip in trashcan.
15. Fastens sticky side of sanitary napkin lengthwise in underwear and presses into place.
16. Pulls up underwear and outerclothes.
17. Flushes toilet.
18. Washes hands as in Step 7.
19. Exits bathroom putting soiled underwear in laundry bag and plastic bag in trash.
20. Places box in bedroom cabinet for storage.

Source: From "Teaching Menstrual Care to Mentally Retarded Women: Acquisition, Generalization, and Maintenance" by G. S. Richman, M. L. Reiss, K. E. Bauman, and J. S. Bailey, 1984, *Journal of Applied Behavior Analysis, 17,* p. 443. Copyright 1984 by the Journal of Applied Behavior Analysis. Reprinted by permission.

forcement or an absence of teaching staff to provide starting cues or corrections. In some cases students will have grooming skills but fail to use them, as Doleys, Stacy, and Knowles (1981) reported with seven clients living in one of two community-based group homes. Bathing, brushing teeth, washing hair, shaving, wearing clean clothes, and dressing appropriately were regarded as essential daily grooming skills. In the morning each client was checked, praised, and awarded tokens that could be exchanged for a variety of reinforcers. The men's faces were checked for whiskers; clothes were judged clean if pressed with no traces of dirt and stains. In order to be dressed appropriately, three criteria had to be met: (a) color and pattern were coordinated, (b) attire was suitable for weather, and (c) clothing was appropriate for daily activity (work, leisure). Whenever a target grooming skill was observed, it was recorded. Results revealed a fairly rapid improvement in grooming after the

implementation of the token program. Though not reported, it would be desirable to fade out the token reinforcement and teach the clients to respond to more natural contingencies. Instead of being given tokens, students could learn to self-monitor their appearance by checking photo charts of themselves dressed appropriately (coordinated, weather and activity suitable) in comparison to their actual appearance in the mirror. Instruction would be directed towards teaching the student to self-check on each criterion and apply self-praise or corrections as needed.

Also of concern during maintenance is the performance of an entire cluster of related skills, which may have been taught separately (getting up, using toilet, brushing teeth, showering, drying, combing hair, and dressing). Freagon and her colleagues (1983) reported the use of an actual house, rented by the school, in which students were taught to improve their rate of performance of daily living skill clusters, their handling of initiation and problem-solving during skill performance, and their ability to perform certain domestic skills during the natural use times of early morning (getting up when the alarm goes off) or late evening (preparing sack lunch for next day).

Jarman, Iwata, and Lorentzson (1983) taught completion of individual grooming skills to 40 adolescents with moderate to severe handicaps who lived in an institutional setting. Only after instituting a *chained contingency* procedure in which tokens were given for completion of *all* six skills involved in the morning routine did the students independently use the entire regimen of skills. By contrast, Snell, Houghton, and Lewis (1985) taught one toothbrushing skill at a time but programmed for maintenance as soon as one of the three toothbrushing skills—opening mouth during brushing, rinsing, and wiping mouth—was mastered. Maintenance programming consisted of having the student perform each mastered skill without help during each session, while teaching focused on the unlearned skill. Both strategies of teaching a student to perform a lengthy chain of related skills appear effective.

If the skill has been taught in realistic places using actual materials, concerns with skill generalization may be limited more to schedule changes (whether the student will use the skill at the times it is needed) and fluctuations in task materials and/or setting (soap dispenser with a crank handle versus a push button nozzle; presence of unfamiliar people or no people in a public restroom). Freagon and Rotatori (1982) contrasted the effects of *natural* training time and setting with *artificial* training time and setting on the learning, retention, and generalization of grooming skills. The adolescents who had severe handicaps mastered more skills when taught at the appropriate times and places in their group home, than when these times and places were unnatural (brushing teeth at the group home's kitchen sink in the afternoon); however, skill maintenance or generalization to a *second* setting was *not* affected by the prior training conditions. Apparently, the relevant stimuli and responses were present in both conditions and not tied to setting and time of day. Still, this study lends support to the practice of teaching at times and in places natural to the performance of the grooming skill.

Clothing Selection

Clothing selection skills follow after the basics of dressing. Although learning to put clothes on and fasten them may continue into adulthood for persons having handicaps, additional skills are needed for an acceptable appearance. These skills include selecting clothes that match in color and design, buying clothes that fit, dressing appropriately for differing places (work, sports, church), and dressing appropriately for the weather. Also, like hairstyling, clothing selection varies, depending on current styles, personal preference, and culture.

Nutter and Reid (1978) solved the problems of differences in styles by teaching the local fashion norms to women with severe and profound retardation. The five women selected for this study all had independent dressing skills but could not select matching clothes. The authors observed more than 600 women in public settings in their community to determine the most popular matches. (By contrast, teachers probably would make informal notation of the clothes worn by their students' peers without handicaps.) Nutter and Reid elected only to teach matching solids for almost half the women they observed wore no patterns. To teach clothing selection, a puzzle body with attachable clothing was used. They chose this simulated training over actual dressing because a greater number of training trials could be included in the alloted time; however, generalization was encouraged by verbal and visual reference to the clothes the women wore and reviews with actual clothes. Also, generalization probes were made of the women's selection of their own clothes. This training was successful; the

women increased their selection of popular color combinations when dressing the puzzle and themselves. To teach these skills meaningfully, teachers applying these methods need to have some of the student's actual clothing available and would be advised to test this skill intermittently at the natural morning dressing time, perhaps using a special overnight training setting as Freagon and her colleagues (1983) suggest for teaching wake-up and nighttime domestic skills.

Cleaning Clothes

In addition to selecting clothes, adults need to keep them clean, which may include learning to use a dry cleaner, sort clothes to be washed, wash in a washer or by hand, dry in the dryer or on a line, fold and hang clothes, and polish shoes.

Cuvo et al. (1981) reported a study focusing on laundry skills. Sorting, washing, and drying were taught to each of five students with moderate retardation individually in a multiple baseline across subjects design. The laundry skills were socially validated through consultation with a home economist and observations of nonhandicapped adults performing the tasks. A system of least prompts described earlier was used to teach most steps. Students were praised when they made progress and were taught to use bar graphs to illustrate and self-monitor their improvements on probes. This program led to rapid acquisition of the laundry skills by all five subjects.

Two academic skills that might further enhance this program are reading and coin selection (for coin laundry). These accompanying functional academic skills are the topic of Chapter 15.

Mending Clothes

The ability to mend clothes can be an asset to any adult. Mending clothes improves personal appearance, adds to the life of the clothes, and thus saves money. Cronin and Cuvo (1979) taught five adolescents with moderate retardation to mend clothes in school. Based on social validation using a sewing text, a home economics professor, and a wardrobe survey, they decided to teach sewing on buttons, hemming, and mending a seam by hand. The easiest, sturdiest hand stitches were selected for instruction. Students were assessed and taught both to identify the mending required and to mend the clothes. The prompts (system of least intrusive prompts) and consequences were similar to those in Johnson and Cuvo (1981); however, visual cues were related to emphasize the sewing discriminations. For example, the stitch length was marked with a dot, and the teacher said, "Poke the needle down at the dot." Each student mastered all mending tasks after instruction and maintained the skills at the 100% criterion in a 2-week follow-up. Some generalization did occur between mending subtasks. Although setting generalization was not measured, the students reportedly used their mending skills at home.

When teachers work to target skills indicated as being important by care providers, it is easier to obtain care providers' support in encouraging students' use of the skills once mastered. An important aspect of teaching useful mending skills is whether students will initiate mending when the need actually arises. Probes should be made of the skill, once learned, to assess the student's ability to recognize the need for mending when, for example, a tear in clothing is discovered, and to apply mending skills to repair the clothing.

Housekeeping

Acquiring some basic housekeeping skills is likely to be essential for many people with severe disabilities. Hiring someone to do all housekeeping is rarely economically feasible. In addition, the person who masters housekeeping skills will have a usable skill to earn additional income or as a main source of employment. Inadequate housekeeping can lead to eviction from an apartment (Crnic & Pym, 1979; Williams & Cuvo, 1986). Unfortunately, in some institutional settings and families, the person is not expected, or even permitted, to help clean the house. This lack of experience makes transition to a supervised or independent living setting where housekeeping is required difficult.

To determine what housekeeping skills to teach, a survey of the tasks most frequently performed by her age peers in similar living situations is often helpful. For example, what chores do nonhandicapped young adult group homes require (off-campus college housing)? Requiring that people with handicaps perform much more housekeeping tasks than their peers, and without pay would be unfair; but requiring less work would also be unfair to the client's need for a normalized life. A second means for identifying skills is to survey the student's current and future residences and the housekeeping requirements and specific materials available.

A long-term housekeeping program should include at least two instructional phases. In the first phase, acquisition, the teacher would be closely involved, providing systematic prompts and feedback. Once the skill is acquired, a maintenance phase should be implemented with gradually decreasing teacher checks and reinforcement for quality of performance, until the student uses the skills routinely under normal conditions (infrequent praise by visitors for a nice apartment). When generalization is built into acquisition and maintenance by teaching in a variety of real, living settings, there will be less need to program separately for skill generalization.

Acquisition of Cleaning Skills

As mentioned previously, the system of prompts selected for training will depend on the student's ability to respond to various cues. If previous work indicates that the student will usually perform a step with verbal instructions, then a least-intrusive prompt system would be appropriate (Cronin & Cuvo, 1979). However, students who do not frequently respond to verbal instruction early in a task and who tend to make errors if allowed to perform independently may need more assistance initially, with gradual fading. An example of this procedure is illustrated in one bed-making study (Snell, 1982). Snell taught four institutionalized young men bed-making skills using time delay of a model plus verbal prompt. The four tasks were making a partially unmade bed, stripping, putting top and bottom sheets on, and putting blanket, pillow, and spread on a bed.

Instruction included teaching all steps of each task simultaneously (total task instruction), error correction procedures, and model plus verbal prompts and physical plus verbal "back-up" prompts. During the initial four trials, the teacher gave a model plus verbal prompt for the first step of the task analysis immediately after the instructional cue ("Make the bed") and then immediately guided the student to perform the step while repeating the verbal prompt. The model was given using a second bed parallel to the training bed. This procedure was repeated for all steps. After four trials, the trainer began to delay the prompts to encourage the student to perform independently.

Reinforcement was praise and a penny token system with age-appropriate materials (Velcro dart board, cassette tape player) and edibles that could be "purchased" at the end of the task. If a student made errors, either by failing to complete a step or by performing it inadequately, the trainer told the student that performance was not acceptable ("No, that's not how you make the bed"), withheld the penny, put the student through the step, and turned away from the student (timeout) for 10 seconds.

A multiple-probe design across students showed a functional relationship between training and the acquisition of the skills. The students acquired from one to four of the skills in the time allocated for the study. Although training was conducted in a classroom, probes indicated that three of four subjects generalized their skills to their own beds. Two of the subjects maintained the skills with their own beds 7 weeks after training ended. Unfortunately, it was institutional policy that the housekeeping staff, *not* the students, make the beds on a daily basis; thus the students' ability to recall their bed-making skills was surprising, since they did not have much chance to use them.

Another study of housekeeping skills also overlaps with vocational preparation in janitorial tasks. Cuvo, Leaf, and Borakove (1978) trained six 13- to 15-year-old students having moderate retardation to clean a school restroom. Social validation of their task analyses was based on observation made of the school janitor and a trained person with handicaps as they cleaned restrooms. They used a least intrusive system of prompts similar to Johnson and Cuvo's (1981). They also used a most-to-least help sequence of prompts for more difficult steps that were frequently performed poorly, like spraying the mirror. Praise and candy, used as reinforcers, were thinned over sessions. All students rapidly acquired the cleaning skills, generalized to a second restroom, and maintained them for 2 weeks. More natural social approval would provide a better alternative to the edible reinforcer used in this study. Other daily living skills studies have supported the effectiveness of reinforcing with praise and self-graphing (Cuvo et al., 1981; Johnson & Cuvo, 1981), which are more age-appropriate for this population and will lead to better skill maintenance.

Finally, Brueske and Cuvo (1985) taught cleaning skills to a blind woman with mild handicaps to prepare her for supervised apartment life outside the institution. The woman's blindness complicated the completion of several housekeeping tasks. The techniques employed to overcome her vision limitations may have particular value to students with severe handicaps with or without vision problems.

First, gauging the amount of cleaning solution presented difficulties that were resolved by teaching the client to count the number of squirts of glass cleaner or bath tub spray. Second, the client was unable to clean a surface without missing places; thus, she was taught a consistent pattern of wiping surfaces and sweeping.

For example, Mary placed her right hand flat against the object in a vertical position with her fingers extended. Her hand always moved horizontally from left to right across the surface and back again in the same path. To help her keep her place while using this pattern, the authors devised a marking procedure. That is, first she placed the index finger of her left hand beside the base of the thumb of her right hand. After she moved her right hand from left to right and back again across the object, the base of her thumb was once again in line with her left index finger. Then she moved her right hand down the object until her fingertips were aligned with the tip of her left index finger, and lowered her index finger to the base of the right thumb. (Brueske & Cuvo, 1985, p. 19)

Repetition of the wiping procedure was programmed to ensure cleanliness of surfaces wiped, since the client could not visually inspect them. When sweeping, the woman was taught to spot-check for dirt by feeling the floor and repeat sweeping only if dirt was discovered. Finally, the training procedures used a least-to-most prompt procedure of no help, minimal verbal instruction, detailed verbal instruction, and physical guidance plus detailed verbal instruction. Because model prompts rely on visual observation to be effective, they were not used.

Apartment upkeep and maintenance often go beyond simple cleaning chores. To most tenants these skills include defrosting and cleaning refrigerators, cleaning stove surface and ovens, operating air conditioners and heaters and upkeep of their filters, and safely restoring power to household electrical appliances. Williams and Cuvo (1986) intervened in these skill areas with six clients of a rehabilitation facility when they demonstrated problems in apartment upkeep and two clients faced possible eviction from their apartment. Instruction was provided to the clients in a vacant apartment identical to their own. A system of least intrusive prompts was applied as they proceeded through the entire task. Once a client mastered a skill, less informative prompts were added to the prompt system (confirmation of a client's verbal description of the next step or nonspecific verbal prompts—"What's next?") and were used *before* more help was given. Results indicated both the acquisition of the upkeep skills and their subsequent retention and transfer to other apartment settings.

Maintenance of Housekeeping Skills

Before a student has mastered housekeeping, she must be able to determine when chores should be performed and then must continue to perform them regularly. Emphasizing during training the naturally occurring cues such as an unmade bed or a trash-littered restroom will encourage later, independent skill performance (Falvey et al., 1980); however, these naturally occurring cues will not automatically serve as potent stimuli for a person with severe disabilities because the cues are numerous and have not all been taught or the cues may be barely discernible ("dirty" sheets).

Picture schedules may be included in instruction as an added, but still normalized cue, which will prompt regular performance of housekeeping chores (Spellman et al., 1978). Bauman and Iwata (1977) taught scheduling by initially reminding clients to follow the posted schedule and then gradually requiring them to meet the schedule. Although their subjects had few or no handicaps, their techniques have relevance for clients having more severe handicaps. Teachers using this strategy probably would substitute photos of the client performing the task for any words used in the schedule. Also, checking and "reading" the schedule would be built into the task analysis as one or more steps to be taught. Chapter 15 addresses further the use of pictures to teach scheduling or time management.

Telephone Skills

The telephone can be used to save time (ordering over a phone), save money (no transportation needed to shop by phone), maintain communications with friends and family, and allow the individual to get aid in an emergency. Telephone operation may require reading a phone book or reading or remembering a number, matching numbers, recalling numbers, dialing, giving social greetings, stating a message, answering questions, using coins (if a pay phone), and mastering dial and digital phone models. For some students, telephone use may enhance academic and language skills.

For less capable students, adjustments can be made to minimize the academic and language requirements and still permit phone use. A personal phone book contains fewer words and pictures than the regular book and thus is easier to use. A card with money pictures showing the coin combination acceptable for a pay call could be useful. Another technique would be to give the caller a set phrase to use in calling for a service, rather than relying on the individual to formulate a message. The studies that follow illustrate ways both to simplify the telephoning task and to teach the skills.

Aids and Organizations

Studies by Leff (1974, 1975) and Smith and Meyers (1979) identify successful instructional arrangements that may have value in teaching any telephone task. Leff (1974, 1975) developed a device called the Dial-A-Phone; Figure 14.2 shows a page from the Dial-A-Phone book. The service or person to be called is illustrated with a picture and word. The number itself is color coded and has a window to guide dialing one number at a time. This device was tested in two studies teaching telephone skills to more than 200 children and adults with moderate retardation. Over 90% of the subjects learned to dial using this device. The device would need adaptation for use with digital phones.

Another possible instructional arrangement for teaching telephone skills is group instruction. Smith and Meyers (1979) compared a practice or control procedure with two teaching procedures to 60 adults with moderate to profound retardation: demonstration with verbal summaries, and demonstration alone (no verbal instruction), using both group (five people) and individual formats. The telephone skills taught included identifying six parts of the telephone, dialing the operator to report a fire, calling for a doctor's appointment, and calling a drug store to ask the closing time. While all procedures improved telephoning skills, in most cases, the group-trained individuals surpassed the performances of those trained individually. Demonstrations and verbal summaries were *not* found to be greatly superior to practice without instruction. However, these cues were *not* step-by-step prompts but were lectures given before the students performed the skills. Based on this study, the teacher might maximize learning by using group instruction and step-by-step prompting rather than an initial verbal description; and, if verbal prompts are used, they should be specific to a step, given only as

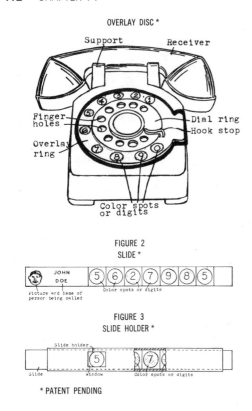

OVERLAY DISC *

Support   Receiver

Finger-
holes   Dial ring
                         Hook stop
Overlay
ring

Color spots
or digits

FIGURE 2
SLIDE *

JOHN
DOE   ⑤⑥②⑦⑨⑧⑤

Picture and name of   Color spots or digits
person being called

FIGURE 3
SLIDE HOLDER *

Slide holder

⑤   ⑦

Slide   Window   Color spots or digits

* PATENT PENDING

FIGURE 14.2 Dial-A-Phone device

Source: From *How To Use the Telephone* by R.B. Leff, 1975, Copyright 1975. Instructo/McGraw-Hill, Paoli, Pennsylvania, 19301. Patent No. 3878623. Published in *Mental Retardation, 13*(3), p. 10. Reprinted with permission of the author and the American Association on Mental Deficiency.

needed, and given just before the step (or following an error on a step to correct performance), rather than in a multiple-step cluster.

Using the Yellow Pages

For some students, using the telephone company directory might be preferable to a teacher-made book, or this instruction might follow mastery of the simplified book. One of the advantages of using the regular directory is access to a greater number of persons and services as well as its availability and accuracy over time. Kittleson and Certo (1975) taught five students with mild retardation and orthopedic impairments to use the local Yellow Pages to secure the delivery of selected goods and services. This program was particularly beneficial because of the students' difficulty in finding transportation to area businesses. The program was taught in six phases that focused on the components of Yellow Pages use, including locating the number (given a written cue), linking a needed product with its generic class (food for supper: grocers-retail), locating the number given a verbal cue, writing the number, dialing the number and making the request, and securing the product or service by performing all the tasks.

Before this program, these students had been taught related skills in reading, math, telephone use, and the use of the Yellow Pages. They could locate the Yellow Pages in the directory and read the guide words. These prerequisite academic abilities will not be appropriate for many of our students. Teaching procedures followed principles described in Chapter 5, including task analysis, verbal and model prompts, reinforcement contingencies (praise and stars on a chart), and group instruction. One strategy this study used that may have been particularly helpful was alphabetical tab markers. These helped the student locate the guide words (cleaners, laundries, pizza, hospital equipment and supplies). Of course such markers would not be available on normal directories.

A second technique employed was the instruction of verbal scripts to order items. A sample of these scripts is shown in Table 14.9. Sample scripts facilitated initial success as they eliminated the need for verbal spontaneity. It seems probable that similar scripts could be used effectively with students who would learn to use a personal telephone directory in place of the Yellow Pages; such a modification would eliminate many academic skills.

Emergency Phone Calls

Perhaps one of the most critical telephoning skills is the ability to call for help in an emergency. To place an emergency call, one must discriminate when help is required, whom to call, how to call, and what information to state. Most localities have or will have a shorter emergency number (911) that may be dialed in place of a specific emergency service for a given locality. Although this practice simplifies the teacher's instructional task enormously, students still must learn to use the system and state clearly the emergency and the location.

Risley and Cuvo (1980) taught three adults with moderate handicaps to place *specific* emergency calls (using specific numbers rather than shorter generic emergency numbers) and to provide the necessary information. As prerequisites, the sub-

TABLE 14.9 Sample script taught for ordering a service by telephone after using the yellow pages

Sample Script

Heading Word: *Cleaners*
Business: Good afternoon. Madison Steam and Dye.
John: *Hello. My name is John Hayes. I would like to have some clothes to be dry cleaned picked up at my school.*
Business: What is the name and address of the school?
John: *Lapham School. 1045 East Dayton Street. Room 117.*
Business: What is your name?
John: *John Hayes. The cleaning will be billed to my teacher, Mrs. Kittelsen.*
Business: When can we pick those up?
John: *Today or tomorrow before three.*
Business: We will take care of it. Thank you. Goodbye.
John: *Thank you. Goodbye.*

Source: From "Teaching Orthopedically Handicapped Adolescents to Secure Selected Products and Services from their Community Through Functional Use of the Yellow Pages and Telephone" by E. Kittleson and N. Certo. In L. Brown, T. Crowner, W. Williams, and R. York (Eds). 1975, *Madison's Alternative for Zero Exclusion: A Book of Readings*, Madison, WI: Madison Public Schools, p. 250. Reprinted with permission.

jects were required to state their name and address and read correctly five, 7-digit numbers. The materials used included modified telephone directories containing a picture of the emergency person (fireman, police, or doctor), printed occupation, and a randomly selected 7-digit number. Also used were disconnected telephones and 18 pictures of emergency situations. These pictures showed scenes like a kitchen stove on fire, someone hurt, or someone in danger. A yellow posterboard "thermometer," showing the steps of the task analyses that were completed independently, was used to give graphic feedback. The task analyses for the three types of calls were validated by watching someone make the calls, consulting the telephone company and the emergency departments, and viewing a telephone company film on dialing.

During the test and training, the trainer showed one picture of an emergency and asked the student to use the telephone book and phone to demonstrate what to do in that situation. The "emergency person" on a second phone asked the vital questions identified earlier by social validation ("What is your name?"). During testing, each step of the task analysis was scored, with no help or feedback provided. During training the prompts used included verbal instruction ("Put your index finger in the dial

hole for the number three"), verbal instruction plus modeling, and verbal instruction plus physical guidance. Reinforcement consisted of praise after a predetermined set of steps and filling in the thermometer at the end of the task. A multiple baseline design across subjects demonstrated the effectiveness of the procedure. Also, after one emergency was trained, generalization occurred to the other two emergencies. Most critical in the development of a teaching program in this area is the validation of task analyses with local telephone emergency procedures and the use of real phones—both dial and digital models, since both are prevalent.

Handling and Preventing Home Accidents

To the extent that a handicapped individual can recognize and escape fires and deal with simple injuries, the possibility of living in the community independently or semi-independently will be more likely. Although telephone skills may contribute to success in these areas, the telephone either may not be needed in such situations or may be insufficient.

In an exemplary study, Haney and Jones (1982) taught fire escape skills to four school-aged children having severe handicaps. The children all were ambulatory and lived in a group home. Props were used to make the training setting (one bedroom in the home) more realistic. For example, hot and cold pads were used to change the touch temperature of the door and a tape recording of house's fire alarm was played. Training was provided individually on four different situations represented in Figure 14.3. In the first situation the student awoke to the sound of the fire alarm, slid out of bed, got into a crawl position, crawled to the door and felt the door. Once there, the student was taught to decide whether the door was cool or was hot and had smoke coming from under it, which, in turn, meant the student would crawl away from the door to a window, open the window, and wait for help. Situation 2 was similar but occurred only when the door was cool and led to different escape behavior.

Prompts were provided only as needed in a least-to-most order. Errors first were corrected with verbal feedback plus modeling that was followed by intensive practice if the students still did not correct their performance. Intensive practice consisted of three to four repetitions of the incorrect portion of

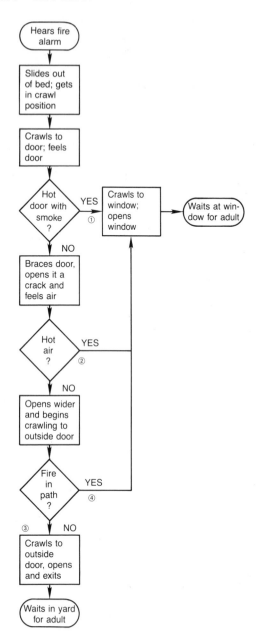

FIGURE 14.3 A flow chart analysis of emergency escape skills from the second floor of the home at night. Ovals represent termination points, rectangles represent responses, and diamonds represent decision points.

Source: From "Programming Maintenance as a Major Component of a Community-Centered Preventive Effort: Escape from Fire" by Janell I. Haney and Russell T. Jones, 1982, *Behavior Therapy, 13,* p. 51. Copyright 1982 by the Association for Advancement of Behavior Therapy. Reprinted by permission of the publisher and the author.

the task and was given with continuous feedback and social reinforcement from the instructor.

To promote maintenance, the authors faded the reinforcement schedule and shifted instructor reinforcement to self-reinforcement during the course of acquisition. Also, once each of the four individual situations was mastered, students received simultaneous presentation of previously learned situations. Generalization was programmed as well through the concurrent use of reinforcement fading, self-reinforcement, and training in a third room once all situations were mastered in the training room. Results indicated relatively fast acquisition of responses once training procedures were instituted as well as retention of learning 6 months after removal of all practice and contingencies.

Because emergency skills cannot be taught without some simulation and role play, the known generalization difficulties of students with severe handicaps requires that teaching programs devise realistic simulations as illustrated by Haney and Jones (1982). This probably includes instruction in an actual home or apartment setting, escape methods validated by reliable fire prevention procedures, and active performance of the emergency procedure (crawling to the door and feeling its temperature) rather than simple verbalization of the procedure.

COMMUNITY DOMAIN

Community skills are described under two major categories: mobility in the community and use of the community. Within the mobility section, the discussion will first address the advantages, the risk, and the goals of instruction. Their specific intervention procedures are described for various forms of mobility: walking, street crossing, and bus use. Research and techniques relevant to teaching people to use community resources focuses first upon shopping and finally upon the use of restaurants.

Community Mobility Skills

Advantages and Risks

Community mobility can be an important asset to an individual with handicaps. Orientation and mobility are critical skills for visually impaired people. Unfortunately, mobility training has not always been considered a priority for the sighted person with handicaps, despite deficiencies in this area and need for these skills (Laus, 1977; Vogelsberg & Rusch, 1980). Walking or taking public transportation frees one from reliance on parents, friends, or special vans for access to employment, services, and recreation, thus providing a more normal life. Further, the financial savings of agencies that teach the use of public transportation, compared with providing special transportation for all clients, can be impressive (Cortazzo & Sansone, 1969). Descriptions of successful, mobility-training programs for people with extensive handicaps document the feasibility benefits of instruction in this area.

The major barriers to a community mobility program often are parental, staff, and community concern for the student's safety. Perske (1972) has defended the handicapped person's right to the "dignity of risk." Overprotection of people with handicaps can bar them from opportunities for normal growth and development. Over the years, people can learn incompetent or "helpless" behavior because service providers unintentionally deprive them of making decisions (Floor & Rosen, 1975).

Given the right to learn skills that involve some risk, it is still the instructor's responsibility to maximize safety. Sowers, Rusch, and Hudson (1979) included several safety precautions in their program to teach an adult with severe handicaps to ride a bus. The client carried an emergency information card; instructors notified the local police about the program; and teaching procedures incorporated the gradual fading of supervision. To fade supervision, the instructor stopped riding the bus with the client after he performed all but one nonessential step independently. At this same point, the client's parents waited at the bus stop to check his arrival on the right bus at the right time. In the next phase, neither parents nor the instructor were present, but an observer unknown to the client rode the bus. In the last phase, the client rode the bus with infrequent follow-up checks by the unknown observer. On one occasion, the client missed his stop and rode the bus to the end of the route. The bus driver notified the police, who returned the client to his home.

Vogelsberg and Rusch (1980) recommend that, because of the risks involved in mobility training, instructors obtain parental or guardian consent, have professional liability coverage, and inform the mass transit system of the program. In their research Vogelsberg and Rusch (1979) used two instructors to teach one client to cross a street so that one could model the response while the other ensured that the client remained on the sidewalk. However, other studies (Horner, Jones, & Williams, 1985; Matson, 1980; Page, Iwata, & Neef, 1976) have used one-to-one training and even small group instruction successfully.

Goals for Community Mobility

Community mobility requires a wide variety of skills: locating the destination, paying bus fares, crossing intersections, and handling variations in routine such as a late bus. Table 14.10 lists some of the community mobility skills, assuming that the student will be taught to travel in the community unassisted; however, the goal for many individuals may be semi-independent travel.

To select a program goal from this list, the instructor should consider the student's age, residence location (current and future), and current and future practice and skill expectations. Vogelsberg and Rusch (1980) recommend first teaching a student to travel to and from work. Younger students can learn to look both ways, to cross with help, and to master short routes in school and at home. Next, the instructor might teach older students to travel to needed services (health center) and then to travel to recreational facilities. Furthermore, the authors emphasized the importance of teaching any academic skills (coin identification) in the context of the mobility program. (This is discussed in depth in Chapter 15.)

If a student is younger, not yet employed, and has some community mobility skills, a more comprehensive program might be taught. For example, Laus (1977) taught mobility skills to students with moderate handicaps in the following order: (a) using stop/nonstop sign intersections; (b) traveling to a specific location, such as a neighborhood business, (c) crossing controlled intersections of many different types; and (d) traveling independently to and from home and on a school bus. Supplemental classroom instruction was provided in color recognition, numeral recognition, personal grooming, verbal communication, basic sign reading, and counting and exchanging money. To enhance generalization, these skills instead might be taught in the context of a bus-riding program.

One other consideration in selecting the mobility program goal is the prior need for reliable pedestrian skills. Generally, programs teaching bus riding to handicapped people with no community-mobility

TABLE 14.10 Skills for community mobility

Use of Public Transportation	Car Pooling (if no public transportation available)	General Pedestrian Skills	Academics
		Cross at Various Intersections	Optional
1. Walk to bus stop (*see* General Pedestrian Skills)	1. Be ready to watch for car	1. Pedestrian light	1. Read bus
2. Identify correct bus	2. Enter car, use seatbelt	2. Traffic light	2. Coin identification and summation
3. Signal bus	3. Social behavior in car	3. Stop sign	3. Read community signs (bus names, numbers, street signs)
4. Board bus (pay fare)	4. Pay share (more than driver's share)	(a) Cars cross pedestrian path	
5. Social behavior during bus ride	5. Indicate destination	(b) Cars same direction as pedestrian	**Essential If Traveling Alone**
6. Knowledge of route (identify landmarks)	6. Exit car	4. Unmarked	1. Leave home or work in time to catch bus
7. Identify stop and pull buzzer		Walking	2. Present prepaid pass or coins for fare
8. Depart bus		1. Within boundaries of sidewalk—correct side of	3. Recognition of correct bus numbers or name
9. Bus transfer		2. To destination (knowledge of route)	4. Use landmarks to follow correct route walking or identify bus departure site
10. Walk to destination		3. Appropriate behavior (posture, absence of unusual movements or noise, etc.)	
11. Handling predictable variations: e.g., Bus does not arrive due to weather; Bus late; Someone stands blocking exit door; No seats on bus.			

skills have taught the related pedestrian skills as a component (cf. Cortazzo & Sansone, 1969; Neef, Iwata, & Page, 1978; Sowers, Rusch, & Hudson, 1979). Gruber, Reeser, and Reid (1979), on the other hand, selected walking to school as the priority goal. This priority was supported by the authors' survey of residences for people with handicaps in 43 states, which indicated that transportation to school was a serious problem.

Once the mobility goal is selected, the teacher must plan an effective program. A review of research on mobility instruction can suggest successful techniques.

Walking to a Destination

Some recent research has validated procedures for teaching children and adults to walk to a destination. The precision of this research, in contrast to earlier references on community mobility, has demonstrated that partial and independent mobility is feasible for students who previously might not have been candidates for this instruction. For example, Gruber et al. (1979) taught independent walking skills to four institutionalized men who had

profound retardation and were nonvocal, had toileting accidents, and exhibited self-stimulatory and self-abusive behavior. The target behavior was to walk from the living area to the school building, staying within defined but unmarked boundaries and without exhibiting inappropriate behaviors. To shape this behavior, the staff used backward chaining by initially bringing the student three-fourths of the way to school and adding one-quarter distances after the student mastered each segment. During the travel to school, the staff intermittently praised correct walking, verbally prompted remaining within boundaries, and reprimanded any inappropriate behaviors. Over training days, the staff faded themselves by increasing their distance from the clients.

Before instruction, the staff obtained a baseline measurement by watching each client walk to school. The assessment ended when the client walked out of bounds or engaged in an inappropriate behavior, at which time the student was returned to the living area. Once intervention began, the same procedure was repeated to probe independent walking at four program points (the four, chaining distances). In a multiple baseline design across subjects, all four students learned to travel to school in 4 to 15 days. Without further training, all were able to walk back to the living area and maintained the travel skills when probed 8 weeks later. Although the intervention procedures were effective, their further use outside the institutional setting probably would have yielded more normalized community mobility skills for the students.

Another school travel program was implemented by Spears, Rusch, York, and Lilly (1981), who taught school bus departure to a nonvocal boy with severe retardation, visual problems, and no self-help skills. A multiple baseline design was employed across three target behaviors: walking to the building from the bus, locating the bedroom and putting down school bag and coat, and locating and entering the playroom. The stimulus cue for this chain of behaviors was the school bus driver's request "Go in the building." The instructor used a least-intrusive prompt system and verbal praise during baseline *as well as* intervention. The actual intervention technique was *pacing prompts* or verbal reminders to prevent pausing on the next step (Bellamy, Horner, & Inman, 1979).

Pacing prompts were introduced on subtasks that required verbal instruction to be completed correctly after other subtasks were consistently performed correctly. Pacing prompts consisted of a verbal instruction to Peter reminding him to complete the task that he consistently missed on previous occasions. Pacing prompts were delivered just prior to completion of the subtask immediately preceding the missed subtask, e.g., just as Peter approached the door (step 2b), the trainer would tell him, "Remember to pound on the door window" (step 3). (p. 42–43)

A reversal design indicated the effectiveness of the pacing prompts. The student acquired the independent arrival (to living area) behavior in 46 days.

Most students will need to learn, in part or total, either to walk or to move their wheelchair or simply to behave appropriately while traveling to various destinations experienced daily. Many will learn to indicate where they wish to go or are expected to go; whereas most will be taught to interact socially along the route with their peers or with adults familiar to them. At times, older students will have the potential for ambulation but will not have the skill, due usually to a lack of systematic intervention (Walker & Vogelsberg, 1985). Walking or being wheeled to and from the schoolbus dropoff point,

the school cafeteria, the playground, the drinking fountain, the bathroom, and the gym are trips common to most students' school day. In the home environment and neighborhood, there are also frequently used routes which, if mastered, would constitute a functional skill. In programs focusing on reaching a destination, the student also should be expected to learn appropriate behavior (refrain from stereotypic behavior, continue moving without noise) and the related social or communication skills. Reid and Hurlbut (1977) taught students to indicate their desired destination by touching a picture before they were wheeled there. Colozzi and Pollow (1984) taught five elementary-aged students to walk from the school lobby to the classroom, but allowed time and reinforcement for appropriate social exchanges along the route. Teaching mobility along with the companion social and verbal behaviors promotes the generalization of these collateral skills.

Pedestrian and Street Crossing Skills

More complex and potentially hazardous than reaching a destination in a building are pedestrian and street crossing skills. Realistically, the two skills must go together, although some students may not need to attain complete independence in either. These people include those who are young, those who use wheelchairs but are unable to operate them, and those who will be accompanied by an adult or a peer without handicaps during trips into the community. Horner (1981) reported intervention with a young man having profound retardation who learned to walk the distance from his residence to work using upright posture, and while accompanied by an adult or peers. The main objective of the program was maintenance of upright posture while walking with others in the community; the objective was *not* completely independent walking skills. This was accomplished through the use of radio music played only when the client held his head 7 degrees or less from upright. By placing a mercury switch, attached to the radio, in the man's cap, this music reinforcement was automatically dispensed. Over a 14-phase period the radio was faded out, peers were added, and additional walking routes were used; during this time the frequency of upright posture fluctuated but generally was retained.

Other research has studied the acquisition of street crossing with students having few or no handicaps to those with extensive retardation. In general, students with more handicaps have learned these skills best when instruction included actual street settings.

Page, Iwata, and Neef (1976) taught students to cross five types of intersections: unmarked, pedestrian lights, traffic light, stop sign with cars crossing the pedestrian's path, and stop sign with cars going in the same direction as the pedestrian. Some students had no mental handicaps whereas others had mild-to-moderate retardation. Instruction occurred in the classroom and included a model representing four city blocks and a doll moved around on the simulated intersections. They also used frequent street probes to assess generalization to a real setting. Simulated training was used to minimize danger, to provide more training opportunities unhindered by weather, and to avoid the time and staff required for *in vivo* training. A multiple baseline across students and behaviors demonstrated that simulated training on each skill led to mastery of the simulated task; however, three of the five clients needed some *in vivo* training before generalizing their classroom learning to a real street. These results emphasize the value of teaching in realistic settings even with students with no mental retardation or with mild handicaps.

Another comparison of pedestrian training in two settings (Marchetti, et al., 1983) demonstrated significantly more skill mastery by 18 adults with mild-to-moderate retardation when group training took place at intersections in the community versus with a table model in the classroom. In a third comparison study (Matson, 1980), 30 adults with moderate-to-severe handicaps were taught pedestrian skills by one of three procedures: no treatment, classroom group training, or independence group training at a mock intersection on an institution's grounds. The independence training involved the same peer instruction and reinforcement strategies used in Matson's other work with showering and dining skills. This form of training proved the most effective, while classroom instruction resulted in far less learning.

In contrast, Vogelsberg and Rusch (1979) also taught street crossing, but their program was conducted entirely *in vivo*, and their adolescent students had severe retardation along with other handicaps. They selected only the first skill identified by Page et al. (1976)—unmarked intersections. The behavior was further analyzed into approach, look, step, and walk. Results of the multiple base-

line design across subjects indicated that instructional feedback (least intrusive prompts) taught the students to approach and walk; however, it was necessary to use repeated practice (five repeated trials) to establish the looking responses. To fade reliance on prompts, the instructor rehearsed the entire skill with the student and then modeled the skill as the student watched. Next, the student crossed the street alone. After 3 1/2 months of daily, 20-minute sessions, the students acquired the skill, then generalized it to similar, untrained intersections.

The decision to use simulated or *in vivo* training may depend partly on the client. The subjects of Page et al. (1976) had fewer handicaps. As a group, Page's clients learned in a simulated setting with minimal *in vivo* training (an average of 5.3 hours). In contrast, the subjects in the Vogelsberg and Rusch (1979) study, who had severe handicaps, required substantially more time to acquire one street-crossing skill *in vivo;* however, they might *never* have learned a useful skill had instruction been limited to classroom or mock street settings. These findings, taken together, lend support to training in the natural environment in order to minimize problems with skill generalization.

The generalization difficulty of our students has been handled in another way as Horner has illustrated in one of several studies taking a *general case instruction* approach. Horner et al. (1985) studied the geographical area in which their three subjects with severe handicaps resided in order to identify a small set of streets, which sampled the entire range of street crossing stimuli and responses [speed of cars, number of cars, changes in lights, number of lanes, traffic direction (1-way, 2-way), angle of crossing required (straight, diagonal), and street type (stop sign, uncontrolled, traffic lights)]. The different variations of crossing the streets from this representative set was trained, one street at a time, using one-to-one instruction, 24 trials daily over a 20-to-40 minute period (with multiple crosses at some streets), verbal and physical prompts, and student reinforcement after each correct crossing. The results of this general case approach were that generalized street-crossing skills were learned once instruction focused on the set of representative street crossings. That is, when students were probed on street crossings that they had never used, they were able to cross safely any street in the community. Along with the other demonstrations of this general case approach with students having severe handicaps for vocational (Horner & McDonald, 1982) and community living skills (McDonald & Horner, 1985; Pancsofar & Bates, 1985; Sprague & Horner, 1984), it appears reasonable that this method yields perhaps the most functional skill since it is fairly impervious to changes in stimulus conditions or response requirements.

The student's safety must be planned for by having adequate coverage by staff or volunteer trainers, by using proven training procedures, and by teaching at isolated or less busy intersections first. At some point during training, students' performance must be tested in the criterion street setting with proper precautions in place, in case errors occur. A failure to test a student's mastery in the natural setting can be as irresponsible as overprotection throughout the training process. Teachers, students, and parents need to know whether the skill is reliable under real conditions or whether its use could be dangerous.

Bus Use

The research on bus usage by people with handicaps mirrors many of these same instructional questions. To be most efficient and effective should training be performed in simulated settings, real settings, or a combination of the two? In addition to the training setting, what other variables may influence the student's safety?

Neef et al. (1978) used both simulated and *in vivo* settings to teach bus riding skills to students with borderline to moderate retardation. Five students were taught with a simulated bus, slides depicting correct and incorrect responses, and a street model identical to the one used by Page et al. (1976) to teach pedestrian skills. Two students were trained *in vivo* in order to compare cost and speed of learning to simulation training. The simulated instruction was less expensive, less time-consuming (9 hours versus 33 hours), and generalized to an actual bus. Students also were able to generalize to a second bus (novel in contrast to the simulated bus) and maintained their skills over a year. All seven students were able to employ their skills when tested in a real bus they had not used before. The five students taught under simulated conditions learned more quickly (9 hours versus 33 hours) than the two taught *in vivo* and with less expense; however, such small numbers *do not*

make these group comparison data very conclusive. The important finding is that *good* simulations may yield learning that will generalize in students with borderline to moderate handicaps. (No students with severe handicaps were included.) *Good* simulations appear to be those requiring responses to critical stimuli that are very similar to those found in the natural environment and may also "minimize irrelevant and distracting features present in the natural environment."

More recently, Neef's study was repeated with a larger group of similar students ranging in age from 15 to 46 years (Robinson, Griffith, McComish, & Swasbrook, 1984). Robinson and his colleagues modified Neef's earlier methodology because there was a lack of correspondence between classroom and community performance of individual students. (Thus, these procedures are likely to be more suitable to students with severe handicaps than Neef's simulation methods.) So as not to delay community training prematurely but to guarantee some familiarity with bus riding, the students trained by Robinson et al. began training on actual buses before they mastered all skills in the classroom. After they could predict at least one upcoming step per sequence when shown slides of each of the three skill sequences (locating the bus stop, boarding and riding the bus, and leaving the bus—Table 14.11), the students began using real buses during training. Few students could read destination names so they were taught to recognize only the key words in the classroom and were tested during bus training. In most cases, classroom training with slides and role play was brief; thus, only partial classroom performance was required before training began on community buses. This *in vivo* training began individually and included nonspecific prompts ("What do you do next?") and specific verbal prompts ("Signal the bus to stop") by the teacher in anticipation of each upcoming response.

Students then performed the rehearsed response "according to the naturally occurring, discriminative stimuli" (p. 39). After two training trials, students either joined small groups of peers for more instruction or were tested on individual bus trials. If test performance (without prompting) was entirely correct, additional training was done individually with no preresponse prompting. Less skilled bus riders were taught in small groups using peer modeling as part of the teaching strategy. If no progress occurred in groups, students received

TABLE 14.11 Response sequence for the skill components of bus riding and the associated types of training-room instruction

Skill Response in Community	Type of Training-Room Instruction
Locating bus stop and signaling bus	
1.1 Subject says which suburb he/she lives in	Slide
1.2 Subject walks to and identifies correct bus stop	Slide and role playing
1.3 Subject waits at bus stop, facing approaching bus	Slide and role playing
1.4 Subject reads destination sign on front of bus	Slide and role playing
1.5 Subject signals bus to stop	Slide and role playing
Boarding and riding bus	
2.1 Subject waits in queue by the front door of bus	Slide
2.2 Subject enters by front door	Slide
2.3 Subject presents driver with ticket to be clipped and returned	Slide and role playing
2.4 Subject sits in any empty seat or stands in rear of bus	Slide
2.5 Subject sits quietly without disturbing others	Slide and role playing
2.6 Subject looks out for landmarks indicating required destination	Slide
Exiting bus	
3.1 Subject pulls cord or pushes buzzer as bus approaches destination stop	Slide and role playing
3.2 Subject stands up and holds onto handrail until bus comes to a stop	Slide and role playing
3.3 Subject moves to rear door and steps down	Slide
3.4 Subject steps onto curb and moves away from bus	Slide

Source: From "Bus Training for Developmentally Disabled Adults" by D. Robinson, J. Griffith, K. McComish, and K. Swasbrook, 1984, *American Journal of Mental Deficiency, 89*, p. 39. Copyright 1984 by the American Association on Mental Deficiency. Reprinted by permission.

more 1-to-1 teaching with pre-response rehearsals. Ultimately after successful performance on two probe trials (one *from* home and one *to* home) students were tested without a trainer present (on all but steps 2.5, 2.6, and 3.1).

These procedures yielded mastery of bus riding skills by all 34 clients, though 20 students needed fewer than 11 training trials and the remaining 14 needed more. Followup results showed accurate retention of the skills used daily, by the clients, for a year following training. Instructional time ranged from 2 to 28 hours with an average cost of $74 per client. The combined classroom-*in vivo* approach proved less expensive and more effective than either approach when used alone. In two other studies, students with severe retardation were taught to ride buses. After first using a simulated bus in the classroom with slides, Coon, et al. (1981) did *not* find that their student generalized her skills to an actual bus. Only after she was trained in the natural environment was she able to ride an actual bus.

Primarily using the natural environment, Sowers et al. (1979) taught bus riding to a man with severe retardation in daily 3-hour sessions with supplemental classroom instruction on identifying the bus number. After 24 days, when the student had acquired all but one nonessential step (pulling the buzzer), training ended and covert observations were made to ensure his skill maintenance and safety. Although no certain conclusions can be drawn from the research on pedestrian and bus-riding skills, simulated training alone appears less effective with students having severe handicaps. Whereas simulated training *may* result in generalization, it more than likely will have to be supplemented with *in vivo* training. If a simulated setting is used initially, similarity to the actual task will enhance generalization (using slides, videotapes of landmarks). Further, Robinson's (1984) work demonstrates that it is better to use less rigorous skill requirements than mastery before training is moved into the community. For students with no community mobility skills, *in vivo* training appears to be well worth the investment of staff and time. Teaching pedestrian skills may be easier to train *in vivo* than bus riding. Teaching bus riding in the classroom may enhance, but will *not* replace, *in vivo* training (cf. Coon et al., 1981).

Community mobility training requires a long period of time. Sowers, et al. (1979) scheduled daily, 3-hour, bus-riding lessons (one trial to and from work) and concluded that more bus trips per day might have resulted in faster acquisition. For safety, staffing may need to be one-to-one or even two-to-one for some clients trained *in vivo;* however, these temporary expenditures may be offset by the long-range savings when the client can travel independently.

Use of Community Resources

Goals for independent mobility probably include traveling to work, procuring community services, and using recreational facilities. Numerous community services might be selected for training, depending on the student's needs (health center, grocery stores, pharmacy, restaurants, clothing stores, and banks). After selecting the service, the teacher writes objectives specifying what items or services the student must learn to obtain. Ford, Opperman, and Weis (1975) listed hierarchies of objectives for teaching people having severe handicaps to use clothing stores, grocery stores, and restaurants. Under clothing stores, they included objectives on getting to the store, finding the correct department, paying for the purchase, and leaving the store. The least sophisticated objective required the student to indicate which of several objects could be purchased there. The most sophisticated skill was to name or select a given clothing item.

For many younger students or students having more extensive handicaps, partial-participation objectives may be more appropriate than those specifying independence in shopping. As shown in Figure 14.4, some students may be accompanied by an adult or a peer during trips to the store because they are young or require physical assistance. The amount of independence required for a shopping skill to be useful to a particular student will be determined through the ecological inventory process.

Direct instruction in shopping is essential for learning. For example, Matson (1981) has shown that even adults with mild handicaps will not acquire shopping skills unless taught to do so. Instead, uninstructed adults with mild retardation will select items randomly or impulsively (Williams & Ewing, 1981). In addition, unless the targeted shopping skills include another person who assists in some way, the teacher must find ways to simplify or bypass the more complex steps involving writing, reading, and math. These complex steps often include: developing and using a shopping list, planning for a set budget, locating food aisles or departments by reading signs, identifying specific brands or ingredients through reading, cost comparison between brands, tallying costs before purchase to keep within a budget, paying the stated price, and checking for correct change. All the applied research on shopping with persons having handicaps involves grocery skills, and, in some ways, has simplified the task to reduce the dependency upon reading and math. Similar practices will be evident in the remaining sections of the chapter with vending machine, cafeteria, and restaurant use.

Grocery Shopping

In groups of five, Matson (1981) taught grocery shopping skills to adults with mild retardation through classroom instruction followed by *in vivo* instruction. The 10 adults who were taught learned more than an untrained control group, maintained the skills for at least 2 months, and generalized the skills to an untrained store. During the first phase, training alternated between the classroom and the store.

Classroom training focused on selecting grocery items from a shopping list, staying within a $10 budget, and locating items using an aisle and department map of the store. By grouping grocery items in cost columns ($1 or $2), each client learned to select a total set of items under $10, since all were capable of counting to 10. In addition, clients rehearsed to the others in their group the 14 grocery-buying steps listed in Table 14.12 and the basics of grocery item selection and location. On alternative sessions, training took place in the store, where food location was the primary skill taught during the first phase. During the second and third phases, clients were taught to buy their own weekly groceries, using the chain of steps. First, the trainer modeled and described shopping tasks, then each client individually performed the task. Clients were asked to evaluate themselves; those that thought they'd done well also were given feedback about the accuracy of their evaluation. A client who stated that she needed to improve was asked to specify how, and was then given feedback on these comments. In addition to trainer modeling, self-evaluation, and trainer feedback, peer reinforcement in each group of five clients was also used. Although these subjects had mild retardation, a similar instructional package (described in

a

b

c

d

e

an earlier section) was applied successfully in teaching showering skills to clients with more extensive handicaps (Matson et al., 1981). Teachers using these procedures would need to modify the verbally dependent methods (verbal rehearsal and evaluation) perhaps by substituting single-word-plus-photo "descriptions" of the steps in the task.

In an effort to reduce training costs, Aeschleman and Schladenhauffen (1984) also used classroom instruction and role playing to teach grocery shopping skills. The subjects were four institutionalized teenagers with severe retardation and many maladaptive behaviors. Instruction took place in a classroom, part of which was arranged to simulate a small grocery store. Because of the surprising effectiveness of simulated training, real grocery stores were only used to test students on the skill sequence. The sequence included: entering the store, using a picture grocery list drawn by the client, selecting and securing items, going to checkout, removing items to counter, greeting cashier only if greeted first, giving proper amount of money rounded to the nearest dollar, pocketing change, and leaving store. Several performance parameters were specified as well to reduce student errors: shopping had to be completed in 10 minutes, only one item was purchased from each lunch food category (lunch meat, salty snack, produce, drink, sweet snack) and no other category purchases were made, and the student had to refrain from initiating social interactions and not make more than one unsolicited verbalization.

Instruction included a variety of strategies. First, students learned to make shopping lists by drawing representative pictures of lunch items they would buy, and to select corresponding luncheon items. Next, shopping skills were taught. Two methods used to teach shopping were verbal instruction of the monetary transaction at a classroom table followed by role playing of the shopping sequence in the simulated store. An analysis of the clients' performances indicated that role-playing in the classroom "store" contributed strongly to learning, whereas verbal instruction outside the "store" (used

to teach the rounding-up to the nearest dollar) resulted in few skill gains.

Given the mobility research findings described earlier, in which training settings are contrasted, the results of Aeschleman and Schladenhauffen's (1984) work is somewhat surprising: the students were able to generalize their shopping skills to three different stores without any *in vivo* training. Training sessions ranged from 8 to 21 in number, with total time lasting from 3.3 hours to 10.5. Several explanations for their success include a sequence of steps which had been validated in nearby stores, the use of "personalized" shopping lists serving clients as mnemonics for the needed items, the purchase of a limited set of products (luncheon items), and the use of small grocery stores as the *in vivo* test sites. Furthermore, the simulated grocery was described as having little physical resemblance to the actual stores, although the key stimulus elements were present: actual food products and fresh produce, real money, realistic placement of products, and realistic physical arrangement of the simulation setting (food arranged on book cases, desk serving as checkout counter, use of basket to carry items).

One final comment on this study warrants mention. Aeschleman and Schladenhauffen noted that the monetary transaction procedure had been simplified from its successful use in other studies with persons having fewer handicaps (van den Pol, Iwata, Ivancic, Page, Neef, & Whitley, 1981), but, still, the procedure was not fully successful with their clients. Although all students began using the method ("Repeat the dollar amount and add one more," p. 257) after role play instruction, average scores did not improve beyond 50% correct. This skill difficulty is an important one in that it has the potential of making the remaining sequence of skills unusable. More study of the rounding up procedure is needed to enable students with severe handicaps to make successful monetary transactions.

A third grocery shopping study programmed instruction in both the classroom and actual stores,

FIGURE 14.4 Aaron is learning to use the 7-Eleven on a semi-independent basis. With his teacher giving prompts only as necessary, (a) he walks from the parking lot into the store, (b) selects a snack, (c) gives the cashier his money (precounted by teacher or parent), (d) receives his change, and then (e) leaves. Aaron is simply learning to give the dollar bill that is in his wallet, rather than to count out the exact change or to count his returned change.

Credit must be given to Community Based Instructional Program of Albemarle County Public Schools in Charlottesville, Virginia and to Trice Lewis and Shara Walters of the Community Integration Program at the University of Virginia.

TABLE 14.12 Checklist of grocery shopping skills

1. *Can Select the Store.* The client was able to pick out the grocery store from other stores on the block.
2. *Go into Correct Door.* The client could walk through the "in" door of the grocery store. (This step was important for decreasing congestion at the entrance of the store. Also, many grocery store doors are automated, making it impossible to go through the "out" door). Discriminative cues taught to the clients included going through the door to the right and identifying the words "in" and "out."
3. *Attend to Traffic Flow.* The client was able to follow traffic flow to the shopping carts. Attempts to go through the checkout area to reach the food shelves were scored as incorrect.
4. *Select a Shopping Cart.* The client was expected to obtain a cart from the storage area. No food items could be present in the cart.
5. *Look at Shopping List.* After obtaining a shopping cart, the client could look at his or her grocery list and determine where selected items were located in the store. Clients were then required to indicate verbally and/or gesturally zones specific foods were in. (A zone was defined as a discrete section of the grocery store, labeled with signs, where canned goods, meats, etc., were stored).
6. *Go to Zone of Store.* The client could successfully go to the store zone where grocery list items were located.
7. *Go to Additional Zones.* The client could go to all zones other than the first one in which food items on the shopping list were stored without trainer prompts.
8. *Find Individual Items.* The client could obtain all foods checked on the grocery list, unless the item was out of stock.
9. *Select Acceptable Quantity.* Based on the need and money available, the client could select an appropriate size and quantity of each item. (Quantities were predetermined and discussed with each resident receiving independence training before going to the store.)
10. *Check Grocery List.* Before checking out the items from the store, the client could review his or her grocery list to ensure that all required items had been selected. This task was checked by the trainer, who observed the client while he or she verbally reviewed items after being asked to do so.
11. *Go to the Checkout Counter.* The client could line up at the checkout counter.
12. *Help Checker.* The client could take items from the grocery cart and place them on the checkout counter.
13. *Handle Money Appropriately.* After all items had been tabulated, the client could give the checker an amount of money greater than that required to pay for items purchased. The client could then wait until he or she received change and could safely deposit it in his or her pocket, purse, and/or wallet.
14. *Take Groceries.* The client could lift the groceries from the checkout counter and carry them out of the store.

Source: From "Use of Independence Training to Teach Shopping Skills to Mildly Mentally Retarded Adults" by J.L. Matson, 1981, *American Journal of Mental Deficiency, 86,* p. 178. Copyright 1981 by the American Association on Mental Deficiency. Reprinted by permission.

(Gaule, Nietupski, & Certo, 1985). Grocery shopping was taught to four adults with moderate to severe handicaps in three skill sequences: preparation of a grocery shopping list, location and securing of items in the store, and purchase of items. The first skill cluster was taught in the classroom and involved use of a prosthetic shopping aid and picture recipes, which were to be prepared later. Students were taught to examine the recipes and check needed items on the picture shopping aid. This aid was a notebook that not only pictured many different food items but indicated cost of each using a set of squares to symbolize each 50-cent unit of the item's price. Finally, students learned to total the price-squares, which had been checked next to needed food items, to obtain the cost of the purchase.

The two remaining skill clusters focused on actual shopping in a grocery store and were taught once or twice weekly, *in vivo,* using a group format, with trials offered one student at a time. Teaching techniques included error correction using models, repeated practice, and verbal reinforcement by the teacher. Students were taught to count out enough dollar bills to match the total cost indicated on the picture shopping aid; thus, they did not use the less involved method that required repetition of the quoted price with rounding up by one dollar. As in all studies reviewed, change was not counted, only pocketed.

Results indicated fairly good skill acquisition by students and partial maintenance after an average of 15 hours training and a per-pupil cost of $6 for food and transportation. Acquisition problems were experienced by two of the three students on locating and obtaining food items. Authors suggested that fewer items be taught initially and that instruction be given in aisle search strategies (use of aisle headings that involves reading or row-by-row scanning) in order to promote better learning.

In another application of the *general case* instructional approach McDonald and Horner (1985) taught eight young adults with moderate to severe handicaps to locate 15 specific grocery items (a type of bread, milk, Tide, Cheerios). Two approaches were used: isolated, *in vivo* training and simulation-plus-*in vivo* training. Teachers using the first method taught students to locate the 15 items using daily sessions in a store located near the school. By contrast, the second method included classroom training with slides of grocery store aisles and shelves along with training in one store. The slides were taken in nontraining or probe stores to illustrate the range of position variation of the items found in supermarkets, packages of non-target items that looked like targeted items, assorted aisles and shelves, variations in size and position of items within aisle.

Results indicated that when students received, through slides, exposure to an increased range of the stimulus variation involved in location of grocery items, they demonstrated generalized, item location skills. Students with combination simulation-plus-*in vivo* training could locate the target items in many untrained grocery store locations whereas other students' performance in these same stores was much poorer after receiving only isolated, *in vivo* training.

As in Horner's other general-case research, the findings strongly support two important teaching practices for promoting generalization. First, the set of examples used, during teaching sessions, *should* sample the range of relevant stimulus variation that the student will encounter after teaching; however, examples *should not* use stimuli that are both irrelevant and consistent across teaching sample items. Perhaps to improve further the simulation-plus-*in vivo* phase, simulation training could be done with real grocery items, *not* limited to pictured items.

Use of Calculators During Shopping

As a possible means of simplifying monetary transaction, two publications have addressed the use of calculators by shoppers having moderate to severe handicaps. Wheeler and her colleagues (1980) used a least-to-most intrusive prompt system to help students to print dictated grocery lists, to locate items in a store, to use calculators for consecutively subtracting item prices from the pre-entered total amount (although tax was not included), to retain only the items they had adequate funds for, to purchase items at the checkout by giving the cashier a rounded-up dollar amount,

and to receive the change and leave. Instruction occurred primarily in a simulated classroom with later phases of the program conducted in real stores. All students were reported to have attained criterion, but, unfortunately, the absence of an experimental design makes it difficult to judge actual intervention effects.

In a second study (Nietupski, Welch, & Wacker, 1983), four young adults with moderate and severe handicaps were taught to use inexpensive pocket calculators and picture prompt-cards of money to purchase grocery items. As in Wheeler's work, initial instruction focused on number skills and took place in the classroom; similarly, students needed to know a fair amount of beginning number skills (number reading of dollar bills and prices, matching a sequence of 1 to 4 digit numbers on the calculator display), though both studies avoided teaching students the nonessential skill of entering the decimal point into the calculator. The Nietupski study used cards picturing xerox copies of bills ($1, $5, $10, $20) along with the actual dollar and cents value *after* sales taxes were removed (one dollar bill equalled 96 cents). Students were taught to use calculators by following 8 steps that allowed each grocery item to be subtracted from the total amount of money actually available for shopping (total dollars minus tax).

1. Turn the calculator on.
2. Press the "clear" key.
3. Enter the amount indicated on the card for the bill denomination given.
4. Press the minus key.
5. Enter the cost of the first item.
6. Press the minus key.
7. Continue 5 and 6 until either:
   A) all items are purchased; or
   B) a negative subtotal is reached, in which case the item is returned.
8. Turn off calculator. (Nietupski et al., 1983, p. 281)

Their results were encouraging in that four students could use their calculator skills in actual stores; furthermore, skill maintenance measured in three of the four students was excellent for two and partial for one. A limitation of this study was its narrow focus on calculator skills and the absence of a phase to teach students to combine their learning with all the other skills involved in supermarket shopping.

Use of Restaurants and Related Skills

Learning to use vending machines and inexpensive fast food restaurants constitute two of the simpler ways a person with handicaps may become more independent in the community. Because most school programs, from preschool through high school, have some type of lunch program, skills targeted for many students will include cafeteria use as well. Cafeteria use is particularly appropriate with younger students when instruction of daily living skills will take place more often in the school than in the community. Many skills are involved when eating in school cafeterias, including behavior among peers who have no handicaps, line-up and wait skills, food selection, payment, eating in the midst of many other people, and cleanup. Mastery of these skills will pave the way for later community-based instruction of restaurant use.

School Cafeterias   Kohl and Stettner-Eaton (1985) taught 3 fourth graders to serve as peer tutors to 3 of their schoolmates who had severe handicaps. The focus of the tutoring was upon a complex sequence of three clusters of cafeteria skills involving the cafeteria line, eating, and clean-up. (Table 13.4 in the last chapter delineates the skills in these clusters.) Following a baseline period, the students were taught by their teachers over 15 to 45 consecutive sessions to use the cafeteria through rather simple error correction and positive reinforcement procedures. They demonstrated gradual but certain improvements, whereupon the peer tutors were given the teaching responsibility after receiving some training themselves in using these procedures. As a result of their tutoring, the student with handicaps either maintained the cafeteria skills learned or continued to improve their performance.

Since their tutees were nonvocal but used either Bliss or picture communication boards, the fourth grade tutors learned to communicate with them through this mode. A staff member provided tutor instruction and monitored the tutors as they taught, thereby making the practice feasible in classrooms with only a teacher and an aide. Unfortunately, no additional measures were taken to document whether attitude changes occurred in tutors, as a result of their experience as teachers, or in their classmates, who simply viewed the tutoring process. Other literature suggests that integration efforts such as these may promote positive feelings toward persons with handicaps, in addition to the benefits realized by the tutored students in learning

useful skills under natural conditions (cafeteria use, communication, and socialization opportunities with peers).

Vending Machines   Three recent studies have focused upon teaching persons with moderate and severe handicaps to use commercial vending machines to purchase snacks and drinks. Because vending machines vary widely in prices, items they sell, and operational steps, and because they will change as better models are introduced, instruction must address the generalization problems that are predictable for our students. Learning to use one machine is not likely to be a very useful skill.

Nietupski, Clancey, and Christiansen (1984) taught three elementary-aged students to use picture-prompt cards in order to simplify the coin selection steps involved in purchasing drinks from a machine. The cards showed the choices of drinks, the printed price, and imprints of the needed coins. Three different machines were selected so that the prices varied, the selection varied, the container was either a bottle or a can, and the machine was either traditional (vertical display with a door from which a bottle was pulled) or a "talking" machine with a push panel selection. Each of the three prompt cards was matched to a machine. Students were taught in pairs first on a traditional machine, located in the school halls, then on a similar machine, located in the junior high they would attend eventually. Finally, they learned to use the "talking" machine located in a nearby mall. The price cards were incorporated into the task so that students learned to match the correct coins to the cards then insert them into the machine. All students mastered the skills but required instruction on all three machines. Although there was partial generalization to untrained machines, no student showed total generalization.

Browder et al. (1985) contrasted *in vivo* instruction with simulated vending machine instruction in the classroom by using different priced drink and snack machines that were matched to the teaching conditions (in the community or simulated). No prostheses were used with the four students who had moderate to severe retardation. Instead time-delay procedures were employed to prompt all the steps in the task, including the more difficult steps of reading the price and selecting the needed coins.

The simulated vending machine consisted of an enlarged photo replica with dowel handles to pull or with spots to push, a slot for coins (with a metal catch box to provide a "clink" noise after the coin was inserted), and a space to retrieve the selected purchase, which the teacher made available. The "machine" appeared to incorporate all the relevant stimuli of the matched "real" machine in the community on which generalization was probed. In the alternating treatment design, students were taught under both simulated and *in vivo* conditions (as well as being probed on a matched but untaught machine in the community) though the prices and machines differed. One student learned to operate a simulated snack machine in the classroom with prices of 25 cents and 40 cents; she *also* learned to operate a drink machine in a nearby YMCA with prices of 30 cents and 50 cents.

Regardless of the location of instruction, students learned to use the machines including the difficult steps (price reading and coin selection) which differed across conditions. Classroom instruction allowed somewhat more training since travel was not involved, an advantage natural to that location.

Sprague and Horner (1984) tackled the anticipated generalization problems by comparing two approaches (single and multiple instance) with a general-case approach to teach vending machine skills to six high school students with moderate and severe handicaps. Training and probe procedures were the same across the three conditions except that the rules for selecting the vending machine(s) differed. The training procedures involved daily individual instruction of students in 30-minute sessions using a massed trial format (3 to 15 trials per session). Verbal and physical prompts were used to ensure correct responding but faded as quickly as possible. Error correction with multiple-step repetition was used for incorrect responses along with praise for correct responses.

The difficult coin selection steps were simplified for students in two ways. First, *students learned only to spend quarters*, one to three, depending on the machine. Second, students were taught to determine the necessary number of quarters by referring to a prosthetic card they carried with them. The card listed all possible prices on its left side and showed the respective number of quarters needed on the right side. Thus, students learned to determine the cost from the machine, match the cost numbers to the card, determine the corresponding number of quarters needed, count out the quarters, insert them, activate the machine, obtain the item, and check the machine for change.

In the *single-instance* training condition, experienced first by *all* students, a vending machine closest to the classroom was used. *Multiple-instance* training involved the same procedures, except training rotated across three machines that were similar to each other. Finally, the *general-case, training phase*, which followed single- and/or multiple-instance approaches, differed only in the rules by which the vending machines were selected. The three machines were chosen so that when combined with the single-instance machine, they sampled all the stimulus and response variations represented by vending machines dispensing drinks in the immediate community. All students were periodically probed on their use of 10 nontrained vending machines which sampled a wider stimulus and response range available in the area (drinks and food; prices 20 and 75 cents). This probe performance allowed a measure of generalized vending machine use by students after exposure to one of the three training conditions.

Results indicated that students took successively longer to master each of the three training conditions (14.8 trials for single-instance, 40.7 trials for multiple-instance, and 41.3 trials for general-case). This was not surprising, as the difficulty level increased as more stimulus and response variations in the task were added. When the students' probe performance for generalization to the 10 untrained machines were examined, however, only the general-case procedures enabled students to use their skill across the entire range of untrained machines. These findings, along with other research using the *general-case, instruction approach*, lend clear support to this strategy for overcoming barriers to skill generalization. Unless teachers plan ways to teach for skill generalization, small fluctuations in the stimulus and response properties of a learned skill are likely to render a skill useless. Although teaching under the criterion conditions is one way to promote skill use and to bypass immediate generalization problems, general-case strategy appears to promote *generalized* learning which ultimately may be more resistant to any task changes; however, it takes longer to teach a generalized response, and the process for selecting the general case examples is also time consuming. Thus, research needs to focus on the overall efficiency of using general-case instruction over less thorough methods of promoting generalization, such as simply teaching multiple exemplars (use of several vending machines, not those chosen to sample the whole class of machines available in a community).

Fast-Food Restaurants Learning to use restaurants, even with varying degrees of independence, will involve many clusters of skills, some of which are rather complex. Prior instruction in areas of domestic skills (eating neatly, clearing table, bathroom use) and community skills (leaving and entering cars and buildings, behavior in crowded public places, line waiting behavior) is likely to contribute to a student's success once restaurant use is actually identified as a useful target.

In addition, portions of the activities involved in using restaurants may be simplified in one or more ways without eliminating participation. Ordering can be planned before reaching the restaurant, then placed (a) by another person, (b) by handing a written note (see Figure 14.5), (c) by pointing to photos, or (d) by playing a tape recording. Paying can also be simplified in numerous ways as shown in the photos in Figure 14.5 and verified in the research. Marholin, O'Toole, Touchette, Berger, and Doyle (1979) taught four adults with moderate and severe retardation to travel to McDonald's and order a meal. This instruction was conducted *in vivo* and incorporated a least-intrusive prompt system, social reinforcement, rehearsal, and brief timeouts (a few seconds withdrawal of teacher attention contingent on incorrect response). These adults increased their number of correct responses and generalized to an untrained fast-food hamburger restaurant. The authors defended the selection of a well-known chain as a target site because of convenient hours, location, and stimulus cues that are present across locations ("golden arches"). Two other considerations also should be addressed when selecting which restaurants to teach students to use: (a) Do the student and her care-providers use the restaurant? (b) Does the restaurant have features in common with other restaurants so that the skills learned may have application in other settings? Fast-food restaurants often fit both considerations.

In a second study that taught the use of a fast-food restaurant, three high school students with mild to moderate handicaps learned to use McDonald's (van den Pol et al., 1981). Classroom training using slides and a simulated ordering counter was combined with periodic *in vivo* probes. Follow-up generalization probes in a second fast-food restaurant (Burger King) were conducted both with and without the subjects' knowledge. Results indicated generalization to a novel restaurant and improved performance as well as extended maintenance a year after training.

SUMMARY

Mastery of the routine, life skills probably should constitute the majority of instruction time for most students with severe handicaps. The literature on deinstitutionalization and community living indicates that success in community-based, supervised, residential settings is clearly facilitated by skills in personal care, food preparation, home and clothing maintenance, and community use. This chapter reviewed some of the recent literature in domestic and community instruction with this population, including preparing food, grooming, selecting and caring for clothes, housekeeping, telephone skills, handling and preventing home accidents, telling time, pedestrian skills, using public transportation, shopping, and using vending machines and restaurants. Some related program planning considerations were also addressed. Although there are many other skills that may be targeted in these two broad domains, besides those with published research, intervention strategies described in this chapter are applicable across many of these other skills. The research reviewed provides clear support for the following general programming considerations:

FIGURE 14.5 There are many ways people with disabilities can learn to use fast-food restaurants. First, (a) standing in line is often made difficult by many distractions and waiting; even this task may require some instruction. Kevin, (b) whose signing cannot be understood by many, hands the cashier a teacher-written note that reflects his lunch order. Then, (c) he pays using one dollar bills, pockets the change, gets his straw and napkin (d), and is ready to eat. For some students, like Darrell (e) getting the precounted money out of the wallet and (f) the change back will require a lot of practice, but can be performed independently.

Credit must be given to Paula Norton of the Community-Based Instructional Program of Albemarle County Public Schools in Charlottesville, Virginia.

a

b

c

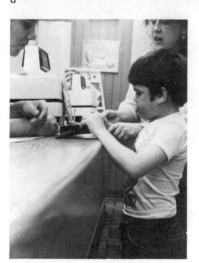

d

e

f

1. Self-management and long-term skill maintenance must be the ultimate goal of each daily
   living program.
2. Program goals should be selected only after a
   thorough inventory of the student's current
   and future environments (vocational, domestic,
   leisure, and community).

3. To maximize skill generalization, teaching
   should be done with multiple realistic materials and in multiple natural settings as often
   as possible; planning instruction to focus upon
   the general case constitutes another successful means of obtaining skill generalization.

a

b

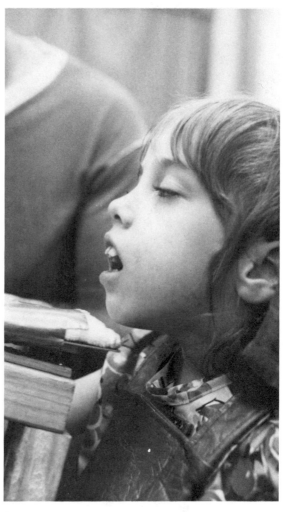

c

FIGURE 14.6 These two students have learned to place their order using a prerecorded tape that reflects the desired items. Prior to the bi-weekly trip to McDonalds and Hardees, the teacher asks for their order using their yes/no communication system; each order is then recorded on a tape that is taken to the restaurant. Once there, John (a) illustrates how he uses his head switch to turn on the recorder and thus to greet, place his order, and finally to thank the cashier. Shelly gets some classroom practice on the days she does not go into the community. As she sees a photo taken at the restaurant and hears the cashier's greeting and request for her order (b) Shelly turns on and off her prerecorded message by pushing a chin switch (c). By stimulating the fast food ordering skill in the classroom, Shelly gets the extra practice she needs to operate the switch at just the right times.

Credit must be given to Community Based Instructional Program of Albemarle County Public Schools in Charlottesville, Virginia and Ron Banks and the Community Integration Project, University of Virginia.

4. To maximize skill maintenance, daily living skills should be targeted that are most likely to be frequently needed and, thus, naturally retained through regular use.

5. Since the development of valid task analyses is central to skill acquisition, teachers should employ validated task analyses as programs are being developed; pre-written or published task analyses must be avoided without validation for the given student, materials, and other pertinent performance conditions.

6. To reduce program expense, teachers may want to probe less frequently than daily, teach after the first error on the probe, and recycle materials whenever possible. Probes must be carried out *in* the actual setting, even if infrequently, in order to monitor learning of the skill under criterion conditions.

7. Group instruction, as well as the active involvement, of students in the teaching process is likely to reduce "down time" and may even facilitate the acquisition and generalization of daily living skills, however, community-based instruction requires that groups be small (one to four).

8. System of least intrusive prompts and time delay appear to be successful systematic prompting and fading methods although they may not necessarily focus upon the critical, natural, task stimuli. Teachers will need to identify these stimuli and emphasize them, possibly through gestural or verbal cues, but certainly by using real materials and settings.

9. "Repeated practice" or repeated, mass trials on the same difficult step appears to be one effective way of teaching a step in a task that is not mastered when the others have been; a most-to-least prompting procedure can also be used.

10. Domestic and community skill instruction should teach the needed collateral skills—social behavior and communication—at the same time, so that a realistic medium for learning exists, and the resulting skill is more *complete*.

REFERENCES

Aeschleman, S. R., & Schladenhauffen, J. (1984). Acquisition, generalization and maintenance of grocery shopping skills by severely mentally retarded adolescents. *Applied Research in Mental Retardation, 5,* 245–258.

Alberto, P., Jobes, N., Sizemore, A., & Doran, D. (1980). A comparison of individual and group instruction across response tasks. *Journal of the Association for Severely Handicapped, 5,* 285–302.

Baer, D., Holman J., Stokes, T., Fowler, S., & Rowbury, T. (1981). Uses of self-control techniques in programming generalization. In S. Bijou & R. Ruiz (Eds.), *Behavior modification: Contributions to education* (pp. 39–61). Hillsdale, N.J.: Lawrence Erlbaum Associates.

Bates, P., Renzaglia, A., & Clees, T. (1980). Improving the work performance of severely/profoundly retarded young adults: The use of the changing criterion procedural design. *Education and Training of the Mentally Retarded, 15,* 95–104.

Bauman, K. E., & Iwata, B. A. (1977). Maintenance of independent housekeeping skills using scheduling plus self-recording procedures. *Behavior Therapy, 8,* 554–560.

Bellamy, G. T., Horner, R. H., & Inman, D. P. (1979). *Vocational habilitation of severely retarded adults.* Baltimore: University Park Press.

Browder, D., Hines, C., McCarthy, L. J., & Fees, J. (1984). A treatment package for increasing sight word recognition for use in daily living skills. *Education and Training of the Mentally Retarded, 19,* 191–200.

Browder, D., & Shapiro, E. (in press). Applications of self-management to individuals with severe handicaps: A review. *Journal of the Association for Persons with Severe Handicaps.*

Browder, D., Snell, M., & Ambrogio, B. (1984). *Using time delay to transfer stimulus control within the behavioral chain of vending machine use with a comparison of training sites.* Unpublished manuscript, Lehigh University, Department of Special Education.

Brown, F., Holvoet, J., Guess, D., & Mulligan, M. (1980). The Individualized Curriculum Sequencing Model (III): Small group instruction. *Journal of the Association of the Severely Handicapped, 5,* 352–364.

Brueske, S. L., & Cuvo, A. J. (1985). Teaching home cleaning skills to a blind client. *Journal of Visual Impairment and Blindness, 79,* 18–23.

Colozzi, G. A., & Pollow, R. S. (1984). Teaching independent walking to mentally retarded children in a public school. *Education and Training of the Mentally Retarded, 22,* 97–101.

Connis, R. (1979). The effects of sequential pictorial cues, self-recording and praise on the job task sequencing of retarded adults. *Journal of Applied Behavior Analysis, 12,* 355–361.

Coon, M. E., Vogelsburg, T., & Williams, W. (1981). Effects of classroom public transportation instruction of generalization of the natural environment. *Journal of the Association of the Severely Handicapped, 6*(2), 46–53.

Cortazzo, A. C., & Sansone, R. (1969). Travel training. *Teaching Exceptional Children, 3,* 67–82.

Crnic, K. A., & Pym, H. A. (1979). Training mentally retarded adults in independent living skills. *Mental Retardation, 17*(1), 13–16.

Cronin, K. A., & Cuvo, A. J. (1979). Teaching mending skills to retarded adolescents. *Journal of Applied Behavior Analysis, 12,* 401–406.

Cuvo, A. J. (1978). Validating task analyses of community living skills. *Vocational Evaluation and Work Adjustment Bulletin, 11*(3), 13–21.

Cuvo, A. J., Jacobi, E., & Sipko, R. (1981). Teaching laundry skills to mentally retarded students. *Education and Training of the Mentally Retarded, 16,* 54–64.

Cuvo, A. J., Leaf, R. B., & Borakove, L. S. (1978). Teaching janitorial skills to the mentally retarded: Acquisition, generalization and maintenance. *Journal of Applied Behavior Analysis, 11,* 345–355.

Doleys, D. M., Stacy, D., & Knowles, S. (1981). Modification of grooming behavior in adult retarded: Token reinforcement in a community-based program. *Behavior Modification, 5,* 119–128.

Falvey, M., Brown, L., Lyon, S., Baumgart, D., & Schroeder, J. (1980). Strategies for using cues and correction procedures. In W. Sailor, B. Wilcox, & L. Brown (Eds.), *Methods of instruction for severely handicapped students* (pp. 109–133). Baltimore: Paul H. Brookes.

Fantuzzo & Clement (1981). Generalization of the effects of teachers and self-administered token reinforcers to nontreated students. *Journal of Applied Behavior Analysis, 14,* 435–448.

Floor, L., & Rosen, M. (1976). Investigation of the phenomenon of helplessness in mentally retarded adults. *American Journal of Mental Deficiency, 79,* 565–572.

Ford, A., & Mirenda, P. (1984). Community instruction: A natural cues and corrections model. *Journal of the Association for Persons with Severe Handicaps, 9,* 79–88.

Ford, A., Opperman, D., & Weis, J. (1975). *Minimum objectives related to teaching severely handicapped students to use selected stores and services.* Unpublished manuscript, University of Wisconsin.

Freagon, S., & Rotatori, A. F. (1982). Comparing natural and artificial environments in training self-care skills to group home residents. *Journal for the Association of the Severely Handicapped, 8*(3), 73–86.

Freagon, S., Wheeler, J., Hill, L., Brankin, G., Costello, D., & Peters, W. M. (1983). A domestic training environment for students who are severely handicapped. *Journal for the Association of the Severely Handicapped, 8*(4), 49–61.

Gaule, K., Nietupski, J., & Certo, N. (1985). Teaching supermarket shopping skills using an adaptive shopping list. *Education and Training of the Mentally Retarded, 20,* 53–59.

Goetz, L., Gee, K., & Sailor, W. (1985). Using a behavior chain interruption strategy to teach communication skills to students with severe disabilities. *Journal of the Association for Persons with Severe Handicaps, 10,* 21–30.

Gollay, E., Freedman, R., Wyngaarden, M., & Kurtz, N. R. (1978). *Coming back: The community experiences of deinstitutionalized mentally retarded people.* Cambridge, Mass.: Abt Books.

Gruber, B., Reeser, R., & Reid, D. H. (1979). Providing a less restrictive environment for profoundly retarded persons by teaching independent walking skills. *Journal of Applied Behavior Analysis, 12,* 285–297.

Hamre, S. (1974). An approximation of an instructional model for developing home living skills in severely handicapped students. In L. Brown, W. Williams, & T. Crowner (Eds.), *A collection of papers and programs related to public school services for severely handicapped students,* (pp. 386–414). Madison, WI: Madison Public Schools.

Hamre-Nietupski, S., Nietupski, J., Bates, P., & Maurer, S. (1982). Implementing a community-based educational model for moderately/severely handicapped students: Common problems and suggested solutions. *The Journal of the Association for the Severely Handicapped. 7*(4), 38–43.

Haney, J. L., & Jones, R. T. (1982). Programming maintenance as a major component of a community-centered preventive effort: Escape from fire. *Behavior Therapy, 13,* 47–62.

Horner, R. H. (1981). Stimulus control, transfer, and maintenance of upright walking posture in a severely mentally retarded adult. *American Journal of Mental Deficiency, 86,* 86–96.

Horner, R. H., Jones, D. N., & Williams, J. A. (1985). A functional approach to teaching generalized street crossing. *Journal of the Association for Persons with Severe Handicaps, 10,* 71–78.

Horner, R. H., & McDonald, R. S. (1982). A comparison of single instance and general case instruction in teaching a generalized vocational skill. *The Journal of the Association for the Severely Handicapped, 1,* 7–20.

Jarman, P. H., Iwata, B. A., & Lorentzson, A. M. (1983). Development of morning self-care routines in multiple handicapped persons. *Applied Research in Mental Retardation, 4,* 113–122.

Johnson, B. F., & Cuvo, A. J. (1981). Teaching mentally retarded adults to cook. *Behavior Modification, 5,* 187–202.

Jones, P. A., Conroy, J. W., Feinstein, C. S., & Lemanowicz, J. A. (1984). A matched comparison study of cost-effectiveness: Institutionalized and deinstitutionalized people. *Journal of the Association for Persons with Severe Handicaps, 9,* 304–313.

Kahn, E. H. (1974). *Cooking activities for the retarded.* Nashville: Abingdon.

Kazdin, A. E. (1977). Assessing the clinical or applied importance of behavior change through social validation. *Behavior Modification, 1,* 427–452.

Kittleson, E., & Certo, N. (1975). Teaching orthopedically handicapped adolescents to secure selected products and services from their community through functional use of the Yellow Pages and telephone. In L. Brown, T. Crowner, W. Williams, & R. York (Eds.), *Madison's alternative for zero exclusion: A book of readings,* (pp. 104–194). Madison, WI: Madison Public Schools.

Kohl, F. L., & Stettner-Eaton, B. A. (1985). Fourth graders as trainers of cafeteria skills in severely handicapped students. *Education and Training of the Mentally Retarded, 20,* 60–68.

Kreutner, A. K. (1981). Sexuality, fertility, and the problem of menstruation in mentally retarded adolescents. *The Pediatric Clinics of North America, 28,* 475–480.

Laus, M. D. (1977). *Travel instruction for the retarded.* Springfield, IL: Charles C Thomas.

Leff, R. B. (1974). Teaching the TMR to dial the telephone. *Mental Retardation, 12*(2), 12–13.

Leff, R. B. (1975). Teaching TMR children and adults to dial the telephone. *Mental Retardation, 13*(3), 9–12.

Livi, J., & Ford, A. (1985). Skill transfer from a domestic training site to the actual homes of three moderately handicapped students. *Education and Training of the Mentally Retarded, 20,* 69–82.

Marchetti, A. G., McCartney, J. R., Drain, S., Hooper, M., & Dix, J. (1983). Pedestrian skills training for mentally retarded adults: Comparison of training in two settings. *Mental Retardation, 21,* 107–110.

Marholin, II, D., O'Toole, K. M., Touchette, P. E., Berger, P. L., & Doyle, D. A. (1979). "I'll have a Big Mac, large fries, large coke, and apple pie," . . . or teaching adaptive community skills. *Behavior Therapy, 10,* 236–248.

Martin, J. E., Rusch, F. R., & Heal, L. W. (1982). Teaching community survival skills to mentally retarded adults: A review and analysis. *Journal of Special Education, 16,* 243–268.

Martin, J. E., Rusch, F. R., James, V. L., Decker, P. J., & Trytol, K. A. (1982). The use of picture cues to establish self-control in the preparation of complex meals by mentally retarded adults. *Applied Research in Mental Retardation, 3,* 105–119.

Matson, J. L. (1980). A controlled group study of pedestrian-skill training for the mentally retarded. *Behaviour Research and Therapy, 18,* 99–106.

Matson, J. L. (1981). Use of independence training to teach shopping skills to mildly mentally retarded adults. *American Journal of Mental Deficiency, 86,* 178–183.

Matson, J. L., DiLorenzo, T. M., & Esveldt-Dawson, K. (1981). Independence training as a method of enhancing self-help skills acquisition of the mentally retarded. *Behaviour Research and Therapy, 19,* 399–405.

McDonald, J. J., & Horner, R. H. (1985). Effects of *in vivo* versus simulation-plus-*in vivo* training on the acquisition and generalization of grocery item selection by high school students with severe handicaps. *Analysis and Intervention in Developmental Disabilities, 5,* 323–343.

Neef, N. A., Iwata, B. A., & Page, T. A. (1978). Public transportation training: *In vivo* versus classroom instruction. *Journal of Applied Behavior Analysis, 11,* 331–344.

Nietupski, J., Clancey, P., & Christiansen, C. (1984). Acquisition, maintenance and generalization of vending machine purchasing skills by moderately handicapped students. *Education and Training of the Mentally Retarded, 22,* 91–96.

Nietupski, J., Welch, J., & Wacker, D. (1983). Acquisition, maintenance and transfer of grocery item purchasing by moderately and severely handicapped students. *Education and Training of the Mentally Retarded, 18,* 279–286.

Nutter, D., & Reid, D. H. (1978). Teaching retarded women clothing selection skill using community norms. *Journal of Applied Behavior Analysis, 11,* 475–487.

O'Neill, J., Brown, M., Gorton, W., & Schonhorn, R. (1985). The impact of deinstitutionalization on activities and skills of severely/profoundly mentally retarded multiply handicapped adults. *Applied Research in Mental Retardation, 6,* 361–371.

Page, T. H., Iwata, B. A., & Neef, N. A. (1976). Teaching pedestrian skills to retarded persons: Generalization from the classroom to the natural environment. *Journal of Applied Behavior Analysis, 9,* 433–444.

Pancsofar, E. L., & Bates, P. (1985). The impact of the acquisition of successive training exemplars on generalization. *Journal of the Association for Persons with Severe Handicaps, 10*(2), 95–104.

Perske, R. (1972). The dignity of risk. In W. Wolfensberger (Ed.), *The principle of normalization in human services.* Toronto: National Institute on Mental Retardation.

Quirk, C., & Janssen, C. M. (1984). *Inservice manual: Training teachers of students with severe handicaps.* Unpublished manuscript. School District of Philadelphia, Division of Special Education.

Reid, D. H. & Hurlbut, B. (1977). Teaching nonvocal communication skills to multihandicapped retarded adults. *Journal of Applied Behavior Analysis, 10,* 591–603.

Richman, G. S., Reiss, M. L., Bauman, K. E., & Bailey, J. S. (1984). Teaching menstrual care to mentally retarded women: Acquisition, generalization, and maintenance. *Journal of Applied Behavior Analysis, 17,* 441–451.

Risley, R., & Cuvo, A. (1980). Training mentally retarded adults to make emergency telephone calls. *Behavior Modification, 4,* 513–525.

Robinson, D., Griffith, J., McComish, L., Swasbrook, K. (1984). Bus training for developmentally disabled adults. *American Journal of Mental Deficiency, 89,* 37–43.

Robinson-Wilson, M. A. (1977). Picture recipe cards as an approach to teaching severely and profoundly retarded adults to cook. *Education and Training of the Mentally Retarded, 12,* 69–73.

Rusch, F. R., Morgan, T. K., Martin, J. E., Riva, M., & Agran, M. (1985). Competitive employment: Teaching mentally retarded employees self-instructional strategies. *Applied Research in Mental Retardation, 6,* 389–407.

Sailor, W., Halvorson, A., Anderson, J., Goetz, L., Gee, K., Doering, K., & Hunt, P. (1986). Community intensive instruction. In R. Horner, L. Voeltz, & B. Fredericks (Eds.), *Education of learners with severe handicaps: Exemplary service strategies.* Baltimore: Paul H. Brookes.

Schalock, R. L., & Harper, R. S. (1978). Placement from community-based mental retardation programs: How well do clients do? *American Journal of Mental Deficiency, 83,* 240–247.

Schalock, R. L., Harper, R. S., & Carver, G. (1981). Independent living placement: Five years later. *American Journal of Mental Deficiency, 86,* 170–177.

Schleien, S. J., Ash, T., Kiernan, J., & Wehman, P. (1981). Developing independent cooking skills in a profoundly retarded woman. *Journal of the Association for the Severely Handicapped, 6,* 23–29.

Shapiro, E. S. (1981). Self-control procedures with the mentally retarded. In M. Hersen, R. Eisler, & P. M. Miller (Eds.), *Progress in behavior modification* (Vol. 12, pp. 265–297). New York: Academic Press.

Smith, M., & Meyers, A. (1979). Telephone skills training for retarded adults: Group and individual demonstrations with and without verbal instruction. *American Journal of Mental Deficiency, 83,* 581–587.

Snell, M. E. (1982). Teaching bedmaking to severely retarded adults through time delay. *Analysis and Intervention in Developmental Disabilities, 2,* 139–155.

Snell, M. E., Houghton, A., & Lewis, A. P. (1985). *Teaching students with severe handicaps to partially participate in toothbrushing.* Unpublished manuscript.

Sowers, J., Rusch, F., Connis, R. T., & Cummings, L. (1980). Teaching mentally retarded adults to time-manage in an vocational setting. *Journal of Applied Behavior Analysis, 13,* 119-128.

Sowers, J., Rusch, F. R., & Hudson, C. (1979). Training a severely retarded young adult to ride the city bus to and from work. *AAESPH Review, 4,* 15-23.

Spears, D. L., Rusch, F. R., York, R., & Lilly, M. S. (1981). Training independent arrival behaviors to a severely mentally retarded child. *Journal of the Association for the Severely Handicapped, 6*(2), 40-45.

Spellman, C., DeBriere, T., Jarboe, D., Campbell, S., & Harris, C. (1978). Pictorial instruction: Training daily living skills. In M. E. Snell (Ed.), *Systematic instruction of the severely and profoundly handicapped* (pp. 391-411). Columbus, OH: Charles E. Merrill.

Sprague, J. R., & Horner, R. H. (1984). The effects of single instance, multiple instance, and general case training on a generalized vending machine use by moderately and severely handicapped students. *Journal of Applied Behavior Analysis, 17,* 273-278.

Staples, K. S. (1975). *Cooking from pictures.* Fargo: North Dakota State University.

Steed, F. R. (1974). *A special picture cookbook.* Lawrence, KS: H & H Enterprises.

Thinesen, P. J., & Bryan, A. J. (1981). The use of sequential pictorial cues in the initiation of maintenance of grooming behaviors with mentally retarded adults. *Mental Retardation, 19,* 247-250.

van den Pol, R. A., Iwata, B. A., Ivancic, M. T., Page, T. J., Neef, N. A., & Whitley, F. P. (1981). Teaching the handicapped to eat in public places: Acquisition, generalization, and maintenance of restaurant skills. *Journal of Applied Behavior Analysis, 14,* 61-69.

Vitello, J. S. (1978). Involuntary sterilization: Recent developments. *Mental Retardation, 16,* 405-409.

Vogelsberg, R. T., & Rusch, F. R. (1979). Training severely handicapped students to cross partially controlled intersections. *AAESPH Review, 4,* 264-273.

Vogelsberg, R. T., & Rusch, F. R. (1980). Community mobility training. In F. R. Rusch & D. E. Mithaug (Eds.), *Vocational training for mentally retarded adults,* (pp. 119-145). Champaign, IL: Research Press.

Wacker, D. P. & Berg, W. K. (1984). Use of peer instruction to train a complex photocopying task to severely retarded adolescents. *Analysis and Intervention in Developmental Disabilities, 4,* 219-234.

Walker, R. I., & Vogelsberg, R. T. (1985). Increasing independent mobility skills for a woman who was severely handicapped and nonambulatory. *Applied Research in Mental Retardation, 6,* 173-183.

Wheeler, J. A., Nietupski, J., Loomis, R., & Brown, L. (1980). Teaching moderately and severely handicapped adolescents to shop in supermarkets using pocket calculators. *Education and Training of the Mentally Retarded, 15,* 105-112.

Williams, G. E., & Cuvo, A. J. (1986). Training apartment upkeep skills to rehabilitation clients: A comparison of task analytic strategies. *Journal of Applied Behavior Analysis, 19,* 39-51.

Williams, R. D., & Ewing, S. (1981). Consumer roulette: The shopping patterns of mentally retarded persons. *Mental Retardation, 19,* 145-149.

Yates, J. (1972). *Look and cook.* Seattle: Bernie Straub Publishing Co. and Special Child Publications.

Perhaps some of the more difficult decisions teachers and careproviders must make when teaching students with severe handicaps concern academic skills. We have come to associate reading, writing, and math with normality and with "being educated." In some of our students, particularly when there is a lot of early intervention, we see some talent in learning academic skills. Trying to decide whether it is best to invest time teaching academic skills depends upon many factors including the student's age and, thus, the number of years of school left, the student's learning history, upcoming skill requirements, and current skill performance.

Teachers and parents need not limit their attention to the decision "to teach or not to teach." If performance in an activity is determined to be functional for a given student, and that activity involves some academic abilities like telling time, reading, or making change, the teacher's job might be to invent academic prostheses (techniques or devices which bypass or simplify activity requirements). How many of us count our change? Do we need to teach this complex skill? Signature stamps, picture recipes, and pocket reference cards with coin-price equivalencies also exemplify acceptable ways to reduce the skills required to participate in an activity that requires writing, reading or monetary transactions.

For many of our students there will be little debate on whether to teach academic skills; these students will be busy with more basic skills; however, when functional academic skills are identified as being important by either parents or careproviders, careful thought and negotiation will help avoid the creation of an IEP battleground. In the next chapter, Diane Browder and I provide some guidelines for making these decisions, and we review the research on teaching partial and generalized academic skills.

Introduction to Chapter 15

15

Functional Academics

Diane M. Browder
Lehigh University

Martha E. Snell
University of Virginia

Formally defined, academic skills are those areas of study such as reading or math that complement vocational or technical skills. An examination of the skills required to live in community settings reveals that academic skills are subcomponents of many daily activities (reading bus names, making purchases, dialing a telephone); however, academic skills can be taught without reference to daily activities and instead with an emphasis on theoretical applications of the concept. Many young children learn computation with worksheet problems that make no reference to what actual items are being added or subtracted. By contrast, the functional academics approach is concerned only with academic skills that are related directly to daily living, including work and leisure pursuits. Thus, functional academics only partially overlap with traditional elementary school subjects in that the skills targeted for students who are classified as severely and moderately handicapped will be those most frequently needed to function in their particular community. Also, the activities for learning will incorporate the academic skill in the community. Generalization will not be assumed, for example, by using a workbook with pictures of money, but will be taught by having students make purchases based on their emerging mastery of money use.

A teacher might take one of four approaches in assisting a student to meet the academic demands of daily life. The *first approach* would simply be *to perform academic tasks for* a student and thus bypass academic instruction (giving an individual exact change to use the bus). (See Chapter 14 for examples.) The *second approach* would involve teaching students to use an *academic prosthesis* to perform an activity independently, again bypassing or limiting the need for academic ability (a rubber name-stamp; prepaid coupons for a fast-food restaurant). In the *third approach*, the academic responses required by the activities identified in the student's domains of daily living would be taught. This *specific, limited academic instruction* might include reading soda names and prices on the vending machines at school or work, reading one's

The authors gratefully acknowledge the staff of the Centennial Life Skills program for the many examples given that their work inspired.

own name to identify a paycheck, dialing one or two telephone numbers such as home and work. *The last* and most time-consuming approach would be to teach *generalized academic skills.*

A student who masters generalized academic skills would be able to use all types of money, read a wide range of materials, tell time, and compute various mathematical problems encountered in daily life. In this fourth approach, a skill sequence is needed to teach the continuum of skills needed to obtain broad application of reading, math, or other academics. This sequence might contain some steps that, when taken alone, have limited daily utility, but are viewed as essential for acquisition of the general functional academic goal; however, each subskill in the sequence is scrutinized for practical use. If neither essential to the ultimate goal nor useful, the subskill will not be taught. Roman numerals, set theory, and geometric shapes, although often included in elementary mathematics, are not essential to the mastery of computation and are rarely used in daily living. Thus, the functional academic skill sequence will be much more streamlined and efficient than those often found in elementary school curricula.

The selection of this fourth approach, *generalized academic skills instruction,* requires careful consideration because of the time required to achieve goals such as telling time or acquiring word analysis skills. The potential benefits of acquisition of these broad skills, however, make this consideration worthwhile. The individual with generalized academic skills need not learn each new academic demand encountered in daily life, but rather can rely on his skills to sound out new words, compute an answer, or count money required for a stated price. Also vocational opportunities may be broadened with the mastery of a generalized scope of academic skills.

Some educators have questioned the ability of students with moderate to severe retardation to learn academics (Gearhart & Litton, 1975; Hishoren & Burton, 1979). This contention has not been supported by research. In the area of reading, students with moderate to severe mental retardation have frequently learned to read sight words (Brown, Hermanson, Klemme, Haubrich, & Ora, 1970; Dorry, 1976; Sidman & Cresson, 1973) and sometimes have acquired passage reading comprehension and/or decoding skills (Domnie & Brown, 1977; Entrikin, York, & Brown, 1977; Nietupski, Williams, & York, 1979). Research with

children having autism and other severe developmental disabilities provides further evidence of academic potential (Browder & D'Huyvetters, 1985; Hewett, 1966; Rincover, 1978).

SELECTION OF AN ACADEMIC APPROACH

Given this range of options for instruction in functional academics, the teacher must decide which approach or approaches would be best for an individual student. The potential benefits of generalized academic skills may lead her to consider this option first. The following criteria may be applied to assist the decision of whether or not generalized academic skills instruction would be appropriate.

What Is the Student's Chronological Age?

Generalized academic skills require years for mastery and, if selected, would usually be initiated in the early elementary years; however, exceptions may be appropriate if the additional criteria apply and if the individual has not had the opportunity to learn academic skills (due to previous institutionalization without an educational program.)

What Has Been the Student's Rate of Learning in Academic Instruction?

The rate of a student's learning can be an important criteria for targeting or continuing instruction in generalized academic skills. Once a skill sequence has been selected, a performance aim can be set for progress on each step in the sequence for mastery to occur. If a time-telling sequence has 20 steps and the teacher thinks this skill should be mastered by the time job training is initiated at junior high age (age 12) and the student currently is 7 years old, the student has 5 years to learn 20 steps. Thus, the student's rate of learning should average at least four steps per year. Because early learning may be slower than later learning, the student may learn two or three steps the first year and four or five steps the next year and still meet the performance aim. By contrast, consider what will happen if the student only learns 2 steps in 2 years (an average of 1 step per year). At this rate of learning, the student would not master the sequence to be able to tell time until he becomes 26 years old. Given such a slow learning rate, the teacher must give serious consideration between starting instruction that will continue into adult education versus teaching an alternative form of telling time (digital watch) or teaching the use of a time-telling prosthesis (picture schedule). Of course, a prerequisite to assessing a student's rate of learning is systematic, daily instruction in the target skill. *Otherwise, slow progress will be a reflection of inadequate instruction rather than slow learning.*

What Are the Parents' and/or Student's Preferences Regarding Academic Instruction?

If parents think a student's potential will not be achieved without an opportunity to learn to read and do other academic skills, their preferences must be considered when planning for academic instruction. Also, a *student* may indicate a preference for this type of instruction either with his communication system or by showing special interest during an introduction to academic instruction.

What Academic Skills Are Needed by the Student in His Current and Future Environments?

The consideration given to academics needs to be anchored in the projections of the student's current and future use of these skills. Is it projected that the student will eventually live alone in a partially supervised apartment and will work with minimal supervision in a competitive setting? If so, academic demands may warrant the current time investment to acquire these skills. Does the student have special potential in a vocational field that requires a particular academic skill (reading for use of computers)? Or, by contrast, is the student's future placement projected to include supervision at work and home where academic skills could be bypassed with a supervisor's assistance?

How Do Academic Skill Needs Compare to Other Skill Needs?

Some students may have priority skill needs that require large investments of instruction that preclude the time investment to acquire generalized academic skills. Teachers can use the skill selection procedures described in Chapter 4 to decide the relative importance of academic skills, such as learning to read versus additional practice in

grooming, communication, or ambulation. After carefully weighing these criteria, a teacher can decide whether generalized academic instruction is appropriate for a particular student. Often a combination of approaches will be selected. Perhaps reading is selected for generalized academic instruction because of the difficulty in designing prosthetics to bypass reading; however, a digital watch is chosen to teach time with specific activities used for time management. Also, calculator use might be taught rather than longhand computation. Consider Randy, a student who exemplifies such a decision:

Randy, now 17 years old, needs to identify starting and lunch time in order to obtain a cafeteria bussing job for which he is being trained. It is likely that he will hold this minimum wage job upon completion of school, and thus recognition of specific times is an important skill for him. In 4 years, no one will be readily available to remind him of the time, however, since Randy does not need to tell time beyond this limited amount, the teacher considers the second academic approach— a prosthesis, and the third academic approach— limited instruction in reading specific times. The teacher decides to combine approaches and teaches reading specific times using a digital watch and following a picture schedule.

In the area of money, Randy prefers to bring his lunch and purchase a drink. He also must take the bus to work. For now, the teacher selects the first academic approach to bypass academic skill needs. Randy's parents are asked to send $1 with Randy each day so he can buy a soda by handing the cashier $1 and pocketing the change. The parents also purchase bus passes so that no money is needed at this point to ride the bus. Both Randy and his parents consider money use to be an important and motivating skill to acquire; therefore, the teacher designs a skill sequence for generalized use of a limited range of dollars (ones, fives, tens) and coins (quarters). The sequence is divided into steps to acquire in each of Randy's last 4 years of school. Cashing the paycheck and making small purchases will be the activities used for instruction.

Regardless of the approach taken to academic instruction, the activities for learning will be those from the student's daily life including home, community, and job activities. To be "functional," academics cannot consist of activities only seen in classrooms (workbooks) but must be blended with other areas of the student's individualized plan.

In the remainder of this chapter, more detail is given to the approaches to teach academic skills:

(a) generalized academic skills, (b) specific, limited academic skills, and (c) academic prosthetics. The *alternative* approach, *not to teach academics at all,* must be considered since the teacher wants to be responsive to the student's needs, instead of being committed to a curricular content area. Prior to presenting more detail in each academic approach, research on stimulus control will be reviewed that can help the teacher design academic instruction. No matter how simple the response selected for the academic instruction, discrimination and generalization will be required. Thus, the following research will help teachers structure tasks to enhance discrimination and generalization.

STIMULUS CONTROL RESEARCH AND ACADEMIC SKILLS

Before reviewing some stimulus control research that may help a teacher improve academic instruction, it may be helpful to review how learning or stimulus control is actually achieved. Teachers want to design instruction to achieve stimulus control—to increase the probability that a particular response will occur in the presence of a specific environmental event called the discriminative stimulus (S^D). For example, the teacher asks, "What is your name?" (S^D) and the student responds, "Tom."

In many skills, including academics, the objective for stimulus control is often broader than making one specific response in the presence of one specific stimulus. Teachers are concerned with discrimination of a *stimulus class* and acquisition of a *response class*. This can be illustrated with the example of stating one's name. To communicate adequately, Tom needs to give his name in response to varied verbal stimuli ("Who are you?" "I didn't catch your name."). These varied stimuli set the occasion for the response "Tom" and are a *stimulus class;* however, Tom does not give his name for other verbal stimuli ("Who is with you?" "Where do you live?"). Thus, Tom has made a *generalization* (the class of stimuli that set the occasion for the response "Tom") and a *discrimination* (not to give his name for stimuli outside of this class). Similarly, Tom might learn *response generalization* or to respond verbally to other questions such as "What did you do last night?" that could set the occasion for a variety of responses. These would constitute a *response class.*

Academic skills can be grouped into similar response and stimulus classes. By planning such grouping, the teacher can instruct for a generalized response. Depending on the academic approach, this generalization may be broad or limited. For example, generalized coin use has a very broad stimulus class (varieties of vending machines); however, generalization of a coin-matching card may be targeted for a limited range of stimuli (the city bus, the work break area vending machine, the shopping mall video games). If the range of generalization to be achieved is defined and assessed (by assessing untaught examples), the teacher can be more certain of the student's actual skill mastery.

The term "general case instruction" has been used to refer to this practice of defining the range of responses and stimuli to be mastered. "The general case has been taught when, after instruction on some tasks in a particular class, any task in that class can be performed correctly" (Becker, Engelmann, & Thomas, 1975, p.325). Although teaching the general case may require more planning time, it may save teaching time by increasing the likelihood that students will use skills regardless of whether there are changes (in requests, settings). Approaches to preplanning generalization to be reviewed include the: (a) sufficient exemplar, (b) best exemplar, (c) equivalence, and (d) comparative. Also, because many academic skills require complex visual discriminations, attention is given to research on developing visual discriminations, including (a) unfaded prompts, (b) time delay, (c) stimulus fading, and (d) stimulus shaping.

Planning for Generalization

The Sufficient Exemplar Approach

One easily implemented strategy to enhance generalization is to teach multiple exemplars of a stimulus or response class (Allen, 1973; Garcia, 1974; Schumaker & Sherman, 1970; Stokes, Baer, & Jackson, 1974). An example of the use of this approach in teaching academic skills is a study by Solnick and Baer (1984), in which they taught number-numeral correspondence to preschool children. Five worksheet formats were selected for instruction requiring both stimulus and response generalization of number-numeral correspondence (the student was to draw a line from the numeral 3 to three buttons; or was given the numeral 2 and told to circle two of a row of apples). The experimenter conducted probe sessions for the five formats and then chose one format for instruction. When this format was mastered, all formats were probed again. If generalization had not occurred, a second format was trained. The children generalized to all five formats when trained in up to three formats. This generalization of formats also extended to new number groups (from 1–3 to 4–6 and 7–9).

Solnick and Baer's research provides an excellent example of preplanning the sequence of instruction to teach and test for generalization, however, to apply the sufficient exemplar sequence to functional academics, the teacher would:

1. Select several (5) exemplars or sets of exemplars of the stimulus or response class to be trained.
2. Probe all exemplars.
3. Train an exemplar to mastery.
4. Probe for generalization to untrained exemplars.
5. Repeat steps 3 and 4 until generalization occurs.

This approach may be applied to functional academics as follows:

- **SKILL:** Name Recognition (specific, limited academic instruction)
  STIMULUS CLASS: First and last name as found in felt pen lettering on clothes, typed on check, raised letters on bottom of lunch box, felt pen lettering on locker label, typed on time card.
  RESPONSE CLASS: Select item from among 1 to 10 distractors; selection may involve opening the locker or picking up the item.
  SETS OF EXEMPLARS: (1) Clothes labels (hat, jacket, gloves), (2) Typed check (3 checks that vary in size and/or color that are typical of area businesses), (3) Raised letters (lunch box, thermos, sandwich container each with raised letters), (4) Locker label (class locker, gym locker, YMCA locker), (5) Time card (punch card, time sheet, sign in board)
  INSTRUCTIONAL SEQUENCE: (1) Probe all exemplars, (2) Teach clothes labels, (3) Probe all exemplars, (4) Teach checks, (5) Probe all exemplars, . . .Continue teaching and testing in order of skill importance until student demonstrates untaught name recognition.

"Best" Exemplars Approach

While using several examples is usually better than a single exemplar approach, Becker, Engelmann, and Thomas (1975) propose that the examples should be carefully selected to sample the range of stimulus variation within the targeted stimulus class. In the previous example on name recognition, the teacher targeted most, if not all, of the stimuli in the class of name recognition the student needed in her community settings. Since the stimulus class was fairly limited, the sufficient exemplar approach easily facilitated preplanning; however, other skills, especially those typical of generalized academic skills, have much broader stimulus and/or response classes. More attention may be needed to select which exemplars will be chosen to teach and test for generalization.

An example of the advantage of careful selection of exemplars can be found in laboratory research by Tennyson, Woolley, and Merrill (1972) who found that correct classification was most likely to occur when irrelevant attributes of exemplars and nonexemplars were matched, and relevant attributes across exemplars were different. These researchers focused on attributes of poetry, but for simplicity, color will be considered. If *red* were the attribute to be mastered, the shade and hue of red would be varied so that the person would learn *redness* rather than only one subtle shade (relevant attribute). Irrelevant attributes (shape, size) would not be varied (all exemplars and nonexemplars would be 2-inch circles). The disadvantage of this approach is that students with severe handicaps may not generalize the classification beyond these matched irrelevant attributes (2-inch circles) until taught to do so.

At least two applications of the best exemplar approach have been made in research with individuals having severe handicaps. In one approach, examples selected for training contained *all* relevant features of the concept (Hupp & Mervis, 1981). For example, Hupp and Mervis found that a picture of a typical table produced better identification of "tables" than did a poor example (desk). In a second approach, a set of exemplars was chosen that sampled the range of stimulus and response variation within a class of items (Horner & McDonald, 1982; Sprague & Horner, 1984). Any one item within the class might itself have been a poor example, but together with other members of the set, an item provides the range of relevant stimulus features. Because it can be difficult to find an example with all relevant stimulus features, this second-best exemplar approach may have more practical utility. This approach has been called "general case instruction" (Horner & McDonald; Sprague & Horner). To apply general case instruction, the teacher would:

1. Define the stimulus and response class,
2. Define the relevant features of the class,
3. Select examples that sample the range of relevant features,
4. Vary irrelevant features of examples in early instruction and/or select nonexamples with matched irrelevant features,
5. Use one set of examples for instructions and a similar set (not taught) to probe mastery of the general concept, and
6. Teach exceptions (poor examples) after mastery of the good examples set.

Identification of the relevant features of a class can be a difficult task. The research by Horner and MacDonald and Sprague and Horner provide examples and further descriptions of this procedure. This approach may be applied to functional academics as follows:

- **SKILL:** State Approximate Time to Nearest Quarter Hour (generalized academic skill) (From O'Brien, 1974)
  STIMULUS CLASS: all standard clocks with 12 numerals, an hour hand, and a minute hand. All possible placements of the hands on the clock.
  RESPONSE CLASS: "It's ___.15." "It's ___:30." "It's ___ o'clock." "It's ___:45."
  RELEVANT STIMULUS FEATURES: numeral the hour hand is on or nearest to; discrimination of whether the minute hand is closest to 12, 3, 6, or 9.
  IRRELEVANT STIMULUS FEATURES: size of clock, typeset of the numerals; for the minute hand, the numerals 1, 2, 4, 5, 7, 8, 10, 11 are irrelevant.
  EXCEPTIONS: digital clocks; clocks without all the numerals.
  INSTRUCTIONAL SET: 1:05; 6:57; 4:03; 8:55 (It's about ___ o'clock); 11:12; 3:17; 7:16; 12:10 (It's about ___-fifteen); 1:35; 7:28; 4:25; 9:36 (It's about ___-thirty); 2:43; 5:49; 12:40; 9:46 (It's about ___-forty-five)
  TEST SET: 2:57; 5:05; 9:04; (It's about ___ o'clock); 1:11; 7:17; 4:13; 9:21 (It's about ___-fifteen); 1:37; 8:29; 10:27; 3:32 (It's about ___-thirty); 11:41; 2:50; 7:43; 9:47 (It's about ___ forty-five)

AFTER MASTERY: Introduce clocks with missing numerals; teach reading exact time with digital clock and watch.

Equivalence Approach

Another generalization approach that considers the selection of items for instruction is based on the mathematical principle of equivalence or "transitivity." This principle states that if "a" is equivalent to "b," and "b" is equivalent to "c," then "a" is equivalent to "c." A demonstration of the application of this principle to childrens' learning was made in a laboratory study by Sidman and Tailby (1982). In earlier studies, Sidman (1971) and Sidman and Cresson (1973) noted this type of transfer of training in teaching sight words to learners with severe mental retardation. The entire sequence of Sidman's and Sidman and Cresson's training is shown in Figure 15.1. Figure 15.2 shows how transfer of training occurred.

Equivalence is especially useful in teaching reading comprehension. This principle would predict that if word analysis is mastered and the language concept is acquired, comprehension would follow. Interestingly, Skinner (1957) proposed three decades ago that deficiencies in reading comprehension are language problems. As shown in Figure 15.2, a person who reads words without comprehension (mastered that the printed word = the stated word) needs instruction in language (the picture = the stated word) as shown in Figure 15.2.

An application of equivalence was made to sight word instruction by Browder and D'Huyvetters (1985). After learning word recognition and object labels, the children in this study (who had been diagnosed as mentally retarded and emotionally disturbed) required no further instruction for comprehension. Similarly, Laitenin, Hall, Daugle, and Reid (1985) found that students with severe handicaps acquired untrained responses when equivalent relations were taught for the names (printed, spoken and pictures) of people and common household objects. Unfortunately, this application of equivalence to obtain comprehension is limited to vocabulary that can be depicted with objects or pictures.

Teaching equivalence relations may be an efficient approach to produce generalization in academics. The following example illustrates the way a teacher might design an equivalence sequence:

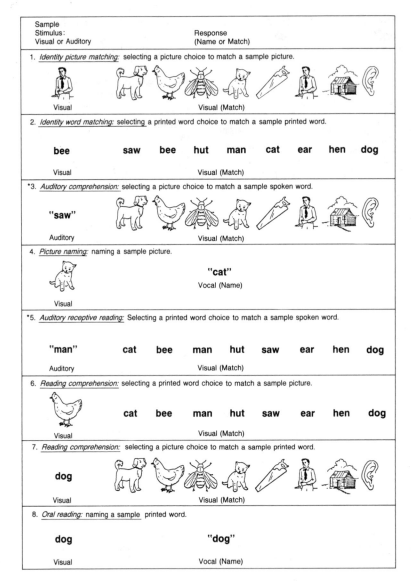

FIGURE 15.1   A task analysis of learning to read by a whole word process. Once tasks 3 and 5 were mastered, subjects demonstrated successful learning transfer to tasks 6, 7, and 8—they demonstrated reading comprehension and oral reading without direct introduction on these skills.

Source of Pictures: From *Peabody Picture Vocabulary Test* by L.M. Dunn, 1959, Circle Pines, Minn.: American Guidance Services. Used with permission.

Source of Task Analysis: Drawn from Sidman, 1971; Sidman and Cresson, 1973.

1. Sketch a triangle. On each point of the triangle write the equivalent classes to be trained. In reading, the points might be actions or pictures, the spoken word, and the printed word. In money skills, the points might be printed prices, money combination, and spoken money values.

2. Select two points for training and a third point to use to test for equivalence. This selection requires considering which subsets will yield the most efficient generalization. For example, it is more logical to teach word analysis and picture identification to obtain reading compre-

1. Teach auditory com-
   prehension of pictures:

   $\dfrac{a}{\text{picture}} = \dfrac{c}{\text{stated word}}$

   = "mop"

2. Teach auditory receptive
   reading:

   $\dfrac{b}{\substack{\text{printed} \\ \text{word}}} = \dfrac{c}{\substack{\text{stated} \\ \text{word}}}$

   MOP = "mop"

3. Probe for transfer of
   learning to reading
   comprehension tasks:

   $\dfrac{b}{\substack{\text{printed} \\ \text{word}}} = \dfrac{a}{\text{picture}}$

   MOP =

FIGURE 15.2   Example of equivalence in acquisition of sight words

hension than to begin by teaching reading comprehension and picture identification to obtain word analysis.

3. Select the specific set of examples to be trained and tested.
4. Train point one; then train point two; and then test for equivalence.

In the following two examples, the transitivity principle applied to functional academics.

- **SKILL:** Following a Recipe
  POINTS OF THE TRIANGLE: the stated word, the printed word, the action denoted by the word
  TRAINING SETS: (1) stated word = action, (2) printed word = stated word
  EQUIVALENCE TEST SET: (3) printed word = action
  EXAMPLE: For the first set, the teacher states the word and has the student perform the action to cook (stir, beat, spread, set oven). For the second set, the teacher has the student read those stated words aloud from printed, adapted recipes (stir, beat, spread, set oven). Then, to test generalization, the teacher gives the student the printed recipe and asks him or her to read and follow it. It is worth noting that in most cooking classes, the cooking technique is demonstrated (taught) before the participant is asked to follow its use in the context of a recipe.

- **SKILL:** Price-Money Matching
  POINTS OF THE TRIANGLE: the stated money value, the printed price, the combination of coins
  TRAINING SETS: (1) stated money value = combination of coins, (2) printed price = stated money value
  EQUIVALENCE TEST SET: (3) printed price = combination of coins
  EXAMPLE: The teacher picks several prices from the student's community training, including bus fare, vending machines, the telephone, and coffee at a restaurant. The teacher first instructs the student to combine the correct coins when she or he states the price ("Show me the 30 cents you need to ride the bus"). Next, the teacher has the student read the prices from photographs of the prices found in the community (picture of the bus coin slot, of the vending machine). Then she tests for equivalence by showing the pictures and asking the student to select the correct change.

Comparative Approach

Some academic skills require discrimination of a stimulus dimension (size, color, shape or other visual feature). Later in this chapter, procedures to teach visual discriminations will be described (time delay, stimulus shaping). Sometimes, the teacher may be interested in not only visual discrimination, but also generalization or classification of that stimulus. To use money, a student needs to know that the written price $4.54 requires dollars and that $0.54 requires only one dollar or change. Thus, the student needs not only to know that the price is "four fifty-four," but also, that it belongs to the class of prices that require 5 ones, a five, a ten, or 4 ones and exact change.

One method to teach classification is known as "continuous conversion" (Weisburg, 1980). In this approach, the stimulus is changed while the learner observes. Weisberg found that when continuous conversion was used, more subtle distinctions were mastered in a laboratory task with college students. Continuous conversion is also one method used to teach comparisons in the DISTAR reading, math and language curricula (Engelmann & Bruner, 1974).

Continuous conversion may be applicable to generalized or specific academic training. This approach helps the learner discriminate between subtle visual differences that set the occasion for different response classes. In generalized academics, the response classes may be quite broad as in the long/short vowel example that follows. Or, in specific academics, the response classes may be more restricted as in the money example that follows.

- **SKILL:** Silent "E" in Phonetic Word Analysis (Generalized academic skill instruction)
  RESPONSE: state the word using either the short or long vowel sound
  COMPARATIVE STIMULI: words with and without silent "e"
  CONTINUOUS CONVERSION: The teacher has the student read the word "pin," then writes an "e" on the end of the word while the student watches. The student then reads the word "pine." This is repeated for several examples. Untaught examples are assessed to determine if the silent "e" rule has been mastered.

- **SKILL:** Discrimination of Dollars and Cents (Specific, Limited Academic Skill)
  RESPONSE: The student selects either one dollar and says, "I can buy this any day," (daily allowance) or the student selects multiples of ten dollar bills and says, "I can only buy this sometimes," (monthly allowance).
  COMPARATIVE STIMULI: dollars and cents

CONTINUOUS CONVERSION METHOD: The teacher shows a price, followed by a "¢," from the store flyer. The student states that it can be bought any day and takes out a dollar. The teacher cuts away the cents sign and tapes on a dollar sign while the student watches. The student then states that it is a monthly purchase and selects the correct number of ten-dollar bills. The teacher tests untrained examples with "¢" and "$" to be sure the student has mastered the discrimination and classification.

General Symbol Identification and Sight Word Reading

Identification of written symbols is a response often required in academic learning. Identifying a symbol's name or "reading" the symbol may be required not only for words but also for prices, clock numbers, money, and community symbols. Usually the teacher will initially prompt symbol identification to assist the student who has not learned the discrimination. If expressive labeling is the target response, the teacher might prompt by modeling the verbal response ("six o'clock") or by pointing to the correct choice, such as the student's name in an array of written names.

Prompting and fading, described in Chapter 5, are reviewed here briefly and their applicability to teaching symbol discrimination is discussed. Etzel and LeBlanc (1979) have recommended a principle of parsimony for use in designing transfer of stimulus control (prompt-fading) procedures. Procedures to fade prompts in symbol identification may be arranged in order of their complexity. Complex procedures, which are not necessarily more effective, are those that require more time to plan or to prepare special materials for each symbol taught.

Unfaded Prompts

The simplest way to teach an individual to read a symbol is to model the word several times and then eliminate the model. The prompt is simply omitted (without gradual fading) after several trials. A response prompt frequently used in teaching oral reading of a printed word is a verbal model. A verbal model has been used to teach subjects who were moderately and severely retarded to read nouns and adjective-nouns (Brown et al., 1979; Brown, Jones, Troccolo, Heiser, Bellamy, & Sontag, 1972; Folk & Campbell, 1978), and prepositions in sentences (Brown & Perlmutter, 1971).

Brown et al (1972) taught two students with moderate retardation, 5 and 5 yr. 9 mo. old, to read nouns. The instruction consisted of three steps and was preceded by a baseline measurement of all steps. The instructional steps taught the subjects to (a) label 12 objects, (b) read 12 printed words (the objects' names), and (c) match each object with its name. To teach oral reading of the printed word, the teacher presented the word, verbally modeled its correct label (response prompt), and asked each student to imitate the verbal model. After three verbal models for each word, the prompt was dropped (no fading). The teacher reinforced correct imitations with praise and correct oral reading (no prompt) with praise and edibles. Incorrect labels were corrected by the teacher. After 15 trials, the subjects reached the goal of reading all 12 words for three consecutive trials. This same procedure was employed by Brown et al. (1970) to teach 17 sight words (various parts of speech), by Brown and Perlmutter (1971) to teach noun-preposition phrases, and by Brown et al. (1974) to teach action verbs.

In teaching sight word reading to two primary-age students with severe reading disabilities, Hendrickson, Roberts and Shores (1978) compared the use of an antecedent model to a contingent or error correction model. The antecedent model was like that used by Brown et al. (1974), in which the teacher labeled the word and required student imitation. In the contingent model, the teacher presented a word, waited for a response, and then modeled the word if the student did not respond correctly. Hendrickson et al. (1978), using a multiple treatment experimental design, found the antecedent model to be superior to the contingent model in that the students required fewer days to reach the goal and made fewer errors. This research suggests the need to present the verbal model with each printed word prior to the student's response and to require an immediate response from the student.

In all of these studies using a verbal model, the model was eliminated all at once rather than faded (Brown et al., 1972; Brown et al., 1974; Brown & Perlmutter, 1971; Hendrickson et al., 1978). Although the procedures were effective, they were probably not errorless. Brown et al. (1972) reported a high error rate for their subjects which *increased* for each new word list introduced, until the last list when errors dropped somewhat. Even though Hendrickson et al. (1978) found fewer errors using

antecedent modeling than contingent modeling, errors were still reported. It is not known how the errors in these studies influenced acquisition or retention of the word lists.

In fact, when prompts are introduced and not faded, acquisition of a skill may not be superior to trial and error learning (Hawker, Geertz, & Shrago, 1964). Hawker et al. and Hawker (1968) compared prompting to confirmation (trial and error learning) in teaching sight words to institutionalized subjects with mental retardation. The prompt employed was a red arrow over the correct word in an array of words. The prompt was never eliminated during training trials and was not present in test trials that were interspersed as every third trial. Although the authors concluded that these studies failed to support the use of prompting, their results actually failed to support the use of an *unfaded* prompt. When a prompt is neither faded nor eliminated, no opportunity is allowed to transfer stimulus control from the prompt to the discriminative stimulus; thus, the learner may not attend to the discriminative stimulus because it is not required in order to make the response and receive reinforcement.

Time Delay

A simple method to fade a prompt like a verbal model or gesture is time delay. Browder, Hines, McCarthy, and Fees (1984) used delay to teach sight words in daily living instruction booklets. The key words selected for instruction were those that would assist in cooking, doing laundry, and using the telephone. Generalization probes were made of the students' ability to perform similar cooking, laundry, and telephone tasks using the key words with new materials. Instruction in each session included repeated practice on reading the key words, followed by instruction on reading the directions to perform the task. All but one of the students mastered the words, used them to perform the task, and generalized to untrained tasks. This same delay procedure was successful in teaching letters and words to young children with severe behavior disorders (Browder & D'Huyvetters, 1985; D'Huyvetters & Browder, 1985) and prices on vending machines to students with moderate mental retardation (Browder, Snell, & Ambrogio, 1985). This procedure is as follows:

- *No Delay.* All words or symbols are presented initially with an immediate model of the response. ("Look at the word. Read the word permanent press.' ") The student is reinforced for imitating the model correctly.

- *Progressive Delay.* A fading schedule is introduced for each individual word or symbol. If the word is read correctly *after* the prompt for two consecutive training trials, the teacher introduces a 2-second delay. After two more trials of correct imitation to read the word, the prompt is given with a 4-second delay. This pattern (two consecutive trials of correctly initiated responses with the model delayed an additional 2 seconds) is continued until an 8-second delay is reached; then the prompt is given at 8 seconds for all subsequent trials until the word is read before the prompt. In this phase, reinforcement is given for correct imitation of the model.

- *Alternative if Read Without Prompts.* If the word is read correctly for two consecutive trials before the prompt is given at any point in the progressive delay schedule, the prompt is eliminated and reinforcement is only given for reading the word correctly without prompting.

- *Alternative if Errors Occur.* If the student makes two consecutive errors, phase one and two are repeated. That is, the teacher reintroduces the immediate prompt for two consecutive trials and then begins the progressive delay schedule again.

- *Types of Trials.* If the words are being taught in a massed trial format, each word on the list is presented until all words have been presented. The entire list may then be reviewed again for two or three rounds. If the words or symbols fall in the context of a daily living skill, the delay procedure is applied when the symbol discrimination is required in the response chain to execute the task. Thus, a trial is an opportunity to read the word which may come in a series of words or in a series of responses in a response chain. The delay schedule and criteria for fading are applied to *each* word. Since the use of the progressive delay on an individual word criterion requires careful data review, an example of these data is shown in Figure 15.3.

Stimulus Fading

Another approach to designing strategies for transfer of stimulus control involves the addition of a visual stimulus prompt (picture) followed subsequently by graphic fading—removing components of the prompt or making it progressively lighter.

This graphic fading technique is most frequently referred to as "fading" in reading research. Several experiments have supported the effectiveness of using stimulus fading with a picture serving as the stimulus prompt (Corey & Shamow, 1972; Dorry, 1976; Dorry & Zeaman, 1973; Dorry & Zeaman, 1975).

Dorry and Zeaman (1973) compared graphic fading to a no-fade condition in training a list of sight words to 18 children who were retarded and could not read. After training and an acquisition test on the list of sight words, a second list of eight words was taught. The group taught using the fading procedure acquired significantly more words, both for word acquisition and transfer to new words.

In a follow-up study, Dorry and Zeaman (1975) compared this same graphic fading technique to three other procedures of teaching sight words to students having moderate and severe retardation. The four procedures used were: (a) a standard no-fade condition, (b) fading the picture out, (c) alternating trials of presenting the word and picture alone, and (d) presenting the word alone or picture alone on alternate trials (control). Two lists of four words were trained for three trials per word (12 trials) using the same procedure for both lists. An analysis of group means on tests of both lists showed the faded condition to be superior to the other three procedures in number of words acquired and retained.

Another study (Dorry, 1976) was designed to determine whether stimulus change itself was responsible for the superiority of the fading procedure. Dorry selected 48 subjects with retardation and assigned them to one of four training procedures: (a) fade picture out, (b) fade word in, (c) double fade: picture out and word in, and (d) standard no-fade condition. Two word lists were trained using these procedures, and a third was trained to assess transfer. An analysis of group means on tests of acquisition, retention, and transfer showed the fading picture out and double-fade conditions to be significantly superior to the other conditions. Dorry concluded that it was not the stimulus change that produced the better performance, but rather the technique of fading the picture. An example of stimulus fading is shown in Figure 15.4. Another example (Figure 5.5) was presented on page 131 of Chapter 5 in which the word was superimposed on the picture.

DAYS

	DAYS 1		DAYS 2		DAYS 3		DAYS 4		DAYS 5		DAYS 6		DAYS 7	
TRIALS	1	2	3	4	5	6	7	8	9	10	11	12	13	14
WARM	⊕ 0	⊕ 0	⊕ 2	⊕ 2	⊕ 4	⊕ 4	⊕ 6	⊕ 6	⊕ 8	⊕ 8	⊕ 8	⊕ 8	+ 8	+ 8
HOT	⊕ 0	⊕ 0	⊕ 2	⊕ 2	⊕ 4	+ 4	+ 6	+ *	+ *	+ *	+ *	+ *	+ *	+ *
COLD	⊕ 0	⊖ 0	⊕ 0	⊕ 0	⊕ 2	⊕ 2	⊕ 4	+ 4	+ 6	+ *	+ *	+ *	+ *	+ *
PERM. PRESS	⊕ 0	⊕ 0	− 2	− 2	⊕ 0	⊕ 0	⊕ 2	⊕ 2	⊕ 4	⊕ 4	− 6	⊕ 6	⊕ 8	⊕ 8
REGULAR	⊕ 0	⊕ 0	⊕ 2	⊕ 2	⊕ 4	⊕ 4	− 6	− 6	⊕ 0	⊕ 0	⊕ 2	⊕ 2	+ 4	+ 4
DELICATES	⊕ 0	⊕ 0	− 2	− 2	⊕ 0	⊕ 0	⊕ 2	⊕ 2	⊕ 4	⊕ 4	+ 6	+ 6	+ *	+ *
HI	⊕ 0	⊕ 0	⊕ 2	⊕ 2	⊕ 4	+ 4	+ 6	+ *	+ *	+ *	− *	+ *	+ *	+ *
LOW	⊕ 0	⊕ 0	⊕ 2	⊕ 2	⊕ 4	+ 4	+ 6	+ *	+ *	+ *	+ *	+ *	+ *	+ *

NUMBERS ARE DELAY LEVEL TEACHER USED

+	CORRECT NO HELP
⊕	CORRECT AFTER VERBAL MODEL
⊖	ERROR AFTER VERBAL MODEL
−	ERROR BEFORE MODEL
*	NO PROMPT

FIGURE 15.3 An example of a time delay schedule for teaching sight words

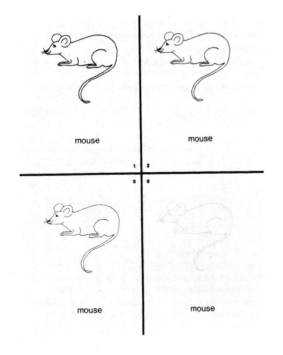

mouse   mouse

mouse   mouse

FIGURE 15.4 An example of stimulus fading

Source: From "Errorless Discrimination and Picture Fading as Techniques for Teaching Sight Words to TMR Students" by B.F. Walsh and F. Lamberts. 1979. *American Journal of Mental Deficiency, 83*(5). p. 474. Reprinted by permission.

Stimulus Shaping

In stimulus shaping, an easy-to-hard discrimination is taught by changing the exemplars and/or nonexemplars in an array of symbols from a maximum to a minimum contrast. The illustration from the Edmark Reading Program shown in Figure 15.5 shows how the materials are prepared for stimulus shaping. The target word is presented in an array of cards with "distractor" symbols. Initially, these distractors have large differences from the target word. Horizontal lines are used as distractors in contrast to the target word. Over trials the distractors acquire more stimulus features of the target word (letters, word length, similar or same letters). By the last trials, the distractors and target word are highly visible, which teaches the learner to attend to every stimulus feature (every relevant letter) of the word in order to make the discrimination between the target word and similar word.

Comparison of Methods

Complex stimulus fading and shaping techniques require making several materials for each word

horse	---	---
ft	horse	un
ros	fuvx	horse
sho	horse	rwao
	horse	

FIGURE 15.5 An example of stimulus shaping

Source: From "Errorless Discrimination and Picture Fading as Techniques for Teaching Sight Words to TMR Students" by B.F. Walsh and F. Lamberts. 1979. *American Journal of Mental Deficiency, 83*(5). p. 474. Reprinted by permission.

to be taught; thus, the teacher must question whether these procedures are more effective than simpler methods like time delay. Stimulus shaping, although more complex than stimulus fading, has resulted in better acquisition of symbols by children who are nonhandicapped than has stimulus fading (Schilmoeller, Schilmoeller, Etzel, & LeBlanc, 1979) and better acquisition of sight words by students with moderate mental retardation than stimulus fading (Walsh & Lamberts, 1979). However, time delay is *less* complex than stimulus fading and also has been more effective in teaching letters and numbers to preschool children (Bradley-Johnson, Sunderman, & Johnson, 1983) and sight words to adults with moderate to severe mental retardation (Browder, 1981). Perhaps due to the complexity of stimulus shaping, no comparisons have been made of this procedure with time delay.

Logistical considerations also favor the selection of delay to teach symbol identification. Time delay has been shown to be quite portable: It can be used to teach reading in the context of daily living activities as demonstrated by Browder et al. (1984). Delay also requires no special materials beyond the picture or word booklets to be taught or reproductions of the words as found in community contexts. By contrast, if a teacher wants to use a published curriculum to teach early sight word reading, the *Edmark Reading Program* is readily available and based on an empirically supported procedure (stimulus shaping) to teach visual discrimination. Research on this curriculum is described later in this chapter.

Summary of Applications of Stimulus Control Research

The research just reviewed can help teachers make two important decisions in planning academic instruction. The first is how to select and sequence instruction for efficient learning with generalization. The second relates to one specific, frequently required academic response: visual discrimination. By applying this research, teachers may develop prompt fading procedures to teach visual discriminations. Later in this chapter some published curricula will be reviewed. Sometimes it may be more efficient for a teacher to use a published curriculum, saving application of research findings for designing more individualized and functional academic activities or for remedial programs when published academic programs are not effective. Existing commercial curricula primarily focus on generalized academic skills. When isolated skills are selected or prostheses are to be designed, the methodology presented on stimulus control may be especially helpful for creating a curriculum for a student. The rest of this chapter is devoted to the various approaches to planning academic instruction, with more suggestions for planning in traditionally recognized academic areas of reading, math, and language arts. As described at the beginning of this chapter, these topics can be considered within the academic approach to be taken: (a) generalized academic skills, and (b) specific, limited academic instruction and prostheses.

GENERALIZED ACADEMIC SKILLS

As mentioned earlier, generalized academic skills require a longitudinal (several year) commitment to an instructional sequence designed to teach broad stimulus generalization; however, the sequence must also be designed to teach academic skills required in daily life, including reading, math skills (computation, money use, and telling time), and language arts skills required for writing.

Reading

"Functional literacy" requires a student to attain about a fourth-grade reading level; however, a broad spectrum of reading skills at a lower "grade level" can also enable the student to perform many daily reading skills. Categories of daily reading have been described by Lichtman (1974) and are shown in Figure 15.6. Some examples of commercial curricula that include daily living reading are listed at the end of this chapter. Achieving the goal of generalized reading, (the ability to analyze and comprehend a large vocabulary of words, phrases, and passages) requires several skills. These include: a sight vocabulary of frequently encountered words, word analysis, and comprehension.

Sight Words

To determine which words to teach in a functional literacy reading program when only a limited number will be taught requires an awareness of word frequency. Word lists such as Fry's list of 300 "Instant Words" (Fry, 1957, 1972), the Dolch list of 200 words (Dolch, 1950), and the revised Dale list of 769 useful words (Stone, 1956) all represent efforts to compile the most frequently appearing words in beginning reading material. Duffy and Sherman (1977) selected words common to the Fry, Dolch, and Stone lists as the most frequently appearing, and therefore most useful, words. Most of these would be taught during the readiness phase. Next, they classified words by their phonetic and structural elements (compound words, words with the *sh* digraph, and those with the *-at* phonogram), ordered each classification in terms of frequency, eliminated words composed of infrequently occurring elements, and matched groups of words with teaching objectives. Words with a certain phonetic or structural element are taught at the time their corresponding rule is taught, whereas some frequently appearing but irregular words (those not employing the identified elements) are taught as sight words. In addition, some regularly spelled words (such as "cat" and "pen") are taught in the prerequisite skills unit as sight words and are used again later as examples of phonetic or structural generalizations. In all, the reader who completes the prerequisite and word recognition skill units learns to recognize or analyze more than 900 words. Figure 15.7 provides an informal test for recognition of one high frequency word list— the Dolch list (Dolch, 1950). This list could be expanded as described by Duffy and Sherman (1977) by adding phonetically regular words.

One problem with such word lists is that, although the words may frequently be encountered in basal reading series, they may be less important to reading for daily living (color words like "red" and "green"). The teacher may wish to scrutinize these lists to eliminate such words. Alternatively,

1 Signs and Labels	2 Schedules and Tables	3 Maps	4 Categorized Listings and Indices	5 High-Interest, Factual Narrative
Road Signs* Clothing Tags Medicine Labels Billboards	T.V. Guide* Bus Schedule Train/Plane Schedule Work/School Schedule	City/Street Road* Global Weather	Yellow Pages Book Indices Want Ad* Dictionary	Sports Events News Report Narcotics Article*

6 Illustrated Advertisements	7 Technical Documents	8 Sets of Directions	9 Fill-in Blank Form
Department Store Yellow Pages Food Store* Magazine	Conditional Sales Contract Insurance Policies Guarantees Apartment Lease*	Recipe (Pizza)* Use of Tools/ Machinery/Equipment Sewing with Pattern	Banking Forms Job Application* Car Registration Credit Application Hospital Entry Form

*For each of these representative reading activities, detailed task analyses have been prepared, including terminal tasks and enabling tasks.

FIGURE 15.6 Categories of commonly used printed materials. [Items marked with an asterisk are included in a test of functional literacy: Reading/Everyday Activities in Life (R/EAL). The test is presented so that its appearance clearly resembles its actual printed form.]

Source: From "The Development and Validation of R/EAL, An Instrument to Assess Functional Literacy" by M. Lichtman, 1974, *Journal of Reading Behavior, 6,* 172. Reprinted by permission.

the list of frequently encountered words could be generated or expanded by reviewing the student's current and future environments to identify words needed in each. Lichtman's (1974) activities suggest a list of words that may be appropriate for some students. Commercial materials with sight words also may be useful if they are validated through environmental inventory for the student's use. For example, the word "poison" is neither functional nor a survival word if it does not appear anywhere in the student's environment. But a symbol of a skull and crossbones or the phrase "Not For Internal Use" might be frequently encountered. Similarly, words on road signs are seldom required for nondrivers. A student who walks will learn to stop at all curbs, not just those with a stop sign.

Word Analysis

Many researchers have recognized the limitations that whole word methods put upon reading achievement. Brown et al. (1974) comment:

It is quite probable that the whole-word method of teaching reading, at least as it has been discussed here, can result in substantial gains in reading achievement. However, it is doubtful that teachers will, by the use of this method, teach their students to read every word, every verb conjugation, and every plural and abbreviation that the students must learn. Hopefully it should be unnecessary to do this. Effective methods of teaching word-attack skills, phonetic, etc., must be delineated and verified empirically for use with this level student. (p. 58)

In order to achieve functional reading goals, the reader with moderate or severe handicaps must learn some word-recognition skills. Some of the laboratory research (Neville & Vandever, 1973), as well as some applied research with people with moderate retardation (Apffel, Kelleher, Lilly & Richardson, 1975; Vandever, Maggart, & Nasser, 1976) and with mild handicaps (Lahey, Weller, & Brown, 1973; Lovitt & Hurlburt, 1974), has indicated the success of teaching readers to analyze words by sound, sight, and context rather than to read by sight alone. To read fluently, a student must instantly recognize a large number of words as well as quickly determine new words. The three different techniques are *phonetic analysis* or sounding out words; *structural analysis* or recognizing meaning units such as parts of compound words, prefixes, suffixes, and parts of contractions; and *context anal-*

ysis or using the meaning of the sentence and preceding sentences to determine an unknown word.

Phonetic analysis includes three subskills: letter-sound correspondence, phonetic generalization, and syllabication (Duffy & Sherman, 1973). The prerequisite letter-sound associations focus upon single consonants and consonant blends and digraphs* but do not teach symbol-sound associations for vowels. "Letter-sound correspondence" at this point focuses upon analyzing vowel sounds. To analyze the sound a vowel makes, one must know the letters that surround that vowel in any given word. Because a single vowel may have many sound associations, depending upon the word it is in, you cannot identify its associated sound apart from seeing its position in a word. Instruction of vowel-sound correspondence proceeds in two stages. First, the student is taught to recognize short-vowel phonograms† (*at, et, ot, ut it*) within known words (c*at*, p*et*, c*ot*, n*ut*, s*it*) and then to replace the initial consonant with another to make a new word (h*at*, s*et*, r*at*, b*ut*, p*it*). Later, the student learns to replace the final consonant or a digraph to make new words with new phonograms (c*at*—c*ap*, c*an*; m*et*—m*en*, m*esh*).

In the English language there are some fairly consistent rules of sounding similar letter combinations in similar ways. These are called *phonetic generalizations*. Examples of these include the silent *e* (in the pronunciation of smil*e*, mak*e*, jok*e*, rid*e*, hol*e*) and the two vowels together—one syllable rule (b*oa*t, pl*ai*n, wh*ea*t, g*oa*t, s*ui*t). Although these rules are not universally true, they are consistent enough to be taught as patterns to attend to in unknown words.

Syllabication is the third part of ph. netic analysis—strategies to analyze sound units in an unknown word as a means of identifying that word. Syllabication breaks large, multisyllabic words into smaller, more manageable units. the instructional progression for teaching various syllabication patterns (vowel-consonant-consonant-vowel: *until, almost, after;* vowel-consonant-vowel; *even, between, tiger*) is first to teach auditory discrimination of the number of sound units, then to teach visual discrimination of the number of sound units, then to teach visual discrimination of the particular pattern of vowels and consonants and the rule for dividing a word into single sound units, and finally to teach generalization of the rule across many unfamiliar words with various patterns of letters.

Whereas in phonetic analysis, the learner focuses on sound units to unlock unknown words, in *structural analysis* the learner must direct attention to those parts that signal meaning as a method to analyze unknown words. Units of meaning that the student is taught to attend include:

1. Root words plus inflectional endings, such as *-s, -ed,* and *-ing;*
2. Root words plus suffixes, such as *-ness, -able,* and *-ly.*
3. Prefixes plus the root word (*un-happy*);
4. Parts of compound words (*back-pack*);
5. Parts of contractions (*couldn't = could not*). (Duffy & Sherman, 1973, p. 169).

To use structural analysis, the reader must be able to look at unknown words and discover known parts, recognize the root word either instantly as a sight word or by sounding it out, sound the prefix, suffix, or the other portion of the compound, and finally blend the parts together as one word.

Context analysis allows a reader to determine unknown words from the meaning of known words and the clues provided by known letter sounds. Context analysis requires the student to read for meaning and, with the assistance of letter-sound analysis guess unknown words. When context clues are used without letter-sound analysis or vice versa, guessing often is inefficient. For example, the unknown word in the sentence "She put the [unknown word] on her head" could be *cap, hat, helmet, scarf, shampoo,* etc. If an initial sound clue (*s . . .*) is recognized, identity becomes more likely. Additional phonetic or structural clues (*s . . . f*) may be used along with context to increase this likelihood (final consonant, syllabication, prefixes).

Entrikin et al., (1977) report a well-defined sequence of objectives directed toward the instruction of elementary word recognition strategies; using picture cues, context clues, and initial consonant sounds to determine an unknown word.

---

*A blend is the sound combination resulting from adjacent consonants without loss of either sound's identity; for example, "*bl*ue st*r*ike." A digraph is two letters in succession which, when pronounced, represent a single sound rather than a blending of both letter sounds; for instance, "*th*irty."

†A "phonogram" is a pronounceable sound unit beginning with a voewl (*-ing, at, of*) frequently found at the end of a word which may be combined with various initial consonants, consonant blends, or digraphs to make new words (s*ing*, br*ing*, th*ing*).

General Instructions:

The following steps should be followed to give an informal test of an individual's ability to recognize frequently used words (Dolch, 1950) in isolation of phrase or sentence context.

1. *Preparing word cards.* Type in primary-sized type or print clearly the high utility words selected for each grade level on separate 3 × 5 inch cards. A minimum of 25 words should be selected for at least each of the following grade levels: preprimer, primer, first, second, third.
2. *Ordering the words.* Order the words by level from preprimer on with a matched listing on which to score the student's responses (see test pages).
3. *Flashed exposure.* Make sure that the student is ready and attending; flash the words to the student one at a time allowing a 1-second exposure to each word. Unless you have information that the student "reads well" at levels above preprimer, start with preprimer words. The best method of flashing words is to hold a blank card over the word and move it up (or down), then back down after 1 second. Another way involves the use of a card with a window-opening in it or a tachistoscope.
4. *Scoring flashed words.* If the word is correctly read in the flashed condition, score a + in the appropriate blank and go to the next word. Immediate self-corrections are scored as incorrect because it indicates that the student's initial perception of the word was not accurate. If the word is not attempted, score a NR for no response to the word. For misread words, write the incorrect response in the blank. These mistakes will be analyzed after the test to detect any patterns in the student's incorrect responses.
5. *Untimed exposure.* Whenever an error is made in a flashed exposure, record the student's performance, then repeat the trial, allowing sufficient time (10 seconds) for the student to examine and analyze the word.
6. *Scoring untimed words.* The student's response to the untimed condition is listed in the untimed column: + for correct, NR for no response, and for errors the misread word is placed in the blank.
7. *Test ceiling.* Testing is stopped as soon as the student misses 10% (or more) at a given grade level (i.e. 2 of 20 words, 4 of 40, etc.). However, if one is interested in obtaining a larger baseline, one may test beyond a 10% error level as long as adequate reinforcement is made available.
8. *Determination of reading levels.* The results of a word list test can be used only to *roughly estimate reading levels* and tend to underestimate these levels because reading words in isolation is more difficult than in context. However, the highest grade level at which 98–100% of the words were correctly read may be regarded as an estimate of the student's independent reading level; 95% corresponds to instructional level and 90% or less signifies frustration level.

Name _____   Examiner _____

Date _____   School _____

	Pre-Primer			Primer			First Grade	
	Flashed	Untimed		Flashed	Untimed		Flashed	Untimed
1. and	___	___	1. all	___	___	1. after	___	___
2. run	___	___	2. am	___	___	2. again	___	___
3. up	___	___	3. are	___	___	3. an	___	___
4. down	___	___	4. at	___	___	4. any	___	___
5. where	___	___	5. ate	___	___	5. as	___	___
6. it	___	___	6. black	___	___	6. ask	___	___
7. come	___	___	7. do	___	___	7. by	___	___
8. red	___	___	8. eat	___	___	8. could	___	___
9. yellow	___	___	9. four	___	___	9. every	___	___
10. big	___	___	10. get	___	___	10. fly	___	___

	Pre-Primer			Primer			First Grade	
	Flashed	Untimed		Flashed	Untimed		Flashed	Untimed
11. see			11. good			11. from		
12. away			12. he			12. give		
13. I			13. like			13. going		
14. me			14. must			14. had		
15. make			15. new			15. has		
16. blue			16. no			16. her		
17. help			17. now			17. him		
18. one			18. on			18. his		
19. for			19. our			19. how		
20. a			20. out			20. just		
21. little			21. please			21. know		
22. funny			22. ran			22. let		
23. go			23. saw			23. live		
24. three			24. she			24. may		
25. two			25. soon			25. of		
26. to			26. that			26. old		
27. said			27. there			27. once		
28. my			28. they			28. open		
29. the			29. this			29. pretty		
30. look			30. too			30. put		
31. here			31. under			31. round		
32. is			32. want			32. some		
33. in			33. was			33. stop		
34. find			34. well			34. take		
35. can			35. what			35. them		
36. you			36. white			36. then		
37. not			37. who			37. think		
38. we			38. will			38. walk		
39. jump			39. with			39. were		
40. play			40. yes			40. when		
TOTAL			TOTAL			TOTAL		
PERCENT CORRECT			PERCENT CORRECT			PERCENT CORRECT		

FIGURE 15.7 Informal word recognition test of Dolch basic words in isolation

Source of Word List: *Teaching Primary Reading,* (2nd ed.) by E.W. Dolch, 1950, Champaign, Ill: Garrard Press. Reprinted by permission.

Three 10-year-old students with moderate mental retardation and varying motor handicaps met the following six entry criteria for training and successfully used basic word recognition strategies with unknown words.

1. Imitation of teacher-provided consonant sounds.
2. Rudimentary speech;
3. A sight vocabulary of at least 50 words;
4. Left-to-right eye movement when reading;
5. A reliable and valid yes-no response;
6. A basic understanding of logical and absurd relationships. (p. 171)

The content of the instruction program is summarized in the skill sequence shown in Figure 15.8. For more definition of teaching procedure, see the original report (Entrikin, York, & Brown, 1973). Many commercial materials also exist to help teachers design instruction for word analysis (see the list at the end of this chapter.)

Comprehension Skills

As mentioned in the discussion of equivalence earlier in this chapter, comprehension is a language skill. If students can analyze the words in a passage and have mastered the concepts of language, comprehension will probably be evident. The teacher might take two approaches to remedy comprehension (language) deficits. One would be to provide direct instruction in answering typical reading comprehension questions. Questions that would address some comprehension areas are:

1. "Wh" questions for factual recall (what, who, when, where)
2. What do you think happens next? (prediction)
3. What happened before (or after). . . ? (sequence)
4. What would be a good title for this story? (main idea)
5. What would (this character) do if. . . ? (inference)

Commercial resources on comprehension provide many examples for practice in this type of question answering skill (*Clues for Better Reading*—see list at end of chapter).

Another approach to comprehension instruction is to have the student compose a story (Stauffer, 1970). This "language experience approach" has the advantage of providing vocabulary from the student's current language concepts. In the language experience approach, the student dictates a

I. Word Analysis through the Use of Pictures and Initial Consonant Sounds·
   1. Name objects and pictures.
   2. Make initial consonant sounds when shown printed letter.
   3. Point to the first letter in the word.
      a. Color coded.
      b. Not color coded.
   4. Make initial consonant sounds when shown first letter in printed word.
   5. Make initial consonant sound when shown a picture.
      a. After teacher names the picture.
      b. After student names the picture.
      c. Without naming the picture.
   6. Identify a picture given the initial consonant sound.
   7. Analyze a new word given an array of pictures and a printed word by matching initial consonant sounds of picture to first letter of the word.

II. Word Analysis through the Use of Pictures and Context
   1. Name pictures.
   2. Discriminate between logical (combing hair with a comb) and absurd pictures (combing hair with a toothbrush).
   3. Discriminate between logical and absurd sentences read aloud by teacher.
   4. Complete a sentence by selecting a picture.
      a. Object.
      b. Action verb.
      c. Subject.
      d. Mixed sentences with either a, b, or c.
   5. Complete a sentence by selecting a printed word.
      a. Sentence read by the teacher.
      b. Sentence on a worksheet, not read by the teacher.

III. Word Analysis through the Use of Pictures, Initial Consonant Sounds, and Context
   1. Name pictures.
   2. Demonstrate comprehension of a new word in a sentence by marking a picture of it (student identifies picture with same first sound as new word and that is logical).

FIGURE 15.8 Skill sequence to teach word analysis
Source: Adapted from "Teaching Trainable Level Multiply Handicapped Students to Use Picture Cues, Context Cues, and Initial Consonant Sounds to Determine the Labels of Unknown Words" by D. Entrikin, R. York, & L. Brown, 1977. *AAESPH Review, 2*, p. 169–190.

story which the teacher records, adding words to make complete sentences if necessary. Reading instruction is focused on this story or passage, which may consist of topics such as classroom activities, community instruction, family events, or other subjects the student initiates. To use this passage for reading instruction, the teacher may (a) put new words on flash cards for sight word instruction, (b) ask comprehension ("wh") questions and underline the phrase or passage in the story with the answer, (c) ask the student to select a picture (photograph) for the story, and (d) have the student type, recopy, or photocopy the story for a permanent story book. Figure 15.9 provides an example of a story composed by an adolescent with moderate mental retardation and a severe behavior disorder.

Commercial Programs

Several commercially available programs are listed at the end of this chapter. Of these programs, only the *Edmark Reading Program* (1972, 1984) was specifically designed for nonreaders with mild and moderate mental retardation (Bijou, Birnbrauer, Kidder, & Tague, 1966; Birnbrauer, Wolf, Kidder, & Tague, 1965). The *Edmark* program uses stimulus shaping to teach word discrimination. The new edition has available computer software, a handbook for signing, and an adaptive device. Thus, this program may be especially appropriate for the young child with physical handicap or who is nonverbal. *The Peabody Rebus Reading Program* (Woodcock, Davies, & Clark, 1969) uses picture symbols to facilitate reading. This program incorporates stimulus fading from pictures to words. Finally, the DISTAR reading program (Engelmann & Bruner, 1974) teaches word analysis and uses principles of learning such as stimulus fading, continuous conversions, and modeling. All three programs have been successful in teaching some

reading skills to students with mild and moderate mental retardation (*Rebus:* Apffel et al., 1975; Woodcock, 1968; Bijou et al., 1966; Birnbauer, et al., 1965; Lent, 1968; Vandever, Maggart, & Nasser, 1976; Vandever & Stubbs, 1977; DISTAR: Apffel et al., 1975; Booth, Hewitt, Jenkins, & Maggs, 1979; Bracey, Maggs, & Morath, 1975; Engelmann, 1967; Williamson, 1970). Unfortunately, few comparative studies allow critical evaluation of each program's effectiveness and identification of ways to match students to programs.

Spelling and Writing

Alphabet reading is *not* a prerequisite for sight-word reading. Adolescents and adults may have limited use for the skill of reading the alphabet. On the other hand, younger children may benefit from mastery of alphabet reading and writing. Alphabet recognition might be introduced along with typing or computer skills. If a computer or a typewriter is available, using either one would provide a logical alternative to handwriting for students who learn slowly and/or whose handwriting is illegible. Handwriting instruction may only be needed for the skill of writing a signature. While Calhoun (1985) used the "hunt and peck" method to teach typing, color cues may be used to teach finger placement typing, as illustrated by the commercial material *Touch to Type* (see list at end of chapter).

If handwriting is taught, letter strokes might be task analyzed for instruction. Figure 15.10 provides an example of a task analysis to teach printing the first name "Benjamin." The figure gives examples of the verbal prompts that might be used. In addition to these, a prompt hierarchy could be used with a model and physical guidance. If laminated paper and a washable felt tip pen are used for instruction, mistakes can be corrected with the next level prompt. Stimulus prompts, such as color cues for

I rode the bus. I went to the store. I bought a flashlight for Father's Day. I rode the bus. It cost 50¢.

FIGURE 15.9 Example of a language experience story composed by a student and used to teach reading passages

B e n j a m i n

Task Analysis	Verbal Prompt
B 1.	1. Pull down
2.	2. Push out and pull curve to the middle
3.	3. Push out and pull curve to the bottom
e 4.	4. Push out
5.	5. Curve around Don't touch
n 6.	6. Pull down
7.	7. Push over. Curve. Pull down
j 8.	8. Pull down below the line
9.	9. Curve up to the line
10.	10. Dot it
a 11.	11. Push around the circle.
12.	12. Pull down
m 13.	13. Pull down
14.	14. Push over. Curve Pull down
15.	15. Push over. Curve Pull down
i 16.	16. Pull down
17.	17. Dot it
n 18.	18. Pull down
19.	19. Push over. Curve Pull down

FIGURE 15.10   Example of task analysis and prompts to teach name writing

left and right (green to signal "go" at the left margin and red to signal "stop" at the right margin), or boxes to cue letter height and spacing may also be introduced and gradually faded.

Math Skills

Besides computation, money use, and telling time, other daily living skills (use of a bank machine or telephone) may require number recognition. Similar to reading, a generalized functional math sequence will include skills closely aligned to daily activities. Inventory of the student's environments, including discussion with parents, can help the teacher decide what to target for this longitudinal instruction.

Computation

Given the current availability of inexpensive calculators, teaching computation may be unnecessary and inefficient for students with severe learning problems. Instead, the teacher may wish to design a skill sequence for generalized computation with the use of a calculator. Horton (1985) compared the computational speed and accuracy of students with mild retardation who used a calculator to students without handicaps who used paper and pencil and found that the calculators enabled the students to exceed the performance of their peers without handicaps. Computational skill sequences have been developed and investigated in research (McClennen & Harrington, 1982; Resnick, Wang, & Kaplan, 1973). Commercial materials also exist to teach basic computation (see list at end of chapter). But again, the teacher may want to weigh the time required to teach computation against investing the time in other instruction. Whereas mastering generalized computation with a calculator could require several years of instruction, it could still be a more efficient approach than teaching paper and pencil computation.

Money Use

One of the most efficient ways to approach money instruction may be to teach generalized dollar bill use and specific, limited coin use. Observations of people without handicaps in public settings often reveal that exact change is rarely given for purchases, and change received after the purchase is rarely counted. To date, research on money use has focused on coin usage (Lowe & Cuvo, 1976; Trace, Cuvo, & Criswell, 1977); however, group home and apartment living requires far more dollar use than coin use. To teach generalized dollar bill use, the teacher might teach the student to discriminate and classify prices by the bills required. The order of instruction might be:

1. Use of one dollar for small, over-the-counter purchases.
2. Discrimination of the number of one dollar bills needed for purchases from less than $1 to $10 based on using the next dollar amount (use 6 ones for $5.43).
3. Discrimination of ten-dollar bills needed to make major purchases like groceries and clothes based on the same rounding up procedure used in #2 for ones (uses 4 tens for $36.48).

4. Classification of mixed purchases as requiring either ones or tens (use ones to purchase a snack or meal at a fast-food restaurant; use tens at the shopping mall for clothes and shoes and at the grocery store).

5. Although most purchases could be made with ones and tens, further generalized money use could be introduced once these amounts were mastered, by teaching bill equivalency using the principle of equivalence described earlier in this chapter (1 twenty equals 2 tens or 4 fives).

Generalized coin use might be selected as early money instruction for the young child. This might be accompanied by teaching use of the one dollar bill as described above. Research by Cuvo and his colleagues provides examples of how generalized coin use could be sequenced and taught.

Coin Summation   Lowe and Cuvo (1976) taught adolescents with mild and moderate mental retardation a finger-counting method to sum coins. The students were taught to place certain fingers on the table and tap them while counting. Nickels were counted by tapping the index finger once for each count by fives, "5, 10, 15 . . ."; dimes were counted by tapping the middle finger once for each count by tens, "10, 20, 30 . . ." All five fingers were tapped in succession for a quarter. Pennies were introduced last and were counted by tapping beside each penny and counting by ones from the amount already totaled (with a nickel and two pennies, "five" by the nickel, "six, seven" beside the pennies). The order of instruction was:

1. Count nickels.
2. Count dimes.
3. Sum nickels and dimes.
4. Count quarters.
5. Sum nickels, dimes, and quarters.
6. Count half dollars.
7. Sum nickels, dimes, quarters, half dollars.
8. Count pennies.
9. Sum all coins.

The instructional procedure was to model the counting while the student watched, to count the coins with the student, and then to require the student to count them alone. This sequence permits functional use from the onset. Teaching students to count pennies first may be less functional since many services, vending machines, and telephones will not take pennies.

Whatever the order of coins selected, teaching counting can be more effective if the student initially displaces or moves the coin while counting. In a comparison of displacement and nondisplacement, Borakove and Cuvo (1976) found superior performance for students with moderate mental retardation taught with the displacement method. This finding is consistent with Resnick et al.'s (1973) counting sequence.

Coin Equivalence   To purchase an item, one must match coins equivalent to a price. To teach this skill, Trace, Cuvo, and Criswell (1977) used an adapted vending machine. Prices were illuminated on the front of the machine. The machine returned incorrect coin combinations and accepted correct coin combinations, for which it dispensed candy. Thus, the machine itself provided realistic feedback. The only exception was a coin equivalency test in which the machine was used to indicate prices only. Students were taught a variety of combinations to represent the prices on the machine beginning with nickels alone and moving to larger coin combinations. Three specific responses were taught for using the machine; naming the price, selecting equivalent coins, and depositing coins. Although not included by Trace et al., the instructor could teach functional reading of the selection buttons—a fourth response required with most vending machines.

Change Computation   Computing change is more difficult than summing coins because it requires either subtraction of counting from one number (price) to another (money given). Change computation is primarily useful to avoid mistakes by salespeople. A study by Cuvo, Veitch, Trace, and Konke (1978) taught change computation to adolescents with moderate mental retardation who were able to sum coins, read prices, and put together equivalent coins. The order of instruction was 1¢ to 4¢, 3¢ to 25¢, 10¢ to 45¢ (using multiples of 5), and 11¢ to 49¢ (not using multiples of 5). The skill was taught by having the students make a purchase with available coins and then compute their change. The "counting back" procedure was used to make change. That is, the student learned to read the price ("10 cents") and count from the price to the coins given for purchase ("15, 20, 25") and then to state the sum of the change ("15 cents").

Telling Time

Many programs designed to teach time telling to people with handicaps require extensive prerequisites (O'Brien, 1974). For example, one of the best designed commercial programs (Bijou, 1973) requires students to (a) discriminate red and green, (b) count from 1 to 60, and (c) read numbers from 1 to 60, (d) write numbers from 1 to 60, and (e) count by 5's to 55. O'Brien designed a program that does not require many prerequisites. To simplify the task, he taught 14 adults with moderate retardation who resided in an institution to tell time to the nearest quarter hour and to say "about" when shown times between quarter hours ("It's about 8:15"). The only prerequisites necessary were adequate vision and some expressive language. A magnetic clock with detachable numbers was used. Reinforcement was praise and moving a slide counter ahead after each step. After eight slides of the counter, the subject received a sip of diet soda. When errors occurred, the trainer, who was a ward attendant, said a loud "No!" and moved the counter to zero. The phases of the O'Brien program are listed in Figure 15.11. Note that the steps are based on an easy-to-hard discrimination sequence and introducing and withdrawing a verbal prompt. It would be possible to fade the verbal prompt more gradually, using time delay. Although O'Brien successfully taught telling time without using delay fading, this technique might enhance learning for other students.

As O'Brien noted, the skill he taught was only one of many possible time-telling skills. An ecological inventory of a student's environment will identify the precise skills needed, which may include reading written times in a movie ad or TV schedule, reading a digital clock (a watch or alarm clock), budgeting time to finish activities by a given time (getting to a bus stop, ending a break at work), and identifying a clock time, given a spoken time ("Take the roast out at 6:00, John"). When time-telling instruction is separate from its natural use in context (as O'Brien did), it will need to be probed and perhaps retrained in the natural situation. For some students it might be more efficient to teach a selected skill in the setting in which it is needed. An adult in a workshop could be taught to return to a work station when "the long hand passes the two" without knowing how to read the time or any other number.

Measurement

Another math skill that might be targeted for generalized use is measurement. This may include measurement of length (ruler), volume (cups, tablespoons), or weight. Smeenge, Page, Iwata, and Ivancic (1980) developed a skill sequence to teach measurement to an adolescent and two adults who were enrolled in a center for people with multiple handicaps. The skill sequence included instruction with specific feedback ("Good, you lined up the ruler") and produced generalized ruler skills for these three individuals, who had been classified as emotionally disturbed and mildly mentally retarded.

Measurement may best be taught if presented in the context of the activity in which it is to be used (sewing, cooking, vocational skills). It would probably be most logical to put these activities in order of their complexity. The sequence might progress from simple discriminations like matching to complex measurement (cups and half cups). The sequence evaluated by Smeenge et al. (1980) provides an example of skill sequencing for the measurement of length.

1. Discrimination of lengths that are the same or different.
2. Discrimination of lengths that are longer or shorter.
3. Match to sample of a 1-foot length.
4. Measure in 1-foot units.
5. Measure in multiple feet.
6. Measure in multiple inches.
7. Measure in feet and inches.

IEP Example for Generalized Academic Skills

Before reviewing an example of an IEP based on generalized academic skills, the reader may wish to review the guidelines presented at the beginning of the chapter for selecting this type of instruction. The objectives presented in this example are designed for a *young* student who has years to master the targeted generalized use of the skill. This student has also shown a *learning rate* for academics that makes this acquisition a realistic, longitudinal goal. Additionally, this student's *parents* consider academic skills to be important for this phase of their child's school instruction. This example is adapted from an IEP developed at the

I. Reading the Hour Hand
   Step 1: Match number to clock face number
          Phase 1: 1,   (numbers on the clock)
                 2: 1, 8
                 3: 1, 8, 5
                 4: 1, 8, 5, 4
                 5: 1, 8, 5, 4, 10
                 6: 1, 8, 5, 4, 10, 9
                 7: 1, 8, 5, 4, 10, 9, 2
                 8: 1, 8, 5, 4, 10, 9, 2, 6
                 9: 1, 8, 5, 4, 10, 9, 2, 6, 11
               10: 1, 8, 5, 4, 10, 9, 2, 6, 11, 7
               11: 1, 8, 5, 4, 10, 9, 2, 6, 11, 7, 3
               12: 1, 8, 5, 4, 10, 9, 2, 6, 11, 7, 3, 12
               13: 1, 8, 5, 4, 10, 9, 2, 6, 11, 7, 3, 12
   Step 2: "Point to the number ___ on the clock face."
          Shown the number, point to its match on the clock.
          In 13 phases (see above), number held farther and farther away from clock.
   Step 3: "Point to number ___ on the clock face."
          (Not shown the number.)
   Step 4: Imitation of number name. "This is number ___.
          What number is this? Say ___." (Point to number on clock face.)
   Step 5: Number naming. "What number is this?" (Point to number on clock face.)
   Step 6: Reading the hour hand. "What number does the hour hand point to?"

II. Reading the Minute Hand
   Step 7: Discrimination of hour and minute hand. "Point to the hour hand." "Point to the minute hand."
   Step 8: Read minute hand—imitation. "What does the minute hand say. Say 'o'clock'." ("o'clock", "30", "15", "45")
   Step 9: Read the minute hand (no verbal prompt.)

III. Read the Nearest Quarter Hour Setting
   Step 10: Read hour hand when not exactly on a number.
           Phase 1: Move hour hand clockwise.
                  2: Only 2 numbers on clock. Hour hand between them. "Which number did the hour hand point to last?"
                  3: All numbers showing.
                  4: Hour hand between and minute hand on 9.
                  5. Hour hand between and minute hand on 3.
                  6: Hour hand between and minute hand on 6.
                  7: Hour hand between or on and minute hand 12, 9, 3, 6.
                    Note S[D]: "What number does the hour hand point to?"
                    "What number does the minute hand read?"
                    'What time is it? Say ___."
   Step 11: Read time to quarter hour. "What time is it?"
   Step 12: Read time between quarter hour as "It's about ___."
           S[D]: "What time is it? Say about ___."
   Step 13: Read time between quarter hours. No prompt. "What time is it?"
          Phase   Distance from nearest quarter hour
           1   1 minute
           2   1, 3
           3   1, 3, 5
           4   1, 3, 5, 7
           5   0, 1, 3, 5, 7

FIGURE 15.11   Steps in the O'Brien program for telling time

Source: From "Instruction in Reading a Clock for the Institutionalized Retarded" by F. O'Brien, 1974, Unpublished manuscript, Southern Illinois University. Reprinted by permission.

Centennial School in Bethlehem, Pennsylvania, in the Life Skills Classroom II. (The student's name and specific objectives have been changed to protect confidentiality.) The entire IEP is not shown (objectives in street crossing, social integration, grocery store use) but rather, only those goals and objectives directly reflecting academic skills are shown.

Lynn is a 9-year-old girl who has received classifications of moderate mental retardation, autism, and severe emotional disturbance in various psychological evaluations.

● MATHEMATICS

I. When given situations that require coin usage (purchase of an inexpensive item), Lynn will select coin combinations to $1 on 2 out of 3 occasions.

Skill Sequence:

1. Nickels
2. Dimes
3. Nickels and dimes
4. Quarters
5. Nickels, dimes, and quarters

Activities for Instruction:

1. Classroom repeated trial practice with real money
2. Purchase crackers at the drug store
3. Vending machine use
4. Purchase soda at a restaurant

For each of these activities, Lynn uses the coin combinations that she is learning in classroom practice (she carries a roll of nickels to the drug store when she is in the first phase).

II. When given activities that require noting the time, Lynn will identify the time correctly on two out of three occasions.

Skill Sequence:

1. Match numbers
2. Discriminate the hour and minute hands
3. Identify ___ o'clock (Fixed minute hand)
4. Identify ___:45, :30, :15 (Fixed hour hand)
5. Identify time to the nearest quarter hour (variable hour and minute hands with minute hand on the nearest quarter hour; next year she will be taught to read times that fall between these quarter hours).

Activities for Instruction:

1. Repeated classroom trial practice with a real clock
2. Picture schedule with times at her current level of instruction (e.g., in phase one this would require number matching) to be used as a reference for new activities during the day
3. Incidental instruction on clocks seen during instruction in the community

● READING

I. When given a 50-word passage with familiar vocabulary, Lynn will read it with 90% accuracy and correctly answer 3 out of 3 comprehension questions about the passage.

Skill Sequence:

1. 5 to 10-word passage
2. 15-word passage
3. 25-word passage
4. 40-word passage
5. 50-word passage

Activities for Instruction:

1. Lynn composes a story weekly about her other instruction (a story about going to the drug store). This story is used for flash card review of vocabulary and comprehension practice daily.
2. The DISTAR reading program is also taught daily to improve Lynn's word analysis and comprehension. Lynn is currently in the first grade level.

Long-Term Goals: These specific objectives were selected for Lynn to help her meet the long-term goals of competitive employment and an independent or partially supervised living arrangement. Because Lynn has begun to make progress in academic skills early in her school career, by age 21 she may master (a) daily living reading (bus schedules, recipes, movie ads, television guides, and job memos), (b) management of a daily or weekly monetary allowance, and (c) management of her time to follow job and social schedules.

SPECIFIC ACADEMIC INSTRUCTION AND PROSTHESES

At the beginning of this chapter, three other approaches to academic instruction were reviewed. One approach requires that no instruction begin because all academic decisions are made for the student (caretaker gives the individual exact change for the bus). The other two approaches require instruction in the specific academic response or in the use of a prosthetic device and are reviewed in this section of the chapter. When the teacher begins to design specific academic instruction, the focus is primarily on the activity rather than the academic response. Thus, this instruction overlaps with daily living, recreation, and vocational skill instruction. To stimulate thought regarding how these daily skills might be enhanced with concurrent academic instruction, the following discussion is organized by academic skill areas. However, in this approach to academics, the teacher would probably not schedule a time for "reading," but rather would teach the reading concurrently with its functional activity (reading recipes while cooking). Also, because the academic instruction differs greatly from generalized academics, some new categories of skills are suggested. For example, rather than addressing a sight vocabulary or word analysis, the teacher would consider skills like picture booklets and package discrimination. The chapters in this book that address domestic, recreational, and vocational skills may also stimulate ideas for specific, academic instruction.

Specific Reading and Writing Skills

The idea of teaching a limited number of sight words for "survival" has been a frequent practice; however, when the words are selected without ecological inventories of activities, they may lack real utility. When a person only learns to read a few words and/or symbols, careful consideration must be given to vocabulary selected and the activities used for instruction. The following are some potential specific reading skills that might be taught.

Specific Reading Skills

Picture-word Instruction Booklets Instruction booklets have been used most widely for cooking (Johnson & Cuvo, 1981; Martin, Rusch, James, Decker, & Trytol, 1982). Recently, Wacker and Berg (1984) found picture instructions to be beneficial to vocational performance. To develop use of picture or word booklets, a method is needed to teach symbol reading and how to use the booklets to perform the task. Each set of instructions may include some core symbols and pictures (the student's name or a symbol for work) as well as the symbols for that particular task. A book may be idiosyncratic to one specific task (making a peanut butter and jelly sandwich) or general to a type of task (making a sandwich with spreads such as peanut butter, jelly,

cream cheese, meat spreads). The following procedure gives an example of how to select the vocabulary and teach use of the books.

Browder et al. (1985) made word and picture booklets for cooking, telephone use, and laundry skills. Each activity had three general task instructions. Cooking instructions were made for preparing a drink, sandwich, and hot muffin. In laundry, instructions were made for setting the washer for white, medium, and dark clothes. For telephone use, instructions were given for social, personal, community, and emergency calls. The booklets were designed to introduce a core vocabulary that could be used across a type of task (various blender drink recipes). Reading the booklets was taught using time delay in a repeated trials practice format. Following this reading practice, the adults in this study received task analytic instruction in the related daily living activities. Reading and following the booklets were incorporated as steps of the task analysis. A prompt hierarchy was used to assist the learner to perform the daily living response and time delay was used to prompt reading the booklet aloud while performing the response. The adults learned to read the booklets and to use them to perform the trained and an untrained task.

Container/product Discrimination Another important discrimination may be the identification of containers such as packages and bottles. Due to the visual discrimination this requires, it may be viewed as a reading skill. A person must be able to discriminate between powdered cleanser and furniture polish in performing cleaning skills. In grocery shopping, the person might prefer to buy a specific brand of an item and thus, would need to discriminate between "Cheerios" and other cereals, for example. These sometimes difficult discriminations might be enhanced through direct instruction in context of the activity and with repeated trial practice in the classroom.

One product discrimination that could be targeted as a "survival" skill is identification of edible versus inedible products. To teach product discrimination, such as of edible items, the teacher might select containers frequently encountered in the student's home, school, and in future settings such as work. These might include: (a) boxes [cereal, crackers, detergent, biscuit mix], (b) cans [vegetables, fruit, baking powder, mothballs], (c) bottles [soda, dishwashing liquid, cooking oil, juice], and

(d) jars [pickles, peanut butter, silver polish, mayonnaise]. The objective might be for the student to classify the items as (a) those we eat, (b) those we cook to eat, and (c) those we never eat. To teach the discrimination, the teacher might display an item and ask, "What can you eat?" If the student picks a correct choice (edible item from category (a) he receives a taste of it. If an inedible is chosen, the teacher might say "No. You never eat this. It makes you sick" and turn away for a few seconds as an error correction procedure. If the student picks a cooking item, the teacher might say, "We have to cook this first. Try again," and allow another choice. To strengthen instruction, the discrimination might be taught initially with an immediate pointing prompt that is faded with time delay. It would be very important in a skill like this to probe many untaught exemplars to be sure the student has learned to discriminate edibles from inedibles.

Reading to Make Choices Another category of daily reading is the use of pictures or words to make choices. Teaching students to read menus, store fliers with photos, soda names on machines, television guides, movie ads, menus, or teacher-made "menus" of free-time activities may enable them to make choices before engaging in activities. These choices may be displayed as word lists, line drawings, photographs or slides (of the fast food menu). To teach reading the choices, a time-delay procedure might be applied in which the student is taught to read all options aloud. Then choice-making could be taught by giving the student a sample of the first item selected when asked, "What do you want?"

Reading for Mobility Another daily activity that can be facilitated by reading is locating one's destination such as the exit, a certain bus, the aisle in a grocery store, restrooms, and the department of a discount department store. Usually there are many "natural cues" to serve as prompts for these discriminations. For example, the same people may board a bus each morning. The sports department of a department store may have a large rowboat visible from the front of the store; however, teaching reading along with the use of these cues may help the student respond in new settings and when natural cues change (the person who serves as a role model for bus selection may become ill and not be at the bus stop). To transport this instruction to the classroom, slides or videotapes may be especially useful, because they will present both

the words from the community setting and the natural cues. The slides could be designed to include novel settings and occasions when the natural cues are absent to ensure the student can respond to either combination of cues. Sometimes the bus driver forgets to turn the bus destination sign on.

Using daily activities to generate word lists is an alternative to "survival words" that are a core vocabulary to be taught in isolation in the classroom. Such words may never be encountered in the student's actual environments ("caution") or never be needed to perform the activity (a stop sign). For students whose reading will be extremely limited, "survival" reading consists of responding to symbols in context or learning to get by with other cues. Classroom practice may be scheduled to supplement community practice by using real materials, slides, pictures, and objects.

Reading Prostheses Some might consider pictures to be a prosthesis to bypass word reading. Pictures do simplify the discrimination, but a picture instruction booklet may require instruction for comprehension; however, this same task may not be easily learned by some students who even find photograph "reading" to be difficult. Sometimes match-to-sample instruction may further simplify the discrimination. The student is sent to the grocery store with a coupon or photographs of the items to be bought. The discrimination is made by matching items on the shelf to the picture.

Writing
In teaching specific skills, writing probably will not be a goal. Instead a student may be taught to make a distinctive mark or to use a rubber stamp for a signature on forms. Earlier typing was discussed as an alternative to handwriting in this computer age. The typewriter or computer could be viewed as a prosthesis to bypass the fine motor skills necessary to write. With word processing on a computer, the demands for motor dexterity are greatly reduced. In specific skill instruction, the student might be taught some specific use of the computer. He might learn to use a simplified budget or to develop a grocery list using a computer program a teacher or caretaker has designed.

Specific Math Skills
In the discussion of teaching generalized math skills, some prostheses such as calculator use were advocated. In specific math skills, even more

attention will be given to selection of prosthetic devices to simplify academic judgments. Also, the math skill selected will be a component of a daily living, recreational, or vocational task analysis that is taught concurrently.

Specific Calculator Use In generalized academic instruction, basic computation is taught with a calculator. By the end of the generalized use skill sequence, the student should be able to perform most math problems encountered in daily activities. In specific calculator use, a more limited repertoire is targeted. The calculator is taught for some specific activity such as adding purchases in the grocery store to ensure that the budgeted amount has not been exceeded. Chapter 14 describes studies that illustrate use of the calculator while shopping. Specific calculator use might also be taught for measurement calculations in a vocational context or to balance a checkbook.

Money Use In using money, people without handicaps rarely give exact change; it is *not* required. To simplify money use, the student may be taught to carry quarters for vending machines and dollars for other purchases. Periodic trips to the bank might be made to convert change back to quarters and dollars for ease of use. *Bank machines* also may help facilitate this simplified money use. When making a slightly larger purchase, the student might be taught to withdraw multiples of 10 and to redeposit the change after making the purchase or to convert the change to quarters and dollars at the next trip to the bank cashier counter. Limited money use instruction might include repeated practice in discriminating between coins and dollars ("Which do you use to buy a soda at the machine?" "Which do you use to buy a snack at the drug store?") and practice in discriminating quarters from other coins. These discriminations would also be included as steps in the task analyses for vending machine use, shopping, and so on.

Time Management Reading a clock aloud is usually a social response to "Excuse me, what time is it?" For daily living, a student often needs to perform an activity at or near a given time. Thus, limited time-telling would be focused on time management rather than reading all potential clock times. For example, Connis (1979) taught time management in a workshop with a picture of the clock time that signaled break

time. Match-to-sample time telling simplifies clock reading. The student might also be taught to identify specific clock times that have different configurations of the clock times (8:00 to leave for work, 12:00 to take lunch; 3:15 to leave for home). Time management might also be taught across a week or month with a picture calendar.

Math Prostheses Math skills can often be bypassed through the use of prostheses. Perhaps one of the most frequently used math prostheses is the counting jig for vocational assembly. A board or chart, developed with one slot for each item can be adapted to home skills. Ingredients to be added to a recipe in multiple quantities (2 cups of flour) might be taught using two pictures of measuring cups in the recipe and two measuring cups for each scoop of flour. An egg carton could be cut to 10 cups and used to count dimes to equal a dollar.

Besides counting jigs, calculators, computers, and digital watches are all technological advances that could be considered to be prosthetics in that they bypass certain academic responses. New technology may bring new opportunities for students with severe handicaps to participate in more decisions through bypass of *academic judgment*. Smeets, Lancioni, and Van Lieshout (1985) designed a prosthetic device for children with mild or moderate retardation to tell time and meet appointments using time formulations in the students' native Dutch language. The prosthesis reduced the number discrimination and time estimation demands typical of using a clock to follow a schedule. Finally, matching may also be used to bypass academic responses. A coin-matching card might be carried in a wallet to aid selection of coins for a bus or vending machine.

IEP Example for Specific Academics and Prostheses

In designing an IEP that includes specific academic skills, the "academic" instruction of the IEP may be difficult to identify. That is, specific skills will be embedded in daily living, recreation, and vocational skill objectives. The following IEP example is also adapted from the Centennial School, Life Skills Class Level IV. Mary is 15 years old and has been classified as moderately mentally retarded and severely emotionally disturbed in different psychological evaluations. Mary's name and specific objectives have been changed to protect confidentiality. The objectives are listed by domain with the academic skill cross-coded to help the reader identify the academic skill. Specific academics are chosen for Mary because of her age and very slow rate in learning academic skills.

- COMMUNITY DOMAIN

  I. When given the opportunity to travel alone, Mary will use the city bus to reach her destination on 5 out of 5 opportunities.

  Skill Sequence:
  1. Ride the bus with group and select 2 quarters alone (Math-money)
  2. Ride the bus with group and select correct bus for the group by reading the bus name (Reading)
  3. Ride the bus with the group and select the time for the group to leave to catch the bus (Math-time management)
  4. Ride the bus alone to a destination

  Activities for Instruction:
  1. Biweekly bus-riding instruction in the community
  2. Classroom bus simulation with slides
  3. Repeated practice on selecting quarters, reading bus names, discriminating time to leave using match to sample schedule

  II. When given an assigned purchase to make for her home or class, Mary will enter the grocery store alone and leave with the stated item on 3 out of 3 trips.

  Skill Sequence:
  1. With group, Mary hands correct bill to cashier (Math-money)
  2. With group, Mary selects correct brand using picture (Reading)
  3. With group, Mary finds correct aisle (Reading markers and noting natural cues)
  4. In classroom, Mary selects pictures and dollars to make her list after being told items that are needed (Reading and money)
  5. Mary plans her trip and at store, goes in alone to make purchase

  Activities for Instruction:
  1. Weekly trip to grocery store
  2. Classroom grocery simulation with slides and tape recorder
  3. Repeated practice on bill discrimination, matching pictures to packages, selecting picture stated
  4. With group, Mary selects item using picture

- RECREATIONAL DOMAIN

  I. When given time to make social plans, Mary will use a personal calendar to plan 4 out of 5 upcoming events.

  Skill Sequence:
  1. Mary puts a picture sticker on 4 out of 5 events (Reading and time management)
  2. When asked if free on any date, Mary consults calendar and response appropriately (Reading)
  3. When asked how many days until a certain event, Mary responds appropriately by counting days (Math)
  4. Mary marks a calendar to show both events and days to plan for events (vacation date and shopping day for bathing suit). (Math-time management)

  Activities for Instruction:
  1. Classroom lesson in planning activities
  2. Cafeteria social conversation with non-handicapped peers to discuss upcoming events (Mary shares calendar).

- VOCATIONAL DOMAIN

  I. When given the opportunity to work as a secretarial assistant, Mary will perform assigned duties to receive a satisfactory rating from the secretary on 9 out of 10 days of work.

  Skill Sequence:
  1. Mary affixes correct postage using a match to sample guide and a scale (Math, Reading)
  2. Mary photocopies papers and collates them in correct page order (Math)
  3. Mary files by student names alphabetically using a filing jig that highlights the first letter in red (clear red ruler) (Reading)

  Activities for Instruction:
  1. On the job training in the school office
  2. Classroom repeated practice for using postage guide and filing jig.

  Long-Term Goals:
  Plans for Mary at this time are for her to continue living with the family after high school; however, her parents and teacher's goals are for Mary to assume adult responsibilities such as making some of the family's grocery purchases and riding the bus to visit friends without a family member escort. Mary and her parents hope she will obtain a job as an assistant to a secretary. At this time it is projected that Mary's office supervisor and family will perform more complex academic skills for

her (filling out forms, managing her money, answering her mail).

SUMMARY

Academic skills may be viewed as a low priority for students with severe handicaps. Through the use of prosthetic devices (picture recipes) and minimal caretaker assistance (giving the student exact fare for the bus) academic demands can often be bypassed, however, when academic skills are bypassed, the student is dependent on others to design and redesign prosthetics and to perform academic tasks. Because academic skills provide greater independence, instruction for generalized academic skills is justifiable when future environments for a student will require their use and when the student's rate of progress makes mastery feasible during the school years. When the decision of how much academic instruction will be introduced is made with the parents and student, the following guidelines can aid in planning this instruction.

1. Generalization of academic skills may be enhanced through careful selection of instructional exemplars and a plan for the sequence of presentation of exemplars.
2. Many academic skills require visual discriminations (of letters, numbers, words) which may be taught with a prompting and fading procedure such as time delay.
3. Even when the goal is mastery of generalized academic skills, this instruction should be related to activities in the student's daily living.
4. Specific academic skill instruction requires identifying daily living activities and then picking academic skills to enhance them. These objectives will blend with the student's objectives for each life domain and may not appear "academic" *per se.*

REFERENCES

Allen, G. J. (1973). Case study: Implementation of behavior modification techniques in summer camp settings. *Behavior Therapy, 4,* 570–575.

Apffel, J. A. (1974). Some TMR's can read. *Education and Training of the Mentally Retarded, 9,* 199–201.

Apffel, J. A., Kelleher, J., Lilly, M. S., & Richardson, R. (1975). Developmental reading for moderately retarded children. *Education and Training of the Mentally Retarded, 10,* 229–236.

Becker, W., Engelmann, S., & Thomas, D. (1975). *Teaching 2: Cognitive learning and instruction.* Chicago: Science Research Associates.

Bijou, S. (1973). *It's about time.* Bellevue, Wash.: Edmark.

Bijou, S. W., Birnbrauer, J. S., Kidder, J. D., & Tague, C. (1966). Programmed instruction as an approach to teaching of reading, writing, and arithmetic to retarded children. *Psychological Record, 16,* 505–522.

Birnbrauer, J. S., Wolf, M. M., Kidder, J. D., & Tague, C. (1965). Classroom behavior of retarded pupils with token reinforcement. *Journal of Experimental Child Psychology, 2,* 219–235.

Bliss, C. K. (1965). *Semantography.* Sydney, Australia: Semantography Publications.

Booth, A., Hewitt, D., Jenkins, W., & Maggs, A. (1979). Making retarded children literate: A five year study. *Australian Journal of Mental Retardation, 5,* 257–260.

Borakove, L. S., and Cuvo, A. J. (1976). Facilitative effects of coin displacement on teaching coin summation to mentally retarded adolescents. *American Journal of Mental Deficiency, 81,* 350–356.

Bracey, S., Maggs, A., & Morath, P. (1975). The effects of a direct phonic approach in teaching reading with six moderately retarded children: Acquisition and master learning stages. *The Slow Learning Child, 22,* 83–90.

Bradley-Johnson, S., Sunderman, P., and Johnson, C. M. (1983). Comparison of delayed prompting and fading for teaching preschoolers easily confused letters and numbers. *Journal of School Psychology, 21,* 327–335.

Browder, D. (1981). *A comparison of a stimulus prompt and a response prompt with four fading procedures to teach sight words to the moderately and severely retarded.* Unpublished doctoral dissertation, University of Virginia.

Browder, D., & D'Huyvetters, K. (1985). Transfer of stimulus control and comprehension in sight word reading for mentally retarded, emotionally disturbed children. Manuscript submitted for publication. Lehigh University.

Browder, D., Hines, C. McCarthy, L. J., & Fees, J. (1984). Sight word instruction to facilitate acquisition and generalization of daily living skills for the moderately and severely retarded. *Education and Training of the Mentally Retarded, 19,* 191–200.

Browder, D., Snell, M., & Ambrogio, B. (1985). Using time delay to transfer stimulus control within the behavioral chain of vending machine use with a comparison of training sites. Unpublished manuscript.

Brown, L., Hermanson, J., Klemme, H., Haubrich, P., & Ora, J. (1970). Using behavior modification principles to teach sight vocabulary. *Teaching Exceptional Children, 2,* 120–128.

Brown, L., Huppler, B., Pierce, L., York, B., & Sontag, E. (1974). Teaching trainable level students to read unconjugated action verbs. *Journal of Special Education, 8,* 51–56.

Brown, L., Jones, S., Troccolo, E., Heiser, C., Bellamy, T., & Sontag, E. (1972). Teaching functional reading to young trainable students: Toward longitudinal objectives. *Journal of Special Education, 6,* 237–246.

Brown, L., & Perlmutter, L. (1971). Teaching functional reading to trainable level retarded students. *Education and Training of the Mentally Retarded, 6,* 74–84.

Buchanan, C. D. (1968). *Teacher's guide to programmed reading* (Book I, Series 1, rev. ed., Sullivan Associates Program). St. Louis, Webster Division, McGraw-Hill.

Calhoun, M. L. (1985). Typing contrasted with handwriting in language arts instruction for moderately mentally retarded students. *Education and Training of the Mentally Retarded, 20,* 48–52.

Certo, N., Schwartz, R., & Brown, L. (1975). Community transportation teaching severely handicapped students to ride a public bus system. In L. Brown, T. Crowner, W. Williams, & R. York (Eds.), *Madison's alternative for zero exclusion: A book of readings.* Madison, WI: Madison Public Schools.

Connis, R. (1979). The effects of sequential picture cues, self-recording, and praise on the job task sequencing of retarded adults. *Journal of Applied Behavior Analysis, 12,* 355–361.

Cooking with Betty Crocker mixes (large type edition) (1970). Minneapolis: General Mills.

Corey, J. F. R., & Shamow, J. (1972). The effects of fading on the acquisition and retention of oral reading. *Journal of Applied Behavior Analysis, 5,* 311–315.

Cuvo, A. J., Veitch, V. D., Trace, M. W., and Konke, J. L. (1978). Teaching change computation to the mentally retarded. *Behavior Modification, 2,* 531–548.

D'Huyvetters, K., & Browder, D. (1985). Now I know my ABCs. Manuscript submitted for publication. Lehigh University.

Domnie, M., & Brown, L. (1977). Teaching severely handicapped students reading skills requiring printed answers to who, what, and where questions. *Education and Training of the Mentally Retarded, 12,* 324–331.

Dolch, E. W. (1950). *Teaching primary reading (2nd ed.)* Champaign, IL: Garrard Press.

Dorry, G. W. (1976). Attentional mode for the effectiveness of fading in training reading-vocabulary with retarded persons. *American Journal of Mental Deficiency, 81,* 271–279.

Dorry, G. W., & Zeaman, D. (1973). The use of a fading technique in paired-associate teaching of a reading vocabulary with retardates. *Mental Retardation, 11*(6), 3–6.

Dorry, G. W., & Zeaman, D. (1975). Teaching a simple reading vocabulary to retarded children: Effectiveness of fading and nonfading procedures. *American Journal of Mental Deficiency, 79,* 711–716.

Duffy, G. G., & Sherman, G. B. (1973). *How to teach reading systematically.* New York: Harper & Row.

Duffy, G. G., & Sherman, G. B. (1977). *Systematic reading instruction (2nd ed.).* New York: Harper & Row.

Easy menu cookbook. (1974). Bristol, IN: Elkhart Jaycees-Auxiliary of the Elkhart Jaycees.

Edmark reading program: Teacher's guide. (1972, 1984). Seattle: Edmark.

Engelmann, S. (1967). Classroom techniques: Teaching reading to children with low mental age. *Education and Training of Mentally Retarded, 2,* 193–201.

Engelmann, S., & Bruner, E. C. (1974). *DISTAR reading: An instructional system.* Chicago: Science Research Associates.

Entrikin, D., York, R., & Brown, L. (1977). Teaching trainable level multiply handicapped students to use picture cues, context cues, and initial consonant sounds to determine the labels of unknown words. *AAESPH Review, 2,* 169–190.

Etzel, B. C., & LeBlanc, J. (1979). The simplest treatment alternative: The law of parsimony applied to choosing appropriate instructional control and errorless instructional control and errorless learning procedures for the difficult-to-teach child. *Journal of Autism and Developmental Disorders, 9,* 361–382.

Folk, M. C., & Campbell, J. (1978). Teaching functional reading to the TMR. *Education and Training of the Mentally Retarded, 13,* 323–326.

Fries, C. C., Wilson, R., & Rudolph, M. K. (1966). *Merrill linguistic reader.* Columbus, OH: Charles E. Merrill.

Fry, E. (1957). Developing a word list for remedial reading. *Elementary English, 33,* 456–458.

Fry, E. (1972). *Reading instruction for classroom and clinic.* New York: McGraw-Hill.

Garcia, E. (1974). The training and generalization of conversational speech form in nonverbal retardates. *Journal of Applied Behavior Analysis, 7,* 137–149.

Gearhart, B. R., & Litton, F. W. (1975). *The trainable retarded: A foundations approach.* St. Louis, MO: C. V. Mosby Co.

Hawker, J. R. (1968). A further investigation of prompting and confirmation in sight vocabulary learning by retardates. *American Journal of Mental Deficiency, 72,* 594–598.

Hawker, J. R., Geertz, U. W., & Shrago, M. (1964). Prompting and confirmation in sight vocabulary learning by retardates. *American Journal of Mental Deficiency, 68,* 751–756.

Hendrickson, J., Roberts, M., & Shores, R. (1978). Antecedent and contingent modeling to teach basic sight vocabulary to learning disabled children. *Journal of Learning Disabilities, 11,* 424–425.

Hewett, F. M. (1966). The autistic child learns to read. *Slow learning child: The Australian Journal of the Education of Backward Children, 12,* 107–20.

Hirshoren, A., & Burton, T. A. (1979). Teaching academic skills to trainable mentally retarded children: A study in tautology. *Mental Retardation, 17,* 177–179.

Horner, R. H., & MacDonald, R. S. (1982). A comparison of single instance and general case instruction in teaching a generalized vocational skill. *Journal of the Association for the Severely Handicapped, 7,* 7–20.

Horton, S. (1985). Computational rates of educable mentally retarded adolescents with and without calculators in comparison to normals. *Education and Training of the Mentally Retarded, 20,* 14–24.

Hupp, S. C., & Mervis, C. B. (1981). Development of generalized concepts by severely handicapped students. *The Journal of the Association of the Severely Handicapped, 6,* 14–21.

Johnson, B. F., & Cuvo, A. J. (1981). Teaching cooking skills to mentally retarded persons. *Behavior Modification, 5,* 187–202.

Kaman, M. (1974). *Cooking activities for retarded children.* Nashville: Abingdon.

Kazdin, A. E. (1977). Assessing the clinical or applied importance of behavior change through social validation. *Behavior Modification, 1,* 427-452.

Kirk, S. A. *Educating exceptional children (2nd ed.).* Boston: Houghton Mifflin, 1972.

Kittleson, E., & Certo, N. (1975). Teaching orthopedically handicapped adolescents to secure selected products and services from their community through functional use of the Yellow Pages and telephone. In L. Brown, T. Crowner, W. Williams, & R. York (Eds.), *Madison's alternative for zero exclusion: A book of readings.* Madison, WI: Madison Public Schools.

Koury, M., & Browder, D. (1985). *Moderately retarded children's use of delay to teach sight words to their peers.* Unpublished manuscript.

Lahey, B., Weller, D., & Brown, W. (1973). The behavior analysis approach to reading: Phonics discriminations. *Journal of Reading Behavior, 5,* 200-206.

Laitenin, R. E., Hall, T., Daugle, N., & Reid, C. (1985). *Equivalency relations and educational tasks for the severely handicapped.* Paper presented to the conference of Applied Behavior Analysis: Columbus, OH.

Lent, J. N. (1968). Mimosa cottage experiment and hope. *Psychology Today, 52,* 51-58.

Lichtman, M. (1974). The development and validation of R/EAL, an instrument to assess functional literacy. *Journal of Reading Behavior, 6,* 167-182.

Lovitt, T. C., & Hurlburt, M. (1974). Using behavior-analysis techniques to assess the relationship between phonics instruction and oral reading. *Journal of Special Education, 8,* 57-72.

Lowe, M. L., & Cuvo, A. J. (1976). Teaching coin summation to the mentally retarded. *Journal of Applied Behavior Analysis, 9,* 483-489.

Martin, J., Rusch, F., James, V., Decker, P., & Trytol, K. (1982). The use of picture cues in the preparation of complex meals. *Applied Research in Mental Retardation, 3,* 105-119.

Matson, J. L. (1980). Preventing home accidents: A training program for the retarded. *Behavior Modification, 4,* 397-410.

McClennen, S., & Harrington, L. (1982). A developmentally-based functional mathematics program for retarded and autistic persons. *Journal of Special Education Technology, 5,* 23-30.

Neville, D., & Vandever, T. (1973). Decoding as a result of synthetic and analytic presentation for retarded and nonretarded children. *American Journal of Mental Deficiency, 77,* 533-537.

Nietupski, J., Williams, W., & York, R. (1979). Teaching selected phonic word analysis reading skills to TMR labeled students. *Teaching Exceptional Children, 11,* 140-143.

O'Brien, F. (1974). *Instruction in reading a clock for the institutionalized retarded.* Unpublished manuscript. Anna State Hospital and Southern Illinois University.

Reed, F. S. (1973). *A special picture cookbook.* Lawrence, KS: H & H Enterprises.

Resnick, L. B., Wang, M. C., & Kaplan, J. (1973). Task analysis in curriculum design: A hierarchically sequenced introductory mathematics curriculum. *Journal of Applied Behavior Analysis, 6,* 697-710.

Rincover, A. (1978). Variables affecting stimulus fading and discriminative responding in psychotic children. *Journal of Abnormal Psychology, 8,* 235-246.

Schilmoeller, G. L., Schilmoeller, K. J., Etzel, B. C., & LeBlanc, J. M. (1979). Conditional discrimination responding after errorless and trial and error training. *Journal of the Experimental Analysis of Behavior, 31,* 403-420.

Schumaker, J., & Sherman, J. A. (1970). Training generative verb usage by imitation and reinforcement procedures. *Journal of Applied Behavior Analysis, 3,* 273-287.

Sidman, M. (1971). Reading and auditory-visual equivalences. *Journal of Speech and Hearing Research, 14,* 5-13.

Sidman, M., & Cresson, O., Jr. (1973). Reading and cross modal transfer of stimulus equivalences in severe retardation. *American Journal of Mental Deficiency, 77,* 515-523.

Sidman, M., & Tailby, W. (1982). Conditional discrimination vs. matching to sample: An expansion of the testing paradigms. *Journal of the Experimental Analysis of Behavior, 37,* 5-22.

Skinner, B. F. (1957). *Verbal behavior.* New York: Appleton-Century Crofts.

Smeenge, M. E., Page, T. J., Iwata, B. A., & Ivancic, M. T. (1980). Teaching measurement skills to mentally retarded students: Training, generalization, and follow-up. *Education and Training of the Mentally Retarded, 15,* 224-229.

Smeets, P. M., Lancioni, G. E., & Van Lieshout, R. W. (1985). Teaching mentally retarded children to use an experimental device for telling time and meeting appointments. *Applied Research in Mental Retardation, 6,* 51-70.

Solnick, J. V., & Baer, D. M. (1984). Using multiple exemplars for teaching number-numeral correspondence: Some structural aspects. *Analysis and Intervention in Developmental Disabilities, 4,* 47-63.

Sprague, J. R., & Horner, R. H. (1984). The effects of single instance, multiple instance, and general case training on generalized vending machine use by moderately and severely handicapped students. *Journal of Applied Behavior Analysis, 17,* 273-278.

Staples, K. S. (1975). *Cooking from pictures.* Fargo: North Dakota State University.

Stauffer, R. G. (1970). *The language-experience approach to the teaching of reading.* New York: Harper & Row.

Sterick, G. (1979). A follow-up study of ten children who learned to read in a class for trainable students. *Education and Training of the Mentally Retarded, 14,* 170-176.

Stokes, T. F., Baer, D. M., & Jackson, R. L. (1974). Programming the generalization of a greeting response in four retarded children. *Journal of Applied Behavior Analysis, 7,* 599-610.

Stone, C. B. (1956). Measuring difficulty of primary reading material: A constructive criticism of Spache's measure. *Elementary School Journal, 6,* 36-41.

Tennyson, R. D., Woolley, F. R., & Merrill, M. D. (1972). Exemplar and nonexemplar variables which produce correct classification behavior and specified classification errors. *Journal of Educational Psychology, 63,* 144–152.

Trace, M. W., Cuvo, A. J., & Criswell, J. L. (1977). Teaching coin equivalence to the mentally retarded. *Journal of Applied Behavior Analysis, 10,* 85–92.

Vanderheiden, G., & Grilley, K. (1975). *Non-verbal communication techniques and aids for the nonvocal severely handicapped.* Baltimore: University Park Press.

Vandever, T. R., Maggart, W. T., & Nasser, S. (1976). Three approaches to beginning reading. *Mental Retardation, 14*(4), 29–32.

Vandever, T. R., & Stubbs, J. C. (1977). Reading retention and transfer in TMR students. *American Journal of Mental Deficiency, 82,* 233–237.

Wacker, D. P., & Berg, W. K. (1984). Training adolescents with severe handicaps to set up job tasks independently using picture prompts. *Analysis and Intervention in Developmental Disabilities, 4,* 353–366.

Walsh, B. F., & Lamberts, F. (1979). Errorless discrimination and picture fading as techniques for teaching sight words to TMR students. *American Journal of Mental Deficiency, 83,* 473–479.

Warren, N. A. (1963). Academic achievement of trainable pupils. *Training School Bulletin, 60,* 75–88.

Weisburg, P. (1980). Adult judgements of differences between positive and negative instances for comparative concepts taught by continuous and noncontinuous conversions. Unpublished manuscript. Cited in Weisberg, P., Packer, R. A., & Weisburg, R. S. (1981). Academic training, In J. L. Matson & J. R. McCartney (Eds.), *Handbook of behavior modification with the mentally retarded.* New York: Plenum Press.

Williamson, F. (1980). *DISTAR Reading—Research and experiment,* Urbana: University of Illinois.

Woodcock, R. W. (1968). The Peabody-Chicago-Detroit reading project: A report of second year results. In J. R. Block (Ed.), *i.t.a. as a language arts medium.* Hempstead, NY: The *i.t.a.* Foundation, Hofstra University.

Woodcock, R. W., Davies, C. O., & Clark, C. R. (1969). *The Peabody rebus reading program supplementary lessons kit: Manual of lessons.* Circle Pines, MN: American Guidance Service.

EXAMPLES OF PUBLISHED CURRICULUM MATERIALS FOR GENERALIZED ACADEMICS

Assessment

Brigance, A. H. (1978). *Brigance diagnostic inventory of early development,* North Billerica, MA: Curriculum Associates, Inc.

Martinez, D. (1983). *Martinez assessment of the basic skills—a criterion referenced diagnostic testing of the basic skills.* Portland, OR: AISEP Education Company.

Math

Kramer, T., Krug, D. A., & Magee, S. (1983). *I can + and – arithmetic program.* Portland, OR: ASIEP Education Company.

Writing/Typing

Magee, S. A., & Krug, D. A. (1983). *I can print.* Portland, OR: ASIEP Education Company.

Nash, K., & Geyer, C. (1983). *Touch to type.* North Billerica, MA: Curriculum Associates, Inc.

Job/Community Skills and Recreational Reading (Low Reading Levels)

Applications and forms and *Personal finance series* (1981). Mt. Kisco, NY: Interpretive Education, Guidance Associates, Inc.

Doyle, E. P., & Beam, J. K. (1983). *DEAL: Daily experience and activities for living.* Allen, TX: Developmental learning materials.

Lifetimes. (1979). Belmont, CA: Fearon Education, Pitman Learning.

The Work series, the Money series, the Health series. Sewickley, PA: Hopewell Books, Inc.

Reading Comprehension and Word Analysis

Durrell, D. D., & Murphy, H. A. (1972). *Sound Start.* North Billerica, MA: Curriculum Associates, Inc.

Edmark Reading Program. (1982, 1984). Bellevue, WA: Edmark Corp.

Engelmann, S., & Brunner, E. C. (1974). *DISTAR reading: An instructional system.* Chicago: Science Research Associates.

Lapp, D., & Flood, J. (1982, 1984). *Clues for better reading.* North Billerica, MA: Curriculum Associates, Inc.

Vash, K., & Geyer, C. (1978, 1981). *Write to read typing.* North Billerica, MA: Curriculum Associates, Inc.

Swain, E. H. (1983). *Swain beginning reading program.* Allen, TX: Developmental Learning Materials.

Woodcock, R. W., Davies, C. O., & Clark, C. R. (1969). *The Peabody rebus reading program supplementary lessons kit: Manual of lessons.* Circle Pines, MN: American Guidance Service.

Recipe Reading

Reed, F. S. (1973). *A special picture cookbook.* Lawrence, KS: H & H. Enterprises.

Staples, K. S. (1975). *Cooking from pictures.* Fargo: North Dakota State University.

Introduction to Chapters 16 and 17

"**P**ost-school," "adulthood,"—these phrases are frightening to many parents of sons and daughters with disabilities, and to teachers it means a "time crunch" or "Will we have enough time to prepare our students?" Other buzz words and phrases—"transition into adulthood" and "life-long planning"—emphasize that the years beyond school can and should be planned for ahead of time.

The transition from school to adulthood has received increased attention over the past few years largely due to the results of recent studies which have examined key factors that have affected the outcomes of special education graduates. For example, Hasazi, Gordon, and Roe (1985) noted that special education students graduating from public school programs are inadequately prepared for employment and generally do not have access to resources and services that would enhance community participation. In addition, McDonnell, Wilcox, and Boles (1986) asked whether we really know enough to plan ahead inasmuch as their nation-wide survey indicated that most states have substantial waiting lists for adult vocational and residential programs. Furthermore they found that (a) significant numbers of students with severe handicaps are leaving schools over the next three years, and (b) states are projecting inadequate increases in their services. If planning is done, will the services even be available?

Earlier in this book Ann Turnbull and Buzz Bronicki discussed the difficulties that facing the future or planning for it may entail for the student's family. This may lead to the resurrection of old expectations and hopes as well as lead to uncertainty and disagreements over what is best; however, little effort has been made to involve parents actively in the transition of their son or daughter from school to adult services despite their critical role in developing appropriate educational programs for their child and in obtaining services after the child's graduation (Halpern, 1985; McDonnell, Wilcox, Boles, & Bellamy, 1985). Previous surveys have shown that parental attitudes may affect not only the type of program that is selected for their child, but also expectations for program placements in the future (Hill et al., 1985; Meyer, 1980). In fact, parental support has been shown to be a critical variable in the success of persons with severe handicaps who have been employed in the community (Kochany & Keller, 1981).

Teachers must work to help facilitate a meaningful transition from school to adulthood. Thus, teachers will need to focus on developing in their students skills needed to function in the community; they will need to become familiar with the services provided by adult service agencies within their local communities and will need to plan systematically for the transfer of programming responsibilities as students approach graduation. In order for this to be accomplished, interagency collaboration, including the active involvement of school staff, parents, and adult-service agency personnel, is essential.

McDonnell and Hardman (1985) have cited three reasons that public schools appear to be the most logical place to begin this transition process. First, schools have the primary responsibility for preparing individuals with severe handicaps to function independently in the community as adults. Second, transition planning is a cumulative process, and schools provide the setting by which parents and teachers can set, evaluate, and refine goals as students near graduation. Third, the individualized education plan (IEP) provides teachers, parents, and adult-service agency personnel with a tool by which they are able to incorporate specific plans related to the transition from school to work.

As a result, leaders in vocational research with students having severe handicaps are emphasizing that the major goals of education should be not only to prepare students to be independent in their daily living skills but also to be employable (Rusch & Chadsey-Rusch, 1985, Wehman, Kregel, & Barcus, 1985). Although future legislation (reauthorization of the Vocational Rehabilitation Act) may create options generally unavailable to most of our students now, parents, teachers, program administrators, and the lay public have not yet embraced what research has shown is possible. Students with severe handicaps, when given adequate training and support, can hold regular jobs that pay competitive wages. In the next chapter, Frank Rusch, Janis Chadsey-Rusch, and Tom Lagomarcino set forth the educators' steps in this process of helping students make the transition from school to employment in the community.

The other half of adult life concerns one's residence and life in the community. As is the case with employment, most people have an inaccurate picture of the potential of people with severe handicaps for living in the community. The barriers toward their living in the community-living settings tend to be exaggerated, and the benefits may be misunderstood. In the final chapter in this book Tom Bellamy and Rob Horner describe the rules of the existing adult service delivery system in our country and trace their implications for transition planning by families and educators.

REFERENCES

Halpern, A. S. (1985). Transition: A look at the foundations. *Exceptional Children, 57,* 479–486.

Hasazi, S. B., Gordon, L. R., & Roe, C. A. (1985). Factors associated with the employment status of handicapped youth exiting high school from 1975–1983. *Exceptional Children, 51,* 455–469.

Hill, J., Seyfarth, J., Orelove, F., Wehman, P., & Banks, P. (1985). Parent/guardian attitudes toward the working conditions of their mentally retarded children. In P. Wehman & J. Hill (Eds.), *Competitive employment for persons with mental retardation: From research to practice* (pp. 285–314). Richmond: Rehabilitation Research and Training Center, Virginia Commonwealth University.

Kochany, L., & Keller, J. (1981). Reasons mentally retarded clients fail in their jobs. In P. Wehman (Ed.), *Competitive employment* (pp. 181–198). Baltimore: Paul H. Brookes.

McDonnell, J., & Hardman, M. (1985). Planning the transition of severely handicapped youth from school to adult services: A framework for high school programs. *Education and Training of the Mentally Retarded, 20,* 275–286.

McDonnell, J., Wilcox, B., & Boles, S. M. (1986). Do we know enough to plan for a transition? A national survey of state agencies responsible for services to persons with severe handicaps. *Journal of the Association for the Severely Handicapped, 11,* 53–60.

McDonnell, J., Wilcox, B., Boles, S. M., & Bellamy, G. T. (1985). Transition issues facing youth with severe disabilities: Parents' perspective. *The Journal of the Association for Persons with Severe Handicaps, 10*(1), 61–65.

Meyer, R. J. (1980). Attitudes of parents of institutionalized mentally retarded individuals towards deinstitutionalization. *American Journal of Mental Deficiency, 85*(2), 184–187.

Rusch, F. R. & Chadsey-Rusch, J. (1985). Employment preparation for persons with severe handicaps: Curriculum development and coordination of services. *Focus on Exceptional Children, 17*(9), 1–8.

Wehman, P., Kregel, J., Barcus, J. M. (1985). From school to work: A vocational transition model for the handicapped. *Exceptional Children, 52*(1), 25–38.

Frank R. Rusch
Janis Chadsey-Rusch
Thomas Lagomarcino

University of Illinois at Urbana

16

Preparing Students for Employment

With adulthood comes certain responsibilities and roles which we are all expected to assume. One of these roles is the role of "contributor to society" which can be carried out in various ways, including finding and maintaining employment. Employment is important to the individual. Through employment one derives monetary rewards which can be used to purchase desired goods and services; employment also provides intangible rewards, such as the opportunity to interact with others, the development of self-worth, and the chance to contribute to society (Turkel, 1972). Employment is significant in our daily lives because it can structure our individual adjustment. Indeed, our residential and recreational opportunities are influenced by our employment status (cf. Rusch, Chadsey-Rusch, White, & Gifford, 1985).

Will (1984) has also suggested that employment is critical to the lives of most Americans, regardless of whether their work is specialized (banking, computer science, medicine), entry-level (maid services, janitorial services, food services), or supported (work crews, enclaves). Will's statement has important implications for students with severe handicaps because these individuals are likely to be employed in entry-level or supported employment positions. Unfortunately, prevailing educational and adult services for persons with severe handicaps have resulted in few employment opportunities for them in this country.

Recently, the United States Commission on Civil Rights (1983) reported that between 50% and 80% of all persons with disabilities are unemployed. These data suggest that a disproportionately large number of disabled persons, and *practically all those labeled severely handicapped by the schools,* do not obtain meaningful jobs. Several recent follow-up studies conducted in Vermont (Hasazi, Gordon, & Roe, 1985), Virginia (Wehman, Kregel, & Seyfarth, 1985), and Colorado (Mithaug, Horiuchi, & Fanning, 1985) indicated that less than 12% of all individuals who are severely handicapped are employed, and that all of these persons are underemployed. It appears that, although there has been considerable recent attention focused upon elementary and secondary education over the past few years, these resources have not resulted in meaningful employment outcomes for graduating students. Consequently, it appears that we are at a crucial point in our education of persons with severe handicaps. It is time to implement the current "best practices" in order to prepare these students for adulthood, particularly if adulthood includes employment. Undoubtedly, more research and development needs to occur to further refine and clarify the "best practices" in employment preparation. In fact, with the exception of a single text (Wilcox & Bellamy, 1982) and a few chapters and articles, educational "best practices" related to employment for students who are severely handicapped appear not to have attained a level of universal adoption that results in meaningful outcomes—employment.

All students with severe handicaps should be prepared for employment. Further, this preparation should take place when the student is in school. In addition, school personnel also need to assume a leadership role to enhance students' meaningful transition from school to work. This chapter provides curriculum guidelines that will enable school personnel to assume such roles. This chapter also presents the *survey-train-place-maintain* or *supported work model* by discussing how to identify job requisites for competitive employment, develop longitudinal curricula, establish community-based vocational training stations, identify placement options, and provide long-term, follow-up services. The term "supported work models" highlights the need for support during all phases of employment (training, placement, and follow-up). In addition, this chapter describes the need for coordinated services so that the transition from school to work is effective and efficient.

GUIDELINES FOR CURRICULUM DEVELOPMENT

This section overviews important curriculum guidelines that have been developed over the past few years. This curriculum model is important because it provides the blueprint for teachers to consider when establishing a program's philosophical commitment. This commitment includes establishing a curriculum that is (a) community referenced, (b) integrated, (c) longitudinal, and (d) community based.

Community Referenced

Community-referenced curricula answer the "what to teach" question by identifying the skills and behaviors students must be able to perform in employment settings in which they are going to be placed. The community-referenced approach does not follow more traditional approaches to curriculum development that are organized along academic sequences (language, reading, math). Instead, this approach focuses upon the basic demands required for adult life (employment, leisure, community participation). This guideline has opened a new arena for curriculum planning that may prove to be as influential to students with severe handicaps as was the identification of goals and objectives in the 1960s and the formation of Individualized Education Plans in the 1970s.

Briefly, developing a community-referenced curriculum requires that the local community be surveyed to determine (a) the types of jobs that are available and (b) the requirements of the jobs identified. Once a listing of potential jobs has been generated, the specific "survival skills" required in each of the potential job sites is identified. *Survival skills* are generally thought of as those behaviors that facilitate functioning in the community (Martin, Rusch, & Heal, 1982). In relation to employment, survival skills are those skills that when acquired increase the likelihood of employment and/or job maintenance (Rusch, 1979). Identifying survival skills is important because this information results in a better understanding of what students should learn in school. The identified survival skills—the actual requirements of the job—can then be used by teachers as a basis for selecting instructional objectives. These objectives, when taught, will likely result in meaningful employment outcomes for students when they leave school.

After teachers have compiled a list of potential jobs, and have identified the critical survival skills needed for job success, they must still decide which type of job is most appropriate for individual students. This decision can be facilitated by assessing parent and student preferences for the specific jobs available in the community, and by determining how well the student's skills match the social and vocational skills needed for the job.

In summary, a community-referenced curriculum consists of specific behaviors, or survival skills, that students must be able to perform in employment settings in which they are going to be placed. Local communities are surveyed for the types of jobs available, and the requirements for the jobs (survival skills) are identified.

Integrated

The traditional occupational choice for students who are severely handicapped has been the sheltered workshop or similar segregated settings (adult day care centers, work activities centers). Typically, these segregated settings offer limited work opportunities, and consequently, little training for specific jobs occur. If work is available, it usually represents work performed in nonsheltered settings in the community by persons who are not handicapped. This work is then subcontracted to the segregated setting for persons who are handicapped. Typically, sheltered workshop employees work at subminimum wages, completing tasks such as assembling, packaging, or sorting "widgets," for periods of less than 2 to 3 hours per day. From a rehabilitative perspective, this work is viewed as therapeutic; from our perspective this work is viewed as demeaning and does not contribute to the individual's growth and development.

It is important for students with severe handicaps to be prepared to work in settings with nonhandicapped persons. Employment preparation in integrated settings allows the student to gain exposure to and experience with the demands and expectations of these environments. Integrated settings also provide employers and coworkers the opportunities to interact with the student with handicaps. Through this symbiotic relationship, the student can more easily learn the appropriate social and vocational skills needed for the job, and the employer and coworkers can learn of the student's potential as a reliable employee and friend. Thus, employment preparation for students with severe handicaps should occur in job situations that are integrated. Often, as a consequence of integrated teaching environments, students may also earn a more competitive wage.

Longitudinal

As students with severe handicaps move from one instructional level to the next (from intermediate to secondary classrooms), they should acquire a range of skills that will eventually lead to employment. One way to ensure that this goal is reached is to begin work on the skills early in the educational sequence. Thus, preschool through high school experiences should include instruction that develops identified survival skills.

Each teacher's major responsibility is to teach skills required in future placements. Acquiring a list of the survival skills that potential employers believe are critical for job entry allows the teacher to develop a coordinated and longitudinal curriculum. Preschool, elementary, and intermediate classroom teachers should develop instructional programs that prepare their students to perform employer-specified tasks. It is important to remember that instructional content should be based on goals that are sequenced and on what is functional for each student. *Functionality* within the context of employment preparation refers to teaching relevant (age-appropriate) applications of survival skills that are identified as important for eventual job entry. A student might learn to move independently around the classroom, from the classroom to the cafeteria for lunch, then to the playground, and eventually from home to work. At the secondary level, all skills need to be taught on placement-specific tasks, such as riding the bus to and from a community-based employment training station.

Community-Based

One of the significant learning problems for students with severe handicaps is that they often do not generalize, or transfer, previously acquired skills across settings, people, behaviors, and/or time. Educational efforts, to date, reflect the assumption that what is learned in the classroom, or during simulated work stations, will also be performed outside of the school or in real work situations. Because this assumption is frequently faulty, it is important for teachers to establish and provide instruction in *community-based training stations.*

Establishing community-based training stations in actual employment settings is one way of providing realistic and functional training for employment. A community-based training station is a vocational training site within an ordinary community work setting (in dishwashing rooms in restaurants, in industrial plants) (Stainback, Stainback, Nietupski, & Hamre-Nietupski, 1986). One of the major implications of community-based instruction is that students will receive less and less instruction in the classroom. In fact, when a student reaches the age of 12, instruction in the community should occur for extended periods of time. This means that school personnel will need to provide instruction on job sites in the community outside of the classroom. It is also important to remember that community-based job sites must be community referenced: they must be established in vocations where there is a potential market for employment.

Community-based training sites have been successfully established and maintained by special education teachers (Alper, 1981; Nietupski, Hamre-Nietupski, Welch, & Anderson, 1983). Compared to sheltered, segregated, and/or simulated work settings, community-based training stations offer many advantages, some of which are listed in Table 16.1. As much as possible, special educational personnel should capitalize on these advantages by trying to establish community work stations as primary settings for vocational training of students who are severely handicapped.

Summary

This section overviewed curriculum guidelines that have resulted in meaningful employment outcomes for students who are severely handicapped. These guidelines included the development of a community-referenced, integrated, longitudinal, and community-based curriculum. A community-referenced curriculum focuses upon the "actual" demands of local communities and jobs and pinpoints objectives that serve to guide the development of students' IEPs. The integrated guideline is important because it directs attention toward equitable opportunities for training and placement. Longitudinal and community-based guidelines refer

TABLE 16.1   Advantages of community-based training stations

1. Training of vocational survival skills ensured.
2. Opportunities to learn social survival skills provided.
3. Coworkers serve as role models.
4. Coworkers begin to understand persons who are severely handicapped.
5. Direct service personnel become familiar with employment.
6. More normalized learning experience.
7. Positively influences community members' expectations.
8. Enhances the likelihood of employment.

Source: From *Competitive Employment Issues and Strategies* by F. R. Rusch (Ed.), 1986b, Baltimore: Paul H. Brookes. Adapted by permission.

to skills being taught in the community that are functional and that share some commonality throughout the student's school years.

The next section of the chapter introduces the supported work model. This model is defined by four major activities that are important in securing employment for students with severe handicaps. These activities include: (a) surveying potential employers to determine "survival" skills that need to be trained, (b) training students to perform these skills, (c) placing trained students into non-sheltered settings, and (d) providing follow-up training until, hopefully, this service is provided by post-school agencies.

THE SUPPORTED WORK MODEL

Survey: Examining Communities for Survival Skills

Identification of possible community jobs and the skills needed in those jobs results in a better understanding of what schools should teach. This section will identify potential job placements to determine job requisites, beginning with a discussion of survival skills and will conclude with a brief discussion of how to develop a community-based employment curriculum.

Survival Skills

Much has been written in the past few years on developing age-appropriate and functional curricula for students who are severely handicapped (cf. Brown et al., 1981). A pivotal concern is identifying relevant and functional skills that can increase the opportunity for people to enjoy the community, to obtain generic services (Kenowitz, Gallaher, & Edgar, 1977), and to interact with persons without handicaps (Brown et al., 1981). We must teach relevant and functional vocational *and* social skills, called *survival skills*, that have direct value to prospective employers. Obviously, curricula and associated instruction should be offered in domestic, recreation/leisure, and general community functioning to help students function in integrated settings (Brown et al., 1979). With respect to vocational preparation, survival skills, such as completing a task or following instructions, are essential for success. *Social survival skills* include interactive behaviors such as exchanging greetings, following directions, and complying with requests; *vocational survival skills* refer to behavior directly related to performing a task, such as completing a sweeping or sorting task (Rusch & Schutz, 1981). Job survival depends upon valued social behavior as well as valued work behavior (Chadsey-Rusch, 1986).

Identifying Potential Job Placements

Acquiring and maintaining a job is usually the result of demonstrating valued behaviors (skills employers identify as important). The two broad categories of social and vocational survival skills should be the focus of employment training, therefore, identifying them must be the initial concern. Logically, knowledge of a community's requirements for job survival is critical to developing a comprehensive employment training program. Because communities differ with respect to what is considered acceptable, survival and related programming may be a "local issue" (Thurman & Fiorelli, 1979). Thus, each community of employers must define what is important for survival, with training programs adjusting to these requirements. The primary role of training should be to prepare an individual for community integration; consequently, when developing programs, it is important to base goals and training objectives upon what the students will be expected to do on the job. Martin (1986) has outlined procedures to follow when surveying employers by mail or telephone. (Specific strategies for surveying employers are discussed later in this chapter.) These surveys are particularly useful because a large number of prospective employers can be contacted at a relatively low cost. Regardless of the approach taken, these initial contacts are fundamental to developing a community-based employment training program.

Surveying Job Requisites

We have identified the job requisites Illinois employers believed would lead to competitive employment (Rusch, Schutz, & Agran, 1982). Specifically, employers representing service and light industrial occupations were surveyed. The combined results of these two surveys and ways they can be used to develop a community-based training curriculum are discussed next.

The Illinois Survey Table 16.2 lists the vocational and social survival skills that 80% of the Illinois respondents agreed were critical for entry into competitive employment.

Vocationally, respondents unanimously agreed that prospective employees must demonstrate the basic skill of addition. Socially, they unanimously agreed that prospective employees must recite their full name verbally upon request and follow at least one instruction at a time. Employers believed that prospective employees should be able to learn new job tasks to minimum proficiency when provided a maximum of 1 to 6 hours of instruction (#49), by watching coworkers perform the task (#35), or when explained by verbal instructions (#43). They also indicated that potential employees should contact supervisors or co-workers (#26) when they cannot perform a job and respond at least 50% of the time appropriately, immediately after receiving an instruction (#9). Regarding compliance, these same employers indicated that potential employees should be able to respond to an instruction that requires compliance within at least 90 to 120 seconds (#36) and with no more than one reminder (#21).

The results of this survey deserve a note of caution. The skills and standards listed in Table 16.2 were obtained from potential employers in Illinois. Although it is quite possible that service and light industrial employers in other states may have similar expectations, it is also possible that they would differ markedly (Thurman & Fiorelli, 1979). Ideally, each community of employers should be surveyed to determine the skills necessary for employment entry. On the other hand, these findings may have general application. Many of these survival skills—such as those that refer to safety, compliance, time management, and grooming—are logical inclusions in any curriculum, however, although they may be universally applicable, the standards may vary. Specific placements may require a shorter time period for compliance or may require that an employee acknowledge a request to comply (Karlan & Rusch, 1982).

Train: Developing Community-Based Vocational Training Stations

It is difficult to simulate a real job with real expectations for real production; consequently, unnecessary training in simulated environments should be avoided. Individuals with severe handicaps often have difficulty generalizing newly acquired skills to new settings (Wacker & Berg, 1986; Horner & McDonald, 1982); therefore, secondary instructional content and training should occur primarily in community job-site settings that have immediate value to the student. Community-based vocational

TABLE 16.2 Competitive employment survival skills ordered by employers' response

Critical Entry Skill	Percentage of Employers
1. Recites verbally upon request full name	100
2. Demonstrates basic arithmetic skills of addition	100
3. Follows 1 instruction provided at a time	100
4. Recites verbally upon request home address	99
5. Recites verbally upon request home telephone number	99
6. Communicates such basic needs as sickness	99
7. Maintains proper grooming by dressing appropriately for work	99
8. Understands work routine by not displaying disruptive behaviors when routine task or schedule changes occur	99
9. Responds appropriately and immediately after receiving 1 out of every 2 instructions	98
10. Demonstrates basic arithmetic skill of subtraction	97
11. Moves safely about work place by paying attention to where walking	97
12. Works without displaying or engaging in major disruptive behaviors (arguments) more frequently than 1 to 2 times per month	97
13. Communicates such basic needs as pain	96
14. Reaches places of work by means of own arrangement (walking, taxi, personal car)	96
15. Maintains proper grooming by cleaning self before coming to work	96
16. Initiates contact with coworkers when needs help on task	96
17. Initiates and/or responds verbally in 3- to 5-word sentences	96
18. Speaks clearly enough to be understood by anyone on the second transmission	96
19. Maintains personal hygiene by keeping teeth clean	96
20. Maintains personal hygiene by keeping hair combed	95
21. Remembers to respond to an instruction that requires compliance after a specified time interval with one (1) reminder	95
22. Works without initiating unnecessary contact with strangers more frequently than 1 to 2 times per day	95
23. Communicates need to use toilet	94
24. Follows instructions with words such as "in," "on"	94
25. Continues working without disruptions when co-workers are observing	94
26. Initiates contact with supervisor when job cannot be done	94
27. Responds appropriately to safety signals when given verbally	93
28. Follows instruction with words such as "under," "over," "through"	93
29. Continues working without disruptions when supervisor observing	93
30. Writes 3- to 5-word sentences	93
31. Corrects work on task after second correction from supervisor	93
32. Communicates by means of verbal expression	92
33. Understands the purpose of money	92
34. Follows instructions with words such as to your right/left	92
35. Learns new job tasks explained by watching coworkers/supervisors perform task	92
36. Responds to an instruction requiring immediate compliance within 90 to 120 seconds	92
37. Works without initiating unnecessary contact with supervisor more frequently than 3 to 5 times per day	92

TABLE 16.2 (continued)

Critical Entry Skill	Percentage of Employers
38. Moves safely about work place by identifying and avoiding dangerous areas	91
39. Wants to work for money	91
40. Manages time by completing an assigned task on time	91
41. Follows 4- to 6- word instructions	91
42. Communicates such basic needs as thirst	90
43. Learns new job tasks explained by verbal instruction	90
44. Wants to work for sense of accomplishment	90
45. Works without initiating unnecessary contact with co-workers (who are working) more frequently than 6 to 8 times per day.	90
46. Recites age verbally upon request	89
47. Communicates such basic needs as hunger	89
48. Moves safely about work place by wearing appropriately safe work clothing	89
49. Learns to minimum proficiency new job task, provided 1 to 6 hours of instruction	89
50. Demonstrates understanding of rules (set down by supervisor) by not deviating from them more frequently than 1 to 2 times per month	89
51. Works without displaying or engaging in minor disruptive behaviors (interruptions) more frequently than 1 to 2 times per month	89
52. Adapts to new work routine, achieving normal levels of productivity within 1 to 5 days	88
53. Follows instructions with words such as press, hold, twist	88
54. Recognizes the importance of attendance and punctuality by not being late or absent from work more than an average of once per month	88
55. Maintains proper grooming by dressing appropriately after using restroom	86
56. Answers the telephone appropriately for self	85
57. Initiates contact with supervisor when a mistake is made	85
58. Participates in work environment for periods of 5 to 6 hours	85
59. Initiates contact with co-workers when needs task materials	84
60. Completes repetitive tasks previously learned to proficiency within 25 to 50% rate	84
61. Works at job continuously, remaining on task for 1- to 2-hour intervals	84
62. Reads 6- to 8- word sentences	83
63. Recites verbally, upon request, name of previous employer	83
64. Tells and follows time on the quarter hour	82
65. Adapts to new work routine, with the number of supervisory contacts being 3 to 4	82
66. Maintains proper grooming by washing after using restroom	81
67. Maintains personal hygiene by using deodorant	81
68. Works alone and increases productivity on own	81
69. Works continuously without leaving job inappropriately (not having a good reason) more than 1 to 2 times per day	81
70. Responds appropriately to safety signals (buzzers, bells)	80
71. Works alone and increases productivity when asked to complete job by a specified time	80

training refers to training community-relevant behaviors (survival skills) in an environment that closely resembles probable job placements, job station selection and organization, and the training and management strategies that might be used to teach social and vocational survival skills follow.

Station Selection   Training stations, which are integrated (co-workers without handicaps are present) and representative likely community job placement options should be selected. Many communities contain hospitals, federal, state, and local government offices; universities or colleges; restaurants; large factories; and other industries. These settings are ideal for training stations. If a local hospital employs a bedmaking staff, a training station could be set up in a similar setting to train bedmakers. Or, if maids are needed in a town, a teacher could approach the manager of a motel or hotel to establish a training program to teach students to perform maid-related tasks.

Typically, employers, supervisors, and most other people have not worked with or seen students who are severely handicapped; therefore, these people need to be informed about the distinguishing characteristics of these students, emphasizing individual differences and abilities. It is important to establish that this population, historically, has been underrepresented in our public schools and that new laws, combined with a developing teaching technology, suggest that they can learn marketable skills. These students are complex people who require more time and, possibly, more innovative teaching methods to learn new tasks. Stress that, with systematic instruction, they can be taught such complex tasks such as riding a bus to and from work (Sowers, Rusch, & Hudson, 1979) and managing their time on the job (Sowers, Rusch, Connis, & Cummings, 1980).

It will also be useful to establish a probationary period between the school and employing personnel so that the school and the employer can have a set period of time (9 months) to evaluate the overall success of their relationship. Topics to be discussed, when the probationary period is established, might also include other items such as the holidays and breaks that are taken by schools but not most other institutions, the number of students to be trained, the number of supervisory staff and hours, and the types of tasks to be performed.

Many of the training stations we have established have included students working staggered hours and performing a variety of tasks during an 8-hour shift. These students typically worked for periods of 3 to 5 hours, receiving training in social survival skills for another 1 to 3 hours. The hours or tasks to be performed would vary depending on the age of the student, physical limitations, or transportation constraints. If two training stations were developed in a performing arts and convention center, one group of students might clean stages, auditoriums, and entry ways in the morning, while a second group might manage a different set of tasks (clean walkways, windows, floors) in the afternoon.

Analyzing Job Tasks

Identifying job tasks is based upon task analyses (Wehman, 1981). The task analysis should list the skills the student will perform and the method or particular way in which each task should be performed (Gold, 1980). For example, the sequence of steps for sweeping and mopping a floor may be determined by directly watching a janitor perform the criterion task(s).

Table 16.3 displays an example of a task analysis for kitchen laborer tasks that three students needed to complete during a work day. This sheet shows the time a task should be started, the tasks to be performed, the number of minutes each should take (based upon data from watching employees perform the task), and a place to mark when the student started, total time spent, and whether the task was completed on time. In this example, Student 1 is working a 4-hour shift; Student 2, a 4½-hour shift; and Student 3, a 2-hour shift. Both Students 1 and 2 are in the final stages of training and are being considered for actual placement. For Student 3, the majority of instruction is based on mobility skills, learning job-related skills (wiping, sorting, drying, carrying), and learning to cook and manage household chores at other times; thus, Student 3 is still in the early stages of training.

Training and Management Strategies

Menchetti, Rusch, and Lamson (1981) assessed college and university food service employers' acceptance of selected training and management strategies, grouping 68 survey items into six procedural categories. Table 16.4 lists the items that 50% or more of the 29 respondents agreed could or could not be used when training on the job. The results of this survey suggest several guidelines for providing training and management in competitive employment settings. These em-

TABLE 16.3 Kitchen laborer task performance sheet

Teacher _____ Date _____

Aide _____

		Min Allowed	Start Time	Total Time	On Time
Student 1					
Ready for work					
9:00 A.M.	Set up steam table	15			
9:15 A.M.	Clean small soup pot	20			
9:35 A.M.	Clean large soup pot	15			
9:50 A.M.	Clean soup drain	6			
9:56 A.M.	Clean windows	@ 3			
10:00 A.M.	Dry dishes	20			
10:30 A.M.	Wash dishes	20			
10:50 A.M.	Polish and/or clean windows	@ 3			
11:45 A.M.	Fill sinks and wash dishes	7;20			
12:25 P.M.	Sweep floor	15			
12:40 P.M.	Mop floor	15			
1:00 P.M.	Clean sink	8			
Student 2					
Ready for work					
9:00 A.M.	Remove items from sink	1			
9:01 A.M.	Scrape pots and pans	2			
9:03 A.M.	Fill sinks w/water	8			
9:11 A.M.	Wash pots and pans—1 load only	20			
9:30 A.M.	Laundry (M-W-F)	10			
9:40 A.M.	Wash dishes—1 load only	20			
10:00 A.M.	Clean refrigerator (T-F)	20			
10:30 A.M.	Dry dishes—1 load only	20			
11:00 A.M.	Wash dishes—1 load only	20			
12:00 P.M.	Clean stove oven	30			
12:15 P.M.	Wash dishes & large plastic containers	20			
1:20 P.M.	Mop kitchen area	15			
Student 3					
Ready for work					
10:00 A.M.	Clean cart	1			
10:01 A.M.	Clean mixer	5			
10:06 A.M.	Dry dishes—1 load only	54			
11:00 A.M.	Wash dishes—1 load only	20			
11:20 A.M.	Empty garbage	10			
11:30 A.M.	Wash dishes—1 load only	20			
11:50 A.M.	Clean sink	10			

ployers indicated that data could be collected, but not more frequently than once a week. Consequently, data should be collected unobtrusively, and the purpose for data collection should be discussed with both employers and workers without handicaps.

These employers also felt that, when an employee made an error, varying levels of instructional assistance could be used, including asking the employee why she was behaving inappropriately.

They also stipulated that employees must be paid money and that if money was paid for work performed, other reinforcers could also be used (points, tokens). These employers indicated that instructions could be repeated, one task could be taught at a time, the easiest jobs could be taught first, and job-related equipment could be color coded.

Employers also specified several training strategies they would not allow. Techniques that they

TABLE 16.4 Selected training and management strategies for use in competitive employment

Employers would allow:
1. Keeping monthly records.
2. Keeping weekly records.
3. Telling the employee what she did wrong.
4. Verbally or physically instructing the employee while she corrects an error.
5. Asking the employee why she is acting socially inappropriately.
6. Allowing a performance rate of faster than 50% when the employee is receiving training.
7. Working for money.
8. Praise from a supervisor.
9. Immediate reinforcement
10. A combination of food, points, access to preferred activities, physical contact, or praise and money.
11. Verbal instruction, demonstrations, and physical assistance when learning a new job.
12. Repeating an instruction.
13. Teaching one task at a time.
14. Teaching the easiest jobs first.
15. Color coding job-related equipment.

Employers would never allow:
1. Ignoring an error.
2. Yelling at an employee.
3. Yelling at the employee when acting socially inappropriately.
4. Ignoring socially inappropriate behavior.
5. Points for work which can later be traded for material objects.
6. Teaching all tasks at one time.

indicated were absolutely inappropriate for use in any job training station included the use of overcorrection (Rusch & Close, 1976). Ultimately the techniques used to control job-related behavior must be very similar to those that are tolerated on the job (Menchetti et al., 1981). Schutz, Rusch, and Lamson (1979) used an employer-validated procedure to teach three individuals to stop verbally abusing their co-workers in an employment training station. The employer's procedure for misconduct on the job, which was a warning and one-day suspension, successfully reduced verbally abusive statements. The goal of this program was to teach potential employees to respond to the contingencies that would eventually be used by the employing agency. Failure to teach potential employees to respond to normal working conditions, such as those related to staff supervision, unnecessarily stigmatizes the new employee.

Place: Matching Student Abilities to Job Requirements

Job placement should be one of the primary outcomes of school-based supported work programs. Job placement requires school personnel to be involved in activities related to transferring students from community-based work stations into competitive employment positions. Realistically determining which job is going to best suit a particular student should be based upon the individual to be placed, the tasks to be performed on the job, and a willingness of the employer and co-workers to allow training to occur on the job. Certain steps are necessary if schools are to be successful in matching student abilities to specific job requirements. These steps include: (a) surveying the local community for potential jobs, (b) evaluating the positions that have been identified through the use of a comprehensive job-analysis survey, (c) comparing the job-analysis information to student assessment data that have been collected at the training stations, (d) involving parents or guardians in discussions related to job placement, (e) making a recommendation on the information received, (f) interviewing for the job, and (g) job placement.

Surveying the Local Community for Potential Jobs
As has been discussed, the purpose of the initial survey is to identify potential jobs in the community and to determine the social and vocational skills related to these positions. This information is used to develop a community-based vocational training program that closely reflects the jobs that have been targeted. The emphasis here is to identify specific jobs for those students who have completed or are nearing completion of training.

Communities often offer limited job opportunities, and frequently several social service agencies, all serving individuals with handicaps, appear to be competing for these jobs. Given this problem, it is important that school personnel work closely with staff from the local rehabilitation agency in coordinating job survey and placement goals. Students who are placed in competitive employment will be likely to need support services even after they have graduated. This support might involve additional training, advocating for an increase in pay or hours, or assistance in locating a new job. Cooperative planning involving school staff and rehabilitation agency personnel is essential in promoting the effective transition from school to work for students with moderate and severe handicaps. In addition, a business advisory council made up of employers and community leaders could provide school and rehabilitation agency staff with information and guidance about the local labor market. This council could help in finding job vacancies; gaining entrance into various job sites; communicating with co-workers, supervisors, and employers; and conducting local surveys.

Mailed surveys and telephone surveys have proven to be successful in finding employment for students with handicaps (Martin, 1986; Rusch & Mithaug, 1980). The obvious advantage of mailing or telephoning is that a very large number of prospective employers can be contacted with very little cost. This method can serve to introduce the school vocational training program to potential employers and, at the same time, acquire feedback from the employers regarding job availability and interest in hiring students. Also, it provides school personnel with an opportunity via letter or telephone conversation to describe how the community-based training program is better able to provide "trained" workers for identified occupations (food service, janitorial). Screening newspaper classified ads for job openings and contacting employers where past graduates have been successful can also be used in identifying prospective employment sites.

Job Analysis

The next step in the placement process is to contact the businesses who have expressed an interest in hiring and conduct a thorough job analysis. Rusch & Mithaug (1980) have outlined four components of such an analysis that need to be considered: (a) work environment (agency overview), (b) tasks to be completed (job task analysis), (c) conditions of employment (work hours per day, pay scale, travel requirement, insurance, and other benefits), and (d) work requirements (educational requirements, reasons for previous firings or abandonments). This information can be gathered by interviews with employers and co-workers, observations, and actually doing the job.

Direct observation of the job provides teachers with a description of the major tasks: the equipment and materials needed to perform the tasks, time frames in which work is to be completed, the level of supervision available, nonvocational skills that are needed, and opportunities for interactions with co-workers and customers. This information is invaluable when attempting to match student abilities to the job requirments that have been identified. We recommend that school staff take the time to review the information that has been included in the job analysis to make sure that the job duties outlined are accurate.

Student Assessment Data

Successfully placing a student in competitive employment rests largely on the school staff's ability to assess the student's strengths and weaknesses based on her work experiences in the training stations. Information on the social and vocational skills addressed in training provide teachers with additional knowledge that can be beneficial in making critical decisions concerning job placement. Moon, Goodall, Barcus, and Brooke (1985) have identified 20 different variables that need to be considered in assessing student ability. Rate, appearance, interaction behavior, independent task sequencing, ability to adapt to change, and time management were just a few of the variables that have been mentioned. Other factors that obviously can't be ignored in considering potential job placements include: (a) the student's vocational interest, (b) available transportation, (c) times available to work, (d) financial and living arrangements, (e) and physical limitations after adaptations have been considered.

Parent Involvement

All aspects of the job placement process should be discussed with parents or guardians. Parent's attitudes toward the employment of their son or daughter can determine the success or failure of a placement (Kochany & Keller, 1981). Parents need to know what the work environment is like, the tasks that are to be completed, hours, wages, and benefits. Also, school staff need to inform parents of the impact employment may have upon public support payments (Social Security Income). Finally, it is important to review with parents the advantages of employment (Rusch & Mithaug, 1980). These advantages include working co-workers without handicaps and the opportunity for their child to develop to her fullest potential through employment in the community. It is the school's responsibility to make sure that parents understand all of the factors in considering job placement so that they are better able to make informed decisions.

Recommending Job Placement

No decisions on job placement should be made until input has been provided by the employer, student, parents, and school staff. The chances of a successful job placement are enhanced by a systematic collection and review of pertinent information related to the student's abilities and job requirements.

Interviewing for the Job

Some students will be capable of participating in job interviews and should be encouraged to do so. When this is appropriate, the primary emphasis of instruction should be on wearing the proper attire for interviews, answering questions by employers, and teaching students the kinds of questions to ask employers about potential jobs. School personnel should accompany students to interviews and should take steps to ensure that lack of independence in job-seeking skills would not lower employer perceptions of the student's ability to independently perform job-related tasks.

Martin (1986) has pointed out that most of the students with moderate and severe handicaps will be unable to participate in a formal interview and recommended that a pre-interview be used instead. School personnel and the employer should have been actively involved in the job placement to this point and will ultimately make the final decision. The pre-interview would provide the student with the opportunity to meet his supervisor and co-workers as well as to learn more about the job site.

Job Placement

Once the student has been placed, school staff need to meet with the employer to once again review responsibilities of the targeted position and to discuss how to help the student adjust to her new job. School personnel should discuss the role they will play in on-the-job training for maintenance and should establish evaluation procedures that will give the employer the opportunity to provide feedback concerning student progress.

Maintain: Providing Follow-Up Services After Job Placement

Many nonhandicapped students graduate and enter the work force when they are 18 years old. Child labor laws in all states require work permits for youths under the age of 16; therefore, as a general rule, students should be placed in employment situations sometime between their 16th and 22nd birthdays. This decision should be based upon the student's competencies, the availability of follow-up personnel, and the selection of an appropriate placement. Most students, however, should receive *at least* 2 years of follow-up services before they graduate. In most (if not all) cases, the period should be longer.

An effective follow-up program has many functions, including identifying problems on the job, providing on-the-job training, seeking validation through significant others, planning intervention by others, and specifying effective strategies to withdraw follow-up services. Identifying problems and providing on-the-job training rely upon general behavior analysis procedures that require precise specification of survival skills needed before training. Once actual work performance standards are listed, a student's level of functioning can be evaluated. This evaluation identifies behavioral excesses or deficits that are then translated into instructional objectives. Mithaug and Haring (1977) proposed a similar approach which included, in part, these steps.

1. Analyzing the skills required to complete a job.
2. Pinpointing behaviors expected by the supervisor.
3. Specifying the motivational system on that job.
4. Encouraging conformity to rules.
5. Discouraging deviant behavior.
6. Assessing skill level relevant to the job.
7. Specifying behavioral objectives for each of the deficiencies identified.
8. Developing and implementing a training program.

These strategies have already been covered in this chapter or elsewhere in this text. Seeking validation from significant others and developing a long-term follow-up program, which includes planning intervention by others and withdrawing services, will be discussed next.

Seeking Validation from Significant Others*

One of four things happen when attempting to determine how well a placement is going (Rusch & Mithaug, 1980). Significant others (co-worker,

---

*Significant others refers to persons who, because of their expertise or contact with the student (employers, supervisors, co-workers) are able to assess whether instructional goals, procedures, and results are appropriate for their intended purposes.

supervisor) either agree or disagree with direct, repeated measures taken by follow-up personnel of people competitively or, these same follow-up personnel either agree or disagree with indirect measures typically provided by supervisors or others on the job who have *designated* evaluation functions.

Discrepancies between objective and subjective measures may be the result of several factors. People who serve as evaluators, like observers, may be influenced by others. Applied researchers have been known to influence the performance of observers in order to confirm their expectations. This same problem can arise when an employer's wishes (either positive or negative) are made known to the evaluator; thus, an employee may receive a negative evaluation based on an employer's perceptions rather than on actual job performance.

Discrepancies between these measures may also be due to the evaluator and the teacher attending to similar, but not exactly the same, dimensions of behavior. Rusch et al. (1981) indicated that work performance evaluators used broader definitions to influence their estimates of how well a target employee was adjusting to the job. Typically, teachers focus upon narrower dimensions of a target behavior. Teachers in the Rusch et al., study obtained the ratings of co-workers in conjunction with their direct measures to determine whether co-workers agreed if preinstructions and feedback resulted in fewer topics being repeated during lunches and breaks in a kitchen setting. Interestingly, at the end of the training period, co-workers indicated that there was no change. Direct measures obtained by the teachers, however, showed the target employee had not repeated topics for almost 3 weeks before the co-worker ratings.

Social validation methodology is a strategy that can be used to help identify these discrepancies, as well as to help decide how placed students are adjusting on the job. Social validation methodology includes subjective evaluation and social comparison. *Subjective evaluation* is a way to evaluate instructional programs by soliciting the judgments or opinions from significant others about the effectiveness of that instruction. Work behavior that has been changed by a teacher might be evaluated by an employer or co-worker who are in a position to judge the effects of their instruction. School personnel should develop a work performance evaluation form along specific behavioral dimensions so employers can give feedback. Typically, employers evaluate staff at least annually, with new staff

evaluated during the first 3 to 6 months of employment. We typically ask employers to complete the work-performance evaluation form once a week for the first month, then once a month for the remainder of the first year. Sometimes work-performance evaluations that already exist in the employment setting may be used by teachers. Often, however, existing forms are not sufficiently expansive or behaviorally oriented to provide information needed to develop training plans; therefore, teachers should establish their own work-performance evaluation form that can be used *in addition* to the form that is used by the employing agency.

The work-performance evaluation form should be completed by an employee who has responsibility for staff evaluations and, possibly, hiring and firing of these same staff. This form should not be completed by co-workers in positions similar to the new employee nor by the new employee (or student) alone. Recent research has indicated that there are gross discrepancies between evaluations done by experienced staff and lower-level employees (White & Rusch, 1983). People with handicaps and their co-workers have been shown to evaluate performance significantly higher than supervisors.

Subjective evaluations may also include verbal reports. Periodically asking significant others how well a student is doing can be helpful in pinpointing areas that may require additional training. In general, however, written feedback is preferrable because it provides a permanent product of evaluation.

Another form of social validation methodology is *social comparison*. Social comparison involves collecting direct measures of acceptable behavior to serve as a norm for adequate functioning, thus, data would be collected to compare the student's target behavior (also their goals and the procedures used to teach them) with that of their peers/co-workers. The primary goal is to determine whether the targeted student's behavior is distinguishable from the behavior of persons whose performance is valued. Social comparison entails directly observing the work performance of a peer/co-worker to compare performance with that of the target student/employee. The goal is *not* to teach the student to work just like employees who are not handicapped. Rather, the goal is to adjust or manage target behavior so that the student works within acceptable performance standards.

In order to use social comparison methodology correctly, one must be familiar with the performance of the target student and then must select an employee who is performing comparable tasks during similar work periods. It is also crucial to collect direct, repeated measures of work performed under very similar conditions. It would be appropriate to collect data on a target employee within 30 minutes of break if the comparison employee is also being observed during the same period. If both are working in the same location, the observer could either observe the target student for a brief period (10 seconds), then the selected employee for the next time period, alternating until the entire work sample is completed. If the student and the selected employee are working in separate locations in the same building, the teacher could watch the student and then the selected employee for exactly the same periods of time (for 10 minutes each), again in alternating fashion. If a selected employee is not working at the same time as the student, the employee should be observed during the same periods the student works except on her days off. For example, if the student works 5 days a weeks with a part-time employee working her days off (or the reverse), observations could be made on both employees but on different days.

Developing a Long-Term Follow-up Program

Recent literature pays considerable attention to maintaining a job (Rusch, 1986a) and evaluating job maintenance (Rusch & Kazdin, 1981). Our discussion provides only an overview of this topic, and will include establishing a schedule to deliver follow-up services, using co-workers to support job maintenance, and withdrawing training and management strategies to enhance job maintenance.*

Rusch (1986a) has suggested two follow-up schedules: (a) the adjusted follow-up schedule and (b) the fixed follow-up schedule. The *adjusted* follow-up schedule is based exclusively on how well the student performs on the job, with less and less time spent on follow-up as the student adjusts to the demands of the job. The *fixed* follow-up schedule is preset by the teacher and reflects decreasing time spent by follow-up staff over an extended time. Because some employers believe they can provide "all necessary training," and therefore may ask the follow-up staff not to help them provide on-the-job training, it is crucial to establish a schedule for the follow-up staff for monitoring performance and providing training.

---

*See Kochany and Keller (1981) for an analysis of the reasons that some individuals placed by Wehman and his colleagues have failed to retain their employment.

A placement should not be made if the employer will not, in advance, allow adjusted or fixed follow-ups. As we have said, people with mild and emotional handicaps have been the primary recipients of vocational rehabilitation, and they have adjusted largely due to their existing skills. Students or adults with severe handicaps have *not* been a target rehabilitation population; consequently, most employers have no experience working with them. Therefore, job advocacy based upon student performance and employer perceptions of that performance will be crucial in determining whether the individual adjusts to a particular job.

Both the adjusted and fixed schedules should include onsite and offsite services over periods of 6 months or longer. The initial months will likely require daily services over the entire work schedule, including getting to and from the worksite. Onsite time will usually be spent training, managing, and evaluating behavior and the perceptions of how others believe a placement is going (subjective evaluation). This time should be divided into periods when the follow-up personnel are observable and not observable to the employee. Existing research suggests that employees react to the observed presence of evaluators (Rusch, Menchetti, Crouch, Riva, Morgan, & Agran, 1984); therefore, teachers should ensure that newly placed students perform in the presence of co-workers and supervisors just as they might perform in your presence.

Using Co-workers to Support Job Maintenance
Typically, follow-up staff observe and evaluate behavior and provide feedback based on their evaluations. To date, very little attention has been paid to job placement follow-up provided by co-workers (Shafer, 1986). Co-workers could be trained in short, in-service workshops to not only evaluate behavior but also to train and manage behavior. Short 10-minute sessions might be scheduled during breaks or before or after work to demonstrate effective training procedures and to allow co-workers the time to practice the techniques that they have learned. Behavior descriptions and the goal of work-performance, evaluation forms also could be discussed. In essence, the follow-up staff have the responsibility to monitor their placements. To this end, some time should be devoted to a well-planned and coordinated schedule of in-service activities directed toward all workers at the site.

Withdrawing Training and Management Strategies
Methods of withdrawing training packages and

evaluating these withdrawals have been discussed in the literature (Connis & Rusch, 1980; Rusch & Kazdin, 1981). Several factors should be considered when estimating how quickly to withdraw staff from the placement setting. Foremost, is determining whether the target employee can perform the job without any feedback from a teacher and in the teacher's absence. Rusch and Kazdin (1981) have suggested using sequential withdrawals to evaluate and maintain behavior. *Sequential withdrawal* entails withdrawing one component of a multiple-component training package initially, then a second, and so on, until all training components have been withdrawn. Rusch, Connis, and Sowers (1978) used this strategy with a woman having mild handicaps who was instructed to attend to task ("look busy"). The attending behavior was developed with prompts, praise, and a token economy. It required the woman to exchange her points twice a day; therefore, the authors withdrew the token economy, the prompts, and then praise, until the training package consisted of payment of wages every 2 weeks.

Withdrawal methods have only recently been introduced, and thus, there are few studies using them; however, the strategies to withdraw training and management procedures are logical. We can say that teachers should evaluate whether the absence of intervention, and the person(s) who introduced intervention, results in loss of behavior. If so, the withdrawal approach must be (a) repeated more slowly so that the new employee eventually does not discriminate between the absence or presence of the trainer or intervention, (b) supplemented with a second strategy (self-monitoring) or possibly, (c) not totally withdrawn (part of the procedures remain). In the last instance, the strategy might include training people on the job to maintain performance (Rusch & Menchetti, 1981).

Summary of Work Model

The supported work model provides special education personnel with specific examples of how to include the curricula guidelines outlined in the previous section (community-referenced, longitudinal, integrated, community based) into a program that will successfully prepare students for employment. The first step of the model, *survey*, requires teachers to identify future community job placements and the social and vocational survival skills associated with each of these jobs. After these survival skills have been socially validated, via the comprehensive survey, community-based training stations are established. These stations provide teachers with the opportunity to *train* the identified, survival skills to severely handicapped students in settings that are very similar to the targeted job placements. The third step, *place*, refers to the transition process during which the student is moved from the community-based training station to a specific job placement. When a placement is made it provides teachers with a criterion by which all previous instructional efforts can be evaluated. *Maintain* is the final step of the model. This step requires school staff initially to provide the necessary follow-up services to assist students in maintaining employment in the community. The follow-up services may be needed for retraining or training of new skills, to advocate for the student, to assist the student in dealing with problems that may result from interaction with new supervisors and co-workers, and to ensure that the expectations outlined for the positions are maintained.

TRANSITION FROM SCHOOL TO WORK

Coordination of Services

Even if school programs are successful in placing students into employment before they leave school, the chances of students with severe handicaps maintaining these positions in the absence of support after graduation are bleak without communication between schools and adult service providers. Educational and rehabilitation programs cannot effectively serve these students until efforts are made by both service providers to plan and coordinate their services. Coordinated services (a) provide a more efficient, effective, and meaningful continuum of services for students, (b) help reduce duplicate efforts, and (c) provide service personnel with additional knowledge and appreciation for each other's roles in service delivery (Hall, 1980).

One of the first steps that can be taken by special education personnel to improve the coordination of services is to become familiar with the adult service alternatives typically available for persons with severe handicaps and the outcomes of these programs. To date, work activity centers and sheltered workshops have served as the primary employment options for this population; however, recent development of new employment options—

supported employment and competitive employment—have provided teachers and adult service providers with alternatives to sheltered employment for severely handicapped persons. An awareness of these various alternatives enables special education teachers to advocate more appropriate vocational services for their students, as well as providing parents with information of potential employment options for their child.

Work Activity Centers

Work activity centers are day programs where between 20 to 60 individuals with handicaps spend their day performing activities that bear little if any relation to employment (coloring, dressing a doll, sitting quietly). Few work activity centers offer employment training or wages; most focus their training efforts on leisure activities such as arts and crafts. If wages are offered, they are generally quite low (less than $300 a year).

Sheltered Workshops

The goal of sheltered workshops is to prepare individuals for competitive employment; however, actual placement out of the workshop seldom occurs. If work is offered and wages are paid, the wages are often very low (about $700 a year). Sheltered workshops, like work activity centers, are segregated and employ large numbers of individuals with handicaps (between 50–100). Few persons who are severely handicapped ever attain sheltered-workshop status; most workshops employ individuals who are mildly or moderately handicapped.

Supported Employment

Supported employment options include work crews and enclaves, which exist in only a few communities. Work crews generally consist of small groups of individuals who are handicapped and who are under the supervision of an individual who is not handicapped. Work crews perform jobs according to specified contracts that are bid upon (yard work or janitorial services at an office building). Work crews usually move from one job to another job throughout a work day. Enclaves, however, are located within a single business or industry performing light industrial or electronic assembly tasks (Rhodes & Valenta, 1985). Similar to work crews, enclaves also consist of a group of individuals with handicaps who are trained and supervised by an individual without handicaps. Both employment options assume that the individual worker will require continuing support throughout the tenure

of employment; thus, this option is a viable one for individuals who are severely handicapped. Supported employment options generally occur in integrated settings and may offer competitive wages for full- or part-time work.

Competitive Employment

An individual who is competively employed performs work that is valued by an employer in an integrated setting making minimum wage or better. Traditionally, competitive employment options have existed in most communities. Agencies, such as Vocational Rehabilitation, offer job placement services to eligible clients. These services are usually offered to individuals who require little training to learn job-related tasks and then once placed on the job require little if any follow-up. Individuals served by Vocational Rehabilitation are placed into competitive and integrated settings. Many individuals using these services are not mildly handicapped, but are considered disadvantaged or displaced workers (workers without handicaps who have lost their jobs).

Competitive employment is also a viable alternative for persons who are severely handicapped if each of the four curriculum guides introduced above (community referenced, integrated, longitudinal, community-based) is followed. Rusch (1986) suggests that competitive employment include intensive job-site training and advocacy, ongoing evaluation, and extended follow-up services. In competitive employment, ongoing services are not necessary for the duration of employment (like the supported employment option), and in fact, services are gradually withdrawn as soon as the individual shows he or she can maintain employment on his own.

Although not all employment options may exist in all communities, parents and school personnel should be aware of innovative employment programs occurring in other communities. The lack of various options should also not stop parents or school personnel from requesting services that they think would be appropriate for their child.

The Transition Planning Team

Transition is a term that has been used for several years (Brown et al, 1981). Recently, Wehman (1984) defined vocational transition as

. . . a carefully planned process, which may be initiated either by school personnel or adult service

providers, to establish and implement a plan for either employment or additional vocational training of a handicapped student who will graduate or leave school in three to five years; such a process must involve special educators, vocational educators, parents and/or the student, and an adult service system representative, and possibly an employer. (pp. 23-24)

According to Wehman's definition, vocational transition must be: (a) a well-planned and systematic process, which (b) occurs well before the student reaches 21 years of age, and combines the efforts of (c) individuals from numerous disciplines and service agencies, and (d) parents and/or students. This coordination is achieved by developing and implementing a vocational transition plan. A vocational transition plan (like the IEP) helps to ensure that educational and rehabilitation personnel meet and pool their resources so that students will obtain employment or additional vocational training after leaving high school.

Transition planning should involve those agencies and individuals who will be playing a role in the transition of severely handicapped students from school into adult services. School staff should make sure that parents, students, and adult service agency personnel are included in the transitioning process.

Parents

Parents are crucial to the transition team because they make the ultimate decision regarding which employment options are the most desirable for their children. Parental choices will vary depending upon their personal values, their expectations for their children, and the information they possess about program options; thus, in order for the best decision to be made for students, parents will need to be well-informed regarding the employment options that exist in their communities.

Students

Students should also be involved in planning their transition from school to work. As much as possible, their interests and needs regarding various employment options should be considered.

Schools

As has been stated above, the schools have the responsibility to prepare students for employment. Classroom teachers should work together with the local rehabilitation agency staff to conduct surveys of communities for potential job training sites as well as permanent employment positions. It makes little sense for classroom teachers and rehabilitation personnel to conduct independent job surveys as well as to establish independent job training sites. This duplicative effort, which often exists in communities, could be eliminated by early coordination of services. This coordination of effort with the local rehabilitation agency ensures that parents will be well informed of the various employment options available for their children when their children leave the school system. This arrangement also enables school staff to provide information to adult service agency personnel relative to specific placement sites and training strategies that have been successful in maintaining students in their jobs.

Adult Service Agencies

Adult rehabilitation agency personnel (and/or employers) should be represented on the transition planning team. Reasons for including these personnel include their need to inform teachers, parents, and students about employment options existing in the community and their need to work closely with the teachers and parents to facilitate entry into the desired employment placements. Also, adult-service providers need to work closely with school staff to ensure job maintenance for those students who are employed at the time of graduation. Further, they should work continually to improve employment options. Expanding their access to community references is important to the continual development of their programs.

In summary, several individuals should be involved in planning the transition from school to work for individuals with severe handicaps. Parents are necessary because they make the ultimate decision regarding which employment option is the most desirable for their children. Students need to be consulted, when possible, so their vocational interests are known. The school is essential because it prepares the student for employment, and adult-service agencies facilitate entry into desired employment placements, and may provide further training and/or follow-up services. The transitional process is further enhanced by formulating a written transitional plan, which is discussed in the next section.

The Vocational Transitional Plan

The *vocational transition plan* is a formal mechanism for making certain that recommendations for

TABLE 16.5 Individualized vocational transition plan

Student's Name _____ Date of Birth _____ Residence _____ Phone _____

Parent/Guardian _____ Address _____ Phone _____

High School _____ Date of Graduation _____ School year _____ Date of plan _____

Participants _____

Issues Related to Vocational Transition	Activities	Product	Date of Initiation	Date of Completion	Personnel Involvement
1.0 Job Placement	1.1 School staff will meet adult-service agency staff and parents to discuss potential employment options for student and discuss level of follow-up services that could be provided after graduation.	Completed Job Placement Plan. Includes vocational interests, times available to work, etc.	September 1	September 1	School staff; Adult-service agency follow-up staff; Parents; Student
	1.2 Student will be placed into competitive employment during the fall semester.	Job Analysis Survey; Vocational Service Plan	September 8	September 1	School staff; Employer; Student
	1.3 School staff will provide initial on the job training.	Task Analyses; Individualized Program Plans, graphs; Work Performance Evaluations; Job Placement Logs	November 1	ongoing	School staff; Adult-Service agency follow-up staff; Employer; Student
	1.4 School staff will meet with adult-service agency staff and the employer to discuss the transfer of follow-up responsibilities	Individualized Follow-up Plan for site. Includes time for cooperative programming and gradual fading of school staff involvement	January 15	ongoing	School Staff; Adult-service agency follow-up staff; Employer; Student; Parent
2.0 Transportation	2.1 School staff will train student to use the city bus to and from work.	Bus pass; Travel Training Task Analysis graph	November 1	November 15	School staff; Student
3.0 Income	3.1 Meet with staff from local security office to discuss how employment will affect student's SSI benefits.	Written letter from Social Security Office outlining the effects on SSI benefits.	September 3	September 3	Social Security staff; School staff; Adult-service agency Case Manager; Parents
4.0 Recreation-Leisure	4.1 Student has time between school and work. Has expressed interest in joining Fitness Center near work.	Membership card	December 1	ongoing	School staff; Fitness Center staff; Student
	Student will go to Fitness Center on Monday, Wednesday, Friday.	Workout schedule	December 1	December 1	Fitness Center staff; Student

employment occur. Essentially, vocational transition plans should be individualized and delineate the necessary steps or procedures (type of training, materials) needed for entry into the employment option selected. They should specify the recommended employment option and should designate the person(s) responsible for implementing the procedures within a specified time period. An example of a transition plan is provided in Table 16.5. The vocational transition plan will ensure that the parents are aware of employment options and adult services, will enable the student to acquire adult services with few disruptions, and will provide school personnel and adult-service agency representatives with a set of procedures and timelines to follow.

Summary

It is essential to coordinate services between parents, the students, schools, and adult-service agency personnel so that students who are severely handicapped can be appropriately placed (attain meaningful employment after leaving school). A lack of planning and coordination is likely to result in less desirable and more restrictive placements. Vocational transition plans serve as written records of the recommendations and the steps necessary to achieve employment.

CONCLUSION

Identifying employers, jobs, survival skills, significant others, and the many other characteristics of a community that may influence the success of a community-based, vocational training program is crucial. We have suggested that placement staff consider a community of employers as a fixed commodity and identify and develop jobs for the purpose of employing workers with handicaps. Communities offer limited job opportunities, and often several social service agencies appear to be competing for these jobs; thus, transition from school to work and adulthood can only be successful if linkages are developed between school and adult-service agency personnel through cooperative vocational training planning.

This chapter has presented the *survey-train-place-maintain* model for preparing students with severe handicaps for competitive employment. We have not, however, discussed the importance of leisure and recreation, domestic, or self-help training as they relate to competitive employment. These topics and the skills they represent interact in a way that appreciably influences individual success. Failure to consider the entire student and the requirements of her future environments will surely result in our failure to serve our students with severe handicaps appropriately.

REFERENCES

Alper, S. (1981). Utilizing community jobs in developing vocational curriculum for severely handicapped youth. *Education and Training of the Mentally Retarded, 16,* 217–221.

Brown, L., Pumpian, I., Baumgart, D., Vandeventer, P., Ford, A., Nisbet, J., Schroeder, J., & Gruenewald, L. (1981). Longitudinal transition plans in programs for severely handicapped students. *Exceptional Children, 47,* 624–631.

Chadsey-Rusch, J. (1986). Identifying and teaching valued social behaviors in competitive employment settings. In F. Rusch (Ed.), *Competitive employment issues and strategies* (pp. 273–287). Baltimore: Paul H. Brookes.

Connis, R. T., & Rusch, F. R. (1980). Programming maintenance through sequential withdrawal of social contingencies. *Behavior Research of Severe Developmental Disabilities, 1,* 249–260.

Gold, M. (1980). *Try another way training manual.* Champaign, IL: Research Press.

Hall, H. B. (1980). The intangible human factor: The most critical coordination variable. In J. O. Elder & P. R. Magrab (Eds.), *Coordinating services to handicapped children: A handbook for interagency collaboration.* (pp. 45–62). Baltimore: Paul H. Brookes.

Hasazi, S. B., Gordon, L. R., & Roe, C. A. (1985). Factors associated with the employment status of handicapped youth exiting high school from 1979 to 1983. *Exceptional Children, 51,* 455–469.

Horner, R. H., & McDonald, R. S. (1982). Comparison of single instance and general case instruction in teaching a generalized vocational skill. *Journal of the Association for the Severely Handicapped, 7,* 7–20.

Karlan, G., & Rusch, F. (1982). Analyzing the relationship between acknowledgement and compliance in a sheltered work setting. *Education and Training of the Mentally Retarded, 17,* 202–208.

Kenowitz, L. A., Gallaher, J., & Edgar, E. (1977). Generic services for the severely handicapped and their families: What's available: In E. Sontag, J. Smith, & N. Certo (Eds.). *Educational programming for the severely and profoundly handicapped.* Reston, VA: Council for Exceptional Children.

Kochany, L., and Keller, J. (1981). An analysis and evaluation of the failures of severely disabled individuals in competitive employment. In P. Wehman (Ed.), *Competitive employment.* Baltimore: Paul H. Brookes.

Martin, J. E. (1986). Identifying potential jobs. In F. Rusch (Ed.). *Competitive employment issues and strategies* (pp. 165–185). Baltimore: Paul H. Brookes.

Martin, J. E., Rusch, F. R., & Heal, L. W. (1982). Training community survival skills to mentally retarded adults: A review and analysis. *The Journal of Special Education, 16,* 243-267.

Menchetti, B. M., Rusch, F. R., & Lamson, D. S. (1981). Employers' perceptions of acceptable training procedures for use in competitive employment settings. *Journal of the Association for the Severely Handicapped, 6,* 6-16.

Mithaug, D. E., & Haring, N. G. (1977). Community vocational and workshop placement. In N. G. Haring & L. J. Brown (Eds.), *Teaching the severely handicapped* (Vol. 2) (pp. 257-284). New York: Grune & Stratton.

Mithaug, D. E., Horiuchi, C. N., & Fanning, P. N. (1985). A report on the Colorado statewide follow-up survey of special education students. *Exceptional Children, 51,* 397-404.

Moon, S., Goodall, P., Barcus, M., & Brooke, V. (1985). *The supported work model of competitive employment for citizens with severe handicaps: A Guide for job trainers.* Richmond, VA: Virginia Commonwealth University, School of Education.

Nietupski, J., Hamre-Nietupski, S., Welch, J., & Anderson, R. (1983). Establishing and maintaining vocational training sites for moderately and severely handicapped students: Strategies for community/vocational trainers. *Education and Training of the Mentally Retarded, 18,* 169-175.

Rhodes, L. E., & Valenta L. (1985). Industry-based supported employment: An enclave approach. *Journal of the Association for the Severely Handicapped, 10,* 12-20.

Rusch, F. R. (1979). A functional analysis of the relationship between attending to task and production in an applied restaurant setting. *Journal of Special Education, 13,* 399-411.

Rusch, F. R. (1986a). Developing a long-term follow-up program. In F. Rusch, (Ed.), *Competitive employment issues and strategies* (pp. 225-232). Baltimore: Paul H. Brookes.

Rusch, F. R. (1986b). (Ed.). *Competitive employment issues and strategies.* Baltimore: Paul H. Brookes.

Rusch, F. R., & Close, D. (1976). Overcorrection: A procedural evaluation. *AAESPH Review, 1,* 32-45.

Rusch, F. R., Connis, R. T., & Sowers, J. (1978). The modification and maintenance of time spent attending to task using social reinforcement, token reinforcement, and response cost in an applied restaurant setting. *Journal of Special Education Technology, 2,* 18-26.

Rusch, F. R., Chadsey-Rusch, J., White, D. M., & Gifford, J. L. (1985). Programs for severely mentally retarded adults: Perspectives and methodologies. In D. Bricker & J. Filler (Eds.). *Severe mental retardation: From theory to practice* (pp. 119-140) Reston, VA: The Division on Mental Retardation of the Council for Exceptional Children.

Rusch, F. R., & Kazdin, A. E. (1981). Toward a methodology of withdrawal designs for the assessment of response maintenance. *Journal of Applied Behavior Analysis, 14,* 131-140.

Rusch, F. R., & Menchetti, B. M. (1981). Increasing complaint work behaviors in a non-sheltered work setting. *Mental Retardation, 19,* 107-112.

Rusch, F. R., Menchetti, B. M., Crouch, K., Riva, M., Morgan, T., & Agran, M. (1984). Competitive employment: Assessing employee reactivity to naturalistic observation. *Applied Research in Mental Retardation, 5,* 313-325.

Rusch, F. R., & Mithaug, D. E. (1980). *Vocational training for mentally retarded adults: A behavior analytic approach.* Champaign, IL: Research Press.

Rusch, F. R., Schutz, R. P., & Agran, M. (1982). Validating entry-level survival skills for service occupations: Implications for curriculum development. *Journal of the Association for the Severely Handicapped, 7,* 32-41.

Schutz, R. P., Rusch, F. R., & Lamson, D. S. (1979). Evaluation of an employer's procedure to eliminate unacceptable behavior on the job. *Community Services Forum, 1,* 4-5.

Shafer, M. S. (1986). Utilizing co-workers as change agents. In F. Rusch (Ed.). *Competitive employment issues and strategies* (pp. 215-224). Baltimore: Paul H. Brookes.

Sowers, J., Rusch, F., Connis, R. T., Cummings, L. E. (1980). Teaching mentally retarded adults to time manage in a vocational setting. *Journal of Applied Behavior Analysis, 13,* 119-128.

Sowers, J., Rusch, F. R., & Hudson, C. (1979). Training a severely retarded young adult to ride the city bus to and from work. *AAESPH Review, 4,* 15-22.

Stainback, W., Stainback, S., Nietupski, J., & Hamre-Nietupski, S. (1986). Establishing community-based training stations. In Frank R. Rusch, (Ed.), *Competitive employment: Issues and strategies* (pp. 103-114). Baltimore: Paul H. Brookes.

Thurman, S. K., & Fiorelli, J. S. (1979). Perspectives on normalization. *Journal of Special Education, 13,* 339-346.

Turkel, S. (1972). *Working.* New York: Pantheon.

U.S. Commission on Civil Rights. (1983). *Accommodating the spectrum of disabilities.* Washington, DC: U.S. Commission on Civil Rights.

Wacker, D. P., & Berg, W. K. (1986). Generalizing and maintaining work behavior. In F. Rusch (Ed.) *Competitive employment issues and strategies* (pp. 129-140). Baltimore: Paul H. Brookes.

Wehman, P. (1981). *Competitive employment.* Baltimore: Paul H. Brookes.

Wehman, P. (1984). Transition for handicapped youth from school to work. In J. Chadsey-Rusch (Ed.), *Conference proceedings document: Enhancing transition from school to the workplace for handicapped youth* (pp. 22-39). Champaign, IL: University of Illinois, Office of Career Development for Special Populations.

Wehman, P., Kregel, J., & Seyfarth, J. (1985). Employment outlook for young adults with mental retardation. *Rehabilitation Counseling Bulletin, 29,* 90-99.

White, D. M., & Rusch, F. R. (1983). Social validation in competitive employment: Evaluating work performance. *Applied Research in Mental Retardation, 5,* 343-354.

Wilcox, B., & Bellamy, G. T. (1982). (Eds.), *Design of high school programs for severely handicapped students.* Baltimore: Paul H. Brookes.

Will, M. (1984). Bridges from school to working life. *Programs for the Handicapped,* March/April, 2.

G. Thomas Bellamy
U.S. Department of Education

Robert H. Horner
University of Oregon

Beyond High School: Residential and Employment Options After Graduation

17

Planning for life beyond high school has become an important part of research and practice in special education for persons with severe disabilities. This emphasis is a natural product of the demographics of special education. Research and development efforts have addressed programming issues with gradually older individuals as the first cohort of students with severe disabilities grew up attending the public schools. The field has progressed from documentation of the potential benefits of and procedures for early intervention (Hayden & Dmitriev, 1975), to development of instructive methods of content for the elementary years (Sontag, Smith, & Certo, 1977), and finally, to innovations in adult-referenced curricula and community-based instruction in the secondary school (Brown, Certo, Belmore, & Crowner, 1977; Wilcox & Bellamy, 1982).

As this first cohort of students begins the transition to work and adult life, professionals face the task of helping them solve the same lifestyle issues that confront other adolescents and young adults in our society: finding meaningful employment, selecting a place to live outside their parents' home, and getting the support that will maintain and continue the personal development achieved during school.

The forces that focus professional attention on transition to adult services also create a crisis for parents and their young adult sons and daughters. The crisis of graduation is apparent in the number of students who leave school to no services at all (McDonnell, Wilcox, & Boles, 1986; Zollers, Conroy, Hess, & Newman, 1984), the prevalence of inappropriate services (Buckley & Bellamy, 1985), and the difference in parent and service-provider perceptions about needed services (Brodsky, 1983). It is not surprising that some states have responded to vocal parent and professional concerns with legislation to formalize the process of planning for postschool services (Nettekoven & Ramsey, 1985).

This chapter was co-authored by Tom Bellamy in his private capacity. No official support or endorsement by the Department of Education is intended or should be inferred.

Together, the professional efforts to address transition issues, family concerns for postschool options, and state mandates for transition planning significantly increase the competencies needed by high school teachers of students with severe disabilities. In addition to fulfilling familiar roles in instruction, community integration, and family support, teachers need both a vision of what is possible in adult life and an understanding of the mechanisms for service funding and delivery that can realize that vision.

The purpose of this chapter is to provide a broad introduction to critical aspects of adult services for persons considered severely handicapped by the schools. The chapter focuses specifically on options for employment and community living and is intended as a resource for teachers, parents, and others as they plan for these critical postschool services for persons with severe disabilities. The chapter begins with an overview of critical differences between school and adult services that affect planning for transition. Employment and residential services are then discussed from the perspective of both current research and existing services. The chapter's focus is on how teachers and parents might apply this information to improve the transition process and prospects for youth with disabilities.

INTRODUCTION TO ADULT SERVICES

Structural and historical differences between school and adult services for persons with severe disabilities create significant barriers as teachers and parents plan for life beyond school. Understanding these differences is a critical first step in postschool planning with, and on behalf of, an individual with a severe disability. This section describes four important characteristics of the adult services system and illustrates the difficulties these can create for school leavers with severe disabilities.

Fragmented Responsibility for Services

Unlike special education, in which a clearly identifiable public agency has responsibility for service delivery, regulation, and funding at the local, state, and federal levels, adult services are authorized by several different federal and state laws and administered by several agencies, each with responsibility for a particular service. By both statute and administration, different programs have different, some-times conflicting goals and provide or fund services to different groups of citizens. A service may be designed for persons who are able to document the presence of a disability, meet a means test, or maintain earnings below a certain level. Different program goals include providing basic financial and medical support for those who are unable to work, assisting persons to enter the workforce, maintaining community residence, and simply meeting the social service needs that are defined by local and state authorities. At the federal level, at least, there is no single agency responsible for coordinating adult services to persons with severe disabilities. This results in a lack of systematic information on the overall effectiveness and efficiency of adult services.

This fragmented and seemingly uncoordinated system makes transition planning difficult. First of all, it means that the pattern of adult services established for any individual is likely to be an incomplete mosaic of programs and supports. Constructing the optimum mosaic for any individual requires both information about the many federal and state programs for which an individual might be eligible, and knowledge of the details of how those programs actually operate in the person's own community. Second, without coordination of most services at the federal level, each state, and indeed, many communities have developed unique program labels. What is called a group home, work activity center, competitive employment program, supervised apartment, or self-advocacy program in one community is often radically different from a program with the same name elsewhere. A third result of this fragmentation of responsibility for adult services across agencies and levels of government is the relative difficulty in advocating for needed expansion or improvement. Unlike the schools, where it is clear what agency must change to achieve a desired service, there are usually many possible targets for advocacy efforts in adult services. For example, parents wishing to expand employment services for adults with severe disabilities might attempt to (a) influence the federal vocational rehabilitation agency to serve more persons who are considered severely handicapped by the schools; (b) influence state Development Disabilities/Mental Retardation agencies, who now fund most of the community day services for this group, but provide mostly nonvocational services; or (c) focus energy on local service providers who may have the descretion to change the kind of services offered.

Definitional Confusion

Compounding the difficulty created by fragmentation of responsibility for adult services is the variety of different uses of the term "severely disabled" or "severely handicapped" across programs and agencies. The primary focus of this book is on those persons who are considered severely handicapped in school. Severe disability in special education is defined by the need for extraordinary services in order to benefit from educational services, and consequently reflects difficulty in learning and behavior in the school (45 Code of Federal Regulations 121.1). Quite different views of severe disability emerge as the frame of reference is shifted from progress in school to employment, independent living, income maintenance, and other concerns of adult living. In the Vocational Rehabilitation program, for example, severe disabilities encompass a much larger group than special education, including those individuals with any level of mental retardation, specific learning disabilities, neurological disorders, musculo-skeletal disorders, and many other conditions which seriously limit functional capacities in relation to employment, but for which an individual can reasonably be expected to benefit in terms of employability from vocational rehabilitation services (31 CFR 361.1). Contrasting assumptions are apparent in the definition that establishes eligibility for income support and most medical assistance services. Here a severe disability is supposed to reflect an inability to do any work which exists in the national economy (20 CFR 416.905). In practice, the definition also includes persons with greater ability levels than would be included in an educational definition of severe disability, but it excludes those whose income is above defined limits, whatever their level of disability. Because federal medical assistance funds are used in many states to support community residential and day services, this same definition may affect access to those services as well.

This definitional confusion affects transition planning principally by making it difficult to obtain accurate information on service possibilities and options. It is not unusual for adult service programs that report successful services for persons with severe disabilities to serve persons who would be considered mildly handicapped or nonhandicapped by the schools. Similar difficulties are encountered in interpreting research and demonstration efforts, unless unusually detailed information is given about persons studied. A frequent result is the perception that procedures and programs are available for persons considered severely disabled by the schools, when in fact, the available services and information often reflect work with much more capable individuals.

Eligibility, Rather than Entitlement Services

Whatever definition of disability structures eligibility for a service, meeting the requirements of the definition does not actually guarantee access to the needed service. Unlike education, where a right to services is established in federal legislation, most community services are available only when the individual qualifies for services *and* those services are available locally. Income support and medical assistance programs represent important exceptions to this lack of entitlements, but these programs seldom meet the critical need for support in residential and employment contexts. Actual entry into needed community services may be affected by the extent to which a state provides funds for these services and the way in which state and local policy or practice give priority to persons awaiting services.

This lack of entitlements has an immediate effect on many persons with severe disabilities leaving the schools: they graduate not to needed services, but to waiting lists for those services. Even before the recent increase in the number of persons with severe disabilities leaving school, Brodsky (1983) and Stanfield (1973) found a significant number of young adults with severe disabilities at home without needed services. A more recent survey of responsible state agencies found long waiting lists for community day and residential services in every state that maintained records of service needs (McDonnell et al., 1986). Even those states that have addressed the problem of transition from school to employment in state legislation have required planning and information exchange processes, without mandating provision of adult services. The New York statute specifically states that nothing about the way it is written should be "construed to create an entitlement to adult services" (New York state transitional law, Chapter 570, 1976, p.4). A second implication of the lack of entitlements is that it creates the need for ongoing local and state advocacy efforts as a fundamental part of all transition planning for school leavers with severe disabilities. Implementation of state of the art services for young adults with severe disabilities requires (a) that states allocate sufficient funds to offer those services to persons in need, and (b) that local programs be designed and managed to use available technology.

Private Sector Delivery System

Unlike schools where a public agency delivers the majority of required services, most vocational, residential, and social services for adults with disabilities are delivered by private, not-for-profit corporations. Responsible public agencies contract with these corporations for service delivery, providing all or some part of the required funding and requiring that the resulting services meet defined standards. Not surprisingly, there are enormous state-to-state differences in the expectations which funding agencies have for corporations providing services, and the extent to which those expectations are enforced through systematic contracting and evaluation processes. It is not unusual for a single community organization to work under contract with several state and federal agencies, so that the clear distinctions among programs that sometimes exists in federal legislation and regulation are blurred in local service delivery. Not-for-profit service delivery organizations operate under the direction of volunteer boards of directors and usually function as tax exempt entities. Within broad guidelines of the tax code and the funding agency requirements, they are free to establish their own policies and procedures; define service objectives, locations, and procedures; set priorities for who will be served; and raise funds through business ventures, donations, or other means. The not-for-profit delivery system is generally believed to be less expensive than publicly provided services, reflecting the potential for both cost sharing and competition among agencies. Community organizations usually do experience direct or potential competition for both funding and service recipients, and as a result may engage in active marketing of their services to both consumers and funders of service. Staffing constitutes one of the most significant issues in the not-for-profit delivery system. Wages are generally lower than in comparable public school or institution positions, turnover is high, and staff have fewer of the benefits and protections associated with employment in the public sector (Conroy & Bradley, 1985).

Reliance on not-for-profit corporations to deliver adult services creates additional considerations for planning the transition from school to adult life for persons with severe disabilities. Whatever the purpose of federal and state programs, so much program discretion and variation is usually present in local services that information about postschool options must be collected in every community. This is often made difficult by the public relations and marketing efforts of local services, which may describe exemplary program goals, but offer little information of how well existing service recipients are achieving those goals. Without standard nomenclature for types of adult services, labels used to describe various services may provide little information about the services actually provided. Because program staffing is somewhat volatile, it is also important to know what systems a local corporation has in place to ensure continuity of its programs across staff and over time.

Together, the fragmented responsibility for services, conflicting definitions of severe disability, general lack of service entitlements, and reliance on a private sector delivery system contribute to the difficulty of planning for postschool options that take advantage of the success achieved in special education. The ways that these issues affect an individual's chances for obtaining needed employment and residential support is the focus of the following sections.

EMPLOYMENT AND RELATED SERVICES

Remunerative employment is an implied promise of American education for all students and a specific objective of most secondary special education programs. Like others in our society, persons with severe disabilities and their families have reason to believe that completing school will enhance their ability to compete for and perform well in selected occupations. Employment and related day services exist because of: (a) the difficulty experienced by persons with disabilities in obtaining and maintaining work, and (b) the public's willingness to provide work-related support and training for these individuals.

Employment typically provides an individual with income and the choices and independence that income can create; social interactions with co-workers and others in the workplace; a structure for daily life; a sense of enhanced personal identity; and an opportunity to contribute to the community (Terkel, 1975). Most employment services offer at least some of these benefits, even when an individual is not engaged in self-supporting employment. It is consequently no surprise that persons with disabilities and their parents rate employment and related services as the most needed service upon graduation, and that lack of access to employment or related services appears related to parent satisfaction with the status of their adult sons or daughters with severe disabilities (McDonnell, Wilcox, Boles, & Bellamy, 1985; Zollers, et al., 1984).

This section describes the employment outlook for persons with severe disabilities from two perspectives, both of which are critical for effective transition planning. First, the results of research and development literature are briefly described to illustrate the possible vocational futures of students with severe disabilities. The administrative basis, program approaches, and results of current services are then presented to clarify what kinds of services and opportunities are likely to be found today in most communities. The section concludes with a brief discussion of how teachers and parents engaged in transition planning might proceed, given the discrepancy between possible and actual services.

Research and Development

Perhaps because it is such a central aspect of adult life, quality employment has been the focus of extensive research. Although review of that literature is beyond the purpose of this chapter, a useful perspective can be gained by a brief look at the five major questions that research and development efforts have addressed.

If persons with severe disabilities can learn to work, what procedures are most useful in developing the required vocational skills? Clear documentation that adults with moderate and severe levels of mental retardation could learn vocational tasks has been available since the mid-1950's (Clarke & Hermelin, 1955). Research since that time has extended confidence about learning potential to persons with more severe disabilities (Crosson, 1966; Gold, 1972) and to more lengthy and complex tasks associated with modern industry (Bellamy, Peterson, & Close, 1975; Gaylord-Ross, Forte, & Gaylord-Ross, 1983). The procedural research has documented the efficacy of procedures for analyzing work tasks (Silvern, 1963), teaching behavioral topographies (Tate & Barhoff, 1967; Walls, Sienicki, & Crist, 1981), establishing

stimulus control over responses where difficult discriminations are required (Irvin & Bellamy, 1977), and showing the utility of procedures for teaching generalized skills needed to accommodate task changes (Horner, Eberhard, & Sheehan, in press; Horner & McDonald, 1982). Results from this research suggests that the vast majority of persons with moderate and severe handicaps can learn work skills when systematic instructional procedures are used.

Are there supervision procedures that allow persons with severe disabilities to perform their work skills in a way that has value to employers? Whatever an individual's skill level, he is likely to maintain remunerative work only if work rate and quality meet job requirements and maintain over time. Several early studies showed the sensitivity of work rates to simple antecedent and consequence manipulations, and demonstrated that vocational skills could be performed at rates that, if sustained, could result in significant wages (Gold, 1973). Later investigations actually documented performance during full work days and over extended periods (Bellamy, Inman, & Yeates, 1978), and a few have systematically evaluated procedures for promoting quality of performance and maintenance of work behavior (Koop, Martin, Yu, & Suthons, 1980). The research makes it clear that most persons with moderate and severe disabilities can work in accordance with quality standards during full work days over extended employment periods. What the research also indicates, however, is that some ongoing support for retraining, contingency management, or crisis intervention is typically needed—support that is seldom available in the truly competitive work setting. For most individuals considered severely handicapped, sustained, high quality, high-rate performance appears to require some ongoing support in the workplace, which may last for as long as they are employed.

What procedures allow persons with severe disabilities to work in regular work settings? The expectation fostered by research on acquisition and performance of employment skills was that persons with severe disabilities could take their place alongside others in normal work places, where they could be free from the segregation, work scarcity, and stigma that often characterize large sheltered work and day programs. Initial efforts in this area involved introducing persons without disabilities into sheltered facilities (DuRand & DuRand, 1978), and studying behavior in vocational training, rather than actual employment settings (Pumpian, Baumgart, Shiraga, Loomis, & Brown, 1980). An increasing number of these studies now are conducted in regular work places where performance requirements are an economic reality, not just a training objective. Regular work places require more than task performance, and the research has addressed such areas as managing one's time while at work (Sowers, Rusch, Connis, & Cummings, 1980), monitoring the quality of one's work over time and soliciting supervisor feedback (Mank, 1985), interacting with co-workers and customers, and managing disruptive behavior in the work setting (Rusch & Menchetti, 1981). Like the research on work performance, investigations in this area support the ability of persons with severe disabilities to work in regular work sites, performing the work support behaviors required in those settings. Segregation in large sheltered facilities appears quite unnecessary when current procedures for developing work and work support behaviors are used; however, it does seem that most persons with severe disabilities may require ongoing support in the work setting—ranging from periodic follow-up visits to continuous supervision—to develop needed work support skills and maintain them over time.

Can service programs be designed that allow persons with severe disabilities to succeed in employment? Information gained from the research on work and work support behaviors became functional for persons with severe disabilities when it was integrated into a plan for program operation that included simultaneous procedures for securing work opportunities, hiring, training, and maintaining staff and managing services within the constraints of public funding and regulation. The needed staff roles, service location, and allocation of available work which are necessary to take advantage of the research results are significantly different from those found in traditional sheltered work and day programs. A series of program development efforts have addressed this difficulty by designing service demonstrations and models that do result in employment results for persons with severe disabilities. Program approaches include enclaves for six to eight persons with severe disabilities within electronics industries (Rhodes & Valenta, 1985), individual placement with on-site training, primarily in service occupations (Wehman & Kregel, 1985; Vogelsberg, 1986), operation of electronics businesses employing a small number of persons with severe disabilities together with persons without apparent handicaps (Boles, Bellamy, Horner, & Mank, 1984), placement in food service occupations after pretraining in a controlled, but integrated setting (Rusch & Mithaug, 1980), and work crews that employ persons with disabilities in small groups at regular work sites (Distler & Watson, 1984).

These programs differ in type of work specialization, strategy for providing ongoing support, and ability levels of persons served, but have common features of (a) use of systematic strategies for training and maintenance of work and work support behaviors; (b) focus on work opportunity, rather than work preparation; (c) emphasis on social integration, either with co-workers, customers, or other persons in the vicinity of the workplace; and (d) definition of program success in terms of wages and related work benefits. There appear to be some differences among the models in the level of earnings, the extent of social integration, the level of disability of the persons served, and the types of jobs which each approach can accommodate (Mank, Rhodes, & Bellamy, in press). Although no full comparison among approaches is available, one can safely conclude from this variety of program approach that available public funding and employment opportunities can be combined in several effective ways to provide real employment opportunities for persons with severe disabilities.

Does employment really benefit persons with severe disabilities, and is it in society's interest to support such employment? Anecdotal reports abound of enhanced quality of life for persons with severe disabilities who are employed, but research data remain limited. Gersten, Crowell, & Bellamy (1986) found that even modest employment success in small electronics enterprises was related to improvements in behavioral adjustment in residential settings. Descriptive reports have shown increased independence in use of public transportation (Hill, Hill, Wehman, & Banks, 1985), movement to less restrictive living settings (Hill et al., 1985), and expansion of social networks and improvement of health status (Mank, 1984). Analyses of the costs and benefits of several different approaches to employment preparation and support demonstrate that society's return on the investment in employment services is substantial (Hill et al., 1985; Kerachsky, Thornton, Bloomenthal, Maynard, & Stephens, 1985).

Summary

The research and demonstration results support optimism about the employment potential of persons with severe disabilities but also show fundamental differences between the employment success achieved with these individuals and the employment success typically acknowledged in publicly funded programs. It is clear that most and perhaps all persons with severe disabilities can learn to perform productive work over time to quality standards, and learn to perform other behaviors needed for work in regular settings. It is also clear that some publicly funded, ongoing support is needed in the work setting if performance is to endure and adapt over time, and that the successful employment achieved by many persons with severe disabilities does not yet constitute self-support. Consequently, public programs that offer only time-limited, employment preparation programs are unlikely to result in employment success for persons with severe disabilities. Current research suggests that support in employment, rather than preparation for employment, should be the goal of federal, state, and local efforts on behalf of persons with severe disabilities.

The Current System

Vocational and day services share with other adult programs the difficulties described in the introduction to this chapter. Responsibility for service funding and regulation is fragmented at the state and federal level and local services are provided by not-for-profit corporations whose programs are only partially determined by public laws and regulations.

Federal and state programs have historically distinguished between short-term vocational services and long-term nonvocational services for persons with disabilities. By practice or by statute, vocational services, including vocational rehabilitation, the Job Training Partnership Act and its predecessor the Comprehensive Employment and Training Act, and vocational education offer time-limited and resource-limited services designed to prepare an individual for his most independent work status. Implicit or explicit eligibility criteria for these services typically give priority to persons who can benefit in terms of employability from these short-term services, so most persons with severe disabilities have not been served by these programs. (See,

for example, the low utilization rates of vocational rehabilitation among special education graduates in studies by Brodsky, 1983; Hasazi, Gordon, & Roe, 1985). For persons not served by these employment programs but who required daytime services, state and federal support is provided through a variety of programs that have historically emphasized or mandated that services be nonvocational in nature. A recent survey of state mental retardation/developmental disabilities agencies, which administer these programs in most states, showed that day programs are provided for an estimated 185,000 persons, with nearly $1 billion annually coming from the Federal Social Service Block Grant, Medicaid, and state appropriations (Buckley and Bellamy, 1985).

Supported Employment

There is quite obviously a direct conflict between these historical program policies and the results of research on employment of persons with severe disabilities. If one needs the long-term support, which appears critical to employment success of most persons with severe disabilities, he is likely to be ineligible for employment-related services, and to be included instead in a nonvocational or prevocational program where work opportunities and work related services are absent. A recent conceptual change in federal and state policy has addressed this problem. The concept of supported employment, which was introduced into both the Developmental Disabilities Act of 1984 (P.L. 98-527) and the Department of Education's regulations affecting transition and adult services offers a new approach to vocational services for persons with severe disabilities. Supported employment is defined in P.L. 98-527 as

paid employment which (i) is for persons with developmental disabilities for whom competitive employment at or above the minimum wage is unlikely and who, because of their disabilities, need intensive ongoing support to perform in a work setting; (ii) is conducted in a variety of settings, particularly worksites in which persons without disabilities are employed; and (iii) is supported by any activity needed to sustain paid work by persons with disabilities, including supervision, training, and transportation., (Developmental Disabilities Act of 1984)

Four features of this definition are especially important, given the current research results on employment of persons with severe disability. First, the definition establishes *remunerative employment* as a program goal for persons with severe disabilities who have typically been served in nonvocational programs. Second, it emphasizes that employment should occur in *integrated work settings*, rather than in large, segregated facilities. Third, the definition recognizes the need for *ongoing support* in the work setting, and specifically encourages a diversity of approaches to providing this support. And, finally, the definition makes it clear that supported employment is for *persons with severe disabilities* who have not been typically served in vocational programs because they required ongoing support. There is, consequently, the clear possibility that supported employment may become the nation's first zero-reject employment program.

As is defined in federal law and regulation, supported employment allows—indeed encourages—a variety of program approaches. Any combination of paid work and ongoing support in an integrated setting qualifies. Instructions to applicants for a related Department of Education grant program provided useful guidelines for what constitutes supported employment: programs qualified if they (1) provided paid work for at least 20 hours per week, (2) in settings where no more than eight persons with disabilities worked together; and (3) with ongoing public funding for support in the work setting. Thus, most of the individual job training and placement models, work crews, enclaves and small businesses documented in the research literature qualify as supported employment approaches.

Because of the fragmentation of responsibility for services, implementation of the supported employment concept will require adjustments in several other federal and state policies and programs. It involves use of funds now spent in day services for employment support and requires development of new state procedures for coordination between agencies that provide vocational and nonvocational day services.

Employment of persons with severe disabilities can be affected by several state and federal programs in addition to the direct support for employment and day services. Regulations and incentives affecting individual income support and medical assistance payments, for example, directly affect whether it is in an individual's best interest to accept particular employment possibilities (Conley, Noble, & Elder, 1986). Similarly, regulations and incentives affecting employers influence the likelihood that available work opportunities will be offered to persons with disabilities. Employers are directly affected by the minimum wage regulations, procedures to certify individuals for sub-minimum wages based on productivity, and incentives like the Targeted Jobs Tax Credit, which temporarily reduces the tax liability of employers of persons with disabilities. Additional federal programs affect the operation of local service provider organizations. These organizations must comply with the provisions of the Fair Labor Standards Act in paying less than minimum wages to employees who are disabled and must operate in accordance with provisions of the Internal Revenue Code if they are to maintain a tax exempt status. Local service providers also receive the benefit of federal and state "set-aside" work, which can be performed for government agencies without going through normal competitive bidding procedures.

Local Service Delivery

Most employment and day services for adults with severe disabilities are delivered by not-for-profit corporations, funded by state or local agencies and regulated by the state and federal programs described above. Historically, services offered by these agencies have been designed as a continuum of programs through which individuals were expected to progress toward employment. Although the names used to describe various services in the continuum vary from state to state, there are typically the following types of services: (a) a nonconventional program where persons with the fewest work related skills are expected to develop readiness for work through leisure skill training and instruction on self care, academic, and other tasks; (b) a work activities center, where some work is performed for piece rate pay, but where, by statute, therapeutic activity, not work is the main purpose, so that the individual can gain the skills required for later sheltered or competitive work; and (c) a regular program workshop, where sheltered work is intended to serve as a medium of job preparation, leading to related employment outside the service system. Although many variations on the exact content and location of services exist within this continuum, the overall effect is that persons with severe disabilities typically have access to one set of services in a community—the day activity and work activities programs, while the available work opportunities are concentrated in other programs that serve more capable persons.

Exactly what can teachers and parents expect now for young adults with severe disabilities leaving school and entering these local services? Data on current services are not encouraging. Long wait lists exist in many states for any employment or day service, so the real possibility exists that school will be followed by a significant period of no service. Studies by Brodsky (1983), Stansfield (1976), and Zollers et al. (1984) found that many former students in classes for persons with moderate and severe handicaps were simply at home without services. That similar periods without services await many special education graduates is now clear from both national surveys (McDonnell, Wilcox, & Boles, 1986) and the public press of many communities.

If they do get into services, persons with severe disabilities are likely to be served in a program that emphasizes nonvocational or prevocational service in a segregated setting. Eighty-two percent of the programs that funded state mental retardation programs were classified as nonvocational, adult day programs in a national survey by Buckley and Bellamy (1985).

Even among service recipients with greater ability level, low wages have been a consistent concern in community programs (Bellamy, Rhodes, Bourbeau, & Mank, in press). Similarly, movement from day programs to be less restrictive and more vocationally oriented services has been widely reported as low, and studies of program movement in various states continue to support this finding (Minnesota Developmental Disabilities Planning Council, 1982; California Department of Finance, 1979). Together, these program results suggest that when persons with severe disabilities gain access to day or vocational services, they are likely to have little access to paid work, minimal income, little opportunity for social integration during the workday, and little chance of moving to a higher level service.

Implications for Transition Planning

The discrepancy between documented employment potential and the current services offered in the average community means that the employment needs of persons with severe disabilities leaving public school programs are unlikely to be met simply by evaluation and placement in existing services. The new federal initiative on supported employment may well promote change in these services, but providing real work opportunities for persons considered severely handicapped by the schools will require major adaptation of most current day programs. Consequently, effective transition planning will require teachers and parents to: (a) advocate for state appropriations to provide needed services for persons leaving school; and (b) work to develop alternative, supported employment services that can provide employment opportunities and ongoing support to persons with severe disabilities.

RESIDENTIAL SERVICES

Among the most significant symbols associated with adulthood in the United States is the establishment of a living space away from "home." Developing a place to live in the community can be especially difficult; however, when a young adult has severe disabilities, his new living space must provide an array of social, instructional, and community-living supports.

The struggle to provide adequate residential support for adolescents and adults with severe disabilities has a rich and controversial history (Bruininks & Lakin, 1985). Questioning continues, however, over where people should live, the level and type of support people should receive, and the measures that can be used to determine if adequate support is being provided. During the past two decades federal courts have kept the focus of residential policy on the return of individuals from institutional settings to their local communities (Bradley, 1985; Conroy & Bradley, 1985; Laski, 1985). Recently, residential services for young adults aging out of high school (and their homes) has been added as a major concern for state and federal policy makers (McDonnell, Wilcox, Boles, & Bellamy, 1985). In many communities graduating students will be greeted with inadequate or nonexistent residential support. Of equal importance, the residential services that will be available are being designed in response to the deinstitutionalization movement. This means parents, advocates, and young consumers of residential support will be more intimately affected by planning for deinstitutionalization than is often perceived. In this section, we examine the status of residential services in the United States, research on the feasibility and impact of community living for people with severe disabilities, and implications for the future.

The Status of Residential Services

There are nearly 300,000 adults with mental retardation receiving residential support in the United States today (Hauber, Bruininks, Hill, Lakin & White, 1982; Landesman & Butterfield, in press). Approximately 41% of these individuals reside in publicly operated institutions; 37% live in community-based residential programs; and the remaining 22% live in county mental hospitals and nursing homes (Landesman & Butterfield, in press). In addition, our best estimates suggest that 9,000 young adults per year will be aging out of public schools for the foreseeable future (McDonnell, Wilcox, & Boles, 1986). Many of these students can be expected to look for appropriate residential options that support their new roles as adults. The need for residential support is at once large, growing, and complex.

To understand the residential options available to mentally disabled citizens in general, and specifically those persons with severe mental disabilities, it is important to examine the types of residential facilities currently available, their funding structure, and their impact on individual lifestyle. The most recent demographic information in the United States comes from a 1982 survey that found 243,669 people identified as experiencing some level of mental retardation living in 15,630 state-financed facilities (Hauber, Bruininks, Hill, Lakin, Scheerenberger & White, 1984). Table 17.1 provides a breakdown of the types of facilities identified, the age of residents, and the level of mental retardation of residents for each type of facility.

The data in Table 17.1 indicate that most of the people receiving residential support are adults (70% between 22 and 62 years old). In addition, the size of a residence appears inversely related to the measured IQ scores of the residents. That is, people with more severe retardation live in larger groups.

What types of residential options exist? Among the most exciting trends in the field of residential support is a growing recognition that people with disabilities can live in the community under a wide array of organizational situations. In the past group homes, nursing homes, foster homes and intermediate care facilities were seen as "the" residential options for people with special needs. Today the old categories are undergoing phenomenal diversification. There is increasing recognition that residential support can occur not only in medical and group home settings, but in apartments and family settings as well. Of even greater importance is the growing recognition that a wide variety of support services are possible in each of the above locations (Taylor, 1985). Depending on their skills, the demands of the setting, and their local social networks, people can live successfully in small, community-integrated settings and with brief, infrequent contact from a support person; with regular support visits; with support from nonpaid members of the community; and with 24-hour supervision.

Where do people with severe disabilities live? To date, people labeled severely or profoundly retarded have been the most likely to live in large, highly structured, nonintegrated situations (Hauber, Bruininks, Hill, Lakin, & White, 1982; Lakin & Bruininks, 1985). Of the 154,000 individuals with developmental disabilities still living in settings of 64 or more, 115,300 (75%) are labeled severely or profoundly retarded (Hauber et al., 1984). Although the last 20 years have witnessed a major reduction in the number of people in state institutions for developmentally disabled persons with lower functioning levels. Most people with severe disabilities still live in settings that are large, segregated from the community, and highly structured (Lakin & Bruininks, 1985).

What does residential support cost, and who pays? The overall cost for residential care in the United States to all 243,669 people receiving support in 1982 was over 5 billion dollars (Hauber et al., 1982). Landesman and Butterfield (in press) report that in 1984 this figure had risen to an annual rate of over 7 billion dollars (4.3 billion in institutionalized settings and approximately 3 billion in community settings). The single largest source of support comes from Title XIX of the Social Security Act (Medicaid). Title XIX supplies nearly half of the costs to operate state-operated institutions, and 70% of the *federal* support of community services (Landesman & Butterfield, in press). The remaining funds come from resident, social security benefits, Section 8 of the Housing and Urban Development Act, and state support.

In general, the rate of funding for residential support varies dramatically by type of program and by state. Hauber et al. (1984) identified patterns of funding, indicating that larger facilities and nursing homes receive daily rates per resident that are double those of small, community-based facilities.

TABLE 17.1 Age and level of retardation of mentally retarded persons in residential facilities: United States, 1982

Resident Characteristics	Special Foster Home (n=17,147)	Group Residence (1–15) (n=42,018)	Group Residence (Private 16+) (n=40,347)	Group Residence (Public 16+) (n=122,971)	Semi-Independent Living (n=2,870)	Board and Care (n=1,264)	Personal Care Home (n=4,070)	Special Nursing Homes (n=12,982)	U.S. Total (n=243,669)
Age[a]									
Birth–4	3.1%	.4%	1.0%	.4%	.0%	.7%	.5%	3.7%	.8%
5–9	6.2%	1.4%	3.8%	1.5%	.2%	.6%	1.6%	8.0%	2.5%
10–14	10.0%	4.0%	9.5%	4.5%	.1%	.6%	2.5%	10.9%	5.8%
15–21	18.1%	14.0%	17.8%	15.6%	7.3%	4.0%	5.6%	15.6%	15.5%
22–39	32.0%	53.3%	41.8%	50.2%	65.4%	38.3%	31.6%	33.6%	47.0%
40–62	23.1%	23.8%	22.1%	22.9%	25.5%	40.5%	41.1%	21.8%	23.3%
63+	7.6%	3.0%	4.1%	5.0%	1.5%	15.3%	17.1%	6.4%	4.8%
Level of Retardation[b]									
Borderline/mild	25.9%	29.3%	26.8%	7.0%	61.8%	47.1%	31.2%	9.2%	16.8%
Moderate	37.7%	37.9%	29.9%	12.9%	32.5%	3.6%	39.8%	16.2%	22.8%
Severe	26.0%	23.2%	24.0%	24.3%	5.3%	17.6%	20.6%	26.2%	24.0%
Profound	10.4%	9.5%	19.3%	55.8%	.4%	1.7%	8.4%	48.5%	36.5%

[a]89.1% facilities reporting representing 91.8% of 243,669 residents
[b]89.2% facilities reporting representing 92.5% of 243,669 residents

Source: From *National Census of Residential Facilities* (p. 51) by F. A. Hauber, R. H. Bruininks, B. K. Hill, K. C. Lakin, and C. C. White. 1982. Minneapolis: University of Minnesota. Department of Educational Psychology. Reprinted by permission.

Across the nation, public residents serving 64 or more people were funded at an average rate of $85.94 per person per day, whereas group homes in community settings serving one to five residents were funded at an average rate of $40.25 per person per day.

Of equal interest is the disparity in pay rates across states; the more generous states (North Carolina, Massachusetts, Pennsylvania and Rhode Island) provide average daily reimbursements per resident (across both institution and community placements) of $80 or more; nearly twice the rates provided by those states with the lowest residential funding levels (the District of Columbia, Minnesota, Mississippi, Oklahoma, and South Dakota).

Research on the Feasibility of Community Living for Individuals with Severe Mental Disabilities

It has long been assumed that community living for people with severe disabilities is not procedurally feasible, will not be in the best interest of the persons with disabilities, or is simply too expensive for states to deliver (Ellis et al., 1981). These assumptions stand in stark contrast to the values of normalization, integration, and fairness that are often looked to as foundations for service delivery (Lakin & Bruininks, 1985). They also stand in conflict with a growing body of research suggesting that community-based residential support is not only desirable, but possible, beneficial, and economically feasible.

Can people with severe disabilities live in the community? Small demonstration projects across the United States are providing repeated examples that it is possible for states to provide community-based, residential support to people with severe disabilities. Hauber et al. (1984) documented that in 1982 nearly 20% of adults labeled severely mentally retarded who were receiving residential support were receiving that support in a community-based setting, housing 15 or fewer persons. Hauber et al. (1984) also indicated that a small percentage of adults diagnosed as profoundly mentally retarded were represented in every community living option examined, including semi-independent living. These broad, demographic data are consistent with individual analyses focusing on the feasibility of small, community living situations for people with severe disabilities (Bruininks, Meyers, Sigford, & Lakin,

1981; Close, 1977; Conroy & Bradley, 1985; O'Neill, Brown, Gordon, & Schonhorn, 1985; Schalock, Harper, Genung, 1981).

Many of the myths about residential support are being called to question as the diversity in residential options for people with disabilities has increased. It has become evident, for example, that the support needed by people with severe disabilities can be delivered in a wide array of community-based contexts. An individual's need for assistance (medical, behavioral, or educational) is no longer a valid barrier to community involvement. Examples such as that in the Bronx where nonambulatory, young adults with severe retardation and multiple physical disabilities are living in apartments (Eirich, 1985) make it difficult to argue that community-based, residential support cannot be provided to people with significant needs. In many ways, however, the question of whether community residential support is possible is much easier to answer than whether this support is in the best interest of people with severe disabilities.

Do people with severe disabilities benefit from community-living settings? The complex nature of a community program, and the nontrivial measurement problems faced by researchers in community settings makes it necessary to adopt extreme caution when interpreting research addressing the effects of community-living programs on the lives of people with disabilities (Butterfield, 1985; Chadsey-Rusch, 1985; Heal, 1985; Landesman & Butterfield, in press; Switzky & Haywood, 1985). In spite of these qualifications numerous studies have documented improvements in adaptive behavior (Conroy, Efthimiou, & Lemanowicz, 1982; Eyman & Borthwick, 1984; Newton, Boles, Romer, Bellamy, & Horner, 1985; Schalock, Harper, & Genung, 1981; Singer, Close, Irvin, Gersten, & Sailor, 1984) medical status, (Landesman-Dwyer, Sulzbacher, Edgar, Keller, Wise, & Baatz, 1980), family contact (Landesman-Dwyer, Berkson, & Romer, 1979), and activity patterns (O'Neill et al., 1985; O'Neill, Brown, Gordon, Schonhorn, & Greer, 1981) following movement from segregated settings into community, residential settings.

No research has addressed the question of whether persons living with their families will benefit from moving into community-living settings. Most researchers and policy makers have assumed that the first question is to assess if individuals currently in institutions will benefit from community placement. If this question is answered in the affirmative, the implication is clear that students who now live at home should not be institutionalized.

A recent and comprehensive analysis of the impact of deinstitutionalization has been undertaken in Pennsylvania. During the past five years, Conroy and Bradley (1985) have been monitoring the deinstitutionalization of mentally disabled residents from Pennhurst State School and Hospital. To determine if moving to the community had an effect on behavior, Conroy and Bradley (1985) used the Behavior Development Survey (BDS) to assess the adaptive behavior of 176 individuals before they left Pennhurst (in 1978 and 1980) and after they left Pennhurst (in 1983 and 1984). The results for these individuals (see Figure 17.1) show that minimal growth occurred during the time the residents were in the institution, but that substantial development was noted after they entered the community.

These results are supported by a second analysis that Conroy and Bradley (1985) conducted in which the gains made by those individuals who left Pennhurst were compared with a group of people who remained in the institution and were selected for analysis because they were similar in terms of age, sex, skill level, etc., to those people who returned to the community. The residents who entered the community demonstrated 10 times the gains in adaptive behavior as their matched "twins" who remained at Pennhurst.

Conroy and Bradley (1985) recognized that "adaptive behavior" is not the sole measure needed to determine if people benefit from community placement. In an effort to broaden their analysis, interviews were conducted with verbal residents of Pennhurst and their family members before and after movement to the community. Results from these interviews indicate that prior to the move, the residents defined themselves as "happy" and satisfied with Pennhurst. Their families were also satisfied with the institution, and were most likely to be in "strong disagreement" with the plan to move to a community placement. When these same people were reinterviewed after placement the residents indicated they were significantly happier in the community and did not want to return to Pennhurst. As can be seen in Figure 17.2, the attitudes of family members also shifted to "strong agreement" with community placement after their family members had been placed.

In summarizing the results of their five-year analysis, Conroy and Bradley (1985) conclude:

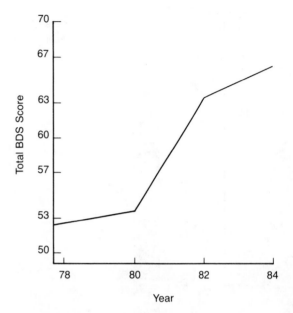

FIGURE 17.1 Adaptive behavior growth (4 observations for 175 people)

Source: From *The Pennhurst Longitudinal Study* (p. 107) by J. W. Conroy and V. J. Bradley, 1985, Philadelphia: Temple University, Developmental Disabilities Center. Reprinted by permission.

On the average, the people deinstitutionalized under the Pennhurst court order are better off in every way measured. This is an uncommon, but welcome, situation in social science. More often, evaluative results are mixed and one must balance gains in one area against losses in another. For the people who have moved from Pennhurst to small community residences, results are not mixed. They are conclusive. . . . It is also important to note that we have observed an unusual community placement process, in that 81% of the people who have moved to community living arrangements were labeled severely or profoundly mentally retarded. That simple fact definitively invalidates the notion that community care for people with severe or profound mental retardation cannot work. (p. 322–323)

The results from Conroy and Bradley's in-depth analysis of one deinstitutionalization effort are supported by a recent review of the past 30 years of research on the effects of community residential programs by Landesman and Butterfield (in press). They indicate that our existing data base provides clear evidence for several broad conclusions about the impact of community residential services for adults with disabilities. Two of these conclusions are:

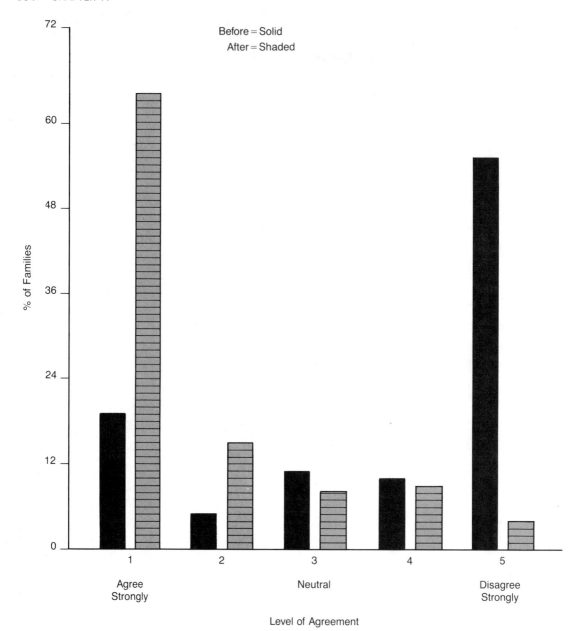

FIGURE 17.2 Agreement with community placement

Source: From *The Pennhurst Longitudinal Study* (p. 179) by J. W. Conroy and V. J. Bradley, 1985, Philadelphia: Temple University, Developmental Disabilities Center, Reprinted by permission.

a. *Given adequate support systems, most severely and profoundly retarded individuals, even some with severe behavior or health problems, can progress in settings other than large, traditional institutions (p. 16),* and
b. *Physical renovation and increased staffing levels in institutions have resulted in modest improve-*

ments compared to more positive changes observed for apparently similar types of individuals who moved to small, independently owned community homes. (p. 16)

Although these two conclusions are extremely encouraging, they are tempered by Landesman and Butterfield's careful emphasis that the data do *not* show that simply being in the community or being in a small residential setting will produce desirable lifestyles (Landesman-Dwyer, Sackett, & Kleinman, 1980). There are ample instances where small, community-based programs have proven ineffective. The message we are left with is that community residential support for people with severe disabilities is possible, and can have a major positive impact. At this time, however, we do not have command of all the variables that will allow prediction or development of effective settings.

Is community residential support for individuals with severe disabilities financially possible? A clear picture of the relative costs of residential support under institutional and community options has not been possible to date. Although Hauber et al. (1984) document that community programs are funded at far below the rates received by institutions, it must be remembered that institutional costs include day program, medical support, and ancillary services that are not covered by residential programs in the community. In addition, the current institutional population clearly represents people who are more severely disabled and would require higher than average support in the community. Parents and advocates of young people graduating from high school should expect to face concern on the part of state managers that the cost of serving people with severe disabilities in the community will be more than state budgets can bear. Once again the main data base in response to this concern comes from studies of people who have left the institution and moved back to their home communities.

The best estimates at this time suggest that high quality, residential support for people with severe disabilities (even severe physical disabilities) can be provided in local communities for at least the same cost as currently being expended in large, institutional settings. Conroy and Bradley's (1985) analysis of community costs for Pennhurst residents indicated that community-based support proved less expensive due to the use of generic services (buses, laundry) in the community, and due to the substantially lower pay of community staff. They caution their readers, however, that the current discrepancy between the pay scale of community and institution staff will likely diminish in response to unionization and other market forces. At this time the best evidence suggests that future costs for residential services in the community will closely approximate those currently paid in school and institutional settings. State managers and advocates should not look to the community as an avenue to save money, but as a strategy for delivering much more valued opportunities for the money that is expended. Whereas the costs may be equal, the benefit of community placement appears far more valuable.

A critical financial issue facing those who would encourage the development of community residential services is whether states will choose to use available funds to improve, expand, and maintain existing institutions, or use those funds to promote community options. Few states have the financial flexibility to support development in both areas. One commonly heard suggestion is to use funds that presently support institutional services to develop community placements. This idea has received considerable support, and led to the construction of the Community and Family Living Amendments, a far-reaching legislative proposal that would allow more flexible use of federal funds to support community residential and vocational options for people with significant disabilities (Chafee, 1983, 1985).

Implications for the Future

Whether or not federal financial incentives are restructured along the lines proposed by the Community and Family Living Amendments, factors within the states' services point to continued expansion of community alternatives to institutional care. A number of states are committed to downsizing or closing institutions under the present financial incentives. The pressure this creates for growth in community residential options is magnified by the increasing number of students with severe disabilities who are leaving high school and looking to the community for living options, employment, and social support.

These pressures to expand community services create an opportunity for states and communities to develop a system of residential services that emphasizes individualized support in local, typically sized settings. Such a system is unlikely to emerge, however, from a simple expansion of existing community options. To assist in development of effective residential support parents of high school students, advocates, and students should be actively involved *today* in the design of residential support plans.

The needed planning and advocacy is unlikely to occur unless a broadly based consensus is forged about exactly what residential services for persons with severe disabilities are for. Fundamental questions about the structure and function of these services are raised by the success of programs like those documented by Conroy and Bradley (1985). While pointing to potential benefits of community living, this and other studies demonstrate the need for conceptual and organizational changes similar to those that have occurred in vocational services.

Traditionally, residential support has been conceptualized within a readiness model, in which students are expected to progress to gradually less restrictive and more normative settings as they develop the skills needed in each subsequent environment. This model creates two difficulties for persons with severe disabilities and the programs serving them: it links service success or quality to movement from one location and level of service to another, and it focuses programming within services on acquisition of skills that are seen as needed in higher level services. The logical and practical problems which such a continuum of services creates in vocational services is equally apparent in the residential arena. Problems of skill generalization, logistics of funding and movement, and excess skill demands when one is trained for generic, rather than specific, competence all work against persons with severe disabilities in readiness-oriented programs.

Not surprisingly, an advocacy and programmatic response to the problems of readiness in residential services mirrors the emerging changes in employment policies and programs. The development of supported employment replaced this readiness emphasis of "preparation for employment" with a support emphasis on "ongoing assistance in employment." A similar focus on supported living is developing. The supported living approach replaces attempts to prepare individuals for independent, integrated living at some future time with programs that immediately deliver the support needed by each of these individuals to live in typical homes and to enjoy typical lifestyle patterns, whatever their skill level.

Supported Living

Supported living means *"people with disabilities living where and with whom they want, for as long as they want, with whatever support is necessary to make that choice possible"* (Fredericks, 1986). The concept of supported living does not raise persons with disabilities above the fiscal and logistical constraints faced by typical members of society. It does assert, however, that within a person's individual resource constraints, he will receive support from the state to enjoy the same type of living options as persons without disabilities. Supported living is a different way of conceptualizing residential services. A supported living approach to residential services is characterized by three main features: lifestyle accountability, individually determined support, and a broadened technology of residential support.

Lifestyle Accountability With the shift in focus from development growth and movement to achieving satisfactory lifestyles in regular settings comes a need for accountability based on lifestyle measures (Bellamy, Newton, LeBaron, & Horner, 1986; Emerson, 1985). Programs that deliver residential support need simple, valid systems for monitoring the impact of support on critical lifestyle measures. Such measures would be of immense value to providers and consumers of service, while providing a basis for internal and external program accountability. Initial efforts to define lifestyle measures suggest that this objective is within the scope of existing technology, and should be pursued as a critical need in residential services today (O'Brien, in press; Newton et al., 1985). Among the most exciting features of supported living is recognition that persons with disabilities can live successfully in as many different situations as persons without disabilities. A person's disability constrains his living options only when adequate support is not available. A system of residential support should not be designed around rules and regulations that pigeonhole people into certain classes of residences because of their disability. Supported living breaks the traditional link between type of setting and level of support, making it possible for consumers with severe disabilities to receive residential services in a much broader array of home situations.

Individually Determined Support The concept of supported living contains a strong emphasis on individualized support that is directed as much as possible by the consumer. To accomplish this, systems are needed to: assess the level of functioning of each individual, establish funding levels for each individual that are consistent with these assessments, and provide a diversity of options from which individuals and their families can choose. The advantage of an individualized rate structure is its potential incentive for providers to offer services to persons with more significant disabilities. Although initial efforts to develop such financing systems do exist, much work is needed to ensure that the new approaches do not simply create a new set of disincentives while overcoming the old set (by punishing programs with automatic withdrawal of funds when exemplary services reduce an individual's support needs).

Individualized funding strategies provide the consumer and family with greater control over the fiscal contingencies in the service system when there are sufficient living options that each individual can choose among several alternative programs.

Broadened Technology of Residential Support An important feature of supported living is the expanded types of support it creates. Too often residential support is viewed as limited to maintaining health and safety, and training new skills. These are important and essential components of residential support. If "lifestyle" is used as the index of support adequacy, however, it becomes clear that other avenues of support such as participation assistance, partial performance assistance, use of community prosthetics, and alternative performance strategies must be added to the arsenal of residential support technologies. Research in these areas with high-school-age students suggests that major changes in community and social integration can be achieved within very reasonable staff commitments (Wilcox & Bellamy, 1982; in press).

The status quo in community residential services will experience considerable reevaluation in the next few years. There are many reasons to expect that new directions, such as those suggested by "supported living," are both possible, and within reach. If positive development of residential support is to occur, however, the involvement of transition-age students and their advocates is needed.

CONCLUSION

The existing system of employment and residential services gives those responsible for transition planning a three-part message. First, the success stories encourage parents and teachers to set optimistic goals for all students leaving school. Supported employment, supported living, and community integration are reasonable expectations, given the demonstrated potential of persons with severe disabilities and the current level of public investment in adult services.

Second, the services needed to support this adult life may not be available when an individual completes school. Long wait lists for services in many states mean that parents have to provide all needed support by themselves for a period of time after graduation. Consequently, planning for this interim period and advocating funding for needed services are important parts of the transition planning process.

Third, the services that are available in many communities fail to take advantage of the potential for employment and integration that students with severe handicaps have demonstrated. Designed for an earlier generation who did not benefit from the right to an education, the existing services available in most communities fail to provide integrated work or residence possibilities. Consequently, simply selecting among existing services the one that best fits an individual student will seldom result in a desirable transition outcome. Instead, involvement to change the objectives and methods of existing adult services is a critical part of transition planning on behalf of students with severe disabilities. Whether this involves changing existing service organizations or creating new ones, it means that transition planning will be successful only when parents and teachers spend the effort to restructure local adult services.

The process of transition planning that emerges from this analysis of employment and residential services is a much more active and demanding one than the popular notion of assessment and placement within the adult service system. Those participating in the transition planning process need first to describe the adult lifestyle that is desired by and for an individual. Formal services and information supports that will enable that lifestyle can then be identified. The process then shifts to ensuring that these services will actually be available, through advocacy for needed resources and efforts to develop the needed local services within existing or new provider organizations. New concepts like supported employment and supported living offer important chances to develop needed local services. Like other adult service priorities, however, supported employment offers an opportunity, not a mandate. Its implementation in any community depends on local implementation effort. The dream that an integrated, productive life can follow special education for all students need not become a mirage for those with severe disabilities. To prevent this, however, teachers and parents need to engage in an active process of planning and advocating for the postschool futures of students in the secondary schools.

REFERENCES

Bellamy, T., Inman, D., & Yeates, J. (1978). Evaluation of a procedure for production management with the severely retarded. *Mental Retardation, 17*(1), 37–41.

Bellamy, G. T., Newton, J. S., LeBaron, N., & Horner, R. H. (1986). *Toward lifestyle accountability in residential services for persons with mental retardation.* Unpublished manuscript. Eugene, OR: University of Oregon, Specialized Training Program.

Bellamy, G. T., Peterson, L., & Close, D. (1975). Habilitation of the severely and profoundly retarded: Illustration of competence. *Education and Training of the Mentally Retarded, 10,* 174–186.

Bellamy, G. T., Rhodes, L. E., Bourbeau, P. E., & Mank, D. M. (1986). Mental retardation services in sheltered workshops and day activity programs: Consumer outcomes and policy alternatives. In F. R. Rusch (Ed.), *Competitive employment: Service delivery models, methods, and issues* (pp. 241–256). Baltimore: Paul H. Brookes.

Boles, S. M., Bellamy, G. T., Horner, R. H., & Mank, D. M. (1984). Specialized training program: The structured employment model. In S. C. Paine, G. T. Bellamy, & B. Wilcox (Eds.), *Human services that work: From innovation to standard practice* (pp. 181–208). Baltimore: Paul H. Brookes.

Bradley, V. J. (1985). Implementation of court and consent decrees: Some current lessons. In R. H. Bruininks & K. C. Lakin (Eds.), *Living and learning in the least restrictive environment* (pp. 81–96). Baltimore: Paul H. Brookes.

Brodsky, M. M. (1983). *A five-year statewide follow-up study of the graduates of school programs for trainable mentally retarded students in Oregon.* Unpublished doctoral dissertation, University of Oregon, Division of Special Education and Rehabilitation, Eugene.

Brown, L., Certo, N., Belmore, K., & Crowner, T. (1977). *Madison's alternative for zero exclusion: Papers and programs related to public school services for secondary age severely handicapped students.* Madison, WI: Madison Public Schools, Department of Specialized Educational Services.

Bruininks, R. H., & Lakin, K. C. (Eds.) (1985). *Living and learning in the least restrictive environment.* Baltimore: Paul H. Brookes.

Bruininks, R. H., Meyers, C. E., Sigford, B. B., & Lakin, K. C. (Eds.) (1981). *Deinstitutionalization and community adjustment of mentally retarded people* (AAMD Monograph No. 4). Washington, DC: American Association on Mental Deficiency.

Buckley, J., & Bellamy, G. T. (1985). *National survey of day and vocational programs: For adults with severe disabilities. A 1984 profile.* Unpublished manuscript, The Johns Hopkins University, Baltimore.

Butterfield, E. C. (1985). The consequences of bias in studies of living arrangements for the mentally retarded.

In D. Bricker & J. Filler (Eds.), *Severe mental retardation: From theory to practice* (pp. 245–263). Reston, VA: Council for Exceptional Children.

California Department of Finance (1979). *A review of sheltered workshops and related programs (Phase II): To assembly concurrent resolution No. 206, Volume II, Final Report.* Sacramento: State of California.

Chadsey-Rusch, J. C. (1985). Community integration and mental retardation: The ecobehavioral approach to service provision and assessment. In R. H. Bruininks, & K. C. Lakin (Eds.), *Living and learning in the least restrictive environment* (p. 245–260). Baltimore: Paul H. Brookes.

Chafee, J. H. (1983, November 4). Community and Family Living Amendments Act. (S. 2053). *Congressional Record,* 98–150, S15480–S15485.

Chafee, J. H. (1985, April 3). Community and Family Living Amendments Act of 1985. (S. 873).

Clarke, A., & Hermelin, F. (1955). Adult imbeciles: Their abilities and trainability. *The Lancet, 269*(1), 337–339.

Close, D. (1977). Community living for severely and profoundly retarded adults: A group home study. *Education and Training of the Mentally Retarded, 12*(3), 255–262.

Conley, R., Noble, J., & Elder, J. (in press). Problems with the services System. In W. Kiernan, & J. Stark (Eds.), *Pathways to employment for developmentally disabled adults* (pp. 67–83). Baltimore: Paul H. Brookes.

Conroy, J. W., & Bradley, V. J. (1985). *The Pennhurst longitudinal study: A report of five years of research and analysis.* Philadelphia: Temple University Developmental Disabilities Center.

Conroy, J., Efthimiou, J., & Lemanowicz, J. (1982). A matched comparison of the developmental growth of institutionalized and deinstitutionalized mentally retarded clients. *American Journal of Mental Deficiency, 86*(6), 581–587.

Crosson, J. (1966). *The experimental analysis of vocational behavior in severely retarded males.* Unpublished doctoral dissertation, University of Oregon, Eugene.

Distler, M., & Watson, M. (1984). *Boatworks and cleansweep mobile work crews: For adults with developmental disabilities.* Oakland, CA: Stepping Stones Growth Center.

DuRand, L., & DuRand, J. (1978). *The affirmative industry.* St. Paul, MN: Minnesota Diversified Industries.

Eirich, B. (1985). Presentation at the 1985 Oregon Residential Conference, "Residential Support for Multiply Handicapped Adults."

Ellis, N., Balla, D. A., Estes, O., Warren, S., Meyers, L., Hollis, J., Isaacson, R., Palk, B., & Siegel, P. (1981). Common sense in the habituation of mentally retarded persons: A reply to Menolascino and McGee. *Mental Retardation, 19,* 221–225.

Emerson, E. B. (1985). Evaluating the impact of deinstitutionalization on the lives of mentally retarded people. *American Journal of Mental Deficiency, 90*(3), 277–288.

Eyman, R. K., & Borthwick, S. A. (1984). A longitudinal study of foster care placement. In S. Landesman-Dwyer (Ed.), *The social ecology of handicapped people.* Baltimore: University Park Press.

Fredericks, H. D. (1986, March). Personal communication.

Gaylord-Ross, C., Forte, J., & Gaylord-Ross, R. (1983). *The community classroom: Technological vocational training for students with serious handicaps.* Unpublished manuscript, San Francisco State University, Special Education Department, San Francisco.

Gersten, R., Crowell, F., & Bellamy, T. (1986). Spillover effects: Impact of vocational training on the lives of severely retarded clients. *American Journal of Mental Deficiency, 19,* 501–506.

Gold, M. W. (1972). Stimulus factors in skill training of the retarded on a complex assembly task: Acquisition, transfer, and retention. *American Journal of Mental Deficiency, 76,* 517–526.

Gold, M. W. (1973). Factors affecting production by the retarded: Base rate. *Mental Retardation, 11*(6), 41–45.

Hasazi, S. B., Gordon, L. R., & Roe, C. A. (1985). Factors associated with the employment status of handicapped youth exiting high school from 1979 to 1983 in Vermont. *Exceptional Children, 51,* 455–469.

Hauber, F. A., Bruininks, R. H., Hill, B. K., Lakin, K. C., Scheerenberger, R. C., & White, C. C. (1984). National census of residential facilities: A 1982 profile of facilities and residents. *American Journal of Mental Deficiency, 89*(3), 236–245.

Hauber, F. A., Bruininks, R. H., Hill, B. K., Lakin, K. C., & White, C. C. (1982). *National census of residential facilities: Fiscal year 1982.* Minneapolis: University of Minnesota, Department of Educational Psychology.

Hayden, A. H., & Dmitriev, V. (1975). The multidisciplinary preschool program for Down syndrome children at the University of Washington Model Preschool Center. In B. Z. Friedlander, G. M. Sterritt, & G. E. Kirk (Eds.), *Exceptional infant: Assessment and intervention* (pp. 193–221). New York: Bruner/Mazel, Inc.

Heal, L. W. (1985). Methodology for community integration research. In R. H. Bruininks, & R. C. Lakin (Eds.), *Living and learning in the least restrictive environment* (p. 199–224). Baltimore: Paul H. Brookes.

Hill, M., Hill, J., Wehman, P., & Banks, D. (1985). An analysis of monetary and nonmonetary outcomes associated with competitive employment of mentally retarded persons. In P. Wehman & J. W. Hill (Eds.), *Competitive employment for persons with mental retardation* (pp. 110–133). Richmond, VA: Virginia Commonwealth University, Rehabilitation Research and Training Center.

Horner, R. H., Eberhard, J., & Sheehan, M. R. (in press). Generalization of table bussing skills with moderately and severely retarded adolescents. *Behavior Modification.*

Horner, R. H., & McDonald, R. S. (1982). Comparison of single instance and general case instruction in teaching a generalized vocational skill. *Journal of the Association for the Severely Handicapped, 7*(3), 7–20.

Irvin, L. K., & Bellamy, G. T. (1977). Manipulation of stimulus features in vocational-skill training of severely retarded individuals. *American Journal of Mental Deficiency, 81*(5), 486–491.

Kerachsky, S., Thornton, C., Bloomenthal, A., Maynard, R., & Stephens, S. (1985). *The impacts of transitional employment for mentally retarded adults: Results from the STETS demonstration.* New York: Manpower Demonstration Research Corporation.

Koop, S., Martin, G., Yu, D., & Suthons, E. (1980). Comparison of two reinforcement strategies in vocational-skill training of mentally retarded persons. *American Journal of Mental Deficiency, 84*(6), 616–626.

Lakin, K. C., & Bruininks, R. H. (Eds.) (1985). *Strategies for achieving community integration of developmentally disabled citizens.* Baltimore: Paul H. Brookes.

Landesman, S., & Butterfield, E. C. (in press). Normalization and deinstitutionalization of mentally retarded individuals: Controversy and facts. *American Psychologist.*

Landesman-Dwyer, S., Berkson, G., & Romer, D. (1979). Affiliation and friendship of mentally retarded residents in group homes. *American Journal of Mental Deficiency, 83*(6), 571–580.

Landesman-Dwyer, S., Sackett, G. P., & Kleinman, J. S. (1980). Relationship of size to resident and staff behaviors in small community residences. *American Journal of Mental Deficiency, 86,* 6–17.

Landesman-Dwyer, S., Sulzbacher, S., Edgar, E., Keller, S., Wise, B., & Baatz, B. (1980). *1979 Rainier School placement study.* Olympia, WA: Department of Social and Health Services.

Laski, F. J. (1985). Judicial address of education for students with severe mental retardation: From access to schools to state-of-the-art. In D. Bricker, & J. Filler (Eds.), *Severe mental retardation: From theory to practice.* Lancaster, PA: Council for Exceptional Children, Division on Mental Retardation.

Mank, D. M. (1984). *Changes in quality of life: Descriptions from the Specialized Training Program.* Unpublished manuscript, University of Oregon, Specialized Training Program, Eugene.

Mank, D. (1985). *Maintaining work rate of youth with severe handicaps: The effects of self-management.* Unpublished doctoral dissertation, University of Oregon, Eugene.

Mank, D. M., Rhodes, L. E., & Bellamy, G. T. (1986). Four supported alternatives. In W. Kiernan, & J. Stark (Eds.), *Pathways to employment for developmentally disabled adults* (pp. 139–154). Baltimore: Paul H. Brookes.

McDonnell, J., Wilcox, B., & Boles, S. (1986). Do we know enough to plan for transition? A national survey of state agencies responsible for services to persons with severe handicaps. *The Journal of the Association for Persons with Severe Handicaps, 11,* 53–60.

McDonnell, J. J., Wilcox, B., Boles, S. M., & Bellamy, G. T. (1985). Transition issues facing youth with severe disabilities: Parents' Perspective. *Journal of Association for Persons with Severe Handicaps, 10*(1), 61–65.

Minnesota Developmental Disabilities Planning Council. (1982, February). *Policy analysis series: Summary of issues, programs and clients in Minnesota Developmental Achievement Centers: 1980–1982.* St. Paul: Department of Energy, Planning and Development.

Nettekoven, L., & Ramsey, E. (1985). Entitlements: One solution to the transition dilemma? In M. S. Gould, & G. T. Bellamy (Eds.), *Transition from school to work and adult life* (pp. 24–56). Eugene, OR: Specialized Training Program.

Newton, J. S., Boles, S., Romer, M., Bellamy, G. T., &

Horner, R. H. (1985) *Final Report: Deinstitutionalization models for severely handicapped children and youth* (Grant No. 300–81–0406). Eugene, OR: University of Oregon, Specialized Training Program.

O'Brien, J. (in press). A guide to lifestyle planning: Using the Activities Catalog to integrate services and natural support systems. In G. T. Bellamy & B. Wilcox (Eds.), *The Activities Catalog: An implementation guide*. Baltimore: Paul H. Brookes Publishing.

O'Neill, J., Brown, M., Gordon, W., & Schonhorn, R. (1985). The impact of deinstitutionalization on activities and skills of severely/profoundly retarded multiply handicapped adults. *Applied Research in Mental Retardation, 6*, 361–371.

O'Neill, J., Brown, M., Gordon, W. Schonhorn, R., & Greer, E. (1981). Activity patterns of mentally retarded adults in institutions and communities: A longitudinal study. *Applied Research in Mental Retardation, 2*, 367–379.

Pumpian, I., Baumgart, D., Shiraga, B., Loomis, R., & Brown, L. (1980). *Vocational training programs for severely handicapped students in the Madison Metropolitan School District*. Madison: University of Wisconsin-Madison, Madison, Metropolitan School District.

Rhodes, L. E., & Valenta, L. (1985). Industry-based supported employment: An enclave approach. *Journal of the Association for Persons with Severe Handicaps, 10*(1), 12–20.

Rusch, F. R., & Menchetti, B. M. (1981). Increasing compliant work behaviors in a non-sheltered work setting. *Mental Retardation, 19*, 107–112.

Rusch, F. R., & Mithaug, D. E. (1980). *Vocational training for mentally retarded adults: A behavior analytic approach*. Champaign, IL: Research Press.

Schalock, R. L., Harper, R. S., & Genung, T. (1981). Community integration of mentally retarded adults: Community placement and program success. *American Journal of Mental Deficiency, 85*, 478–488.

Silvern, L. C. (1963). Object analysis and action synthesis methods in developing a program for the assembly of a television antenna in a sheltered workshop. *Mental Retardation, 1*, 140–147.

Singer, G. H. S., Close, D. W., Irvin, L. K., Gersten, R., & Sailor, W. (1984). An alternative to the institution for young people with severely handicapping conditions in a rural community. *Journal of the Association for the Severely Handicapped, 9*(4), 251–261.

Sontag, E., Smith, J., & Certo, N. (1977). *Educational programming for the severely and profoundly handicapped*. Reston, VA: Division on Mental Retardation, The Council for Exceptional Children.

Sowers, J., Rusch, F. R., Connis, R. T., & Cummings, L. E. (1980). Teaching mentally retarded adults to time-manage in a vocational setting. *Journal of Applied Behavior Analysis, 13*(1), 119–128.

Stanfield, J. S. (1973). Graduation: What happens to the retarded child when he grows up? *Exceptional Children, 39*(7), 548–552.

Switzky, H. N., & Haywood, H. C. (1985). Perspectives on methodological and research issues concerning severely mentally retarded persons in D. Bricker, & J. Filler (Eds.), *Severe mental retardation: From theory to practice*. Council on Exceptional Children, Division on Mental Retardation.

Tate, B. G., & Baroff, G. S. (1967). Training the mentally retarded in the production of a complex product: A demonstration of work potential. *Exceptional Children, 33*, 405–408.

Taylor, S. (1985, April). In J. Knoll (Ed.), *The Community Integration Project*. Syracuse, NY: Syracuse University, The Center on Human Policy, Division of Special Education and Rehabilitation.

Terkel, S. (1975). *Working*. New York: Avon.

Vogelsberg, R. T. (1986). Vermont's employment training programs. In F. R. Rusch (Ed.), *Competitive employment: Service delivery models, methods, and issues* (pp. 35–50). Baltimore: Paul H. Brookes.

Walls, R. T., Sienicki, D. A., & Crist, K. (1981). Operations training in vocational skills. *American Journal of Mental Deficiency, 85*(4), 357–367.

Wehman, P., & Kregel, J. (1985). A supported work approach to competitive employment of individuals with moderate and severe handicaps. *Journal of the Association for Persons with Severe Handicaps, 10*(1), 3–11.

Wilcox, B., & Bellamy, T. (1982). *Design of high school programs for severely handicapped students*. Baltimore: Paul H. Brookes.

Wilcox, B., & Bellamy, G. T. (in press). *The Activities Catalog: An implementation guide*. Baltimore: Paul H. Brookes.

Zollers, N., Conroy, J., Hess, C., & Newman, E. (1984). *Transition from school to work. A study of young adults and their families in Pennsynvalia*. Philadelphia: Temple University, Developmental Disabilities Center/UAF.

Name Index

Subject Index